1894. 2:30 Book and Table of Sires

Gocher, W. H. (William Henry)

1894

⇒2:30⇐

BOOK AND TABLE OF SIRES

CONTAINING

*ALL TROTTERS WITH RECORDS OF 2:30 OR BETTER, ALL PACERS
WITH RECORDS OF 2:30 OR BETTER, ALL SIRES OF 2:30
PERFORMERS AND THEIR PERFORMERS, WORLD'S
RECORDS, BIG MONEY-WINNERS, WINNING
SIRES, CHAMPION TROTTERS AND
PACERS, UP TO THE
CLOSE OF 1894.*

COMPILED BY

W. H. GOCHER,

Editor of THE AMERICAN SPORTSMAN.

PUBLISHED BY COMPILER.
CLEVELAND, O., 1894.

CONTENTS

ILLUSTRATIONS.

═PREFACE═

A work of this character requires but little introduction. Each page tells its own story, as it is a history of the best performances made by trotters and pacers to harness from the earliest time up to the close of 1894. In it will be found all of the 2:30 trotters, all of the 2 30 pacers and all stallions that have sired 2 30 performers, together with their performers under them. In the 2:30 list of trotters and pacers the color, age, sex, sire and dam, as well as sire of dam is given where known. In placing this work before the public my aim has been to condense matters so that the price of the book would not be exorbitant. Of late years many have avoided a publication of this character from the fact that the composition bill was so high and because there is such a limited field, as is the case with all class publications. Should this book, however, meet with the approval of the public, it will be followed at the close of 1895 with one that will be much more complete and also contain more statistical matter.

That there are errors in this 2:30 Book is not denied. Absolute correctness is impossible in a work of this magnitude. Those who have handled statistical matter know that the trip from the copy hook to the press is a very hazardous one, and that even the most careful proof reading will not detect all errors. Individual knowledge of horses will bring such faults to light and information of their existence will be thankfully received. By referring to the book it will also be found that there are a great many horses whose ages are not given, from the fact that they are not registered. Many of their pedigrees are also incomplete. Information on either of these points will be very acceptable. In other words, I want the assistance of every one on the turf papers, and every one who has occasion to consult these pages, to help in making this book more complete than it is at present. Turf writers, of all others, have occasion to refer to such a work frequently, and the more accurate it is the more acceptable it will be to them.

The basis of records used are those accepted by the National Trotting Association and the American Trotting Association. In other words, the records that appear here are the ones that each horse would be expected to start under should his owner decide to campaign him. This has made a number of changes in the performers credited to a few stallions, and has also made several changes in the table of champions

In making the announcement of this book through the press I stated that it would be a work of about three hundred pages. Now that it is completed, I find that it contains three hundred and thirty-four pages. This includes the illustrations, which have not been folioed. There are, however, two hundred and ninety-six pages of printed matter.

CLEVELAND, OHIO, DECEMBER 31, 1894.   W. H. GOCHER.

P. P. JOHNSTON, Lexington, Ky.
President of National Trotting Association.

W. P. IJAMS, Terre Haute, Ind.
President of American Trotting Association.

PART 1

THE 2:30 TROTTERS.

The following are all of the horses that have made records of 2:30 or better to harness to the close of 1894.

A. A., b s, 1890, by Almont Aberdeen—Ringlet, by Ringgold 2:26
A. A. A., b m, 1891, by Azmoor—Abbess, by Mohawk Chief 2:25
Aaron S., br s, 188—, by California Lambert 2:29
Abanteeo, b m, 1889, by Anteeo—Abbotine, by Abbotsford 2:17½
Abbadonne, b m, 1889, by Wilkes Boy—Lulu Patchen, by Tom Patchen 2:23¼
Abbie, b m, by Hambletonian Prince 2 29½
Abbiedeen, b m, 1888, by Aberdeen—Kate Thompson, by Ericsson 2:29¼
Abbottsford, b s, 1872, by Woodford Mambrino—Columbia 2:19½
Abbottsford Jr., br s, 188—, by Abbottsford, dam by American Boy... 2:25
Abby, b m, 1877, by George Wilkes—Mattie Wilder, by American Clay.. 2:26
A. B. C., br g, 1883, by Warwick Boy—Capitola, by Bay Billy 2:29¼
A. B. C., b s, 1886, by Chief—Molly A., by Romeo 2:28
A. B. C., blk g, by Jim Crow, dam by Dick Edwards 2.24¼
Abdallah (Goldsmith's), b s, 1863, by Volunteer—Martha, by Abdallah . 2 30
Abdallah Boy, b s, 1870, by Abdallah Messenger—Motto, by Corbeau ... 2:24¼
Abdallah Clay, blk s, 1884, by Lakeland Abdallah—Kitty Clay, by Strader's Cassius M. Clay Jr .... 2·20¼
Abdallah Medium, b s, 1882, by Happy Medium—Lady Reynolds, by Jackson's Sir Archy 2:27¼
Abdamed Allen Jr., b s, 1885, by Abdamed Allen—Kit 2.26½
Abdol, blk s, 1883, by Grand Moor—Black Bess 2:28
Abe Downing, b s, 1875, by Joe Downing, dam by Harrison.. ... 2:20½
Abe Edgington, gr g, 186—, by Stockbridge Chief Jr.—Dooley Mare.... 2:23¾
Abe G., b g. (ringer?) 2:29½
Abel, b g, 1877, by Messenger Chief—Lucy, by Vermont 2.24¼
Abel Muscovite, b g, 1891, by Muscovite 2 29¾
Abercrombie, ch s, 1886, by Ambassador—Fearless, by Western Fearnaught 2:21¼
Abe Smith, b g, 1885, by Artemas, dam by Combination 2:24¾
Aberdeen Wilkes, ch m, 1884, by Wilkie Collins—Aberdale, by Aberdeen. 2·26
Abner F., b g, 1876, by Dr. Maxwell —Nancy Fenn 2,24¼
Abnet, b m, 1892, by Ambassador—Emblem, by Empire 2:29¼
Abraham L., b g, by Naham, dam by Red Buck 2:18
Abram, br g, 1885, by Goldemar—Mary Foss 2:25
Absolute, blk s, 1884, by Dictator—

Ida Elliott, by Allie West 2:30
Accident, ch s, 188—, by Alexander H. Sherman 2:26½
Acclamation, b s, 1889, by Elector—Ollie Ray, by Reliance 2:24¼
A. C. K., ch g, 1889, by Michigan Boy—Queen, by Prince Albert 2:29½
Acme Girl, b m, 18—, by Almont Ford 2:29¼
Acolyte, b s, 1884, by Onward—Lady Alice, by Almont 2 21
Action, ch m, 1888, by Onward—Sahara, by Challenger 2:28
Actor, b g, 1888, by Richwood—Queen Patchen, by Mambrino Patchen Jr. 2:26¼
Actress, b m, 1882, by Knickerbocker, dam by Edsall's Hambletonian..... 2:26¾
Actress, ch m, 188—, by Triceps... 2 28¾
Actress, blk m, 1885, by Star Wilkes —Lizzie C., by Star Hambletonian . 2.27¼
Ada, br m, 1886, by Alcantara—Admiration, by Administrator 2:28¼
Ada, b m, 1878, by Sir Denton—Sweetheart, by Magna Charta 2.29¼
Ada, gr m, 1885, by Fairy Gift—Nelly's daughter, by Live Oak... 2.29½
Ada B., b m, by Bourbon Wilkes—Morette, by St Elmo 2:26¾
Ada D., blk m, 1881, by Elial G.—Belle Wilson, by Lovely's Priam... 2:21¼
Ada De Clare, b m, 1886, by Lord Russell—Aida, by Rysdyk's Hambletonian 2 26½
Adah Look, ch m, 1887, by Look, dam by Gen. Stark 2:29¼
Adair, b g, 1879, by Electioneer—Addie Lee, by Culver's Black Hawk 2:17¼
Ad Alene, blk m, 1891, by Coeur d'Alene—Lakeland Queen, by Lakeland Abdallah 2 26
Adalia, br m, 1876, by St Clair—Addie Lee, by Culver's Black Hawk 2.27
Ada M. b m, 1879, by Corsair—Rhinehart Mare, by Muzzy Morgan 2:29½
Adam Index, b g, 1886, by Index Jr., dam by Nero 2:29½
Ada P., b m, 188— by Bloodmont... 2:25½
Ada Paul, ch m, 1875, by Stone's Red Buck—Maggie Morgan, by Young's Morgan .... 2·26
Adbel, b s, 1893, by Advertiser—Beautiful Bells, by The Moor..... 2:23
Addie C., b m, 1881, by Rysesuke—Miss Wilson, by Blue Bull, pacing 2·29 .... 2:30
Addie De, ch m, 1887, by Nutwood—Adelaide, by Phil Sheridan 2:25¾
Addie E, ch m. 1883, by Algona—Lady Stewart, by A. T. Stewart... 2:19
Addie E C, b m. 1872, by Burger—Fear'ess, by Bellbrino 2:28½
Addie Fitz B b m. 1890, by Charley B.—Addie E. B, by Charley B.... 2:26¼
Addie G., b m, 1877, by Young Voluu-

Albani, ch m, 1886, by Hermit—Mississippi Maid, by Anglo Saxon..... 2:21¼
Albany, ch m, 1888, by Hamlin's Almont Jr.—Jenny Bate, by Cuyler... 2:30
Albany Boy, b s, 1885, by Smuggler Jr.—Nelly Crow, by Mambrino Eagle 2:23
Albemarle, gr g, 1868, by Tom Hunter, dam by Wadsworth's Blucher...... 2:19
Albert, blk g, 186—, pedigree not traced. Bought out of a sale stable 2:24¾
Albert, b s, 1888, by Alcryon—Nelly O., by Louis Napoleon........... 2:29¼
Albert Bretwood, b s, 1891, by Bretwood 2:26¾
Alberta France, b g, 1878, by George Wilkes—Alley, by Hambletonian... 2:20¼
Albert M., b s, 188—, by Favorite Wilkes 2:29¼
Albert S., br s, 1888, by Wilkes Boy—Windom Belle, by Mambrino Foster 2:30
Albert S., blk s, by George Sprague.. 2:30
Albert S., gr g.................... 2:26½
Albert T., ch g, 1888, by Albert W.—Tobin mare, by Whipple's Hambletonian 2:19¼
Albert W., b s, 1878, by Electioneer—Sister, by John Nelson 2:20
Albion, br g, pedigree not traced.... 2:29¼
Albion, br g, 1883, by Bostick's Almont Jr.—Mattie C., by Trouble.... 2:25¼
Albion, b s, 1883, by Gen. Benton—Amy, by Messenger Duroc 2:26½
Albion, b s, 1886, by Wilkes Boy—Admiration, by Administrator 2:25½
Albion, br g, by Winooski............ 2:27¼
Albion Medium, b s, 1885, by Happy Medium—The Witch, by Almont.... 2:30
Albright, b s, 1891.................. 2:23
Albrina, b m, 1887, by Albrino—Hippenheimer, by Volunteer 2:27
Alcagetta, gr m, 1885, by Alcantara—Lady Daggett, by Logue horse, died 1888 .... 2:25
Alcaide, gr g, 1878, by Alroy—Nelly M., by Joe Hooker 2:28¼
Alcander, ch s, 1884, by Alcantara—Cleopatra, by Abdallah Prince...... 2:20½
Alcandre, blk s, 1883, by Alcyone—Lady Carr, by American Clay....... 2:26¼
Alcantara, b s, 1876, by George Wilkes—Alma Mater, by Mambrino Patchen 2:23
Alcantarus, blk s, 1889, by Alcantara—Grace Medium, by Happy Medium 2:20¼
Alcantine, b s, 1886, by Alcantara—Net Medium, by Happy Medium.... 2:29
Al Carroll, gr s, 188—, by Alcryon.. 2:24¼
Alcavala, b g, 1880, by Alcantara—Leah, by Blue Bull 2:29
Alcazar, b s, 1883, by Sultan—Minnehaha, by Bald Chief............. 2:20½
Alcazar, blk s, 1883, by Alcantara—Galatea, by Fearnaught............ 2:24½
Alcazar Belle, ch m, 1888, by Alcazar—Kate Russell, by Mambrino Russell 2:24¼
Alerdalle, b m, 188—, by Sir Walter Jr.—Comee's Sister, by Daniel Lambert 2:30
Alchemist, b s, 1882, by Almont—Willetta, by Strader's Cassius M. Clay Jr. 2:30
Alcolyte, br s, 1886, by Onward—Godiva, by Egmont 2:27¼
Alcona Jr., b s, 1881, by Alcona—Madonna, by Strader's Cassius M. Clay Jr. 2:19
Al Cooper, b g, by Kenelin.......... 2:28¼
Alcryon, gr s, 1882, by Alcyone—Lady Blanche, by Privateer 2:15
Alcyona, b m, 1883, by Alcyone—Cutter, by Coaster 2:29
Alcyone, br s, 1877, by George Wilkes—Alma Mater, by Mambrino Patchen 2:27
Alcyone Belle, ch m, 188—, by Alcyone 2:29¾
Alcyone Jr., ch s, 1887, by Alcyone—Lady Garfield, by Young Jupiter.. 2:18¾
Alcyonium, b s, 1886, by Alcyone—Sister, by Almont 2:24¼
Alcyrene, blk s, 1888, by Alcyone—Serene, by Nutwood 2:28¾
Alcyrene, blk m, 188—, by Alcyone.. 2:27¾
Alcy Wilkes, b s, 1883, by Alcyone—Daisy, by Stanhope's Blood Hawk.. 2:16
Aleck B., b g, 1882, by Electioneer—Alvaretta, by George Lancaster ... 2:24¾
Aldeana, b m, 1882, by Electioneer—Eliza Dolph, by Wildidle 2:25
Alden, br s, 1883, by Alden Goldsmith—Jenny, by Swigert 2:26
Aldine, br m, 1873, by Almont—Mother Hubbard, by Johnston's Toronto ... 2:19¼
Alejandri, blk m, 1886, by Dexter Prince—Princess, by Nutwood...... 2:15¾
Alencon, ch s, 1885, by Lord Russell—Alice West, by Almont........... 2:23¼
Alert, b g, 1879, by Ensign—Outlaw, by Martin's Eclipse 2:18½
Alex, b g, 1883, by Alexander........ 2:26
Alexander, b s, 1868, by Goldsmith's Abdallah—Bay Fanny, by Bellfounder 2:28¾
Alexander, blk s, 1874, by Ben Patchen—Jenny Martin, by Canada Jack 2:19
Alexander, b g, 187—, by Happy Medium—Mary Patchen by Bully King. 2:26¼
Alexander, br s, 1877, by Robinson—Nelly Williams, by Copperbottom .. 2:25
Alexander Button, b s, 1877, by Alexander—Lady Button, by Napa Rattler 2:26½
Alexander Button Jr., br s, 1886, by Alexander Button—Kate Kearney, by John Nelson 2:26¾
Alexander D., b g, 188—, by Williams' Idol—Bell Wilson, by Lovely's Priam 2:20
Alexander McCord, b g, 1883, by Gladiator 2:29¼
Alexander S., rn g, 1873, by Silliman Morgan 2:28¼
Alexander Stewart, ch g, 18—, breeding unknown 2:29¼
Alex C., b g, 1887, by Alert—Crymble Mare, by Marksman 2:21
Alex C., b s, 1890, by Belmont Chief.. 2:28¼
Alexie Sherman, b m, 1890, by Sherman, dam by Messenger Duroc.... 2:25¼
Alexis, b s, 1885, by Prince All—Nelly 2:21½
Alfonso, br s, 1886, by Baron Wilkes—Alma Mater, by Mambrino Patchen 2:29¾
Alfred, b s, 1887, by Hambletonian Gem—Lady Richelieu, by Richelieu. 2:26
Alfred, b s, 1880, by Gen. Benton—Alice, by Almont 2:25
Alfred, b g, 187—, by Cloud Mambrino 2:26½
Alfred G., b s, 1885, by Anteeo—Rosa B., by Speculation 2:19¾
Alfred S., b g, 1873, by Elmo—Nora Marshall, by Union 2:16¼
Alfretta, b m, 1876, by Mambrino Gift—Blondie 2:26¼
Alf Taylor, br s, 1887, by Capt. Cook—Jewel, by Blood Chief Jr..... 2:24½

—Alex, by Allie West 2:15

Allie Wilkes, ch m, 188—, by Red Prince 2 28

Allhmore, blk m, 1887, by Altamore—Lizzie H., by Hinkston Boy 2:29¾

Allo, br s, 1881, by Altoona—Nelly... 2:22½

Allorita (Lena H), ch m, 188—, by Altoona—Neily 2:16¾

All Monarch, ch s, 1888, by Almonarch—Lady Bostwick, by Prince of Wales 2:19½

All Right b s, 1891, by Gogebic ... 2:21

All Right Jr., b s, by All Right..... 2:29½

All So, b s, 1884, by Blackwood Jr.—So So, by George Wilkes......... 2:20¼

Alma, blk m, 1886, by Almont M.—Barrett mare 2:28½

Alma, br m, 1872, by Rysdyk's Hambletonian—Clara, by American Star. 2:28¾

Alma, b m, 1883, by Electioneer—Alvaretta, by George Lancaster.... 2:28½

Alma Alto, b m, 1891, by Palo Alto.. 2:30

Almambro, br s, 1881, by Alar Clay—Nigger, by Stanhope's Mambrino Pilot Jr 2:28½

Almarch, ch s, 1883, by Almonarch.. 2:30

Almater, ch m, 1884, by Hambrino—Alma Mater, by Mambrino Patchen. 2:24¼

Almira Highwood, b m, 1891, by Highwood—Sally Cossack, by Don Cossack 2:23¼

Almo, b s, 1880, by Hamdallah—Topsy, by Alexander 2:30

Almonarch, b s, 1875, by Almont—Hi, by Asteroid 2:24¾

Almonette, b m, 1881, by Altamont—Favorite, by Post's Hambletonian.. 2:29¼

Almonition, blk s, 1888, by Alcona—Pansy, by Strader's Cassius M Clay 2:24¾

Almont, b g, 1877, by Alburn—Lutie Ware, by Stanhope's Blood Hawk.. 2:17½

Almont, b g, pedigree not traced.... 2:28¼

Almont, br g, 18—, by Morris' Almont 2:25

Almonta, b m, 1884, by Tilton Almont—Susie 2:25

Almont Aberdeen, b s, 1884, by Aberdeen—Brightness, by Almont 2:22½

Almont Brunswick, b s, 1881, by Almont Chief—Affliction, by Duke of Brunswick 2:25¼

Almont Eagle, br s, 1872, by Almont—Mag Ferguson, by Mambrino Chief 2:27

Almont General, b g, 1879, by Hamlin's Almont Jr.—Mrs. Pratt, by Niagara Champion 2:24½

Almont Gift, b s, 1878, by Almont Chief—Shoo Fly, by Hall's Mohawk 2:27¼

Almont Gift Jr., b s, 188—, by Almont Gift 2:29¼

Almont Hambletonian, gr s, 1884, by Romulus—Delusion, by Almont..... 2:23½

Almontine, b m, 188—, by King Almont 2:19¼

Almont Jr. (Bostick's), b s, 1871, by Almont—Belle Forrest, by Edwin Forrest 2:29

Almont Jr (Hamlin's), b s, 1872, by Almont—Maggie Gaines, by Blood's Black Hawk 2:26

Almont King, br s, 1885, by Al West—Nelly Lee, by Mambrino Gay...... 2:29¼

Almont M., b s, 187—, by Bostick's Almont Jr.—Dutch mare, by Vermont Boy 2:30

Almont Maid, ch m, 1885, by Gen. Withers—Winona, by Winthrop Morrill 2:26

Almont Medium, b s, 1882, by Happy Medium—Lady Chiles, by Almont... 2:18¼

Almont Patchen, b s, by Hamlin's Almont Jr.—Kit, by Hamlin Patchen 2:29¼

Almont Star, b s, 1881, by Almont—Blanche Star, by Conklin's American Star 2:28¾

Almont Star, b s, 1885, by Almont Pilot—Star Maid, by Magnolia...... 2:25

Almont Wagoner, b s, 1884, by Almont Chief—Kit Patchen, by Wild Wagoner 2:29½

Almont Wilkes, br s, 1883, by Wilkie Collins—Almontress, by Hamlin's Almont Jr. 2:20

Alonzo Hayward, gr s, 187—, by Billy Hayward—M'liss 2:30

Alpha, blk m, 1880, by Alcantara—Jessie Pepper, by Mambrino Chief.. 2:23½

Alpha, ch m, 1887, by Pilot Champion—Nell, by Hatfield's Jake Weaver... 2:25¾

Alpha, b g, 1872, by Whalebone Knox, dam by Sanborn horse 2:29¼

Alpha, b g, by Armagh............. 2:21¾

Alpheus, b s, 1880, by Mambrino Wilkes—Rose, by Major Mono...... 2:25

Alphington, b s, 1886, by Pilot Medium—Nell Buckman, by Masterlode.. 2:16½

Alpine, b s, 1886, by Hambrino—Gwendolen, by Harold 2:30

Al Q. Chase, b g, 1888, by Onslaught—Dolly Carter, by Hambletonian Bashaw 2:24¾

Al R., b g, 1879, by Frank Nichols—Flora, by Coomb's Black Hawk.... 2:27½

Alrich, blk s, 1890, by Altus—Namouna, by A. W. Richmond 2:30

Alroy, b g, 1879, by Peacemaker—Mason Girl, by Arabian Chief 2:22¼

Alsie, ch m, 1882, by Kentucky Prince—Beatrice, by Rysdyk's Hambletonian 2:29

Alspur, b s, 1887, by Don Carlos—Alice, by Mambrino Dudley 2:21

Alta, blk m, 1886, by Allie Gaines—Malinda Weeks, by Star of the West 2:17½

Alta, br m, 1872, by Almont—Lady, by Bourbon Chief 2:23¼

Alta, b m, 1880, by Altamont—Maud, by Mike 2:23½

Alta, b m, pedigree not traced...... 2:29¼

Alta A., b g, 1883, by Altamont, dam by Autocrat 2:29¼

Alta Boy, b s, 1887, by Billy Wilkes—Flocee, by Louis Napoleon...... 2:26½

Alta May, b m, 1887, by Herschel—Trapeze, by Tramp 2:27

Alta May, b m, 1891, by Auctioneer—Marie, by Greenbacks (dead)...... 2:28½

Altamont, b s, 1875, by Almont—Sue Ford, by Brown Chief 2:26¾

Altamont, b g, 188—, by Almont Star Birthday, by Daniel Lambert 2:29¾

Altamura, br m, 1883, by Harold—Alice West, by Almont 2:30

Altao, b s, 1886, by Altamont—Sally M., by Oregon Pathfinder........... 2:16

Alta Patchen, ch s, 1885, by Seneca Patchen—Nelly Daniels, by Seneca Chief 2:24½

Altar, ch s, 1881, by Abdalbrino—Laureta, by Daniel Lambert...... 2:16¼

Altaree, b m, 1891, by Alturas 2:30

Alta Reina, b m, 1890, by Atto Rex—Jay, by Jim Hawkins 2:27

Alta Rose, b m, 188—, by Highlawn.. 2:28¾

Altena, blk m, 1884, by Altamont—Sleepy Kate, by Mike 2:26½

Althaia, b m, 1890, by Altamont—Venetia, by Almont 2:27½

Althard, b m, 1888, by St. Gothard—Alicia, by Harold 2:28¼
Althea, b m, 1886, by Ben Franklin—Susie Riker, by Blackstone....... 2:24½
Altissimo, blk g, 1890, by Grandissimo—Kate, by Toronto Chief Jr....... 2:25¼
Altitude, b s.......................... 2:27¼
Altitude, b s, 1872, by Almont—Molly, by Cantrell's Sir Archy........... 2:28
Altivo, b s, 1890, by Electioneer—Dame Winnie, by Planet 2:18½
Alto, dn s, 1884, by Antar—Lowville, by Green Mountain Boy 2:26½
Altogether, gr g, 1885, by Hamlin's Almont Jr.—Kitty Stack, by Stephen A. Douglas................ 2:19¼
Alton Boy, ro s, 186—, by Honest Allen 2:29½
Altoona, b m, 188—, by Menelaus (pacing 2:16¾) 2:22¾
Altoneer, br s, 1891, by Sphinx—Pilotena Wilkes, by Pilot Wilkes.. 2:25
Altus, b s, 1885, by Alcantara—Gossip, by Mambrino Patchen.......... 2:25¼
Alvan, b s, 1883, by Bostick's Almont Jr.—Vanity, by Enfield........... 2:26½
Alvary, b s, 1887, by Alvarado—Victoria, by Stockbridge............... 2:30
Alvin, ch s, 1885, by Orpheus—Nancy, by Toronto Chief Jr.............. 2:11
Alvira, b m, 1876, by Stillson—Fanny, by Harry Clay 2:29¼
Alviso, br g, by Brown Jug.......... 2:20
Alzippa, ch g, 1885, by Alroy—Goldie, by Rifleman 2:14¼
Amani, blk m, 1889, by Wilton—Alma Mater, by Mambrino Patchen........ 2:28¾
Amaranth, ch s, 188—, by Ambassador 2:27¼
Amazon, ch m, 1886, by Ambassador—Bishop mare, by Mohawk Jackson.. 2:29¾
Ambassador, blk s, 1875, by George Wilkes—Lady Carr, by American Clay 2:21¼
Amber, b s, 1871, by Clear Grit—Jenny Jinks, by Royal Revenge..... 2:25¼
Amber, b m, 1888, by Nelson—Nellie Rampart, by Rampart............. 2:24
Amber F., ch s, 188—, by Amber.... 2:30
Amberlou, gr m, 1888, by Black Hawk McGregor—Polka, by Pocahontas Boy 2:27¼
Amberlyte, b s, 1889, by Acolyte—Louella, by Amber 2:30
Ambler, b g, 1871, by Wood's Hambletonian 2:30
Amboy, ch g, 1884, by Heptagon—Lady Burchard, by Rysdyk's Hambletonian 2:13¾
Amboy, ch s, 1865, by Green's Bashaw—Fan, by Spread Eagle...... 2:26
Ambrosial, b s, 1889, by Tom Pugh—Miss Harrington, by Regulator..... 2:17¼
Amboies, b s, 1892, by Altheus—Hattie R., by Andy Johnson........... 2:26½
Ameer, b s, 1890, by Nephew—America, by Rysdyk's Hambletonian.... 2:27
Amelia, ch m, by Rustic—Petaluma.. 2:22½
Amelia C., b m, 1876, by Dexter—Bradford, dam by Volunteer 2:19¼
Amelia Rives, blk m, 1886, by King Richard—Wanda 2:27¾
Amender, b s, 1884, by Meander—Lady Anna, by Woodford Mambrino 2:25¼
America, blk s, 1886, by Kentucky Prince—Alma, by Rysdyk's Hambletonian 2:23½
American Girl, b m 1862, by Amos' Cassius M. Clay Jr. (dead)....... 2:16½
American Jay, ro s, 1888, by Eagle Bird—Our Mary, by Lelaps 2:24¾
American Lad, b s, 1885, by Ethan Wilkes—Rarity, by Messenger Bashaw (pacing 2:17¼) 2:26½
Amherst Boy, b s, 1887, by Elyria, dam by American Boy 2:24½
Amigo, b s, 1885, by Electioneer—Nadine, by Wildidle (died 1892).... 2:16¾
Amorel, blk m, 1889, by St. Bel—Adonai, by Dictator 2.26
Amoskeag, ch s, 1887, by Ambassador—Maud 2:23
Amurath, b s, 1887, by Sultan—Smuggler Girl, by Smuggler 2:23
Amy, b m, 1865, by Volunteer—Belle Brandon, by Rysdyk's Hambletonian (dead) 2:20¼
Amy Arney, b m, 1887, by Montgomery—Coalie, by Rob Roy 2:22½
Amy B., b m, 186—, by Frank Dunn—Daisy Dean, by Black Jack (dead). 2:24¼
Amy King, ch m, 1879, by Mambrino King—Belle Clay, by Kentucky Clay 2:22½
Amy Lee, ch m, 1882, by Bay Star—Nell, by Scott's Hiatoga 2.14
Ana, blk m, 1882, by Kentucky Prince—Starbeam by Rysdyk's Hambletonian 2:28½
Ancient Order Boy, ch g, 186—, by Gen. Morgan, dam by a son of Brown's Bellfounder 2:27
Andante, ch s, 1882, by Bostick's Almont Jr.—Mary M., by Bassinger 2:20½
Anderson, b g, 188—, by Baron West. 2:29¾
Anderson Wilkes, b m, 1884, by Onward—Magnet, by Strathmore 2.22¼
Andrew Allison, b s, 1886, by Andante—Kate K., by Trouble 2:22½
Andrew C., b g, 1884, by Harlan—Bess, by Robert Whaley 2:26¼
Andes, g s, 1885, by Clay Cuyler—Elsie Wilkes, by George Wilkes... 2:27½
Andy Cutter, gr g, 1888, by Cyclone—Gray Maid, by Major Downing.. 2:19¼
Andy Ensign, b s, 1891, by Ensign—Linda, by Supervisor............... 2:26½
Andy K., b g, 188—, by Barkis ....: 2:25½
Andy Mershon, gr s, 1870, by Curtis' Hambletonian—Lucy Mershon, by Kavanaugh's Grey Eagle.......... 2:25½
Andy Pogue, b s, 1887, by Harry Pulling—Sarah, by Coriander 2:29¼
Angelina, b m, 1886, by Wilkes Boy—Molly, by Kentucky Clay 2:12
Angus, blk s, 188—, by Wilkes Boy. 2:29¼
Anita, br m, 1887, by Baron Wilkes—Mary F., by Mambrino Boy 2:29¾
Anita, br m, 1886, by Le Grand—Hannah Price, by Arthurton........ 2:25½
Anita, gr m, 1886, by Rockwood Jr.—Lucy, by Vermont 2:23½
Angelica, ch m, 188—, by Young Fullerton 2:25¼
Angelus, ch g, 1891, by Whitby—Winnifred, by Brennan 2:23½
Anglin, b g, 1876, by George Wilkes—Betty Brown, by Mambrino Patchen 2:27½
Anna B., gr m, 1887, by Dirkee V.—Lucy, by Petoskey 2:27
Annabel b m, by Herschel, dam by Star Hambletonian 2:29¾
Annabelle, ch m, 1888, by Dawn—Pacheco, by Hubbard 2:27½
Annabel Lee, ch m, 1880, by Aberdeen—Betty Martin, by Mambrino Time 2:26
Anna C., b m, by Hambletonian

Tranby—Imogene 2:27½
Annacander, ch m, 1888, by Alcander—Leona 2:28¾
Anna K. b m, 1887, by Haw Patch—Ella B., by Aldrich Morgan. 2:28¾
Anna Knowlton (Annie), ch m, 1877, Broken Leg—Zulu Z, by Daniel Lambert 2:27¼
Anna M., blk m, by Tom Allen. . . 2:30
Anna Mace, gr m, 1889, by Robert McGregor—Mattie H, by Blue Bull. . . 2:29¼
Anna May, b m, 1885, by Delmonico Sprague—Nelly, by Jiggler 2:27¼
Anna May, b m, by Delmonico Sprague 2:27¼
Annette, ch m, 1887, by King Rene—Lady Pride, by Hamlet Jr 2:27½
Annette, b m, 1874, by Sentinel—Minnie, by Kentucky Clay 2:25½
Annie, b m, pedigree not traced . . 2:29¼
Annie B, b m, 1887, by Abdallah Mambrino—Clip, by Hamlet Denmark 2:29½
Annie Bennett, ch m, by Bayonne Prince, dam by Royal Fearnaught. . 2:26¼
Annie Boone, b m, 188—, by Daniel Boone 2:25¼
Annie C, b m, 188—, by Commander. 2:28¾
Annie C., gr m, by Melrose 2:27½
Annie C, b m, 188—, by C M Clay Jr, dam by Mambrino Black Hawk. 2:23¼
Annie Collins, br m, 1862, by Paul Jones—Morgan Belle (dead) 2:23½
Annie D., b m, 1884, by Port Leonard—Dolly, by Wilson's Capt Walker. . 2:29½
Annie E, b m, 1886, by Tilton Almont—Nippy, by Henry Belmont. . . 2:23
Annie G., br m, 1870, by Dictator—Annie Laurie, by Harris' Hambletonian (dead) 2:28
Annie H. (Susie Walton), b m, 1884, by Gen. George H Thomas—Edgefield Girl, by Enfield 2:20
Annie Hazen, ch m, 188— by Robert McGregor, dam by Onward 2:22¼
Annie K., gr m, by Happy Medium, dam by Mercer Patchen 2:28¾
Annie L., ro m, 1890, by Prince Orloff, dam by son of Harold. 2:29¾
Annie Laurie, b m, 1877, by Echo—Black Swan, by California Ten Broeck 2:30
Annie Laurie, ch m, 1878, by Daniel Lambert—Never Mind, by a son of Young Moscow 2:27¾
Annie Lou, b m, by Daniel Lambert—Brown Nelly, by a son of Vermont Black Hawk 2:30
Annie McGregor, b m, 1890, by Robert McGregor—Annette, by Young Jim 2:24
Annie Only, ch m, by George H Hazzard 2:27¾
Annie Ossian b m, 188—, by Ossian. 2:25
Annie P., b m, 1887, by Patchen Volunteer—Kitty C., by Landmark . . . 2:25¾
Annie Page, b m, 1872, by Daniel Lambert—Fanny Jackson, by Stonewall Jackson 2:27¼
Annie Pixley, b m, 188—, by Stocking Chief 2:29½
Annie Rooney, b m, 1884 by Springfield—Kate 2:24¼
Annie S., ch m, 1877, by Almont—Blanche Star, by Conklin's American Star 2:26¼
Annie Stevens, b m, 1887, by Kentucky Prince—Lady Horton, by Sweepstakes 2:18¼
Annie W., ch m, 1875, by Bostick's Almont Jr—Mary M by Bassinger. 2:20
Annie Wilkes, b m, 1881, by Wilkie Collins—Fanny, by King George . . 2:21½
Annie Wilkes, b m, 1889, by Arthur Wilkes—Belle Barnard, by Dr. Herr. 2:24½
Annine, ch m, 1891, by Warlock—Puella, by Harold 2:21
Annorean, b m, 1889, by Cyclone—Neoma C, by Twilight 2:26½
Anodyne, ch g, 1863, by Ross colt, dam by Young Hogarth 2:25
Ansel, b s, 1880, by Electioneer—Annette, by Lexington 2:20
Anselma ch m, 1885, by Ansel—Elaine, by Messenger Duroc 2:29½
Ansel W, rn g, 188—, by Harbinger 2:29¾
Anson, b g, 188—, by Landmark, dam by Rough and Ready 2:25¼
Ansonia, br s, 1875, by Jay Gould—Lady Ella 2:27¼
Answer, b g, 1887, by Ansel—Flora, by Whipple's Hambletonian 2:14½
Antarees, b s, 188—, by Anteeo—Bay Flora, by Skenandoah 2:27½
Antecedent, gr s, 1889, by Wilton—Anna Lotta, by Red Wilkes. 2:29½
Anteeo, b s, 1879, by Electioneer—Columbine by A. W. Richmond . . . 2:16½
Anteeo Jr, b s, 1884, by Anteeo—Lady Signal, by Signal 2:25¼
Anteeo Richmond, gr s, 1888, by Anteeo—Queen, by A. W. Richmond. . 2:21¼
Antella, b m, 1890, by Ansel—Garaphelia, by Gen Benton 2:26½
Antelope, ch s 1880, by Nutwood—Fanny, by Jerseyman 2:23½
Anteeoyne, b s, 1890, by Anteeo—Anna Lotta, by Red Wilkes 2:23
Anterose, b m, 1888, by Anteros—Ruby F, by Harry B 2:25
Antevolo, br s, 1881, by Electioneer—Columbine, by A W. Richmond. . . . 2:19½
Anthelia, b m, 1890, by Anteeo—Wilksie G, by Robert McGregor. . 2:18
Antinous, b s, 1882, by Electioneer—American Girl, by Toronto Sontag. . 2:28½
Antioch, br s, 1889, by Antevolo—Fanny, by Mambrino Wilkes. 2:21¼
Antonina, b m, 1888, by Antonio—Kitty Morgan, by Sam Purdy 2:26¾
Antonio, b s, 1880, by Messenger Duroc—Green Mountain Maid, by Harry Clay 2:28¾
Anvil, b s, 1889, by Manville—Ance, by Amber 2:23¾
Aparka, b s, 1887, by Onward—Lizzie K, by Magic 2:22
Apex, b s, 1882, by Prompter—Mary, by Flaxtail 2:26
Apollo Wilkes, b s, 1883, by Alcantara—Kit, by Gov Banks 2:28¾
Appanoose, b s, 1885, by Egbert—Hope, by Magic 2:26½
Aquarius, ch s, 1882, by Pancoast—Doris, by Cuyler 2:26
A. R, b g, 1881, by Gold Leaf Jackson 2:27½
Ara, ch m, 1883, by Masterlode—Fanny, by Magna Charta 2:29¼
Arab, b g, 1878, by Arthurton—Lady Hamilton 2:15
Arabella, b m, 1887, by Arabesque—Nell, by Scott's Hiatoga 2:26½
Arabesque, b s 1882, by King Rene—Alco, by Princeps 2:29¾
Arago, br s, 1885, by Steele—Jenny

Patchen, by Tom Patchen 2:22½
Arasene, b m, 1887, by Arabesque—
Fantine, by Altorf 2:28¼
Aravant, b s, 1887, by Arabesque
—Maggie Miller, by Auditor 2:24¼
Arbiter, blk s, 1878, by Administra-
tor—Alma Mater, by Mambrino
Patchen 2:22¾
Arbogast, b g, 1879, by Jack Shep-
pard 2:29¼
Arbutus, blk g, 1882, by Electioneer
—Amy, by Messenger Duroc 2:26½
Arcadian, blk s, 1883. by Egbert—
Yaura, by Almont 2.23½
Archbishop, ch s, 1886, by Wood-
ward's Ethan Allen Jr.—Nutshell,
by Nutwood 2:19½
Archie, b s, 1870, by Garibaldi—Lady
Mischief 2:24½
Archie B., ch g, by Thought....... 2:18½
Archie Sherman, b s, 1888, by Sher-
man—Maggie, by Mambrino Howard 2:29¼
Archlight, blk s, 1886, by Rampart—
Gypsy, by Robert R. Morris 2:19¾
Arctic B., gr s, 188—, by Aristos........ 2.24
Arctic B., b s, 1885, by Squire Tal-
mage—Belle, by Stephen A. Douglas 2:17¾
Arden, br s, 1884, by Detractor—
Music, by Goldenbow 2:29¾
Ardent, b s, 1890, by Alcazar—Nelly
D, by Echo 2:30
Ardoch 2:26
Areida, ch m, 1884, by Favorite
Wilkes—Aria O., by Neill Robinson.. 2.26
Arena, b s, 1890, by Alcantara—Mar-
tense, by Gen. Knox............. 2·15¼
Argent, b s, 1882, by Sterling—Madam
Buckner, by Tom Hal 2:24½
Argentine, ch g, 1882, by Sweepstakes
—Lady Deyo, by Hasbrook's Black
Hawk 2:21¼
Argo, br g, 1885, by Jerome Eddy—
Alice White, by Walker's Denmark 2:25½
Argo A., b s, 1882, by Wood's Ham-
bletonian—May, by Dandy 2:28
Argomont, ch s, 188—, by Argomont.. 2:29¼
Argonaut, b s, 1873, by Fearnaught... 2:23¾
Argonaut, br g, 187—, by Wood's
Hambletonian—Hackett Mare ... 2:23¼
Arguile, b s, 1887, by Alcantara—Miss
Alice, by Squire Talmage.......... 2·25
Aria, b m, 1891, by Bernal—Ashby,
by Gen. Benton 2:16¾
Arial, b s, 1890, by Wildnut—Nina,
by Piedmont .... 2·27¾
Ariana, b m, by Ansel—Rebecca, by
Gen. Benton 2.26
Arias, b g, 1888, by Mambrino Clark—
Adele Wilkes, by Abdallah Wilkes. 2.29¾
Arion, b s, 1889. by Electioneer—Ma-
nette, by Nutwood 2:07¾
Aristall, b s, 1891, by Energy ...... 2·25¾
Aristides, b s, 1886, by Red Wilkes—
Monie West, by Almont .... 2·20¾
Aristomont, b g, 1882, by Aristos—Al-
monia, by Almont 2:27¾
Aristos, b s, 1870, by Daniel Lambert
—Fanny Jackson, by Stonewall
Jackson 2.27¾
Aristotle, br s, 1885, by Aristos—Lady
Herbert, by Waltham 2:22½
Arlene Wilkes, ch m, 1888, by Ham-
bletonian Wilkes—Lady Beach, by
St. Lawrence 2:22¼
Arline, b m, 1888, by Noble Harold—
Zilla Golddust, by Glencoe ...uddust 2:25
Arlington, b g, 1886, by Fleance—
Dolly .... 2·24½
Arlino, b s, 1885, by Jerome Eddy—

Fanny Prewitt, by Mambrino
Patchen 2:29½
Aristos Chief, blk s, 18—, by Aristos,
dam by son of Black Tiger. 2:30
Armand, blk s, 1885, by Egbert—Dixie,
by Richelieu 2:23
Armenian, b s, 1892, by Pelletier.... 2.27¼
Armory, b s, by Artillery—Calliope,
by Onward 2 20¾
Arnutta, b m, 1887, by Nutbourne—
Arabell, by Aristos 2:27¼
Arol, br m, 1880, by Electioneer—
Aurora, by John Nelson (dead) ... 2:24
Arona, ch m, 1890, by Hermit—Miss-
issippi Girl, by Anglo Saxon. .. 2:24¾
Aroon, b s, 1889, by Brown Wilkes—
Athene, by Harold 2:27¾
Arpansa, ch m, 1888, by Pancoast—
Arabell, by Aristos (pacing 2.23¾).. 2·30
Arrival, b s, 1886, by Charley Wilkes
—Aspasia, by Alcantara 2:24½
Artemas B., br g, 1883, by Artemas—
Dolly Clay, by Honest Royal George 2:25¾
Artemesa, b m, 1889, by Arbiter—Star
Queen, by Whipple 2:29¾
Arthur, gr g, 1869, by Columbus—
Lasher Mare, by Milliman's Bell-
founder 2.27½
Arthur, ch g, 1872, by Dorsey Gold-
dust—Sylvia Pearl, by George Leigh-
ton 2.28¾
Arthur, b, 1872, by Ethan Allen—
Arcadia, by Canadian Grey Eagle.. 2:26½
Arthur, blk g, 1866, by Lexington .. 2·28¼
Arthur, b g, 1880, by Wichita—Lady
Litchfield, by Clark Chief 2.26½
Arthur Dodge, b g, 18—, by Albert W
—Rosa Mary, by Re-Echo ...... 2·20¾
Arthuretta, b m, 1886, by Hannis.... 2:29¼
Arthur M., gr g, 188—, pedigree not
traced 2:20½
Arthur Sprague, br s, 1887, by Walker
Sprague—Molly Merrill, by Dakota 2:27½
Arthur T., br g, 1869, by Col Ells-
worth, dam by Hector 2.27
Arthur T., b g, 1891, by Count Louis. 2.29
Arthur Wilkes, b s, 1884, by Guy
Wilkes—Gracie, by Arthurton ... 2:28½
Arthur Wilkes, b g, 1882, by Mam-
brino Wilkes—Princess, by Honest
Allen 2:19
Artilla, br m, 1889, by Artillery—Sym-
pathy, by Gen Washington 2 20
Artilley, b s, 1873, by Rysdyk's Ham-
bletonian—Wells' Star, by Seely's
American Star 2.21½
Artisan, b s, by Onward—Monette,
by Bonnie Bay 2:18¾
Artist, blk g, 1880, by McCracken's
Golddust, dam by Dave Hill Jr... 2.26½
Artist, b s, 1885, by Dictator Chief—
Belle Morrow, by Belmont 2:29
Ashby, br s, 1883, by Dictator—Filly,
by Bald Chief 2:27¼
Ashby, b s, 1890, by Vatican—Wilkes
Bird, by Mambrino Boy........... 2.19¼
Ashby Girl, br m, 1887, by King
Wilkes—Lady Ashby, by Morgan
Black Hawk 2 25
Ashland Boy, br s, 1882, by Fergus Mc-
Gregor—Bird, by Frank Bird 2:28¾
Ashland Girl, b m, 188—, by Ashland
Boy 2:22¼
Ashland Kate, ch m, 1869, by Ashland
Chief, dam by Capt. Walker..... 2·29¾
Ashland Prince, b s, 1883, by Happy
Medium—Josie Kenny, by Standard
Bearer 2:26¾
Ashland Wilkes, b s, 1882, by Red

Baby Bunting, blk m, 1889, by Waxford—Miss Crook 2:28½
Baby Lambert, b g, 1880, by Daniel Lambert—Melrose, by Melbourne Jr. 2:27¼
Baby Mine, rn m, 1873, by Stonewall Jackson—Dolly McIntire, by John Edwards 2:27¼
Baby Mine, b m, 1884, by Paramount—Flora, by Gifford Allen 2:22
Baby Mine, blk m, 1881, by Nephew—Lady Burns, by Black Boy 2:27
Baby Mine, ch m, 1878, by Stillson.. 2:29¼
Baby S., b m, by Cromwell.... 2:24½
Bachelor Wilkes, 1890, by Victor Wilkes—Nancy B., by Ben Franklin 2:30
Backman Maid, b m, 1876, by Charles Backman, dam by Godfrey Patchen. 2:25¼
Bad Actor, b g, 1888, by Black Ambassador—Georgie, by Latham's Royal George 2:21¼
Baden, gr g, 1886, by Steinway—Bloomfield Maid, by Whipple's Hambletonian 2:24¾
Badger Boy, gr s, 1882, by Swigert—Badger Girl, by Black Flying Cloud (dead) 2:27¾
Badger Boy, b g, 1872, by Leon, dam by Vermont Hero (dead) 2:29
Badger Girl, gr m, 1866, by Black Flying Cloud (dead) 2.22½
Badger State, b s, 1884, by Billy Sprague—Nelly Lefler 2:30
Badouna, b m, 188—, by Gideon, dam by Gen. Knox 2:26¼
Baker, b g, 1890, by Sphinx, dam by Pilot Medium 2:19¼
Balance All, b m, 1883, by Brigadier—Nellie McCracken, by Billy McCracken 2:29¾
Baldwin, ch g, by Bacon's Ethan Allen 2:24¼
Baldy, b g, 188—, by Baird's Hambletonian Prince, dam by Victor 2:29¼
Baldy T., b g, 1879, by Squire Talmage—Glasseye 2:29¾
Balkan, br s, 1885, by Mambrino Wilkes—Fanny Fern, by Jack Hawkins 2:15
Ballast, b s, 1887, by Onward—Miss Redmond, by Bourbon Wilkes 2:29¼
Ballona, br m, 1889, by Stranger—Lady Banker, by Rysdyk's Hambletonian 2:11½
Balmoral Boy, br g, 1885, by Griffard, dam by Columbus 2:29½
Baltimore, b s, 1891, by Bellman, dam by Lancewood 2:30
Battullo, br s, 1890, by Sphinx—Florence, by Brilliant 2.25
Balzac Chief, b s, 1886, by Matterhorn—Bicara, by Harold 2:26¼
Balzarine, b s, 1886, by King Rene—Crape Lisse, by George Wilkes 2:27
Bamboo, br s, 1886, by Lumps—Oria Wood, by Wildwood 2:28¼
Bamboo, blk g, 1888, by Nutwood—Emma, by Mambrino Boy 2:29¼
Bandoline, b m, 1884, by Ambassador—Ida Miller, by Blue Bull 2:28½
Banner Bearer, b s, 1886, by Standard Bearer—Maggie Clay, by American Clay 2:28½
Banner Boy, ch s, 1887, by Jefferson Star—Kitty F., by Bacon's Ethan Allen 2:23¼
Banner Boy, b g, 1881, by Standard Bearer—Mattie, by Norman 2:25
Banner Mark, b s, 1888, by Victor Bismarck—Moonlight, by Alcyone . 2:17¾
Bannockburn, ch s, 1888, by Aberdeen—Abdalletta, by Strader's Cassius M. Clay Jr. 2:29¾
Banquet, ch s, 1884, by Mambrino Patchen—Podie, by George Wilkes. 2:24
Banquo, b g, 1870, pedigree not traced (dead) 2.21
Baptism, b s, 1889, by Sunolo—Lady Mambrino, by North Star Mambrino 2:30
Barbara Patchen, b m, 1874, by Akers' Idol—Lady Patchen, by George M. Patchen 2:24½
Barberine, ch m, 1882, by Bullion—Josephine, by Mambrino Pilot .. 2:27½
Barbero, gr s, by Len Rose, dam by Crichton 2:29½
Barclay, b g, 1885, by Monte Cristo—Doris, by George Wilkes 2:20¼
Barkirola, b s, 1887, by Barkis—Kit, by Glencoe Golddust 2:26¼
Barada, br s, 1888, by Nutbreaker—Lavinia, by Cuyler 2:22½
Barderah, br s, 1890, by Brown Wilkes—Miss Lewis, by Nugget 2:26¾
Barkis, b g, 1872, by Whirlwind—Collona, by Green Mountain Black Hawk 2:25½
Barnetta, b m, 1892, by Barnhart—Orianna, by Onward 2.27¾
Barney, b g, 1868, by Mike—Kate 2:25¼
Barney Allen, blk g, 1879, by Panic—Fairy Morgan, by Gifford Regulator 2:26½
Barney B., b g, 187—, by Budd Doble. 2:27¼
Barney Clay, gr s, 1885, by Abdalbrino—Fanny Clay, by American Clay 2:28
Barney Clay, ch g, 1880, by Black Douglas 2:29½
Barney Egbert, b s, 1890, by Egbert—Genevra, by Barney Wilkes 2:27½
Barney F., ch s, 1886, by Achilles—Patti, by Wheeler's Hambletonian Star 2:29¼
Barney H., ch g, 186—, pedigree unknown 2:30
Barney K., ch g 2:25
Barney Kelly, b g, 1865, by Holland's Ethan Allen—Morrill Mare 2:25
Barney Lee, ch g, 1880, by Case's Dave Hill 2:25
Barney Wilkes, b s, 1884, by Red Wilkes—Avalanche, by Administrator 2:23¾
Barney Wilkes Jr., b g, 188—, by Barney Wilkes 2:26½
Barnhart, b s, 1887, by Jay Bird—Gussie Wilkes, by Mambrino Boy. 2:22¾
Barolite, b s, 1889, by Baron Wilkes—Lamberta, by Daniel Lambert 2:21½
Baron, b s, 1882, by Hersey—Phillis, by Young Golddust 2:29¼
Baron Brown, blk s, 1892, by Bermuda 2:24½
Baron Brown, br s, 1887, by Baron Wilkes—Brownie, by Daniel Lambert 2:26¼
Baron Crisp, b s, 1891, by Baron Wilkes—Maria, by Cuyler 2:24
Baron Dillon, b s, 1891, by Baron Wilkes—Mattie Nutwood, by Nutwood 2:16¾
Baroness, gr m, 1886, by Hambrino—Zephyr, by Mambrino Patchen .. 2.30
Baronet, b s, 1890, by Baron Wilkes—Lamberta, by Daniel Lambert .. 2:11½
Baron Jean, b s, 1890, by Baron

Wilkes—Jean, by Kentucky Prince.. 2:30
Baron Luff, b s, 1869, by Happy Medium—Belle Boyd, by Sherman Black Hawk 2:27
Baronmore, br s, 1890, by Baron Wilkes—May Wagner, by Strathmore 2:17½
Baron Posey, b s, 1888, by Baron Wilkes—Neva, by Nutwood 2:21½
Baron Rogers, br s, 1890, by Baron Wilkes—Ashland Maid, by Ashland Chief 2:17½
Baron Rose, b s, 1888, by Stamboul—Minnehaha, by Stevens' Bald Chief 2:29¾
Baron Russell, b s, 1886, by Baron Wilkes—Alpha Russell, by Mambrino Russell 2:24¼
Baron Wilkes, br s, 1882 by George Wilkes—Belle Patchen, by Mambrino Patchen 2:18
Barry Golddust, br s, 1882, by Highland Golddust—Kit Jarrard, by Harwood's Turk (dead) 2:24½
Barrmore, blk s, 1884, by Leland—Bessie, by Victor Bismarck 2:29¾
Bartholdi, b s, 1884, by Belvidere—Goshen Maid, by Rysdyk's Hambletonian 2:30
Bartholdi Patchen, ch s, 1886, by Seneca Patchen—Nelly Daniels, by Seneca Chief 2:22¾
Bashaw (Butler's), b s, 1880, by Green's Bashaw—Dolly 2:28¼
Bashaw Bill, ch s, 1882 by Harold C.—Sally, by Green's Bashaw...... 2:26
Bashaw Jr., ch s, 1860, by Green's Bashaw—Fanny Foss, by Young Green Mountain Morgan 2:24¾
Bashaw Maid, ch m, 1866, by Plow Boy 2:30
Bashawmont, b s, 1886, by Egmont—Lady McCoy, by Amboy 2:22½
Basil Duke, rn g, 186—, by Garrard Chief, dam by Copperbottom......... 2:28¼
Bassileen, b m, 188—, by Nutbreaker 2:27½
Bassinger Boy, br g, 1880, by Black Bassinger—Dot by Addison Jr. 2:23
Bassora, br s, 1887, by Greenbacks—Bella B., by Pasacas 2:22¼
Bateman, b g, 186—, by Black Harry Clay—Nell, by Rysdyk's Hambletonian (dead) 2:22¼
Bay, b g, 1868, by Gideon—Fanny Knox, by Gen Knox 2:27½
Baybrino, b g, 1872, by Swigert—Bonazella 2:28
Bay Cedar, b s, 1887, by Red Cedar—Kate Barr, by Broughton 2:30
Bay Charley, b g, pedigree and history unknown 2:28½
Bay Chieftan, b g, 1874, by John F. Payne—Fanny Williams, by Alexander's Abdallah 2:28¼
Bay Dick, b g, 1872, by Howser's Hiatoga, dam by a son of Duff Green 2:29½
Bay Fanny, b m, 1869, by Nigger Baby—Franchise 2:28
Bay Frank, b g, 1877, by Tornado—Grover 2:20
Bay Frank, b g, 1881, by Commodore Vanderbilt, dam by Reddick's Mambrino 2:28¾
Bay Henry, b g, 185— by Mambrino Chief—Orange Blossom (dead) 2:28½
Bay Henry, b s, by Mambrino Swigert 2:29¼
Bay Hull, b g, 1886, by Hull—Flora, by Black Squirrel 2:29¼
Bay Jack, b g, 1863, by Victor 2:30
Barney K., ch g.................... 2:26¼
Bay Mate, b g, 1876, by Pacing Abdallah—Lottie, by Parson's Abdallah 2:30
Bayonne Prince, blk s, 1879, by Kentucky Prince—Emily C. (dead)... 2:21¼
Bay Rose, b s, 1881, by Sultan—Madam Baldwin, by The Moor 2:20½
Bay Rum, br s, 1887, by John Sevenoaks—Kitty S., by Quien Sabe..... 2:19½
Bay State Morgan, b g, by Sherman Morgan 2:25
Bay Sultan, b s, 1887, by Sultan—Annie Cook, by Pacing Abdallh... 2:29½
Bay Thorn, b g, 1885, by Hawthorne—Brown Nelly, by Gen. McClellan. 2:23½
Bay Thornwood, b g, 1883, by Keystone—Thorndale Princess, by Thorndale 2:24½
Bay Tom, b g, 187—, by Honest John, dam by Grey Jack 2:21¾
Bay Tom, b g, 188—, by Aberdeen..... 2:29¼
Bay Victor, b s, 1887, by Black Victor—Elnora, by Administrator......... 2:30
Bay Whalebone, b g, 1862, by Whirlwind (dead) 2:26¼
Bay Wilkes, b g, 188—, by Black Wilkes 2:25¼
Bay Wilkes, b s, 1883, by Bourbon Wilkes—Anwood, by Forrest Patchen 2:26¾
Bay Wilkes, b s, 1886, by Mambrino Wilkes, dam by Frank Hunter...... 2:16¼
Baywood, b s, 1884, by Nutwood—Lady Cuyler, by Cuyler............ 2:27
Baywood, b s, 1885, by Blackwood Mambrino — Lucy Woodruff, by Hiram Woodruff 2:29½
Bayzant, b s, 1889, by Bezant—Fanny Payne, by John F. Payne 2:26¼
B. B. (Billy Barlow), blk g, 1875, by Millman's Bellfounder—Blackey, by Vermont 2:21½
B. B. Custer, b g, 1879, by Bostick's Almont Jr.—Lady Belle, by Ethan Allen 2:22½
B. B. P., b s, 1891, by Pilot Medium, dam by Schuyler Colfax........... 2:13½
Beaconsfield, b g, 1878, by Dean Sage—Cricket, by Happy Medium 2:25½
Beaulak, blk m, 188—............... 2:28
Beaufort Girl, blk m, 188—, by Beaufort 2:27¼
Beaumont, ch s, 18—, by Bostick's Almont Jr. 2:28¼
Beaumont, ch s, 1885, by Le Grand—Oakgrove Belle, by Arthurton 2:23½
Beauregard, ch g, 1878, by Mohican—Nelly Mack 2:21½
Beaury Mc, b g, 1886, by Nephew—Nelly, by Gen. McClellan. 2:14½
Beautiful Bells, blk m, 1872, by The Moor—Minnehaha, by Stevens' Bald Chief 2:29½
Beautiful Chimes, b m, 1889, by Chimes—Maid of Honor, by Mambrino King 2:22½
Beauty, b m, 188—, by Chismore........ 2:29½
Beauty (Effie G.), b m, 1874, by Blue Bull—Cora 2:28
Beauty Bells, b m, 188—, by Bell Boy—Vera 2:28½
Beauty Bright, b m, 1878, by John Bright—Tennie C., by Young Pacelot 2:21¼
Becky Sharp, br m, 1882, by Coriander—Judy O'Can, by Evan Dhu... 2:23½
Beconian, rn s, 1890, by Jay Bird..... 2:30
Bedah, b m, 188—, by Nutwood—

Belle of Montour, b m, 1887, by Mohawk Chief—Lady Weed, by Buckley's Clay ... 2:29¼
Belle of Navarre, ch m, 1881, by Ambassador, dam by Scott's Hiatoga ... 2:28¼
Belle of Portland, b m, 1850, by Witherell Messenger (dead) ... 2:26
Belle of Saratoga, br m, 184—, by Vermont Black Hawk—Poll Roe (dead) ... 2:29
Belle of Shelby, gr m, 1887, by Fisk's Belmont ... 2:28¾
Belle of Toronto, gr m, 1863, by Toronto Chief (dead) ... 2:30
Belle Ogle, br m, 1878, by Mohawk Jr.—Hall's Lady Ogle, by Tom Tucker 2:21½
Belle Pedro, b m, 188— by Don Pedro 2:29¼
Belle Pepper, b m, 188— by Pepper.. 2:28¾
Belle Red, b m, 1891 by Red Wilkes—Ermine G., by Almont ... 2:28¼
Belle Pedro, br m ... 2:29¼
Bellerene, ch m, 1882, by Tremont—Lady Wilkes, by George Wilkes.... 2:26¾
Bellronial, b m, 1892, by Baronial—Belle Clay by Strader's C. M. Clay Jr. ... 2:29¼
Belle S, b m, 1875, by Andy Johnson—Flora Dunn, by Champion Fox-hunter ... 2:28½
Belle S, b m, 1880, by Menelaus—Belle, by Red Cloud ... 2:25
Belle Shacket, ch m, 1876, by Abraham—Cloverfed, by De Long's Ethan Allen (pacing record 2:27¾) ... 2:27½
Belle Smith, ch m, 1869, by Bearce Horse (dead) ... 2:29
Belle Spencer, b m, 1875, by Black Ralph, dam by Langford ... 2:26¼
Belle Stanton, br m, 1887, by Gen Stanton—Jenny, by Gilderoy... 2:24½
Belle Strickland, ch m, 1860, by Merrow Horse—Welch Mare, by Witherell Messenger (dead) ... 2:26
Belle Thorne, b m, 1886, by Hawthorne—Gail McMahon, by McMahon 2:27
Belletone, b m, 1892, by Bellman, dam by Othello ... 2:30
Bellette, b m, 1892, by Bellman, dam by Lancewood ... 2:24¼
Belle Truitt, gr m, 1885, by Hazel Bashaw—Hale Mare, by Telegraph 2:23½
Belle Truxton, blk m, 1889, by Truxton—Miss Preston, by Prince Orloff 2:30
Belle Underhill, b m, 1884, by Walter Lewis—Flora, by John Bull ... 2:26¼
Belle Unrue, b m, 1884, by Ajax—Jennie, by Blue Bull ... 2:29¼
Belle Ure, b m, 1888, by Hambrino—Fashion, by Curtis' Hambletonian.. 2:19½
Belle Vara, b m, 1887, by Vatican—Nell, by Estill Eric ... 2:08¾
Bellevue Wilkes, ch s, 1887, by Red Wilkes—Lady Cassell, by Shelby Chief ... 2:27¾
Belle W, blk m, 1885, by Selkirk—Juno, by Sawdust ... 2:19¼
Belle W., b m, 188—, by Highland Chief ... 2:29¼
Belle Werne, b m ... 2:29¼
Belle Whitney, gr m, 1887, by Whiteline—Hotspur Girl, by Hotspur Jr. 2:30
Belle Wilkes, b m, 1883, by Young Wilkes—Belle of Johnson, by Narragansett ... 2:28¼
Belle Wilson, ch m, 1876, by Blue Bull—Kate Jennings, by St. Lawrence II ... 2:23½
Belle Wilson, gr m, 1886, by Jim Wilson, dam by Thomas A. Scott ... 2:20
Belle Wilson, b m, 187—, by Mambrino Bruce—Miss Wilson ... 2:24¼
Belle Wilson, ch m, 1880, by George Wood ... 2:28¼
Belle Wythe, b m, 1882, by Toronto Patchen—Lady Lightfoot, by Flaxtail ... 2:27½
Bellini, br s, 1887 by Artillery—Merry Clay, by Harry Clay ... 2:13¼
Bellman, b s, 1886, by Indiaman—Lulu F., by Ericsson ... 2:14¾
Bellman, b s, 1888, by St. Bel—Daisy D., by Goldstone ... 2:28¾
Bellona, br m, 1889 by Brown Wilkes—Lottie D., by Homer ... 2:29¼
Belle Peters, b s, 1885, by Sterling Boy, dam by American Clay ... 2:29
Bellton, b s, 1888, by Belden Boy—Mollie Miner, by Steinbok ... 2:24¼
Bell Town, br s, 1888 by St Bel—Rosa Blackwood, by Blackwood ... 2:20¼
Bellwether, ch s, 1888, by Viking—Christine, by Wood's Hambletonian 2:19¼
Bellwood, b m, 1887, by Nutgrove—Lady Gay, by Volunteer Star ... 2:30
Belmont, b g, 1882, by Belmont—Dolly 2:28½
Belmont Prince, b s, 1888, by Waxford—Maggie Shea, by Jefferson Prince ... 2:17¼
Bel Onward, blk m, 1889, by St. Bel—Hildegarde, by Onward ... 2:23
Belva B., b m, 188—, by Artemas. . 2:20¼
Belva May, ch m 188—, by St. Clair . 2:29¼
Ben Ali, b g, 187—, by George M. Patchen Jr. ... 2:22
Ben Anna, b g, by a Drennon horse. 2:29
Ben B, b g, 1885, by Ridgewood—Jess, by Young Warrior ... 2:17½
Ben Bolt, dn g, 1884, by Giltedge—Trouble by Gus Henry ... 2:27½
Ben Butler, b g ... 2:29
Ben Buxton, b g, 188—, by Bartholomew Wilkes, dam by Rolly Seymour 2:26¾
Ben Cole, b g, 1884, by Ben Lomond Jr.—Molly Cole, by Cardinal ... 2:23¼
Ben Corbitt, b s, 1888, by William Corbitt—Jessie M., by A. W. Richmond ... 2:21
Ben Davis ch g, 1885, by Great Tom—Lena ... 2:19½
Ben Downs, b g, 1889, by Allie Wilkes—Madge, by Case's Dave Hill ... 2:29¼
Ben Duroc, br g, by Duroc ... 2:26¼
Benedicta, gr m, 1889, by Waterloo—Young Nelly Haynes, by Harry Wise 2:29½
Benediction, ch s, 1887 by Benefactor—Abutilon, by Belmont ... 2:27¼
Benefactor, ch s, 1882, by Egbert—Mary, by Woodford Mambrino... 2:28
Benefactor, b s, 1884, by Gen. Benton—Frolic, by Harry Clay ... 2:29¾
Ben Flagler, gr g 186—, by Niagara Chief (dead) ... 2:26½
Ben Franklin, ch s, 1873, by Daniel Lambert—Black Kate, by Addison.. 2:29
Ben Gage, b g, 187—, by Swigert ... 2:30
Ben Gaines, b g, 188—, by Allie Gaines, dam by Star of the West... 2:27¼
Ben H. b g, 1887, by McCurdy's Hambletonian Jr—Old Gal ... 2:16½
Ben H, b s, 1888, by Star Ethan—Merse, by Isham Morgan ... 2:30
Ben H., b g, 1890, by Elyria, dam by Hotspur Jr ... 2:25¼
Ben Haden, ch s, 1885, by Robert Burns—Irene, by Almont Rattler ... 2:30
Ben Hulett, b s, 1882, by Louis Napo-

leon—Mattie Hulett, by Bay Middle-
ton.... ....:............ 2.26¼
Ben Hur, b s, 188—, by Elial G....... 2.29½
Ben Hur, b s, 1884, by Hambrino—
Pearl, by Hero of Thorndale....... 2 24
Ben Hur, ch g, by Jefferson Prince—
Bobbie, by Bacon's Ethan Allen... 2 29¼
Ben Hur, ch g, 1888, by Howard's
Champion, dam by Golddust ... 2 24¼
Ben K., br g, 1881, by Ozark, dam by
Abdallah Boy.................... 2 27¾
Ben Kinney, b g, 1888—, by Black's
Hambletonian.................. 2 21½
Ben Lambert, ch g, 1883, by Daniel
Lambert—Lady Malcomb.......... 2 27
Ben Lomond Jr., ch s, 1877, by Ben
Lomond, dam by Morgan Sumpter
(dead) 2 27
Ben McClellan, ch g, by Drew Horse
(dead) 2 30
Ben Morrill, br s, 1868, by Winthrop
Morrill, dam by Columbus........ 2.27
Benny B., ch g, 1888, by Butler's Ba-
shaw—Alfarata, by Somonauk 2 24
Benny O., b g, 1888, by Indianapolis
Jr—Clipper, by Albert........... 2.22½
Benoni, b s, 1886 by Pretender—
Sport, by Onward............... 2.22½
Ben-no-nie, b s, 1884, by Joe Gavin—
Napoleon Maid, by Louis Napoleon. 2.25
Ben S, b g, 1886, by Indiaman, dam
by Hampton 2 25
Ben Smith, gr g, 186—, by Young
Columbus, dam by Vermont Hamb.e-
tonian...................... 2 27
Ben Star, b g, 1876, by Tom Hazzard
—Dolly Buxton, by John Richards
Jr (pacing record 2.19¼) (dead) .. 2 21¾
Benteer, b g, 1886, by Kentucky Vol-
unteer—Ben Bay, by Ben Lomond Jr 2 30
Benton, b s, 1885, by Gen Benton—
America, by Rysdyk's Hambletonian 2:20¾
Bentoneer, b s, 1885, by Gen Benton
—Guess, by Electioneer 2 28½
Benton M, ch s, 1888, by Gov. Benton
Sadie M., by Dauntless.......... 2 16¼
Benton Wilkes, b s, 1889, by Alcone—
Jessie Benton, by Jim Scott....... 2 22
Ben V., b s, 1886, by Red Wilkes—
Rena C., by Messenger Chief....... 2 29½
Ben Wallace, b g, 1886, by Hamenger
—Nettie, by Mambrino Pilot Jr . . 2.19¼
Ben Williams, b g, 18— (Inger?), by
Iron Duke? 2 29¼
Ben Wilkes, blk g, 188—, by Defender,
dam by Motion 2 26
Ben Wright, br s, 1879, by Royal
Fearnaught—Mag Peterson, by Mas-
terlode 2:30
Benzoni, b s, 1891, by St Bel—Beulah
West, by Abdallah West.. ..... 2.30
Berceto, ch s, 1890, by Antevolo—
Nelly Rose, by Sacramento 2.29
Bergen, b g, 1877, by Messenger
Duroc — Belle of Richmond, by
Rysdyk's Hambletonian 2.26¾
Berkshire Belle, b m, 1886, by Alcyone
—Belle Brasfield, by Viley's Cripple. 2:22¼
Bermuda, bl s, 1883, by Banker—Pat-
tie Patchen, by Mambrino Patchen 2.20¼
Bermuda Boy, ro s, 1889, by Bermuda
—Baby Mine, by Stonewall Jackson. 2 20¾
Bermuda Girl, br m, 1892, by Ber-
muda—Annie McKee, by Red Wilkes 2·21¼
Bermuda Chief, b s, 188—, by C. F
Clay—Juanita, by Messenger Chief 2:29¼
Berna Dotte, b s, 1890, by Wilton—
Mary Morn, by Hambrino.......... 2:29½
Bernal, b s, 188—, by Electioneer—Re-

becca, by Gen, Benton............ 2 17
Bernice Medium, blk m, 1891, by
Riley Medium 2:27¾
Berry, bl s, 188—, by Delmarch. .. 2 26¼
Bert B, ch g, 1881, by Dan Brown—
Flora S., by Zero. 2:29½
Bertha, b m, 1884, by Egmont—Polka
Dot, by Senator Madden.......... 2:29¼
Bertha, ch m, 1877, by Blue Bull—
Kit, by Wolf Cockspur 2.23¼
Bertha, br m, 1879, by Hambletonian
Downing—Belle Clay, by Strader's
Cassius M Clay Jr 2 27¼
Bertha C, ch m, 188—, by Warlock... 2 29¼
Bertha C., ch m, 187—, pedigree not
traced 2:30
Bertha D, blk m, 1890, by Durango,
dam by Fairy Gift.... ..... 2 22½
Eertha Clay, bl m, 1874, by Henry
Clay Jr—Rosekranz, by Edwin Fo-
rest . ... 2·30
Berthard, b m, 1880, by St Gothard—
Grace Bertram, by New Jersey. 2 29
Bertha S, b m, 1878, by Bonnie Bay
—Belle of Cayuga, by Post's Ham-
bletonian Prince.............. 2 29¼
Bertie, gr m, 1867, by Blue Bull, dam
by Tom Crowder............... 2 27
Bertie Girl, b m, 1889, by Jay Bird—
Kate, by Abdalbrino 2:23¾
Bertie M, gr m, 188—, by Iowa Chief. 2:27¼
Bertie R., b m, 1888, by Wilkomont—
Red, by Red Eagle 2 15¼
Bettie Sprague, b m, 188—, by Gov.
Sprague 2 24
Bertnot, br g, 188—, by Billy Wilkes 2 29¾
Bert Oliver, b s, 1889, by Ashland
Wilkes—Ione Wilkes, by Red Wilkes 2 19¼
Bertrace, b m, 1871, by Rysdyk—Polly
Barber, by Bully King 2.27½
Bertrace Patchen, br m, 1885, by Sen-
eca Patchen—Bertrace, by Rysdyk.. 2 29
Bertrina, br m, 1885, by Jerome Eddy
— Miss Bryant, by Mambrino
Patchen 2 23
Bert Sheldon, br g, 187—, by War-
wick Boy—Cole, by Priestman.... 2 29¼
Bert Sheldon Jr, blk g, 1883, by War-
wick Boy—Cole, by Priestman. .. 2:16¼
Burwick, b g, 188—, by Ned Wilkes,
dam by Lambert Chief 2 30
Berwick Boy, gr g, 1884, by Pilot
Medium—Sparta Girl (dead) ... 2:24½
Besor, b g, 1877, by Bartholomew
Wilkes — Puss Cook, by Mambrino
Clay 2 28¾
Bess, ch m, 1887, by Elmo—Miss Mor-
rill, by Winthrop Morrill......... 2.29¼
Bessie, ch m, 1876, by Blue Bull—Os-
burn 2 17½
Bessie, br m, 1875, by Marmaduke—
Fanny 2.26¼
Bessie, b m 1881, by Ben Franklin—
Gypsy, by Bay Lambert 2 29¾
Bessie Allen, b m, 1888, by Dresden—
Fanny Parvin, by Green's Bashaw.. 2:26½
Bessie Bell, g m, by Green's St. Bel—
Belle D, by Dempsey's Belmont... 2:29¾
Bessie Benton, ch m, 1888, by Gov.
Benton—Dolly Varden by Clarence 2 26¾
Bessie Burton, b m, 1885, by Nut-
wood—Motto, by Cuyler.......... 2 22½
Bessie C., ch m, 1881, by Red Wilkes
—Belle, by Stockbridge Duke 2 30
Bessie C, bl m, claimed to be Old
Maid, by Monogram 2 29¼
Bessie Cecil, br m, 1888 by Gulvallis
Lucy Cecil, by Driftwood 2 29½
Bessie Chimes, b m, 1889 by Chimes

dam by Hamlin's Almont Jr....... 2:27½
Bessie D., b m, 188—, by Aberdeen.. 2:20
Bessie F., br. m, 1886, by Athlete—Lady Graves (dead) 2:29½
Bessie G., br m, 1878, by Almont Boy—Bird, by Stansifer's Clay 2:25½
Bessie H., b m, 188—, by Abraham.. 2.25¼
Bessie Jordan, b m, 1891, by Gambetta—Lucy's Last, by Danville Wilkes 2:25¼
Bessie M., b m, 187—, by Messenger Chief—Lady Elgin 2:30
Bessie P., bl m, 1884, by Lumps—Nettie Howell, by Ashland Chief 2:29½
Bessie R., b m, 188—, by Webb's Hambletonian Bashaw 2:29½
Bessie R., b m, 188—, by France.... 2:25¼
Bessie S., b m, 1884, by Prince Albert, dam by Vick's Ethan Allen Jr..... 2:29¼
Bessie S., b m, 188—, by Clayford.. 2:26
Bessie Sheridan, bl m, 1879, by Phil Sheridan—Puss 2:23½
Bessie Thorne br m, 188—, by Hawthorne—Bessie Sedgwick by Joe Daniels 2:22½
Bessie Trego, ch m, 1889, by Trego—Preston Mare, by Frankfort Chief.. 2:26½
Bessie W., ch m, 188—, by Como 2:28¾
Bessie Wilkes, bl m, 1886, by Sealskin Wilkes—Iette, by Mambrino Patchen 2:24
Bessie Wilkes, b m, 1884, by Young Wilkes—Bessie, by Bristol.......... 2:29¾
Bessie Wilkes, b m, 1886, by Wilkes Boy—Lucy Thorn, by Mambrino Thorne 2:29¼
Bessie Wilkes, b m, 1889, by Major Fowler—Ella Wilkes, by Red Wilkes 2:24¼
Bessie Wilkeswood, ch m, 1889, by Wilkeswood—Silkie A., by Golden Bow 2:20
Best Way bl g, 1891, by Prince Red—Claypso, by Steinway............. 2:29¾
Bethel, b m, 1885, by Beauclerc—Nelly K., by Black Ranger............. 2:16¼
Bethlehem King, br s, 1887, by The King—Lena Gist, by Almont Sentinel 2:24¼
Bethlehem Star, b s, 1882, by Volunteer Star—Grey Eaglet, by Dick Hambletonian 2:20¾
Betina, b m, 188—, by Egbert 2:29¼
Bet Madison, b m, 1891, by James Madison—Betsy Trotwood, by Abbottsford 2:30
Betsey Ann, ch m, 187—, by Hoagland Horse, dam by Marshall Chief 2:22½
Betsey Baker, b m, 1879, by Dictator—Mother Hubbard, by Johnston's Toronto 2:30
Betsy Belle, b m, 1890, by Belmont—Betsy Baker, by Dictator........... 2:28¼
Betsey Braun, bl m, 1881, by Masterlode—Minnie, by Winthrop Morrill.. 2:21¾
Betsy Britton, br m, 1888, by Egotist—Crepon, by Princeps 2:20¾
Betsy C., b m, by Mohawk Hambletonian 2:25¾
Betsy Cotton, rn, m, 1886, by Jay Bird—Flora Pilot 2:16¾
Betsy Trotwood, bl m, 1883, by Atlantic 2.26½
Betterman, ch g, 188—, by Betterton 2:27¼
Betty, b m, 1887, by Dictator Chief—Annie by Nelson's Onward 2.28¼
Betty B., b m, 1873, by Enfield Jr.—Midnight by Crim's Black Hawk .. 2·29¼
Betty Battle, b m, 188—, by Jessie James 2:28½
Betty Jones, b m, 1880, by Abdallah Mambrino—Charlotte, by John Bright 2:19½
Betty K., ch m, 1881, by Mambrino Lexington—Nelly .... 2·26¼
Betty King, b m, 1890, by Betterton—Mambrino Beauty, by Mambrino King .... 2·23¼
Betty Mac, ch m, 188—, by Abdallah Mambrino .... 2·29
Beulah, b m, 188—, by La Crosse.... 2 26¾
Beulah, b m, 188—, by Onawa ..... 2·26
Beulah, ro m, 1880 by William Rysdyk—Curiosity, by Enquirer 2 29¼
Beulah, b m, 1882, by Gen. Knox—Lucia, by Jay Gould.............. 2·19½
Beulah C., ch m, 1891, by Badger Clay, dam by Gov. Wilkes (dead) (pacing record 2:28½) 2:27
Beuzetta, b m, 1891, by Onward—Beulah, by Harold ....
Beverly, br, s, 1890, by Sable Wilkes Huntress, by Arthurton 2:24½
Belwilder, b g, by Baywood 2:28½
Bezant, b s, 1885, by Chichester—Bicara, by Harold 2:21½
Bezant Rule, b s, 1889, by Bezant—Kate Kelly, by Backman's Idol 2 30
B. F. Solon, br s, 188—, by Glenalen 2 22
B G., gr m, 188—, by Plumstone 2.24½
B. G., b m, 188—, by Puritan .... 2·27½
Biwabic, b s, 1892, by Bezant 2 28½
Bianca, b m, 1889, by Hampshire—Echo, by Don J. Robinson 2:29¼
Bianca, b m, 1888, by Brown Wilkes Nicotera, by Nugget (dead) 2.19¼
Bickford, dn g, 186—, by Black Chief dam by Gen. Taylor 2 29¼
Biddy B., b m, 188— by Amboy 2 26¼
Biddy Boru, bl m., 1882, by Iowa Star Railroad Maid, by Bonner 2 26¼
Biddy Donovan, b m, 1887, by Allie Wilkes—Kit, by Yankee Dan (dead) 2.27
Bifty Duck, b m, 1889, by Bezant—Bay Duck, by Guide 2.25
Big Ben, b s, 188—, by Confederate Chief—Maid of Beverly, by Jupiter Abdallah 2.28¼
Big Bone, gr g, 188—, by Gambetta .. 2:23½
Big Brown Jug, br g, 1885, by Referee—Lilly, by Doble 2 29½
Big Charley, b g, 1884, by St. James—Cynthiana, by Goldsmith Boy 2.23¼
Big F., b g, 1883, by Broken Leg—Myers Mare 2:16½
Big Fanny, bl m, 1879, by John E. Rysdyk—Mag, by Davis' Black Hawk Morgan 2 26¼
Big Fellow, br g, 1865, by Edward Everett 2:23½
Big Four, ch g, by Hambletonian Mambrino 2.26¼
Big Fox, b s, 1889, by Onslaught—Kapiolani, by Mainspring 2.22½
Big Frank, b g, 1880, by Sultan—Gibson Mare 2:30
Big Ike, gr g 1873, by Nick Wall—Daisy Looker 2 29¼
Big Jim, b g, 1881, by Gen Benton,—Dame Winnie, by Planet 2:23¼
Big John, b g, 187—, by Pilot Duroc 2·24¼
Big Lize, b m, 1873, by George M. Patchen Jr.—Long Island Maid, by a son of Long Island Black Hawk.. 2·24¼
Big Mc., b s, 1886, by McMahon—Molly Good, by Blue Bull 2:25¾
Big Rock, b g, by Little Rock ...... 2·29¼
Big Soap, b g, 1870, by Honesty—

Betty ... 2:23
Bijou, b m, 188— by Fred Arnold ... 2 24
Bijou, br g, 1878, by Abdallah Messenger—McNeil Mare, by Farmer's Glory ... 2 24½
Bill Cody, br s, 1886 by Sprague—Fanny Bright, by John Bright ... 2.29
Bill Ed, b g, 186—, by Gen. Washington (dead) ... 2.28
Bill Granger, b g, 1888, by Hambletonian Wilkes—Linnie, by Tom Hunter ... 2.26
Bill Lindsay, gr g, 1889, by Vasco—Albino, by Albion ... 2:17½
Bill Thunder, b g, 1864, by Robin Clay—Betsey Thunder, by Alexander's Abdallah, (dead) ... 2 25
Bill of Expense, b g, 188—, by Hambletonian's Last ... 2 27½
Billy, ch g, 185—, pedigree not traced (dead) ... 2 30
Billy, br g, 1871, by Victor Denmark—Kate Bradley, by Clifton Pilot ... 2:29¼
Billy, bl g, 188—, by Durango ... 2:23¾
Billy A., b g, 1884, by Bay Tom Jr.—Fidele, by Gibson's Tom Hal ... 2:13¼
Billy Acker, b g, 1881, by Squire Talmage—Sally Fox, by Seniours' Davy Crocket ... 2 24½
Billy Allen, b g, 188—, by Bacon's Ethan Allen ... 2·27
Billy B, b g, 188—, pedigree not traced 2 27½
Billy B., gr g, 1883, by Artemas—Blue Mare, by Combination ... 2:23¼
Billy B, b s, 1887, by Little Billy—Belle Harris, by Billy Cook ... 2.19¼
Billy Bachelor, br g, 1883, by Buckeye Chief ... 2 21½
Billy Barefoot, bl g, 1866, by King Herod, dam by Young Green Mountain Morgan (dead) ... 2·28½
Billy Barr, dn g, 185—, by Ethan Allen (dead) ... 2 23¾
Billy Bashaw, ch s 1881, by Golden Star—Jenny, by Black Flying cloud 2·29½
Billy Bashaw, bl g, 188—, by Harry Bashaw ... 2 28½
Billy Bell, b g, by Red Wilkes—Lucy by Royal George ... 2·25¾
Billy Beverly, bl g, 188—, by Jerry—Jule ... 2 21
Billy Bird, ro s, 1887, by Jay Bird—Emma G., by Almont ... 2 26¼
Billy Blackburn, b g, 188—, by Joe Blackburn ... 2 26½
Billy Bolton, br g, 188—, by Almont Pilot ... 2:15¾
Billy Boy, b g, 187—, by Mambrino Temple—Mary Harney, by St. Lawrence Jr. ... 2 26¼
Billy Burr b g, 187—, by Walkill Chief ... 2·29½
Billy Burton, b g, 1883, by Gypsy Boy—Lady Burdett ... 2 25¼
Billy Button, b g, 188—, by Alexander Button ... 2 27
Billy Button, ch g, 1876 by Baird's Hambletonian Prince—Logan Maid, by Page's Logan ... 2·18¼
Billy C b g, 188—, by Volley ... 2 23¼
Billy C, b g, by Middletown Jr, dam by Gen Benton ... 2·20¼
Billy Cramer, b s, 1886, by Egmont—Hattie M., by Flaxtail ... 2 26¼
Billy D, b g, by Tarantalus ... 2.21¼
Billy D, b g 187—, by Squire Talmage—Lucy Pilot, by Roscoe Jr ... 2 17½
Billy D, b g, 188—, by Tempest ... 2 18½
Billy D, b g, 187—, by Daniel Lambert—Capt. Moore's Mary, by Mazeppa ... 2 26
Billy D., blk g, pedigree and history not recorded ... 2:26¼
Billy Dayton, b g, 187—, by Archy Mambrino, dam by Black Hawk 2d 2 27¼
Billy Dolan, b g, 188—, by Golden Seal 2.27
Billy Dow, b g, 186—, pedigree not traced (dead) ... 2·27
Billy F., b g, 1887, by Morgmont ... 2.22¼
Billy F., b g, 188—, by Dandy Boy ... 2·24¼
Billy F., br g, 1881, by Mike Logan ... 2.28¾
Billy Ford ch g, 187—, by Blondin—O'Brien Mare ... 2:26¼
Billy Freer, gr g, 1879, by Western Fearnaught—Grey Nell ... 2·24¼
Billy G., b g, 188—, by Brilliant Golddust—Ryestraw ... 2.17¼
Billy G., b g, 1886, by Hotspur Chief—Winnie ... 2.27¼
Billy Gaines br g, 1885, by Allie Gaines—Fan ... 2.23
Billy H., br g 188—, by Dick Executor ... 2 28
Billy H., b g, 1885, by Don Pedro dam by Donerail ... 2 27¼
Billy H, br g, 1884, by Mambrino Dick—Dolly ... 2 29¼
Billy Hoskins, gr g, 1861, by Edwin Forrest—Santa Maria, by Pilot Jr. (dead) ... 2 26¼
Billy Holmes, b s, 188— by Black Douglas ... 2 27
Billy Hustler, b g, 188—, by Charles Caffrey—Nanny, by Long Island Chief ... 2 27
Billy Hood, ch g ... 2 25¾
Billy K, ch g, 188—, by Rysdyk ... 2 25¾
Billy I, blk g, 187—, by Harry Knox, dam by Beale's Horse ... 2:29¾
Billy L., b g, 187—, pedigree and history unknown ... 2:28¼
Billy L., br g, 1889, by Platte—Flora L. by Jack Bambol ... 2:13¾
Billy Lambertson, b g, 186—, by Cloud Mambrino—Fox, by Farmer (dead) ... 2 28¼
Billy Leach, b g, 1882, by Strang's Joker—Kit ... 2 29¾
Billy M., b, s, 188—, pedigree not traced ... 2 25
Billy McGregor rn g, 188—, by Fergus McGregor ... 2 28¼
Billy Marshall, bl g, 1877, by Mambrino Patchen—Maggie Marshall, by Bradford's Telegraph ... 2·27½
Billy Mack, ch g, 1879, by Burger, dam by Golddust ... 2 19
Billy McGregor, ro s, 188—, by Robt. McGregor ... 2 28¼
Billy McGregor, b s, 1883, by McGregor Chief—Madam Kirkwood Jr., by Captain ... 2·21½
Billy McMahon, ch g, 1886, pedigree not traced ... 2·25
Billy Miller, b s, 1886, by George Miller—Nellie German, by Satellite ... 2·26½
Billy Mitchell, br g, 1884, by C. W. Mitchell—Wild Duck, by Pearsall ... 2 28¾
Billy Oaks, gr s, 188—, by John Sevenoaks ... 2 30
Billy O'Neil, b g, 186—, pedigree not traced (dead) ... 2·27
Billy Parks, gr s, 1891, by Dauntless—Cleopatra, by War Call ... 2·26½
Billy Platter, gr g, 186—, pedigree not traced (dead) ... 2·26

CHARLES MARVIN, MEADVILLE, PA.

(THE MAN IN GRAY.)

Marvin cut the world's record for trotters to 2:08¼ with Sunol, the
world's record for trotting stallions to 2:15¼ with Smuggler and 2:08¾ with Palo Alto, and the two-
year-old record for trotters to 2:10¾.

R. CURTIS, Greendale, Ky.

(THE STUDENT.)

The young man who was out with Pamlico 2:10,
David B. 2:10½ and Miss Nelson 2:12¾.

Billy Q. (Columbus), b g, 1875, by
Bayard—Flora, by Blanco 2 29½
Billy R., b s, 188—, by Billy Stranger. 2 29¼
Billy R., gr g, 188—, by Young Volun-
teer 2 24½
Billy R, b g, 1873, by Clay Pilot—
Fanny, by Seely's American Star 2 25½
Billy Ray, ro g, 186—, by Wood's
Hambletonian (dead) 2.23¾
Billy Red, b s, 1889, by Red Wilkes—
Columbia, by Dixon 2:28½
Billy Rysdyk, bl s, 1878, by William
Rysdyk—Lady Annie, by Henry B.
Patchen 2.27½
Billy S, b g, 1874, by Regulus, dam by
Tillott's Hambletonian 2:28¼
Billy Shedd, b s, 188—, by J. R. Shedd 2.30
Billy Terrill, b g, 1880, by W P Max-
well—Birdie Clay, by Terrill's Clay. 2 28¼
Billy Thomas 2:25¾
Billy Thomas, gr g, 1888, by Kellar
Thomas—Double Lick, by Mambrino
Templar Jr. 2 23
Billy Thornhill, b s, 1884, by Beverly
Wilkes—Emily, by George Wilkes. 2 24½
Billy Tompkins, b s, 1883, by Gen
George H Thomas—Ella, by Enfield 2·21½
Billy W, gr g, ... 2.25¼
Billy W, br g, 188—, by Antar 2 25¾
Billy Warren, b g, 188—, by Albert. 2.24½
Billy White, gr g, 187—, by Maury
Chief 2 28½
Billy Wilkes, br s, 1880, by Harry
Wilkes—Dora Seldon, by Clark Chief 2·20¼
Billy Wilkes, b g, 1882, by Georgia
Wilkes—Miller Mare .... 2·20¼
Billy Wilton, bl s, 1889, by Wilton—
Patchen Lass, by Mambrino Patchen 2.20
Billy Woods, ro s, 1884, by Wood's
Hambletonian—Fan 2 20½
Billy Worthington, gr s, 1883, by
Roger Hanson—Rushville Maid, by
Blue Bull 2 27¼
Billy Young, bl s, 188—, by Joe Young. 2.29¼
Bion, br s, 1890, by Gen Beverly—Lu-
laneer, by Piedmont 2 24¾
Bud, br m, 1882, by Starlight—Topsy,
by Frank Forrester 2 22
Bird Allerton, ch m, 1889, by Allerton
—Bird, by Mambrino Royal 2.20½
Bud Button, gr s, 188—, by Alexander
Button—Lettie, by John Nelson 2 29¾
Birdseye, ch m, 1889, by Fred—Queen 2 29½
Birdie, b m, 1888, by Egotist—Ber-
nice, by Harold 2 27¾
Birdie, b m, 1884, by Whirlwind Chief
—Splinter, by Beattie's Norman . . 2.28½
Birdie, bl m, 1886, by Sidney—Annie
G, by McClellan Duke 2:28
Birdie C, b m, 1872, by Garibaldi—
Minnie, by Edward Everett 2.28¼
Birdie Egmont, br m, 1884, by Egmont
—Coly Stone, by Black Timoleon. . 2.29
Birdie Ensign, b m, 188—, by Ensign 2 25½
Bird McGregor, ro s, 1887, by Jay
Bird — Crosspatch, by Robert Mc-
Gregor 2 23¼
Bishop Dudley, ch s, 1889, by Egotist
—Belle Dudley, by Belmont . . 2.27
Bishop Hero, b s, 1883, by Bishop—
Lida Kendall, by Hero of Thorndale. 2·24¼
Bismarck, gr g 188—, by Joe Gavin . 2 28
Bismarck, gr g, 1886, by Young Joe. . 2·26¼
Bismarck, ch s, 1873, by Index—Lady
Weeks, by Williamson's Belmont. . 2 29¼
Bismarck, ch s, 1884, by Hirsch Bel-
mont 2 22¼
Bismarck Monroe, b s, 1885, by Victor
Bismarck — Miss Monroe, by Jim

Monroe 2.25
Bismont, b s, 1885, by Victor Bis-
marck—Ducky Almont, by Almont. . 2:18½
Bismuth, b s, 188—, by Bourbon
Wilkes—Spot, by Westwood ...... 2·30
Bismuth, br m, 188—, by Ellerslie
Wilkes 2:23¼
Bither, b s, 1892, by Kremlin—Kan-
taka, by Bay State.............. 2:28¾
Bitter Root, b s, 1890, by Lord Byron
—Easel, by Commodore Belmont.... 2 25
Black Amble, bl g, 1881, by Joe Irving
—Flakey, by Gen. Knox.......... 2 26¼
Black Beauty, blk m, 188—, by Heath-
wood 2 24
Black Bess, blk m, 188—, by Edict. . 2.30
Black Bass, gr m, 1888, by Monroe
Chief—Bessie, by Gibralter 2 25¾
Black Bess, blk m, 188—, by Edict.... 2.30
Black Bess, bl m, 187—, by St. Elmo 2 30
Black Bess, bl m, 1888, by Wellington
—Strathlene 2d, by Strathmore.... 2:22½
Black Bess, bl m, 188—, by Algardia 2.26¼
Black Bird, bl m, 188—, pedigree not
traced 2 29½
Blackbird, bl s, 1862, by Simpson's
Blackbird — Jane Smith, by Capt.
Lightfoot (dead) 2.22
Black Captain, bl s, 1881, by Mazeppa
—Fillie Lawrence, by Robert Bonner 2 29¼
Black Cloud, bl s, 1872, by Ashland
Chief—Mrs Cluke, by Pilot Walker 2:17¼
Black Cloud Jr., bl g, 1876, by Black
Cloud—Nelly Neff 2 25
Black Diamond, bl g, 1878, by Pe-
gasus—Lady Taylor, by Stockbridge
Chief 2 19½
Black Diamond, bl g, 1889, by Scott—
Lady Kale, by Black Damon...... 2:18¾
Black Diamond, bl s, 1879, by Gen.
Lee—Black Bess, by Enterprise 2.20¾
Black Diamond, bl m, 1877, by Dicta-
tor—Puss Prall, by Mark Time..... 2.29¾
Black Dick, bl g, 188—, breeding un-
known 2 27¼
Black Douglass, bl g, 184—, by Henry
Clay (dead) 2 30
Black Frank, bl g, 1860, by Frank—
Becky (dead) 2 23¼
Black Frank, bl g, 186—, by Pony
Frank (dead) 2.30
Black Frank (Frank), bl g, 186—, by
Wild Wagoner 2 24½
Black Frank, bl s, 188—, by Mam-
brino Swigert 2:27¼
Black George, bl g, 188—, breeding
unknown 2 30
Black Hal, blk s, 188—, by Onslaught 2·29¼
Black Hawk, bl g, 1890, by Orphan
Boy—Dolly R., by Billy R........ 2·20¼
Black Hawk McGregor, g·s 1883, by
Robert McGregor—Lizzie Drew, by
Grey Eagle (Blind Eagle) 2:28
Black Ide, bl m, 1882, by Cyclone—
Madam Beatty, by Monroe Chief .. 2.17
Black Jack, bl g, 1882, by Sweep-
stakes—Emma, by Wilkins Micawber 2.22¼
Black Jim, bl g, 188—, by Reconstruc-
tion 2:20¾
Black Joe, bl s, 1883, by Black Frank
—Mag Kern, by Nichols' Tempest 2 29½
Black Joe, bl s, 1886, by Altitude—
Lottie Lee, by Herman D. Patchen.. 2:27¼
Black Johnny, bl g, 187—, pedigree
not traced 2.30
Black Jug, bl g, 1875, by Bonnie Scot-
land—Miss Drum, by Black Morgan 2:27¼
Black King, bl s, 1886, by The King—
Toddie, by Pilot Mambrino. 2 29¼

Goldie, by Mambrino King ... 2.22¾
Blue Bell, ch m, 187—, by Blue Bull, dam by Bennett's Red Oak ... 2.26¼
Blue Bell, b m, 188—, by Tramp ... 2.30
Blue Bell, ch m, by Overseer ... 2.30
Blue Bells, blk m, 1887, by Quartermaster—Belle Medium, by Fairview Chief ... 2:18¼
Blue Blood, b s, 1888, by Baron Wilkes—Mary A. Whitney, by Volunteer ... 2.22¾
Blue Bug, br s, 1888, by Brignoli Wilkes—Lady Schofield, by Blue Bull 2.21¾
Blue Bull (Grove's), blk s, 1878, by Blue Bull — Myra Shaw, by Tom Lang (dead) ... 2.26¼
Blue Charley, gr g, 1884, by Wapsie—Fanny Munger, by Panic ... 2.22
Blue Cloud, ro g, 1876, by Ashland Chief—Belle Clay, by American Clay 2.27
Bluecoast, br s, 1887, by Pancoast—Young Maid of Erin, by Blue Bull . 2.29¼
Blue Dawn, ro s, 1888, by Jay Bird—Widow's Mite, by Waveland Chief .. 2.21½
Blue Dick, ro s, 1883, by Pretender—Fanny, by Dougherty's Rob Roy ... 2.30
Blue Grass Hambletonian, b s, 1883 by Victor Bismarck—Hamletta, by Hamlet ... 2.19¾
Blue Grass Maid, br m, 1884, by Dictator, dam by Long Island Bashaw. 2.30
Blue Jay, ro g, 187—, by Ben Lomond Emma, by Tom Hal ... 2.29¼
Blue Jay, ro s, 1887, by Jay Bird, dam by son of Honest Allen ... 2:29¾
Blue John, ro g, 1884, by Young Rolfe 2.26¼
Bluelight, gr g, 188—, pedigree not traced ... 2.26¼
Blue Mare, ro m, 186—, by Wood's Hambletonian—Betts (dead) ... 2.23
Blue Knight, ch g, 1890, by Happy Day, dam by Blue Bull ... 2.23
Blue Prince, blk s, 188—, by Blue Blood ... 2.26
Blue Queen, br m, 1889, by Blue Blood—Jessie ... 2.29¼
Blue Stem, b s, 1889, by Damo—Nancy B., by Richmont ... 2.28
Blue Wing, ro m, 1883 by Jay Bird—Ella Clay, by Springfield ... 2.29¾
Bluewood, dn s, 1886, by Tom Kirkwood—Belle Hamilton, by Hamblehawk ... 2.24½
Boabdil, blk s, 1890, by Bermuda—Carrie Mack, by Champ Ferguson .. 2.23¼
Boaz, b s, 1884, by Onward—Ruth, by Pasacas ... 2.17½
Bob, ch g, 1882, by Rob Roy McGregor—Kate, by Little Johnny 2.30
Bob, b g, 188—, pedigree not traced 2.26¾
Bob Acres, ch g, 1876, by Honest Allen—Caro Nomo, by Rysdyk's Hambletonian ... 2.28½
Bob Allen, ch s, 188—, by Judge Salisbury ... 2.27¼
Bob Burdette, b s, 187—, by Ensign—Lady Stowe by a son of Henry Clay ... 2.30
Bob Curtis, br s, 1887, by Bob Sprague—Bird, by Billy Shaker ... 2.23¼
Bob Ford, b g, 188—, by Rocky Ford . 2:28¼
Bob Henderson, gr g, 1883, by Sacramento—Belle ... 2:29¼
Bob Johnson, b g, 187—, by Hero of Thorndale ... 2.28¼
Bob's Jug br g, 1877, by George Wilkes—Amiability, by Honest Allen 2.22¾
Bob M. b g, 1882, by Orange Duroc—Lady May, by Marshal Ney ... 2.26¼
Bob Mason, b s, 1879, by Echo—Belle Mason, by Williamson's Belmont .. 2.27¼
Bob Mason Jr., b s, 188—, by Bob Mason, dam by Inca ... 2.27½
Bob Pinkerton, br g, 1880, by Polonius — Zelipha, by Rysdyk's Hambletonian ... 2.30
Bob Sprague, b s, 1877, by Gov. Sprague—Kitty Lyons, by Honest Abe ... 2.24¼
Bob Swigert, b s, 1885, by Swigert—Merrimac, by Richard's Bellfounder. 2.26½
Bobby Howard, b s, 1886, by Circulator—Lady Frankfort, by Frankfort Chief ... 2.30
Bodine, b g, 1865, by Volunteer, dam by Harry Clay ... 2.19¼
Bogardus, b g, 1886, by Lebel, dam by Stephen A. Douglas ... 2.29¼
Bohemian, b m, 1887, by Onward—Kansas, by William Rysdyk ... 2.22½
Bohemian Boy, b g, 1888, by Pilot Medium, dam by Beby Horse ... 2.24½
Bolly Lewis, b g, 185—, by Seely's American Star (dead) ... 2.29½
Bomba, br m, 1884, by Beverly Wilkes—Jenny, by Messenger Duroc ... 2.29¼
Bon Accord, b s, 1885, by Dictator—Mazourka, by Administrator ... 2.26
Bon Ami, b m, 1889, by Nugget—Thorndale Princess, by Thorndale .. 2.23¾
Bonanza, ch s, 1883, by Arthurton—Sister, by John Nelson ... 2.29½
Bon Bon, b m, 1886, by Fieldmont—Ellen Belle, by Mambrino Patchen 2.29¾
Bon Bon, b m, 1884, by Simmons—Bonnie Wilkes, by George Wilkes ... 2.26
Boneset, blk g, 1891, by Don Marvin—Nelly Bly, by Alpheus ... 2.27½
Bonesetter, b s, 1870, by Brooks—Jenny, by Stump the Dealer (dead) 2.19
Bonhomme, b m, 1887, by Red Wilkes—Venus Almont, by Star Almont ... 2.17¼
Boniface, b s, 1880, by Altorf—Wyandot Queen, by Greever's Mambrino Chief ... 2.22½
Boniface, blk, 188—, by Baron Wilkes, dam by Happy Medium ... 2.29¾
Bonita, b m, 1879, by Electioneer—Mayfly, by St. Clair ... 2.18½
Bon Mot, b m, 1886, by Baron Wilkes—Mary A. Whitney, by Volunteer .. 2.25¼
Bonner, ch g, 1867, by Star of Catskill, dam by Skenandoah ... 2.23
Bonner Boy, b g, 1868, by Gill's Vermont ... 2.23
Bonner N. B., b s, 1888, by Daly—Nancy, by Gen. McClellan ... 2.17
Bonner Steele, gr g, 188—, by Steele . 2.30
Bonnibel, b m, 1890, by Azmoor—Bonnie, by Gen. Benton ... 2.17¾
Bonnie, br m, 1879, by Gen. Benton—America, by Rysdyk's Hambletonian ... 2.25
Bonnie A., b m 1887 by Stanley—Bon Doon, by Legal Tender Jr. ... 2.25½
Bonnie Annie, b m, 1883, by Rooker—Blink Bonnie, by New York Black Hawk ... 2.26¼
Bonnie Dean, gr s, 1889, by Aberdeen—Bonnie Belle, by Almont ... 2.30
Bonnie Donne, b m, 1886, by Rooker—Blink Bonnie, by New York Black Hawk ... 2.29¼
Bonnie F., gr s, 1889, by Willie McMahon—Cricket, by Grundy ... 2.26
Bonnie G., br m, 188—, by Regulator 2.28
Bonnie Josie, ch m 1887, by Bonnycastle—Josie Logan, by Joe Logan. 2.24½

Bonnie L., ch g, 1876, by Charley B.—Juliet, by Cayuga Star........... 2:27¼
Bonnie McGregor, b s, 1879, by Robert McGregor—Fanny, by Reconstruction 2:13½
Bonnie M. George, br s, 1886, by William H. Vanderbilt—Brown Nib, by Lovejoy's Flying Cloud 2:30
Bonnie Mack, b s, 1886, by Bonnie McGregor—Malvina, by Fearnaught Spy.................................. 2:20¼
Bonnie Medium, blk m.................. 2:27¼
Bonnie Nutwood, b s, 1887, by Nutwood—Bonnie Wilkes, by George Wilkes 2:29¼
Bonnie Phallas, b s, 1888, by Phallas—Bonnie Doon, by Aberdeen.......... 2:29
Bonnie S., br s, 1892, by Bonnie McGregor 2:30
Bonnie Wilkes, ro m, 188—, by Adrian Wilkes........................ 2:15¾
Bonnie Wilkes, br m, 1876, by George Wilkes—Betty Viley, by Bob Johnson 2:29½
Bonnie Wilmore, b s, 1886, by Wilmore—Molly R., by imp. Bonnie Scotland 2:14½
Bonny Bon, br m, 188—, by Director, dam by George Wilkes............. 2:29¾
Bon Ton, br s, 1886, by Richwood—Louisiana 2:29¾
Bon Ton, br m, 1890, by Wilton—Belle Bowen, by Richelieu.......... 2:28½
Boodle, b s, 1886, by Stranger—Bride, by Jay Gould 2:19¼
Boone Wilson, gr s, 1887, by Jim Wilson, dam by Daniel Boone (pacing 2:13) 2:20½
Booth-Barrett, br s, 1890, by Ross S., dam by Sultan.................... 2:29½
Borden, ch s, 1885, by Cuyler—Silence, by Alexander's Abdallah..... 2:24¾
Borden, ch g, 1884, by Mansfield—Coralie, by Rysdyk's Hambletonian. 2:29½
Border Wilkes, b s, 188—, by Jay Bird—Lizzie Mills, by Homer 2:25½
Boreal, b s, 1892, by Bow Bells—Rosy Morn, by Alcantara 2:17¼
Borneo, b s, 1889, by Sphinx—Judea, by Mambrino Archy 2:23
Bosque Bonita, b m, 1885, by Thomas K.—Susie W. 2:26¼
Boss, b g, 188—, by Gladiator, dam by Consternation 2:29¼
Boss H., b g, 187—, by Emulus, dam by Seely's American Star 2:25¼
Boston, b g, 1873, by Daniel Lambert—Flyaway, by Patrick Henry 2:27¾
Boston, b g, 188—, by Don Wilkes .. 2:26¼
Boston, ch s, 188—, by Orient—Hattie Lewis, by Forrest Chief 2:29½
Boston Davis, blk g, 1874, by Atlantic Chief—Fly, by Black Flying Cloud 2:26½
Boston Girl, b m, 1877, by Gideon—Stickney, by Gen. Sherman 2:25¼
Boston Globe, ch s, 1886, by Red Wilkes—Lizzie H., by Star Almont.. 2:24
Boulanger, blk s, 1886, by Mambrino Startle—Kate West, by Enterprise 2:28½
Bouncer, b m, 1891, by Hummer—Musette, by Mambrino Patchen ... 2:18½
Bourbon Russell, b s, 1884, by Mambrino Russell—Steinette, by Steinway 2:30
Bourbon Wilkes Jr., ch s, 1886, by Bourbon Wilkes—Ashurst mare, by Black Prince 2:12¼
Bow Bells, b s, 1887, by Electioneer—Beautiful Bells, by The Moor 2:19¼
Bowman, b s, 1881, by Mambrino Paris—Belle B., by Green's Bashaw 2:30
Boxwood, ch s, 188—, by Hull 2:26
Boy Blue, ro g, 1880, by Grove's Blue Bull, dam Topsy, by Blue Bull 2:23¼
Boy Blue, blk s, 1889, by Chimes—Bobolink, by Mambrino King 2:25¼
Boyer, blk s, 1888, by Rumor—Bijou, by Gen. Knox 2:29¼
Bozeman, b s, 188—, by Mambrino King, dam by Hamlin's Almont Jr. 2:17
Bracelet, b m, 1879, by Auditor—Olio, by Dick Hambletonian 2:25
Brad, b g, pedigree not traced 2:23½
Bradford, b s, 188—, by Fugleman—Mollie McGregor, by Robert McGregor 2:17¾
Bradstreet, b s, 1887, by Banker—Fanny D., by Star Almont 2:27¼
Bradtmoor, br s, 1888, by Fallis—Ethel H., by Sultan 2:26¼
Bramblette, b m, 1891, by Marvin ... 2:24½
Brandoline, b s, 1886, by Brown Wilkes—Abbess, by Wedgewood .. 2:28½
Brandy Boy, b g, 1876, by Admiral Patchen Jr.—Flower, by Delaware Mingo 2:20¼
Bran Slack, b g, 188—, by Mambrino Hannis 2:27¼
Brantford, b g, 1882, by Little Billy .. 2:29¼
Brava, b m, 1885, by Baron Wilkes—Mary A. Whitney, by Volunteer .. 2:14½
Bravado, br s, 1887, by Kentucky Wilkes—Alicia, by Messenger Duroc 2:16½
Braxton, b s, 18—, by Onward 2:30
Brazil, b s, 1888, by Jorunalist—Fantine, by Altorf 2:16¼
Brazilian, b s, 1889, by Brown Wilkes—Olive, by Lakeland Abdallah 2:24¼
Breadwinner, b s, 1887, by Pancoast—Nelly L., by George Wilkes 2:29¼
Break O'Day, blk m, 1890, by Darknight—Clarion, by Rumor 2:11½
Breastplate, b s, 1884, by Hawthorne—Ryan Mare, by McCracken's Black Hawk 2:23½
Breeze, b g, 1867, by Rysdyk's Hambletonian—Kate, by Bellaire (dead) 2:24
Breeze Medium, b m, 1876, by Happy Medium—Net, by Frank 2:22¼
Brenda, b m, 1886, by Nelson—Elise, by Fearnaught Jr. 2:28¼
Brewster, br s, 1879, by Hotspur Chief—Fashion, by Toronto Chief .. 2:26
Brewster F., br g, 1886, by Brewster Flash, by Marmaduke ... 2:24¼
Brian Boru, b g, 1880, by Iowa Star—Railroad Maid, by Bonner 2:27¾
Bric-a-Brac, gr m, 1889, by Alcazar—Blanche T., by Nephew 2:28½
Bridal Bells, b m, 1889, by Bell Boy—Trousseau, by Nutwood 2:22½
Bridal Gift, br m, 1888, by Ambassador—Silver Gift, by Grand Sentinel 2:28½
Brigadier, (Doty's) b g, 1885, by Brigadier—Maud D., by Challenge 2:29¼
Brigadier, b s, 1873, by Happy Medium—Lady Turner, by Frank Pierce Jr 2:21¼
Brightmarck, b s, 1887, by Victor Bismarck—Lulu Bright, by John Bright 2:24¾
Brightmont, b s, 1883, by Montagu—Brightness, by Pearsall 2:27½
Brighton, ch g, 1873, by Lippincott's Jack Stewart—Lucy 2:28¼
Brighton, b s, 1882, by Brougham—

Flip, by Ti Boy 2:28½
Bright Rattler, br s, 1880, by John Bright—Roxie, by Alexander's Norman 2:19¾
Brightwood, b s, 1884, by Cromwell—Topsey Morgan 2:29½
Brignolia, br s, 1855, by Mambrino Chief—Sally Woodford (dead) 2:29¾
Brignolia, b s, 1883, by Brigadier—Princess 2:29¼
Brignoli Wilkes, br s, 1883, by George Wilkes—Patsey, by Brignoli 2:14½
Brilliant, blk s, 1881, by Swigert—Annie Goldsmith, by Volunteer ... 2:17½
Brilliant, b m, 1883 by Electioneer—Bright Eyes, by General Benton .. 2:23
Brillantine, b m, 1885, by Nutwood—Crepon, by Princeps 2:29½
Brinhild, b m, 1889, by Viking—Daisy Wilkes, by Mambrino Wilkes 2:19¼
Brinker Sprague, br s, 1882, by Governor Sprague—Lizzie Brinker, by Brinker's Drennon 2:28
Briscom, b g, ... 2:28
Bristol Bill, gr g, 186—, pedigree not traced (dead) 2:29
Bristol Girl, b m, 187—, by Jim Ervin, dam by Capt. Walker 2:28¾
Brittle Silver, b g, 1881, by Hamdallah—Belle S., by Star of the West .. 2:25½
Broadway, b s, 1881, by Robert Smith—Volunteer Maid, by Volunteer 2:20½
Brocade, ch s, 1885, by Tramp—Burrie, by Captain.................. 2:28
Brogan, ch s, 1885, by Rolf Duke—Lady, by Australian H. 2:29½
Bromo, br, s, 1886, by Brougham—Belle of Clarence, by Finch's St. Lawrence 2:26
Bronco, b g, 188—, by Defiance 2:26¼
Bronze, b m, 1878, by Morgan Messenger Jr.—Kate, by Christie's Blacksnake 2:21¼
Brookie, b m, 1884, by Knickerbocker—Belle Archer, by Fred Pierson 2:29¼
Brooklawn, b s, 1888, by Chesterwood—Constance, by Hamlet 2:28¼
Brooklyn, br g, 1887, by Lawrence—Lillian Brooks, by Pilot Hutchinson 2:24
Brookside b g, 188—, by West Chester 2:26
Brookside Flora, br m, 1871, by Hamlet 2:29
Broomal, b s, 1888, by Stranger—Brooch, by Jay Gould 2:15
Brother Dan, ch g, 1882, by Joe Bassett—Cary Mare by Swetting's Ned Forrest 2:23½
Brother G., b s, 1887, by Sentinel Wilkes—Sister G., by Mambrino Boy 2:25¼
Brother Jim, b s, 1887, by Intrigue—Minnie, by Windsor 2:22¼
Brother Jonathan, b g, 1862, by Potter Horse, dam by Beattie's Norman (dead) 2:24
Bourbon Belle gr m, 188—, by Bourbon Prince 2:26¾
Brown, br s, 1884, by Combat—Gauntlette, by Dictator 2:18¾
Brown Bess, br m, 1885 by Culpepper Allen—Black Bess, by Cox's Stump the Dealer 2:25½
Brown Billy, br g, 187—, by Corbeau 2:29
Brown Cedar br s, 1887, by Red Cedar—Polly Duck, by Guide 2:22
Brown Daisy, br m, 1886, by Iron Duke, Jr., dam by Filken's Morgan 2:25
Brown Dick, br g, 1888, by St. Cloud—Maud R., by Escort 2:12
Brown Dick, br g, 1866, pedigree not traced (dead) 2:24½
Brown Dick, br g, 1871, by Anthony Wayne—Lucy Mason, by Vermont Hero 2:29¼
Brown Dick, br g, 1849, by son of Selly's American Star, (dead) 2:25¼
Brown Donna, br s, 1890, by Brown Wilkes—Nellie Lambert 2:20¼
Brownie, b g, 188—, by Wilkes 2:24¾
Brown Jim, b g, 1885, by Con—Lettie Miller, by Honest John 2:22½
Brown Jim, br s, 1884, by Voltaire, dam by Lexington Chief 2:27¾
Brown Joe, br g, 1880, by Buck 2:29½
Brown Lace br m, 1889, by Volmer—Point Lace, by King Rene 2:28½
Browmark, br s, 1883, by Victor Bismarck—Lucy Patchen, by Mambrino Boy 2:24
Brown Mat, br m, 188—, by Maximus 2:29¼
Brown Richmond, br s, 188—, by Brown Chief 2.28½
Brown Russell, br s, 1891, by Kentucky Russell—La Mascotte, by Robert McGregor 2:29¼
Brown Silk, br m, 1887, by Baron Wilkes—Nanny Etticoat, by Bellwood 2:22½
Brown Thorne, br g, 188— by Hawthorne 2:27¾
Burnstone, br g, 188—, by Freestone 2:28½
Brown Velvet, br s, 1889, by Vatican—Terrell Mare, by Tommy Wilkes.. 2:28¼
Brown Wilkes, br s, 1876, by George Wilkes—Jenny Irving, by Henry B. Patchen 2:21¾
Bruce, b g, 1884, by Black's Hambletonian—Mitt, by Yeiser's Norman .. 2:27¼
Bruce King, blk s, 1886, by The King—Bertha, by imp. Saxon 2.28¾
Bruno, b s, 1889, by Junio—Dolly, by Mozart 2:19
Bruno, br g, 1861, by Rysdyk's Hambletonian—Kate, by Bellaire 2:29½
Brunswick, b s, 1885, by Walkill Prince—Bonnie Lass, by Blue Bull.. 2:25
Brushy John, blk, g, 186—, by Rappahannock, dam by Owen Dale (dead) 2:27
Brutus Girl, blk, m, 188—, by Sheffield's Andrew Jackson 2:21¼
Bryan Girl, b m, 1887, by Glen Miller—Emma, by German Boy (dead) .. 2:26¼
Bryan McGregor, ch s, 1883, by Robert McGregor—Thora, by Hambrino 2:23¾
Bryson, br s, 1890, by Simmons—Lena, by Bramolet's Clark Chief Jr. 2:20¾
Bub McLaughlin, b g, 1882, by Charles Dickens—Rikert Mare, ... 2:29
Buccleuch, blk, s, 1884, by Scott's Thomas—Lady Strong, by Mambrino Patchen 2:29½
Bucephalus, ch g, 1879, by Niagara Chief—Lady T., by Champion 2:28¼
Bucephalus, ro s, 1877, by Wood's Hambletonian—Beauty, by Fish's Bertrand 2:30
Buck McGregor blk s, by Robert McGregor 2:29½
Buck Morgan, ch g, 188—, by Buckeye Bayard—Morgan by Blind Tom 2:20¼
Buckshot, gr g, 1885 by Pilot Medium—Alice Thornton, by Shelby Chief.. 2:20¼
Buckskin Dick, b g, 1879, by Byerly Abdallah—Flora, by Downy's Royal George 2:23¼
Bucyrus b g, 1892, by Wilton—Nutgall by Nutwood 2.23¼

Bud Ewing, ch s, 1891 by Don McGregor, dam by Fleetfoot .... 2·25
Budd Flax, ch g 1886, by Flaxmont—Julia, by Frank .... 2·24½
Buddinger, ch s, 1886, by Butler's Bashaw—Petal, by Colporal .... 2·24
Bud L., blk s, 1889, by Don L.—Johanna, by Maxim .... 2·29¾
Buffalo Bill, ro g, 187—, by Limber Bill 2.29½
Buffington, b s, 1892, by Sable Wilkes—Annie G., by Le Grand 2:20½
Bullet, b s, 1887, by Lumps—Relic, by Mambrino Chief Jr .... 2·25¼
Bullion, ch s, 187—, by Blue Bull—Kate, by Archie Lightfoot 2:28
Bully Brooks, b g, 1861 by Dirigo—One Eye by Whitney Horse .... 2·28
Bulwer, ch g, 1877, by Blue Bull, dam by Sorrel Tom .... 2·23
Bulwer, br g, 188—, by Buccaneer .... 2·26½
Bumps, blk s, 1887, by Lumps—Lorina, by King Rene .... 2·29½
Bunnie G., b m, 188—, by Elial G—Morley Girl, by Commonwealth .... 2·23¾
Burdetta, blk m, 1885, by Kentucky Ruler—Belle Chase, by Long Island Bashaw .... 2·30
Burglar, b s, 1879, by Auditor—Pantalette, by Princeps .... 2·24¾
Burleigh, br s, 1888, by Chelton—Maid of Racine, by Surfeit .... 2·28½
Burlesque, ch s, 1884, by Hambrino—Roan Fanny, by Mambrino King... 2·25¼
Burns, b s, 1870, by Kirkwood—Kate, by Mambrino Eclipse .... 2·30
Burns McGregor, b s, 1887, by Robert McGregor—Birdie J., by Young Jim (dead) .... 2·29
Burt, b g., 1884, by Bonnie McGregor, dam by Romulus .... 2·26½
Burt G., b g, 1887, by Prince L.—Griffin Mare, by Dick Linderman... 2·25¾
Busbey, b g, 1873, by George Wilkes—Dame Tansey, by Daniel Lambert 2:29¼
Bush, blk m, 1886, by Alcyone—Lady Garfield, by Young Jupiter 2.14¼
Bushnell Chief, b g, 1885, by Mambrino Messenger—Smick Mare. ... 2·29¼
Bushwacker, b s, 186—, by Joe Hooker—dam by Jupiter .... 2·29½
Business, b g, 186—, by Gossip Jones 2·28
Butte, b g, 1883, by Red Wilkes—Naunearle, by Messenger Chief..... 2·29¾
Buttercup, dn m, 1878, by Belmont—Topsey, by St Elmo .... 2·28
Butterfly, br m, 1879, by Young Jim—Tansey, by George Wilkes.......... 2·19¼
Butterscotch, br g, 1876, by Panic—Maid of the Mist, by Cummings' Davy Crocket .... 2·20
Button, b g, 1883, by Polonius—Dubois 2:26
Buzz, b g, 1868, by Toronto Chief—Lady Fulton, by Stubtail (dead).... 2·28½
Buzz Medium, b m, 1873, by Happy Medium—Rockefeller Mare, by Nonpareil .... 2·20¼
Byron, ch s, 186—, by Royal George—O'Brien Mare (dead)..............., 2.25½
Byron Sherman, b s, 1880, by Saturn—Kitty Clyde, by Pasacas.......... 2:28
Byron Smith, b s, 1882, by Reporter—Jessie, by Roberts' Royal George . 2·29¾
C. A. B., ch g, 188—, pedigree not traced .... 2·29¼
Cabash, ch s, 1880 by Bashtine—Cachuca, by Eugene .... 2·27¼
Cad, ch s, 1883, by Bayonne Prince—Emma K., by Burger (dead). .... 2·27¾
Cadmonia, blk m, 1887, by Cadmus Hambletonian—Hosier, by George Rolfe .... 2·25
Cadmus Hambletonian, br s, 1880, by Squire Talmage—Lena, by Clay Cadmus .... 2·29¾
Cadmus Jr., blk s, 1888, by Cadmus Hambletonian—Daytona, by Trouble 2·26
Cad Wade, b m, 1884 by New York—May Day, by Pacing Abdallah... 2·20
Caesar, b g, 1885, by Norwood Chief—Kit, by Col. Walter .... 2·23¼
Caesar, b s, 1876, by Caesar .... 2·29
Caesar, b g, 188—, pedigree not traced 2:29¼
Cairo, b g, 187—, by Chieftain...... 2:26
Calamus, b m, 1872, by Swigert—Merrimac, by Richards' Bellfounder.... 2,24¼
Calwell Maid, b m, 188—, pedigree not traced 2.29¼
Caledonia Chief, ch s, 1865, by Howe's Royal George—Jule, by Coates' Eclipse (dead) .... 2·29½
Calhoun, b s, 1885, by Pilot Medium—Topsy, by Bay Middleton .... 2·24¾
Calhoun, b g, 188—, by Sam Purdy... 2·29¼
California Damsel, ch m, 1852, by Andrew Jackson Jr. (dead) .... 2·24½
California Lambert, b s, 1883, by Ben Franklin—Maud, by Daniel Lambert .... 2·27
Calinda, ch m, 1884, by Harold—Claytona, by American Clay .... 2·26¼
Cal. Kotch, b s, 188—, by California—Mary, by Bloomfield .... 2·30
Callahan Maid (Chicago Maid), ch m, 1872, by Revenge—Illinois Maid, by Black Donald 2.25
Called Back, ch g, 1884, by Mark Field—Daisy, by Revenge 2.27¼
Callie K., b m, 188—, by Kirby's Cadmus, dam by Hambletonian Pilot... 2·30
Calliopsis, b m, 188—, by Montgomery 2.29¼
Callino, b s, 1890, by Wildrino, dam by Rooker 2.20½
Callisto, b s, 1886, by Alcantara—Annie Page, by Daniel Lambert .... 2·26½
Calmar, b g, 1889, by Bourbon Chief, dam by March's Boliver 2.22
Calvo, b s, 1888, by Rumor—Cigarette, by Gen Washington 2:29¼
Cambria Wilkes, br s, 1884, by Clay Wilkes—Nubia, by Harold .... 2·29¼
Cambridge Girl, ch m, 188—, by Ben Franklin .... 2·28½
Cameo, ch m, 1888, by Amender—Camptown, by Messenger Duroc.. . 2.28¼
Camilla, b m, 1887, by Indiaman—Lulu F., by Ericsson........ 2·24¼
Camille, b m, 1880, by Happy Medium—Bess, by Volunteer .... 2·20¼
Camille, b m, 1882, by Monmouth B .. 2.27¼
Camille, b m, 1888, by Harbinger—Abbie B., by Hambletonian Knox. . 2·24½
Camlet, ch g, 188—, by Andante...... 2·20½
Cammie L., b m, 1885, by Harold—Pera, by Belmont .... 2·21
Camors, blk g, 1864, by Gen. Knox.. 2.19¾
Camors, b g, 1871, by Dirigo........ 2·25¼
Canary Bird, ro m, 1888, by Jay Bird—Blue Bells, by Gov. Sprague (dead) 2·19½
Candidate, blk s, 1885, by Electioneer—Norah, by Messenger Duroc .... 2·26½
Caneland Wilkes, b s, 1887, by Young Jim—Augusta, by Allie West .... 2·29
Canemah, b m, 1887, by Altamont—Ophelia Chiles, by Almont .... 2·19¾
Cantella Wilkes, b m, 188—, by Barony .... 2·25½

Cantrell, ch s, 1886, by Tennessee Wilkes—Latona, by McCurdy's Hambletonian . . . 2:29¾

Capadura, b s, 1874, by Pearsall—Sally Jones, by Rysdyk's Hambletonian . . . 2:30

Capplee, b g, 1888, by Reveille . . . 2:30

Capitalist, b s, 1888, by Happy Medium—Etona, by Almont . . . 2:29½

Capitana, blk s, 1889, by Young Wilkes—Mill Girl, by Jay Gould . . . 2:20½

Capitola, b m, 1862, pedigree not traced (dead) . . . 2:26½

Capitola, b m, 1878, by Colonna—Flora . . . 2:24¼

Capitola, b m, 1880, by Ensign—Peoria Belle, by Partridge's Star of the West . . . 2:24¼

Capitola, blk m, 1872, by Gilbreth Knox—Bridgham Mare, by Young Bundy . . . 2:22½

Capitola Fisk, b m, 1890, by Dictator Almont—Lady Fisk by Masterlode . . . 2:30

Capoul, br s, 1874 by Sentinel—Rosa Clay, by American Clay . . . 2:28

Cappie Woodline, b m, 1892, by Woodline—Venture, by Voltaire . . . 2:28¼

Caprice, b m 1888 by Kentucky Wilkes—Betty Adams, by Almont . . . 2:14¼

Caprivi, br s 1887, by Woodbrino—Belle Blackwood, by Blackwood . . . 2:28

Capson, ch s, 1886, by Baldman's Idol—Susan, by Guide . . . 2:25¼

Captain, b s, 186–, by Billy Denton—Seward Mare, by De Kay's Bellfounder (dead) . . . 2:28

Captain, b g, 1879 by Tom Patchen, dam by Keene's Brandywine . . . 2:21½

Captain, b g (same as Deck, 2:29½, and Prince E, 2:30) . . . 2:28½

Captain, gr g, 1878, by Kansas Rattler, dam by Robert Bonner . . . 2:24

Capt Ben, b g, 1876, by King Philip—Borden . . . 2:27

Capt Bowman, ch s 1887, by Ned Wilkes—Kathrine, by Daniel Lambert . . . 2:28¾

Captain Crouch, ch s, 188–, by Gen Smith . . . 2:25

Capt Douds, ch g, 187—, by Bishop . . . 2:27¾

Capt Edwards b s, 1884, by Dick Edwards—Nelly Grant, by Como Chief . . . 2:25¾

Capt. Emmons, ch g, 1871 by Continental—Nelly, by Tiger Morgan . . . 2:19¼

Captain F., b g, 188— by American Star . . . 2:29½

Capt. Gill, br g, 186—, pedigree not traced (dead) . . . 2:30

Capt Hamner, ch g, 1882, by Albion—Molly, by Grey Norman . . . 2:30

Captain Hare b s, 1887, by Col. Hare—Orphan, by Captain . . . 2:25

Capt. Herod, ch s, 1870, by Old Ringham . . . 2:25¾

Capt. Jack, b g, 186—, by Fisher Patchen, dam by Black Douglass . . . 2:26

Capt. Jenks, ch g, 186—, pedigree not traced . . . 2:30

Capt Lee, b s, 1887, by Mambrino Startle—Indianapolis Maid, by Indianapolis . . . 2:25

Capt Lewis, ch g, 187—, by Spink, dam by Wallace's Pheuomenon . . . 2:20¼

Capt Lyons, b s, 1882, by Sweepstakes—Maggie, by Edward Everett . . . 2:17¼

Captain Mac, b s, 1887, by Nutwood—Rapidan, by Dictator . . . 2:20

Captain Macey, b s, 1890, by Macey—Thorn'eaf, by Hero of Thorndale . . . 2:19½

Capt. O. (San Diego, pacing, 2:21), b g 188—, by Victor . . . 2:25¼

Captain Retter, br s, 1888, by Retter—Lady H, by Joe Young . . . 2:26¼

Capt. Seth, ch s, 1882, by Tramp—Black Sally, by Barnard's Muscatine 2:27

Capt. Smith gr g, 186—, by Fenian Chief—Minnie Ralston . . . 2:28½

Capt Smith, br g, 1876, by Locomotive—Maid of Clay, by Henry Clay . . 2:29

Captain Tom b s, 1889, by Col Tom—Maggie H., by Magna Charta . . . 2:26½

Captain Wade, gr g, 1888, by Reveille—Caprana by Daniel Lambert . . . 2:30

Capt. Walbridge, b s, 1890, by Arsaces—Ruth Medium, by Happy Medium 2:18¼

Captain Watters, br s, 1883, by Judge Folger—Mary S. by James R. Reese 2:25½

Captain White, blk s, 1890, by John G—Jane Mosley by Mambrino Patchen . . . 2:29

Captain Wilkes, br s, 1887, by Allie Wilkes—Jenny Redwood, by Redwood . . . 2:25¼

Capt Wilkes, b s, 1888, by Hambletonian Wilkes or Gov. Hayes—Maggie M., by Magna Charta . . . 2:26½

Captor, gr g, 188—, by Capri . . . 2:26½

Cara Mia, b m, 1888, by Electioneer—Bicara, by Harold . . . 2:29½

Carbolic b g, 187—, by Logan Jr., dam by Bashaw Jr . . . 2:24¼

Cardinal, b s, 188—, by Redfield . . . 2:27

Cardinal, gr g, 185—, by Cardinal (dead) . . . 2:30

Careless Boy, b g, 1869, by Brandywine (dead) . . . 2:28

Carilla, b m, 1887, by Nugget—Cascarilla, by Shelby Chief . . . 2:22¼

Carillon, b s, 1890, by Chimes—Charmer, by Mambrino King . . . 2:27¼

Carl, ch g, 1878 by Hidalgo—Lotta Swigart, by Edenborough . . . 2:23¾

Carl, b g, 1885, by Chevron—Daisy Golddust . . . 2:30

Carl G., gr g, 188—, by French's Bashaw . . . 2:27¾

Carldon, ch s, 1888, by Don Carlos—Lizzie Smith, by Scott's Thomas . . . 2:10¼

Carleton br s, 1885, by Mambrino King—Barbara, by Kentucky Prince 2:28

Carleton Chief, b s, 1885, by Gen Washington—Nettie Hambletonian, by Aberdeen . . . 2:21¼

Carlisle, ch s, 1884, by Piedmont—Idabelle, by Rysdyk's Hambletonian 2:22¼

Carlisle McGregor, blk s, 1884, by Fergus McGregor—Bird, by Frank Bird 2:29¾

Caryl Carne, gr g 1891, by Hambletonian Mambrino dam by Confederate Chief . . . 2:25

Carlos, ch s 1886, by Don Carlos—Clara Dudley, by Mambrino Dudley 2:27

Carlotta, ch m, 188—, by Bob Lee . . . 2:29¼

Carlotta, ch m, 1885, by Aristos—Emma Abbott by Broken Leg . . . 2:26

Carl S., b g . . . 2:30

Carl Redwood b g, 188—, by Redwood, dam by Detective Patchen . . . 2:20¼

Carmencita, b m, 1890, by C. F. Clay—Messenger Princess, by Messenger Clay . . . 2:27½

Cannello, br s, 1891, by Sidney—Pansy, by Berlin . . . 2:21¼

Carrie, gr m, 1881, by George Wilkes—Bashaw Belle, by Green's Bashaw 2:29¾

Carrie, b m, 1867, by Volunteer, dam by Seely's American Star . . . 2:24¼

rest—Grey Goose, by Nottingham's Norman 2:30

Champion, ch g, 188—, by Gooding's Champion, dam by Magna Charta.. 2:26¼

Champion Jr., br s, 186—, by Mambrino Champion, dam by Eureka... 2:24

Champion Girl, br m, 188—, by Gooding's Champion 2:28

Champion Medium, b s, 1882, by Happy Medium—Tamora, by Almont 2:22¼

Champion Morrill, br s, 1867, by Vermont Ranger, dam by Vermont Champion II (dead) 2:27

Champion Wilkes, b g 1878, by Barney Wilkes—Enconstance, by Blue Bull 2:22¼

C. F. B., gr g 2:28½

C. F. Clay, b s, 1881, by Caliban—Soprano, by Strathmore 2:18

Chance, ch g, 1870, Blue Bull—Molly, by Pete Guffin 2:20½

Chance, ch g, 1882 by Royal Fearnaught—Nance, by Western Chief Jr 2:23¼

Chance, b g, 1889, by Mohican—Folly, by Hambletonian Tranby 2:19¼

Chancert, gr s, 1891, by Pilot Medium—Lucy Montgomery, by Montgomery (dead) 2:29¼

Chancellor, ch s, 1884, by Bismarck—Lucy, by George B. Patchen Jr ... 2:16

Chancewood, b s, 1887 by Nutwood—Lucia, by Hambletonian 2:25

Chandler, b s, 1881, by Louis Napoleon—Belle Isle, by Young Dictator 2:28

Chandos, ch s, 1879, by Strathmore—Arline, by Almont 2:28¼

Chantilly, br m, 1886 by Nephew—Hazel Green 2:20¼

Chanter, b g, 1880, by Cuyler—Augusta, by Rysdyk's Bellfounder 2:20¾

Chantward, br s, 1890, by Shadeland Onward—Saxtena, by Enchanter.... 2:21

Charity, b m, 1888, by Bob Link—Zoa, by Dauntless 2:20¼

Charlemagne, b s, 1888, by Gambetta Wilkes—Martha, by Rothschild ... 2:27½

Charles A., blk g, 1878, by Leighton Horse—Nelly Edgerly 2:27¼

Charles Anderson, ch g, 188—, by Wilkes Chief 2:22½

Charles B., b g, 188—, by Bay Middleton 2:24¼

Charles C., br g, ... 2:29¼

Charles Derby, br s, 1885, by Steinway—Katie G., by Electioneer ... 2:20

Charles Dickens, gr g, 188—, by Dictator 2:29¼

Charles Dorsey, b g, 188—, by Green Boy 2:20½

Charles E. Loew, blk s, 185—, by George M. Patchen, dam by Dutchman (dead) 2:25½

Charles F., b s, 1889, by Seth P.—Nettie Smith, by Ozark 2:20¾

Charles F. Iseminger, b g, 1884, by Othello 2:19¾

Charles H., br s, 1882, by Old Charley—Fly 2:21½

Charles Henson, gr g, 187—, pedigree not traced 2:25

Charles Hilton, b g, 1879, by Louis Napoleon—Dolly Bryant, by Ned 2:17½

Charles H. Hoyt, b s, 1880, by Newmont—Reel, by Blue Bull 2:21½

Charles James, b g, 1880, by Le Grand—Hannah Price, by Arthurton 2:22¼

Charles P., 188—, by Gamaleon 2:19¼

Charles M., b s, 1888, by Subscriber.. 2:29¼

Charles R., b g, 188—, by Edgar Wilkes 2:29½

Charles R., br g, 1868, by Gilbreth Knox, dam by Witherell Messenger. 2:27

Charles Reade, ch s, 1886, by Woodard's Ethan Allen Jr.—Princess Dagmar, by Daniel Lambert 2:24¼

Charleston, ch s, 1884, by Bourbon Wilkes—Mary Thomas, by Abdallah Mambrino 2:12¼

Charles W., gr g, 1872, by Honest Dan—Lasher Mare, by Millman's Bellfounder 2:29½

Charles W. Wooley, b g, 1868, by Crazy Nick—Molly, by Morgan Messenger 2:22½

Charles Z., gr g, 188—, by Legal Tender Jr. 2:28¼

Charley, b g, 188—, pedigree not traced 2:26¼

Charley Anderson, ch g, 188—, by Wilkes Chief 2:22¼

Charley B., b s, 1869, by King's Champion—Old Jane, by Magnum Bonum. 2:25

Charley B., ch g, 186—, by Chickamauga 2:30

Charley Baldwin, blk s, 1883, by Iowa Chief, dam by American Eagle 2:23¼

Charley Boy, ch g, 187—, by I. J., dam by Vermonter (dead) 2:25¾

Charley Burch, b s, 1885, by Artemas—Kate, by Blue Bull 2:23½

Charley C., gr g, 1882, by Sam Purdy—Bessie O'Malley, by Davis O'Malley 2:13½

Charley C., b g, 187—, by Woodard's Ethan Allen 2:28½

Charley C., b g, by Accidental 2:29¼

Charley C., br g, 188—, by Brown Jug—Nellie C., by Napa Rattler........ 2:14¼

Charley Champlin (Home Rule), b g, 1874, by Messenger Duroc—Mary Hulse, by Seely's American Sta-... 2:21¾

Charley D., b s, 188—, by Henry Clay 2:29½

Charley D., b g, 187—, pedigree not traced 2:20¼

Charley D., ch g, 188—, pedigree not traced 2:28½

Charley Douglas, b g, 187—, by Tom. 2:30

Charley Downing, ro g, 1886, by Hambletonian Downing—Nancy Carney, by Carney's Sam Hazard 2:29¼

Charley Ellis, br s, 1888, by William Rysdyk—Miss Steel, by Oceana Chief 2:27¼

Charley Ford, gr g, 187—, by Cheney's Grey Eagle—Sadie M. 2:16¾

Charley G., rn g, 188—, breeding unknown 2:24¼

Charley Gibson, gr g, 1877, by Brown Douglas—Lady Grey, by Blue Dick.. 2:21½

Charley Gilbird, ch g, by Gibbin's Sprague—Waterloo, by Coleman's Abdallah J 2:29¾

Charley Green, b g, 186—, by Careless 2:26¾

Charley Green, ch g, 1884, by Praetor—Nob, by Gen. Stark 2:19¼

Charley H., b g, 188—, pedigree not traced 2:28¾

Charley H., b g, 1888, pedigree not traced 2:29¼

Charley H., g g, 188—, by Sam Purdy, dam by Davis' O'Malley 2:20¼

Charley H., br s, 1888, by Pompadour—Laura, by Rodolph 2:22¼

Charley Hogan, b g, 1876, by Virgo Hambletonian—Seybolt 2:18¾

Charley Hood, b g, 187—, by Pearsall. 2:29½

Charley K., b g, 1882, by Oak Hill—Fenton Mare 2:29¾
Charley K., b g, 188—, by Dictator .. 2:30
Charley Kalle, b g, 1885, by Sweepstakes—Oceola, by Middletown ... 2:28
Charley M., ch g, 187—, pedigree not traced (pacing record 2:25) ... 2:24¼
Charley M., b g, 188—, by Dictator ... 2:26¼
Charley Mac, ch g, 1868, by Holsbird's Ethan Allen—Stone Mare, by North American 2:25
Charley Mitchell, br g, 1882, by Allright—Jenny, by Gen. Williams 2:28¼
Charlie Moore, b g, 188—, by Nuthunter 2:21¾
Charley P., gr g, 1882, by Gov. Sprague — Martha, by Rothschild (pacing 2:11¼) 2:25½
Charley R., ch g, 1884, by Madrid—Speed, by War Dance 2:30
Charley R., b g, 188—, by Gen. Wilkes 2:27¾
Charley Ray, ch s, 1883, by Ben Franklin—Ray Mare 2:29
Charley Rolf, ch g, 188—, by Bay Rolf 2:29¼
Charley Ross, blk s, 1884, by John A. Kasson—Pet R. 2:29¾
Charley S., b g, 187—, by Snowstorm 2:27¾
Charley Shepherd, b g, 188—, by Batch 2:27½
Charley Sprague, gr g, 1885, by Gov. Sprague Jr.—Lady Jane, by Brady's Bellfounder 2:28¼
Charley Startle, blk g, 188—, by Startle Hambletonian 2:29¼
Charley T., ch g, 187—, pedigree not traced 2:29¼
Charley Thorne, gr g, 187—, by John Green — Fanny Hopkins, by Young Otsego 2:25½
Charley Tipton, b g, 188—, pedigree not traced 2:27¾
Charley Van, ch g, 1877, by Strang's Joker—Lady Purdy 2:29¼
Charley West, ch s, 1876, by Allie West—Clayette, by Strader's Cassius M. Clay Jr. 2:27
Charley Wheeler, ch g, 1891, by Blitzen—Sally Allen 2:19½
Charley Wilkes, b s, 1882, by Red Wilkes — Kate Bradley, by Clifton Pilot 2:21¾
Charlie Rolfe, b g, 188—, by Bay Rolfe 2:29¼
Charmer, blk m, 188—, by Burns' Black Cloud—Lady Knox, by Gen. Knox 2:27
Charmion, b m, 1889, by Spectator—Lady Lisle, by Ensign 2:20½
Charming Chimes, blk s, 1891, by Chimes, dam by Mambrino King .. 2:18½
Chartamount, b s, 1887, by Trouble—Lady Powers, by Magna Charta 2:28
Chatterton, ch s, 1885, by Crittenden—Sally Southworth, by Mambrino Patchen 2:18
Charter, b m, 1888, by Onward—Hecla, by Strathmore 2:24
Chastelard, b s, 1884, by King Rene—Sally Wilkes, by George Wilkes ... 2:29¾
Chatsworth, br s, 1889, by Dictator—Virgie Wilkes, by George Wilkes . 2:24¾
Chattel, b g, 1887, by Chatham—Nelly K., by Black Ranger 2:29½
Chauncy M. Bedle, b g, 1871, by Gooding's Champion 2:30
Chauncy H., br g, 187—, by Robert Bonner 2:27¼

Chazey Maid, b m, 1878, by Chazey Patchen 2:28
Checkmate, b s, 1885, by Competitor—Miss Egbert, by Egbert 2:29½
Cheerful Charlie, b g, by Broadway . 2:28¼
Chelsea D., ch g, 1883, by Index ... 2:18¾
Cheltenham, b s, 1884, by Oxmoor—Hildegarde, by Harry Clay 2:28
Cherokee, b s, 1884, by Jefferson Mambrino—Cumberland, by McFerran Cuyler 2:29½
Cherokee, gr g, 1888, by Pilot Medium—Minnie Medium, by Happy Medium (dead) 2:29½
Chester, b g, 1866, by Hambletonian—Julia Machree, by Seely's American Star 2:27
Chester, ch g, 1867, by Patrick Henry—Molly 2:28¼
Chester, br s, 1888, by Wilkes Spirit Jr.—Delilah, by Black Jake 2:17¼
Chester A., ch g, 188—, breeding unknown 2:30
Chester Allen, b g, 1885, by Mohawk Hambletonian—Wyandotte Maid, by Robert Fillingham Jr. 2:22¾
Chester F., ch g, 1875, by Mercury—Mary Ann, by Magnolia 2:30
Chester Morris, ro g, 188—, by Mount Morris 2:27¼
Chestnut 2:24¼
Chestnut Boy, ch s, 1875, by Burger—Lady, by Addison 2:28¼
Chestnut Hill, b s, 1872, by Strathmore—Polly Barber, by Bully King (dead) 2:22½
Chestnut Wilkes, ch s, 1885, by Red Wilkes—Fanny D., by Star Almont 2:26½
Chestnut Wilkes, ch m, 1884, by Favorite Wilkes — Kate Downing, by Joe Downing 2:29½
Chet Wilkes, br s, 188—, by Alcantara Prince 2:25
Chetwood, gr s, 1884, by Chichester—Vanity Fair, by Alexander's Abdallah 2:27
Chevalier, br g, 1882, by Chevalier—Barbara, by Green's Bashaw 2:27
Chevalier Ensign, b s, 1889, by Ensign—Lady, by Chevalier ... 2:29¾
Chevalita, ch m, 188—, by Extra—Frosty 2:25½
Cheyenne, b s, 1885, by Nutbourne—Jeanette, by Messenger Duroc..... 2:14¼
C. H. H., b g, 1883, by Chosroes—Long Mary, by Derby's Bashaw ... 2:27¼
Chicadee, blk s, 1885, by Mambrino Boy—Satinette, by Sentinel........ 2:29
Chicago, b g, 1850, by Ole Bull (dead) 2:24¾
Chicago Jack, b g, 185—, by Sherman Black Hawk (dead) 2:30
Chichester, b s, 1881, by Harold—Rosebush, by Woodford Mambrino 2:25¼
Chick Bills, b g, 1888, by Black Mack, dam by Star Hambletonian 2:26¼
Chico, b s, 188—, by Monroe Chief—Orphan Girl, by Reavis' Black Bird 2:20½
Chide, b m, 1891, by Chimes, dam by Bourbon Wilkes 2:26¼
Chief, b g, 188—, pedigree not traced . 2:23¼
Chief, b g, 188—, by Daubigne.. 2:27¾
Chief (ringer?), br g, 188—, pedigree not traced 2:27
Chief Medium, b s, 1882, by Happy Medium—Molly Crutcher, by Clark Chief 2:24½
Chief Onward, b s, 1889, by Right Onward—Flora, by Cleveland Chief.. 2:22¼
Chief Wilkes, b s, 1889, by Hinder

Claude, g g, 1887, breeding unknown 2 20½
Clatana b s, 188—, by Daly, dam by Gen. McClellan 2.27½
Clatina, b m, 1887, by Clay—Melissa, by Mohawk Chief 2 28¼
Claudia, b m 1882, by Sir Walkill—Merry Maid, by Abdallah Prince .. 2 29
Claudius, b s, 1886, by Landmark—Lady Lambert, by Daniel Lambert 2.25
Claudius, ch g, 188—, pedigree not traced 2 21¼
Claudius, b s, 1886, by Fairy Gift—May Day, by Harrison Chief 2:29¾
Claudius, ch g, 188—, by Hambletonian Tranby 2·21¼
Claudius, b s, 188—, by Artemus 2 29¾
Claus Almont, b g, 1888, by Santa Claus—Belle Byron, by Bowman's Clark Chief 2 26½
Clay, br s, 1879, by Electioneer—Maid of Clay, by Henry Clay 2·25
Clayberta, br m, 1886, by Egbert—Arnie Clay, by Tom Clay 2:30
Clay Cross, b s, 188—, by Royal Windsor—Belle of Happy Medium 2 30
Clay Davis, ch s, 187—, by Cassius M Clay Jr. 2 28¼
Clay Duke, b s, 1883, by Alcona—Metamora, by Duke of Orange Jr 2 29
Clay Duroc, b s, 188—, by Glen Duroc 2.30
Clay France, b s, 188—, by France ... 2:26½
Clay Forrest, ch s, 1884, by Clay Davis, dam by Edwin Forrest 2·24¼
Clay Herr br s, 1886, by Dr. Herr—Mattie Clay, by Whip Clay 2:16¾
Clay King, br s, 1884, by King Clay—Amy, by Volunteer 2.27¾
Claymore, b g, 1880, by King Clay—Time Enough, by Mambrino Time .. 2:17¾
Clayola, b m, 1885, by Allie Clay—Jessica, by Bellwood 2·21¼
Clayone b s, 1891, by Clay—Nelly Stout, by Mambrino Time 2:27¼
Clayton, b s, 1886, by Perduro—Molly Clay, by Neely's Henry Clay 2:20½
Clayton, b g, 1882, by Harry Clay—Star Maid, by Jupiter Abdallah 2.19
Clayton Edsall, br s, 1876, by Major Edsall, dam by Andy Johnson .... 2·22¾
Claytonia, ch m, 1884, by Hambletonian Downing—Belle Clay, by Strader's Cassius M Clay Jr 2 21½
Claytonian ch s, 1883, by Hambletonian Downing—Belle Clay, by Strader's Cassius M. Clay Jr 2 27¼
Claytonian, b m, 187—, by Haven's Harry Clay Jr 2.27¼
Clayton Lee, br s, 1888, by C F. Clay—Prescott Belle by Rysdyk 2:24¾
Clay Toska, b s, 188—, by King Toska 2 26¾
Clearmont, ch h, 188—, by McGinnis 2 28
Clegg Wright, br s, 1888 by Aristos—Jenny V., by Almont Eagle 2.29
Clematis gr m, 1889, by Barkis—Bessie Benton, by Major Benton 2 21¼
Clementine b m, 1888, by C. F. Clay—Delilah, by Administrator 2 29¼
Clementine, b m, by Addison Jr, dam by Young Emigrant (dead) 2·21
Clemmie G., ch m, 1877, by Magic—Ned 2 15½
Clemmie G II, ch m, 1888, by Post Boy, dam by Phillips Blackwood .. 2 18¼
Clendon, blk s, 1884, by Crittenden, dam by Richelieu 2 26
Cleo, b m, 1888, by Gambetta—Sue Harden, by Thomas K 2 19½
Cleo, b m, 1879 by Badger—Bird Grant, by Gen Grant 2·21
Cleon, b g, 1882, by Heptagon—Nelly Hoyt, by Norwood 2·22
Cleopatra, blk m 1890, by Dark Night—Florine, by Administrator .. 2 29½
Cleora, blk m, 1875, by Menelaus—Thornleaf, by Mambrino Patchen .. 2 18¾
Clermont, ch g, 1873, by Almont—Jean Wood, by Melbourne Jr. (dead) 2 29¼
Cleta Wilkes, b m 188—, by Wilkes Boy 2·29¼
Cleveland, b s, 1883, by Zilcaadi Golddust—Rosa, by Mambrino Reliance 2.29¼
Cleveland ch s, 188—, by Sir Walter 2 26½
Cleveland b g, 1869, by Hughes' Edwin Forrest—Mary Elmore, by Mambrunello 2·28¼
Cleveland Boy, b g, 188—, by Lothair Jr 2:23
Cleveland Boy, ch g, 1886, by Hambletonian Tranby—Belva, by William's Blue Bull 2 20¾
Cleveland S., b s, 1884, by Montgomery—Topsy, by Tippoo Saib (pacing record 2 11¾) 2.24
Client, br s, 1887, by Climate—Matt, by Gill's Vermont 2:24
Clifton, ch g, 1882, by Signet—Eliza Jane, by Morgan Rattler Jr. 2:27
Clifton Bell, b s, 1883, by Electioneer—Clarabell, by Abdallah Star (dead) 2:24½
Clifton Boy, b g, 1869, by Joe (dead) 2 23
Clifton Boy br g, 1872, by Major Winfield—Lady Irwin, by George Wilkes 2 30
Clifton Boy, br s, 1877, by Squire Talmage—Nelly Draco, by Draco 2 26¼
Clifford K., blk m, 1890, by Norwood Wilkes—Goldie T., by Washington Jr. 2.29¼
Climatize, b s, 1886, by Climate—Carrie Pachen, by Mambrino Patchen.. 2 24¾
Cling, b g, 188—, by Grey Jim 2.29¼
Clingstone, b s, 1880, by Star Hambletonian—Fly 2 30
Clingstone, b g, 1875, by Rysdyk—Gretchen, by Chosroes 2 14
Clingstone, 2d, b s 1884, by Rysdyk—Gretchen, by Chosroes 2.29½
Clinker Jr, b s, 1883, by Clinker—Bird 2 24
Clinton Wilkes, b s, 188—, by Red Wilkes 2·26
Clio Wilkes blk m, 1888, by Guy Wilkes—Directress, by Director .. 2.30
Clipper, b g, 187—, by Lex 2 23½
Clipper, ch g, 1887, by Melville Chief—Stockard Mare 2·24¼
C L K., ch g, 188—, by Gov Benton 2 29¼
Clochette, ch m, 1885, by Chester Chief—Abdahne, by Goldsmith's Abdallah 2·17¼
Clonmore, b s, 1882, by Connaught—Hopeless, by Hermes 2 21
Clontarf, b s, 1885 by Nutbourne—Duroc Cuyler, by Messenger Duroc 2 22
Clorine, ch m 1888, by C. F. Clay—Lady Pepper, by Onward 2:18¼
Clotilda, ch m, 1887, by Argonaut—Clotyde, by Almont 2 28½
Clover, b g, 186—, by Hindoo 2.25¾
Clover Leaf, b s, 1889 by C. F Clay—Lassie, by Kentucky Prince 2:21¾
C M P., blk g, 188—, by Junior .. 2·26½
Coalburg, br g 1886, by Com. Wilkes—Coalburg Kit, by Oakwood 2:30
Coast Boy, blk s, 1885, by Bourbon Wilkes—Alaatress, by Coaster 2·21

Coaster, b s, 1870, by Caliban—Sal, by Canada Chief 2:26¼
Coaticook Boy, b s, 188—, by Page's Hambletonian 2:26¼
C. O. B., b g, 188—, by Mambritonian 2:26¼
Cobee, ch g, 188—, pedigree not traced 2:27¾
Cobdellah, ch m, 188—, by Cobden ... 2:26½
Cobden, ch s, 1874, by Daniel Lambert—Clara, by Ethan Allen (dead).. 2 28¾
Cobden, II., ch g, 188—, by Cobden.. 2.24
Cobwebs, ch g, 1888, by Whips—Molly Cobb, by Gen. Benton 2.12
Cocoon, blk m, 1887, by Cyclone—Fanny Conner, by Bourbon Wilkes.. 2·15
C. O. D., ch g, 1888, by Simmons—Miss Linder, by Triumvir........ 2 30
Code, b s, 1879, by Dictator—Crop, by Pilot Jr........ 2.22¼
Cœur d'Alene, b s, 1887, by Dexter Bradford—Belle H., by Williamson's Belmont 2 19½
Cohansey Boy, b g, 188—, by Messenger Chief Jr........ 2 24¼
Coincident, b m, 1891, by Calabar—Daphne, by Kentucky Prince....... 2:20
Colbourne, gr g, 186—, pedigree not traced (dead) 2:30
Colden Belle, b m, 1884, by Hamlin's Almont Jr.—Nell, by son of imp Lapidist (dead) 2:20¼
Coleridge, b s, 1888, by C. F. Clay—Susie Wilkes, by Red Wilkes (pacing 2 09¾) .... 2·23½
Collinwood, b s, 1887, by Mambrino Startle—Sarah C., by Metropolitan.. 2 21¼
Colma, gr m, 1886, by Electioneer—Sontag Mohawk, by Mohawk Chief 2 25¼
Colonel, blk g, 1869, pedigree not traced 2.27
Colonel, blk s, 1884, by Riley's Administrator, dam by Ellington Boy. 2 29½
Col Arthur Wilkes, gr s, 188—, by Mambrino Wilkes 2 29½
Col. B., blk g, 188—........ 2.29½
Col Barnes, ch g, 186—, by King's Champion .... 2·28½
Col. Bismarck, b s, 1883, by Victor Bismarck—Lucy Thornton, by American Clay 2 24
Colonel Briggs, br s, 1885, by Hambleton—Bessie, by Floramour 2 22
Col Bullitt, b s, 1887, by Squire Talmage—Black Maria, by Bostick's Almont Jr. 2 18¼
Col. Burr, ch s, 1887, by King William—Louie T., by Greenback........ 2 25½
Col Colgrove, b g, 188—, by Jim Hill. 2 29¼
Col. Crockett, b s, 1878, by Ripple—Belle Green, by Green's Bashaw ... 2 20¼
Col. Crownble, b s, 1888, by Alcande—Kitty, by Billy Bow Leg 2 26¼
Col. Dawes, b g, 187—, pedigree not traced 2 24¼
Col. Dickey, b s, 1889, by Pilot Medium—Mady L., by Honest Dick 2 16¾
Col. Dorsey, b s, 1885, by Conner's Almont—Betsey, by Golddust. .. 2 25
Col. Egbert, b s, 1881, by Egbert—Maisie, by Shelby Chief.. .... 2 30
Col H., ch h, 1890, by Don McGregor—Queen, by Bonnie Scotland........ 2 22¼
Col. Hawkins, br s, 1877, by Echo—Thetis, by Morgan Black Hawk Comet 2 29¼
Col. Hickman, gr s, 188—, by Nevada 2 25¼
Col. Kip, b s, 1883, by Kenwood—Agnes, by Hamlet 2 20¼
Col Kip, blk s, 1884, by Aristos—Laura 2.24¼
Col. K. R., br s, 188—, by Bay Rose—Addie E., by Algona........ 2·22¼
Col. Kuser, br s, 1890, by Stranger—Inez, by Jay Gould .... 2·16½
Col. Lamont, b s, 1886, by Bostick's Almont Jr.—Grand Duchess, by Mambrino Patchen 2 26¼
Col. Lewis, gr g, 1870, by Rifleman... 2:18¾
Col. Lillard, b s, 1884, by Jay Bird—Kitty, by Durant 2:25½
Col. McNasser, ch g, 1886, by Starlight—Lady Dexter, by Whipple's Hambletonian .... 2·19
Col Matson, blk s, 188—, by Chance.. 2:27
Col. May, br g, 1885, by May Boy—Fanny Bicknell, by imp. Hercules .. 2:17
Col. Moss, ch g, 1885, by Mambrino Russell—Hattie Fuller, by Strathmore 2 27¼
Col. Moulton, ch s, 1861, by Daniel Lambert—Jenny, by Bigelow Horse (dead) 2 28½
Col Neal, b s, 1883, by Squire Talmage—Lizzie, by Clark's Mohawk Jr. 2 25¾
Col. Nuttingham, br s, 1888, by Nuttingham—Lou, by Western Fearnaught 2:22½
Col. Osgood, b s, 1887, by Wilkes—Kitty Almont, by Constellation..... 2:18¾
Col. Owen, br g, 1887, by Spink's Clark Chief—Topsey, by Confederate Chief 2.15½
Col. P., b s, 1887, by Paramount—Flora, by Gifford Allen........ 2 24¼
Col. Pike, b g, 1860, by Young Cassius (dead) 2.29½
Col. Pitt, b s, 1889, by Wilkes—Hesperia, by Constellation 2:19¼
Col. Russell, b g, 1865, by Louis Napoleon (dead) 2 25¼
Col Simmons, b s, 1887, by Simmons—Lena, by Bramblett's Clark Chief Jr 2:22¾
Col Sterling, b s, 1883, by Sterling—Meigs, by Robert Fillingham Jr. ... 2 28½
Col Stevens, b g, 1888, by Administrator—Coquette, by American Clay.. 2 28½
Col. Taylor, b g, 188—, by Thomas K. 2 21½
Col Tom, b s, 1884, by Lumps—Lulu Morton, by Whip Clay........ 2:22
Col. Walker, b g, 1881, by St. Cloud—Minnie, by Gould Clay........ 2·24¼
Col. Wood, b g, 1878, by Billy Patterson—Flora Andrews, by Gooding's Champion. .... 2·21¼
Col. Young, b s, 1885, by Young Jim—Emily, by George Wilkes........ 2.23½
Col. Young, br s, 1887 by Joe Young—Della, by Sam Balch........ 2·29¾
Colonia, ch g, 188—, by Flaherty's Fearnaught 2 24¼
Colored Girl, blk m, 1881, by Viktor Knight—Beauty, by Trophy. 2:25½
Colored Man, blk s, 1887, by Celadon—Kate Lee, by Harold 2 23
Colossus, b g, 187— (ringer?) 2 29
Columbia, b m, 1879, by Dixon, dam by Robert Bonner 2 30
Columbia Chief blk s, 186—, by Mambrino Black Hawk—Lady Jackson by Kemble Jackson (dead). 2 28¼
Columbus Hambletonian, b s, 1873, by Ajax—Orphan Girl, by Young Columbus 2 26
Columbus S., b s, 1889, by McDonald Chief—Fanny Rose, by Vick's Ethan Allen Jr........ 2 27½
Colvina Sprague, blk m, 1880, by Gov

Cora, b m, 1887, by Hamlin's Almont Jr.—Coraline, by Almonarch 2:26
Cora Belle, b m, 1878, by Joe Gavin—Owosso Belle, by Louis Napoleon . 2:29½
Cora Belmont gr m, 1872 by Belmont—Miss Russell, by Pilot Jr . . . 2:24½
Cora C., b m, 1880, by Coriander ... 2:28¾
Cora F., gr m, 186—, by Brown Harry—Cora, by French Tiger 2:28
Cora F., b m, 1885, by Kentucky Prince—Topsey, by Walkill Chief . 2:20½
Coral b m, 1887, by Electioneer—Columbine, by A W Richmond . . . 2:18½
Coraline, gr m, 1890, by Coralloid—Meg E B, by Banker Rothschild . 2:26¼
Coralloid, blk s, 1886, by Simmons, Coral, by Clark Chief 2:13½
Coral Queen, b m, 1891, by Coralloid 2:28½
Cora McGregor, ch m, 1885, by Fergus McGregor—Coranda, by Coriander . 2:23¼
Cora R, b m, 188—, by Crazy Nick Jr. 2:25¾
Cora R, b m, 188— by Kent 2:19½
Cora Riggs, b m 1884, by Bourbon Wilkes—Emma, by Westwood 2:28¼
Cora Ashwood, ch m, 188—, by Ashwood, dam by Tattersall 2:21¾
Cora Sterling, blk m, by Sterling Boy 2:26½
Cora S, b m, 1886 by Elector 2:19¼
Cora S, gr m, 1884, by Harold—Cora Belmont, by Belmont 2:25½
Cora Woodward, b m, 1884 by Mohican—Adele Tyler 2:25¼
Cora Barlum, b m, 1885, by Louis Napoleon—Home Maid, by Royal Fearnaught 2:23½
Corena ch m 188—, by Aberdeen 2:24¼
Coriander Maid, b m, 188—, by Coriander 2:29½
Corinne br m, 1889, by Ambassador—Lucy Lincoln, by Masterlode 2.24½
Coriander, b s, 1873, by Iron Duke—Clara Wood, by Harry Clay 2:29¾
Corie McGregor, b s, 1888 by Robert McGregor—Coriander Maid, by Coriander 2:21
Corinne, b m, 1887, by Robert McGregor—Constine, by Conductor . 2:14½
Corinne, ch m, 1890, by Valdemeer—Nelly West, by Charley West . 2:20
Corisande, br m, 1869 by Iowa Chief 2:24½
Corisco, b s, 1884, by Frank Noble—Mary Safford, by Combat . . 2:21
Corna, blk g, 1889, by Patchen Wilkes—Corneta, by Coronet 2:26¼
Cornelia blk m 1888 by Wilton—Corrella, by Col Bonner 2:25¼
Cornelia, blk m, 1875, by Col. Bonner 2:21¼
Cornelia Howard, b m, 1890 by Wilton—Lilith, by Robert McGregor (dead) 2:29¼
Cornelia Wilkes, ch m 1887 by Wilkes Spirit—Silver Tail, by Jupiter Pilot 2:23¼
Cornelius M, b s, 188—, by Cornelian, dam by Blue Bull 2:30
Corner Belle b m, 1890 by Bell Boy—Four Corners, by Mambrino Time (dead) 2:23
Cornwall, b s, 1887, by Kentucky Prince—Atlanta, by Messenger Duroc 2:20
Corona, b m 1880, by Baird's Hambletonian Prince—Flora, by State's Rights 2:24½
Corrie, br m, 1886, by Belvour—Leda, by Nobby 2:28½
Cortez, br s, 188—, by Madrid . . 2:30
Coshet, b s, 1881, by Capoul—Lola, Administrator 2:30
Cossart, b m, 188—, ... 2:29½
Cottage Girl, ch m, 1870, by Mambrino Star—Lady Franklin 2:29½
Cottonette, b m, 1880, by Western Chief—Cotton Picker, by Red Buck 2:25
Cottonwood Chief ch g, 1887, by Jaywood 2:29¼
Cottonwood Chief ch s 1879, by Clark Chief Jr 2:29
Counsellor, b s, 1881, by Onward—Crop, by Pilot Jr ... 2:21¼
Counsellor, (Sabin's) b s, 1887, by Counsellor—Julia, by Chickamauga 2:26½
Count Folsio, b s, by Onward—Viola, by King Rene 2:26¾
Countess Eve, b m, 188—, by Norval 2:29¼
Countess, br m, 1889, by Count Waldemar—Mattie S, by Lumps . .. 2:27
Count Robert, b s, 1888, by Robert McGregor—Christine, by Monte Christo 2:13½
Country Boy, br g, 1882, by Regalia—Belle, by Danville Boy 2:23½
Counterfeit, b m, 1886, by Greenback—Madge, by Trophy 2:30
Country Medium, b s, 1884, by Happy Medium—Country Maiden, by Country Gentleman 2:25¼
Count Waldemar, b s, 1884 by King Rene—Evadne, by Long Island Bashaw 2:21½
Coupon, blk c, 1892 by Director Chief, dam by Phallas . . . 2:26¼
Coupon, dn g, 1875, by High Jack—Nig, by Nigger Dick 2.26¾
Courier, b s 1887 by Crittenden—Tillie C, by Jay Bird 2:15
Courtland, b s, 1882, by Kentucky Prince—Harriette, by Messenger Duroc 2:24¼
Covey, b s, 1883, by Steinway—Katy G, by Electioneer 2:25
Cow Boy, br g, 187—, , Harper 2.30
Coxcomb, ch s, 1888, by Madri—Miriam, by Egbert 2:25½
Coxsackie King, ch g, 188— by Young Jupiter 2:29¼
Cozette, blk m, 1863, by Black Bashaw, dam by Star Gazer .. . 2:19
C. P. C, b s 188—, pedigree not traced 2:28¼
C P R., b g, 188—, by All Right . 2.26½
Cranston, b g, 1884, by Sweepstakes—Miss Eager, by Post Boy 2:27½
Crayon, b s, 1887, by Cuyler—Dainty, by Contractor 2:29¼
Credo, b m, 1891, by Jersey Wilkes . 2.29¾
Creel, br s, 1890, by C. F. Clay—Springway, by Harkaway 2:29¼
Cremonia, b m, 1883, by Ansonia—Cream, by Messenger Duroc .. 2:23
Crepe McNett, b m, 1886, by Turk—Nelly 2:28¼
Crescent b m, 1884 by Belmont—Chinchilla's dam by Alexander's Norman 2:25½
Crescent, b m, 1888, by Favorite Wilkes—Seabolt, by Wacker . 2:25
Crescendo ch s, 1883, by Mambrino Dudley—Mayenne, by Wedgewood (dead) 2:24
Cresson, b s 1885, by Hambrino—Emma by Belmont . . . 2:21½
Crete, ch m, 1885, by Dictator Chief, dam by Daniel Lambert . 2:27¼
Crete, br m, 1888 by Onmore—Belle

of Dubuque, by Mambrino Boy ... 2:29¾
Cricket, b m, 1878, by Selkirk—Nelly Woodmansee, by St. Lawrence 2:24½
Criterion, blk m, 1884, by Crittenden—Mamie, by Star Almont 2:29¾
Crimrose, b s, 1890, by Gamaleon—Hebe, by Guide 2:29½
Crome, b g, 188—, by Motion—Lucy, by Foote's Black Hawk 2:26
Crossman, b g, 1885, by Mcdiid—Mary, by Mambrino Hatcher 2.26
Crown Imperial b s, 1873, by Imperial—Lady Bryant, by Brignoli 2:27½
Crownmont, b g, 188—, by Montello.. 2:24¼
Crown Point, ch s, 1870, by Speculation—Young Martha, by George M. Patchen Jr. 2:24
Crown Prince, ch g, 1886, by Dexter Prince—Clara by Chieftain 2.17½
Crown Prince, gr g, 1862, by Logan's Messenger—Lady Messenger, by Warrior (dead) 2:25
Croxie, b m, 1872, by Clark Chief—Molly Whitefoot by Little Priam .. 2:19¼
Cruiser, b g, 1880, by Coaster—Polly, by John Dillard 2:28¼
Crusader, b g, 1878, by Dauntless—Sally Hall, by Young America 2:29½
Crysolite, ch m, 1890, by Acolyte—Allanah by Red Wilkes 2:27¼
C. T. L., ch g, 1880, by Gen Withers—Lady Gilbreth, by Gilbreth Knox 2:23¼
Cuba, b g, 187—, by George Wilkes, dam by Gen. Knox 2:27¾
Cuba, b m, 188—, by Bonnie Doon .. 2:25½
Cubic, b g, 1883, by Electioneer—Cuba, by imp Australian 2:28½
Cubit, br s, 1882, by Caliban—Camlet, by Hamlet 2:27½
Cuckoo, 1878, by Frank Wolford—Jenny, by Corbeau 2:28
Cuckoo, b m, 188—, by Cunard Jr. ... 2:19¾
Cudahy, b s 1890, by Allandorf—Nora Mapes by Furor 2:21
Cumberland, blk g, 188—, by Maplehurst 2:21¼
Cunard, b s, 1885, by Virgo Hambletonian—Slybolt, by Wacker 2:26¼
Cunard, b g, 1873, by Von Moltke, dam by Gen. Knox 2:30
Cunard Jr. ch s, 1881, by Cunard—Pet Morris, by Young Hiram Drew 2:28¼
Cupid, b s, 1885, by Sidney—Venus, by Capt Webster 2:18
Curfew, b s, 1889, by Chimes—Mabel L., by Victor 2:24¼
Curio, b m, 1890, by Alcantara—Cigarette, by Gen. Washington 2:25
Currie D, b m, by Happy Medium, dam by Almont 2:26
Currier, b g, 1883, by McVeigh—Weeks' Mare, by Mudget Horse... 2:27
Currito, b s, 1887, by Idol Gift—Star Maid, by Jupiter Abdallah 2:17¾
Currer Bell, b m, 1883, by Belmont—Bertha, by Harold 2:29¾
Cuthbert, b s, 1881, by Cuyler—Marcia S., by Williams' Mambrino . 2:23¾
Cuthbert H., b s, 188—, by Cuthbert.. 2:21¼
Cuylercoast, b s, 1886, by Pancoast—Hilda, by Cuyler 2:16½
Cut Glass, b m, 1891, by Onward—Crystal, by Crittenden 2:17
C. V. B., b s, 1884, by Ensign, dam by Gen Fletcher 2:15½
C. W. S., b s, 188—, by Abbottsford—Muldoon, by George M. Patchen.... 2:26¼
Cyclone, blk s, 1876, by Caliban—Camlet, by Hamlet 2:23½
Cyclone, blk g, 187—, by Godfrey Patchen 2:30
Cyclone, ch g, 188—, by Toronto Chief Jr. 2:27¼
Cyclone, blk g, 1884, by Tony Ensign—Sorrel Nelly 2:25
Cyclone, br g, 18—, by Brigadier...... 2:26¾
Cyclone, ch g, 188—, by Whipple's Hambletonian 2:26¼
Cyclone Jr., b g, 1885, by Hawthorne—Lizzie Patchen, by Bully King ... 2:27
Cyclone Wilkes, ro g, 1886, by Cyclone—Ella Wilkes, by Favorite Wilkes.. 2:23¼
Cyclops, b s, 1873, by Marshal Ney—Kitty Puss, by Frank Pierce Jr.... 2:27
Cypress, ch s, 1881, by Kentucky Prince—Lady Hilton, by Sentinel... 2.18¼
Cypress, b s, 1882, by Cyclops—Fanny Fern, by Worden's George M. Patchen Jr.......... .... 2:30
Cypress, b m, 1881, by Strathmore—Aspinola, by Belmont 2.22½
Cyprus R., blk s, 1881, by Nutwood—Belle, by Jack Roberts 2:17¾
Cythera, ch m, 1890, by Jersey Wilkes—Huma, by Connaught 2:20¾
Czar, ch s, 1889, by Russia—Bon Doon, by Legal Tender Jr.......... 2.12½
Czarina, b m, 1882, by Egbert—Dolly, by Mambrino Chief 2:21
Dacia, br m, 1868, by Woodford Mambrino—Dahlia, by Pilot Jr.......... 2:29½
Deciana, blk m, 1873, by Harold—Dacia, by Woodford Mambrino..... 2:27½
Daconis, b s, 1886, by Norwood Star—Lady Grace, by Hamlet 2:24
Daddy K., b g, 1888, by Wellington—Molly, by Kentucky Prince Jr. (dead) 2:28½
Daghestan, b s, 1890, by Stamboul—Alta Belle, by Electioneer.......... 2.25½
Dahlia Wilkes, b m, 188—, by Almont Wilkes, dam by Abdallah Chief..... 2:24½
Daily News, b s, 188—, by Sagerser.. 2:25
Dainty, b m, 1879, by Dictator—Vic, by Mambrino Chief 2:26¾
Daireen, gr m, 1881, by Harold—Dahlia, by Pilot Jr. 2:21½
Daisy, ch m, 1885, by Tecumseh—Daisy, by Mambrino Abdallah...... 2:23¼
Daisy, b m, 188—, by Wellington.... 2:28¼
Daisy, g m, 1891, by Conundrum...... 2:28
Daisy, br m, 188—, by Miltonian...... 2.28
Daisy B., dr m, 1887, by Iowa Harold—Maud, by Hiatoga Jr. 2:29¼
Daisy Blackwood, br m, 1879, by Blue Bull 2.29¼
Daisy Burns, b m, 1857, by Skenandoah, dam by Harden Horse (dead) . 2:29¾
Daisy C., b m, 1882, by Mountain Boy—Smith Mare, by Darkie.... .. 2:22¼
Daisy C., b m, 1887, by Hambletonian Bashaw—Warfield Mare, by Green's Bashaw 2:23¾
Daisy D., b m, 1882, by Parmenus—Lady, by Pat Maloy.. .... 2:30
Daisydale, b m, 1872, by Thorndale—Daisy, by Washington (dead) 2.19¾
Daisy Dean, br m, 1876, by Damon.. 2:29¼
Daisy Dee, ch m, 188, by Sigma Nu—Fanny, by Truesdale's Abdallah Jr. 2:27
Daisy Drew, b m, 1880, by Horace... 2.30
Daisy Eyebright, b m, 1876, by Kirkwood—Quackenbush Mare, by Voorhees' Abdallah Chief 2.27
Daisy G., ch m, 1888, by Norwood Chief—Kit, by Col. Walter......... 2:25½
Daisy Gardner, br m, 1875, by Hawk-

BUDD DOBLE, Chicago, Ill.

(THE FIELD MARSHAL).

Doble placed the world's record for trotters at 2:17¼ with
Dexter, at 2:14 with Goldsmith Maid and
2:04 with Nancy Hanks.

W. MALONEY, KALAMAZOO, MICH.
The Canadian boy that conditioned and drove Dancourt 2:16¼
when he won The Horseman Stake at Detroit in 1894.

eye—Peerless, by Defiance.. .... 2:28¼
Daisy Garfield, b m, 1886, by Garfield—Osborn Mare, by Reconstruction .. 2:27
Daisy Hamilton, b m, 1874, by Blackstone—Lady Hamilton (dead) 2:28½
Daisy Hartshorn, ch m, 1878, by Aberdeen—Emeline, by Henry B. Patchen 2:24½
Daisy J., b m, 1867, pedigree not traced 2:27
Daisy J., ch m, 1886, by Golden Wing—Lucy 2:24¼
Daisy Kelly, b m, 188—, by Don J. Robinson 2:29¼
Daisy Kenmore, ch m, 1885, by Kenmore—Little Wonder 2:25½
Daisy L., b m, 188, by Lawrence 2:27¾
Daisy Lambert, ch m, 1885, by Motion—Dolly, by DeLong's Ethan Allen.. 2:23½
Daisy M., b m, 188—, by Morris' Almont 2:25
Daisy Mac 2:25
Daisy N, ch m, 188—, by Nutwood ... 2:26½
Daisy P., b m, 188—, by Gov. Seymour 2:22¼
Daisy Queen, gr m, 1883, by Sir Walter Scott—Kitty Scott, by Jim Scott. 2:24½
Daisy R., br m, 1881, by Lexington Chief—Kate 2:25½
Daisy Rolfe, b m, 1881, by Young Rolfe—Gretchen, by Gideon 2:20¼
Daisy S., ch m, 187—, by Tilton Almont, dam by Rattler (dead)..... 2:23½
Daisy W., blk m, 188—, by Onawa.... 2:23¼
Daisy Ward, b m, 188—, by Ward's Lambert 2:23¾
Daisy Wilkes, br m, 1880, by George Wilkes—Daisy Dean, by Gov. Clark.. 2:30
Daisy Wood, b m, 1891, by Silkwood.. 2:27
Dakoma, b m, 1886, by De Soto—Concord Maid, by Hamlet..... 2:27½
Dakota Maid, ch m, 187—, pedigree not traced 2:26¼
Dallie Wilkes, gr m, 1886, by Red Wilkes—Ida, by Alta 2:14
Dalphia D., gr m, 1889, by Nutwood—Dalphine, by Harold 2:29¼
Damania, ch g, 1887, by Nutmeg—Maud R., by Mambrino Sultan...... 2:22¾
Daly, b s, 1883, by Gen. Benton—Dolly, by Electioneer 2:15
Dame Trot, blk m, 1870, by Messenger Duroc—Green Mountain Maid, by Harry Clay 2:22
Damon, br s, 1869, by Palmer Bogus—Old Grey, by Grey Eclipse 2:23¾
Damosella, b m, 188—, by Nelson—Flora S, by Gideon..... 2:25
Dan, ch g, 1874, by Bay Billy (Wild Willie) 2:25¼
Dan, ch g, 188—, pedigree not traced. 2:24½
Dan, br s, 1880, by Flaxtail—Wild Wolf 2:30
Dan, b g, 188—, by Electioneer 2:20¾
Dana Wilkes, b s, 188—, by Victor Wilkes 2:29½
Dan B., b g, 188, pedigree not traced.. 2:26¼
Dan Backman, b s, 1884, by Charles Backman—Thalia, by Bashaw Messenger 2:22½
Dan Bailey, b g, 188—, by J. W. Bailey 2:28½
Dan Berry, ch g, 188—, by Guarantee 2:23½
Dan Brown, b g, 188—, by Anteeo—Miss Brown, by Brown's Volunteer.. 2:24¾
Danbry, b s, 1884, by Catch Colt—Maggie B., by Menelaus..... 2:30
Dan Bryant, ch g, 186—, by Plow Boy, dam by Rappahannock (dead).. 2:24

Dance', b s, 1886, by Alarm—Omaha Maid, by Fisk's Mambrino Chief Jr.. 2:25½
Dancourt, blk s, 1890, by Ambassador—Lowland Girl, by Legal Tender Jr. 2:16½
Dan Cupid, b s, 1888, by Barney Wilkes—Astermore, by Strathmore.. 2.00½
Dan Donaldson, ch g, 187—, by Bonnie Scotland 2:24¾
Dandy, b g, 1884, by Atlantic—Fancy, by Blazing Star 2:14¾
Dandy (See Taylorson).
Dandy, b s, 1887, by Karatus—Flora, by Novelty 2 30
Dandy Boy, br s, 1881, by Almont Rattler—Nelly Tole, by Baker Horse 2.29¾
Dandy Boy, br g 2 29
Dandy Boy, b g, 187— 2.30
Dandy C., b g, 1886, by Almont Chief—Joqua, by Glenn's Hambletonian.. 2:21¾
Dandy Dan, ch s, 1886, by Attorney—Topsy, by J. L. 2 24¼
Dandy Jim, gr g, 1885, by Young Jim—Caprara, by Daniel Lambert...... 2 10½
Dandy L., b s, 188—, by Albington. .. 2:29¼
Dandy L., ch g, 188—, by Antar Jr.... 2:29¼
Dandy R., b g, 188—, by Bay Billy ... 2:27¼
Dandy R., b s, 188—, by Alley Russell 2:27¼
Dandy Salisbury, ch s, 1889, by Judge Salisbury—Belle A., by Shelby Chief. 2:24¼
Dandy Sprague, b s, 188—, by Ashland Sprague, dam by Blue Bull 2 25
Dandy Time Jr., b s, 1880, by Dandy Time—Fly Warwick, by Warwick .. 2:25
Dandy Whitestockings, ch g, 1879, by Rocket Jr.—Magga 2:27¼
Dandy Wilkes, b g, 1888, by Wilkesmont, dam by Black Frank...... 2.28½
Dandy Wilkes, blk s, 1885, by Ambassador—Kentucky Whip, by Tiger Whip 2:23¾
Dandy Wilkes, br g, 1886, by Star Wilkes—Nelly B., by Esperango..... 2:29½
Danforth, b g, 188—, by Dauntless.... 2.27
Danger, b g, 1883, by Oddfellow—Fanny G. 2 26¼
Danger, b g, 188—, by Nil Desperandum 2:27
Dan H., b g, 1881, by Grantham Chief 2:26½
Dan H., b s, 1890, by Brod Walnut—Peach Blossom, by Bruce..... 2 27¼
Dan Howell, b g, 1864, by Young Highlander, dam by Brown's Bellfounder (dead) 2 29½
Daniel Boone, gr g, 186—, pedigree not traced (dead) ..... 2·28¼
Daniel Lambert, ch s, 1879, by Aurora—Lady Sherman, by Milliman's Bellfounder 2:28
Daniel the Prophet, b g, 1870, by Red Eagle—Flora, by Napoleon 2:27
Daniel Webster, b g, 1873, by American Ethan—Nora Welsh, by Toronto Chief Jr. 2:29¼
Dan Jenkins, gr s, 1879, by Joe Brown—Ann E., by Chalmer's Jupiter (dead) 2:28
Dan Jennings, b g, 1884, by Luke Brodhead, dam by Aaron Pennington 2.25
Dan L., ch g, 188—, by Sherman..... 2:26¾
Dan Mace, b g, 1885, by Dunham Abdallah—Hannah D., by Erie Abdallah 2.23
Dan Mace, ch g, 1855, pedigree not traced (dead) 2 30
Dan Mack, b g, 188—, by Mammont... 2·27¾
Dan Miller, ch g, 1884, by Daniel Lambert—Lucy Miller, by Administrator (dead) ..... 2·23¼

Dannemora, blk s, 1883, by Kernwood—Lady Anna, by Woodford Mambrino 2:29
Dan N., b s, 188—, by Dan B........ 2:28¼
Dan Neville, b s, 1887, by Hamdallah—Esther, by Silas Wright 2.28
Dan O., ch g, 188—, by Edwin Pilot.. 2:25¼
Dan Phallamont, ch s, 1888, by Phallamont—Lady Miles, by McAlmont.. 2 24½
Dan S., blk g, 1885, by Young Almont. 2.20
Dan S., ro g, 1879, by Wood's Hambletonian—Nancy S., by a son of Black Hawk 2:24¼
Dan Smith, b g, 187—, by Reporter, dam by Trustee 2:21¼
Dan Velox, br g, 188—, by Black Prince 2:16½
Danville Wilkes, b s, 1879, by Lyle Wilkes—Flora, by Skedaddle 2:27
Dan Voorhees, b s, 1880, by Dauntless—Bay Bessie, by Tom Hunter 2:30
Dan Vorhees, ch s, 186—, by Gen. McClellan—Fisher Mare (dead) 2.23¼
Dan Voorhees, ch s, 1877, by Black Frank Turdey Mare 2.30
Dan Wilkes, gr g, 188—, by Mambrino Wilkes 2:24¼
Dan Wilson, blk g, 188—, by Dan Logan 2 23¼
Daphne, b m, 1889, by Onward—Lady Alice, by Almont 2:25
Daphne, b m, 1885, by Col. Hambrick Belle Monroe, by Nick Monroe ... 2:16¼
Dora H., b m, 1891 .... 2:26
Parlee, gr g, 188—, by Almonarch .. 2:23¾
Darby b g, 188—, pedigree not traced 2:30
Darby, b g, 1872 by Delmonico—Black Bess, by Cox's Stump the Dealer 2:16½
Darkness, blk m, 1877, by Mountain Boy—Fanny Walker 2.21½
Darkey Wilkes, blk s, 188—, by Billy Wilkes, dam by Rock Island Bashaw 2:28½
Dark Night, b m, 1886, by Fieldmont—Night, by Herod 2.25½
Darkwood, blk s, 1887, by Right Onward—Lilly Pepper, by Pepper 2 27¼
Darling, b g, 188—, by Dan Mitchell.. 2.24½
Darlington, b s, 1882, by Wellington—Boadicea, by Rysdyk's Hambletonian 2:18¼
Darwinna br m, 1887, by Meredith—Filgate, by Milliman's eBllfounder (dead) 2:23½
Dashwool, b s, 1888, by Sentinel Wilkes—Nutwood Queen, by Nutwood 2:22
Dashwood, blk s, 1889, by Simmons 2:30
D. A. T., ch g, 1880, by Dorsey Golddust—Montgomery Mare, by Smith's Emperor .... 2·23¼
Dauntess, br m, 1885 by Dauntless, dam by Tramp 2:28½
Dauntless, (Parkis Abdallah) b s, 186—. by Taggart's Abdallah...... 2:26¾
Dauntless, L., ch g, 1888, by Dauntless Jr.—Black Mag 2:20¼
Dave Cook, b g, 1890, by Valdemeer 2:24¾
Dave Cox, b g, 188—, by Eagle Bird, dam by Hambletonian Mambrino.. 2:29¼
Davenant, gr s, 1879, by Belmont—Dahlia, by Pilot Jr. 2:26¼
Dave Highland, ch s, 1890, by Thistle 2:30
Don D'Loid, b g, 1890, by Conaloid 2:26
Dave Palmer, gr g, 188—, by Buch's Patchen (dead) 2:26½
Dave Salisbury, ch s, 188—, by Judge Salisbury 2:29¼
Dave Wilson, b g, 1886, by Hamlet—Fanny 2 24¼
Dave Young, ch g, 187—, by Stephen A Douglas 2 23
David B., b g, 188—, by Forrest Prince, dam by Baird's Hambletonian Prince 2:28
David B., ch g, 1889, by Young Jim—Rosa Clay, by American Clay 2:10¼
David C., b g, 1872, by Case's Dave Hill—Miss Heath, by Young Napoleon 2:25
David H., b g, 1888, by Young Wilkes—Rosetta, by Pickering 2:29¾
David Jones, b g, 188—, by Pearsall.. 2.17¼
David L., blk g, 187—, by Fuller Wilkes—Fields Mare, by Rysdyk's Hambletonian 2:19½
David P., b g, 188—, by Almont Revenge 2 24¼
David R., br g, 187—, by Swigert—Kate, by Blue Bull 2 29¼
David Wallace, ch s, 187—, by Mambrino Pilot 2:28
Davy B., b g, 188—, by Davenant.. 2.27¼
Davis Boy, blk g, 188—, ... 2:29½
Davy Crockett, ch g, 188—, by Golddust Chief 2:29½
Dawn, ch s, 1881, by Nutwood—Countess, by Whipple's Hambletonian 2.18¾
Dawnland b g, 188—, by Dauntless.. 2:30
Dawn R., br s, 1887, by Alcantara—Dainty, by Dictator 2:22¾
Dawson, b g, 1884, by Mansfield—Louie, by Rysdyk's Hambletonian 2:19¼
Dayball, ch g, 1885, by Banker Rothschild—Daisy 2:30
Daybreak, ch s, 188—, by Green Boy 2.25¼
Day Dream, ch m, 1879 by Cuyler—Lucia, by Rysdyk's Hambletonian.. 2:21¾
Daylight, br g, 1887, by Eros—Crazy 2:27¾
Daylight, b g, 1888, by Chief of Echo 2:21½
Daylight, b s, 1885, by Gen. Benton—Ameriquita, by Electioneer 2:26¾
Daylight, b g, 1884, by Starlight—Boadicea, by Rysdyk's Hambletonian 2:19¼
Dayton Belle, ch m, 187—, by Blue Bull—Dayton Belle, by Hall's Mohawk Jr. 2:29¾
Dazzle, b m, 1887, by Slander—Daphne, by Jay Gould 2:29½
D. C., b s, 1884, by Dictator—Jane Carlisle, by Antar 2:23
D. C. S., b g, 1874, by Joe Elmo—Alice Drye, by May's Sir Wallace 2:22¼
Deacon, ch g, 1884, by Jefferson Prince 2:28
Deadwood, br s, 188—, pedigree not traced 2:28¾
Dean Wilkes, b m, 1885, by Sherman Wilkes—Saucy Dean, by Paladine .. 2:25¼
Dearest, b m, 188—, by Thomas K... 2.26¼
De Barry, b g, 1879, by Nil Desperandum—Susie, by Happy Medium .. 2:13½
Deborah b m, 188—, by Sable Wilkes, dam by Le Grande 2:21½
Deceit, br g, 1869, by Jean Baptiste, (dead) 2:30
Decider, br s, 1885, by Detractor, dam by Live Oak........ 2·29¼
Deceiver, br g, 188—, by Ethan Allen 2d 2:20¼
Deceiver, blk g, 188—, by Rampart 2:30
Deception, gr g, 186—, pedigree not traced (dead) 2:22½
Deck Wright, b g, 1869, by Hinsdale Horse—Doll Wicks, by Young North

Briton (dead) 2:19¾

Decorah, b s, 1884, by Mambrino Patchen—Hattie Allen, by George Wilkes 2:26¼

Decorum, ch g, 1890, by Victor Wilkes, dam by Blitzen Jr.......... 2:28½

Decorator, ro s, 1882, by Masterlode—Pet Ferguson, by Mingo Chief 2:22½

Defender, blk s, 1877, by George Wilkes—Mist, by Ward's Flying Cloud 2.26

Defiance, br s, 1880, by William Rysdyk—Begum, by Alcalde 2:27¼

Defiance, br g, 186—, by Chieftain (pacing 2.17¾) (dead) 2 24

Delavan, gr s, 1887, by Pilot Medium—Belle Paddock, by Magna Charta 2·25½

Delaware, ch g, 186—, by Morgan Black Hawk—Fanny, by Gen Taylor 2 28

Delaware, b s, 1886, by Chestnut Joe—Merry Lass, by Rysdyk's Hambletonian 2:29¼

Delaware Medium, b s, 1882, by Happy Medium—Dolly, by Richelieu ... 2 30

Delbert, br s, 1891, by Gamaleon—Altama, by Attorney 2.21

Delcho, b s, 1885, by Oneco—Dolly, by Edward 2.23¼

Delectus blk, s, 1887, by Dictator—Patchen, by Mambrino Patchen ... 2·18½

Delegate, b g, 1880, by Dictator—Bertha, by Blackwood 2:27¾

Delegate, br s, 1884, by Dictator—Fanny H., by Red Wilkes 2 19½

Delegate, b s, 1888, by Hamlin's Almont Jr—Toy, by Hamlin Patchen 2.21¼

Delegate, b g, 1887, by Decorate—Molly P., by Chester 2:29¼

Delhi b g, 186—, pedigree not traced (dead) 2:29½

Della Shipp, b m, 188—, by Major Landers 2 21

Dell, br g, 1886, by Rowdy Boy—Dolly 2.27

Della, b m, 1884, by Little Dan—Della 2 28

Della McGee, ch m, 1886, by Walkill Prince—Kate McGee, by Blue Bull.. 2 28-

Dell Brown br s, 1888, by Boston Wilkes—Venus, by Abdamed Allen 2 29½

Del Mar, b s, 1887, by Electioneer—Sontag Dixie, by Toronto Sontag.. 2 16¾

Delmarch, b s, 1884, by Hambrino—Ella G., by George Wilkes 2 11½

Delmas, ch s. 1886, by Almoon—Queen 2 25¾

Delmont, b g, 1884, by Howe's McGregor—Belle, by Young Defiance.. 2·30

Delmont b s, 1891, by Delmarch, dam by Royal Chief 2:18¾

Del Monte, br g, 1879 by Fire Fly—Susan 2:21½

De Long, br s, 1891, by Gambetta Wilkes—Miss Moulton, by Nutwood 2.30

Del Paso ro s, 1885, by Dexter Prince—Daisy D., by Electioneer 2.24½

Delph, b g, 1888, by King Almont—Beck, by Hutchinson Chief (pacing record 2·24¾) 2.27½

Del Ray, ch s, 1886, by Clay Duke—Madonna, by Strader's Cassius M. Clay Jr. .... 2·24¾

Del Sur, blk s, 1876, by The Moor—Gretchen, by Mambrino Pilot .... 2·24

Dembert b s, 188—, by Wabash, dam by Egbert .... 2·30

Democrat, b g, 188—, by Sam Harris 2.24½

Democrat, b g, 1882, by Kisbar—Kate 2:24½

Demonstrator, b s, 188—, by Walkill Prince 2:30

Dennis Ryan, br s, 1880, by Berlin—Lady Washington, by American Boy Jr. 2 29

Denmark blk g, 1864, by Country Boy, dam by Hawkeye (dead) 2.30

Dennis, blk s, 188—, by Dennis Ryan 2:27¾

Dennis, b g, 188—, by Fairholm 2 24¼

Dennis H, b s, 188—, by Ben Franklin 2.28

Dennis P., b s, 1884, by Abdallah Woodford—Hannah, by Volunteer.. 2:29¼

Deposit, ch s, 1888, by Madrid—Gleaner, by Onward 2.29¾

Deputy, b s, 1884, by Echo, Marie Rose, by Inca 2:19½

Derby, b g, 1859, by Rough and Ready, dam by Wilcox's Dragon (dead) 2:25½

Derby Princess blk m, 1892, by Charles Derby—Princess, by Administrator 2:25

Deronda, b m, 188—, by Strathmore, dam by Kentucky Prince 2.27¼

Desdemona, b m, 1876, by Old Joe—Toss, by Louis Napoleon 2 27

De Soto, ch s 188—, by Ranchero, dam by Country Gentleman 2 24

Despardo, b g, 18—, by Richard's Elector 2:29½

Despatch, (Windsor) ro g, 1872, by Lewiston Boy—Nelly, by Berry Horse 2:24¼

Desperation, b s, 1887, by Nil Desperandum—Lizzie, by Goldsmith's Abdallah 2.30

Despot, ro s, 1878, by Dictator—Spray by Bay Munson 2:29

Dessie Wingate, b m, 1884, by Onward—Dora, by Bayard Jr. 2.28

Deucalion, b s, 1867, by Rysdyk's Hambletonian—Trusty, by Marlborough 2:22

Deuxmillion, ch s, 1885, by Deucalion—Blanche B, by Holabird's Ethan Allen 2 29½

DeWitt C., b g, 1884, by Doncaster—Lulu, by Erie Abdallah 2:29¼

De Wulff, ch g, 1886, by Henry Gilbert—Lida Bliss, by Toronto Patchen 2 21½

Dexter, b s, 1886, by Mambrino Jester 2:27

Dexter, br g, 1858, by Milliman's Bellfounder, dam by Sumpter ..... 2·27

Dexter, br g, 1858, by Rysdyk's Hambletonian—Clara, by Seely's American Star (dead) 2.17¼

Dexter, b g, 188—, by Peter Blair.. 2 25

Dexter, b g, 186—, by Volunteer, dam by Seely's American Star (dead) .... 2·27

Dexter C., b g, 188— by Dick Edwards .... 2·24½

Dexter H., b g, 187—, by Banker Messenger, dam by King Faro..... 2·29¼

Dexter L., gr g, 188—, by Abdamed Allen 2 25

Dexter Princess, b m, 1887, by Dexter Prince—Queen Wilkes, by Mambrino Wilkes 2.24¼

Deyo b s, 188—, by Dauntless 2:24

D G B, br g, 188—, by Stillson..... 2·29¼

Diadem, b s, 1886, by Diadem—Nancy, by Col. Ellsworth 2.25¼

Diamond, blk g, 1890, by Forrest Bismarck 2 24¼

Diamond, blk s, 1874, by Wild Bashaw—Debra by Wapsie 2 28

Diamond, b g 1883, by Vandergriff

Colt—Mayfly Drennon 2 15¼
Diamond, ch g, 188—, pedigree not traced 2 30
Diamond Joe, b g, 1886, by Maplehurst, dam by Young Cabell... 2:18
Diana, b m, 1887, by Claimant—Josie H, by Talleyrand 2 29¼
Diana, ch m, 188—, by Harbinger. . 2.24½
Diatonic, br s, 1883, by Fairy Gift—Nelly, by Gage's Logan 2 27¼
D I C, b g, 188—, by Taunton 2 28½
Dickard, ch g, 1873, by Daniel Lambert—Doane Mare, by Young Columbus 2 23¼
Dick, b g, 1882, by Major Benton—Topsey, by Bacon's Ethan Allen.... 2:26¼
Dick, b g, 1887, by William H. Vanderbilt 2 29
Dick Brown, br g, 188—, pedigree not traced 2 29¼
Dick C, b g, 1887, by St. Cloud—Nelly 2:30
Dick Dimple, b g, 1886, by Peoria—Flora 2:30
Dick Eddy, b s, 1886, by Jerome Eddy—Daisy, by Index 2.21½
Dick Flaherty, ch g, 188— by Fearnaught (?) 2.29¼
Dick French, ch g, 188—, by Little Hamilton 2:19½
Dick Garrett, b g, 1877, by Tramp—Sylvia 2:29¼
Dick H, b g, 1884, by Hunt's Blue Bull—Hunt Mare 2 29½
Dick Hardin, b s, 1888, by Shawmut—Beauty, by Dictator 2 29
Dick Hartford, br s, 1885, by Bay Dick—Belle Hartford, by Hartford Hambletonian 2:23
Dick Jamison, b g, 186—, by Joe Downing (dead)...... ...... 2 26
Dick Jay, b g, 187—, by Gen McClellan Jr. (?) 2 30
Dick Johnson, br g, 187—, by Swigert, dam by Phelps' Bellfounder....... 2 29¼
Dick Mitchell, b g, 188—, by Gov. Stanton 2 28¼
Dick Moore, ch g, 1871, by Belmont—Mary, by Monmouth Eclipse (dead). 2:22½
Dick Organ, blk g, 1873, by Commodore—Campbell, by Tom Hal 2.24¼
Dick Richmond, gr s 1882, by A W. Richmond—Belle, by Ben Wade .. 2:20
Dick Roach, gr g, 188—, by Port Leonard 2 24¼
Dick Smith, ch g, 1883, by Luke Brodhead—Calaway Maid by Rockaway. . 2:17
Dick Stauffer, ch g, 188—, by Blue Bull 2 20¼
Dick Swiveller, b g, 1870, by Walkill Chief—Madam Swiveller, by Henry Clay Jr 2 18
Dick Taylor, gr g, 1869, by Bob Didlake 2:24¼
Dick Wilkes, b g, 188—, by Sentinel Wilkes, dam by son of Lexington. 2·30
Dick Wills, b g, 188—, by Wilkesonian, dam by Indian Chief (pacing 2 16¼) .... 2·25¼
Dick Wood, blk g, 188—, by Ellal G. 2:26½
Dick Richmond, br s, 1888, by Pretender—Namouna, by A W Richmond .... 2·27½
Dictator, b g, 1869, by Goldsmith's Abdallah—Fanny, by Blood Royal . 2:27
Dictator (Huckleberry), blk g, 1864, by Comet (dead) 2 22¼
Dictator, ch g, 1883 by Rooker—Big Bird, by John E Rysdyk 2 27¼

Dictator Chief, b s, 1882, by Dictator—Judy, by Plato 2 21½
Dictator G, br s 1885, by Prince Dictator—Fanny Play, by Toronto . 2:30
Dictator Prince, b s, 1889, by Dictator—Vineland, by Kentucky Prince 2 29
Dictator Sidney, b s, 188—, by Sidney, dam by Dictator 2 25
Dictionary, b s, 1884, by Dictator—San Waw by Administrator 2.30
Dictum, br s, 1888, by Dictator Almont—Hetty, by Frank Moscow. . 2·20½
Diddle, b m, 188—, by Brown Mark—Fanny 2.25¼
Dido, b m, 1885, by Judge Gould—Russie, by Joe Young 2 20¼
Die Vernon, rn m, 1888 by Jay Bird—Young Winnie, by Woodford Mambrino 2 27¼
Digma, b s, 1889, by Rumor—Daisy, by Socrates 2.25¼
Diligent, b s, 1883, by Dictator—Jane Carlisle, by Antar 2 28½
Dillard Alexander, br s, 1883, by Alexander—Moonbeam, by John Dillard.. 2 30
Dilleman, b m, 188—, by Eros, dam by Grenadier .... 2·26
Dinah, blk m, 188—, by Norway Knox—Fanny Patchen, by Tom Patchen.. 2 28½
Dinah, b m, 1887 by Israel—Scofield Mare, by Scofield Nelson 2.21¾
Dinah, rn m, 1865, by Young Flying Cloud—Dinah, by Vermont Hambletonian 2 30
Dinah, b m, 1882, by Little Billy, dam by Ontario 2 27½
Dinah Cossack, b m, 18—, by Don Cossack 2 25¾
Dinnie, b m, 1880, by Rochester—Miss Coons, by Clark Chief 2 25
Dio, b g, 1870, by Gen Sherman—Fanny, by Ethan Allen (dead) . 2 30
Diplomacy, b m, 1885, by Don Cossack—Luella, by Hero of Thorndale. 2·27
Direct, blk s, 1885, by Director—Echora, by Echo (pacing record 2.06) 2 18¼
Directa, blk m, 1886, by Director—Alida, by Admiral 2.28
Direct Line, b s, 1889, by Director—Lida W by Nutwood 2 29
Director, blk s, 1877, by Dictator—Dolly, by Mambrino Chief 2 17
Director's Flower, b m, 1891, by Director—Sunflower, by Elmo 2 20
Director's Jug, blk s, 1885, by Director—Lizzie, by John Netherland 2.29½
Directress, br m, 1886, by Director—Aloha, by A W Richmond 2 28¾
Directum, blk s, 1889, by Director—Stem Winder, by Venture ...... 2·05¼
Dirego, br s, 1888, by Principe, dam by Belmont 2 18½
Dirigo, br s, 1856, by Drew Horse (dead) 2 29
Dirigo, b g, 186—, by Foxhunter, dam by St. Clair 2 27
Disputant, b s, 1886, by Harold—Debutante, by Belmont ...... 2·18
Distaff, ch m, 1888 by King William—Tricotrin, by Stillson 2 28¼
Dixie, b m, 1887, by Allegro, dam by Eureka 2 26¼
Dixie, gr m, 1858, by Pilot Jr—Jenny Lind, by Bellfounder (dead) 2:30
Dixie Sprague, b m, 1877 by Gov Sprague—Dixie, by Pilot Jr 2 25¼
Dixie V., br g, 1880, by Dixie—Wickle, by Green's Bashaw .... . 2·27¼

D. K. W. (See Monte Christo)
D. Monroe, b s, 187—. by Jim Mon-
roe—Betty, by Duvall's Mambrino.. 2:28¾
D. N. T. ch g, 1880 by Masterlode
—Kate Hunter, by Pierre Holse.... 2:27¾
Doble, blk s, 1870, by Ericsson—Belle,
by Scrugg's Davy Crocket 2:28
Doc F., blk g, 1882, by Scotch Prince 2·26
Doc M., b g, 1886, by C. A. Niles—
Flora G. .... 2·28¾
Doc McLaughlin. b s, 1871, by Mor-
gan Messenger—Flora, by Getaway 2:30
Dr. Almont, ch g, 1881, by Almont
Boy—Enchantress, by Trouble..... 2:21¾
Dr. Barth. b s, 188—, by Eagle Bird. 2.30
Dramatist, b s, 1889, by Egotist—
Worthea. by Harold 2:20½
Dr. C., b s, 1887, by Swigert—Al D,
by Alden Goldsmith 2:27½
Dr C., b g, 188—, ... 2:26
Dr. Carver, b s, 1885, by New York
Dictator—Kitty Morgan, by Joe
Downing Jr. 2:20¼
Dr Caton, b s, 1888. by Ganymede—
Atalanta, by Don Cossack 2:18½
Dr Cronin, b s, 1889, by Brown Frank
—Lady Gray, by Hambletonian
Chief 2:27½
Dr. Day, b s, 1886, by Seneca Patchen
—Lady Hamblet, by Administrator. 2:27
Doctor E., br s, 1886. by Hambletonian
Downing—Roda, by Morgan Mes-
senger .... 2·28
Dr. Dix, br g, 188— 2.30
Dr. Forest, ch g, 188—, by Forest
Mambrino 2:22¼
Dr. Frank, rn g, 1877, by George Hall
Kit, by Gen Taylor 2:27½
Dr. Franklin Jr., blk s, 188—, by Dr.
Franklin, dam by Hamet 2:26
Dr. French, b s, 1888, by Fred S.
Wilkes 2:23¼
Dr Fritts, b g, 1889, by Garnet
Wilkes—Daisy .... 2·25
Doctor H., rn s, 1889, by Mambrino
Dick—Fanny, by Bashaw Pilot..... 2·28
Doctor Hooker, b s, 1890, by Vatican
—Mary Ann, by White's Hamble-
tonian 2:23¾
Dr. Kidd, blk g, 188—, by Count—
Wilkes. dam by Vindex .... 2·24½
Dr. Lewis, ch g, 1871, by Marshal
Chief .... 2·24
Dr. McFarland, b g, 1883, by Sterling,
dam by Robert Fillingham Jr ...... 2·21¾
Dr Miller. b g, 1878, by Young Volun-
teer—Dolly .... 2·27½
Dr Morland, b s, 188—, by Lewis Na-
poleon 2:28½
Dr Norman, b g, 1877, by Col Moore
—Bay Liz, by McDonald's Hiatoga.. 2:19¾
Dr. Puff, b s, 1892, by Bay Bird—
Polly Puff 2.29
Dr. S., ch s, 1888. by Altitude—Molly,
by Allegro .... 2·29¼
Dr Sheppard, b s, 1875, by Blue Bull
—Bird .... 2·29¼
Dr. Smith. gr g, 1879, by Gov. Mor-
rill—Dixie 2:26½
Dr Sparks. b s, 1887, by Cyclone—
Lilly. by Monroe Chief .... 2·12¼
Doctor T. b g. 188—, by Duquesne—
Kit, by Young Toronto .... 2·27½
Dr. Tilton. b g, 1885, by Twilight—
Lady Tilton, by Abdallah Mambrino 2:25½
Doctor C., b g, 188—, by Crayford.. 2·26¾
Dodger, ch s 1886 by Arminius—City
Girl 2.18

Dodgeville. b g, 1888, by Oberlin—
Country Girl, by Country Boy ..... 2·14¼
Dohrman, br s, 1890, by Abbottsford
—Eureka Belle, by Dexter Bradford 2:27
Dollikans, g m, 18—, by Robert Mc-
Gregor 2.26½
Dolly, br m, 1884, by Mambrino Dia-
mond—Maggie, by Live Oak........ 2:25
Dolly, b m, 186—, by Frank 2:30
Dolly B., b m, 1884, by Austerlitz—
Roxy St. Law ence, by Charter Oak 2 27½
Dolly B., b m, 188—, by Alaric...... 2.21½
Dolly C., b m, 1888, by Gen Stanton
—Lady Collins, by St. Lawrence
(dead) .... 2·19
Dolly Davis, ch m, 1871, by Almont—
Annie Eastin, by Morgan Rattler... 2·29
Dolly H., b m, 1888, by Abdallah
Hambletonian, dam by Lord Earl-
ington .... 2·20¼
Dolly H., b m, 188—, by Kennebeck
Knox .... 2·25¼
Dolly M., b m, 1888, by Copper Duke 2 23¼
Dolly Rene, b m, 1886, by King Rene
—Florine, by Administrator........ 2·29
Dolly S., dn m, 188—, by Bolton
Sprague 2:25½
Dolly Withers, b m, 1887, by Aber-
deen—Annabel, by George Wilkes... 2·29½
Domestic, b s, 1890, by Volunteer—
Godiva, by Godfrey Patchen (dead).. 2 20½
Domineer, b s, 1887, by Red Wilkes—
Lizzie H., by Star Almont 2 18¼
Dom Pedro, ch g, 1872, by Blue Bull. 2 27
Don, b s, 188—, by Almont Ledo..... 2.19¾
Don, b g, 188—, pedigree not traced.. 2.22¼
Don, gr g, 1870, by Aker's Idol—Mary
Weaver, by Black Hawk Vermont.. 2·22½
Donala, blk s, 188— 2 29¼
Donald, b g, 1875, by Dictator—Burch
Mare, by Brown Pilot .... 2·27
Donald, blk s, 1886, by George Wilkes
Jr.—Sonora 2:19½
Donald McKay, gr g, 1885, by Allegro
—Minnie, by Harrodsburg Boy ... 2 22½
Don Anteros, b s, 1890, by Anteros
—Bonnie Bee, by Harry B. 2:30
Don Aristos, blk s, 1885, by Aristos
Jr.—Dessie Lotta, by Haw Patch.... 2 29¾
Don C., b g, 1886, by Don Carlos—
Bryn Maur Maid, by Gen. Lee..... 2 18¼
Don Carlos, b s, 1880. by Cuyle·Clay
—Lady Abdallah, by Alexander's Ab-
dallah .... 2·23
Don Carlos, gr g, 1877, by Highland
Grey—Polly Daly. by Ed 2 28¼
Doncaster, b s, 1880, by Com. Belmont
—Virginia, by Mambrino Champion.. 2 28¼
Don Cossack, b s, 1876, by August
Belmont—Laytham Lass, by Alex-
ander's Abdallah (dead) 2 28
Don Cossack Jr., b s, 1887, by Tubal Cain
—Kate Wilson 2 30
Don Cossack Jr., br s, 1887, by Don
Cossack—Etta May, by Charley
Hammet 2 30
Don Donnan, b s, 1888, by Dictator
Wilkes—Maggie Berne, by Totoway 2.29¾
Don Elipha, b g, 186—, pedigree not
traced 2.30
Don Felix, b s, 1884, by Electioneer
—Adelaide, by Black Donald 2:27¼
Don H., ch s, 188—, by Tramp Jr..... 2·30
Don Gothard, b s, 1884, by St.
Gothard—Crescent, by Contractor.. 2:27
Don Governor, ch g, 188— 2 27½
Don L., b s, 188—, by Fieldmont—Nut-
meg Maid, by Thomas Jefferson... 2·28¾
Don L., br s, 188—, by Col Tom...... 2·23¼

Dundee, br s, 1876, by Jay Gould—
Meta, by Mambrino Pilot 2 25
Dundee, blk s, 188—, by Clifton 2 27½
Dunnette, b m, 1884, by Rienzi—Kate
Gano, by Garrard Chief 2:22¼
Duplex, b g, 188—, by Woodward's
Ethan Allen, dam by Daniel Lam-
bert ......, ... 2·25¼
Dupree, blk s, 1888, by Rumor—Daisy,
by Socrates 2.29½
Duquesne, ch s, 1875, by Tippoo Ba-
shaw—Wild Rose, by Rysdyk's Ham-
bletonian (dead) 2.17¼
Durado, blk m, by Clay King, dam
by Mambrino Time 2:27½
Durango, br s, 1877, by Strader's
Cassius M Clay Jr —Mattie West,
by Almont 2.23¾
Durango Belle, br m, 1888, by Dur-
ango—Gazelle, by Lofty....... 2 22¾
Durango Maid, br m, 1883, by Dur-
ango—Polka Dot, by Senator Mad-
den .... 2·28½
Duroc, br s, 1869, by Banker Messen-
ger—Lady Parker, by Young Ameri-
can 2 26¼
Duroc Gothard, br s, 1887, by St
Gothard—Maggie Duroc, by Messen-
ger Du'oc .... 2·29¼
Duroc Maid, ch m, 1875, by Messenger
Duroc—Fanny Sleight, by Ethan
Allen 2 29¼
Duroc Wilkes, blk s, 1884, by Sher-
man Wilkes—Duroc Pet, by Messen-
ger Duroc 2 28½
Duroc Wilkes, ch s, 1888, by Garnet
Wilkes—Molly Duroc, by Iowa
Duroc 2 18¾
Duster, ch g, 188—, by Cunard Jr.,
dam by Live Oak 2 21¼
Duster Wilkes, blk s, 1886, by Young
Wilkes—Nelly 2.27¼
Dusty Heels, ch m, 1888, by Rush-
ville—Bulla Mare .... 2·27½
Dusty Miller, ro m, 1882, by Triceps.. 2.20¼
Dutchess Boy, br g, 187—, pedigree
not traced 2 29¼
Dutch Girl, rn m, 1874, by Ab-
dallah Boy—Flora, by Black Doug-
las 2 27¾
Dutch Girl, gr m, 1858, by Dusty
Miller (dead) 2 29½
Dutch Girl, gr m, 1877, by Silvertail
—Wild Jin, by Wild Tom 2.27
Dutchman, gr g, 186—, pedigree not
traced (dead) 2 30
Dwight S., ch g, 1886, by Mohawk
Chief—Topsey 2 26¼
Dwyer, ch s, 1888, by Diplomat—
Maggie Twain, by Mark Twain.. 2 27¼
Dynamite, br g, 1887, by Teak Black-
wood Jr.—Ida, by Bob 2 30
Dynamite, b s, 1882, by Hambletonian
Downing—Maude, by Mambrino
Patchen Jr 2 28
Dynamite, blk g 1884, by Ben Frank-
lin—Bess, by Blackstone .... 2·20¾
Dynamite, blk g, 18—, by Gaviota .. 2 29½
Eager, b s, 1889, by Aristocrat—Kath-
leen, by Pilot Jr. 2.28
Eagle Bird, ro s, 1882, by Jay Bird—
Tansey, by George Wilkes .... 2·21
Eagle Lake, b m, 188—, by Walkill
Prince .... 2·27½
Eagle Pass, b g, 1891, by Haskew—
Winnie Lee, by Abdallah West . 2 29¾
Eagle Pass, rn g 1892, by Eagle Bird
Bell, by Uncle Gyp .. .· 2 23½

Eagle Plume, gr g, 1874, by Bayard—
Speed, by Thomas Jefferson .. ... 2·29¼
Earl, b s 1880, by Princeps—Juno, by
Rysdyk's Hambletonian .... 2·23¾
Earl, ch g, 187—, by Revenue 2 29½
Earl Baltic, b s, 1887, by Baron
Wilkes—Alpha Russell, by Mam-
brino Russell 2 25¼
Earl Belmont, b s, 1888, by Belmont
—Betsy Baker, by Dictator 2 26½
Earldom, b s, 1887, by Mambrino
Startle—Bell, by Stockbridge Duke.. 2 30
Earl Finch, b g, 188—, by Robin-
son's Blue Bull 2 26½
Eallie, blk s, 188—, by Guy Wilkes · 2.27¾
Earline, b m, 1885, by Earl—Pioletta,
by Woodford Pilot 2:24½
Earlite, ch m 1887, by Earl—Devo-
tion, by Cuyler 2.29¼
Earl King b s, 1889, by Viking—Bess
Blight, by John Blight 2 27
Earl McGregor, ch s, 1879, by Robert
McGregor—Leona, by Bay Billy .. 2.21½
Earlmont, b s, 1885, by Almont Gift
—Allie S by Ethan Allen Jr. .. 2.21
Earle's Lad, ch s, 1886, by Earl—
Helen Walker, by Pilot Mambrino 2 25½
Earle's Laddy, b s, 1886, by Earl—
Daisy Volunteer, by Volunteer .. 2:24¼
Earl's Lassie, b m, 1885, by Earl—
Flora 2:30
Early Bird, rn s, 1886 by Jay Bird
—Beulah, by Harold 2 12½
Early Bloom, br m, 1888, by Hermes
—Lillybloom, by Daniel Lambert ... 2:29¾
Early Dawn, b m, 1880, by George
Wilkes—Lady Frank, by Mambrino
Star .... 2·21½
Early Rose, ch m, 1875 by Almont—
Jenny, by Ward's Flying Cloud ... 2:20¼
Earnscliff br s, 1884, by Messenger
Chief—Minnie Helm, by American
Boy 2 29
Easter, b m 1886, by Intrigue—Belle
Lyons, by Balsora 2 23¼
Easter Boy, b g, 188—, by Abdaliah
Thorne 2:30
Eastern Boy, br s, 188—, by Gen.
Knox—Jessie, by Beal's Horse.... 2·29½
Eastern Boy, b g, 1881, by Little East-
ern—River Lily, by Gen. Benton.... 2:27¼
Easter Wilkes, b g, 1886, by Wilkes
Spirit Jr.—Ora by Young America.. 2.21¼
Fast View br g, 1887, by Alcyone—
Iredewica, by Oxmoor .... 2·23¾
Eastwood, b g, 1888, by Nuthunter—
Idlewood, by Blackwood Jr 2:24¼
Easy Billy, b g, 1873, by George M.
Patchen Jr —Miss Miller, by Tom
Kimball Jr................ 2·29½
Ebony Job, blk g, 1885 by Melrose—
Ingraham mare .... 2·28¼
Ebony Spink, blk s, 1884, by Spink—
Fanny, by Greyhound 2 29¼
Ebony Wilkes, blk s, 1886, by Adrian
Wilkes—Lady Patchen 2 19¼
Ebony Wilkes, blk s, 1883, by Am-
bassador—Nettie E, by Joe Hooker 2.29¼
Echo, br g, 187—, by Regulus 2:28¼
Echo Medium b g, 1886, by Starin
Medium—Winesap, by Van Dyke.. 2 21¼
Echo Chief, ch s, 1877, by Octibbeha
—Lady Bounce, by Orr's Mambrino 2·21¼
Echo Del Paso, b g, 188—, pedigree
not traced 2 28¼
Echora, br m, 1872, by Echo—Young
Mate, by Jack Hawkins 2 23½
Eclipse ch m, 1888 by Guy Wilkes

—Manon, by Nutwood 2.25¾
Eclipse, b g, 1876, by Edward Everett—Dolly Varden, by Imp Eclipse 2:24½
Economy, b m, 1884, by Echo—Lady Berkey, by Muldoon 2 30
Ecru, b m 1886, by Nephew—Ritchelders, by Messenger Chief 2 30
Ecru, dn m, 1880, by Belmont—Topsey, by St. Elmo 2 27½
Ed, b g, 188—, by Erwin Davis 2 26
Ed Biggs, br s, 188—, by Brigadier 2 28½
Ed Clarkson, b s, 1886, by Idol Wilkes—Maud X, by Mambrino Pet Jr 2 20¾
Ed Cook ch g, 188—, by Warwick Boy—Maggie Boylon, by Mercury 2·24½
Ed Davis, b g, 188—, by Counsellor 2.24¼
Eddie B., br g 1885, by Plato Jr—Fanny 2 29¼
Eddie G, b g, 188—, by Jefferson Prince 2 27½
Eddie Hayes, blk s, 1888, by Charles Caffrey—Eva, by Tippoo Bashaw 2 23½
Eddie Medium, b g, 1878, by Happy Medium—Lizzie Lee by Edwin Booth 2 29¼
Eddie Wilkes, blk g, 187—, by Commonwealth—Lady Wilkes, by Jimmy Rattler 2 23¼
Eddy, b s, 188—, by Damo 2 19½
Eddy Sherman, b s, 1889, by Sherman—Alma Eddy, by Jerome Eddy 2:29½
Ed Eaton gr g, 185—, by White Ghost—Fanny Phelps (dead) 2.28
Edelweiss, b m, 1880, by Colonna—Eliza, by Hartman Horse 2:30
Edenia, ch m, 1888, by Endymion—Empress, by Abdallah Mambrino 2:13½
Ed Fay, b g, 188—, by Chrisman Patchen, dam by Whipple's Hambletonian 2 28¾
Edgar, b g, 188— by Egbert 2 30
Edgar, ch g, 187—, by Col. Winfield—Molly McWhorter, by Young Daniel Webster 2:30
Edgar A b g, 1882, by Collins' Denmark, dam by Collins' Denmark 2 23¼
Edgardo, b s, 1885 by Rumor—Lucia, by Jay Gould 2·13¾
Edgar Dudley, b s 1887, by Ion—Heiress, by Administrator 2·17¾
Edgar Herr, b s, 188—, by Edgar Wilkes 2 29¼
Edgar Moody, b s 1888, by Moody—Durango Maid by Durango 2 21¼
Edgar P b s, 1889 by Nutbreaker—Lady Kate Sprague, by Gov Sprague 2 24¾
Edgar W., b g, 188—, by Manchester 2 24¼
Edgar Wilkes, b s, 1885, by Ethan Wilkes—Callie T, by Kentucky Prince 2 24¼
Edgecliff, b g 1875, by Baybrino—Moll, by Ward Horse 2 27
Edgehill br s, 1878, by Dictator—Sue, by Thorndale 2:25½
Edgemark b s, 1885 by Victor Bismarck—Edgewater Belle, by Edgewater 2 16
Edgerton, b s, 1885, by Blackwood—Enterprise, by Onward 2·26½
Ed Getchel, br g, 1869, by Winthrop Morrill 2·27
Edgewood, rn g 1885 by Tom Rogers—Little One, by Corbeau 2·21
Edgewood, br g, 1878, by Black Ranger—Doll 2 27¼
Edgewood b g, 187—, by Aberdeen 2·25¼
Ed Graham b g, 188—, by Gen George H Thomas, dam by Mambrino Cloud 2·24¼
Edifice, b s, 1888, by Jerome Eddy—Verney, by Haw Patch 2 21
Edina, br m, 1885, by Jerome Eddy—Dolly Bryant, by Regular 2 25¼
Edison, b g, 1878, by Gen. Knox—May Bug, by Aberdeen 2.27¾
Edith, b m, 1878, by Happy Medium—Black Bess by Black Oscar 2 22¼
Edith Almont, b m, 1882 by King Almont—Mary Ann, by Magnolia 2:26½
Edith F, b m, 188—, by Stephen A Douglass 2 28½
Edith Gard, b m, 188—, by Shadeland Onward 2 27½
Edith H, gr m, 1888 by Deucalion—Patti, by Nutbourne 2 12½
Edith N. b m, 1891, by Durango, dam by Laclede 2 27½
Edith R., b m, 1883, by Monaco—Augusta Schuyler, by Aberdeen 2.17¼
Edith Sprague, gr m, 188— by George Sprague—Kitty Hines 2 15¾
Edith V b m, 1888, by Little Ben—Laura G., by Flying Duke 2 24
Editor, b g, 1880, by Princeps—Duroc Maid, by Messenger Duroc 2 25½
Edleen, gr m, 188— by Jerome Eddy 2 27½
Ed Mack, br g 1880, by Hambletonian George—Flora, by Johnny Slasher 2 26¼
Ed Marsh, b g 188—, by Reliance 2 23¼
Edmonita, b m, 1878, by Dictator—Wingate, by Blackwood 2 30
Edmore, b s, 1881, by Louis Napoleon—Fanny Mapes, by Alexander's Abdallah 2 29¼
Edna, ro m, 186—, by a son of Wisconsin Tiger—Mary Barden, by Hobkirk's Sir Henry Jr (dead) 2 29¼
Edmund Burke, b s 1882, by Solicitor—Monette, by Bonnie Boy 2·30
Edna C., br m 1880, by Warwick Boy—Fanny Talmage, by Squire Talmage 2.29½
Edna M., b m, 1888, by Egbert—Grace G., by Petoskey 2·26
Edna W., b m, 1887, by Brougham—Belle of Clarence, by Finch's St Lawrence 2·29
Ed Sutherland, b s 1884, by Egbert—Lizzie Winn by Ericsson 2:29½
Ed Turner, ch s, 1887, by Crittenden—Jettie, by Gibson's Bay Pilot. 2 17¼
Edward, ch g, 1872, by Masterlode—Dolly 2 19
Edward, b g, 1884 by Volney—Daisy. 2 21¼
Edward B, ch g, 1878, by Blue Bull—Jenny Curtis, by Morgan Messenger 2 26½
Edward K br g, 1880, by Knox—Nelly Walker, by Mohawk Chief 2:23¼
Edwardo, b s, 1890, by Epaulet—Edith G., by Young Volunteer 2 26½
Edwin H, ch s, 1879, by Alert—Stencil by Stillson 2 27½
Ed White, b g, 1863, by Jim Scott (dead) 2·27
Ed Wilder ch g, 186—, pedigree not traced (dead) 2 30
Ed Wilkes blk g, 1885, by Bartholomew Wilkes—Bell Lindsey, by Girard Stockbridge 2 28½
Ed Wilkes b s 1882, by Young Wilkes—Flora Bush 2 26¼
Edwin ch g 188—, by Gooding's Champion—Fanny 2 29¼
Edwin A, b s, 1872, by Gooding's Champion—Miss Pratt by Henry Clay 2.24¾

—Midnight, by Pilot Jr............ 2·17¾
Electric King, b s, 1887, by Election-
eer—Mamie C., by imp. Hercules... 2 24
Electrina, b m, 1888, by Richard's
Elector—Stemwinder, by Venture... 2 20
Electrix, b m, 1887, by Electioneer—
Lady Russell, by Harold.......... 2·28½
Electro Bell, b m, 1890, by Electro-
type—Preamble, by Pancoast.. ... 2:27¾
Electrobenton. b s, 1889, by Election-
eer—Nettie Benton, by Gen. Benton. 2:24½
Electroid, b s, 1890, by Eros—Rosa
Bonheur, by Erwin Davis.......... 2:30
Electryon, b s, 1886, by Electioneer—
Lina K., by Don Victor............ 2:24¾
Electuary, b s, 1887, by Electioneer
—Maria, by Don Victor............ 2:27
Electwood, b s, 1886, by Electioneer-
Amrah, by Nutwood 2:30
Elegance, ch s, 1889, by Sidney—Dell
Foster, by A. W. Richmond 2:30
Elena, b m, 1888, by Capoul—Barbara,
by Egbert 2 24¾
Elevator, b s, 188—, by Sim's Clark
Chief 2.22¾
Elfinwood, ch s, 1889, by Nutwood—
Amora, by Attorney 2.15¼
Elfrida, b m, 1890, by Candidate—
Gladness, by Nutwood 2.18½
Elgin, b g, 188—, by Lothair Jr... 2:24¼
Elgin, b g, 188—, by Locomotive.... 2 27
Elgin Girl, blk m 2 27¼
EJ, br g, 1885, by Black Hawk Harry
—Pickle 2:23½
Bil, b g, 1880, by Lothair, dam by
Ethan Allen .... 2·28¼
Eli, dn g, 1877, by a Gypsy horse—
Belle of Clarence, by Finch's St.
Lawrence 2:30
Eli, b g, 1882, by Signal—Worten
Mare 2.18¾
Eli, ch g, 188—, by Melrose, dam by
Wright Horse 2:26
Eli Almont, ch g. 1885, by Almont
Pilot—Flash, by Orlando 2:22½
Elina, blk m, 1885, by Messenger
Duroc—Green Mountain Maid, by
Harry Clay 2:28
Elista, blk m, 1883, by Messenger
Duroc — Green Mountain Maid, by
Harry Clay .... 2·20¾
Elita Russell, b m, 1888, by Lord Rus-
sell—Elite, by Messenger Duroc.... 2:20¼
Elite, b m. 1887, by Messenger Chief
—Laura Thompson, by Dictator.... 2 30
Elixir, cr g, 1886, by Elyria, dam by
son of Stranger 2.22¼
Eliza Jane, b m, 1886, by Thomas K.
—McKenna Mare 2.26½
Eliza T., b m, 188—, by Vitruvian 2 19¾
Elkhorn, b s, 1887, by Onward—Long
Lane, by Long Island Patchen 2:28¼
Elkin, ch s, 1886, by Abdallah Mam-
brino, dam by Berkley's American
Clay 2.22¼
Elkmont, ch g, 188—, by Bostick's
Almont Jr...................... 2:30
Elko, br m, 1885, by Lumps—Katie
O, by Mambrino Patchen 2:17
Ella, b m, 1884, by Electioneer—
Lady Ellen, by Carr's Mambrino .. 2:29
Ella, b m, 1885, by Melrose—Belle
Hammond, by Honest Dan 2:28¼
Ella B., b m, 188—, by Guy Miller ... 2 26½
Ella Belmont, b m, 1888, by Belmont—
Ella Clay by American Clay 2:24¾
Ella Clay, b m, 1882, by Wilkus Clay 2·23¼
Ella Clay. b m, 1869, by American
Clay, dam by Mambrino Chief

(dead) 2:27½
Ella D., b m, 1887, by Azim—Maud
Walker 2:28½
Ella Doe, ch m, 1871, by Daniel Lam-
bert—Sticknose, by Cook's Colum-
bus .... 2·23½
Ella E., gr m, 188—, by Chicago Vol-
unteer 2.25
Ella E, b m, 1882, by Prince Elma—
Coaley 2.22
Ella Earl, br m, 1872, by Almont—
Suse, by John C. Breckinridge 2.25
Ella Elwood, b m, 1860, pedigree not
traced (dead) .... 2·29
Ella Lewis, b m, 1860, by Vermont—
Kate McDonough 2 27
Ella M., b m, 188—, by Richard's
Elector 2:28¾
Ella M., b m. 188—, pedigree not
traced 2 28½
Ella May, ch m, 1891, by Nephew—
Theora, by Gooding's Champion ... 2:28
Ella Madden, b m, 1868, by Rysdyk's
Hambletonian—Lady Vail, by
Drew's Hambletonian............ 2 25¾
Ella McGee, br m, 1887, by Elevator
—Valdue, by Vallive 2 29¼
Ella Norwood, b m, 1878, by Norwood
—Lady Winfield, by Edward Everett 2.22¼
Ello O, blk m, 1887, by Declaration
—Nelly Draco, by Draco......... 2:24
Ella O K., b m, 1887, by Wilkes Boy
—Daisy, by Daubigne 2:29
Ellard, b s, 1888, by Charley Wilkes
—Daisy, by Fearless 2:09¾
Ella Rene, b m, 1889, by Chastelard
—Anita, by Stockbridge 2 25
Ella Vertner, b m, 1889, by Epaulet
—Ella Medium, by Happy Medium 2:19½
Ella W., b m, 188— 2.29
Ella Wilkes, ro m, 1884, by Favorite
Wilkes—Betty Higgins, by Joe
Downing 2 26¼
Ella Wilson, bm, 1866, by Blue Bull—
Fanny Benson, by Jerry 2 30
Ella Woodline, br m, 1891, by Wood-
line—Venture, by Voltaire ...... 2·23½
Ella Wright, b m, 1863, by Trojan,
dam by Hercules .... 2·24¾
Ellemac, b m, 188—, by Alvan 2.27
Ellen Cooper, b m, 1877, by Star of
Catskill—Nelly Haynes, by Vol-
unteer 2:29¼
Elleneer, b m, 1888, by Electioneer—
Lady Ellen, by Carr's Mambrino.. 2:21½
Ellen Mayhew, blk m, 1886, by Direc-
tor—Lady Earnest, by Speculation. 2:22
Ellerslie Wilkes, blk s, 1880 by
George Wilkes—Aileen, by Mam-
brino Boy 2:22½
Ellington D., gr s, 1884, by Ellington
Boy—Lady D., by Norman D..... 2:26¾
Ellis, b g, 1886, by Zack Chandler—
Kit 2:26¼
Ellis Medium, b s, 188—, by Frank
Ellis 2.24
Elloree, ch m, 1890, by Axtell—Flora
McGregor, by Robert McGregor .. 2:18
Elma, b m, 1891, by Quaker Boy—
Lady Motor, by Mambrino Motor... 2:20¾
Elma Sontag, b m, 1890, by Elec-
tioneer—Sontag Dixie, by Toronto
Sontag .... 2·29
El Mahdi, ch s, 1885, by Onward—
Lady Bunker, by Mambrino Patchen 2:25½
Elmbrook, ro s, 1885, by Hamble-
tonian Chief—Pet Knox, by Gil-
breth Knox 2:26¼

Elmer, br g, 1875, by Gooding's Champion—Belle, by Rysdyk's Hambletonian 2:22¼
Elmer Wilkes, ch s, 1883, by Favorite Wilkes—Alma, by Almont Rattler.. 2:28
Elmo, ch s, 186—, by Wise's Mohawk 2:27
Elmo, b s, 1876, by St. Elmo—Jenny, by Tiger 2:27¼
Elmo Echo, br s, 1889, by Stoughton J. Fletcher—Alma, by Elmore 2.30
Elmo Maid, b m, 1885, by Joe Elmo—Nelly, by Doherty Horse 2:23¼
El Monte, gr g, 1882, by Echo—Lightfoot, by Hubbard 2:29
Elmore Everett, b g, 185—, by Andrew Jackson—Falka (dead) 2:30
Elmwood Chief, br g, 1875, by Black Ranger—Doll 2:18¾
Eloise, blk m, 1886, by Kentucky Prince—Camille, by Rysdyk's Hambletonian 2:15
El Pastore, b s, 188—, by Waterford 2:29
El Rami, ch g, 1891, by Wildnut—Nellie Benton, by Gen. Benton 2:29¾
E. L. Robinson, b s, 1889, by Epaulet —Lizzie M., by Thomas Jefferson... 2:17¾
Eliza S., b m, 188—, by Alcantara Jr. —Kataline, by Friday McCracken .. 2:16½
Elsie, ch m, 1887, by Regent—Maud, by Black Ranger 2:26½
Elsie B., br m, 1884, by Springstein's Bashaw 2:29¼
Elsie Good, ch m, 1871, by Blue Bull —Molly Patterson, by Alexander's Abdallah 2:22½
Elsie Groff, ro m, 1874, by Danville (dead) 2.25
Elsie Harris, blk m, 1889, by Scarlet Wilkes—Miss Limestone, by Limestone 2:25½
Elsie Manager, gr m, 1886, by Sample —Josie Ferris, by Altorf 2:30
Elsie S., ch m, 1888, by DuBois' Superior—Ruth 2:21½
Elsie Sprague, ch m, 1885, by Rounds' Sprague—Lady Rodman, by Belmont 2:18½
Elsie Wilkes, gr m, 1890, by Thorne Wilkes—Elsie, by Greenwood 2:24¾
Elsie Wood, blk m 1885, by John E. Wood, dam by Kentucky Whip... 2:30
Elsie Y., br m, 1876, by Whirlwind—Maud 2:29¾
Elsinore, ch s, 1888, by Jersey Wilkes —Lottie Patchen, by Mambrino Patchen 2:25
Elton, br s, 1890, by Egotist—Spring Time, by Nutwood 2:21
El Trebizond, br s, 1887, by Stambond—Ellwood, by A. W. Richmond 2:26½
Elvira, blk m, 1880, by Cuyler—Mary Mambrino, by Mambrino Patchen (dead) 2:18½
Elwina, b m, 1890, by Electioneer—Esther, by Express 2:27¼
Elwood, b g, 188—, by Alaric 2:30
Elwood, br g, 1889, by Kentucky Wilkes—Melinda, by Oxmoor 2:26½
Elwood Medium, b s 1874, by Happy Medium—Blanche, by Hopkins' Abdallah 2:24¾
Elyria, ch s, 1882, by Mambrino King —Maggie Marshall, by Bradford's Telegraph 2:25¼
Elvrina, b m, 1887, by Elyria—Minnie Hicks, by Garibaldi 2:20¼
Ely See, br s, 1888, by Talavera—Maud E., by McMahon 2:27½

Emaline, b m, 1884, by Electioneer—Emma Robson, by Woodburn...... 2:27½
Emaline K., ch m, 1885, by Redden's Lancewood Jr.—Magna 2:30
Embassador, blk s, 1880, by Ambassador—Julia Anderson, by Highland Morgan 2:25
Embassy, b m, 1885, by Ambassador—Jenny, by Robert Fillingham Jr. ... 2:21¾
Emblem, ch s, 1886, by Ambassador—Nettie, by Mambrino Patchen Jr... 2:27¼
Emeline K., ch m, 188—, by Lancewood Jr. 2:29
Emerald, b g, 187—, pedigree not traced 2:29¼
Emerald, gr g, 187—, pedigree not traced 2:30
Emerson King, blk s, 1887, by Mambrino King—Mandrake, by Blackwood Chief 2:27¼
Emily, b m, 1888, by Judge Hayes—Alice, by Menelaus 2:30
Emin Bey, b s, 1888, by Guy Wilkes—Tempest, by Sultan 2:21½
Eminence, b m, 1884, by Empire—Soprano, by Strathmore 2:18¼
Emma Armstrong, ch m, 1884, by Starmont—Belle Hines, by Hylas .. 2:28¾
Emma B., gr m, 1872, by Bayard, dam by Brown Harry 2:22
Emma B., ch m, 1883, by Highland Grey—Kathrina, by Daniel Lambert 2:26¼
Emma B., b m, 188—, by Sherman's Hambletonian—Little Mag, by Little Woeful 2:29¼
Emma B., br m, 188—, by Hambletonian Bashaw 2:26¼
Emma Balch, ch m, 1885, by Nabob—Jenny Lind, by Saxe 2:20¾
Emma Carroll, b m, 188—, by Charley Ross 2:27
Emma E., br m, 187—, by Tom Moore 2.29
Emma E., b m, 1881, by Jim Fisk—Nelly, by Magna Charta 2:19¼
Emmaetta, b m, 1887, by Antioch—Volunteer Maid, by Volunteer 2:20
Emma G., ch m, 1881, by Elmo—Lilly Shear, by Whipple's Hambletonian (dead) 2:27¼
Emma Hayes, gr m, 1886, by Alaric—Lucy, by Grey Eagle 2:24
Emma J., b m, 188—, by Platte 2:27¼
Emma Nutwood, b m, 1880, by Nutwood—Lady Emma, by McCracken's Black Hawk 2:24
Emma R., b m, 1887, by Electioneer —Emma Robson, by Woodburn 2:28¼
Emma T., b m, 1887, by Socrates—Patsy Labor, by Abdallah Pilot 2:17½
Emma Temple, b m, 1883, by Jackson Temple—Lizzie R., by Emigrant (dead) 2:21
Emma Westland, b m, 1892, by Westland 2:29¼
Emma W., b m, 1881, by Boxer ... 2:25½
Emma Wilkes, b m, 188—, by Wilkesonian, dam by King William 2:23¼
Emmett, blk g, 187—, by Mambrino Time—Nelly, by Ashland Chief 2:29½
Emmett, gr g, 188—, pedigree not traced 2:30
Emmett, B., b g, 1877, by Strathmore—Miss Spaulding, by Spaulding's Abdallah 2:29¾
Emmet B., blk s, 1887, by Ellerslie Wilkes—Minnie A., by Young Jim.. 2:28¼
Emmons, b g, 188—, by Forest Prince 2:29¼

Emoleta, b m, 1887, by Sealskin Wilkes—Rosedale, by Almont Pilot 2:24¼
Emory, b g, 1887, by Ethan Wilkes, dam by Peavine 2:30
Emperor, blk s, 1865, by Newman Horse, dam by Lewiston Boy (dead) 2:29¼
Emperor, b g, 1860, by Rollins Horse (dead) 2:30
Emperor Wilkes, b s, 1886, by William L.—Pilot Anna by Pilot Jr 2:20¾
Emperor William, b s, 1867, by Gen Knox—Lady Hollis 2:27½
Empire Wilkes, b s, 1882, by George Wilkes—Jane Moseley, by Mambrino Patchen 2:29¼
Empress, b m, 1852, pedigree not traced (dead) 2:30
Empress, ch m, 1875, by Whipple's Hambletonian—Katy Tricks, by Colonel 2:24
Empress, br m, 1878, by Flaxtail—Lady Narley, by Marion 2:29¾
Empress ch m, 1870, by Panic—Coot Mare, by Yorkshire Whig 2:30
Emulation, ch m 1882, by Onward—Santa Claus, by Magic 2:21
Enchantress, b m, 1874, by Happy Medium—Kitty Clover by Hero 2:26¾
E. N Cook, ch s, 1887, by Wilkie Collins—Nelly F by Mohican 2:26¼
Encore, blk m, 1883, by Kentucky Prince—Maggie Duroc, by Messenger Duroc 2:24¼
Endeavor, b s, 1889, by Counsellor—Evermine, by Evermond.......... 2:29¼
Enderby, b s, 1887, by Victoria—Electra, by King Philip.......... 2:29¾
Endymion, blk s, 1879, by Dictator—Annie Eastin, by Morgan Rattler... 2:23¼
Energy, b s, 1886, by Onward—Fanchon, by Hamlin's Almont Jr 2:24¾
Enfield, b s, 1868, by Rysdyk's Hambletonian—Julia Machree (dead)..... 2:29
Enfin, b m, 1890 by Baron Wilkes—Effie, by Enfield.......... 2:28¼
Enigma, blk m, 1889, by Shermont—Little Maggie, by Victor 2:21
Enigma, b m, 1864 by Alcalde—Leila, by Downing's Vermont 2:26
Enola, ch m, 1883, by R F Galloway dam by Hoagland's Sam.......... 2:21½
Enright, b s, 1885, by Nutwood—La Gracie, by Cuyler 2:18¼
Ensign, b s, 1873, by Enchanter—Oneta, by Volunteer 2:28½
Environ, br m, 1886, by Envoy—Belle Green, by Green's Bashaw 2:26½
Envoy, br s, 1871, by Gen Hatch—Dolly, by Iowa 2:28
Eola, ch m, 188—, by King Clay 2:24¼
Eoline b m, 1890, by Anteeo—Myriad, by Strange: 2:14¾
Epaulet, b s, 1880 by Auditor—Pantalette, by Princeps 2:19
Eph, ch g, 1881, by Zachariah—Lady Carpenter, by Rysdyk's Hambletonian (dead) 2:24¾
Ephraim, br g, 188—, by Dauntless .. 2:29¾
Epithet, b m, 1880, by Princeps—Fautress, by Hamlet 2:29¾
Epitaph, b m, 188— by Billy Stanton. 2:30
Equinox, br s, 1882, by Strader's Cassius M. Clay Jr—Sally M., by Almont 2:27½
Equivalent, b s, 1890, by Reserve Fund—Misdeal, by Sherman Wilkes 2:29¼
Erelus, blk g, 1873, by Scott's Hiatoga—Fanny Moore, by Salsbury Sam .. 2:28¼
Erector, br s, 1888, by Director—Millie D., by Mambrino Gift.......... 2:25
Erena, gr m, 1886, by Alcyone—Estelle, by Clark Chief 2:19¾
Ergot, b m, 1888, by Wilkeswood—Pet, by Haw Patch 2:23½
Eric, b g, 1872, by Ericsson—Jenny Bryan, by John Dillard.......... 2:28¼
Erica, blk m, 1889, by William L.—Canta, by Egbert 2:24
Erie Girl, b m, 1883, by Lord Almont—Erie Maid, by Star Hambletonian 2:23
Erin, b g, 188—, by Dexter Prince.... 2:25½
Erin, b s, 1880, by Belmont—Eventide, by Woodford Mambrino 2:24¾
Erma, blk m, 1886, by Director—Mahiss, by Werner's Rattle 2:25½
Ermine, blk m, 1886, by Plymouth—Fan, by Hugeley's Pilot 2:13¼
Erminie, b m, 1886, by Gen. Washington—Erema, by Socrates 2:30
Ernest B., b g, 1889, by Hambletonian's Last—Zilla, by Trojan Jr. ... 2:27½
Ernestine, b m, 188—, by Byerly Abdallah 2:29¼
Ernest Maltravers, b g, 1879, by Happy Medium—Priceless, by Volunteer. 2:22½
Ernest Wilkmont, b s, 1888, by Bob Link—Fanny H., by Ira Wilkes...... 2:29¼
Ernest Wilton, blk s, 188—, by Wilton 2:27¾
Ernsie, b m, 1891, by Wilkes Boy—Einsiedora, by Sir Walter 2:28
Eros, gr g, 1881, by Haw Patch—Diane, by P. H. Baker.......... 2:29
Eros, br s, 1879, by Electioneer—Sontag Mohawk, by Mohawk Chief 2:29½
Eros, br s, 1883, by Onward—Alva, by Administrator 2:30
Ersilla, ch m, 1886, by Simmons—Beck Bedford, by Brown Ericsson .. 2:26¼
Ervin, b g, 1883, by Jim Ervin—Sally by Thomas A Scott 2:26½
Esca, b g, 1881, by Lexington Boy .. 2:25½
Escalanti, blk s, 1883, by Pathfinder Jr —Molly Nixon, by Post Boy Frank 2:29½
Escape, b m, 1884, by Victor Bismarck — Miss Buchanan, by Clark Chief 2:26½
Escort, br s, 188—, by Guide 2:23
Eskimo, br s, 1889, by Greenlander—Pittie Sing, by Electioneer.......... 2:18¾
Esmeraldo, b m, 1889, by Hambrino—Erma, by Belmont 2:30
Esmeralda, ch m, 1884, by Rattler Jr 2:29½
Esmond blk s, 1887, by Nutwood—Trix Esmond, by Ericsson 2:29¼
Esperanza, b m, 1888, by Phallamont—Mattie, by Dave Bonner.......... 2:23¼
Esperto Rex b s, 1891, by Piedmont—Extra, by Electioneer 2:29
Essex, br g, 1868, pedigree not traced. 2:29
Essex, ch s, 1883, by Aristos—Nelly, by Black Diamond 2:29
Essex Jr., b s, 1888, by Essex Hambletonian 2:26¼
Essex Maid, b m, 1860, by Wild Wagoner (dead) 2:30
Estabrook, b g, 1885, by Alcantara—Rosetta, by Strader's Cassius M Clay Jr. 2:29¼
Estelle, b m, 1883, by Zilcaadi Golddust—Florence by Comet Jr...... 2:26
Estelle, ch m, 1888—, by Star Almont 2:26½
Estelle, b m, 1884, by Nutwood—Starling by Cuyler 2:19
Etelka, br m, 1883, by Hamlin's Almont Jr —Ursula, by Lagow.......... 2:21¼
E T H, b s, 1888, by Victor Bismarck—Minnie King, by Mambrino

King 2.16¼
Ethan Allen, b s, 1849, by Black
Hawk (dead) 2.25½
Ethan K., b s, 1889, by Ethan Wilkes
—Rita Patchen, by Mambrino Patch-
en 2.27¾
Ethan McGregor, b s, 1885, by Robert
McGregor — Akers Pet, by Ethan
Allen 2 29¾
Ethel, g.· m, 1872, by Blue Bull—Guss,
by Tom Crowder (dead) 2.23
Ethel, ch m, 1884, by Happy Thought,
dam by Pathfinder 2:19¾
Ethel B., ch m, 1889, by Bonnie Mc-
Gregor—Blue Bells, by Gov. Sprague 2·16¼
Ethelbert, b s. 1886, by Egbert—Mag-
gie Lee, by Blackwood 2 27¼
Ethel Downes, blk m, 1890, by
Boodle, dam by Nutwood....... .. 2:24½
Ethel H., ch m, 1885, by Beaumont—
Fanny, by Allen Sontag........... 2.20
Ethel Lambert, ch m, 1886, by Col.
Harry Lambert—Bessie Snow 2:20¾
Ethel Mack, b m, 1887, by Anteeo—
Lou Milton, by Milton Medium..... 2 21½
Ethel Medium, b m, 187—, by Happy
Medium 2.25½
Ethel T., blk m, 188—, by Gambetta
Wilkes .... 2·29¼
Ethelwyn, b m, 1887, by Wedgewood
—Ethelberta, by Harold 2:20½
Ethelyn Far laun, b m, 1891, by Fair-
l w n Medium 2 29¼
Ethel X., b m, 188—, by Mohican, dam
by Doughe ty's Royal George....... 2·20
Etiquette, ch m, 1888, by Alcantara—
Flaxy, by Kentucky Clay 2 28
Etolle, b s, 1883, by King Rene—
Ozella, by Regular 2 26¼
Etta, ch m, 1882, by Alcantara—Molly,
by Vindex 2:28½
Etta B., gr m, 188—, by Great Tom.. 2·25¼
Etta Jones, br m, 1869, by Davy
Crocket 2 20
Etta K., b m, 1886, by Douglass—Lady
McCue, by Kent 2 21¼
Etta Wilkes, ch m, 1882, by Red
Wi'kes—Lizzie, by Harrodsburg Boy. 2.28¼
Euchre, b s, 1885, by Euclid—Molly
H by Rothschild................ 2 30
Euclare, b m, 1885, by Euclid—Lady
Hocker, by Lexington Golddust. .. 2:29½
Euclid, ch s, 1880, by Glenview—Reina
Victoria, by Rysdyk's Hambletonian 2 28½
Eugene, b g.................. 2:30
Eula G., b m, 1886, by Pretender—
Lottie Wall, by Strathmore... ... 2·24
Eula Lee, br m, 1882, by Gen. George
H. Thomas—Juanita, by Pilot Jr... 2:29½
Eulalia, b m, 188—, by Robert Mc-
Gregor, dam by Allie West....... 2:29½
Eunice, blk m, 1889, by Jim Lambert
—Maud, by Black Cloud.......... 2 24¾
Eura, ch m, 1888, by Walkill Prince—
Lilly L., by John Black.......... 2:18¼
Eureka, blk g. 187—, by Gen. Grant.. 2:23
Euroclydon, b s. 1888, by Baron
Wilkes—Astria, by Nutwood 2:25
Ensign, b s, 1888, by Ensign—Bessie
O., by Ben Hershey............. 2.25½
Eva, b m, 188—, by Crozier......... 2:29¼
Eva, ch m, 1884, by Amboy—Lilly, by
Amber................... 2:26¾
Eva, br m................... 2:29¼
Eva, b m. 1865, by Gooding's Cham-
pion — Kitty, by Seely's American
Star................... 2 25¼
Eva, b m, 1879, by Sultan—Minne-
haha, by Stevens' Bald Chief....... 2 23½

Eva, gr m, 1879, by George H Low. 2:23¾
Eva Clay, b m, 188—, by Fire Clay... 2 24¾
Evaline Wilkes, b m, 1887, by Olm-
stead's Young Wilkes—Flaxie Fear-
naught 2:27¼
Evangeline, b m, 1888, by Director—
Fanny H., by Red Wilkes (dead).... 2.11¾
Eva M, gr m, 1891, by Florida (dead). 2·25½
Eva T., b m, 188—, by Almont Med-
ium, dam by Alwood.............. 2:26½
Eva S., b m, 1880, by Pascacas—Nelly
R, by Magna Charta............. 2 30
Eva W., ch m, 1882, by Nutwood—
Alice R., by Naubuc.............. 2.25½
Eva Wilkes, b m, 1886, by Star Wilkes
—Maggie West, by Star Hambleton-
ian 2:22½
Eva Wilkes, b m, 188—, by Guy
Wilkes—Libbie B., by Winthrop... 2:25¾
Eva Wilkes, b m, 1887, by Ethan
Wilkes—Lady Landesdown, by Stand-
ard Bearer 2.28½
Eve br m, 1870, by Black Dutchman
—Phoebe .... 2·27
Evening Star, blk m, 1881, by Commo-
dore Belmont—Twilight, by Dictator 2·29
Eventide, blk s, 1884, by Egbert—Net-
tie Time, by Mambrino Time....... 2:29¾
Everett Ray, b g, 186—, by Edward
Everett 2 25
Everett Wilkes, ch s, 188—, by Bou-
bon Wilkes 2:30
Evergood, br s, 188—, by Evermond. 2 24½
Evermond, b s, 1881, by Harold—
Eventide, by Woodford Mambrino
(dead) 2:24½
Ewing, b g, 187—, by Primus—Lady
Washington, by American Boy Jr... 2 21½
F W. L., blk g, 188—, by Arsaces.... 2·25½
Exarch, ch s, 1887, by Ambassador—
Lilly-bloom, by Daniel Lambert..... 2 23½
Excellence, b s, 1885, by Mambrino
King—Windsweep, by Hamlin's Al-
mont Jr:................... 2.19½
Exception, b g, 187—, pedigree not
traced 2 26½
Executor, b s, 1875, by Adminis-
trator—Chestnut, by American Clay 2·24¾
Exit, b m, 1885, by Konantz—Aflak,
by Contractor .... 2·21¼
Expedition, br s, 1889, by Electioneer
—Lady Russell, by Harold......... 2:15¾
Expert, b g, 188—, pedigree not
traced 2:29¾
Express, b g. 1882, by Electioneer—
Esther, by Express (dead) 2:21
Expressive, b m. 1891, by Electioneer
—Esther, by Express .... 2·12½
Extralight, b s, 1889, by Starlight—
Violet, by Volunteer .... 2·27
Eyesee, b g, 188—, by Landmark 2:30
Extravagant, ch m, 1889, by Woodnut
—Economy, by Echo 2:28½
Ezra L., ro g. 1874, by Gideon—Grey-
ling, by Tom Benton 2:21½
Ezra T., b g, 1887, by Woodbrino—
Lady Goldsmith, by Volunteer 2:30
Factory Boy, gr g, 1879, by Billy Ba-
shaw. dam by Schofield 2 20¼
Factory Girl, b m, 1861, by Rysdyk's
Hambletonian, dam by Green's Boli-
var (dead) .... 2·29¼
Faika, b m. 1890, by Stamboul—
Blanche T., by Nephew 2:26
Fairest, ch s, 1883, by McCurdy's
Humb'etonian—Georgie Go'ddust, by
Messenger Golddust (dead) 2.18
Fairhaven. b s. 1889 by Wilton—
Lady France. by Red Wilkes 2:19¼

M. E. McHENRY, Freeport, Ill.

(THE DEMON DRIVER.)

Last season McHenry placed the world's record for pacing stallions
at 2:03¾ with John R. Gentry. and in 1893 he drove May Marshall in 2:08¼, the world's record for pacing mares.

W. K. SMITH, Tiffin, Ohio,
An Ohio boy that placed the half-mile track race record at 2:12¼
with Kitty Bayard.

Fly, br m, by Electricity—Mecca, by Mohawk Chief 2:29¼
Fly-a-Way, blk m, 1886, by Joe Mack —Fanny Poor 2:29¼
F. O. Batch, br s, 188—, pedigree not traced 2:29¼
Focus R, blk s, 1885, by Adrian Wilkes—Maud....................... 2:27¼
Foggy, b g, 1884, by Alcantara— Thalmier Mare, by Hamlet......... 2:27½
Folly, b m, 1885, by Happy Medium— Oriole, by Strader's Cassius M. Clay Jr............................... 2:15½
Folly, blk m, 188—, by All Right..... 2:27
Forest Boy, ch g, 1884, by Forest Mambrino—Dell, by Tempest....... 2.16¼
Forest Boy, b g, 188—, by Walker Morrill 2:26½
Forest King, b g, 1870, by Honest Dan, dam by Wildair 2.27
Forest King, b s, 188—, by Arcadian 2.29¾
Forest King, b s, 1879, by Woodford Knox—Dolly 2:30
Forest Mambrino, ch s, 1886. by Mambrino Patchen 2:29¾
Forest Prince, b s, 1882, by Baird's Hambetonian Prince—Majolica, by Harry Clay 2:17¼
Forest Queen, ch m, 1881, by Forest King—Lucy B., by Star Hamble- tonian 2:29¼
Forest Wilkes, b s, 1882, by Bourbon Wilkes—Ned 2:24¼
Forget-me-not, b m, 188—, pedigree not traced 2:27½
Forrest D., b s, 1886, by Senator N. —Bird, by Billy Jacobs Jr 2.27¾
Forrest Girl, ch m, 188—, by West Liberty 2:30
Forrest Patchen, br g, 1875, by King Patchen, dam by Smith's Flying Cloud 2:19½
Forsee, ch s, 1881, by Colman's Ab- dallah Jr.—Missouri Girl, by Morey's Lath 2:27
Fortunate, b g, 188—, ... 2:30
Fortuna, b m, 1886, by Florida— Emily, by George Wilkes 2:22
Fortunia, b m, 188—, pedigree not traced 2:20½
Foster, b g, 188—, pedigree not traced 2:27½
Four Corners, ch m, 1880, by Mam- brino Time—Laura Wynn, by Hurst & Thornton's Abdallah 2:20¼
Four Lines, b s, 1888 by Western Sprague—Egotism, by Princeps ... 2:20½
Fowler Boy, b g, 1883, by Electioneer —Gazelle, by Primus 2.26
Fox ch g, ... 2:30
Fox, b g, 186—, by Peacock (dead).. 2:30
Foxhunter, ch g, 1888, by Foxwood— Mattie O., by Trouble 2:30
Foxie, ch m, 1883, by Mansfield— Heiress, by Alexander's Abdallah.. 2.28½
Foxie V., ch m, 1870, by King Herod, dam by Green Mountain 2:23¾
Foxmont. b s, 1890, by Egmont—Fox's Baby, by Gage's Logan 2:27½
Foxwood, ch s, 1884 by Nutwood— Lady Foxie, by Daniel Lambert ... 2:24½
Foxy Lambert, b s, 188—, by Daniel Lambert Jr. 2.29¾
France, b s, 1881, by France's Alex- ander—Molly F., by George Wilkes 2:26
Franceps, b s, 1894, by France—Gos- sip, by Princeps 2.24½
Frances, gr m, 1866, by Harry W. Genet—Miss Bean 2.27

Frances O., b m, 1882, pedigree not traced 2.30
Frances O., b m, 188—, by Lotus ... 2:28¼
Frances M., b m, 188—, by Motor ... 2:22¼
Frances P., ch m, 188—, by Sir Nut- Wood—Florence, by Oxmoor 2:28¼
Frank, b g, 186—, pedigree not traced 2.28
Frank, b g, 1876, by Abraham—Root, by Green Mountain Boy 2:19½
Frank, b m, 1867, by Colton Horse, dam by Westfall Horse (dead) 2:27¼
Frank, blk g, 1867, by Young Oneida 2.20
Frank, b g, 187—, (ringer?).......... 2:28½
Frank Allen, b s, 188—, by Greenwood 2:30
Frank Allison, b s, 1868, by Ather- ton's Blackbird—Lucy Pope, by Har- ris' Morgan 2:28¼
Frank B., br s, 1887, by Coligne— Molly, by Eugene Casserly 2.30
Frank B., blk g, 1885, by William M., —Topsey, by Ripton 2:23½
Frank B., br g, 1884, by Bog Oak— Belle, by Stephen A. Douglas 2:17¼
Frank Bellows, b s, 1889, by Herschel —Bessie Turner, by Harry Turner 2:22
Frank Brown, b g, 188—, pedigree not traced 2:25¼
Frank Buford, b s, 1883, by Abdallah Almont Jr.—Sleepy Lize, by Pat Ma- lone 2.20
Frank C., blk g. 2:30
Frank C., b g, 1878, by Mambrino Pilot—Lilly Murray 2:27¼
Frank Dana, b g, 1880, by Aristos ... 2:29¾
Frank Davis, b g, 186—, pedigree not traced 2.20
Frank E., ch g, 1883, by Abdallah Hambletonian—Daisy, by Gifford Black Hawk Jr..................... 2:20½
Frank Ellis, b s, 1871, by Happy Med- ium—Dutch Girl, by Edwin For- rest 2.26¼
Frank Ellis, b s. 1879, by Hermes— Jane Early, by Stranger 2:29¼
Frank Irwin, b s, 1891, by Goodwood Jr., dam by Flaxmont 2.29¼
Frank F., b g, 1887, by Emperor Wil- liam, dam by John Bright 2:26¼
Frank F., b g, 1887, by Sir Folko— Dolly 2:20½
Frank Ferguson, br g, 186—, by Billy Glenn, dam by Romulus (dead) ... 2:26
Frank Fisk, ro g, 186?, by Bertrand Black Hawk (dead) 2:29
Frank Forrester, b g, 1841, by Ab- dallah (dead) 2.30
Frank Forrester, b s, 1872, by Marks- man—Strayer, by Hiagota 2d 2:27½
Frankfort, blk s, 1886, by Pretender Lizzie M., by Magic 2:27¾
Frank G., b g, 1876, by Sweepstakes —Sally Downs, by Edward Everett 2:27½
Frank H., b g, 188—, by Highland Grey 2:21¼
Frank H., b s, 188—, by Laclede 2:25½
Frank H., b s, 1882, by Ben Frank- lin, dam by Gen. Sheridan 2:27½
Frank Hill, b s, 1888, by Edga Hill- Belle, by Ledger 2:18¾
Frank Hull, br g, 1874, by Touch- sone—Jessie J., by Main Sweep- stakes 2:27
Frankie H., ch m, 1880, by Spink (dead) 2.27½
Frank J., dn g, 186—, pedigree not traced 2:23¾
Frank Jones, b s, 188—, by Prince Charles 2:19¼

Frank K., blk g, 188—, by Stephen A Douglas 2:28
Frank Kernan, b g, 186—, pedigree not traced 2:26½
Frank Kober, br s, 1887, by Gat Van Wagner 2:28
Frank L., blk s, 1889, by Sentinel Wilkes—Patty Haydon, by Mambrino Foster 2:14½
Frank L., b g, 188—, by Donny Brook 2:28
Frank L., blk g, 1884, by Beaufort, dam by Black Ralph 2:27¼
Frank Landers, b g, 1871, by Saddling Buck—Roany, by Copperbottom Jr. 2:18¾
Franklin, b g, 188—, by Gen. Reno . 2:19¼
Franklin, br g, 188—, by Goldleaf .. 2:27¾
Franklin, blk g, 1884, by Tobe Jr.—Fanny Farmer, by American Farmer 2:19½
Frank M., blk g, 1877, by Sweepstakes—Beauty 2:29¼
Frank M., ch s, 1888, by Phantom—Belle Hulbut 2:27
Frank M., ch g, 1884, by Priam, dam by Gen. Dana 2:17¼
Frank McCune, ch g, 187—, by William Miner—Miller Mare, by King Pharaoh 2:25¼
Frank McDonald, b g, 1888, by C. L. Martin 2:26½
Frank McGregor, (Joe S) b g, 1880, by Robert McGregor—Susie Thorne, by North Star Mambrino 2:24½
Frank McMahon, b g, 1885, by McMahon—Susie Bostwick, by Aroostock Boy 2:30
Frank Middleton, ch g, 1876, by Bay Middleton—Betsey Allen, by King's Champion 2:20¾
Frank Moscow, ch g, 1871, by Frank Moscow—Draper Mare 2:27½
Frank Munson, ch g, 1868, by Paragon—Fanny, by Zimmerman's Duroc 2:25
Frank Nelson, blk s, 188—, by Flying Dutchman 2:29½
Frank O'Neil, br g, 1881, by Whippleton—Flight, by Gilparic 2:29
Frank P., ch g, 1883, by Black Harp—Fan 2:19¼
Frank P., b g, 188—, by Merchant.. 2:28
Frank P., blk s, 1882, by Darwin—Nelly, by Sims' Morgan 2:25
Frank Palmer, b g, 186—, pedigree not traced 2:26¼
Frank Patchen ch g, 1875, by Seneca Patchen—Maggie, by Andy Johnson 2:24¾
Frank Potts ch g, 188—, by Bonnie Boy 2:30
Frank P. Porter, b s, 1884, by Egbert—Puss, by Brown Chief 2:27½
Frank Quirk, ro g, 1884, by Defiance—Donegan Mare 2:18¼
Frank R., b g, 187—, by Black Dutchman, dam by John B. Patchen 2:23¾
Frank Reeves, b g, 186—, by Skedaddle, dam by Black Hawk 2:23¼
Frank S. (Red Jim), b g, 1874, by Abdallah Pilot—Lucy Lee, by Alexander's Norman 2:25½
Frank S., ch g, 1880, by Taylor Horse 2:22
Frank S., br g, 1884, by Dr. Franklin—Canada Belle, by Don Alonzo 2:29¼
Frank S., b g, 188—, by St. Gothard. 2:30
Frank S., ch g, 188—, by Madrid—Minnie, by Redwood 2:18¼
Frank Sprague, br g, 1880, by Gov. Sprague—Minnie Crawford, by Goldsmith's Abdallah 2:29
Frank T., br g, 1880, by Hill's Duroc—Belle Brandon 2:23¼
Frank Walkill, b s, 188—, by Sir Walkill 2:24¼
Frank Wilkes, br g, 1882, by George Wilkes Jr.—Houghton Mare.......... 2:27¾
Frank Wood, b g, 186—, by Volunteer—Kipp Mare, by Lefevre's Star. 2:24
Frantic, b s, 1886, by Strathmore—Serene, by Sentinel 2:22¼
Fraulein, ro m, 188—, by Autograph—Miss Stewart, by Grey Norman.......... 2:29½
Frazee, ch g, 1881, by Brussels—Jenny, by Coulter's Davy Crocket.......... 2:29½
Frazier, b s, 1887, by Zulcaadi Golddust—Nelly, by Shelbyville Chief... 2:27¾
Freckles, gr s, 1889, by Wilton—Grey Diana, by Administrator.......... 2:30
Fred, b g, by Polonius, dam by Guy Miller 2:28
Fred, ch g, 186—, pedigree not traced (dead) 2:30
Fred, b g, 187—, pedigree not traced.. 2:28¾
Fred, b g, 187—, by Democrat, dam by Rysdyk's Hambletonian 2:30
Fred B., br g, 187—, by Tyler's Black Hawk 2:28½
Fred B., br g, 1886, by Reveille, dam by Black Squirrel 2:16¼
Freda C., b m, 1891, by Princeer.......... 2:30
Fred C., b g, 188—, pedigree not traced 2:29½
Fred Casey, ch g, 1870, by Fessenden—Fanny Allen, by Bacon's Ethan Allen 2:23¼
Fred Crocker, b g, 1878, by Electioneer—Melinche, by St Clair 2:25¼
Fred D., b g, 1881, pedigree not traced 2:29¼
Fred D., gr g, 188—, pedigree not traced 2:30
Fred Douglas, ch s, 1873, by Green's Bashaw—Nancy Bell, by Gale's Morgan (dead) 2:20¼
Fred Douglas, blk g, 1872, by Black Fraank—Boggy, by Billy Cass (dead) 2:24¼
Fred Drake, b s, 1882, by Joe Gavin—Minnie Drake, by Louis Napoleon.. 2:26¾
Freddy, b g, 1888, by Alert—Flora, by New Jersey Volunteer 2:24¼
Freddy B., b s, 188—, by Strathlan.. 2:29¾
Freddy C., b g, 188—, by Ferguson, dam by Volunteer 2:26½
Freddy J., b g, 1880, by Sterling—Miss Saltsman, by Houser's Hiatoga 2:26½
Fred E., br g, 188—, pedigree not traced 2:26¼
Fred Ensign, b g, 188—, by Sir Folko. 2:26½
Frederica, blk m, 1881, by Almonarch—Jenny Lind, by Young Sir Walter. 2:20¼
Frederick L., br s, 1888, by Herschel—Lady Dingman, by Favorite Wilkes. 2:29¼
Fred Folger, b g, 1881, by Kentucky Prince—Flora Gardiner, by Seely's American Star 2:20¼
Fred G., ch g, 188—, by Indicator.... 2:30
Fred Golddust, ch s, 1875, by Fancy Golddust, dam by Donerail 2:27½
Fred H., gr g, 188—, by Rebel Hardee 2:20¼
Fred Hambleton, ch s, 1881, by Hambletonian Mambrino—Springfield Maid, by Lakeland Abdallah 2:26
Fred Hooper, b g, 186—, by Royal Revenge (dead) 2:23
Fred Hull, br g, 1878, by Hull, dam by McClure's Hambletonian.......... 2:29½
Fred Judson, gr g, 188—, by George

L. Napoleon 2:28¼
Fred K., br s, 1884, by Shennan Medium—Polly 2:24½
Fred Lothair, ro s, 1877, by Lothair—Mary Ann 2:29¾
Fred M., blk g, 1883, by Daniel Boone—Snip, by Knox Boy.............. 2:28¼
Fred Mac, b g, 188—, by Golden...... 2:24¼
Fred McGregor, b s, 1880, by Robert McGregor—Belle W., by Romulus... 2:29¼
Fred McGregor, b s, 1887, by Robert McGregor—Lilla, by Mambrino Eagle 2:30
Fred Medium, b g, 187—, by Happy Medium 2:23¼
Fred Neil, b g, 1878, by Bay Tom—Mary Neil, by Luke................ 2:24¼
Fred Nelson, b g, 188—, by O. F. C... 2:24½
Fred O., b g, 188—, by Almont Eagle. 2:29½
Fredonia, ch g, 1887, by Black Cloud, dam by Hambletonian Hunter 2:21½
Fred S. Wilkes, ro s, 1887, by Hector Wilkes—Tillie, by Tattler Chief.... 2:11¾
Fred Wilkes, b g, 1888, by Wilkes—Randall Mare, by Nelson's Onward.. 2:17¼
Fred Wilkes, b s, 1883, by Red Wilkes—Black Princess, by Mambrino Patchen 2:26¼
Fred Wilkes, blk s, 188—, by The King 2:25
Fred Wilkes, b s, 188—, by Bourbon Wilkes 2:26
Fred Wilkes, b s, 188—, by Conn's Harry Wilkes 2:21½
Free, b m, 1888, by St. Bel—Nelly Y., by Stephen G.................. 2:25
Free Coinage, b g, 188—, by Abbottsford—Agnes, by Jim Lick........... 2:18¼
Freedom, b s, 1889, by Sable Wilkes—Laura Drew, by Arthurton........ 2:29¼
Freeland, b g, 1891, by Alfonso—Net Medium, by Happy Medium......... 2:17¾
Freedom, b g, 188—, by Maxim—Chicago Maid 2:28½
Freeman, blk g, 1872, by Macedonian 2:29
Freeman, b g, by Hambletonian Knox 2:29¼
Freestone, b g, 1883, by Capt. Webster, dam by Owen Dale.......... 2:29
Freestone, b g, 1877, by Republic—Fanny Dodge, by Dodge's St. Lawrence 2:25
Freestone, b s, 1881, by Gatling—Gretchen, by Chosroes.............. 2:25½
Free Trade, blk g, 1883, by Young Wilkes—Kitty, by Sorrel Tom...... 2:29¾
Free Trade, b g, 1882, by Smuggler Gift—Prudence, by Plato........... 2:24½
Fremont, br g, 1880, by Almont Eclipse—Celia C., by Taggart's Abdallah 2:30
Fremont, ch s, 1886, by Almont Star—Bonny Doon, by Beaufort.......... 2:29¼
Frenaldo, br s, 188—, by Rinaldo..... 2:27¼
French Girl, ch m, 188—, pedigree not traced 2:28
Frenchman, b g, 1885, by McDonald's Frenchman—Jingle 2:24¾
French Plate, br s, 1888, by Wedgewood—Mary B., by Alcalde......... 2:26¼
Frenzie L., b m, 1890, by Bay Ethan—Daisy L., by Dr. Herr............ 2:20¼
Frenzy, gr m, 1887, by Florida—Patience, by Young Jim.............. 2:27¼
Friday, ch g, 1878, by Blind Tom.... 2:27¼
Friday Jr., gr g, 1886, by Blind Tom, dam by Tom Telegraph............ 2:29¼
Friendship, b g, 188—, pedigree not traced 2:28
Frisco, blk s, 1890, by Quartermaster—Lady Schofield, by Tippoo Saib.... 2:27¾

Fritz, b g, 187—, by Bay Richmond.. 2:27½
Fritz, b g, 1882, by St. Gothard—Fan, by Ralph 2:29¼
Frontier, b s, 1891, by Pioneer Clay—May B., by Western Fearnaught.... 2:29¾
Frou-Frou, ch m, 1890, by Sidney—Flirt, by Buccaneer 2:22
Fugleman, b s, 1881, by Princeps—Miss Fanny, by Hamlet............. 2:28¾
Fugleman, b g, 1882, by High Private—Lady Forrest, by Edwin Forrest.. 2:27¼
Fugle, b m, 1880, by King Rene—Fuga, by George Wilkes (dead)..... 2:19¼
Fulano, ch s, 1889, by El Mahdi—Bay Hambletonian, by Rysdyk's Hambletonian 2:22½
Fulda, b m, 1886, by Hambrino—Mabel, by Middletown.............. 2:19¼
Full Prince, b g, 1887, by Young Fullerton — Lida, by Hambletonian Prince 2:23¼
Fulton Maid, b m, 1871, by Clay Pilot—Old Bashaw, by Green's Bashaw 2:29¼
Furniture Boy, b g, 1883, by Polonius—Nelly, by Major Edsall 2:22½
Future Gilbert, b s, 1886, by Henry Gilbert — Red Wing, by Toronto Patchen.................. 2:26¾
Futurity, b s, 1891, by Hinder Wilkes—Maggie S., by Arnold............ 2:19
Gabrielle, ch m, 1889, by Star Duroc—Loretta, by Strathmore............ 2:20¼
Gail, b m, 1881, by Lakeland Abdallah—Abigail, by Alexander's Abdallah.. 2:26¼
Galata, b m, 1888, by Stamboul, dam by A. W. Richmond.............. 2:28¼
Galatana, ch m, 1891, by Muscovite—Benedicto, by Hero of Thorndale... 2:24½
Galatea, b m, 1873, by Fearnaught—Grand Duchess, by Handley's Hiatoga 2:24¾
Galatea, ch m, 1885, by Lockwood—Coleus, by Iron Duke.............. 2:27¾
Galatea, gr m, 1886, by Pilot Medium—Kit Wheeler, by Cady's Champion 2:25¾
Gale, b m, 1883, by Commodore Belmont—Irene, by Dictator 2:27¼
Galena, blk m, 1887, by Gambetta Wilkes — Lady Yeiser, by Garrard Chief 2:28½
Galen Prince, b s, 1885, by Judge Folger—Mary S., by James R. Reese.. 2:19
Galette, blk m, 1891, by Jud Wilkes—Gale 2:23½
Galilee, b m, 1889, by Col. Hambrick—Fragolett, by Juggler............ 2:26¼
Galion Prince, b s, 188—.............. 2:30
Gamaleon, blk s, 1887, by Gambetta Wilkes—Lady Pepper, by Onward... 2:25¼
Gamarza, br s, 1888, by Gambetta Wilkes — Winnie Wilkes, by Red Wilkes 2:27½
Gambart, b s, 1890, by Gamaleon—Zorah, by Backman's Idol.......... 2:27¾
Gambetta Wilkes, blk s, 1881, by George Wilkes—Jewel, by Gill's Vermont 2:19¼
Gambonito, blk s, 1887, by Gambetta Wilkes—Maud, by Garrard Chief.... 2:19¼
Gambruno, br s, 1887, by Gambetta Wilkes—Deallah, by Administrator. 2:29½
Gam Byron, b s, 1887, by Gambetta Wilkes—Ada Byron, by Enfield...... 2:19¼
Gammer, br s, 1889, by Gambetta Wilkes—Annie Patchen by Mambrino Patchen 2:23¼
G. and M., b s, 1888, by Anteeo—Rosa

B., by Speculation 2:29½
Gardner H., b s, 1887, by Butler's Bashaw 2:25½
Garfield, blk g, 1881, by Durango—Dixie (dead) 2:29¼
Garland, ch s, 1890, by Nuthurst, dam by Metropolitan 2:29¼
Garland M., b s, 188—, by Garland... 2:29¼
Garnet, ch g, 1881, by Young Jim—Snipnose, by American Clay 2.19
Garnet, br m, 1887, by Pancoast—Ruby, by Dictator 2:13½
Garnett Girl, ch m, 1887, by Simmons—Mag, by Hambrino 2:27
Garnishee, b g, 1886, by Prairie King—Lucy Elmo, by Elmo Adams...... 2:22 /4
Garrett L., br s, 1886, by Saxony—Kit Lowry, by Mambrino Royal .. 2:19½
Garrison, b s, 1880, by Orange Blossom—Queen Bess, by Backman's Idol 2:25½
Gas, br g, 188—, by a Copperbottom horse 2:22½
Gascoigne, b s, 1888, by Gambetta Wilkes—Gondula, by Princeps...... 2:24¾
Gautier, b g, 1878, by Red Bank—Flora N., by Dolphin 2.27¼
Gavaroche, b g, 1884, by Wilkins—Dolly 2:28¼
Gazelle, b m, 1865, by Rysdyk's Hambletonian—Hattie Wood, by Harry Clay 2:21
Gazelle, blk m, 1888, by Prompter.... 2:25
Gazelle, blk m, 1891, by Gossiper—dam by Edwin Booth 2:16½
Gazette, b s, 1887, by Onward—Siren, by Dictator (pacing record 2.09¼)... 2:23¾
G. B., b g, 1879, by Dom Pedro—Blanche, by Red Eagle 2:20¼
G. D. S., b g, 1880, by Tattler Jr.... 2:29¼
Gean Smith, blk g, 1878, by Dauntless—Nelly Hero 2:15½
Geb b g, 1888, by Vigil Rene—Lady Whitelaw, by Mambrino Clay (dead) 2:20¼
Gebhardt, ch s, 1887, by Kentucky Prince—Langtry, by Messenger Duroc 2:23
Gee Whiz, b s, 1890, by Billy Stanton 2:30
Gene, b m, 1885, by Bonafide—Nelly L., by Darkey 2.30
Gene Briggs, br s, 1888, by Messenger Wilkes—Straw Girl, by Almont 2:19½
General Alger, blk s, 1889, by Ambassador—Lowland Girl, by Legal Tender Jr. 2:24
Gen. Banks, b s, 1882, by Gen. Brock—Minnie Woods, by imp. Blinkiron 2:29¼
Gen. Bartholomew, b s, 1888, by Onward—Fanny Alley, by William Rysdyk 2.27½
Gen, Beamish, gr g, 187—, by Daugherty's Royal George (dead) 2:26¼
Gen. Benham, b g, 1884, by Gen. Washington—Susie 2:28¼
Gen. Boyle, b s, 1888, by Gambetta Wilkes—Silly, by Alert 2:24¼
Gen. Buford, b g, 1882, by Harry Pulling—Amy, by Black Ben 2:24
Gen. Butler, blk g, 1853, by Smith Burr—Isadora (dead) 2:23¼
Gen. Custer, br s, 1885, by Lenawee Chief—Lady Wilcox, by Mambrino Hambletonian 2:20¼
General Cass, gr s, 1888, by Dauntless—Clyburn mare 2:18¼
General Denver, b s, 1886, by William M.—Lizzie O'Connor, by Harrison Chief 2:22½
General Don, b s, 1889, by Dauntless—Minnie Rowell, by Gov. Tilden 2.27¼
General Grant, b g, 188—, by H. W. Beecher 2.30
General Herkimer, b s, 1889, by Knick Wilkes—Libbie, by Hambletonian Prince 2:24½
General Macey, b s, 1888, by Macey—Thornleaf, by Hero of Thorndale 2:25¼
General Sphinx, b s, 1890, by Sphinx—Ada, by Sir Denton 2:28¾
General Sprague, br s, 188—, by Brinker's Sprague 2.26¼
General Wiles, b s, 1886, by Black Hawk McGregor—Molly Young, by Joe Young 2:19½
Gen. Ewing, b s, 1876, by Windsor, dam by Tullytown (dead) 2.27¼
Gen. Garfield, b g, 186—, by Kentucky Black Hawk—Molly Walker, by Capt. Walker 2.21
Gen. George A. Ballard, blk s, 1874, by Young Rex—Ida Whalebone, by Whalebone 2.30
Gen. Grant, ch s, 1869, by Wapsie—Belle Wilson, by Handley's Hiatoga 2:21
Gen. Grant, blk g, 188—, by Steel's Walkill 2:26¼
Gen. Hancock, b g, 1872, by Lightning—Miss Jones, by Perkins' Morrill .. 2:24¼
Gen. Hardee, rn g, 188—, by Gen Hardee 2:27¼
Gen. Howard, br g, 186—, by Badger Boy (dead) 2:26¼
Genie L., blk m, 1892, by Arcadian.. 2:25¼
Gen. James A. Garfield, ch s, 1881, by Mohawk Gift—Emma B., by Fowler's Star Hambletonian 2.25½
Gen. Lee, ch g, 186—, pedigree not traced 2.29
Gen. Lee, ch s, 1875, by Green's Bashaw—Belle Wilson, by Handley's Hiatoga 2:26½
Gen. Logan, b s, 1886, by Alexander Button—Winnie, by Deitz's St. Clair 2:23¼
Gen. Love, ch s, 1865, by Field's Royal George (dead) 2.30
Gen. Mack, b s, 187—, by Hickey's Happy Medium 2:29¾
Gen. McClellan, b s, 1854 by Drew Horse, dam by Shark (dead) 2:29
Gen. McClellan, dn g, 185—, by Montauk (dead) 2:29
Gen. Marion, b s, 1883, by New Jersey Volunteer—Fleety, by Baywood..... 2:27½
Gen. Picton, gr g, 186—, by Rattler, dam by Sumner Morgan (dead) 2.30
Gen. Russ, gr s, 1876, by Blue Bull—Christina, by Tom Crowder 2.29¼
Gen. Sherman, gr g, 1860, by Pilot Jr. (dead) 2:28¾
Gen. Sibley, b g, 1876, by Swigert—Dollabel, by Richards' Bellfounder. 2:30
Gen. Smith, ch s, 1886, by Albion—Nelly Dewar, by Royal Revenge ... 2:20
Gen. Stark, ch g, 187—, pedigree not traced 2:27¼
Gen. Storms, b g, 187—, by Logan... 2:27½
Gen. Turner, b s, 1881 by Harold—Claytona, by American Clay (pacing record 2:25¾) 2.26¾
Gen. Tweed, ch g, 186—, by Myron Perry, dam by Hill's Black Hawk (dead) 2:26½
Gen. Wellington, b s, 1884, by Electioneer—Waxana, by Gen. Benton.. 2:30
Gen. Wiles, b s, 1886, by Black Hawk

McGregor—Molly Young, by Joe Young 2:15
Gen. Wilkes, gr s, 1881, by George Wilkes—Grace Goodman, by Peacock 2:21¾
Geneva, b m, 1882, by Princeps—Ozone, by Rysdyk's Hambletonian.. 2:17½
Geneva, ch s, 1887, by Leland—Bessie Forrest, by Edwin Forrest 2:14
Geneva S., ch m, 1883, by Abdallah Mambrino—Ella Hopkins, by Octoroon 2:19¼
Geneva Wilkes, blk m, 1883, by Bartholomew Wilkes—Matt, by Rolla Seymour 2:23¼
Geneve, blk m, 1885, by Nephew, dam by Jack Hawkins 2:26¾
Genevieve, b m, 1888, by Brougham—Belle of Clarence, by Finch's St. Lawrence 2:26¾
Genevieve, b m, 188—, by Startle.. 2:28¾
Genevieve, br m, 1889, by Egotist—Genoa, by Princeps 2:29¾
Genevra, b m, 187—, by Butt's Monroe Chief, dam by Perrin Horse.. 2:24¼
Genevra, b m, 1888, by Abby, dam by Hawthorne 2:20
Gense, br m, 1886, by Longfellow—Frolic, by Corbeau Chief 2:19
Genteel, blk g, 1887, by Gambetta Wilkes—Susie Cheek, by Lightheart 2:29¾
Gentile, br m, 1889, by Col. Hambrick—Belle Monroe, by Nick Monroe.... 2:30
Gentle Annie, rn m, 1888, by Wiggins, dam by Scott's Hambrino 2:26
Gentle Harry, b s 188—, by Honest Charley 2:30
Gentry, b g, 1887, by Gambetta—Virginia Grigsby, by American Boy 2:30
George, b g, 1883, by Bullet 2:27¼
George, b g, 186—, pedigree not traced 2:24½
George, b g, 188—, by Dick Jones .. 2:26¼
George, br g, 1885, by Scott's Thomas—Laura, by Forester 2:20¼
George, blk g, 187—, pedigree not traced 2:24½
George A., b g, 1891, by Glencoe Wilkes 2:29
George A., b g, 1875, by Daniel Lambert—Pacing Kate 2:24¼
George A., b g, 1876, by Truesdale's Abdallah Jr.—Kitty Foster, by Silliman Morgan 2:21¾
George Allen, b s, 1883, by William H. Allen—Quickstep, by Foster Horse .... 2·28
George Anthony, b s, 1889, by Nutalwood—Arthur, by Arthurton 2:29¼
George A. Ayer, gr g, 1871, by Woodford Mambrino—Diana, by Pilot Jr. 2:30
George B., gr g, 187—, by Winfield Scott—Black Nina, by Waddell..... 2:29¼
George B. Daniels, ch g, 1869, by King's Champion—Mamie Daniels, by Greyhound (dead) 2:24
George C., ch g 2:30
George C., b g, 1881, by Sweepstakes—Maidy, by Jupiter Abdallah...... 2:23¾
George C., blk s, 1883, by Ben Franklin—Flora Cozzens, by Honest Dan.. 2:28¼
George Condit, blk s, 1892, by Gambetta Wilkes—Lady Watson, by Indianapolis 2:29¼
George Cooley, b g, 1853, by Neave's Cassius M. Clay Jr., dam by Friday (dead) 2:27
George Dexter, br s. 1890, by Dexter Prince—Nelly C., by Kilrush...... 2·18¼
George D. Sherman, blk g, 187—, by Black Ralph 2 29¼
George F., b s, 1887, by St. Gothard—Lotta, by Chester 2.28¼
George F. Smith, b g, 1865, by Niagara Chief—Peggy, by State of Maine (dead)......................... 2:28
George Gift, b s, 1884, by Fairy Gift—Topsey Talbott, by Long Island Patchen 2.29¼
George Gray, br s, 1885, by Redwood—May, by Dolphin 2:27
George H., br g, 188—, by Gen. Benton 2:26¼
George H., rn g, 186—, by Godfrey Patchen (dead) 2:25
George Hait Jr., b g, 187—, pedigree not traced 2:29¼
George Henry, b g, 186—, pedigree not traced 2:27
George H. Mitchell, b g, 1865, by American Ethan, dam by Long's Tornado (dead)....................... 2:26
George Judd, rn g, 186—, pedigree not traced (dead) 2:26¼
George K., b g, 1884, by Coronet—Kitty Morgan, by Bartlett's Morgan 2:29½
George K., gr g, 1872, by Swigert.... 2:25¼
George K., ch g, 188—, by Hambletonian George 2:22
George L., b g, 1880, by Harrison Chief—Miss Ewalt, by Washington Denmark 2:26½
George L., br s, 188—, by Adjutant—Letta, by Rush 2:24½
George Lee, b g, 1879, by All Right, dam by Prince Edward 2:23¼
George L. Napoleon, br s, 1883, by Louis Napoleon—Flora R., by Stonewall 2:24¼
George M., br g, 1885, by Deceive—Kit, by Bacon's Ethan Allen 2:25½
George M., b g, 1875, by Westfield Boy—Flirt, by Champion King 2:24
George Miller, b g, 186—, by Boston Boy (dead) 2:30
George M. Patchen, b s, 1849, by Cassius M. Clay, dam by Head'em (dead) 2:23½
George M. Patchen Jr., br s, 185—, by George M. Patchen—Belle, by Top Bellfounder (dead) 2:27
George M. Rysdyk, b g, 1878, by Rysdyk—Lady Patchen, by George M. Patchen 2:25
George O., ch s, 1880, by Lakeland Abdallah—Fanny B., by Autocrat.. 2:21½
George O., b g, 1876, by Hambletonian Chief, dam by Gen. Knox... 2:24¼
George P., ch g, 1886, by Gettysburg—Dolly, by Success 2:26¼
George Palmer, br g, 1861, by Palmer Bogus (dead) 2:19¼
George R., ch g, 187—, by Getaway, dam by Davy Crocket 2:27¼
George R., b g, 1878, by Daniel Lambert—Brown Fanny, by Young Black Hawk 2:24
George R., b g, 1875, by Bacon's Ethan Allen—Haven mare 2:27½
George Salisbury, b s, 1888, by Judge Salisbury—Gertrude G., by Almont Lightning 2:30
George St. Clair, b s, 1888, by Betterton—Ill Wind by Young Jim (pacing record 2:22½) 2:15¼
George Simmons, b s, 1884, by Simmons—Crip, by Mambrino Time.... 2·28

George S. James, ch g, 1884, by Highland Boy Jr.—Lady Stanton by Gen. Stanton (dead) 2:22½
George Treat, br g, 1868, by McCracken's David Hill Jr.—Kit, by McCracken's Black Hawk 2:25¼
Georgette, blk m, 1884, by Count Wilkes—Nell, by Estill Eric 2:27
George V., ch g, 1874, by Masterlode—Nelly, by Magna Charta 2:20
George W., br g, 1877, by Mambrino Pilot Jr. 2:23½
George W., ch g, 187—, by Lincoln Abdallah 2:30
George W., b g, 188—, by George K.—Dawley mare, by Great Tom.... 2:24½
George W., blk g, 188—, by Mambrino Hippy 2:24½
George Washington, b s, 1886, by Smith's Mambrino Chief Jr.—Fanny Rose, by Vick's Ethan Allen Jr.... 2:16¾
George W. Davis, b g, 1878, by Glencoe Golddust—Jenny, by Eastman Morgan 2:26¼
George Wilkes, br s, 1856, by Rysdyk's Hambletonian—Dolly Spanker, by Henry Clay (dead) 2:22
George Willis, br s, 1887, by Belmont—Mona Wilkes, by George Wilkes.. 2:29¼
George Wolf, b s, 1879, by Shelden Messenger—Chloe, by Charley...... 2:30
Georgia, b m, 188—, by De Soto..... 2:24½
Georgia, b m, 1887, by Nutlane—Molly Armstrong, by Hosman's Pasha 2:24¾
Georgia H., b m, 188—, by Wilton... 2:26½
Georgiana, br m, 1880, by George Wilkes—Kittie Patchen, by Mambrino Patchen 2:26¼
Georgie, gr m, 1884, by Pilot Medium—Kitty, by Marshall Chief 2:28¾
Georgia H., b m, 1888, by Alcantara—Rosa R. 2:16½
Georgie Lee, blk m, 1890, by Gambetta Wilkes—Nutmontie, by Nutwood 2:12¾
Georgie Moshier, ch g, 1882, by Strathmore—Topsey, by Williams' Mambrino 2:22¼
Georgie W., br m, 1878, by New York—Pet, by Blazing Star............ 2:23¼
Georgie Woodthorpe, gr m, 1884, by Altamont—Puss, by Baldy 2:19¼
Geraldine, b m, 1888, by Alcyone—Alice Stoner, by Strathmore.... .. 2:21
Geraldine, b m, 1878, by Gen. Stanton, dam by Blue Dick 2:28¼
Geranium, b m, 1883, by Com. Belmont—Bouquet, by Woodford Mambrino 2:28½
Germaine, b s, 1888, by Mambrino King—Verdant, by Hamlin's Almont Jr. 2:20
German Boy, ch g, 1871, by Old Nig—Nell Wing 2:28¼
German Girl, b m, 1881, by German Boy—Nelly, by Anthony Wayne ... 2:27¾
Geronimo, b g 1881, by Inca—Molly, by Sacramento 2:24½
Gertrude, ch m, 1887, by Elyria—Jenny D., by Tom Hunter........ 2:12
Gertrude, br m, 1887, by Egalite—Lizzie Tevis, by Harry Wilkes.... 2:26
Gertrude Russell, b m, 1883, by Electioneer—Dame Winnie, by Planet... 2:23½
Gestela Atwood, blk m, 188—, by Atwood 2:20½
Gettysburg, b s, 1883, by Gen. Hancock—Nelly 2:20

G. H. F., b g, 1889, by Falcon—Gipsey, by Beaufort 2:23½
Gibber, b g, 188—, by Gibraltar.... 2:29¼
Gibraltar, b s, 1872, by Echo (dead). 2:22½
Gideon, b g, 188— 2:28¾
Gift Jr., b s, 1874, by Mambrino Gift—Little Dolly, by Young Bonnie Scotland 2:27½
Gift O'Neer, ch s, 1889, by Sphinx—Lizzette, by Mambrino Gift (dead). 2:20
Gilbert, b s, 1891, by Gambonito—Mabel, by Messenger Chief 2:28½
Gilbirds Sprague, blk s, 1870, by Gov. Sprague—Bohemian Girl, by Sir Charles 2:21¾
Gilbreth Knox, blk s, 1862, by Gen. Knox—Cahill Mare (dead) 2:26¾
Gilbreth Maid, blk m, 1871, by Gilbreth Knox—Kate, by Ivanhoe 2:25½
Gilfillan, b s, 1888, by Gambetta Wilkes—Jeannie C., by Nutwood ... 2:26½
Gill Boyle, b s, 1887, by Gambetta Wilkes—Gondula, by Princeps 2:27¼
Gillette, blk g, 1886, by Cyclone—Madam Beatty, by Monroe Chief ... 2:11¼
Gillig, br s, 1885, by Aristos—Alice, by Pearsall 2:23½
Gilmore, b g, 1883, by Hamlin's Almont Jr.—Long Mary (dead) 2:21¼
Gilpatrick, b s, 188—, by Junio, dam by Gilpatrick 2.29½
Gilroy, blk s, 1876, by Messenger Duroc—Lady Finch, by Harry Clay. 2:28¾
Gimcrack, ch s, 1884, by Mambrino King—Hyacinthe, by Hamlin's Almont Jr. 2:27
Giovanna, ch s, 1889, by Red Wilkes—Lady Withers, by Aberdeen 2:28¼
Gipsy, b m, 1875, by Winthrop Morrill Jr. 2:24¼
Gipsy A., blk m, 1882, by Star of the West—Pet, by Derbyshire's Flying Cloud 2:25¾
Gipsy Boy, blk s, 187—, by Stonewall Jackson—Fanny Bashaw, by Green's Bashaw 2:28
Gipsy Belle, blk m, 188—, by Atlantic. 2:25½
Gipsy Girl, blk m, 1883, by Junius—Flora, by King William 2:17¼
Gipsy Girl (Sally Howard), b m, 1880, by Aaron Pennington—Calaway Maid, by Rockaway 2:22
Gipsy Maid, b m, 188—, by Chicago Volunteer 2:23¼
Gipsy Patchen, blk m, 1885, by Fred Forrest—Perkins Mare 2:30
Gipsy Queen, b m, 1877, by Gen. Benton—Clara, by Corning's Cassius M. Clay Jr...... .... 2:26¼
Gipsy Queen, b m, 1888, by Bomont—Ella, by Enfield 2:22¼
Gipsy Queen, ch m, 1883, by Rushville—Bulla Mare.................. 2:19¾
Girard, b g, 188—, by Louisville...... 2:26¼
Girfiue, gr g, 1885, by Pilot Medium—Ida, by Golden Dawn 2:22¼
Gladiator, b g, 1875, by Blue Bull, dam Kit, by Cockspur 2:22¼
Gladiator Jr., blk g, 1880, by Tom Patchen—Molly, by Kentucky Clay.. 2:27½
Gladstone, b s, 1884, by Hambrino—Fashion, by Curtis' Hambletonian.. 2:28¼
Gladstone, blk g, 1887, by Wilmont—Kate Gilmore, by Tom Bingham.... 2:28¾
Gladys, b m, 188—, by Jersey Prince.. 2:23¼
Gladys, br m, 1891, by Inveterate—May, by Charles G. Hayes 2:29¾
Gladys, ch m, 1879, by Royal Fearnaught—Kit Harris, by Knott's

Gold Ring, ch s, 1884, by Eden Golddust—Nelly Ingersoll, by Fearnaught Gift ... 2:12¼

Goldsmith Maid, b m, 1857, by Alexander's Abdallah—Old Ab, by Abdallah (dead) ... 2:14

Gold Star, ch s, 1883, by Mambrino Patchen—Golden Lake, by Lakeland Abdallah ... 2:29¾

Goldstone, ch s, 1881, by Masterlode—Chicago Belle, by Sterling ... 2:27¼

Goldzil, ch s, 1891, by Zilcaadi Golddust—Victoria, by Jefferson Mambrino ... 2:30

Golita, br m, 1888, by Guy Wilkes—Cora, by Buccaneer ... 2:27¼

Gondola, b m, 1883, by Belmont—Betsey Baker, by Dictator ... 2:25¼

Gonzales McGregor, b g, 1885, by Norton McGregor—Cora ... 2:16¼

Good-bye, b s, 1884, by Egbert—Circe, by Bell Morgan ... 2:19¼

Good Gift, blk s, 1881, by Fairy Gift—Restless, by Kentucky Clay ... 2:28

Good Morning, b m, 1873, by Harold—Lady Limp, by Toronto ... 2:28½

Good Time, ch s, 1886, by Mark Time—Maggie C., by Felter's Hambletonian ... 2:18

Goodwin Jr., br s, 1886, by Goodwin Hambletonian—Stella, by Brown Chief ... 2:27½

Goodwood Jr., ch s, 188—, by Goodwood—Kitty Morrill, by Young Morrill ... 2:23¼

Go On, ch g, 1884, by Jimmy Gift—Tenney Draper, by Albert Draper. 2:28¾

Gordon Sim, b g, 1888, by Uncle Sim—Lady May ... 2:20½

Gossiper, b s, 1885, by Simmons—Lady Bryan, by Smuggler ... 2:14¾

Gordon, b g, 1883, by Sorrento—Belle of Pawlett, by Warr Hulett... 2:26¼

Go Some, b m, 188—, by Happy Thought ... 2:26¼

Gotell, b m, 1882, by Axtell—Godelia, by Aberdeen ... 2:29¼

Gotham, ch s, 1884, by Nutwood—Eden Lassie, by Golddust ... 2:29¼

Gothatum, b s, 1886, by Dictatum—Ruby Gothard, by St. Gothard... 2:29¼

Governor, gr g, 187—, by Green's Bashaw—Lady McNair ... 2:24

Governor, gr s, 187—, pedigree not traced ... 2:28

Governor, b g, 1866, by Clark Chief—Ware Mare, by Canada Chief (dead) 2:30

Gov. Benton, ch s, 1882, by Major Benton—River Lily, by Gen. Benton 2:22¼

Governor D, blk s, 1881, by Swigert—Dolly Dutton, by Black Douglass.. 2:21

Gov. F., b s, 1888, by Royalty—Elfrida, by Stocking Chief ... 2:21

Gov. Hendee, ch s, 1886, by Duke of Brunswick—Whirlcloud, by Jay Gould ... 2:23

Gov. Hill, b g, 1881, by Star Edmund—Old Maid ... 2:18¼

Gov. Hill, b g, 1885, by Gov. Benton—Lady P., by Buell's Pathfinder... 2:25½

Governor Hogg, b s, 1891, by Obstacle—Star Maid, by Bethlehem's Star.. 2:30

Gov. Plaisted, br g, 1876, by Grey Dan—Daisy, by a son of Drew horse 2:29¼

Gov. Powell, blk s, 1888, by Col Hambrick—Big Mary, by D. Monroe ... 2:25

Governor Riddle, gr g, 188—, by Norman Medium—Puss Barber, by Tiger Morgan ... 2:23

Gov. Rusk, b g, 1888, by Phallas—Changelet, by Volunteer... 2:27¼

Gov. St. John, ch s, 1880, by Amboy—Crazy Jane, by Little Snip Printer 2:27½

Gov. Sprague, blk s, 1871, by Rhode Island—Belle Brandon, by Rysdyk's Hambletonian (dead) ... 2:20½

Gov. Sprague Jr., br s, 1887, by John B. Sprague—Molly Scammon, by Robinson horse ... 2:30

Gov. Stanford, ch g, 186—, by John Nelson ... 2:27½

Gov. Stanford, b s, 1885, by Electioneer—Barnes, by Whipple's Hambletonian ... 2:21

Gov. Strong, b s, 1889, by Dr. Strong—Julia Wilkes, by Governor Wilkes. 2:21

Gov. Wood, ch s, 1879, by Amboy—Bird, by Billy Shaker... 2:29

Grace, br m, 1886, by Redwood—Kitty Dean, by Gideon ... 2:26½

Grace, b m, 1869, by Knickerbocker—Lady Denton, by Seely's American Star ... 2:27

Grace, ch m, 1888, by Sidney—Marguerite, by Speculation ... 2:29

Grace, gr m, 186—, by Lexington—Jenny, by Sorrel John Richards (dead) ... 2:27¼

Grace B., gr m, 188—, by Detractor. 2:26

Grace Bertram, ch m, 186—, by New Jersey, dam by Marshal Ney (dead) 2:29

Grace Darling, b m, 188—, by Alburn. 2:26½

Grace Darling, b m, 1880, by Grand Sentinel—Molly Bawn, by Sir Henry 2:26

Graceful, b m, 1880, by Happy Medium—Lady Grace, by Hamlet ... 2:23¼

Grace Gothard, b m, 1884, by St. Gothard—Grace Bertram, by New Jersey 2:20

Grace Hasting, ch m, 1888, by Bayonne Prince—Kate K., by Burger.. 2:24

Grace Lee, b m, 1885, by Electioneer—Addie Lee, by Culver's Black Hawk ... 2:20¼

Grace Medium, blk m, 1887, by Administrator Jr.—Pattie, by Happy Medium ... 2:20½

Grace Napoleon, b m, 1885, by Louis Napoleon—Kate Wilson, by Scott's Hiatoga ... 2:14½

Grace Simmons, blk m, 1889, by Simmons, dam by Pacing Abdallah... 2:19½

Grace Thorne, b m, 188—, by Egthorne ... 2:28¾

Grace W., br m, 1884, by Blackwood Mambrino—Lucy Woodruff, by Hiram Woodruff ... 2:21¼

Grace Walker, b m, 1886, by Royal Fearnaught—Miss Johnson, by Beaumont ... 2:23½

Grace Wilkes, rn m, 188—, by Adrian Wilkes ... 2:17¾

Gracewood, blk m, 1887, by Nutwood—La Gracie, by Cuyler ... 2:27½

Gracie, b m, 1878, by Landmark ... 2:27

Gracie Almont, blk m, 1886, by Almont Mambrino—Fashion ... 2:30

Gracie B., b m, 1882, by Blackwood Jr.—Littlefield, by Enfield ... 2:22¼

Gracie S., ch m, 1882, by Speculation—Jenny, by Bull Pup ... 2:22

Gracie V., ch m, 1887, by Crittenden—Lula D., by Woodford Abdallah.. 2:30

Grafton, ch g, 1879, by Almont Boy—Lucy B., by Canadian Mohawk ... 2:20½

Grafton, ch g, 1868, by Waxy—Gyp, by Kavanaugh's Gray Eagle ... 2:22¼

Granby, b s, 1882, by Princeps—Hamlite, by Hamlet ... 2:19½

Gram C., b g, 188—, by Hambletonian's Last, dam by Tom Wonder.. 2:23¾

Grand Central, b g, 1882, by Hinsdale Horse, dam by Bacon's Ethan Allen 2:30

Grandee, b g, 1885, by Le Grand—Norma, by Arthurton 2:23½

Grandee, ch s, 1884, by Grenadier—Flora 2:29½

Grandee, b g, 1888, by Hamlin's Almont Jr.—Majorie, by Kentucky Prince 2:27¾

Grand Duchess, b m, 1858, by Handley's Hiatoga—Johnson Mare, by John Richards (dead) 2:26½

Grand Duke, b g, 1877, by Shelby Chief—Molly 2:29¼

Grand George, ch s, 1889, by Hambletonian Wilkes, dam by Magna Charta (pacing record 2:20½) 2:24½

Grand Isle, b g, 1884, by Winooski—Leona 2:24¼

Grandissimo, b s, 1886, by Le Grand—Norma, by Arthurton 2:23½

Grandly, blk s, 1888, by Gambetta Wilkes—Effie Faulkner, by Abdalbrino 2:23¾

Grandmont, br s, 1882, by Almont—Badoura, by Strader's Cassius M. Clay Jr. 2:25½

Grand R., b g, 188—, by Hamlin's Almont Jr. 2:24¼

Grand Turk, b s, 1889, by Connaught—Lurline, by Mambrino Patchen... 2:29¼

Grand Sentinel, b s, 1873, by Sentinel—Maid of Lexington, by Mambrino Pilot (dead) 2:27¼

Grand Sentinel Jr., b s, 1887, by Grand Sentinel—Lucy K., by Dauntless 2:30

Granger B., ch g, 1881, by Hamblehawk—Kitty Haldeman 2:30

Granieta, br m, 1888, by Rockefeller—Maud L., by Messenger Knox ... 2:25½

Granite, gr g, 187—, by Major Grant—Nelly 2:24¾

Grannette, b m, 1889, by Granby—Maggie C., by St. Mark 2:21¼

Granny, b m, 1881, by Abdallah Hambletonian—Black Bess, by Ketchum Horse 2:28

Grant Sherman, b s, 1887, by Sherman—Katie C., by Mambrino Patchen 2:29

Grassee, b s, ... 2:25¼

Granville, ch g, 1868, by American Clay—Lady Abdallah, by Alexander's Abdallah 2:26

Grasshopper, ro g, 1882, by Princeps—Brocade, by Volunteer 2:29½

Grateful, ch g, 1867, by Brown Horse, dam by Crawford Horse (dead) ... 2:28½

Grateful, gr s, 1888 by Gen. Wilkes—Oxford Lass, by Mambrino Ledger 2:30

Grattan, blk s, 1887, by Wilkes Boy—Anna Almont, by Bostick's Almont Jr. 2:13

Gratz, b g, 1882, by Bourbon Wilkes—Kate Henderson, by Cazique 2:17¼

Gravel, br s, 1886, by Haw Patch—Hortense, by Tramp 2:29¾

Graves, ch g, 187—, by Whipple's Hambletonian—Rose Austin 2:19

Graydon, gr s, 1887, by Hambrino—Zephyr, by Mambrino Patchen 2:17¼

Grayfield, gr g, 1887, by Greenfield .. 2:17½

Great Stakes, b s, 1887, by Billy Thornhill—Sweetstakes, by Sweepstakes 2:24½

Great Eastern, b g, 1869, by Walkill Chief—Hammil Mare, by Riley's Consternation (dead) 2:18

Great Eastern, b g, 1885, by Sweepstakes—Annie Hough, by Kentucky Prince 2:23½

Great Western, blk g, 1870, by Superb 2:29

Green B., b g, 188—, by Abdalbrino, dam by Cornwall 2:29¼

Greenbacks, b s, 1882, by Princeps—Lorette, by Rysdyk's Hambletonian 2:23¼

Green Boy, b s, 1877, by John Green—Unis Green, by Green's Hambletonian 2:27¾

Green Bird, b g, 188—, by Lucas Brodhead 2:24¼

Greenbriar, b s, 1888, by Gambetta Wilkes—Nutwood Belle, by Nutwood 2:22¼

Greenbush Star, b s, 1883, by Greenbush—Mabel, by Byron 2:25½

Greenceps, b g, 1888, by Greenbacks, dam by Trophy 2:18½

Green Boy Jr., rn g, 188—, by Green Boy 2:28¼

Green Charley, blk g, 186—, by Green's Bashaw 2:26¼

Greenfield Girl, g m, 188—, by Jim Wilson 2:29½

Green Girl, b m, 1879, by Artemus—Brigham, by Jay Gould 2:21¼

Greenlander Boy, br s, 1887, by Greenlander—Aurelia, by Electioneer 2:21¾

Greenlander Girl, blk m, 1890, by Greenlander—Aurelia, by Electioneer 2:21

Greenleaf, b s, 1887, by Gold Leaf, dam by Case's Dave Hill 2:22½

Greenleaf, br g, 1886, by Simmons—Nelly Monroe, by Jim Monroe 2:10½

Greenlight, b g, 1884, by Signal—Tannie 2:24¾

Greenlander, 1882, by Princeps—Juno, by Rysdyk's Hambletonian 2:12

Green Mountain Boy, b s, 1873, by Thomas Jefferson—Belle 2:28¼

Green Mountain Maid, ch m, 1845, by Harris' Hambletonian (dead) 2:28½

Green River, b s, 1887, by Principe—Maria, by Marabout 2:22¼

Greenway, br s, 1888, by Greenlander—Aurelia, by Electioneer 2:25

Greenwood, b s, 1886, by Greenbacks, dam by Butler Horse 2:20

Greenwood, br g, 188—, by Fergus McGregor 2:29

Greenwood, b g, 188—, by Jaywood.. 2:30

Greenwood, ch g, 187—, by Goodwood—Shoo Fly, by Young Morrill 2:30

Greenwood Belle, b m, 1885, by Caliban—Greenwood Maid, by Strathmore 2:29¾

Greever, br s, 1889, by Picco—Queen Sprague, by George Sprague 2:23¼

Gregorian, ch s, 1888, by Prince George—Beltina, by Mansfield 2:30

Gregory, br g, 1884, by Bishop—Ethel, by Contractor 2:30

Grenadier, b g, 188—, by Messenger Wilkes—Modjeska, by Redwood 2:26¼

Gretchen 2:28¾

Gretchen, b m, 1886, by Schuyler—Nelly, by George D. Patchen.... 2:16¼

Gretna, b m, 1884, by Mambrino Dudley—Bodil, by Peacemaker 2:22¼

Grex, blk s, 1888, by Gambetta

Wilkes—Walie Sprague, by Gov. Sprague 2:28
Grey Bashaw, gr s, 188—, by Charley Bashaw 2:30
Grey Belle, gr m, 188—, by Anteeo.. 2:27
Grey Bill, gr g, 1869, by Brandywine, dam by State of Maine (dead)..... 2:30
Grey Charley, gr g, 186—, pedigree not traced (dead) 2.29
Grey Chief, gr g, 1868, by Louis Napoleon 2:24¾
Grey Cloud, gr s, 1871, by Blue Grass 2.23½
Grey Cloud, gr s, 188—, by Gilt Edge—Comet, by Rattler 2:20¾
Grey Cloud, gr s, 1885, by Reveille—Maud C., by Rex Hiatoga 2:25
Grey Dan, gr g, 187—, pedigree not traced 2:30
Grey Dave, gr g, 1878, by Hotspur Chief—Miss Mason 2.22¼
Grey Dawn, gr g, 1888, by Major White—Belle, by Volga Jim......... 2 20
Grey Dawn, gr m, 1889, by Startle—Daybreak, by Harold 2:22¼
Grey Duke, gr g, 1874, by Hall Colt. 2·29¾
Grey Eddy, gr g, 186—, by Blue Colt.. 2 27
Grey Eddy, gr g, 184—, by Morse Horse (dead) 2 30
Grey Hawk, gr g, 1853, by Hawkeye, dam by Black Archy (dead) 2:28¾
Grey Jack, gr g, 1860, by John Carrier—Madam Huntley (dead) 2.28¼
Grey Jim, gr g, 1885, by Strawn—Grey Nell, by Hurst & Thornton's Abdallah 2.22
Greylight, gr g, 1882, by Starlight—Young Daisy, by Strideaway 2:10⅓
Grey Mack, gr g, 1860, by Black Hawk Hero (dead) 2 25½
Grey Ned, gr g, 1882, by Goodhue's Patchen .... 2·25
Grey Prince, gr g, 188—, pedigree not traced 2:29¼
Grey Salem, gr g, 187—, pedigree not traced .... 2·24
Greystone, gr g, 1881, by Altitude—Lady Miller, by Creeper 2 28½
Grey Swigert, gr g, 1886, by Mambrino Swigert—Molly .... 2·29¼
Greywood, gr s, 188—, by Jim Mulvenna 2.27
Griffin, b s, 1883, by Messenger Duroc—Gimp, by Princeps 2.29¼
Grimsby Gi l, b m, 1886, by Hager's Stanton—Greg, by Winfield Scott . 2.26¾
Griselda, b m, 188—, by Gambetta Wilkes—Lady Yeiser, by Garrard Chief 2.29¼
Grit, b s, 1886, by Onward—Griselda, by William Rysdyk 2.29¾
Grosis, b s, 1889, by Grosjean—Minnie Benton, by Gen. Benton. 2 25¼
Grosjean, blk s, 1883, by Belmont—Sue Dudley, by Edwin Forrest .... 2·24¾
Grover, br g, 1885, by Ed Kimble—Blaze, by Frank Reynolds 2:28½
Grover C., ch s, 1884, by Gilt Edge—Berneda 2 30
Grover C., b s, 1888, by Sarcenett—Lizzie H., by Ralston 2:26¼
Grover C., b g, 1884, by Altar, dam by Britton 2 30
Grover Clay, b s, by Electioneer—Maggie Norfolk, by Norfolk 2.23¼
Grover Cleveland, b g, 1884, by Redwood, dam by Sherwood 2 18¾
Grover Cleveland, b g, 1880, by Bunco—Lady Woods, by Monte 2 24
Grover Cleveland, b s, 1883, by St. Arnaud—Ontario, by Watchman.... 2 30
Grover Wilkes, dn g, 188—, by Newton's Allie Wilkes 2:30
G. T Pilot, dn g, 1868, by McDonough—Jarod 2 24
Guard, b s, by Guide—Lady King, by Hambletonian King 2.27
Guard, b m, 1891, by Clay King—Hannah D., by Abdalbrino......... 2 28¼
Guardian, b g, 188—, by Epaulet ... 2·24¼
Guardsman, b s, 1885, by Alcyone—Qui Vive, by Sentinel 2 23½
Guelph, br s, 1882, by Princeps—Merry, by Messenger Duroc 2:16¼
Guelph Jr., br s, 1887 by Guelph—Trumpeter, by Honesty 2.26¾
Guess, b g, 1885, by Landmark, dam by Palmer Bogus 2:16¼
Guess Not, br m, 187—, by Baird's Hambletonian Prince—Maxwell mare 2:27½
Guido, gr g, 188—, by Ensign 2:21½
Guiado, b s, 1889, by Pistachio—Primrose, by Alexander's Abdallah. 2:30
Guide, br s, 1885, by Director—Imogene, by Norwood 2.16¼
Guilford Dudley, gr s, 1890, by Egotist—Belle Dudley, by Belmont 2 30
Guinea, blk m, 1881, by Egbert—Norma, by Alexander's Norman.... 2.29
Guitar, b m, 1882, by Princeps—Trio, by Volunteer 2 29¾
Gula, ch m, 1885, by Royal Fearnaught, dam by Tom Hunter 2 27½
Gus, b s, 186—, by Millman's Bellfounder—Jenny Noyes 2 26¾
Gurney, ch g, 1885, by Kentucky Prince—Lady Horton, by Sweepstakes 2:28¾
Gus Fellows, b g, 188—, by Charles Caffrey .... 2·29¼
Gussie Leonard, b m, 1890, by George Simmons—Jessie Miller, by Magic.. 2·29¼
Gussie M., b m, 1889, by Moody—Stockings, by Young Amboy..... .. 2 22¼
Gussie T., b m, 1881, by Paragon—Anna Long .... 2·26½
Gus Spreckles, b s, 1879, by Speculation—Jenny, by Blue Pup.. ...... 2 30
Gus Voltz, b s, 1887, by Phal'as—Grace Murray 2 29¾
Gus Wilkes, b g, 1880, by Mambrino Wilkes—Fancy by Bonner 2 22
Guy, blk g, 1880, by Kentucky Prince—Flora Gardiner, by Seely's American Star 2 09¾
Guy, ch s, 1889, by Robert Rysdyk—Red Rose, by Jester D........ 2 15¼
Guy Lambert, b s, 188—, by Sir Thomas .... 2·22
Guyon, b s, 1882, by Princeps—Roma, by Golddust 2.30
Guy Princeton, br s, 1887, by Princeton—Wait-a-bit, by Basil Duke...... 2:28¼
Guy Rene, br s, 188—, by Guy Darrell .... 2·25
Guy Sheridan, br s, 1885, by Chas. Caffrey—Nelly Wooly, by Yeoman.. 2:22½
Guy Vernon, gr s, 188—, by Guy Wilkes, dam by Patchen Vernon .. 2 28
Guy Wilkes, b s, 1879 by George Wilkes—Lady Bunker, by Mambrino Patchen 2 15¼
Gyp, gr m, 188—, by Trouble, dam by Jim Sherwood .... 2·26¾
Guyon b s 1882, by Princeps—Roma, by Golddust 2:27¾
Gypsy Maid, b m 188— by Chicago Volunteer 2:24¼
Gypsy Earl ch m 1890, by Earl, dam

by Leland ... 2:19¾
Gypsy H., b m, 188–, by Sam Sharply ... 2:29¼
Gypsy K., ch m, 188–, by Billy Knox 2:29¼
G. W. Howe, b s, 1891, by King William L.—Envie, by Phallamont ... 2:25¾
Hackberry, b s, 1886, by Harold—Alice Maud, by Belmont (dead) ... 2:25¼
Hades, blk m, 1880, by Leland—Aralon, by Young Woful ... 2:27¾
Hagar, b m, 1887, by Nutwood—Hilda, by Cuyler ... 2:25
Ha Ha, br s, 1880, by Nephew—Ryan Mare, by McCalkins' Black Hawk .. 2:22¼
Haldee B., ch m, 1888, by Charles G Hayes—Silent Friend, by Menelaus.. 2:26
Hailstorm, b g, 1888, by Anteeo Jr.—Star, by Geo. M. Patchen Jr. ... 2:30
Haldane, b s, 1883, by Mambrino Russell — Brownie, by Daniel Lambert (dead) ... 2:26½
Haley, b s, 1889, by Nelson—Greynose, by Fearnaught ... 2:18¾
Halifax, b s, 1888, by West Egbert—Flora Payne, by John F. Payne ... 2:25½
Hal J., b s, 188–, by Limber Jim ... 2:29
Hallie, ch m, 1887, by Harbinger, dam by Monte Christo ... 2:20
Hallie B., b m, 1882, by Alcyone—Elenora, by American Clay ... 2:26¾
Hallie Harris, ch m, 1890, by Combination—Miss Attorney, by Attorney 2:23½
Hallidan, br g, 188–, by Haldane ... 2:28
Hallington, b s, 1889, by Haldane—Lilly Lexington, by Lexington Star 2:30
Hall Terrell, b g, 186–, pedigree not traced ... 2:28¾
Halo, b s, 1887, by Haldane—Cora C., by Buckingham ... 2:27
Hal Pointer, ch s, 1891, by Luke Brodhead, dam by Cottontail ... 2:18¼
Halvan, gr g, 1889, by Haldane—Shena Van, by Daniel Lambert ... 2:22½
Hambleton, br s, 1875, by Florida—Lady Woodhull, by Rysdyk's Hambletonian ... 2:26¼
Hambletonian (McCurdy's), ch s, 1874, by Harold — Belle, by Mambrino Chief (dead) ... 2:26½
Hambletonian (Worley's), ch s, 1880, by Squire Talmage—Fanny Rolfe, by Tom Rolfe ... 2:28½
Hambletonian (Bailey's), b s, 1886, by Thomas K., dam by Mambrino Priam ... 2:29¼
Hambletonian Bashaw, b s, 1870, by Green's Bashaw — Lady Byron, by Gage's Logan ... 2:21¼
Hambletonian Bashaw, b s, 1876, by Fellers' Hambletonian—Lady Dutch, by Hermit ... 2:29¼
Hambletonian, b s, 1873, by Masterlode—Lady Emma, by Canada Champion ... 2:29
Hambletonian Knox, br s, 1873, by Gilbreth Knox, dam by Gideon ... 2:28
Hambletonian Mambrino, b s, 1871, by Curtis' Hambletonian—Topsy ... 2:21¼
Hambletonian's Last, br s, 1876, by Rysdyk's Hambletonian—Lady Russell, by Seely's American Star ... 2:25¼
Hambrino, b s, 1869, by Edward Everett—Mambrina, by Mambrino Chief. 2:21¼
Hambrino Belle, b m, 1874, by Hambrino — Sally Neal, by Mambrino Chief ... 2:25½
Hambrino Pilot, blk s, 1885, by Hambrino—Forest Queen, by Mambrino Pilot ... 2:29½
Hambrino Prince, b g, 188–, by Hambrino ... 2:26
Hamdallah, b s, 1879, by Hambrino—Linda, by Alexander's Abdallah ... 2:23
Hampden Girl, b m, 188–, by Banquo. 2:27½
Hamdallah (Aiken's), b s, 1884, by Hamdallah—Flora, by DeGraff's Alexander (dead) ... 2:24¾
Hamdallah Star, b s, 1885, by Hamdallah—Lady Gregor 2d, by Star of the West ... 2:23
Ham Jr., b s, 188–, by Ham. ... 2:24¼
Hamletta, blk m, 1882, by Bourbon Wilkes—Lady Hamlet, by Hamlet.. 2:27¾
Hammond, b s, 1881, by Tom Scott—Jury, by Hambletonian Bashaw. ... 2:26½
Ham Morrison, b g, 187–, by Masterlode ... 2:30
Hamoun, blk s, 1886, by Watchmaker—Nell, by Pilot Knox ... 2:28¾
Hamperion, b s, 186–, by Rsydyk's Hambletonian—Fanny ... 2:29½
Hampshire, b s, 1885, by Woodford Wilkes—Rosilla, by Swigert ... 2:22½
Hamrock, br g, 1889, by Hambletonian Mambrino—Daisy James, by Rockwood ... 2:21
Hancock, b g, 187–, by Hambletonian Jr.—Young Martha, by George M. Patchen Jr. ... 2:29
Hancock Wilkes, b s, 1884, by Georgia Wilkes—Daisy ... 2:29¼
Handicap, gr g, 187–, by Stephen A. Douglas—Howard Mare ... 2:22
Hannah D., b m, 186–, by Magna Charta ... 2:22¼
Hannen, b g, 188–, by St. Arnaud.. 2:29¼
Hannah Dustin, b m, 188–, by Elial G., dam by Dutton Horse ... 2:29¾
Hannibal Jr., gr g, 1883, by Hannibal—Molly Welsh, by Paul Jones ... 2:27¼
Hannis, ch s, 1870, by Mambrino Pilot—Lady Stuart (dead) ... 2:17¾
Hannis Jr., ch s, 1883, by Hannis—May Queen, by Creeper ... 2:26¼
Happiness, b m, 1886, by Happy Medium—Brightness, by Almont ... 2:29¼
Happy, ch s, 1889, by Happy Prince—Viola, by Vermont Abdallah ... 2:27½
Happy, gr m, 1870, by Mazeppa—Cinderella ... 2:27
Happy Bee, br m, 1887, by Happy Russell—Beeswing, by Kent ... 2:15¾
Happy Courier, b s, 1888, by Happy Medium—Lady Chiles, by Almont.. 2:16¾
Happy Damsel, ro m, 1888, by Happy Medium—Maggie Keene, by Mambrino Hatcher ... 2:26½
Happy Day, gr s, 1886, by Happy Medium—Eye See, by Nutwood ... 2:29½
Happy Doctor, b g, 188–, by Happy Home ... 2:21½
Happy Earl, b s, 1890, by Happy Russell ... 2:29¾
Happy George, b s, 1891, by Happy Russell—Lady Washington, by Gen. Washington ... 2:24½
Happy Girl, ro m, 1880, by Happy Medium—Berks County Maid ... 2:27½
Happy Glen, b s, 1890, by Union Medium—Capicola, by Royal Medium. 2:30
Happy Go Lucky, b s, 1885, by Happy Thought, dam by Wanderer 2:29
Happy Gothard, b s, 1884, by St Gothard—Mignon Medium, by Happy Medium ... 2:29¾

Happy Home, b g, 1884, by Happy Thought, dam by Palmer's Norman 2:24¼

Happy Jack, ch g, 186—, by Andrew Jackson Jr., dam by Seely's American Star 2:30

Happy Jack 2:28

Happy Lady, br m, 1889, by Happy Russell—Lady Washington, by Gen. Washington 2:16¾

Happy Maid, b m, 1877, by Happy Medium—Rosa Bonheur 2:30

Happy Man, b g, 188—, by Masterlode 2:27¼

Happy Minnie b m, 1890, by Happy Russell—Minnie Rifle by Arbuckle's Rifle 2:17½

Happy Pilot b s, 1888, by Pilot Medium—Lady Corrigan, by Milwaukee 2:22¼

Happy Princess, b m, 1876, by Happy Medium—Black Bess, by Black Oscar 2:23¼

Happy Promise, b s, 1888, by Happy Medium—Bonny Belle, by Almont.. 2:13¾

Happy Thought, b s, 1872, by Happy Medium—Lady Duval, by Strader's Cassius M. Clay Jr. 2:22½

Happy Traveler, b s, 1873, by Baird's Hambletonian Prince—Lady Larkins, by Little Jack 2:27½

Happy Volunteer, b s, 1885, by Volunteer—Molly Medium, by Happy Medium Jr. 2:27¼

Happy Wanderer, br s, 1884, by Happy Medium—Cornelia O., by Ohio Volunteer 2:20½

Hardiman, b g, 188—, by Knickerbocker, dam by Panic 2:28¼

Hardshell, br g, 1887, by Com. Wilkes —Molly C., by Contractor 2:28

Hard Tack, b g, 1891, by Joe Humphreys—Sue Crockette 2:26½

Hardwood, blk s, 1875, by Blackwood Jr.—Irene, by McKimmen's Columbus 2:24¾

Harkaway, b s, 1880, by Strathmore —Wait-a-bit, by Basil Duke 2:28¼

Harmonia, b m, 1885, by Memory—Bliss, by Western Chief 2:25¼

Harold Jr. ch s, 1885, by Harold—Maiden, by Belmont 2.25

Harold Chief, b s, 1884, by Harold—Lady Jane, by Banker Rothschild .. 2:24¼

Haroldine, b m, 1888, by Harold Jr.—Bertha, by Almont Rattler 2:23¼

Haroldson, b s, 1884, by Prescott—Queen, by Walker Horse 2:25¾

Harold M., b g, 188—, by Dr. Franklin 2:27¼

Harrie, blk m, 1886, by Elial G.—Kate Claxton, by Joslyn Horse 2:28¼

Harriet, b m, 1886, by The King—Lady Harmond, by Democrat 2:28¾

Harrietta, br m, 1888, by Alcyone—Harriet Clay, by Harry Clay 2:09¾

Harrison, b s, 1886, by Ottawa Chief —Mary Wood, by Richard Wheelock (pacing record 2:19½) 2:18¼

Harrison b g, 1882, by Harrison Chief—Fanny, by Joe Downing (dead) 2:26¼

Harrop's Tom, b g, 1877, by Almont Prince—Maggie Lyons, by Gen. Lyons 2:26½

Harry, b g, 1871, by Happy Medium 2:26

Harry, blk g, 188—, pedigree not traced 2:28

Harry, b g, 188—, pedigree not traced 2.22¼

Harry Admire, b s, 188—, by Bay Henry 2:26

Harry Almont, br g, 188—, by Almont Eclipse 2.24¼

Harry Arlington, gr s, 1871, by Prince Albert—Mac, by Price's St. Lawrence 2:29¼

Harry Arthur, b g, 1882, by Toronto Chief Jr.—Nelly Traveler, by Tom Traveler 2:25½

Harry B., b g, 188—, by Almonarch . 2:29½

Harry Bacchus, ch g, 1886, by Wilkie Collins—Almontress, by Hamlin's Almont Jr. 2:23¼

Harry Baldwin, br s, 1885, by Reveille —Roxy, by Cook's Bulrush Morgan 2:24¼

Harry Belmont, b g, 1884, by Kentucky Belmont—Jennie Clute, by Louis Napoleon 2:29

Harry C., br g, 1875, by Taylor's Red Buck 2:21

Harry C., blk g, 1886, by Green Boy —Nora C, by New York 2:15

Harry Cardinal, b g, 1881, by Cardinal—Kate 2:27¼

Harry Chief, b s, 1883, by Harrison Chief—Peg, by Green Walker Morgan 2:30

Harry Clay, blk s, 1853 by Neave's Cassius M. Clay Jr.—Fan, by imp. Bellfounder (dead) 2:29

Harry Clay, blk g, 1871, by Strader's Cassius M. Clay Jr.—Zephyr 2:23¾

Harry O. Midnight, blk g, 1881 by Mambrino Patchen, dam by Harrodsburg Boy 2:20½

Harry Conklin, b g, 187—, by Superb 2:26

Harry D., b g, 1885, by Black Cloud —Pony Mare 2:27

Harry D, b g, 1879, by Mott's Independent 2:29¼

Harry Eddy, b g, 188—, by Jerome Eddy 2:29¾

Harry Ensign, br s, 1884, by Ensign —Capitola 2:19¾

Harry G., b g, 188—, by James A. Garfield 2:19½

Harry Gilbert, ch g, 1866, by Jupiter (dead) 2:24

Harry Gould, b s, 1885, by Jay Gould —Hester, by Young Jim 2:28¾

Harry H., br g, 188—, by Sweepstakes 2:23¾

Harry Harley, b g, 1863, by Young Columbus—McGee Mare, by Barney Henry (dead) 2:25¾

Harry Hill, ch g, 188—, by Edge Hill 2:25¼

Harry Howe, b g, 1883, by Swigert—Amanda, by Western Chief 2:27

Harry Hylas, ch s, 1882, by Hylas—Belle Garfield 2:26¼

Harry K., blk s, 1887, by Consul—Maud K., by Saturn 2:22

Harry L., br g, 188—, by Gold King 2:28¾

Harry Laird, b g, 1879 by Legal Tender Jr.—Rushville Maid, by Blue Bull 2:29¼

Harry Lambert, b s, 1885, by Ward's Lambert—St. Mary, by Tattersall . 2:22

Harry Lee, b g, 187—, by Legal Tender 2:26

Harry Magee, b g, 1886, by Gen. Magee—Belle, by Gooding's Champion 2.27¼

Harry McGregor, b g, 1881, by Martin McGregor—Martin Mare 2:28

Harry McNair, ro g, 188—, by Allegheny Boy 2:18

Harry Medium, b g, 1884, by Happy Medium—Dolly Varden, by Bob Lee 2:21½

Harry Mills, br g, 1875, by Sweepstakes—Taglioni, by Eureka 2:25½

Harry Mitchell, b g, 186—, by Foster's St Lawrence 2:28¾

Harry Noble, b s, 1885, by Frank Noble—Stell Storms, by Mambrino Excelsior (dead) 2:17½

Harry N., br g, 188—, by Belding's Hambletonian 2:23½

Harry P., blk g, 188—, by Pascarel (dead) 2:25¼

Harry P., b g, 1886, by Bay Middleton, dam by Magna Charta 2:29¾

Harry Parker, blk g, 1876, by Post's Hambletonian Prince, dam by Tom McRabbie (dead) 2:25

Harry Pelham, gr g, 1876, by Thomas Jefferson—Lady Jane, by Rysdyk's Hambletonian.......................... 2:28½

Harry Pennington, b s, 188— by Aaron Pennington Jr., dam by Brandt's Messenger Golddust 2:15½

Harry Phallamont, b g, 1887, by Phallamont—Topsey 2:30

Harry Phelps, b s, 188—, by Crumley Hiatoga (pacing 2.22¼) 2:27½

Harry Pulling, b s, 1875 by Menelaus—Bird, by Smith's Ethan Allen 2:29¼

Harry Reid, ch s, 1883, by Corbin Bashaw—Dolly, by Warrior 2:24

Harry Roberts, b g, 187—, pedigree not traced 2:20

Harry S., gr s, 1884, by Backman's Idol—Sebois, by Orange Duroc 2:27½

Harry Sherman, ch s, 1886, by Alexander H. Sherman—Lady Vidette, by Vidette Boy 2:25

Harry Spanker, b g, 1865, by Gen. Knox—Lady Gay Spanker, by French Tiger (dead) 2:30

Harry Strideaway, blk g, 1882, by Strideaway—Molly, by Continental 2:24¼

Harry T., br g, 1890, by Pelletier—Zella, by Byron 2:28¾

Harry T., ch g, 188—, by Knick Wilkes 2:24½

Harry Velox, b g, 187—, by Velox—Ariosa 2:24½

Harry W., b g, 1881, by Edgewater—Bertie Amos, by Blue Bull 2:27¼

Harry W., ch g, 188—, by The Marquis 2:26½

Harry Wade, b s, 1886, by Reveille—Idalia, by Strathmore 2:19

Harry W. Genet, b s, 186—, by Godfrey Patchen—Lady Danvers, by Rocky Mountain (dead) 2:25½

Harry Wilkes, b g, 1876, by George Wilkes—Molly Walker, by Capt. Walker 2:13½

Harry Wilkes, b g, 1888, by Fitzgerald—Nimrod 2:29¼

Harry Winchester, b s, 1889, by Stamboul—Jessie Ballard, Archie Hambletonian 2:26¼

Harry Y., ch g, ... 2:27

Hartford, b s, 1880, by Harold—Judith, by Mambrino Chief 2:22¼

Hartford, blk s, 1882, by Peacock—Kate Patchen, by Hamlin Patchen 2:30

Hartland, b g, 188—, by Hartland 2:29½

Harvest Queen, b m, 1863, by Rysdyk's Hambletonian, dam by Seely's American Star 2:29½

Harvey, gr g, 1876, by Tom Hunter—Cypher, by Magna Charta 2:24¼

Harvey, b g, 1885, by Kentucky Volunteer—Lucy, by Kentucky Chief... 2.21

Harvey Russell, b s, 188—, by Harbinger 2.29½

Harvey Wilkes, b g, 188—, by Red Wilkes 2:26½

Hasdrubal, gr g, 1885, by Dillingham—Fanny, by Paragon 2:27½

Hastings, b g, 1877, by Clarion Chief, dam by Tippoo Chief.............. 2.28½

Hat Sprague, b g, 188—, by Sprague.. 2:29

Hathaway, b m, 188—, by Regalia.... 2:29¼

Hattie, ch m, 1862, by Trojan (dead).. 2:30

Hattie, b m, 1872, by Dixon—Fan, by Sackett's Hambletonian 2:29¾

Hattie Arnold (Lady Daniels), b m, 187—, pedigree not traced......... 2:26

Hattie B., b m, 1886, by Alexander Button, dam by Don.............. 2:20¾

Hattie Belle, b m, 1887, by Brown Wilkes—Policy, by Harold......... 2:25¼

Hattie D., b m, 1886, by Electioneer—Maple, by Nutwood 2:26¾

Hattie H., br m, 1884, by Alleghany Boy—Hall Mare, by Young Consul.. 2:26½

Hattie Hawthorne, b m, 1879, by Sentinel—Christy Morgan, by Hunter Lexington (dead) 2.23½

Hattie Hull, ch m, 1886, by Hull—Hattie Sparks, by Sweepstakes..... 2:30

Hattie K., b m, 1886, by Phallas—Dutch Girl, by Abdallah Boy....... 2.24¾

Hattie L., ch m, 188—, by Tom Hal.. 2:27½

Hattie L., ch m, 1885, by Motion—Lady Grey 2:25½

Hattie S., ch m, 1886, by Alar Clay Jr.—Nina S., by Bay Middleton..... 2:16¾

Hattie T., ro m, 1877, pedigree not traced 2:29¾

Hattie Woodward, b m, 1871, by Aberdeen 2:15½

Haviland, b g, 1869, by Mountain Chief, dam by Bundy Horse........ 2:29½

Havilla, b m, 1888, by Earl—Daisy Eyebright, by Kirkwood 2.29¾

Hawthorne, ch s, 1883, by Black Arthur—Lady Miller, by Creeper....... 2:29½

Hawwood, ch s, 1888, by Woodnut—Fanny, by Admar.................. 2.30

Haydon, b g, 1885, by Ogden's Hambletonian Mambrino — Daceus, by Duncan's Black Hawk............ 2:26½

Hazel, br g, 1886, by Clay—Aurora, by John Nelson 2:28

Hazel, br m, 188—, by Indianapolis Chief 2:29¼

Hazel, br m, 1890, by Royal Fearnaught—Emo, by Masterlode......... 2:30

Hazel, b m, 1886, by Wilkes—Daisy Rolfe, by Young Rolfe.............. 2:28¼

Hazel O., b m, 188—, by Count Folsio. 2:30

Hazel Dell, b m, 1889, by Stranger—Hazel, by Jay Gould.............. 2:24¾

Hazel King, ch s, 1887, by King Monte Marlo—Sisson Mare, by Black Dan 2:21¼

Hazel Kirke, b m, 1879, by Brigadier—Fancy, by Jim Brown............ 2:24

Hazel Maid, b m, 1886, by Charles G. Hayes—Toney, by Coupon.......... 2:29¼

Hazel N., b s, 1886, by Decatur Chief—Alloa, by Abdallah Mambrino..... 2.26

Hazel Thorne, br s, 1882, by Fairy Gift—Hawthorne Belle, by Lexington Hambletonian 2:29¼

Hazel Wilkes, ch m, 1885, by Guy Wilkes—Blanche, by Arthurton 2:11¼

Hazel Wilkes, b m, 188—, by Wayne Wilkes 2:21¾

Hazelwood, b m, 1891, by Atwood, dam by Dr Talmage............... 2:29½
Hazor, gr g, 186—, by Young America (dead) 2.27
H. B., blk g, 1887, by Winship Jr.—Lady Hackett 2:18¾
H. B. Lambert, ch g, 188—, by Tom Lambert 2:30
H. B. M., b g, 1887, by Belladonna—Lake Mare, by Bay Billy........... 2 20¾
H. B. Winship, blk s, 1876, by Aristos—Willful, by Col. Moulton....... 2 20¼
H. C., b g, 188—, by Wellington, dam by King Faro 2:22
H. C. Hill, b g, 1800, a catch colt by a grey pacer 2.25½
H. Clay, ch g, 188—, by Grey Eagle, son of Walker Morrill..... 2 28¾
H. C. T., b s, 1887, by King Almont—Black Bess, by Frank Wolford..... 2.17¼
Header, ch g, 186—, pedigree not traced 2:28
Headlight, ch g, 187—, by Scott's Hiatoga—Miss Woods, by Flying Hiatoga 2.30
Headlight, b g, 188—..... 2.27½
Headlight, ch s, 1883, by S. R. Lamont—Belle Brandon 2:26¾
Headlight, ch m, 188—, by DeLong's Ethan Allen 2:29¼
Hebron, b s, 1883, by Princeps—Florence, by Volunteer 2:30
Heckothrift, br s, 1884, by Hermes—Katie Middleton, by Mambrino Patchen 2:29
Hector, b g, 187—, by Otego Chief.... 2:23
Hector, gr g, 187—, pedigree not traced 2:25¼
Hedgethorne, b s, 1889, by Hawthorne — Ella Boggs, by Tilton Almont 2.27
Heir-at-Law, blk s, 1888, by Mambrino King—Estabella, by Alcantara. 2·12
Heiress, b m, 1885, by Woodford Wilkes — Hambletonian Maid, by Charles Backman ..... 2·27
Helen, ch m, 1877, by Baird's Hambletonian Prince—Faith Derrick....✓2.28
Helena, b m, 1889, by Ben Franklin—Maggie Myers, by Phil Sheridan... 2:26¼
Helena, b m, 1889, by Electioneer—Lady Ellen, by Carr's Mambrino.... 2:21
Helena B., gr m, 188—, by Coun's Harry Wilkes 2:27
Helene, ch m, 187—, by Baird's Hambletonian Prince—Maxwell Mare.... 2.21
Helen G., b m, 1883, by Ensign—Maid, by Norcross Horse 2:28¼
Helen Goodson, b m, 1886, by Goodson—Nelly Crichton, by Crichton Jr. 2:25
Helen H., b m, 1886, by Earl—Meta, by Thorndale 2.30
Helen Houghton, b m, 1878, by Happy Medium—Molly Sheppard, by Jack Sheppard 2:20¼
Helen K., b m, 1890, by Patron—Wedding Bell, by Nutwood............. 2:22½
Helen Leyburn, b m, 1890, by Onward —Mamie, by Star Almont........... 2:14
Helen Luce, b m, 1882, by Robert Bonner Jr.—Glimpse, by Coupon.. 2.26½
Helen M., gr m, 1887, by Cobden—St. Lawrence Maid, by Laundry Horse (pacing 2:17) 2:27
Helen M., b m, 1889, by Sherman—Liza Jane, by Gooding's Champion.. 2:29¼
Helen R., b m, 1880, by Pickett—Florence, by Quinton's Magnet......... 2 27¼
Helen Wilkes, b m, 1877, by Carlton

Colt, dam by Holland's Ethan Allen 2:25¼
Hellas, b s, 1888, by Phallas—Helen, by Nutwood 2:24½
Helmsman, b s, 1887, by Pilot Medium — Lady Gerster, by Western Pathfinder 2:28¼
Henderson, ch g, 187—, by Strathmore—Brignola, by Brignoli..... 2·27¼
Hendryx, gr g, 1882, by Dauntless—Fan, by Comet 2.17¼
Henrico, blk s, 1889, by Patchen Wilkes—Jenny West, by Allie West. 2:15
Henrietta, b m, 1883, by Mambrino King—Bay Hambletonian, by Rysdyk's Hambletonian 2:17
Henrietta G., ch m, 1887, by Elyria—Maud, by Star Hambletonian....... 2:19¼
Henry C., ch s, 1890, by Midas—Maggie V., by Revenue Jr......... 2:26¼
Henry, b g, 188—, by Bassett's Blue Bull 2:30
Henry, b g, 186—, pedigree not traced 2:29¼
Henry, b g, 185—, by Canadian Lion (dead) 2:27¼
Henry, b g, 1861, by Harry Lathrop—Flora (dead) 2:20¼
Henry Arnold, b g, 1883, by Pyeatt's Brown Henry—Mattie J., by Miller's Frenchman 2:28¼
Henry Bruce, b s, 188—, by Onward.. 2:26½
Henry Colby, blk g, 188—, by Charles G. Hayes 2:27½
Henry Esmond, br g, 1883, by Gov. Sprague—Minnie Crawford, by Goldsmith's Abdallah 2:30
Henry G., b g, 1889, by Harold—Molly Friend 2.28
Henry G., ch s, 1887, by Albert Mack Mary B...... 2:28
Henry Grady, b g, 188—, by Barney Wilkes 2:28
Henry H., b g, 188—, pedigree not traced 2:27¾
Henry L., b g, 188—, by Tony Ensign 2:29¼
Henry L., ch g, 188—, by Mohawk Hambletonian 2:29¼
Henry Middleton, b s, 1878, by Bay Middleton—Maggie Adams, by Holcomb Horse 2:26¼
Henry O., b g, 1879, by Resolute—Doll, by Kemble Jackson 2:25¼
Henry R., br g, 1884, by Gen. Stanton—Kitty Hudson, by Frank Porter 2:25¼
Henry W., b g, 188—, by Reveille..... 2:20½
Hera, b m, 1889, by Mambrino Wilkes —Kitty, by Conductor 2:23
Heresy, b m, 1881, by Hermes—Jessie Douglas, by Stephen A. Douglas. 2:27
Herkimer, b s, 188...... 2:29¼
Herman H., br g, 1879, by Embassador—Felicity, by Enchanter 2:21¼
Herman Nutwood, blk s, 1887, by Nutwood—Hermia, by Woodford Mambrino 2:22¾
Hermes, br s, 1871, by Harold—Hermosa, by Edwin Forrest......... 2:27½
Hermetic, b s, 1886, by Ira Wilkes—Lady Gift, by Hambletonian Gift... 2:23¼
Hernani, b s, 188—, by Electioneer—Gypsy, by Paul's Abdallah......... 2:29¾
Hero, ch s, 1882, by Stoner Boy—Fanny, by Blue Bull 2:28
Herod, blk s, 1866, by King Herod—Hilliard, by Green Mountain Boy.. 2:24½
Heros, br s, 1890, by Eros—Cyrene, by Cyrus R...... 2:26¼
Hersey, br s, 1874, by Macedonian—

Homestead, b s, 1886, by Nutwood—Precept, by Pancoast 2:30
Homewood, ch s 1878, by Hambletonian Tranby—Belle Warman, by Fred Pierson 2:23½
Honest Billy, b g, 186—, by Green Mountain Morgan—Beach Mare, by Ashelot Morgan (dead) 2:29¼
Honest Billy, ch g, 1886, by Tom Jefferson—Nelly Young, by Little Hamilton 2.27½
Honest Byerly, b s, 1887, by Byerly Abdallah—Nina K., by Honesty 2:24¼
Honest Clay, br s, 1889, by C. F. Clay—Chance, by Tom Stamps 2:29¾
Honest Dutchman, ch s, 1862, by Grey Messenger, dam by Bellfounder (dead) 2:26½
Honest George, b g, 1885, by Albert—Fanny Crowler 2:14½
Honest Harry, ro g, 1869, by Winthrop Morrill 2:22½
Honest Jake, b g, 188—, by Honest John 2:27¼
Honest Joe, b g, 188—, by Fred Boone 2:24½
Honest Lyon, ch g, 1870, by Gen. Lyons 2:30
Honest Tommy, blk g, 188—, by Dudley Buck 2:26¾
Honesty, ch s, 1877, by Priam—Western Girl, by Chieftain 2:25¾
Honey B., b m, 1881, by Charley B., Flora Andrews, by Gooding's Champion 2:25¼
Honey Dew, br m, 1889, by St. Bel—Lonely, by Volunteer 2:29½
Honeywood b m, 1890, by St. Bel—Shelbourne Maid, by Hollbird's Ethan Allen 2:19½
Hoodwink, b m, 1881, by Hermes—Charmis, by Belmont (dead) 2:25
Hooka, b m, 1886, by Messenger Chief—Minerva, by Strathmore 2:30
Hoosier Girl, blk m, 1873, by Blue Bull—Kate, by Darley Arabian..... 2.25¾
Hope, ch g, 186—, by Telegraph 2:28
Hopeful, gr g, 1866, by Godfrey Patchen—Kate, by Bridgham Horse (dead) 2:14¾
Hopemont, br m, 1877, by Col. Cross—Miss Robinson 2:28
Horicon, br g, 1881, by Hospodar—Mary, by Darkey 2:19¼
Hornell Wilkes, b s, 1886, by Red Wilkes—Laura, by Capt. Sykes 2:27¾
Hornet, ch m, 1880, by Gooding's Champion—Fanny 2:29¼
Hornpipe, blk s, 1883, by Banker—Jeannette, by Mambrino Howard .. 2.22¾
Hortense, b m, 1890, by Quartermaster—Saratoga, by Grand Sentinel.. 2:21½
Hortense, b m, 188—, by Judge Advocate 2:26½
Horton, b g, 1883, by Polonius—Maggie Horton, by Major Edsall Jr.... 2:25¾
Hot Shot, ch g, 188—, by Deucalion.. 2:21¼
Hotspur, b g, 1861, by Ethan Allen, dam by True John (dead) 2:24
Hotspur Chief b s, 1871, by Hotspur (dead) 2:29
Hotspur Girl, b m, 1878, by Hotspur Jr.—Flora 2:29¼
Hotspur King b s, 1883, by Hotspur Jr.—Lilly 2:27¾
Houri, b m, 1884, by Onward—Jessie Turner, by Mambrino Patchen..... 2:17
Howard, b s, 1887, by Vermont Abdallah—Vernet, by Edward Everett 2:20
Howard, b g, 187—, by George Wilkes—Lady Adams, by Amos' Cassius M. Clay Jr. 2:27¼
Howard Jay, ro g, 1876, by Wood's Hambletonian—Emma Moutour, by Seneca Chief 2:21¼
Howard L., ro g, 1887, by Monarch Jr.—Tiney B., by Black Pilot 2:20½
Howard Medium, b s, 188—, by Saxony 2:19¼
Howard S., b s, 1888, by Western Boy—Smith Mare 2.28½
Howell, b s, 1889, by Haldane—Shena Van, by Daniel Lambert (pacing record 2:24¼) 2:26¼
H. P. E., br g, 188—, by Gen. Garfield 2:25¼
H. R. C., b g, 188—, by Independence, dam by Swigert 2:21¼
Hudson, b g, 187—, by Tippo 2:29
Hudson, b g, 1881, by Kinlock—Flora 2:27
Hugh G., blk g, 188—, by Governor D. 2:28
Hugh McLaughlin, b s, 1873, by Aberdeen—Lady Ham (dead) 2:23
Hugh Patrick, gr g, 187—, pedigree not traced 2:23¼
Hugo, b g, 1889, by Hope So, dam by Coaster 2:22½
Hugo, b s, 1887, by Electioneer—Helpmate, by Planet 2:27½
Hugo H., blk g, 1885, by Hugo Prince, dam by Bonnie Scotland 2:25½
Huguely, b s, 1889, by Vatican—Edna C., by Hogan's Mambrino 2.24
Hulbert, br s, 1888, by Sherman's Hambletonian—Alice G., by Allie West 2:17½
Hulda, b m, 1888, by Guy Wilkes—Jenny, by Bull Pup 2:08½
Huldy B., ch m, 1886, by Ben Franklin—Topsey, by Green Mountain Banner 2:21¾
Humbert, b g, 1878, by Bona Fide—Belle of Paylet, by Warr Hulett.... 2:28½
Humboldt, b g, 187—, by Stockton Chief, dam by Parish's Davy Crocket 2 20
Humbolt Maid, b m, 1891, by Waldstein 2:27
Humbug, gr g, 188—, by Billy Knox, dam by Major Goldsmith 2:21¼
Hundley, ch s, 1887, by Harkaway—Burton Mare, by Peavine 2:20¾
Hunter, ch g, 1867, by Black Dutchman, dam by Walters' son of Saladin (dead) 2:29
Hunter, br g, 1878, by Jerry Ladd 2 25½
Hunter, gr g, 1877, by Banker Rothschild, dam by Glencoe 2:23¼
Hunter Rye, b g, 1884, by Orange Blossom—Carrie, by Andy Johnson 2:26¼
Huntress, ch m, 1878, by Admiral—Black Flora, by Black Prince...... 2:28
Huntress, b m, 1864 by Volunteer—Lady Sears, by Seely's American Star (dead) 2:20¾
Huntsman, b s, 1887, by Heptagon—Big Head Mary, by Virgo Hambletonian 2:30
Huon, b s, 1879, by Hamlin's Almont Jr.—Polly, by Hamlin Patchen 2:28¼
Hurlingham, br s, 1887, by Wilkesdale—Loretta, by Bostick's Almont Jr. 2:19½
Hurly Burly, ch s, 1886, by Rumor—Lucia, by Jay Gould 2:16¼
Huron Boy, ch s, 1885, by Pasacas—Jenny Bell 2:16¼
Hurricane, gr s, 1877, by Ringwood—Maggie Mitchell, by Phil Sheridan... 2:20¼

JOHN SPLAN, Glenville, Ohio.
(THE ORATOR.)
Splan cut the world's record for trotters to 2:13¼ with Rarus,
and the world's record for pacers to 2:06¼ with Johnston.

FRANK DOBLE, Elyria, Ohio.
The member of the Doble family that marked Gertrude 2:12
and Peveril 2:14¼.

Huseholt, br s, 188—, by Reno Defiance 2:25
Hussar, b s, 188—, by Sweepstakes—Lady Power 2:29½
Hussar, b s, 1886, by Jersey Wilkes—Lady Swiveler, by Walkill Chief.... 2:18½
Hustler, ch g, 188—, by Haldane—Lady Pearl, by Abraham (pacing record 2:27½) 2:20½
Hustler, b s, 1890, by Hummer—Musette, by Mambrino Patchen........ 2:20¾
Hustler, ch g, 188—, by Rustler...... 2:29¼
Huxham, ch s, 1887, by Nest Egg—Hagar, by Woodford Mambrino Jr.. 2:18½
Hyacinthe, b m, 188—, by Pasacas... 2:20½
H. W. Beecher, blk s, 1872, by Phil Sheridan—Lady Clement.............. 2:28¼
Hydrogen, b s, 188—, by Nitrogen.... 2:27¼
Hylas, ch s, 1869, by Alcalde—Santa Maria, by Pilot Jr.................. 2:24½
Hylas Boy, b g, 1884, by Hylas, dam by Indian Chief........................ 2:23
Hylas Maid, b m, 1880, by Hylas, dam by Robert Bonner............. 2:29½
Hyperion, ch s, 1886, by Piedmont—Mamie, by Hambletonian Jr......... 2:21¾
Hyson, b s, 188—, by Hyperion....... 2:26½
H. Z. Leonard, b s, 1878, by DuBois's Hambletonian Prince — Leonard Maid, by New York Boy........ 2:30
Iago, b g, 188—, by Tempest—Eulogy, by Commodore Belmont 2:15
Ianthe, b m, 1887, by Bostick's Almont Jr—Littlefield, by Enfield...... 2:16
Ibis, b m, 1884, by Princeps—Lorette, by Rysdyk's Hambletonian........ 2:19¾
Ice Cream, dn g, 188—, by Swigert Chief 2:26
Ichi Ban, b s, 1883, by Belmont—Primrose, by Alexander's Abdallah..2:20¼
Ida, gr m, 1875, by Belmont—Molly Quick, by Scott's Blue Bull......... 2:29½
Ida A., b m, 188—, by Princeer 2:25
Ida B., ch m, 188—, by Ashland Chief 2:28¾
Ida B., b m, 188—, by George Brooks, dam by Key's Miller............... 2:17¼
Ida Belle, b m, 1880, by Maj. Miller—Lady Konkle, by Wood's Hambletonian 2:23
Ida C., b m, 188—, pedigree not traced 2:27¼
Ida D., br m, 1883, by Maxim—Nutmeg Maid, by Thomas Jefferson..... 2:17¾
Ida D., ch m, 188—, by Doncaster.... 2:30
Idah, br m, 1892, by Sidney—Juno, by Buccaneer 2:30
Ida H., br m, 1876, pedigree not traced 2:30
Ida K., b m, 1891, by Robert McGregor 2:29¾
Idaho Patchen, b s, 187—, by Henry B. Patchen—Kate Wallen, by Lusby (dead) 2:26½
Ida May, br m, 1885, by Hawthorne—Baron Tempest, by Chieftain....... 2:28
Ida Norwood, b m, 1881, by Norwood—Arabian Girl, by Arabian Chief... 2:26½
Ida P. J., br m, 1882, by Dread—Fanny Castleman, by Punch......... 2:29¼
Ida S., b m, 188—, by Indiaman...... 2:24½
Ida T., b m, 188—, by Dauntless—Lady Tramp, by Tramp.............. 2:25
Ida T., b m, 188—, by Wagner Bashaw 2:27
Idavan, b s, 1885, by Earl—Meta, by Thorndale.................................... 2:19½
Idia, b m, 1891, by Duquesne........ 2:30
Ideal, b m, 1889, by Onward—Idyl, by Challenger 2:29¼
Idelia, b m, 1886, by Electioneer—Clarabel, by Abdallah Star......... 2:30
Idleweise, b m, 1889, by Idolater—Lady Rownd, by Square Dealer..... 2:24¼
Idle May, b m, 1885, by Electioneer—May, by Wildidle 2:27½
Idle Thought, b m, 188—, by Happy Thought.................................... 2:29½
Idlewild, blk m, 1878, by Glenair—Lady Henkley, by Bartlett's Black Hawk (dead) 2:29¼
Idler, rn m, 188—, by Raymond — Abbie, by Onderdonk................ 2:28
Idol, ch m, 1857, by Bob Ridley—Friendship, by Gossip Jones......... 2:27
Idol, br m, 1869, by Stephen A. Douglass, dam by Seely's Black Hawk... 2:23
Idol, b s, 1887, by Gambetta—Molly, by St. Elmo 2:27½
Idolater, ch s, 1884, by Backman's Idol—Nelly B., by Brougham 2:28½
Idolf, b s, 1885, by Backman's Idol—Molly Jackson, by Stonewall Jackson 2:13¾
Idol Gift, blk s, 1881, by Aker's Idol—Lady McKenny, by Sweepstakes ... 2:24
Idol Jackson, blk s, 1886, by Backman's Idol—Mary Jackson, by Stonewall Jackson 2:27¼
Idol Stone, b g, 188—, by Backman's Idol 2:20¼
Ignaro, b s, 1884, by Princeps—Olio, by Dick Hambletonian 2:25½
Ignis Fatuus, b s, 1884, by Editor—Lulu Wilkes, by George Wilkes..... 2:20½
I Jay S., ch s, 1883, by Tramp—Delancy, by Green's Bashaw.......... 2:21¾
Ike Shultz, b g, 187—, by Vosburg—Kitty Burson, by Rainbow......... 2:30
Ike Wilkes, b g, 1887, by Grand Wilkes—Fanny, by Blue Bull......... 2:17¼
Illinois Egbert b g, 1882, by Egbert—Hippy, by Bowman's Clark Chief... 2:16¼
Ilma Cossack, b m, 1888, by Don Cossack—True Blue, by Blue Bull...... 2:21¾
Ilton, b s, 1885, by Tempest—Bonetta, by Commodore Belmont............. 2:28½
Image, b m, 1890, by Delmarch—Bright Light, by Autocrat Jr....... 2:19
Imitator, b s, 1881, by Delineator.... 2:23½
Immense, ch g, 1890, by Stockwell—Alice W., by Black Chief.......... 2:25¼
Imogene, b m, 1884, by Princeps—Ozone, by Rysdyk's Hambletonian.. 2:22
Imogene, blk m, 1890, by Inmaus, dam by Shooting Star 2:26¼
Impetuous, blk m, 1892, by Dictator—Ethelwyn, by Harold 2:15¼
Ina, b m, 188—, by Ridgeway........... 2:25¾
Ina G., b m, 1875, by Blue Bull...... 2:24½
Inca, br s, 1872, by Woodford Mambrino—Gretchen, by Mambrino Pilot.-2:27
Inca Jr., ch s, 1881, by Inca—Black Hawk Belle 2:20½
Incas, br s, 1884, by Inca—May Day, by Ballard's Cassius M. Clay Jr... 2:14½
Incense, b m, 1885, by Young Jim—India, by Happy Traveler.......... 2:17¾
Independence, gr s, 1871, by Gen Knox—Skip, by Gideon............. 2:21¼
Independence, b s, 1873, by Young Hindoo—Fanny Fern, by Tom Howard 2:23¼
Independence, blk g, 188—, by Edward Everett 2:19¼
Independence B., br s, 1885, by Thunder—Dumpty, by Mambrino Thatcher 2:29¾
Independent, ch s, 1889, by Lincoln—

Wilkes—Minnie Patchen, by Mambrino Patchen 2:13¾
Islam, b s, 1889, by Sphinx—Maggie Hubbard, by Magna Charta 2:26
Isreal, b s, 1884, by Rampart—Jessica, by Bellwood 2:19¼
Issaquena, br m, 1881, by Pancoast—Laytham Lass, by Alexander's Abdallah 2:21¼
Item, b s, 1882, by Artillery—Godiva, by Auditor 2:26¼
Ithuriel, b s, 1888, by Red Wilkes—Topsey, by Strathmore 2:29¾
Ivanhoe, b s, 1883, by Amber—Lysander Maid, by Lysander 2:27¼
Ivica, b s, 1884, by DeGraff's Alexander—Genoa, by Cuyler 2:24¼
Ivo b s, 1887, by Electioneer—Victoria, by Don Victor 2:26
Ivy E., b m, 1887, by Electioneer—Ivy, by Don Victor 2:29½
Ivy Medium, b m, 188—, by Prince Medium 2:24¼
Ivy Princess, ch m, 1886, by Jersey Prince—Fanny Fern, by Wood's Hambletonian 2:30
I. York, b g, 188—, by Gen. Thomas 2:29¼
I X. L., b g, 1883, by Walker Morrill—Sesesh, by Atkins' Trustee 2:25¼
Jack, br g, 188—, by A. W. Richmond 2:26
Jack, b g, 188— by Aristos 2:29¼
Jack, gr g, 1883, by Pilot Medium—Carrie Russell, by Magna Charta... 2:11½
Jack B., br g, 188—, by Annapolis—Hippitaca, by Hermes 2:28½
Jack Barry, b g, 186—, pedigree not traced 2:29
Jack Cade, b s, 1885, by Coriander—Judith, by Robert McGregor 2:26½
Jack Clark, blk g, 1884, by Antar—Yankee, by Ace of Diamonds........ 2:27¼
Jackdaw, br s, 1888, by Jay Bird—Biddy McGregor, by Robert McGregor 2:28¼
Jack Dawson, blk s, 1888, by Director—Favorita, by George Wilkes .. 2:30
Jack Draper, b g, 186—, by Humbird 2:27
Jack Heyden, b g 187—, pedigree not traced 2:23¾
Jack Lewis, b g, 185—, by Clifton Pilot (dead) 2:28½
Jack Offutt, ch s, 1887, by Nantucket—Euclid Maid 2:26
Jack Raleigh, br g, 188—, by Blackstone Prince—Waldo Mare, by Sherman Horse 2:23½
Jack Riley, b s, 1888, by Dan McGregor—Sunset, by Solferino....... 2:25½
Jack Roth ro g, 188—, pedigree not traced 2:28¼
Jack Sailor, br g, 1874, by Sweepstakes—Fanny D, by Black Morgan 2:25¼
Jack Sheppard, b s, 1887, by Anderson Wilkes 2:14½
Jack Sheppard Jr. b g, 1879, by Jack Sheppard—Baby, by Ethan Allen.. 2:29¼
Jack Slade, ch s, 1885, by Prince Monroe—Daisy, by Stockbridge Chief.. 2:29¼
Jackson, b s, 1865, by Fine Cut 2:27¾
Jacksonian, b s, 1887, by Longstride—Kate Tiffany, by Monarch 2:22½
Jacksonian, b g, 1889, by Autograph—Miss Fanny Jackson, by Bay Lambert 2:19¾
Jacksonian, br s, 1889, by Schuyler Colfax—Lady Jackson, by Mohawk Jackson 2:22½
Jacksonville Boy, b g, 186—, pedigree not traced 2:28
Jack Splan, b s, 1876, by Almont—Jenny Martin, by Star Denmark .. 2:26¾
Jack Spratt, b g, 188—, by Tinder . 2:27¼
Jack Spratt, b g, 1888, by Hambletonian Wilkes—Water Lily, by Magna Charta 2:23½
Jack Spratt, br g, 1875, by Tom Patchen—Fowler 2:22¼
Jack the Ripper, b g, 188—, pedigree not traced 2:27½
Jack Wiman, b g, 1888, by Haroldmont, dam by Culbreth Knox 2:20¼
Jaco, blk s, 1888, by Patchen Wilkes—Lida Patchen, by Mambrino Patchen 2:29
Jacobin b s, 1885, by Princeps—Lulu Wilkes, by George Wilkes 2:23½
Jadie Allen, b m, 188—, by Petoskey, dam by Freeman 2:17½
J. A. K., ch g, 188—, pedigree not traced 2:25¼
Jake, b s, 1884, by Messenger Chief—Sal Swope, by Bourbon Chief 2:22
J. Alba, b g, 188—, by Glen Knox ... 2:29½
Jalisco, b s, 1882, by Durango—Purl, by Haw Patch 2:19¼
James, ch g 188—, pedigree not traced 2:26¼
James A. Garfield, blk g, 188—, pedigree not traced 2:29¼
James D., b g, 188—, by Mambrino Pilot 2:23¼
James D., ch g, 1886, by Clay Abdallah—Field Mare 2:30
James D McMann, b g, 186—, by George M. Patchen Jr (dead) 2:28¾
James F., b g, 1883, by Reporter—Jessie, by Roberts' Royal George . 2:22½
James G., ch s, 1881, by Royal Chief—Sunbeam, by Alhambra 2:20
James G. Blaine, blk g, 1866, by Messenger Hunter—Lally Mare, by Call Horse 2:28¾
James H., b g, 1873, by Amboy, dam by Finch's St. Lawrence 2:21¼
James H., b g, 1876, by Gladiator—Fanny Collier, by Collier 2:21
James H., b s, 1887, by Nil Desperandum—Maggie, by Thorndale 2:28½
James Halfpenny, b g, 1875, by Blue Bull, dam by Pearsall 2:29¼
James H Burke, blk g, 186—, by Tippoo (dead) 2:27½
James Howell Jr. br g, 1866, by Rysdyk's Hambletonian—Jessie Sayre, by Harry Clay (dead) 2:24
James L., b g, 1887, by Dexter Prince, dam by Tom Vernon 2:16¼
James M., b g, 1885, by Landmark—Lady Haskins, by Haskins Horse 2:21¼
James Madison, b s, 1884, by Anteeo—Lucy Patchen, by George M. Patchen Jr. 2:17¾
James Morrison, b g, 188—, by Gov. Sprague 2:25¼
James P., b s, 1887, by Princeps—Gracie Van Cott, by Jay Gould..... 2:25
Jane L., br m, 1879, by Hambletonian Mambrino—Molly Welsh, by Paul Jones 2:19½
Jane R., b m, 1879, by Alden Goldsmith—Medora, by Bayard 2:26¼
Janesville, b g, 186—, by Robert Fulton, dam by Gen McClellan 2:29¼
Janet, br m, 188—, by Black Rolfe.. 2:24¼
Janet, b m, 1886, by Bourbon Boy—Lady Wellington, by Wellington 2:27¼

Jame (Opal), b m, 1879, by Jay Gould Ruby—Allen, by Ethan Allen....... 2:21¼
Janifer, br m, 1883, by Red Wilkes Stella O'Neal, by Pacing Abdallah 2 22
Jasper, b g, 1881, by Altimont 2:25¼
Jasper, b g, 1875, by Jasson 2:26½
Jaunita b m, 1887, by Sultan—Beulah, by Harold 2:29
Jay Bird, b m, 1975, by Kent—Molly, by Warchester 2 30
Jay Caldwell, b s, 1887, by Hamdallah—Molly, by Oliver Goldsmith.... 2:22¼
Jay Cook, blk g, 1869 by Joe Hooker—Spy, by Sweet Owen (dead) 2:27
Jay-Eye-See, blk g, 1878, by Dictator—Midnight, by Pilot Jr. (pacing record 2 06¼) 2:10
Jayfoot, ro s, 1888, by Jay Bird—Fleety, by Baywood 2:28
Jay Gould, b s 1864, by Rysdyk's Hambletonian—Lady Sanford, by Seely's American Star (dead) 2:21½
Jayhawk, b s, 1888, by Jaywood—Grenadine, by Grenadier 2:29¾
Jaw Hawker, ro s, 1890, by Jay Bird Sorrento, by Grand Sentinel 2.14¾
Jay See Bee, b s, 1886, by Paramount—Molly B, by Panic 2:28½
Jay See Ell, blk s, 1891, by Round's Sprague 2 24½
Jay U. See, ch s, 1883, by Vermont Abdallah 2 23¾
J. B., b g, 1880, by Dick Turpin—Lady Belle, by Emigrant 2:24½
J. B. C., b m, 188—, by Strait's Superior 2:27¼
J B. Richardson b g, 1877, by George Wilkes—Tullahoma, by Almont 2 16¾
J. B S, br g, 188—, by White's Ethan Allen, dam by Black Ralph 2:29¾
J B. S. b g, 1882, by Allie Gaines—Belle S., by Star of the West 2.19¼
J B Thomas b g, 1874, by Sterling—Lady Hooker, by Defiance 2.18½
J C, b g, 188—, by Oshkosk 2:29¼
J. C. (Frederick) b g, 1882 by Winnebago Chief—Kit 2 20
J. D. C, gr g, 1883, by Roscoe C.—Lady Bromley 2:30
J. D. Creighton, blk s, 1890, by C. F. Clay — Gambettina, by Gambetta Wilkes.... ....2:25½
J. D. L, br g, 1886, by Mambrino King, dam by Stephen A. Douglas.. 2:29¼
Jeanette, b m, 1886, by The King—Jenny, by Young Columbus 2:29½
Jean Look, b m, 188—, by Look....... 2:30
Jeannette, b m, 1882, by Don Cossack—Lotta, by Bashaw Drury 2 26¼
Jeannie, b m 1877, by Abraham—Old Sorrel, by Breed Horse 2 27¼
Jeannie C, b m, 1884, by Nutwood—Delilah, by Administrator 2.22
Jean Valjean, b g, 1883, by Crittenden—Fantine, by Alcaide........... 2:14
Jean Wilkes, b m, 1884, by Red Wilkes—Belle Brino, by Hambrino.. 2 27¼
Jean Wilkes, b m, 1889, by Guy Wilkes—Rosalie, by Sultan....... .. 2:24¾
Jean Wilkes, b m, 1888, by Young Wilkes—Jeanette, by Messenger Duroc.... .... 2 29¼
Jeff Davis, b s, 188—, by Wedgewood. 2:27½
Jeff Davis, br g, 1884, by Atlantic—Doxy Morgan, by Red Lion....... 2:17¼
Jeffersonian b g, 1889, by Ajax—Fanny, by Gray's Tom Hal 2.27
Jefferson Wilkes, blk s, 1891, by Alcone 2 26
Jeffie Lee, ch m, 1887, by Red Pilot, dam by Cramer.. .... 2.22
Jeff Smith, b g, 1881, by Ohio—Doll, by Manchester Tuckahoe (pacing record 2 29¼) 2 27¼
Jeff Wilkes, b g, 1879, by George Wilkes—Lady Adams, by Amos' Cassius M Clay Jr................ .... 2 29¼
Jellyby, b s, 1885, by Walsingham—Nonie, by Golddust................ 2 26
Jenny, b m. 1865, by Red Eagle—Topsy Reamy, by Patalaska (dead).. 2 22½
Jenny, ch m, 1871, by Dandy—Nichette, by Guest Horse............... 2.29¼
Jenny, b m, 1881, by Richwood—Hannah, by Don J. Robinson 2.18¼
Jenny B., b m, 1882, by Blue Bull—Lady Hassin 2.29½
Jenny B, gr m, 1880, by Dan Brown—Jenny Lind, by Tucker's Good Ike.. 2 24
Jenny Bell, b m, 188—, pedigree not traced 2:28¼
Jenny C., b m, 1884, by Kent—Sorrell Lambert, by Daniel Lambert 2 24½
Jenny D., blk m, 1887, by Lake Erie—Nelly, by Star of Ulster.......... 2.26½
Jenny Hill, blk m, 188—, by Egthorne 2·29¼
Jenny Holton, b m, 1868, by Billy Bacchus 2 22¼
Jenny June, br m, 188—, by Motor... 2.19¼
Jenny K., b m, 1887, by Phallas—Dutch Girl, by Abdallah Boy....... 2:15½
Jenny Kirk, ch m, 1877, pedigree not traced.. .... 2:27¼
Jenny L., gr m, 1869, by Terhune Horse—Emma, by Grey Messenger (dead) 2 27¼
Jenny M., ch m, 1880, by Joe Hooper—Hull Mare, by Von Moltke 2 25½
Jenny M., br m........ .... 2.29¼
Jenny Q., gr m, 1890, by Gen Wilkes—Miss Barlow, by Dr Keene....... 2 30
Jenny R., b m, 188—, by Como..... . 2 26¼
Jenny Rolfe, b m, 188—, by Young Rolfe, dam by Summerset Knox ... 2 27½
Jenny R., blk m, 188—, by Warwick Boy 2.28¼
Jenny Sprague, ch m, 1882, by Rounds' Sprague — Kit, by Gage's Logan 2.15¼
Jenny Star, br m, 1885, by Masterlode—Star Maid, by Magnolia 2 24¼
Jenny Thombs, b m, 1887, by Senator—Jenny, by Corbin Bashaw.... . 2·25½
Jenny W., br m, 1870, by Brown Harry—Blackbird, by Black Hawk.. 2:30
Jenny Wilkes, b m, 1885, by Coronet—Kitty Morgan, by Bartlett Morgan . 2 25½
Jenny Wilkes, b m, 1887, by Woodford Wilkes — China Wilkes, by Adrian Wilkes...................... 2.12½
Jenny Wren, b m, 188—, by Coligne . 2 25¼
Jenny Wynne, br m, 188—, by Wade Hampton 2:26¼
Jeremiah, b g, 1879, by William Welch—Lady Gregory, by Corbeau 2:21½
Jericho (Everett), b g, 1867, by Henry Clay—Jenny, by Grinnell's Champion (dead) 2:30
Jerome, b g, 188—, pedigree not traced 2:29¾
Jerome, b g, 1880, by Caesar......... 2·26¾
Jerome, b g, 1870, by Rysdyk's Hambletonian—Fanny Fiske, by Young Almack 2 27
Jerome, b g, 1873, by Hamilton—Blonde, by Ashland 2 23¾

Jerome, ch g, 186—, by Keokuk....... 2:27
Jerome Eddy, b s, 1875, by Louis Napoleon—Fanny Mapes, by Alexander's Abdallah 2:16½
Jerome Turner, b s, 1879, by Byerly Abdallah—Nettie, by Gray's Tom Hal........................ 2:15½
Jerry, b g, 1888, by Garnet Wilkes—Hazel, by Iowa Duroc.............. 2:27¼
Jerry, b g, 188—, by Henry B. Patchen.......................... 2:28¾
Jerry Almont, blk g, 1882, by Almontonian, dam by Ericsson........... 2:26¼
Jerry L., gr g, 1879, by Stonewall Jackson Jr., dam by Bayard........ 2:13¾
Jerry M., b g, 1885, by Bright Clay—Dolly 2:30
Jerry W., ch g, 188—, by Hannis....... 2:22¼
Jerry Wilkes, b s, 1888, by Wilkes Spirit Jr.—Jessie.................. 2:30
Jersey Boy, b g, 1870, by Young Volunteer—Libby, by Gen. Taylor...... 2:21¼
Jersey Belle, blk m, 188—, by Jersey Wilkes, dam by Star of the West... 2:18½
Jerseyman, br s, 1885, by Jersey Prince—Lulu K., by Goldsmith's Star 2:23¼
Jersey Prince, ch s, 1879, by Kentucky Prince—Emeline, by Henry B. Patchen (dead) 2:27¼
Jersey Wood, b s, 1885, by Jersey Prince—Nelly B., by Billy Patterson 2:27¼
Jesse, b g, 187—, pedigree not traced. 2:26¼
Jesse, gr g, 187—, by Deucalion....... 2:21
Jesse Hammond, b g, 1880, by Signal—Jenny Amos, by Middleton's Golddust 2:25½
Jesse Hanson, b g, 1884, by Roger Hanson—Nelly Mac, by Blue Vein... 2:13¾
Jesse James, ch g, 1883, by Don J. Robinson—Black Flora............. 2:29½
Jessie, ch m, 1874, by Vernol's Black Hawk 2:21
Jessie, br m, 188—, by Dexter Prince—Lady Fracture 2:22
Jessie B., ch s, 1885, by Gen. Grant—Lady McBeth 2:21
Jessie B., b m, 1880, by Don J. Robinson—Novice 2d, by Fisk's Mambrino Chief Jr. 2:24¼
Jessie Ballard, b m, 1877, by Archie Hambletonian 2:25
Jessie C., b m, 1889, by Civilization.. 2:24¾
Jessie Clark, b m, 1889, by Norwood Star—Lady Sutherland, by Clark Chief 2:27½
Jessie D., ch m, 1888, by Elyria—Kate, by White Line............... 2:19¾
Jessie Dixon, b m, 1872, by Mambrino Patchen 2:28¼
Jessie Fly, br m, 1886, by Swigert—Lady Lambert, by Mambrino Medley 2:29¼
Jessie Gaines, br m, 1883, by Allie Gaines, dam by Shakespeare 2:15½
Jessie Gould, b m, 1881, by Jay Gould—Dolsey, by Shaeffer Pony.......... 2:29¼
Jessie Hayes, b m, 1868, by Ned Forrest, dam by Highlander........... 2:24
Jessie Hood, b m, 188—, by W. H. Cassidy 2:25½
Jessie K., b m, 1885, by Landmark—Nelly, by Haskins Horse.......... 2:26½
Jessie Maud, gr m, 1870, by Regulus—Quakeress, by Washington 2:29
Jessie McCorkle, ch m, 1889, by Amboy—Lilly, by Amber (dead)..... 2:15
Jessie Sheridan, b m, 1888, by Elial G. Jr.—Chestnut Fan, by Phil Sheridan 2:21¾

Jessie Wales, blk m, 1859, by West's Ajax (dead) 2:30
Jessie Wilkes, b m, 1886, by Pilot Wilkes—Notre Dame, by Hurst and Thornton's Abdallah (dead) 2:28½
Jessie Wilkes, br m, 1888, by Algeria Wilkes—Alice G., by Black Knight.. 2:19¼
Jettie, blk m, 1890, by Bonnie Boy—Lady Cooper, by Andrew Jackson.. 2:18¾
Jewell, ch g, 1882, by Clayton Edsall—Fanny Crawford 2:27¼
Jewell, br g, 1875, by Buckingham—Kate Coe, by Rhode Island....... .. 2:24¾
Jewell, ch g, 1882, by Clayton Edsall—Fanny Crawford 2:29½
Jewel C., b m, 1887, by Kentucky Ruler—Hazel Kirke, by St. Almo (dead) 2:24½
Jewel Wilkes, b m, 1887, by Woodford Wilkes—Pearl, by Ashland Patchen. 2:28½
Jewett, blk g, 1876, by Allie West—Heel and Toe Fanny (pacing record 2:14) 2:20
Jewmont, b s, 1888, by King Almont—Jewel, by Gill's Vermont.......... 2:30
J. G. Morrill, ch g, 1872, by Winthrop Morrill, dam by Eaton Horse....... 2:29
J. H. McCormick, ch g, 187—, by Wagner Bashaw—Lucy, by Flaxtail..... 2:29
J. H. S., ch g, 188—, by Naubic...... 2:30
Jilt, ch m, 1854, by Allegheny Chief—Jenny Lind (dead) 2:28½
Jim, ro g, 1874, by Daniel Lambert—Pacing Kate 2:23½
Jim, gr g, 1882, by Billy Norfolk—Irene.............................. 2:22½
Jim, b g, 188—, by Electioneer....... 2:27¼
Jim Alone, ch s, 188—, by Eolus..... 2:20½
Jim Anderson, b g, 1879, by Robert McGregor—Nelly 2:28½
Jim Blaine, b g, 1884, by Dundee—Ora, by McKinney 2:30
Jim Blaine, b s, 1891, by Eastwood.. 2.30
Jimbone, ch g, 188—, by Bonesetter.. 2:29¾
Jim Bowman, b g, 187—, by a son of Ericsson 2:26
Jim Burns, br g, 188—, by Belmont Chief................................ 2:24¼
Jim Burns, blk g, 1889, by Temperance—Flora, by Harrington Hunter 2:25½
Jim C., b g, 1885, by Jim Swigert—Darkness 2:22½
Jim Crandall, dn g, 187—, pedigree not traced 2:30
Jim Crow, blk s, 188—, by Abbottsford, dam by Lumps.................. 2:23¾
Jim Dean, gr s, 1888, by Dr. Spurr—May, by Bayard 2:20¾
Jim Deyo, ch g, 188—, by S. J. Fletcher 2:20
Jim Dunn, ro g, 1885, by Mambrino Startle—Flora, by Lanigan......... 2:20¼
Jim Early, ch g, 1875, by Fitzsimmons' Champion—Nelly Early, by Pilgrim Eclipse 2:22¼
Jim F., b s, 1886, by Intrigue—Minnie, by Windsor.................... 2:26
Jim Fuller, b g, 1880, by Golden Bow—Maggie, by Fletcher 2:19¼
Jim Golden, blk g, 1880, by Alaric—Jenny Ross 2:30
Jim Graham, b g, 1883, by Harry Franklin—Patterson Girl 2:26½
Jim Irving, b g, 1865, by Wilson's Snowstorm—Lear Mare, by Sir William (dead) 2:23
Jim Knox, ch s, 188—.................. 2:29¾
Jim L., ch s, 1881, by Dan Voorhees—Gracie B., by Uncle Sam.......... 2:20

Jim Lane, b g, 187—, by Dauntless—Kitty Hunter, by Harrington's Hunter............................. 2 29¼
Jim Leach, b g, 1879, by Inca—Molly, by Sacramento 2:28½
Jim Matt, b g, 1884, by Young Jim, dam by American Clay.............. 2 28¼
Jimmy O, b g, 188—, pedigree not traced 2:20½
Jimmy C, b g, 1879, by Col. M,—Fanny Griffinstein 2:23¼
Jimmy Puzzler, b s, 187—by Whirlwind Jr 2:30
Jimmy Steward, b g, 187—, by Daniel Lambert 2:24¼
Jimmy Temple, blk g, 1882, by George Wilkes—Lady Patchen, by Mambrino Patchen (pacing record 2.23¾) ... 2 22½
Jim Nutwood, b g, 188—, by Cornelius 2:21¼
Jim Raven, blk g, 186—, by Star of the West (dead) 2:30
Jim Riddle, ch s, 1887, by Pilot Wilkes—Emma Armstrong, by Starmont 2:25¼
Jim Savery, b g, 1892, by Blitzen 2 29¼
Jim Schriber, gr s, 1872, by Rhode Island—Dutch Girl, by Dusty Miller 2:21½
Jim Smith, b s, 1886, by L J. Sutton—Hattie B., by Don J. Robinson .. 2 22¼
Jim Sneaks, b g, 188—, by McLeod—Molly Graydon, by Green's Bashaw 2.23½
Jim Star. gr s, 1882, by Star of the West—Emma, by Flying Gypsy .. 2 29
Jim Ward, b g, 1871, by Young Columbus—Black Star, by Darkey .. 2 23½
Jim Wilkes, b g, 1885, by Young Jim —Anna P., by Stockbridge Chief Jr 2 19¼
Jim Wilkes, blk s, 188—, by Young Jim—Kate Scott, by Clark Chief ... 2:15¾
Jim Young, b s, 1886, by Young Jim—Cricket, by Mambrino Abdallah .. 2:26½
Jingles, b s, 1886, by Baron Wilkes—Lamberta, by Daniel Lambert . 2·28¾
Jingo Jim, br g, 188—, by Bemis' Black Cloud 2.26½
J. Irving O, b g, 188—, pedigree not traced 2 27¾
J. J. Audubon, ch s, 1887, by Alcyone—Dolly Pomeroy, by Highland Grey 2:19
J. J. Bradley, b g, 186—, pedigree not traced 2 25½
J J Douglas, br g, 1880, by Mambrino St. Lawrence, dam by Getaway 2.20½
J. M. b g, 188—, by Cornell, dam by Lothair Jr.............................. 2 22¼
J M B, b s, 1882, by Selenite—Capiola .... 2·26¾
J. M. D., b g, 188—, by Harry Hamilton, dam by Little Oak 2:13¼
J M G., gr g, 188—, by Whiteline .. 2·20
J. M K., gr g, 1888, by Jet—Nelly Grey, by Jack Splan 2:18
J M T., b g, 188—, pedigree not traced 2 22½
Joan. b m, 1880, by Waveland Chief, dam by Joe 2:30
Jockey, b g, 188—, by Powers Hambletonian 2 30
J. O. blk g, ... 2:27½
J O O gr g, ... 2·25
J. O D., ch m, 1889 by Earl 2 30
Joe, ch g, 188—, by Tom Hunter .. 2 30
Joe, ch s, 1886 by Canonicus—Nelly Ferguson, by McKesson's Gray Eagle 2 19
Joe ch g, 1860, by Young Plenipo

(dead) 2 25¼
Joe, b s, 1887, by Marco—Kate, by Milliman's Bellfounder .... 2·29¼
Joe, b g, 188—, by Elial G,—Jones' Mare, by son of Tom Jefferson .. 2·29¼
Joe, b g 1881, by Sweepstakes, dam by Jupiter Abdallah 2 30
Joe Arhurton, b g, 1878, by Arthurton—Flora, by Langford 2.20½
Joe Bassett Jr., b s, 1883, by Joe Bassett—Cary Mare, by Sweeting's Ned Forrest 2.18¼
Joe Barney, b g, 188—, by Barney Monroe 2 26
Joe Bluffer, b s, 1882, by Wilkesonian—Kitty, by Washington Hambletonian 2:27½
Joe Brown, gr s, 1863, by Woodward's Rattler, dam by Burdick's Engineer (dead) 2 22
Joe Bunker, gr g, 1874, by George Wilkes—Lady Dunn, by American Star 2:19¼
Joe D., b g, 187—, by Cafferty Horse —Fancy Fairbanks, by Hines' Black Hawk Morgan 2.27¼
Joe Davis, br g, 1877, by Dr Herr—Molly, by Mambrino Pilot Jr 2.17¾
Joe Dayton, br s, 187—, by Puzzler, dam by Honest Tom 2.25¾
Joe Eastman, b s, 1883, by Robert McGregor—Josephine, by Gen. Grant.. 2 29¼
Joe Fifer, b s, 1889, by Bloomfield—Dell by Bay Joe 2:18
Joe Gaines, b s, 1889, by Allie Gaines—Lucy Bird, by Abdallah Bird 2 25
Joe Gales, ch g, 1889, by Elyria—Shoo Fly, by Young Tippoo Sultan 2·29¼
Joe Gilbirds, b s, 1885, by Gilbirds Sprague 2.20½
Joe Green, b g, 186—, pedigree not traced 2.26½
Joe H., blk g, 188—, by Canadian Champion .... 2·26¼
Joe Hal, br s, 1879, by Blood Chief Jr—Babe 2.30
Joe Holmes, ch s, 1888, by Sir Walter dam by Blackwood 2 26½
Joe Hooker. ch g, 186—, by Andy Johnson (dead) .... 2·30
Joe Jefferson br s, 1878, by Hambletonian Downing—Mila Thomas, by Blue Bull 2:27¾
Joe Kellogg, b g, 186—, by Tuckahoe Post Boy 2:30
Joe Kinney, b g, 188—, by Alwood, dam by Milliman's Bellfounder. 2 26½
Joe M., br g 1882, by Joe Cool—Dolly M 2 23½
Joe Mark, b s 1887, by Victor Bismarck—Miss Monroe, by Jim Monroe 2 28¼
Joe McLaughlin, b g 1885, by Red Luke—Dolly, by Duroc .... 2·26½
Joe Moreland, b s 1881, by Woodburn—Lottie Lee by Herman D Patchen 2·22
Joe Pettit. b g. 1868, by Ashland—Belle of Fairfield by Toronto Chief 2 30
Joe R., br g. by Kirk .... 2·17¾
Joe R. Lambert, ch g, (ringer) ... 2.30
Joe Ray, b g, 188—, pedigree not traced 2 30
Joe Rhea, b g, 187—, pedigree not traced 2 23
Joe Ripley, b g 1868, by Sawin's Hambletonian dam by Black Arrow 2·25
Joe S, b g, 1869 by Daniel Lambert 2·30
Joe S, dn s, 1883, by Creole—Mary McMolly 2 30

Joe Thorndale, b s, 1882, by Young Thorndale 2:30

Joetta Wilkes, b m, 1889, by Woodford Wilkes—Kate Griffith, by Alden Goldsmith 2:29¾

Joe Udell, b g, 186—, pedigree not traced (dead) 2:30

Joe W., b g, 1887, by Stanton Jr.—Fanny, by Brant 2:26¼

Joe Wilkes, br s, 1885, by Alcantara—Kit, by Belmont Hambletonian.. 2:30

Joe Wonder, b g, 1885, by Bonnie Richards—Bay Doll 2:17¼

Joe You See, b s, 1885, by Joe Young—Lucy, by Antar 2:17¼

Joe Young, blk s, 1876, by Star of the West—Lady Gregory, by Green's Bashaw 2:19½

John A., b g, 188—, pedigree not traced 2:29½

John A. Logan, b g, 188—, by Major Ringgold (pacing record 2:26½)..... 2:30

John A. Logan, b g, 1884, by Tornado M.—Kitty M., by Mosher's Clay 2:25

John B., b g, 1869, pedigree not traced 2:27

John Bascomb, b s, 1886, by Wilkie Collins—Josephine, by Wood's Hambletonian 2:25

John Bury, b g, 1891, by Antinous, dam by George M. Patchen Jr. 2:22

John Carter, b s, 1887, by Regulator—Dolly Fritts, by Marshall Chief ... 2:30

John C. Shelly, b s, 1884, by Hawthorne—Old Tempest, by Morgan Rattler 2:29¾

John Cody Jr., b g, 188—, by Sir Wallace 2:29¼

John D., gr g, 1884, by Royalston—Canadian Girl 2:28¾

John D., b g, 188—, by Dr. Downing.. 2:30

John D., b g, 1874, by Messenger Duroc—Lady Kate, by Kemble Jackson 2:23½

John Dickson, b s, 1882, by Monarch Jr.—Jessie Dixon, by Mambrino Patchen 2:28

John Doddridge, gr g, 188—, by John A. Allen 2:23½

John E., ro g, 1868, by Clark Chief, dam by Alexander's Abdallah 2:28¾

John E., gr s, 1887, by Moody—Lady Olmstead, by Young Wilkes 2:29½

John F., b s, 1880, by Seneca Prince—Bandy Heyl 2:30

John F., b g, 1883, by Mohawk Hambletonian 2.30

John Ferguson, b g, 1880, by Forest Mambrino—Lady Scott, by Winfield Scott 2:25¼

John Fero (Western Boy), b g, 1862, pedigree not traced 2:27½

John F. Phelps Jr., b s, 1873, by Almont—Sue Monday, by Conscript ... 2:26

John G., gr g, 188—, ... 2:29¾

John Goldsmith, br s, 1866, by Volunteer—Ida, by Marlborough 2:28½

John Grant, gr g, 187—, pedigree not traced 2:25½

John G. Carlisle, b s, 1890, by Norval—Mete, by Idol Patchen 2:20

John H., b g, 186—, by Black Bashaw, dam by Morgan Hunter 2:20

John Hall, b g, 187—, by Daniel Lambert, dam by American Ethan 2:24¼

John Hall, blk g, 1869, by Gen. Howard 2:25

John Head, gr g, 1885, by St. Elmo.. 2:26½

John Henry, ch g, 1880, by Pilot Mambrino—Sada Belle, by Stark's Morgan 2:26½

John I., b s, 188—, by Aristos 2:26½

John I Cook, g g, 186—, by Star of the West—Fanny Jewett 2:29½

John L., b s, 188—, by Hermit........ 2:27¾

John L., b g, 1874, by Marshall's Patchen—Kate, by Daniel Webster 2:29¼

John L., b s, 1886, by Bourbon Wilkes—Elsie by Westwood 2:19¼

John L., ch s, 1887, by Al West—Fanny Barge 2:29½

John L., b g, 1887, by Landmark, dam by Bett's St. Lawrence 2:29¼

John Love, b g, 1872, by Billy Denton—Trusty, by Marlborough 2:28½

John McDougall, b g, 187—, by Bay Billy 2:29

John Merrill, b g, 188—, pedigree not traced 2:28½

John Mitchell, b g, 1884, by C. W. Mitchell—Pearsall Mare, by Pearsall 2:26¼

John Morgan, ch g, 1854, by Pilot Jr.—Croppy, by Medoc (dead) 2:24

John Morrill, b g, 1874, by Winthrop Morrill 2:27½

John Murphy, b g, 188—, by Clipper 2:28¼

John M., b g, 187—, (ringer.) 2:29¼

John M., ch g, 1881, by Greenback .. 2:27½

John W., ch g, 188—, by Appleby.. 2:29¼

Johnny A., ro g, 1886, by Ben Lomond Jr.—Fidele, by Gibson's Tom Hal .. 2:22¾

Johnny B., gr g, 1881, by St. Omer—Moss Rose, by Man Eater 2:27¼

Johnnie B., b g, 188—, by Handy B. Cora B., by Artemas........ 2:25¼

Johnny Boggs, b s, 1887, by King of the West—Maggie Gift, by Mambrino Gift 2:23

Johnny Bull, b g, 1886, by Jim Wilson—Daisy Boone, by Daniel Boone ... 2:27

Johnny H., b g, 187—, pedigree not traced 2:30

Johnny Hayward, gr g, 188—, by Poscora Hayward—Mabel, by The Moor 2:26

Johnny Golddust, br g, 1886, by Thompson's Golddust—Fanny, by Toronto Chief Jr. 2:17

Johnny Gordon, ch g, 1869, by Toronto Chief Jr., dam by St. Lawrence.. 2:25¼

Johnny Knott, br g, 1883, by Mohawk Hambletonian—Flora Belle 2:22

Johnny R., ch s, 1886, by Egmont—Daisy 2:25¼

Johnny Skelton, g g, 188—, by Milton Medium 2:30

Johnny Wilkes, b s, 188—, by Wilkes. 2:27½

John R., b g, 187—, by Aker's Idol—Kate Smith, by Spaulding's Abdallah 2:23

John R., blk g, 187—, pedigree not traced 2:25¼

John R. Wise, ch g, 1878, by Hambletonian Tranby—Lizzie Brown, by Belmont 2:23¼

John S., blk g, 1884, by Jersey Prince—Lady Augusta, by Rysdyk's Hambletonian 2.21¾

John S., g g........ 2:29¾

John S., dn g, 1886, pedigree not traced 2.29¼

John S. Clark, ch g, 1873, by Thomas Jefferson—Annie, by Scott's Hiatoga 2:19¾

John S. Heald, br g, 1868, by Whalebone Knox—Cooney, by Stewart Morgan 2:27¼

Johnson, br g, 1885, by Storm—Lady Washington 2:27

John Stewart, b g, 186—, by Tom Wonder — Park Mare, by Harris' Hambletonian (dead) 2.30
John Taylor, b g, 1869, pedigree not traced (dead) 2:25
John Thomas, b s, 1885, by Egmont—Phallas Maid, by Phallas............ 2:28¾
John Virgin, ch g, 1870, by Dirigo.... 2:29
John W., b g, 1877, by Knight—Chance Mare, by Morgan Black Hawk 2.23¾
John W., b g, 1881, by Messenger Duroc—Astraea, by Asteroid.......... 2:24¼
John W., b g, 1883, by John Wentworth—Bay Jenny, by Colonel...... 2:17¼
John W., b g, 188—, by Senator N.... 2:29¾
John W. Conley, b s, 1862, by Tom Wonder, dam by Abdallah.......... 2:24
John W. Hall, ch g, 1866, by Independence, dam by Monarch......... 2:25
John Wilkes, blk s, 188—, by Young Wilkes 2:27
Joker, b s, 1886, by Johnston's Gen. Lee Jr.—Lady Gay, by Prescott's Sambo 2.20
Joker, br g, 186—, by Parris' Hambletonian—Gleason Mare, by Andrus' Hambletonian 2:22½
Joker, b m, 1890, by Aladdin......... 2:24
Jolly Wilkes, b s, 188—, by Bartholomew Wilkes — Puss Patchen, by Patchen Chief 2:30
Joker H., br g, 1888, by Maplewood Chief—Blaze, by Magna Charta Jr... 2.30
Jokton, b s, 1892, by Lord Jenkinson.. 2:24¾
Jonesville, b s, 1886, by Haroldson—Olivia, by Woodburn Pilot.......... 2.29¾
Joseph, b g, 1871, by Blue Bull—Josephine 2.29¼
Joseph A., b g, 1870, by Sackett's Hambletonian 2:24
Josephine, blk m, 1880, by Kentucky Prince—Madam Felter, by Happy Medium 2.24¼
Josephine, b m, 188—, by Rienzi, dam by Magic 2:24¼
Josephine, blk m, 1888, by C. F. Clay—Maud, by Bell Brino 2:29¼
Josephine, blk m, 188—, by Secretary. 2:28½
Josephine, b m, 187—, by Green's Bashaw—Seely, by Cassius 2:30
Josephine, b m, 1884, by Castillian, dam by Yorkshire Lexington......... 2:19¼
Josephine S., blk m, 1874, by Guy Miller—Swartz, by Ethan Allen..... 2.24½
Joseph R., br g, 188—.................. 2:28½
Joseph See, b g, 1884, by Egmont—Jessie Farwell, by Bell Clay......... 2:27¼
Josephus, ch g, 1873, by Green's Bashaw—Simmons Mare 2:10¾
Jose S., gr m, 1878, by Landmark..... 2:22½
Josh Billings, ch g, 186—, by Mott's Independent—Scofield Mare.......... 2:29¾
Josh Morse, blk g, 1880, by Wilson's Messenger Duroc—Nelly, by Henry Clay 2:29¼
Josie A., b m, 188—.................... 2.23¼
Josie B., br m, 1888, by Lew Wann—Bess, by Fred Douglas 2:17¾
Josie B., ch m, 188—, by Watchmaker. 2:28¼
Josie Bates, blk m, 1880, by Almont Prince—Josie, by King William..... 2:27¼
Josie Campbell, b m, 1880, by Dom Pedro—Kitty Morrill, by Winthrop Morrill 2:20¼
Josie Chimes, b m, 1890, by Chimes—Josephine, by Mercury 2:20¼
Josie D., ch m, 1879, by Charley Wicker—Miss Brown 2:30
Josie J., b m, 1887, by Edge Hill—Diamond Maid, by Diamond........ 2:21¾
Josie King, blk m, 1884, by The King—Kincora, by Mambrino Patchen .. 2.20¼
Jourdan Wilkes, b s, 1886, by Jersey Wilkes—Carrie R., by Jay Gould.... 2:20¾
Joy Wilkes, b s, 188—, by Woodford Wilkes 2:23¼
J. P., b g, 1883, by Louis R.—Flora Belle, by Black Horse 2 26¼
J. P. Morris, br g, 1873, by Robert R. Morris—Brown Bess, by Billy....... 2:20¼
J. Q., blk g, 1880, by Kentucky Prince Jr.—Kitty Clyde, by Skinner's Joe.. 2:17¼
J. R. (Joslyn), br g, 1886, by Elector—Topsey, by a son of St. Lawrence... 2:20
J. R. Shedd, b s, 1882, by Red Wilkes—Belle Ericsson, by Ericsson ...... 2·19¼
J. S., b s, 1883, by J. W. South—Rosemont, by Egmont 2.16½
J. S. C., b s, 188—, by a son of Echo.. 2 22½
J. S. Young, b g, 186—, (dead)......... 2.29¾
J. T., blk g, 188—, by Melrose........ 2:24½
Jube, b g, 1887, by Stillman—Zolia, by Confederate Chief 2:26
Jubilant, b s, 1885, by Princeps—Humming Bird, by George Wilkes.. 2:22
Jubilee, b s, 1872, by Satellite—Enchantress, by Volunteer 2.30
Jubilee, ch m, 188—, by Melbourne King 2.23¼
Jubilee, gr s, 1885, by Princeps—Olio, by Dick Hambletonian 2.26
Jubilee de Jarnette, b s, 1883, by Jubilee Lambert—Lady de Jarnette, by Indian Chief 2 29¼
Jubilee Lambert, br s, 1863, by Daniel Lambert — Harvey Mare, by Taft Horse .... 2·25
Jubilee Lambert Jr., b s, 1882, by Jubilee Lambert, dam by Joe Downing 2:27½
Judd Boy, gr g, 1880, by Marlborough—Kit, by Bajardo (dead)........... 2.29¼
Judd's Baby, ch m, 1885, by Roscoe Conkling—Daisy, by Greenleaf's Bashaw 2:19¼
Judean, b s, 1885, by Princeps—Hamite, by Hamlet 2:29¾
Judge Austin, gr g, 188—, by McCurdy's Hambletonian Jr........... 2 12¼
Judge Brown, br s, 1889, by Brown—Addie Hayes, by Judge Hayes...... 2:20¼
Judge Conway, gr g, 1888, by Conway—Finey, by Searcher Jr. 2:28¼
Judge Davis, b g, 1876, by Joe Brown—Lady Sherman, by Millman's Bellfounder 2 18¾
Judge Fisher, ch s, 1888, by Linkwood Chief—Linkwood Maid, by Tripolitan Chief .... 2·14
Judge Fullerton, ch g, 186—, by Edward Everett (dead) 2.18
Judge G., ch s, 1888, by Sidney, dam by Lynwood 2 21¼
Judge Hampton, br g, 188—, by Frank Hampton 2.27¾
Judge Hawes, b g, 187—, by Jim Monroe — Laura Logan, by American Clay 2:24
Judge Keeler, blk s, 1888, by St. Arnaud—Mabel L., by Victor......... 2:21¼
Judge Lindsey, b g, 1880, by Bostick's Almont Jr., dam by Clifton Pilot... 2:21¼
Judge McCue, b s, 188—, by Douglas—Lady McCue, by Kent 2.25½
Judge Parsons, b g, 1876, by Power's Hambletonian—Miss Doty, by Sweet Owen (dead)....................... 2.23½

Judge Pollard, ch g, 1871, by Brown's
   Tom Crowder 2 29½
Judge Purple, b g, 1880, by Sir Wal-
   kill — Mohawk Dixie, by Mohawk
   Chief 2.28½
Judge Rider, b s, 1886, by Billy
   Wilkes—Miss Bemis, by Mambrino
   Patchen .... 2·26
Judge Rysdyk, br s, 1883, by Judge
   James—Lucy Plumb, by Rysdyk.... 2 26
Judge Wilkes, ch s, 1885, by Bourbon
   Wilkes — Leona Patchen, by Mam-
   brino Patchen 2 20½
Judgment, b· g, 1870, by Black Milo,
   dam by Morgan Rattler............ 2:26¾
Judy, gr m, 188— 2.24½
Jud Wilkes, b s, 188—, by Ira Wilkes
   — Champion Maid, by Champion
   Messenger 2 20
Juggler Boy, b s, 1883, by Jubilee
· Lambert—Hattie, by Smuggler..... 2:27
Julia O, b m, 187—, by Phil Sheri-
   dan—Sherline, by Johnny Heanan... 2:23¼
Julia C., gr m, 187—, pedigree not
   traced 2:29
Julia Coulter, br m, 1889, by Wilkes
   Boy—Birdie, by Egbert 2:27
Julia D., ch m, 188—, by Robert Ful-
   ton 2 27
Julia G, b m, 188—, by Daly, dam by
   Gray McClellan .... 2·23¼
Julia H, ch m, 1883, by Monaco—
   Kitty Merchant 2:20½
Julia Jackson, b m, 1885, by Mam-
   brino Startle — Kate Stanhope, by
   King Rene .... 2·25¼
Julia L., b m, 188—, by Landmark... 2·25¼
Julia M., b m, 188—, by Clifton's Kent
   —Violetta, by Young Morrill........ 2:26¾
Juliana, blk m, 1886, by Patchen
   Wilkes—Jenny West, by Allie West. 2.30
Julian, b s, 1883, by Mambrino Boy,
· dam by Surprise 2 30
Julia O, br m 2 24½
Julietta, gr m, 1886, by Fieldmont—
   Cropear, by Pilot Duroc........... 2:21¼
Jumbo Wilkes, ch s, 1888, by Victor
   Wilkes—Daisy, by General Sherman. 2.22¾
June Bug, b m, 1889, by Chimes—
   Lady Bug, by Hamlin's Almont Jr.. 2:29¼
June France, b m, 1885, by France—
   Kit Hoyt 2:29½
Junelight, b s, 188—, by Vatican, dam
   by Lexington Hambletonian........ 2:29¼
Junemont ch s, 1883, by Tremont—
   Fanny Carey, by Jack Rosey....... 2:14
Jungfrau, ch m, 1888, by Matterhorn—
   Jontile, by Hambletonian Prince.... 2.28¾
Junio, b s, 1882, by Electioneer—Nel-
   ly, by Granger 2 22
Junius, blk s, 1879, by Dictator—Con-
   stine, by Conductor 2.27¼
Juno Wilkes, ch m, 1889, by Victor
   Wilkes—Nelly Lambert, by Daniel
   Lambert 2:29
Juno Withers, ch m, 188—, by Gen.
   Withers Jr........................ 2·27¼
Jupiter, b s, 1887, by Stillman—Net-
   tle S., by Raples' Hiram Woodruff.. 2:30
Jupiter Jr., blk s, 188—, by Jupiter
   Abdallah, dam by St Lawrence..... 2:23
Jura, b s, 188—, by Billy Wilkes 2 22½
Jura, ch m, 1881, by Sir Walkill—
   Middletown Belle, by Middletown... 2:26¼
Juror, b s, 1885, by Pilot Mambrino—
   Florence, by Volunteer 2 24¾
Justina, b m, 188—, by Baymont
   (dead) .... 2·25
Justina b m, 1879, by Hamlin's Al-

mont Jr.—Black Golddust, by Ham-
   lin 2:20
Justinette, b m, 188—, by George W.
   Shakespeare 2:28½
Justinian, b s, 1882, by Solicitor—
   Capitola, by Knickerbocker 2:27
J. V. C, ch g .... 2·28
Just Right, ch g, 188—, by Haldane... 2 25¼
J. W. Gould, ch g, 1874, by Jay Gould
   —Idol, by Bob Ridley 2 28¼
J. W. O., b g, 1889, by Princeps—
   Bromide, by Volunteer 2:28
J. W. South, b s, 1880, by Princeps—
   Roxie, by Melbourne Jr. .... 2·29¼
J. W Tedford, g· g, 1882, by Ensign—
   Peg, by Bill Shaker. 2.19¾
J W. Thomas, ch g, 1874. by Scott's
   Thomas—Belle W., by Herr's Black
   Hawk 2.27½
J. Y G., b g, 1883, by Harvester 2 24¼
Kadijah, br m, 1886, by Red Wilkes—
   Our Mary, by Lelaps 2 28¾
Kaffir, b s, 1887, by Alcazar—Flower
   Girl, by Arthurton................ 2:29¼
Kaiser, br s, 1882, by George Wilkes—
   Fair Lady, by Dictator............ 2 28½
Kalula, b m, 188—, by Constellation.. 2:28¼
Kansas Boy, b s, 1884, by Tendoy—
   Prairie Queen, by General McClellan 2 29¾
Kapolina, g m, 188—, by Little Billy 2:25¼
Kansas Chief, b g, 186—, by Young
   Josephus—Ella, by Young Copperbot-
   tom (dead) 2:21¼
Kansas Wilkes, b s, 1881, by George
   Wilkes—Puritana, by Almont 2:30
Kaota, blk m, 188—, by Sir Knight
   (pacing 2:15¼) 2:28
Karl K, blk g, 1889, by Prophet
   Wilkes—Jenny R., by Pilot Medium 2 28¾
Kate, blk m, 1887, by Woodbridge Jr.
   —Dolly Ahart, by Capt Goodwin.. 2·22¾
Kasper, b s, 1887, by Kensett—
   Orphan Queen, by Lakeland Abdal-
   lah 2:27¼
Kate, ch m, 1877, by Morrill Drew,
   dam by Grey Fearnaught .. .. 2·29¼
Kate Agnew, gr m, 1883, by Hamble-
   tonian Chrisman—Nelly, by Oakland
   Boy 2 28½
Kate B. b m, 1886, by Lucas Brod-
   head—Dutch Kate by Jimmie 2.26
Kate Bennett, ro m, 1868, by Blue
   Bull—Jane Oliver, by Gen Taylor.. 2:29¼
Kate Bradley, b m, 1892, by Axtell—
   Ola Moore by Onward .... 2·30
Kate C., ch m, 1879. by Cuyler—Ash-
   land Kate, by Ashland Chief.... 2·27½
Kate C., ch m, 188—, by Gilbirds
   Sprague .... 2·27½
Kate C., b m, 1885, by Phoenix—Lady
   Forrester, by Field's Royal George 2 24
Kate Caffrey, blk m, 1887, by Charles
   Caffrey—Eva, by Tippoo Bashaw... 2·18½
Kate Campbell, b m, 1862, by un-
   named horse, claimed to be a son of
   Ethan Allen, dam by Blind Tucka-
   hoe (dead) 2:25½
Kate Castleton, ch m, 1885, by Kel-
   ly's Ethan Allen—Athol, by Ashland
   Jr 2 26½
Kate Clark, b m, 1881, by Thomas
   Jefferson—Lady Goldsmith, by Rys-
   dyk's Hambletonian 2:29½
Kate Cloud, blk m, 1881, by Harry
   Clay—Kate, by St. Lawrence 2:26¼
Kate Cuyler. b m, 1887 by Cuyler—
   Kate Middleton, by Mambrino
   Patchen .... 2·26

Kate Dillard, ch m, 1885, by Hamenger, dam by John Dillard 2:22½
Kate Ethan, b m, 1887, by Ethan Wilkes—Kate Westwood, by Westwood 2:25
Kate Ewing, br m, 1879, by Berlin—Lady Washington, by American Boy Jr 2:21¼
Kate F., b m, 1885, by Fugleman—Katie Bashaw, by Rinaldo 2:16¼
Kate Hall, ch m, 1870, by Blue Bull—Little Nell, by Proud American Jr. 2:24½
Kate Ham, b m, 1888, by Glen Miller—Rilee, by Hotspur Jr. 2:28½
Kate Hamilton, b m, 1888, by Ravenswood—Laura Wilson, by Smuggler 2:30
Kate Isler, gr m, 1878, by Munsey, dam by Rebel 2:22¼
Kate Jordan, br m, 187—, pedigree not traced 2:28¼
Kate Keener, br m, 1880, by Messenger Golddust—Fanny Keener 2:29¼
Kate McCall, gr m, 1874, by Blue Bull—Carol, by Democrat 2:23
Kate O'Brien, b m, 188—, ... 2:50
Kate Owen, b m, 1877, by Lee's Edwin Forrest 2:26¼
Kate Phallamont, b m, 1887, by Phallamont—Flora McVeane 2:17¼
Kate Preston blk m, 1878, by Pacing Pilot—Lizzie 2:27½
Kate Rowell, b m, 1880, by Byerly Abdallah—Lou Rowell, by Louis Napoleon 2:29¾
Kate Sparks, blk m, 1888, by Mambrino Diamond—Lizzie, by Jubilee Lambert 2:19
Kate Sprague, br m, 1875, by Gov. Sprague—Fan, by Lance 2:18
Kate Taylor, b m, 1872, by Aberdeen—Emeline, by Harry B. Patchen .. 2:23¾
Kate Thomas, rn m, 188—, by G. C. 2:24½
Kate V., br m, 1888, by Heptagon—Cripple, by Orange County 2:23
Kate Wilton b m, 1888, by Wilton—Kate Wilkes, by George Wilkes 2:27
Katharina, b m, 1873, by Flying Hiatoga—Kit Alfred, by King Alfred ... 2:30
Katherine, b m, 188—, by Jerome Eddy 2:29¼
Katherine S., ro m, 1883, by Messenger Chief—Forest Maid by Forest Vermont 2:17¾
Kathleen, b m, 1887, by Stranger—Carmen, by Socrates 2:25¼
Katie B., b m, 1879, by Lord Nelson—Nelly, by Fowler Brandy 2:22¼
Katie B., b m, 1876, by Legal Tender—Rody, by Copperbottom Jr. 2:28¼
Katie Cahill, b m, 1884, by Ogden's Hambletonian Mambrino—Lilly Cahill, by Albert Dudley 2:26½
Katie Drew, blk m, 1885, by Castelar—Lona G., by Crozier 2:28
Katie Earl, ch m, 1888 by Earl—Kitty Wilkes, by Red Wilkes (dead) ... 2:16½
Katie Jackson, b m, 1873, by Almont—Fanny, by Iron's Cadmus........ 2:25¾
Katie L., b m, 1884, by True Bred—Pacing Bessie by Victor Bismarck 2:23¾
Katie Lee br m, 1884, by Rockwood—Lady Kisbar, by Kisbar 2:29¼
Katie, b m, 188—, by Knight Templar 2:30
Katie M., ch m, 1879, by George M. Van Norte—Lilly, by Daniel Lambert 2:25½
Katie Mack, b m, 1889, by Robert McGregor—Celia, by Sealskin Wilkes .. 2:19¾
Katie Middleton, ch m, 1873, by Mambrino Patchen—Flora, by Alexander's Abdallah (dead) 2:23
Katie R., b m, 188— by Landmark, dam by Bacon's Ethan Allen 2:21½
Katie S., blk m, 188—, by Director—Alpha Medium 2:19¼
Katie Wood, b m, 1884, by John E. Wood—Anna, by Hambletonian Downing 2:26½
Katisha, br m, 1886, by Ben Franklin—Pixie, by Pratt's Rifleman 2:26¾
Katrina, b m, 1889, by Conn's Harry Wilkes—Elsie V., by Sir Charles ... 2:25¾
Katrina Bel, blk m, 1892, by St. Bel—Katrina, by Nephew 2:26¼
Kay S., ro m, 1889, by Spectator—Fly, by I. J. 2:29¼
Kebir, b s, 1889, by Alcazar—Yerba Santa, by Santa Claus 2:28¼
Keeler, b s, 1884, by King Rene—Ada Wilkes, by George Wilkes.... 2:13¼
Keeler, br s, 1884, by Dictator—Sally Fox, by Senour's Davy Crockett .. 2.29
Keene Jim, ro g, 1873, by Lookout—Laura Fair by Rattler 2:19¼
Keepsake, b s, 188—, by Black Ralph 2:29¼
Keewaydin, br s, 1889, by Brown Wilkes—Idlewild by Nugget 2:28¼
Keller Thomas, gr s, 1885, by Pilot Duroc—Ida T., by Dictator 2:12¾
Keller V., ch s, 188—, by Abdallah Mambrino—Josie, by Gen Wayne .. 2:21¾
Kelsie, b g, 1872, by Iron Duke—McWhorter Mare 2:23¼
Kemble Maid, br m, 1878, by John Goldsmith, dam by Harry Clay 2:28¼
Kendall, b s, 188—, by Kent, dam by Daniel Lambert 2:20½
Keney, ch g, 187—, pedigree not traced 2:20½
Kenilworth, br g, 187—, by Woodford Abdallah—Mary, by Wilkes Booth (dead) 2:18¼
Kenmar, b s, 1889, by Goldemar—Sally Brass, by Florida 2:20½
Kenneth, b g 1883, by Kentucky Prince—Mary A., by Messenger Duroc 2:28¼
Kenneth, b s, 1886, by Kensett—Princeton Belle, by Woodlawn 2:28
Kenneth, blk s, 1884, by Strathlan—Kate Cooper, by Joe Cooper . .. 2:29½
Keno, b g, 188—, by Greenbacks . 2:24¼
Keno, b g, 1873, by Magic—Lady, by Black Jeff 2:23½
Keno F., ch g, 1883, by Mohawk Hambletonian—Fan 2:17
Kensett F., b m, 1878 by Kensett—Dolly 2:22¼
Kensett Maid, ch m, 1881, by Kensett, dam by Pomp Shafer Horse.. 2:30
Kenton Belle, blk m, 1879, by Denmark Jr.—Coaly W., by Rino Welf.. 2:30
Kentuckian, ch s, 1871, by Balsora—Nonesuch, by Brignoli ... .!... 2:27¼
Kentucky Bird, br s, 1887, by Jay Bird—Kate Clay, by Kentucky Clay (dead) 2:26
Kentucky Blanche, b m, 1879 by Kentucky Prince—Blanche by Railsplitter 2:26¼
Kentucky Boy, b s, 1883, by Victor Bismarck—Bourbon Girl, by McDonald's Mambrino Chief 2:28
Kentucky Dictator, br s, 1882 by Dictator—Nettie Time, by Mambrino

Time 2:29½
Kenucky Girl, b m, 1874, by Edward G.—Kitty Clover by Tom Hal 2:28¼
Kentucky Hambletonian, b s, 1883, by Victor Bismarck—Jenny Wallace, by Joe Downing (dead) 2:27
Kentucky Jim, b s, 1883, by Black Diamond, dam by Bailey's Star Denmark 2:28
Kentucky Lew, b s, 1890, by Wilkes Boy—Annie Almont, by Bostick's Almont Jr. 2:24½
Kentucky Ruler, b s, 1881, by Egbert Lady Almont, by Almont (dead).. 2:29
Kentucky Russell, ch s, 1885, by Mambrino Russell—Annie Steele, by Fearnaught 2:18½
Kentucky Star, b g, 1884, by Volunteer Star—Sally Hamlet, by Peacock 2:21½
Kentucky Union, ch m, 1880, by Aberdeen—Kentucky Central, by Balsora 2:11¾
Kentucky Wilkes, br s, 1874, by George Wilkes—Minna, by Red Jacket 2:21¼
Kenwood, b g, 1885, by Fairy Gift.. 2:17
Keokee, ch m, 1884, by Ambassador—Fearless, by Western Fearnaught 2:20½
Kepler, b s, 1884, by Kensett—Princeton Belle, by Woodlawn 2:29¾
Kent, b s, 1890, by Sable Wilkes—Macola, by Le Grand 2:28
Kerneer, b s, 1888, by Electioneer—Frolic, by Harry Clay 2:23¾
Kerwin, b s, 1887, by Slander—Cigarette, by Gen. Washington 2:20¼
Kesterson, b s, 188—, by Seth P.—Jessie Hunter, by Mambrino George. 2:27
Ketch, blk g, 1882, by unknown sire—Kate Wright, by Abraham 2:18¾
Keturah, ch m, 1885, by Kensett—Golden Era, by Countersign 2:30
Keystone, b s, 1883, by Guarantee—Black Mare 2:28¼
Key West, ch s, 186—, pedigree not traced 2:28½
Keywood, ch s, 1886, by Onward—Mary K., by Ericsson 2:21
Khedive, b s, 1884 by Landseer—Lady Orion, by Orion 2:24½
Kiki, b g, 186—, by Henry B. Patchen (dead) 2:28
Kilburn Jim, b s, 1865, by Wood's Hambletonian, dam a Canadian Mare (dead) 2:23
Kildee, b m, 1883 by Happy Medium—Sally Clay, by American Clay 2:29½
Killona, b m, 1892, by King Wilkes—Chenille, by Crittenden 2:20
Kilrain, b s, 1886, by Hawthorne—March Forth, by Whipple's Hambletonian 2:23¾
King, blk s, 188—, by The King, dam by Bob Sprague 2:28¾
King Almont, b s, 1874, by Almont—Jenny, by Crockett's Arabian 2:21¼
King Bird, ro g, 1884, by Jay Bird—Bonnie 2:27¾
Kingbolt, b s, 1887, by The King—Marba, by Young Jim 2:27¼
King Cardinal, ch s, 1885, by Cardinal—Pilot Queen, by Hylas.......... 2:26¼
King Charles, b s, 1883, by Sir Charles—Lady D'Archy, by Robert R. Morris 2:22¼
King Charles, blk s, 1883, by Pocahontas Boy—Rapalee, by Seneca Chief . 2:29½
King Chester, b s, 1887, by Prairie King—Lady Prince, by Hambletonian Prince 2:19¼
King Clifton, gr g, 1881, by Volante—Lady Naylor 2:22
King D., b s, 188—, by Red Wilkes .. 2:29¼
King Darlington, b s, 1887, by King Wilkes — Marguerite, by Kentucky Prince (dead) 2:16
King Forest, b g, 188—, by Forest Mambrino, dam by Mat Cameron... 2:21½
King Gaines, b s, 1887, by King of the West—Victoria Gaines, by Allie Gaines 2:29¾
King Goldemar, b s, 1891, by Pelletier 2:25¾
King Gillig, ch s, 1892, by Gillig, dam by Aristos 2:26½
King Golddust, b s, 1890, by Indicator, dam by Special Hambletonian 2:30
King Grover, br s, 1886, by Herod—Dolly, by Andrew Burnham......... 2:28½
King Harry, b s, 1889, by Red King—Beulah S., by Sweepstakes.......... 2:22
King Herod, ch s, 1887, by Fayette Chief—Siloam, by Capt. Brooks.... 2:16½
King Holliday, b s, 1887, by Holliday—Ada May, by Maxie Cobb......... 2:22¾
King Mambrino, b s, 1888—, by Hambrino 2:30
King Midas, br g, 187—, by Woodford Pilot, dam by Whirlwind........... 2:28¼
Kingmoor, b s, 1888, by Endymion—Josie Wilkes, by George Wilkes..... 2:28¼
King Nasir, b s, 1889, by Ambassador—Envie, by Phallamont 2:21¼
King of the Ring ch g, 1889, by Silver King—Knight Hawk, by Brigadier 2:23¼
King of the West, b s, 1879 by Hamdallah—Belle S., by Star of the West 2:27
King of Wales, b s, 1883, by Mambrino King — Miss Burton, by Governor............................. 2:30
King Orry, ch s, 1887, by Alcona Clay—Pansy, by Strader's Cassius M. Clay Jr. 2:21½
King Patchen, br s, 1887, by The King—Hatcher, by Mambrino Hatcher.................................. 2:16¼
King Patchen, ch s, 1883, by Mambrino King—Kitty Patchen, by Hamlin Patchen 2:23½
King Philip, ch s 1876, by Mambrino King — Lady Rothschild, by Mambrino Patchen 2:26¼
King Philip b s, 1870, by Jay Gould—Factory Girl, by Rysdyk's Hambletonian 2:21
King Piedmont, b s, 1888 by Piedmont—Daisy D., by Electioneer..... 2:30
King Princeps b s, 1888, by Count Princeps—Lady Almont, by Almont Lightning 2:23¼
King Rex, br s, 1887, by King Rene—Molly, by Sweepstakes............ 2:23½
King Rock, b s, 1882, by Alden Goldsmith — Fanny Dunlap, by Black Rock 2:30
King Russell b s, 1886, by Lord Russell—Mist, by King Rene........... 2:26¼
Kingsbury, b g, 1883, by Kentucky Clay Jr. 2:28¼
Kingsley, b g, 187—, by Wilkins Micawber—Lady Bellfounder, by Rysdyk's Bellfounder 2:26¼
King Sprague blk s, 1882, by Gov. Sprague—Molly Whitefoot, by Little Priam 2:12
King Star, blk g, 188—, by Startle—Venus, by Jupiter.............. 2:26½

Kingston, b g, 188—, by Ed Ellis..... 2:18¼

King Sultan, b s, 1890, by Sultan—Kitty Wilkes, by Red Wilkes 2:23

King Walkill, br s, 1886, by Sir Walkill—Lady Brownell, by American Ethan 2:24¼

King Warlock, ch s, 1890, by Warlock—Lady C, by Corbin Bashaw......... 2:24¼

King Wilkes, b s, 188—, by Ready Money, dam by King Tom.......... 2:25¼

King Wilkes, b s, 1876, by George Wilkes—Missie, by Brignoli 2:22¼

King William, blk g, 1877, by King William—Lizzie Abdallah, by Pacing Abdallah 2:20¾

Kingwood, br s, 1886, by Kentucky Dictator—Burchwood, by Blackwood 2:17¼

Kinsman, ch g, 1880, by Stranger—Jenny, by Young Country Boy (pacing record 2:17¼)............ 2:23¼

Kinsman Boy, b g, 1870, by Case's Dave Hill—Lady Trumbull, by Vermont Trotter 2:28½

Kioto, b s, 1883, by Marmion Golddust—Mischief, by Volunteer 2:20¾

Kiowa, b s, 1888, by Midas—Jessie P., by Administrator................. 2:29¾

Kirkwood, br s, 1860, by Green's Bashaw—Madam Kirkwood, by Young Green Mountain Morgan (dead)..... 2:24

Kisbar, b s, 1873, by Rysdyk's Hambletonian—Lady Fallis, by Seely's American Star (dead) 2:27¾

Kismet, b s, 1882, by Sultan—Saucebox, by Samson (dead) 2:25½

Kitchen Belle, b m, 1885, by King Almont—Jane Hubbell, by Roland . 2:21½

Kitty B., br m 1888, by Volunteer Swigert—Trojan Maid, by Barleycorn 2:29½

Kitty B, b m, 188—, by Nutgold.... 2:29¼

Kitty B, b m, 188—, by Sidney....... 2:24½

Kit Baker, b m, 188—, by Meander.. 2:27¼

Kit Clover, b g, 187—, pedigree not traced 2:25¾

Kit Curry, br m, 1880, by Mambrino Bruce—Kate Curry, by Dave Highlander 2:18½

Kitefoot, b m, 1878, by Landmark—Lucy, by Rough and Ready 2:17¼

Kitewood, ch m, 1886, by Brentwood 2:23

Kit Sanford, b m, 1873, by Wood's Hambletonian—Polly Denton, by Billy Denton 2d.................. 2:21¼

Kit Webber, b m, 1891, by Fast Mail 2:30

Kitty, b m, 1870, by Billy Bowlegs—Eddy Mare, by Byington's Young St Lawrence 2:30

Kitty Abbott, b m, 1874, by Abbott—Lady Franklin, by Eureka 2:26¾

Kitty Almont, blk m, 1880, by Tilton Almont 2:22¾

Kitty B., br m, 1880, by Magna Chief—Kicking Kate 2:27¼

Kitty B., br m, 1883 by Silverheels—Brown Pet 2:29¼

Kitty B, b m, 1885, by Sweet Meats—Pauline, by Roland 2:25½

Kitty B., ch m, 1881 by Rego..... 2:29¼

Kitty Bates, gr m, 1868, by Jim Monroe—Popcorn 2:19

Kitty Bayard, gr m, 1885 by Bayard—Dell by Billy Campbell.......... 2:12¼

Kitty Burch, ch m, 187— by George B McClellan—Kitty Burch 2:24¼

Kitty C., b m, 1877, by Dauntless—Lady Welch, by Jupiter 2:30

Kitty C., ch m, 1882, by Attorney—Helen, by Green's Bashaw........ 2:30

Kitty Can, blk m, 188—, by Elial G.. 2:30

Kitty Clyde, b m, 187—, by Sam Kirkwood—Molly 2:29¼

Kitty Clyde, b m, 1886, by Phallamont—Lady Coakley, by Wagner Golddust 2:28¼

Kitty Clyde, br m, 1873, by Reed's Splendor—Jenny, by McMahon's Boston 2:30

Kitty Cook, b m, 1869, by Abraham, dam by Ethan Allen 2:26

Kitty Cook, blk m, 188—, by son of Godfrey Patchen 2:28¾

Kitty D., br m, 1861, by Rattler Tuckahoe—Mary Hup, by Consul (dead).. 2:26¼

Kitty Edsall, rn m, 1882, by Clayton Edsall—Cheney Mare, by Fortune.. 2:28½

Kitty Fisher, b m, 1874, by Glenn's Hambletonian 2:29¼

Kitty Frazier, br m, 188—, by Peacemaker—Kitty Frazier 2:21¼

Kitty Greenlander, b m 1890, by Greenlander—Kitty Hetzel, by Hetzel's Hambletonian 2:23½

Kitty Grey, gr m, 1881, by Grey Bill—Kate Wilson 2:29¼

Kitty Ham, br m, 1882, by Hambletonian Mambrino—Kitty Lewis, by Silver Duke 2:26

Kitty Hayes, b m, 1884, by Judge Hayes—Laura Swigert, by Swigert. 2:25½

Kitty Hiatoga, b m, 1883, by Harry Phelps—Bawley, by Blanco........ 2:18½

Kitty Hooker, b m, 1886, by Egbert—Laura, by Joe Hooker 2:29¼

Kitty Hudson, ch m 188—, by Hudson, dam by Ironwood 2:25

Kitty Ives, gr m, 1872, by Dolan (Canadian)—Kinkora, by Alger Horse 2:28¼

Kitty Kilburn, g m, 1877, by Kilburn Jim Jr—Belle by Honest John... 2:21

Kitty L., b m, 188— by Paddy Magee 2:27¼

Kitty Lynch, br m, 187—, by Millman's Bellfounder, dam by Morgan Sumpter 2:26¼

Kitty Mills, b m, 188—, by Horry Mills 2:28¾

Kitty Morris, b m, 1872, by Lon Morris 2:30

Kitty M Patchen, b m, 1878, by George D. Patchen, dam by Sir Henry 2:30

Kitty Patchen, ch m, 187—, by Jeb Stuart—Lady Jones, by Hefling's Hiatoga 2:21¼

Kitty Silver, ch m 1876, by Mambrino Patchen—Silk Ribbon, by Joe Wonder 2:27¾

Kitty Story, b m, 188—, by Everett Clay, dam by Roland 2:22½

Kitty Van, b m, 1876 by Walker Morrill—Belle Hastings, by Magna Charta 2:24

Kitty Vera b m 1887, by Talavera—Kittie Lisk by Seneca Chief .. 2:23½

Kitty Waite br m, 188—, pedigree not traced 2:26½

Kitty Wilkes b m, 1877, by George Wilkes—Gilbert Mare, by Clifton Pilot 2:30

Kitty Wood, rn m 1871 by Wood's Hambletonian—Fame, by Chancy Moore Horse 2:24¼

Klamath, b g, 1883 Morookus—Bob, by Ophir 2:13

Kluto, br s, 1890 by Pluto—Belle King, by Mambrino King 2:28¼

Kluxie, rn g, 1881, by Klux 2:24¼

Knight, gr g, 1882, by Pilot Medium—Daisy Dean, by Magna Charta .. 2:29½

Knight, br s, 1888, by Woodford Wilkes—China Wilkes, by Adrian Wilkes 2:28½

Knightmare, b m, 1888, by Sir Knight—Lady Austin, by Envoy.......... 2:12½

Knightmont, ch s, 1889, by Sir Knight—Actress, by Alroy.... .... 2:24

Knighthood, b s, 1885, by Aberdeen—Ophir, by Alamo 2:29½

Knight Templar, br s, 1884, by Egbert—Laura, by Billy Adams....... 2:27

Knita, b m, 188—, by Sir Knight..... 2:23¼

Knotty Boy, blk g, 188—, by Clay.... 2:24½

Knotwood, b s, 1883, by Monaco—Annie Birch, by Almont 2:29

Knox, blk s, 1875, by Gen. Knox—Clementine, by Logan.. .... 2:20½

Knox Boy, br s, 1868, by Gen. Knox—Juniata 2:23½

Knoxie Magnet, blk m, 188—, by Magnet 2.30

Knoxie Walker, ro m, 188—, by Jay Bird......... 2:25¼

Koaline, b m, 1888, by Montgomery—Volga, by Sobol 2:16

Kokomis, b s, 1886, by Victor Bismarck, dam by Goldsmith's Abdallah......... 2:21

Kolena, b m, 1890, by Kokomis—Laura Hatcher, by Mambrino Hatcher 2:22½

Konantz, b s, 1881, by Lyle Wilkes—Lady Gregory, by Corbeau 2:28

Konie, ch m, 1889, by Konantz—Orna, by Woodford Mambrino Jr.......... 2:28½

Konovalinka, ch s, 188—, by Chestnut Wilkes 2:25

K. P., b g, 1881, by Young Padlock—Mohawk Belle, by Mohawk Jackson 2:29¼

Kratz, b s, 1890, by Cyclone—Neoma C., by Twilight......... 2:21½

Kremlin, b s, 1887, by Lord Russell—Eventide, by Woodford Mambrino.. 2:07¾

Kris Kringle, b s, 1883, by Santa Claus—Toto, by Princeps 2:28¼

La Bessa 2:24¼

La Bel, br s, 1888, by St. Bel—Ella Jackson, by Hamlin's Almont Jr. .. 2:27

La Belle, ch m, 1892, by Sidney—Anna Belle, by Dawn 2:16

Lace Dealer, b s, 1880, by Smuggler—Tullahoma, by Almont 2:25

La Crosse Jr., b s, 1890, by La Crosse 2:19¾

Lady Alcy, b m, 1892, by Alcyo—Annie Rooney, by Lothair 2:19

Lady Alert, ch m, 1878, by Mambrino Lance—Queena, by Sampson 2.24½

Lady Alice b m, 186—, pedigree not traced (dead) 2:29¼

Lady Almont, b m, 1885, by John Burdine—Ruby, by Mingo Chief .. 2:27¾

Lady Anderson, b m, 1889, by Anderson Wilkes—Bird, by Edgewater.. 2:28¼

Lady B., ch m, 188—, by Springtime 2:25¾

Lady B., ro m, 1885, by Clark Chief—Puss, by Vinco 2:22¼

Lady B., ch m, 188—, by Goldemar . 2:27

Lady Augusta, b m, 1857, by Rysdyk's Hambletonian (dead) 2:30

Lady B., ch m, 188—, by Warwick Boy 2:23½

Lady Babcock, b m, 188—, by Happy Medium Jr. 2:30

Lady Banker, b m, 1865, by Rysdyk's Hambletonian—Banker Mare, by Boston (dead) 2:23

Lady Barefoot, br m, 1877, by Kent—Dolly, by Ballard's Cassius M. Clay Jr. 2.26½

Lady Beach, blk m, 1885, by Altamont—Hollywood, by Hambletonian Mambrino 2:26½

Lady Belle, gr m, 1887, by Pilot Medium—Minnie Hoag, by Bay Middleton 2.14¼

Lady Blanchard, gr m, 1864, by Whipple's Hambletonian—Lady Livingston, by Gen. Taylor (dead) 2:26¼

Lady Blanche, b m, 188—, by Don Carlos 2:26¼

Lady Blanche, b m, 186—, pedigree not traced (dead) 2:28¼

Lady Blessington, b m, 1868, by Middletown—Jenny Hawkins, by Seely's American Star 2:28

Lady Bomont, b m, 1891, by Bomont. 2.29¼

Lady Bonner, b m, 1875, by Honest Allen—Ledger Girl, by Rysdyk's Hambletonian 2:24¼

Lady Brooks, b m, 1873, by Whitcomb's Fearnaught, dam by Bigler's Bashaw 2.25¾

Lady Bug, blk m, 188—, by Green Boy 2.24¼

Lady Bug, b m, 1881, by Burton—Lucy White, by Young Toronto Chief .. 2 22¼

Lady Bullion, b m, 1884, by Pilot Medium—Hattie Hoyer, by Bullion 2:16¾

Lady Burton, b m, 1887, by Col. Burton 2.28

Lady Byron, blk m, 1861, by Royal George, dam by Sir Lovell (dead).. 2:28

Lady Clare, ch m, 1888, by Elyria—Lou, by Mambrino Sterley 2:18¾

Lady Capom, b m, 1879, by Capoul—Nelly 2:28

Lady Clark, ro m, 1874, by Clark's Mohawk Jr.—Fanny Cox, by Kossuth 2:27

Lady Collins, b m, 188—, by Goodwin's Hambletonian 2:30

Lady Connaught, b m, 1888, by Connaught, dam by Boston 2:30

Lady Crossan, b m, 187—, by Sussex Chief 2:28

Lady Daggett, gr m, 1867, by Logue Horse—Lady Johnson (dead) 2:26

Lady Dahlman, b m, 1865, by Robert Bonner—Miss Seeley, by a son of Hill's Black Hawk 2:28

Lady Daphne, blk m, 1888, by Altamont—Nell, by Duroc Prince 2:21¼

Lady Dawson, b m, 1876, by Jay Gould—Daisy Burns, by Skenandoah 2·28

Lady De Jarnette, b m, 1874, by Indian Chief—Belle, by Lytton's Warfield 2:28

Lady Dinsmore, b m, 186—, pedigree not traced 2:30

Lady Don, b m, 187—, by Don A. ... 2:20½

Lady Douglas, b m, 188—, by Arlington 2:24¼

Lady Douglas, b m, 1865, by Vermont Hero—Sal by Dicky 2:30

Lady Douglass, ch m, 1884, by Clayton Edsall—Stebbin's Mare, by a son of Stephen A. Douglass 2:29½

Lady Egmont, b m, 1887, by Egmont Chief—Nelly S., by Wichita 2:30

Lady Elgin, b m, 1876, by Legal Tender Jr.—Nelly, by Blue Bull.... 2:25¼

Lady Ellen, b m, 1875, by Carr's Mambrino—Ida May Jr., by Owen Dale. 2:29½

Lady Emma, blk m, 1883, by Alcantara—Advantage by Administrator 2 23½

Lady Emma, ch m, 1855, by Jupiter—

Empress, by Abdallah (dead) 2:26¼

Lady Emma, ch m, 1866, by Canada Champion, dam by imp. Consternation (dead) 2:28

Lady Escott, ch m, 1881, by Arthurton—Young Lady Vernon, by David Hill 2.26½

Lady Ethel, br m, 1887, by Baron Wilkes—Princess Ethel, by Volunteer 2:24¾

Lady Euclid, b m, 1885, by Euclid—Maud, by Keene George 2.25

Lady F., gr m, 1878, pedigree not traced 2.29¾

Lady Fairlawn, b m, 1889, by Fairlawn Medium—Iolanthe, by Oceanic Chief 2.28¼

Lady Fargo, b m, 188—, by Happy Medium 2:24¼

Lady Fern, b m, 1890, by Red Fern... 2:29¼

Lady Fay, ro m, 188—, pedigree not traced 2.29½

Lady Finch, b m, 1880, by Star Patchen—Polly, by Winslow Horse. 2:30

Lady Finch, br m, 188—, by Jim Finch 2:27½

Lady Fox, ch m, 1863, by Drury's Ethan Allen—Lady Partington..... 2:30

Lady Foxie, ch m, 1869, by Daniel Lambert—Foxie, by Breed Horse.. 2.24¼

Lady Franklin, b m, 188—, by Ben Franklin, dam by Brown Harry.... 2.25¼

Lady Franklin (Carrie), ro m, 1847, pedigree not traced (dead) 2.29¾

Lady G., b m, 1890, by Antonelle... 2.29¼

Lady Garfield, b m, 186—, pedigree not traced (dead) 2.28½

Lady Gay, ch m, 1883, by Sir Walter—Lady Almont, by Abdallah Mambrino 2.27¼

Lady Gilbert, gr m, 189—, by Red Wilkes—Annie B., by Hambletonian Mambrino 2:25¼

Lady Governor, b m, 188—, by Goldsmith 2:25

Lady Griswold, gr m, 186—, pedigree not traced (dead) 2:29

Lady Griswold, blk m, 188—, by Midnight 2:30

Lady Groesbeck, gr m, 1869, by Star of the West—Old Fly (dead) 2:25½

Lady Grosvenor, b m, 1885, by Grosvenor—Lady Nutwood, by Nutwood 2:27

Lady H., gr m, 1868, by Manchester Tuckahoe 2:27

Lady Hamilton, gr m, 1859, by Toronto Chief—Kate King, by Sir Tatton Sykes (dead) 2:30

Lady Hamilton, b m, 1884, by Ralston—Sally H., by Weedman's Dexter.. 2:25¾

Lady Hamilton, b m, 188—, by Gen. Hatch 2:24¼

Lady Hannis, b m, 1885 by Hannis—Miss Trotwood, by Enfield 2:25

Lady Hare, ch m, 188—, by Col. Hare 2:16¾

Lady Hassan, b m, 1885, by Mambrino Hassan—Lady Penrose, by Moscow Jr. 2:30

Lady Havoc, b m, 1882, by Havoc—Kit 2:23

Lady Helen, ch m, 1879, by Woodburn Chief—Princess, by American Clay 2:22

Lady Hendryx, br m, 1880, by Dauntless, dam by Tom Hunter 2:30

Lady Houk, b m, 1887, by Ambassador—Flora West, by Scott's Hiatoga 2:20½

Lady Hughes, b m, 1860, by Jupiter, dam by Webber's Tom Thumb (dead) 2:30

Lady I., b m, 1882, by Billy Norfolk 2:29

Lady Idol, b m, 1887, by Idol Wilkes—Net Star, by Spencer's Vicar of Wakefield 2:25

Lady Independence, blk m, 1872, by Black Dutchman—Fanny, by Voorhees' Abdallah Chief 2:29¼

Lady J., b m, 1889, by Darknight—Belle Oakwood, by Black's Hambletonian (pacing record 2:20)...... 2:30

Lady Jane, b m, 1885, by Mambrino Swigert, dam by Bismarck 2:17¼

Lady Jane, b m, 184—, pedigree not traced (dead) 2:30

Lady Jefferson, blk m, 188—, by Thomas Jefferson 2:22¼

Lady Jerauld, b m, 1878, by Billy Denton Jr.—Bay Golddust, by Golddust 2:24¼

Lady Juno, blk m, 1890, by Quartermaster—Electa, by Electioneer .. 2:30

Lady Jupiter, ch m, 1874, by Jupiter 2:30

Lady K., ch m, 1885, by Hunter—Virginia Kemper, by Woodmansee's Tuckahoe 2:30

Lady K., b m, 1873, by Gen. George H. Thomas—Lady Crane, by Fazoletta 2:29½

Lady Kate Sprague, b m, 1879, by Gov. Sprague—Bonnie Smyle 2:27¼

Lady Kelso, gr m, 1872, by Belmont—Diana, by Pilot Jr 2:29

Lady Kensett, b m, 1878, by Kensett—Prouty 2:21¼

Lady Kerns, b m, 1876, by Amboy, dam by Blacknose 2:29½

Lady Kildeer, b m, 1862, by Black Dutcheman, dam by Sterling's May Day (dead) 2:28

Lady Lightfoot, b m, 1888, by Almoneer—Weasel 2:28½

Lady Lannon, br m, 188—, by Austerlitz 2:25½

Lady Lear, gr m, 1872, by Morgan Horse—Wiley, by Nelson 2:24½

Lady Lemmon, b m, 1872 by Knickerbocker—Lemmon Mare, by Paul Clifford 2:27

Lady Linda, ch m, 1879, by Haven Star—Kate 2:26

Lady Lockwood, b m, 1853, by Neave's Cassius M. Clay, dam by Rediker's Alexander W., (dead) 2:25

Lady Low, ch m, 1869, by Justin Morgan 2.28

Lady Loye, b m, 1879, by Confederate Chief, dam by Ethan Allen 2.23½

Lady Lumber, blk m, 1870, by Lumber, by Iron Duke 2.29¼

Lady M., ch m, 1878, by Dick Preble—Sabin Mare, by St. Lawrence (Thunderbolt) 2:24

Lady M., b m, 1878, by Hamlet—Nell, by Conant's Black Hawk 2.23

Lady M., gr m, 1870, by Vermont Hero—Loveland, by Night Hawk— 2:30

Lady M., br m, 1885, by Indiaman—Daisy, by Volunteer 2:21

Lady M., gr m, 1886, by Billy H.—Brister, by Brister Horse 2:21¼

Lady M., b m, 188—, by Black's Hambletonian 2:23¼

Lady Mac, b m, 1878, by Mapleton—Susan, by Wheeler's St. Lawrence 2:29½

Lady Mac, b m, 1885, by Lemont—Codicil, by Administrator 2:23½

Lady Mac, b m, 1878, by Mambrino

King, dam by Mambrino Pilot 2:25¼

Lady Mac, b m, 1868, by Whirlwind—Madonna 2:23

Lady Mac, b m, 186—, pedigree not traced 2:30

Lady Mack, b m, 1884, by Chismore Lady Mac 2:25½

Lady McCune, br m, 1882, by Maitland, dam by Babcock Horse 2:28¼

Lady McFatridge, b m, 1868, by Woodford Mambrino—Bayadere, by Bay Chief (dead) 2:29

Lady McGregor, b m, 1887, by Robert McGregor—Leda, by Aberdeen 2:25½

Lady McGregor, br m, 1888, by Gilman Mc Gregor—Lady Almont, by Royal Almont 2:30

Lady McKeen, b m, 188—, by Mohican, dam by Dr. Herr 2:29½

Lady Majolica, b m, 1878, by Dictator—Lyd, by Brown Chief 2:25

Lady Marie, b m, 1876, by Windsor, dam by Voorhees' Abdallah Chief.. 2:29

Lady Martin, ch m, 1878, by Davis' Honest Allen—Lady Ling, by Taggart's Abdallah 2:29½

Lady Martin, b m, 187—, by Downing Abdallah 2:23

Lady Mascotte, b m, 1882, by Red Wilkes—Belle, by Alcalde 2:25½

Lady Maud, br m, 1882, by Rockwood—Lady Clark, by Kisbar 2:23½

Lady Maud, br m, 1867, by Gen. Knox—Fanny, by Sabek 2:18¼

Lady Maxim, b m, 1885, by Maxim—Lady Graves, by Smuggler 2:26½

Lady Mills, b m, 1871, by Chosroes, dam by Othello 2:24¾

Lady Monroe, gr m, 1870, by Jim Monroe, dam by Bald Stockings.... 2:26¼

Lady Monroe, b m, 1884, by Sagerser—Lucy, by Old Morg..... 2:29

Ladymont, b m, 1889, by King Almont—Baughman Girl, by Messenger Chief 2:28½

Lady Moore, br m, 1870, by Peacemaker—Nelly Moore, by Westchester 2:25

Lady Morrison, b m, 1867, by Volunteer—Stella, by Seely's American Star 2:27½

Lady Moscow, br m, 183—, pedigree not traced (dead) 2:30

Lady Nelson, ch m, 1886, by Nelson, dam by son of Emperor William.... 2:21¼

Lady Nutwood, b m, 1891, by Nutwood Francis—Medium, by Happy Medium 2:25¾

Lady O., br m, 188—, by T. O. M.—Baby 2:24

Lady O., gr m, 1884, by Young Prince—Nell 2:28½

Lady of Lyons, b m, 1882, by Argyle—Miss Lyons, by Blue Grass.. ... 2:21½

Lady Onward, b m, 188—, by Game Onward..... 2:28

Lady Passmore, ch m, 188—, by Peter Pinder 2:25½

Lady Peek, ch m, 1885, by Star Duke, dam by State Rights..... 2:26

Lady Potter, gr m, 1891, by Young Fullerton—Mary, by Harry Long... 2:27

Lady Powell, b m, 1888, by Hope So, dam by Annapolis 2:25½

Lady Preston, ch m, 1877, by Dr. Herr—Kitty Preston, by Mambrino Pilot Jr..... 2:30

Lady Prewitt, br m, 1871, by Clark Chief—Lady Wallenstein, by Lexington 2:30

Lady Pritchard, ch m, 1868, by Green Mountain Banner—Pritchard Mare, by Flying Morgan 2:21

Lady Red, b m, 1891, by Glenelg..... 2:24¼

Lady Redwood, br m, 1885, by Redwood—Belle 2:27

Lady Reid, b m, 188—, by Corbin Bashaw 2:28¼

Lady Richards, ro m, 1880, by Bucephalus — Etta Knox, by Roan Prince..... 2:26¾

Lady Richards, b m, 1886, by Swigert—Lady Star, by Goldsmith's Star.. 2:21¼

Lady Richwood, b m, 1876, by Richwood—Oriana, by Ericsson 2:29½

Lady Robert, br m, 1890, by Robert L.—Mina, by Ajax.. 2:17¼

Lady Rooker, b m, 188—, by Rooker.. 2:26½

Lady Rolfe, b m, 1874, by Tom Rolfe—Nelly, by Montezuma (pacing record 2:23) 2:22¼

Lady Ross, b m, 1860, by Vergennes Black Hawk, dam by Neave's Cassius M. Clay Jr..... 2:29¾

Lady Rowena, ch m, 188—, by George 2:29½

Lady Russet, ch m, 1891, by Joe You See—Lady Homer, by Homer..... 2:30

Lady Sampson, b m, 1872, by Dolphus, dam by a Copperbottom horse... 2:28¾

Lady Sargeant, b m, 1873, by Gooding's Champion—Lady Allen 2:27¼

Lady Savage, b m, 188—, by Hinkston Boy 2:25

Lady Scud, b m, 186—, by Edward Everett 2:29¼

Lady Shannon, gr m, 1845, by Harris' Hambletonian (dead) 2:23½

Lady Shepard, b m, 1884, by Scobey's Fearnaught—Molly Allen, by Woodard's Ethan Allen Jr..... 2:28½

Lady Sheridan, b m, 186—, pedigree not traced (dead)..... 2:28¾

Lady Sherman, br m, 1874, by Gen. Sherman, dam by Darkey..... 2:25½

Lady Snell, b m, 1865, by Godfrey Patchen—Lady Stevens, by Biggart's Rattler (dead) 2:23¼

Lady Spanker, b m, 1878, by Wide Awake—Swift, by Richard's Colt... 2:26½

Lady Spencer, b m, 1888, by Idol Wilkes—Lizzie Howes, by Harrison Chief 2:27

Lady Star, b m, 186—, by Sir Henry.. 2:24

Lady Stillman, blk m, 1879, by Hiram Woodruff—Dolly, by Trojan Jr..... 2:29¾

Lady Stout, ch m, 1871, by Mambrino Patchen—Puss Prall, by Mark Time 2:29

Lady Suffolk, gr m, 1833, by Engineer, dam by Don Quixote (dead)..... 2:29½

Lady Sutton, blk m, 1880, by Dashwood—Sutton 2:29½

Lady Sutton, br m, 1839, by Morgan Eagle (dead) 2:30

Lady Tessa, ch m, 1883, by Alcantara—Miss Bluff, by Wilkins Micawber. 2:27¼

Lady Thistle, b m, 1878, by Pineapple—Fanny, by Volunteer 2:27¼

Lady Thompson, gr m, 1886, by Simmons—Lady Humphrey, by Victor.. 2:23¼

Lady Thorn, b m, 1856, by Mambrino Chief—Rhodes Mare, by Gano (dead) 2:18¼

Lady Thorne, b m, 1873, by Darlbay—Sally Messenger, by Starlight (dead). 2:25

Lady Thornton, b m, 1871, by Mapes Horse, dam by Edsall's Jupiter..... 2:26¼

Lady Tighe, b m, 1874, by Felter's Hambletonian—Spider Legs 2:20

Lady Triceps, b m, 1878, by Triceps—Goodwin Mare, by Dolan (Canadian) 2:28
Lady Turpin, blk m, 1869, by Bell Morgan — Nonesuch, by Brignoli (dead) 2:23
Lady Ulster, b m, 1885, by Clay Hambletonian—Maggie S., by Gallagher's Prince of Orange 2:20
Lady Underhill, br m, 188—, by Mike Logan 2:20½
Lady Upton, b m, 1870, by Gen Grant (Canadian) — Nancy, by American Eagle 2:29
Lady Van, b m, 1887, by George Steck—Reubie Newman, by Magic........ 2:28
Lady Vernon, gr m, 1845, pedigree not traced (dead)........ 2:29½
Lady Voorhees, ch m, 1870, by Manchester Tuckahoe 2:23½
Lady Walker, br m, 188—, by Captain Walker Jr., dam by Flaco........ 2:30
Lady W., b m, 188—, by Weisbaden.. 2:18¾
Lady Warren, b m, 188—, by Royal Fearnaught 2:29¾
Lady Washington, b m, 188—, by Onslaught 2:25¼
Lady Washington, b m, 1887, by Princeps—Ella, by Enfield 2:24¾
Lady Watson, blk m, 188—, by Sim Watson 2:20¾
Lady Weeks, ch m, 1884, by Dow S.—Dolly Stover, by Honest Dan..... 2.25¼
Ladywell, b m, 1886, by Electioneer—Lady Lowell, by Shootz's St. Clair. 2:16½
Lady Wellington, blk m, 1882, by Victor—Fanny Crafts 2:25¼
Lady Whitefoot, b m, 1881, by William M. Rysdyk—Nelly, by Matthews' Black Hawk 2.18¼
Lady Whitman, b m, 1861, by Seely's American Star—Nance, by Durland's Young Messenger Duroc 2:30
Lady Wilkes, blk m, 1889, by Ellerslie Wilkes—Lady Eclipse, by Abdallah Eclipse 2:16½
Lady Wilkes, b m, 1882, by Red Wilkes—Grey Nelly, by John Dillard 2:29¾
Lady Williams, br m, 1886, by Lumps—Betty, by Red Chief........ 2:29¾
Lady Williams, ch m, 1867, by Parson's Horse—Logan Maid, by Page's Logan 2:28¼
Lady Wilson, b m, 188—, by Wild Wagoner 2.29¾
Lady Wilton, br m, 1888, by Wilton—Lemonade, by Kentucky Prince Jr. 2:21¼
Lady Winship, br m, 1881, by H. B. Winship—Daisy, by Black Ralph.... 2:23½
Lady Wonder, ch m, 1878, by Little Wonder—Pet, by Whitehall Jr...... 2:25
Lady Wonder, ch m, 188—, by Fergus McGregor—Nell, by Manhattan 2:23½
Lady Woodhull, b m, 1879, by Cornwall—Warwick Star........ 2.29¼
Lady Woodruff, b m, 1851, by Washington, dam by Gen. Coffee (dead).. 2.29
La Ferme, b s, 1889, by Garnet Wilkes—Daisy Wilson, by Lucknow Jr.... 2:23½
La France, b s, 1891, by France.... 2.26¼
La Grange, blk g, 1879, by Sultan—Georgiana, by Overland........ 2.23½
La Grippe, b m, 1886, by Lumps—Black, by Protos 2:17¾
La Haute, b m, 1891, by Re-Election—Elite, by Messenger Duroc........ 2:24¼
Lah-da-dah, b m, 1876, by Ferdinand C.—Laconia 2:26
Lakeside Norval, b s, 1889, by Norval — Mattie, by Rysdyk's Hambletonian 2:13
Lakewood, b s, 1889, by Norwood—Jet, by Ravenswood 2.23
Lakewood Maid, b m, 1882, by Wilkesonian — Mirabeth, by Woodford Mambrino 2:29
Lakewood Prince, b s, 1884, by Wilkesonian — Mirabeth, by Woodford Mambrino (dead)........ 2:13½
Lakoto, br s, 1886, by Bourbon Wilkes—Ella Ellis, by Westwood........ 2:27¾
Lallah Wilkes, blk m, 1889, by Sable Wilkes—Susie Hunter, by Arthurton 2:26
Lamar, br g, 1881, by Baker Pilot—Kate 2:24¼
Lamartine, b s, 1886, by Egbert—Annie, by Cottrill Morgan........ 2:27½
Lambert B., b s, 1884, by Daniel Lambert — Lotta B., by Messenger Chief 2:22¼
Lammermoor, b g, 1884, by Rumor—Lucia, by Jay Gould 2.23
La Mode, ch s, 1887, by Nantucket, dam by Almont Smith........ 2.26
Lamont, b s, 1883, by Redwood—Nelly F., by Coupon 2:19
Lamp, ch g, 1884, by Lively—Nelly, by Hickory Boy 2:26
Lanark, blk s, 1885, by Egbert—Kitty Gibson, by Alcalde........ 2:29½
Lancelot, b s, 1887, by Messenger Duroc—Green Mountain Maid, by Harry Clay........ 2:23
Lancet, blk g, 1849, by Vermont Black Hawk — Old Squaw, by Lee Boo (dead)........ 2.27½
Lancewood, ch g, 1875, by Lancewood—Kate, by Young Napoleon... 2.29¼
Landmark, ch g, 187—, pedigree not traced 2:28¼
Landmark Maid, gr m, 188—, by Landmark—Lysander Maid, by Lysander. 2:23¼
Langton, ch s, 1887, by Alfred—Laura C., by Electioneer 2:21¾
Langtrey, br m, 1882, by Administrator—Fanny Osborne, by Volunteer.. 2.26½
Lanier, b s, 1890, by St. Just—Dora, by Bayard Jr........ 2:27
Langford, b g, 1886, by Mansfield Medium 2:28¼
Laomi, b m, 188—, by Anderson Wilkes 2:24¼
La Oscaletta, br m, 1874, by Dictator—Lady Ketchum, by imp. Osirus... 2:29¼
La Petite Bel, blk m, 1891, by St. Bel—Pet Cub, by Administrator 2:28½
Laprairie Girl, br m, 1880, by Ben Morrill 2:29¼
Laporte, ch g, 1885, by Jappo, dam by Slasher 2:26¼
Laputa, ch s, 1888, by Royal Fearnaught—Maggie Roys, by Shurtz Magna 2.27¼
Larco, gr s, 188—, by A. W. Richmond, dam by Overland 2:28
Largesse, b m, 1874, by Scott's Thomas—Fanny Howard, by Woful 2.25
Larkin, b g, 1871, by Young Woful—Lady Forrester, by Field's Royal George 2:30
Larry, b g, 1883, by Beaufort—Aiken Mare 2.23¼
Larry, b g, 1883, by Tangle 2:29¼
Larry Boy, br g, 1880, by Stockholm—Leary Girl 2:29½
Larry C., b s, 1892, by Ponce De Leon 2:29½
Lasella, b m, 1887, by Grand Sentinel—Governess, by George Sprague ... 2:20

ED. GEERS, Buffalo, N. Y.
(THE SILENT MAN FROM TENNESSEE.)
In 1894 Geers placed the world's record for pacers at 2:01½
with Robert J., and gave Fantasy a four-year-
old record of 2:06.

P. SHANK, Litchfield, Ohio.

An Ohio product that was out last year with Eloise 2:15. In 1895
he will wear the colors of the Two-Minute Stock Farm.

Lasis, b m, 1884, by Champion—Sisal, by Harold 2:20¾
Lassie, b m, 1887, by Masterlode—Ester, by Fisk's Belmont 2:30
Last Chance, b g, 1892, by Regal Wilkes, dam by Arthurton 2:26¼
Last Chance, b m, 1885, by Victor Bismarck—Dicta, by Dictator 2:28¾
Lath, blk g, 1881, by Gypsy Boy—Lady Burdett 2:29¼
Latitude, b s, 1886, by Walsingham—Easel, by Princeps 2:15
Laundry Girl, br m, 1889, by King Rene—Good Morning, by Harold ... 2:29¼
La Tosca, b m, 1888, by Madrid—Fantasy, by Onward 2:15¾
Laura, b m, 188—, by Beaver 2:29¼
Laura B., b m, 1887, by Prairie Star—Ione, by Wapsie 2:27½
Laura B., b m, 188—, by Willie Schepper 2:27
Laurabel, ch m, 1885, by Belmont—Laura, by Joe Hooker 2:27¾
Laura C., b m, 1881, by Electioneer—Fanny Lewis, by imp. Buckden ... 2:29¼
Laura E., b m, 1881, by Swigert—Blucheretta, by Richard's Bellfounder 2:28
Laura F., blk m, 188—, by Bostick's Almont Jr.—Black Maid, by Blackwood Jr. 2:19½
Laura M., b m, 1874, by Washington—Laurel 2:27
Laura McGregor, ch m, 1888, by Robert McGregor—Laura Forrest, by Forrest Golddust 2:22
Laura R., b m, 1885, by Electioneer—Lady Farmer, by Leachmen's Lexington 2:21¼
Laura S., ch m, 188—, by Starmont Jr. 2:23¼
Laura Williams, gr m, 1870, by Holabird's Ethan Allen—Stone Mare, by North American 2:24½
Laura Z., br m, 1886, by Alexander Button—Black Dolly 2:18¼
Lauretta, b m, 1891, by Patchen Wilkes—Dinnie, by Rochester 2:30
Lavender, b m, 1887, by Alcantara—Modjeska, by Royal Fearnaught ... 2:28¼
Lavina, b m, 1889, by Woodford Wilkes—Pearl, by Ashland Patchen 2:28
Lavoca, b m, 188—, by Anderson Wilkes 2:22¼
Lawrence, br s, 1882, by Dr. Franklin—Miss Morrill, by Morrill Champion 2:25½
L. B. R., b g, 188—, pedigree not traced 2:29¼
Lea, ch m, 1890, by Sidney—Venus, by Capt. Webster 2:23¼
Leap Year, b m, 1888, by Tempest—Eulogy, by Com. Belmont 2:26¾
Leck, br g, 1887, by Elector 2:29
Leckwood, b s, 1886, by John E. Wood—Bessie Lee, by Siberian 2:28½
Le Count, b s, 1880, by Sweepstakes—Maggie, by Edward Everett 2:29
L. D., b s, 188—, by South Jersey Patchen, dam by American Jackson 2:25¼
Leda, b m, 1871, by Aberdeen—Pattie W., by Brandywine 2:25½
Leda Wood, br m, 1879, by Blackwood—Fanny Goldsmith, by Edward Everett 2:30
Lee, ch g, 188—, by Gen. Lee—Sister, by Gen. Taylor 2:17¼
Lee Forester, b g, 1886, by Kentucky Belmont, dam by Halsey's Hambletonian 2:22½
Lee Hope, br s, 1882, by Kentucky—Maud 2:26
Lee M., gr g, 188—, by Osier Horse 2:28¼
Lee R., b g, 1879, by Mountain Bird—Maggie, by Snip Printer 2:24½
Lee Russell, b s, 1888, by Lord Russell—Myra, by Electioneer 2:16¼
Leesee, br m, 1887, by Quartermaster—Nelly 2:23¼
Lee W., b g, 187—, by Bourbon Blue—May Fly 2:23¼
Legacy, br m, 1888, by St. Bel—Lonely, by Volunteer 2:30
Legal R., b g, 1876, by Legal Tender Jr.—Betty Hudson, by Frank 2:30
Legal Tender, b g, 187—, by Legal Tender—Liza Boston, by Boston ... 2:27¼
Legal Test, b s, 1886, by Electioneer—Maria, by Don Victor............. 2:29¾
Le Grand, b g, 188—, by Le Grand—Henrietta, by Bell Alta 2:28½
Leicester, ch s, 1884, by Deucalion—Lady Winship, by H. B. Winship.. 2:17¼
Leighton, gr g, 188—, by Jay Bird .. 2:24
Lelah H., b m, 1880, by Homer—Lady Sentinel, by Sentinel 2:24½
Leland, b g, 188—, by Senator 2:29¾
Leland Medium, br s, 1887, by Fairlawn Medium—Kit Ackman, by Judge Leland 2:23¼
Leland Stanford, b s, 1884, by Strathmore—Chum, by Duke's Norman ... 2:24½
Lelawah, blk m, 1885, by Ambassador—Bird, by Orr's Flying Cloud 2:29¼
Lem, b s, 187—, by Orange County—Clara, by Tom Thumb 2:27½
Lemonce, b m, 1890, by Wilton—Lemonade, by Kentucky Prince Jr. 2:18¾
Lemonade, b m, 1879, by Kentucky Prince Jr.—Susie Melbourne, by Melbourne Jr. 2:27¼
L'Empress, blk m, 188—, by L'Emperor—Belle Stevens, by Stevens' Bald Chief 2:20½
L'Empereur, b s, 1883, by Alcyone—Fair Lady, by Dictator 2:25
Lena D., blk m, 1883, by Stephen A. Douglass, dam by Springville Chief 2:30
Lena H., blk m, 1883, by Alaska—Drew Girl, by Winthrop 2:29½
Lena Holly, ro m, 1889, by Direcor—Steinola, by Steinway 2:18¾
Lena Miller, ch m, 1885, by Onward—Long Lane, by Long Island Patchen 2:26¼
Lena Sprague, blk m, 1883, by Gov. Sprague—Helene, by Administrator 2:29¼
Lena Swallow, b m, 1877, by Blue Bull, dam by Aachy Lightfoot...... 2:19
Lena V., b m, 188—, by William H. Vanderbilt 2:28¼
Lenawee, br s, 1884, by Sickle Hambletonian—Fanny Patchen, by Fisk's Mambrino Patchen Jr 2:22¼
Lena Wilkes, b m, 1883, by Barney Wilkes—Gin Burner, by Frank Allen 2:29¼
Lenity, b m, 1885 by Hiram Woodruff—Jessie, by George M Patchen Jr. 2:29¼
Lenmar, b s, 1882, by Admar—Lenore, by Gladiator 2:16¼
Lenore Moody, blk m, 1888, by Moody—Lauretta, by Durango 2:26½
Lenox, br s, 1888, by Quartermaster—Lorna, by Enfield 2:22¾
Lent, b s, 1886, by Electioneer—

Lizzie, by Wildidle................. 2.26½
Leo, b g, 1884, by Pluto—Miss Sibley, by Swigert 2:22½
Leola, m, 1890, by Rockefeller—Modena, by Messenger Wilkes 2.30
Leola, b m, 1888, by Quartermaster—Nelly 2.30
Leon, gr g, 1886, by A. W. Richmond—Nelly, by Grant 2.22¼
Leona, ch m 1887, by Almoon—Daisy, by Bob Woodring 2:28
Leon Boy, ch g, 1877, by Springville Chief—Fanny Greeley, by Peter Jones 2.29¾
Leone, ch m, 1891, by Lancelot—Nida, by Monon 2:28¼
Leon H., blk s, 1888, by Young Wilkes—Nettie Hawkins, by Belvidere 2:29¼
Leonor, b m, 1884, by Dashwood—Geraldine, by Echo 2:24
Leontine, b m, 1874, by Hamlet—Bet, by Clark Chief 2:23¼
Leopard Bob, ch g, 1889, by Little Wonder—Bess Sparks, by Parsons' Abdallah 2:28
Leopard Rose, sp m, 1882 by Kilbuck Tom—Flora Green, by Thorpe's Guerney 2:15¼
Leo Wilkes, b s, 1889, by Brown Wilkes—Maggie Monroe, by Monaco 2:25¼
Leo Wilkes, br s, 1885, by Guy Wilkes—Sable, by The Moor 2:29¾
Leroy, b g, 1881, by Trample 2:29¼
Leroy, ch g, 188—, pedigree not traced 2:29½
Leroy, blk s, 1887, by Joe Young ... 2:25¼
Lesa Wilkes, br m, 1890, by Guy Wilkes—Hannah Price, by Arthurton 2:11½
Leslie Boy, br s, 188—, pedigree not traced 2:26½
Le Simmons, b s, 1888, by Simmons—Clara, by Strathmore 2:26
Leta Howe, b m, 1886, by Balaklava—Lella S, by Sweepstakes 2:27¾
Letcher, gr s, 1888, by Director—Alice Grey, by Signal 2:18¾
Letell, ch s, 188—, by Axtell—Amy Lee, by Bay Star 2:29¼
Letta C., ch m, 1886, by Walkill Prince—Kitty Wilson, by Blue Bull 2:16¼
Letter B, b m, 188—, by Ward B—Brown Irish, by Judge McKinley... 2.27½
Lettie D., gr m, ... 2.28¼
Letitia, b m, 1885 by Louis Napoleon—Maud, by Garibaldi 2 27½
Lettie Watterson, gr m, 188—, by Jim Schriber 2:21¾
Levi Aristos, br s, 1882, by Aristos—Lady Snip, by William Tell 2 26½
Lewand, br g, 1884, by Legal Tender Jr.—Luan, by Sovereign Glencoe .. 2.25¾
Lewellyn, ch s, 1887, by Aberdeen—Selina, by Strader's Cassius M. Clay Jr. 2:19¼
Lewe S, ch s, 188—, by McCurdy's Hambletonian 2.26¾
Lewinski, b g, 186—, by Mambrino Messenger (dead) 2 25¼
Lewis, blk g, 188—, by Brown Rolf 2 28¾
Lewis R, ch s, 1880, by Mammont—Lady Powers, by Davis' Boston . 2 23
Lew Ives, b g, 186—, by Bacon's Ethan Allen, dam by Studtail 2:28
Lew Pettee, b g, 1860, by Benson Horse (dead) 2 29
Lew Sayers, ro g, 185—, by Neave's Cassius M Clay Jr. (dead) 2 28¾
Lew Scott, b g, 186—, by Scott's Hiatoga (dead) 2.23
Lew Wann, br s, 1883, by Egmont—Lady Samson, by Rover 2:25¾
Lew Wallace, blk s, 188—, by Gold stone 2 23½
Lexington, br s, 1883, by King Philip—Diana Patchen, by Mambrino Patchen 2.24½
Lexington Belle, b m, 1888, by Lexington Chief Jr.—May Hamilton, by Little Hamilton 2:24¼
Lexington Boy, b s, 1884, by Egbert—Dixie, by Richelieu 2:23
Lexington Chief, sp g, 188—, by Aristos—Dolly Varden (pacing record 2:23¼)................................ 2 30
Lexington King, b s, 1888, by Hunter Chief—Daisy T., by Governor Hayes 2:28¼
Libby S., ro m, 187—, by Walker's Corbeau—Dolly, by Drennon (dead). 2.19¼
Liberty Bell, b s, 1890, by Bell Boy—Prefix, by Pancoast (dead) 2.24
Liberty Boy, b s, 1881, by Amboy—Kate 2:27
Libretto, br s, 1887, by Mambrino Swigert—Fannie Harris Cutler, by Grey Major 2:30
License, ch g, 1859, pedigree not traced (dead)........................ 2:26
Lida Bassett, b m, 1871, by Forest King—Belle, by Alcalde 2:20½
Lida D., b m, 188—, by Brilliant Golddust 2:24½
Lida Picton, br m, 186—, pedigree not traced (dead) 2:27½
Lida Wilkes, b m, 1888, by Young Wilkes — Lida, by Hambletonian Prince 2 29½
Lifemark, b s, 1890, by Edgemark—Gipsy M., by Eclair................. 2:26¼
Lightfoot, b g, by Bostick's Almont Jr.................................... 2:30
Light Hall, ro s, 1888, by Vatican—Nell, by Estill Eric................. 2:25¾
Lightning, b m, 1887, by Alcantara—Portia, by Startle 2:11
Lightning Maid, blk m, 1880, by Almont Lightning—Grisette, by Draco. 2:27½
Lightwood, b m, 1886, by Nutwood—Belle Lightning, by Lightning...... 2.25¾
Likewise, br s, 1889, by Gideon Chief—Nelly Boone, by Daniel Boone.... 2:17½
Lilac, br m, 1889, by Clay—Lizzie Miller, by St. Clair................ 2.29¼
Lillian, ch m, 1876, by Almont—Lilly Shields, by Cadmus 2:23
Lillian D., br m, 1881, by Wilgus Clay, dam by Edwards' Cadmus.... 2.30
Lillian Smith, ch m, 1888, by Clay Duke, dam by Brightwood......... 2:29
Lillian Wilkes, br m, 1886, by Guy Wilkes—Flora, by Langford......... 2:17¾
Lillis H., b m, 1885, by Chesterfield—Kate 2:23¾
Lilly, ch m, 186—, pedigree not traced. 2.26½
Lilly B., b m, 1885, by Foster Palmer. 2:28¾
Lilly O., blk m, 1880, by Dr. Herr—Mattie Clay, by Whip Clay........ 2:21¾
Lilly Dale, b m, 1877, by Alden Goldsmith—Queen of Meadow Lawn, by Goldsmith's Abdallah 2:25¼
Lilly Dale, b m, 188—, by Conductor.. 2:27½
Lilly H., b m, 1886, by Nutwood—Lottie, by Sentinel 2:20
Lilly Irwin, b m, 1876, by Virgo Hambletonian—Lady Huggins, by Volunteer 2:30
Lilly J, blk m, 1875, by Bayard—

Speed, by Thos. Jefferson 2:25½
Lilly Kahn, b m, 188—, by Star of the West 2:27¾
Lilly Langtry, b m, 1877, by Mambrino Hambletonian—Cream Mare, by Seneca Chief 2:23¼
Lilly McCarthy, ch m, 188—, by Dick Flaherty—Mollie McCarthy 2:30
Lilly Mack, b m, 1886, by Auctioneer Johnny—Ole Sue 2:24¼
Lilly Moreland, b m, 1888, by Red Wilkes—Neva, by Squire Talmage.. 2:26½
Lilly Q., ch m, 1890, by Keywood—Kittie S., by Dispatch 2:29¼
Lilly Rysdyk, ro m, 1882, by William Rysdyk—Curiosity, by Enquirer 2:25¼
Lilly Shields, ch m, 186—, by King's Cadmus—Jane Shields, by Snowstorm (Canadian) (dead) 2:29½
Lilly D., g m, 188—, by Giltedge..... 2.28¼
Lilly Stanley, b m, 1881, by Whippleton—Dolly McMann 2:17½
Limonero, b s, 1891, by Piedmont—Lulaneer, by Electioneer........ 2:15¾
Limber Jim, b g, 188—, by Alhambra. 2:30
Lime Bullard, b g, 187—...... 2:30
Limestone, b g, 1884, by The King—Curd Mare, by Marshall........ 2:19½
Linda, b m, 1882, by Volunteer Boy—Lady Franklin, by Eureka......... 2.20½
Linda Fister, br m, 1888, by Gambetta Wilkes—Bess Wilkes, by Harry Wilkes 2:27½
Linda Sprague, b m, 1881, by Gov. Sprague—Mary Coleman, by Grey's Mambrino Chief 2:17½
Linden Wilkes, b s, 188—, by Woodford Wilkes 2:25
Lindie, br s, 1886, by Pretender—Meta, by Idol Patchen..... 2:20¾
Linkwood, br s, 1886, by Walsingham—Ermine, by Princeps.... 2:20¼
Linkwood Chief, ch s, 1883, by Hannis—Myrtle, by Norman D......... 2:18¾
Linkwood Maid, ch m, 1883, by Tripolitan Chief—Mrs. Rhoades 2:20
Linmont, b s, 1886, by Almont Medium—Livonia, by Almont 2.23½
Linnet, br m, 1888, by Electioneer—Lizzie Whips, by Enquirer 2:29½
Linnette, b m, 1883, by Onward—Josie Sellers, by Mambrino Time........ 2:29¼
Linnette, dn m, 1886, by Reveille—Nelly, by Jones Acuff..... 2:28¼
Linnie, b m, 1885, by Egbert—Mary Cap, by Mambrino Time.......... 2.25
Linwood, b m, 1880, by Mercury—Stroud Mare 2.30
Lion Moscow, ch s, 1890, by Muscovite—Epiphanie Girl 2:21¼
Lisette, b m, 1887, by Laclede—Myrtle Herr, by Dr. Herr (dead).... 2·22¼
Liska, b m, 1889, by Electioneer—Lizzie, by Wildidle........ 2:28¼
Lissa, dn m, 1888, by Patchen Wilkes—Lady Shaw, by Rochester........ 2:16¾
Lister, b g, 187—, by Almont—Mother Hubbard, by Johnston's Toronto... 2:25¼
Litchfield, ch s, 1887, by Mansfield—Heiress, by Alexander's Abdallah... 2:20¾
Litta, b m, 1885, by Haw Patch—Mattie, by Bourbon Chief Jr. 2.22
Little Albert, ch g, 1884, by Albert W.—Star Mare, by Roach's American Star 2:10
Little Belle, b m, 1885, by Chestnut Hill Jr.—Fanny C., by Black Diamond 2:22½
Little Belmont, b g, 1885, by Gratz's Edwin Forrest—Molly Gordon.. .... 2:30
Little Ben, blk g, 187—, by Ben Morrill 2:28¼
Little Betz, ro m, 1888, by John W. Daniel—Betz Springer, by Captain.. 2.23½
Little Billy, b s, 1874, by Clear Grit—Molly, by Thornburn's Royal George (dead)..... 2:23¼
Little Billy, b g, 188—, by Antar..... 2:21½
Little Billy, b g, by William Irvin.... 2.30
Little Crocker, b g, 1890, by Will Crocker—Lady Inca, by Inca...... 2:30
Little Crow, blk s, 1871, by Reconstruction—Dolly Wright, by Sherman Black Hawk.... 2.28¼
Little D., spt g......... 2 23¼
Little Daisy, br m, 1879, by French's Bashaw—Kate, by Magna of Avon. 2:20¼
Little Dan, b g, 188—, by Star Ethan.. 2:19¼
Little Dan, b g, 188—, by Blackwood Chief.... 2:21¼
Little Dick, b g, 1884, by The Banker, dam by Ohio..... 2:29¼
Little Dick, ch g, 1874, by Holabird's Ethan Allen—Josie, by Golddrop (dead) 2:24½
Little Ethan, b g, 1886, by Ashley's Ethan Allen, dam by Holabird's Ethan Allen 2:19½
Little Eva, b m, 1879, by Post's Hambletonian Prince—Kit, by Joe Bates. 2:20½
Little Frank, ch g, 186—, pedigree not traced 2:30
Little Frank, b g, 1883, by Ira Wilkes—Idlewild 2:25
Little Frank, b g, 1880, by Swanbrough's Hambletonian Prince...... 2:30
Little Frank, b g........ 2:27¾
Little Frank, b g, 1882, by Autocrat.. 2.24¾
Little Fred, b g, 1860, by Dirigo (dead) 2:26¾
Little Fred, blk s, 1882, by Star of the West—Dolly 2:30
Little Fred, b g, 187—, pedigree not traced 2:30
Little Fred, b g, 186—, by Eastman Morgan — Frederica, by Simpson's Blackbird 2:20
Little Gem, b g, 187—, by Henry B. Patchen 2.20½
Little George, ch g, 188—, by Hurst & Thornton's Abdallah. 2:25½
Little George, br g, 188—, by Morgan Wilkes....... 2:27¼
Little Gift, b s, 188—, by Fairy Gift.. 2.29¾
Little Gipsy, b m, 186—, by Gray's Tom Hal 2:22
Little Goldie, ch g, 1881, by Little Frank—Dolly G., by Golden Bow... 2:27
Little Harry, ch g, 1878, by Young Banner, dam by Ballard's Cassius M. Clay Jr. 2:29¼
Little Harry, br s, 1885, by Potter's Hambletonian—Nelly, by Leo ...... 2·29¼
Little Ida, b m, 188—, by Kentucky Prince 2:29¼
Little Jake, ro g, 186—, pedigree not traced (dead)...... 2:30
Little Jersey, ch g, 1885, by Jersey Prince—Fanchon, by Ajax......... 2:29¼
Little Jim, b g, 188—, by Wildbrino.. 2:23¾
Little Joe, br g, 1876, by Bob Hunter, dam by Fitzsimmons' St. Lawrence. 2:21½
Little Joe, blk s, 1875, by Joe Bates.. 2:25¼
Little Johnny, b g, 188—, by Highland Jr. 2:30
Little Kahn, ch m, 188—, by Salamon 2:27¾
Little Leo, blk g, 188—, by Leo....... 2:26¾
Little Longfellow, ch g, 186—, by Flying Morgan (dead)..... 2·29¼

Little Mac, b s, 188—, by Stone's Election............................... 2:28
Little Mack, br s, 1867, by McKimmin's Columbus—Old Fly 2:28½
Little Mack, b g, 188—, by Harry Plummer.............................. 2:29¾
Little Mack Jr, b s, 188—, by Little Mack................................. 2·27½
Little Mag, b m, 188—, by Prince Orloff...................................... 2:26
Little Mary, ch m, 1868, by Billy Mustapha............................. 2·25
Little Mat, b g, 1880, by Iron Duke—Maggie Anderson, by Rourke's Cadmus...................................... 2:28¾
Little Maud, b m, 188—, by Patchen.. 2:26¼
Little Mike, b g, 188—................... 2:24
Little Mike, ch s, 1887, by Champion Prince—Nelly, by Gen. Burnside.... 2:23½
Little Miss, b m, 1876, by Goldsmith's Abdallah—Old Lady, by Capt. Walker 2:26½
Little Nancy, rn m, 188—, by Henry O., dam by Macbeth............... 2:29
Little Ned, ch g, 1875, by Hotspur Jr. —Nell Johnson 2:29¼
Little Ned, br g, 1884, by Hampton—Nelly Green, by Green's Bashaw... 2·29¼
Little Nell, b m, 1881, by Jefferson Prince—Musa, by Hugo........... 2:19½
Little Nell, blk m, 1882, by Romulus—Polly Perkins, by Blue Bull..... 2:29½
Little Rock, b g, 1884, by Bullet (pacing record 2:26)...................... 2:29½
Little Sam, ch g, 186—, by Hall Horse —Concord Girl (dead).............. 2·29
Little Sioux, b g, 1873, by Monitor—Eugenia, by Ben Roodhouse....... 2·22½
Little Snap, gr g, 1890, by Kellar Thomas—Maud M., by Crazy Nick Jr...................................... 2:17½
Little Sport, gr g, 1884, by Happy Thought, dam by Palmer's Norman. 2:25¼
Little Tobe, b s, 188—, by Pamlico... 2:19½
Little Thorne, b g, 1879, by Dauntless—Nannie Thorne, by Hamlet....... 2:23¼
Little Tommy, b g, 187—, by Blackwood Jr................................. 2:27¼
Little Walter, b g, 187—, by Clarion Chief.................................... 2:29¼
Little Witch, ch m, 1884, by Ben Franklin — Grey Bessie, by Woodstock .... 2·29
Little Witch, gr m, 188—, by Director, dam by Capt. Hanford 2:27
Little Wonder, gr g, 1895, by George B. Swan—Nellie Hackett, by Whalen's Grey Eagle 2.24¼
Little Wonder, ch g, 188—, by Star Ethan 2:24½
Little Wonder, ch s, 1872, by Blue Bull—Polly, by Sovereign Glencoe .. 2:30
Little Wonder, b s, 187—, by Tom Wonder, dam by May Day.......... 2:30
Little Wonder, ch g, 1879, by Chipmuck—Mag, by William's Magna Charta 2:27¼
Liva, b m, 188—, by Patchen Wilkes—Rosa, by Rochester 2:25¼
Live Oak Girl, b m, 188—, by Deadwood 2.22¾
Lizzie 2d, b m, 1874, by Trouble—Lizzie Craig, by Paragon Morgan.. 2·23½
Lizzie Chapin, ch m, 188—, by Emperor William 2:30
Lizzette, ch m, by Chestnut Joe 2:25
Lizzie F., ch m, 1875, by Windsor, dam by St. Charles 2:27¾

Lizzie F , b m, 1887, by Elector, dam by Duke McClellan 2:16¼
Lizzie Gibson, b m, 1884, by Gen. Stanton—Mattie, by Major Macon (dead) 2:29¼
Lizzie H , b m, 1884, by Winooski—Lady Walkill, by Walkill Chief 2.24¼
Lizzie H., b m, 1883, by Don Robinson—Novice, by Fisk's Mambrino Chief Jr. 2:27¼
Lizzie H , b m, 1881, by Orange County—Bessie, by Middletown 2:28½
Lizzie Harold, b m, 1887, by Manetho —Belle Mambrino, by Ashland Chief 2:28¾
Lizzie K., ch m, 1882, by Deucalion—Emblem, by Minchin's Tom Moore.. 2:26½
Lizzie L., blk m, 1886, by Thomas Carlyle—Clytie, by Young Champion 2:27¼
Lizzie Lansing, b m 1889, by Princeton—Maud Stonestreet, by Conn's Harry Wilkes .... 2·22¼
Lizzie M., b m, 1873, by Thomas Jefferson—Queen Pin, by Legal Tender (dead) 2:20¼
Lizzie M., b m, 1885, by Nutwood—Lucina, by Cuyler 2.24
Lizzie O., b m, 188—, by St. Gothard 2:27½
Lizzie O'Brien, ch m, 187—, pedigree not traced 2:23¼
Lizzie R., br m, 1877, by Mambrino Boy—Ella, by Cripple 2:23½
Lizzie S , br m, 1885, by Iowa Chief —Blanche 2:22½
Lizzie S. b m, 1883, by Honest Dick —Kit 2:30
Lizzie S , blk m, 1886, by Wildfire —Kit 2:22¼
Lizzie S., b m, 1880, by Wild Wagoner, dam by Foote's Bellfounder.. 2·27½
Lizzie Wilkes, blk m, 1880 by George Wilkes—Laura, by Joe Hooker 2:22¾
L. L. C., b g, 188—, pedigree not traced 2:28¾
L. L. D., b s, 1889, by Woodford Wilkes—China Wilkes, by Adrian Wilkes .... 2·24¼
L. M. Wing, b s, 1887, by Glenview—Clayette, by O. B. Gould 2:26½
Loafer, ro g, 186—, pedigree not traced (dead) 2 24½
Loafer P., b g, 188—, by Inspector .. 2:24¼
Lobasco, b s, 1886, by Egmont—Fleta Maid, by Gen. Hatch (dead) ...... 2·10¾
Lobelia, ch m, 1887, by Alcazar—Malia, by Sir Walkill 2.24¼
Lock Boy, br g, 188—, by Dorsey Golddust 2:22¼
Lockheart, b s, 1886, by Nutwood—Rapidan, by Dictator 2:13
Locomotive, ch g, 1887, by Ben Wright—Clara Lincoln, by Masterlode 2:29¼
Lodina, b m, 1889, by California—Belle of Lodi, by Antar 2:27¼
Logan ch s, 1860, by Wadleigh's Logan 2:28
Logan B., br g, 1881, by Wineman's Logan—Madam Jenne, by Green's Bashaw 2.22¾
Logan Chief, blk s, 1878, by L J—Fanny by Vermonter 2 23¼
Logan Grant, ch s, 1881 by Gen. Grant—Olive Logan, by Sage's Logan 2:29
Lohengrin, b g, 1882, by Echo—Vixen, by George M. Patchen Jr .... 2·27¼

Lola, ro m, 186–, by Kenyon's Kemble Jackson Jr. 2:30
Lula Anderson, b m, 188—, by Woodburn Hambletonian 2:29½
Lola D, b m, 1881, by Copperbottom Horse—Nettie, by Flying Bird.. 2.29¾
Lottie T., b m, 1872, by Vermont—Nance, by Red Fox 2:28¼
Lompoc, b g, 188—, by Dan Rice 2 24½
Lona Guffin, b m, 1876, by Blue Bull—Queen Guffin, by Pete Guffin 2.23½
Lonely Medium, b m, 188—, by Shannon Medium 2:28
Lone Star, b s, 1890, by Memento Wilkes—Golden Measure, by Golden Bow 2 29½
Londema Wilkes, b m, 1891, by Ashland Wilkes 2.26½
London, ch g, 1876, by Mambrino Patchen—Beckey, by Edwin Forrest 2 20½
Longfellow, ch g, 1877, by Whipple's Hambletonian—Revere 2:24¼
Longfellow Whip, br s, 1877, by Kentucky Whip—Bessie Brown, by Bird 2 20¼
Longford, b g, 1881, by Chosroes—Long Mary, by Derby's Bashaw .. 2.20¼
Long John, b g, 1884, by Mambrino Templar Jr.—Nelly H. 2:28½
Lon M., blk g, 1879, by Bonnie Scotland—Fanny Lee 2.30
Lonsbury, b g, 188—, by Pickering ... 2.28¼
Lookaway, b s, 1888, by Look—Rosalind, by Harry Clay 2:22½
Lookout, b g, 1881, by Arab, or Stanford .... 2·25
Lookout, b g, 1873, by Gen Lightfoot—Shoo Fly, by Rising Sun ... 2.28½
Loraneer, b m, 1890, by Electioneer—Lora by Piedmont 2:26½
Lora J., gr m, 1885, by Gloster, dam by Fred 2:19½
Lord Brino, blk s, 1889, by Woodbrino—Flirtilla, by Ballard 2 25½
Lord Byron, b s, 1885, by Gen. Benton—May Day, by Wissahickon .... 2·17
Lord Caffrey, blk s, 1887, by Charles Caffrey—Patsy, by Brougham 2 21¼
Lord Clinton, blk g, 1885,, by Denning Allen—Fanny .... 2·08¾
Lord Nelson b s, 1882, by Wellington—Miss McLeod, by Holbert Colt .. 2·26¼
Lord Nelson, b s, 188 - by Bashaw . 2 29½
Lord Palm, b s, 1886, by Mambrino Startle—Lady Palm, by Thomas Jefferson 2:29½
Lord Shelburne, b s 1890, by Homestead—Sister, by Holabird's Ethan Allen 2:19
Lord Stanley, br s, 1889, by Nephew—Susette, by Electioneer 2 28½
Lorella, b m, 1888, by Jerome Eddy—Nanny Payne, by Homer 2 30
Lorena blk m 1887 by Jim Mulvenna—Elmorene, by Elmo 2:30
Loretta, ch m 1881, by Strathmore—Ella, by Cripple 2:30
Loretta, b m, 187—, pedigree not traced 2:29½
Loretta B., b m, 188—, by Greenbacks 2:28
Loretta F. b m, 1877, by Hamlet—Lady Grayson by Col Grayson.. 2:18¾
Lorita, ch m 1883 by Piedmont—Lady Lowell, by Shootz's St. Clair 2 22¾
Lorna Doone, b m, 1884, by Hambrino Star—Vexation, by Belmont Prince.. 2 24¼
Lorody, ch s 1884, by Harold—Nata, by Woodford Mambrino .... 2·24½
Los Angeles, b s, 1891, by Woodlark 2.23½

Lothair, blk s, 1867, by Gilbreth Knox—Bunker Mare, by Eaton Horse 2 29½
Lothair Jr, b s, 1877, by Lothair—Topsy, by Young Drew 2.30
Lot Slocum, b g, 1882, by Electioneer—Glencora, by Mohawk Chief 2:17¼
Lotta, b m, 1877, by Florida—Kate Porter, by Daniel Lambert 2.24½
Lotta Prall, b m, 1875, by Mambrino Patchen—Puss Prall, by Mark Time 2·28¾
Lottery, gr g, 186— by Rysdyk's Hambletonian—Jane Murray .... 2·27
Lottery Ticket, b s, 1887, by Dexter Prince—Emma Nutwood, by Nutwood 2:19½
Lottie, blk m, 1890, by Luminator, dam by Atlantic 2:25¼
Lottie, b m, 188—, by Thompson.... 2:21
Lottie, b m, 1870, by Potter's Foxhunter 2 29½
Lottie, br m, 1866, by Rysdyk's Hambletonian—Molly, by Long Island Black Hawk 2 28
Lottie C., b m, 1879, by Seneca Chief—Rosalind, by Strader's Cassius M. Clay Jr 2.29¼
Lottie E., br m, 1892, by San Diego—Flora B, by Whippleton 2:26¼
Lottie E., b m, 1880, by Blind Tom—Nelly 2 29½
Lottie G., b m, 188—, by Gibraltar ... 2:25½
Lottie K., b m, 187—, by American Emperor Jr—Lady Konkle, by Hetzel's Hambletonian 2 27
Lottie K., gr m, 1879, by Squire Talmage—Varina, by Strader's Cassius M Clay Jr. 2 26¾
Lottie M. b m, 187—, by Nephew—Lucy, by Chieftain 2:24
Lottie Moore, b m, 1890, by Red Wilkes—Lady Backman, by Kentucky Prince 2:29¼
Lottie P., b m, 183—, by Volney . 2·30
Lottie Thorn, b m, 1879, by Mambrino Patchen—Lady Ayres, by Redmon's Abdallah 2 23¾
Lottie W., b m, 1880, by Clark Chieftain—Judea, by Mambrino Archy . 2 21
Lottie Williams, b m, 1887, by Pilot Medium, dam by Jefferson Mambrino 2·27
Lottie Woodruff, b m, 188—, pedigree not traced 2 28¾
Lou, b m, 1890, by Ira—Electra, by Newland's Hambletonian .... 2·27
Lou Edsall, ch m, 188—, by Edsall Star 2 26
Louetta, b m, 187—, by Romulus—Pickelominia, by Bashaw Drury .. 2 24¼
Lou Gates, b m, 1880, by Al West—Dolly Bruce, by Robert Bruce .... 2·29¼
Loughran W., br g, 1887, by Newton's Allie Wilkes—Belle of Peru .... 2·17¾
Louie C., b g, 188— by George Milo 2 28½
Louisa Almont, br m, by Bostick's Almont Jr.—Lady Ella 2 25
Louis D., b g, 187—, by King William 2·24¾
Louise, b m, 1873, by Volunteer, dam by Ethan Allen 2.29¼
Louise, blk m 2.28
Louise B b m, 1887, by Young Fullerton—Stella, by Blackstone 2 29¼
Louise Kellogg, b m, 188—, by Almont Star 2 27¼
Louise Macey, b m, 1887, by Thomas K—Lucy Avent, by Peavine 2 27½
Louise N., b m 187—, by Alpine—Little One, by Columbus 2.20¼
Louise Watt, blk m, 1891, by Wal-

Lula F., b m, 187—, by Ericsson—Mary Messenger, by Downing's Bay Messenger 2:29
Lula Hambletonian, b m, 1877, by McCurdy's Hambletonian—Sue McCurdy 2:27
Lulie C., b m, 1883, by Nutwood—Lottie, by Sentinel.... 2:16½
Lulo, blk m, 188—, by Atlantic, dam by St. Omer.... 2:27½
Lulu, b m, 188—, by Bayonne Prince, dam by Blue Medium 2:26¼
Lulu B., b m, 1885, by Bassett M.—Lucinda, by Haw Patch 2:24¼
Lulu B., b m, 1880, by Louis Napoleon—Libbie.... 2:29¼
Lulu C., b m, 1889, by Alcona—Mother Taylor, by Gen. Taylor.... 2:29¾
Lulu F., b m, 188—, by Christmas ... 2:25
Lulu H., gr m, 1874, by Quaker General—Vickey Mare.... 2:24¼
Lulu Judd, blk m, 1878, by Royal Duke—Moscow Belle, by Field's Royal George 2:26½
Lulu Wilkes, b m, 1890, by Onward—Lulu Harold, by Harold.... 2:22½
Lump, blk s, 188—, by Ruby.... 2:26½
Lumps, br s, 1875, by George Wilkes—Mother Lumps, by Pearsall.... 2:21
Lulu P., b m, 1889, by Sankey.... 2:20½
Lulu Stanton, b m, 188—, by Gen Stanton 2:19¼
Lumpson, br s, 188—, by Lumps.... 2:29½
Lumpwood, b s, 1890, by Cedarwood—Absinthe, by Lumps 2:21¾
Luna, b m, 1887, by Phallamont, dam by Tyler's Patchen 2:21¾
Luner, b m, 188—, by Beamer.... 2:29¾
Lunette, b m, 1883, by Lumps—Lady K., by Gen. George H. Thomas.... 2:25¾
Lurline, blk m, 188—, by Dexter Prince.... 2:23½
Lurline, br m, 1888, by Paramount—Flash, by Hambletonian Bashaw.... 2:17¼
Lustre, b s, 1888, by Fallis—Patti, by Nutwood 2:23½
Luzelle, b m, 1890, by Patron—Rachel Ray, by Overstreet Wilkes 2:16¼
Luzerne, b g, 1879, by Gen. Washington—Martha Nutwood, by Hamlet . 2:27½
Lycurgus, b s, 1884, by Aberdeen—Zoette, by Almont Prince.... 2:15½
Lycurgus, br s, 188—, by Lumps 2:25
Lydi, blk m, 1890, by Joe You See—Idyl, by Chadwick 2:30
Lydia C., b m, 1886, by Bay Rose—Lofty, by Algona 2:27
Lydia Thompson, b m, 1861, by Wild Wagoner, dam by Saladin 2:26¼
Lyman, dn g, 1871, by Bay Chief, dam by Canadian Redbuck 2:25¼
Lynde, ch m, 188—, pedigree not traced 2:29¼
Lyndon, ch s, 1884, by Egbert—Nelly Stout, by Mambrino Time.... 2:29¾
Lyndon Boy, blk g, 1884, by Black Morrill—Rundel Mare.... 2:26¼
Lynne Bel, blk s, 1890, by St. Bel—Vashti, by Bayonne Prince.... 2:27¼
Lynette, b m, 1887, by Lynwood—Lady Belle by Skenandoah.... 2:22½
Lynn Sprague, blk m, 1881, by Governor Sprague—Windom Belle, by Mambrino Foster 2:28
Lynn W., blk g, 1879, by Sponseller Tuckahoe—Topsy, by Rollman Horse 2:21¼
Lynwood, gr s, 1879, by Clinker—Belton Maid, by Stuart Lindley.... 2:20½
Lynwood, b s, 1890, by Guy Wilkes, dam by Sultan Jr.... 2:20½
Lynnwood, b s, 1889, by Look—Flirt, by Baird's Hambletonian Prince.... 2:27¼
Lynx, br g, 1885, by Lexington Chief Jr. (dead).... 2:28
Lyra, blk m, 1877, by Antenor—Morning Star, by Peacemaker.... 2:28¾
Lyric, b m, 1891, by Launcelot—Lyre, by Arthurton 2:26¼
Lysander Boy, ch g, 1870, by Lysander, dam by Wine Creek Black Hawk.... 2:20¾
McCurdy Jr., blk s, 188—, by McCurdy's Hambletonian.... 2:30
Mab, blk m, 1885, by Defiance—Queen, by Republic 2:21
Mabel A., ch m, 1881, by Attorney—Sally, by Tramp 2:23¼
Mabel C., b m, 188—, by Gloster.... 2:25¼
Mabel F., gr m, 1880, by Monahan's Patchen—Blue Bell, by Harry Bluff 2:29¼
Mabel H., b m, 1888, by Alexander Button—Winnie, by Dietz's St. Clair. 2:17¼
Mabel H., ch m, 1879, by Col. West—Nelly Gray, by White Mountain Jr.. 2:26
Mabel H., blk m, 188—, by Lambert Chief 2:22¼
Mabel M., b m, 1882, by Athlete.... 2:30
Mabel Mack, b m, 1885, by Sweepstakes—Lady Bowman, by Star Mambrino 2:25
Mabel Mack, blk m, 188—, by son of Gen. Knox.... 2:29¼
Mabel Parmeter, br m, 1883, by Hambletonian Gift.... 2:29½
Mabel R., br m, 1883, by Deceive—Old Frankie, by Trojan 2:27¾
Mabelle, ch m, 1890, by Betterton—Queen Sweepstakes, by Sweepstakes 2:25½
Mabel S., b m, 1881, by Landmark, dam by Niagara Champion.... 2:22½
Mabel W., br m, 188—, by Thought.. 2:27¼
Maby, b m, 1889, by Oxford Boy—Lady May, by Marshal Ney.... 2:16¼
Mac Ivor, br s, 1889, by Harry Plummer—Trixey, by Deucalion 2:27
Mac, dn g, 1885, by Giltedge—Bell Fall 2:26¼
Mack, br g, 1843, by Morgan Caesar, dam by Bush Messenger 2:28
Mack, b s, 1885, by Thought—Topsey, by Billy Ring.... 2:20½
Macleay, blk s, 1889, by Sable Wilkes—Mamie Comet, by Nutwood (pacing 2:29¼).... 2:22¼
McClelland Stewart, b g, 188—, by Director 2:29¼
McAlister, b g, 1883, by Black's Hambletonian—Katie James, by Waterloo 2:24¼
McAllister, b s, 1885, by Egbert—Laura, by Billy Adams.... 2:27
McCready, blk s, 1882, by Arnold—Mattie Stockbridge, by Stockbridge Chief Jr.... 2:29¾
McCullough, ch s, 1887, by Robert McGregor—Laura, by Joe Hooker.. 2:30
Mac D., ch s, 1883, by Robert McGregor—Gipsy 2:30
McDoel (Sedalia Boy), ch g, 188—, by Fred—Pony 2:15¼
McDuff, b g, 1885, by Fergus McGregor—Judy O'Can, by Evan Dhu.. 2:23
McDuff, b g, 1887, by Flying Hiatoga Jr.... 2:22¾
McElree, b g, 188—, by Martine.... 2:24¼
McEwen, ch s, 1885, by McCurdy's Hambletonian—Mary M., by Bassinger 2:18¼
McFarland, br s, 1881, by Charles Caffrey—Eva, by Tippo Bashaw . 2:29¼

McGinty, br s, 1889, by Inveterate—Nelly, by John A. Rawlins 2:29¼
McGinty, b g, 188—, by Jim Mulvenna ... 2:26
McGinty ... 2:20½
McGlynn, br g, 188—, by Bishop 2:25
McGregor (Hood's), ch s, 1888, by Robert McGregor—Sally Denmark, by Star Denmark ... 2:26¾
McGregor Boy, ch s, 1880, by Robert McGregor—Lydda, by Romulus 2:29½
McGregor Time, ch s, 1888, by Robert McGregor—Ollie Stout, by Mambrino Time ... 2:30
McGregor Wilkes, b s, 1887, by Robert McGregor—Dewey Eve, by George Wilkes ... 2:27¼
McGregor Wilkes, ch s, 1887, by Robert McGregor—Alice Wilkes, by Red Wilkes ... 2:21
McGuire, b s, 1888, by Egbert—Sue Monday, by Tattler Jr ... 2:23½
McIntosh, b s, 1885, by Mountain Boy—Sister Cawley, by Northrup's Rattler ... 2:27½
McKean, b s, 1883, by Volunteer—Black Meg, by Kentucky Prince .. 2:27½
McKee, b g, 188—, by Calamity Dick 2:30
McKelvey, ch s, 1884, by McGregor Jr.—Fanny, by Strathmore ... 2:29¼
McKenna, b g, 188—, ... 2:29¼
McKenzie, gr g, 187—, by Antenor—Silver Islet, by Young Columbus .. 2:25¼
McKinney, b s, 1887, by Alcyone—Rosa Sprague, by Gov. Sprague .. 2:11¼
McKinney Belle, ch m, 188—, by Belmont Chief ... 2:29½
McKusick, b s, 1885 by Olympus—Lady Burns, by Burn's Trotting Childers ... 2:26¾
McLane, g s, 1889, by Pilot Medium—Stella Paddock, by Magna Charta 2:28¾
McLeod, b g, 1877, by Mambrino Blitzen—Jenny Bryan, by John Dillard 2:21¼
McLeod, ch s, 1879, by Saturn—Madge, by Vermont Hero ... 2:19½
Maclure, blk g, 1871, by Messenger Duroc—Nelly Wilmarth, by Raven . 2:30
McMahon, br s 1876, by Administrator—Mattie West, by Almont 2:21
McMillan, ch g, 1883, by Kensington—Lizzie Stillson, by Stillson ... 2:29½
McMinnville Maid, blk m, 1888 by Altamont—Hollywood, by Hambletonian Mambrino ... 2:22
McMullen Boy, br g, 188—, by Sweepstakes ... 2:29¼
McMyatt, ch s 1885, by Ben Franklin—Myatt, by De Long's Ethan Allen ... 2:25½
McVale ch s 1888, by McCurdy's Hambletonian—Fernvale, by Enfield 2:29
McVera, b s, 1889, by Talavera, dam by McMahon ... 2:21¼
McZeus, br s, 1891, by McKinney—Grace Kaiser, by Kaiser ... 2:29¼
Macaroon, b s, 1889, by McCurdy's Hambletonian—Susie G., by Scipio 2:21¾
Madawaska Maid, ch m, 1862, pedigree not traced (dead) ... 2:29½
Madeleine, b m, 1875, by Rysdyk's Hambletonian—Nancy Whitman, by Seely's American Star ... 2:23¼
Mad Eye, ch s, 1886 by France's Alile Wilkes—Meg, by Sir Henry ... 2:26½
Madge D., b m, 1882 by Case's Dave Hill—Kate C., by Young Waxey ... 2:30
Madge Fullerton, b m, 188—, by Young Fullerton—Lucy, by Big Dan 2:30
Madge Hatton, br m, 1885, by Glencoe Jr.—May Waddle ... 2:17¼
Madge Wilkes, ch m, 1890, by Victor Wilkes—Nelly Lambert, by Daniel Lambert ... 2:21¾
Madison, b s, 1887, by Leland—Young Gypsy, by Mambrino Pilot ... 2:24
Madison Chief, b s, 1888, by Madison Wilkes—Fanny Mambrino, by Harris' Mambrino Chief ... 2:21¼
Madison Wilkes, b s, 1878, by George Wilkes—Minna, by Red Jacket ... 2:24¾
Madras, b g, 188—, by Madrid ... 2:25¼
Mad River Belle, b m, 188—, by King of Belair ... 2:29¼
Madwood, b s, 1887, by Nutwood—Ella Madden, by Rysdyk's Hambletonian ... 2:20¼
Maestro, blk s, 1889, by Rumor—Bangle, by Slander ... 2:29½
Magdalene, b m, 1890, by Bermuda—Maggie C., by Hailstorm ... 2:20
Magdallah, ch m 1873, by Primus—Maud, by Mambrino Rattler ... 2:23½
Magenta, b m, 1870, by Woodford Mambrino—Madge, by Alexander's Abdallah ... 2:24½
Maggie, ch m, 1891, by Jerome Heath—Maggie, by Edmore ... 2:29¼
Maggie, b m, 188—, by Dexter Prince 2:20
Maggie B., blk m., 1880 by Shelbyville Chief—Buck, by Red Buck ... 2:20
Maggie B., b m, 1885, by White Line Jr.—Ianthe, by Oceana Chief ... 2:26
Maggie Briggs, b m, 1869, by American Clay—Jenny Morgan, by Sebastapol ... 2:27
Maggie C, b m, 187—, by Whipple's Hambletonian, dam by Eldred .. 2:25
Maggie C., b m, 1880, by Joe Hooper—Pattie, by Bush's Messenger ... 2:27¼
Maggie C., ch m, 1879 by St. Almo—Puss, by Jehu Morgan ... 2:29¾
Maggie C., br m, 188—, by Gen Stanton ... 2:29½
Maggie Campbell, br m, 188—, by Pamlico ... 2:25½
Maggie Dot, b m, 188—, by Tornado 2:24¼
Maggie E, b m, 1880, by Nutwood—May, by George M. Patchen Jr. ... 2:19¼
Maggie F., b m, 1876 by Menelaus—Molly King, by Yorkshire Lexington 2:27
Maggie F., b m, 1873, by Newry—Flora ... 2:26
Maggie F. b m, 1882, by Young Jim—Molly, by Young Diamond ... 2:22¼
Maggie G. Middleton, b m, 1879 by Bay Middleton—Gyp, by Magna Charta ... 2:20¾
Maggie H., gr m, 1876, by Iron Duke—Jordan, by Stonewall ... 2:28¼
Maggie H., b m, 188—, by Nero ... 2:27¼
Maggie H., b m, ... 2:24
Maggie H., b m, 1885, by Barney Wilkes—Alice ... 2:28½
Maggie K., br m 1874, by Brown Chief—Doll Burger, by Myer's Foxhunter ... 2:29¼
Maggie K., b m, 188—, by Deceiver . 2:26
Maggie Kevin, b m, 1879, by Star of the West—Kit Kevin, by Waddington's Simpson ... 2:25½
Maggie Knox, ch m, 1877, by Oceana Chief—Molly Bawn, by Sir Henry .. 2:24¼
Maggie Lambert, br m, 1876, by Daniel Lambert—Brown Fanny, by Young Black Hawk ... 2:25¼

Maggie Lewis, blk m, 1887, by Stranger—Irene Fell, by Mambrino Abdallah 2:28¼

Maggie M., blk m, 1869, by Patrick Henry, dam by Prince Moscow.... 2:27½

Maggie M., b m, 1881, by John Bright 2:28¼

Maggie May, b m, 1881, by Volunteer —Lizzie R., by Emigrant 2:29½

Maggie Miller, br m, 1878, by Harry Knox, dam by Bay State 2:26½

Maggie Miller, br m, 188—, by Auditor 2:29

Maggie Mitchell, br m, 1882, by C. W. Mitchell—Pearsall Mare, by Pearsall (dead) 2:21¼

Maggie Monroe, b m, 1885, by Monaco —Fanny Monroe, by Jim Monroe.. 2:20¼

Maggie Morrill, ch m, 1876, by Charley B.—Maggie Lee 2:29¼

Maggie N., ch m, 1886, by Cupid—Dock 2:16¾

Maggie S., b m, 187—, by Roland..... 2:30

Maggie S., blk m, 18—, pedigree not traced (dead) 2:26½

Maggie S., b m, 1889, by Shawmut—Maggie H., by Homer 2:29

Maggie Sherman, ch m, 1888, by Alexander H. Sherman—Bernice, by Smiser's Mohawk 2:16¼

Maggie's Last, b m, 188—, Pappalee —Maggie 2:29¼

Maggie Sprague, b m, 1889, by Bolton Sprague—Kittie, by Young Woful.. 2:29½

Maggie Sultan, br m, 1887, by Sultan Maggie Prescott, by Jim Monroe .. 2:30

Maggie T., b m, 1884, by St. Charles —Maggie 2d, by Tom Patchen 2:18½

Maggie Wilkeswood, b m, 1888, by Wilkeswood—Maggie, by Magna Charta 2:28

Maggie Wilton, b m, 1891, by Wilton, dam by Homer 2:28½

Maggie Wilton, b m, 1887, by Wilton —Maggie Prescot, by Jim Monroe .. 2:30

Maggie Wright, ch m, 1885, by Silas Wright—Maggie Gift, by Mambrino Gift 2:22½

Magic, blk g, 1874, by Jim Fisk, dam by Sam Slick 2:25¼

Magic Wilkes, b s, 1885, by Onward —Santa Claus, by Magic 2:29¼

Magna Medium, br s, 1889, by Chief Medium—Gyp, by Magna Charta .. 2:24¾

Magna Sphinx, b s, 1890, by Sphinx—Belva Ann, by Magna Charta 2:29

Magna Wilkes, b g, 1880, by George Wilkes—Molly, by Magna Charta.. 2:23½

Magnet, b s, 1875, by Magnolia—Mischief, by Alexander's Abdallah (dead) 2:27¼

Magnetta, b m, 1888, by Cornelian—Magnet, by Strathmore 2:21½

Magnolia, b m, 1887, by Haw Patch —Mag, by Bourbon Chief Jr. 2:09¼

Magnolia, gr g, 186—, by Magnolia.. 2:26¼

Magnoma, blk m, 1886, by Alhambra Chief—Nettie Forrest, by Forrest King 2:30

Mahala, blk m, 1887, by Cyclone—Madam Beatty, by Monroe Chief.... 2:19¾

Mahaska, b s, 1887, by Advance—Bay Sally, by Corsair 2:25

Mahlon, blk s, 1888, by Alcantara—Blanche Jefferson, by Thomas Jefferson 2:13¾

Mahogany b s, 1889, by Bayonne Prince—Sandal, by Jay Gould 2:12¼

Mahomet, b s, 188—, by Mambrino Clay Jr., dam by son of Planet .. 2:20

Mahomet, b g, 188—, by Constellation 2:28¼

Maiden, b m, 1884, by Electioneer—May Queen, by Alexander's Norman 2:23

Maid of Monti, b m, 1871, by Comet—Monti 2:28

Maid of Oaks, ch m, 1880, by Duke McClellan—Oregon Nell 2:23

Maid of the Wilderness, br m, 1888, by Sherman Aristos—Silvertail, by Hadwin Horse 2:25¾

Maidstone, b m, 188—, by John E. Rysdyk 2:30

Majella, b m, 1886, by Counsellor—Alcalde 2:29

Majester, b s, 188—, by Sterling 2:24

Majolica, b g, 1876, by Startle—Jessie Kirk, by Clark Chief 2:15

Major, gr g, 1876, by Gen. Putnam—Kate, by Flying Cloud Jr 2:24¾

Major, b s, 1888, by Don McGregor, dam by Fleetfoot 2:11

Major, b g, 188,— pedigree not traced 2:26¼

Major, ch s, 1890, by Goff's Mohawk, dam by Gould Clay 2:22

Major Brown, br g, 188—, by Philosopher 2:28

Major Brown, b s, 1886, by Tennessee Wilkes—Aline, by Allie West 2:27

Major Ewing, b s, 1889, by Strathmore—Miss Kirksey, by Mambrino Le Grand 2:18¼

Major F., b g, 1883, by Jersey Prince —Jessie, by Henry B. Patchen ... 2:30

Major Lacey, b s, 1887, by Mogadore —Lucy, by Flaxtail 2:30

Major Mapes, b s, 1888, by Bonnie Wilkes—Nora Mapes, by Furor 2:29¾

Maj. A., ch g, 1880, by Maj. Edsall.. 2:29¼

Maj. Allen, ch g, 1864, by Frank Allen.. 2:24¼

Maj. Buford, gr g, 1884, by Charles Caffrey—Lady Belle, by Tip Cranston 2:28½

Maj. Edsall, b s, 1859, by Alexander's Abdallah, dam by Harris' Hambletonian (dead)............................. 2:29

Maj. Flowers, ch g, 1884, by Bourbon Wilkes, dam by Caliban............ 2:21¼

Maj. King, ch g, 186—, by Careless (dead) 2:30

Maj. Lord, dn g, 1870, by Edward Everett—Phoenix Mare................ 2:23¾

Maj. Lynn, ch g, 1881, by Young Bashaw—Snow Flake 2:23¼

Maj. Root, br g, 186—, pedigree not traced (dead).......................... 2:27

Maj. Ross, br s, 1890, by Anteros—Blanche H., by Blue Bull.......... 2:24¼

Maj. S., b g, 188—, by Knick Wilkes.. 2:20¼

Maj. S., b g, 186—, pedigree not traced 2:29

Maj. Thorne, blk s, 1886, by Hawthorne — Old Tempest, by Morgan Rattler 2:30

Maj. Ulrich, b g, 188—, by Vermont Abdallah 2:24¼

Malabar, b s, 1884, by Wedgewood—Kitty Abbott, by Abbott.......... 2:21¼

Malacca (Carrie B.), br m, 1875, by Elial G.—Country Maid, by Hinsdale Horse 2:24½

Malachi, b s, 1886, by Monaco—Dolly Varden, by Daniel Lambert........ 2:20

Malheur, b s, 1888, by Altamont—Belle Price, by Doble................. 2:27

Malvina, b m, 1874, by Fearnaught Spy.. 2:21¼

Mambrinette, b m, 1876, by Mambrino Gift — Lady Alice, by Mambrino Chorister 2:21

Mambrino (Graham's), blk s, 1882, by Mambrino Bashaw—Kitty Clay, by Kentucky Clay.... 2:27¼

Mambrino Archy, br s, 1876, by Mambrino Boy, dam by John Dillard..... 2:24¾

Mambrino Belle, dn m, 188—, by Mambrino Chief Jr 2:23

Mambrino Boy, blk s, 1868, by Mambrino Patchen — Roving Nelly, by Strader's Cassius M. Clay Jr (dead) 2:26½

Mambrino Clay Jr., br s, 1875, by Mambrino Clay—Lousch, by Searcher.... 2:25

Mambrino Diamond, blk s, 1873, by Mambrino Patchen—Lucy, by Strader's Cassius M. Clay Jr.... 2:26

Mambrino Dick, br s, 1879, by Mambrino Time—Scottish Maid, by imp. Bonnie Scotland 2:24

Mambrino Dudley, b s, 1874, by Woodford Mambrino—Sue Dudley, by Edwin Forrest 2:19¾

Mambrino General, br g, 186—, by Fisk's Mambrino Chief Jr.—Black Sal.... 2:25½

Mambrino George, b s 1871, by Fisk's Mambrino Chief Jr.—Bay Wiley, by Royal George 2:30

Mambrino Gift, ch s, 1866, by Mambrino Pilot—Waterwitch, by Pilot Jr. (dead).... 2:20

Mambrino Girl, b m, 1883, by Victor Bismarck — Lady Mambrino, by Walker's Mambrino.... 2:30

Mambrino Jefferson, br s, 188—, by Thomas Jefferson 2:30

Mambrino Kate, gr m, 1869, by Mambrino Patchen, dam by State of Maine 2:24

Mambrino Lambert, ch g, 1881, by Merry Boy—Shadow, by Daniel Lambert 2:29½

Mambrino Lumps, b s, 188—, by Lumps 2:28¼

Mambrino Maid, ch m 1880, by Chief—Hetty, by Case's Frank Moscow.. 2:29¾

Mambrino Maid, b m, 1885, by Mambrino Startle — Winnie Wilkes, by Red Wilkes.... 2:15¼

Mambrino Maud, blk m, 1884, by Mambrino Duke—Daisy C.... 2:28½

Mambrino Medium, b s, 1883, by Happy Medium—Kate Keene, by Mambrino Champion 2:28½

Mambrino Patchen (Flack's), blk s, 188—, by Mambrino Tuckahoe ... 2:30

Mambrino Payne, b s, 1884, by King Mambrino — Katy B., by John F. Payne 2:30

Mambrino Prince, br s, 1885, by Jefferson Prince—Mambrino Lizzie, by Harris' Mambrino Chief Jr.... 2:22

Mambrino Queen, ch m, 1889, by Elyria—Schaible Girl, by Bobby.... 2:13¼

Mambrino Queen, b m, 1884, by Nobby—Beauty, by Sim's Prophet 2:26¼

Mambrino Sotham, blk s, 1874, by Mambrino Gift, dam by Young Black Hawk.... 2:26¾

Mambrino Sparkle, b m, 1878 by Fisk's Mambrino Chief Jr. — Kate Sparkle, by Sparkle (dead).... 2:17

Mambrino Star (Leggatt's), b s, 1862, by Mambrino Chief—Lady Fairfield, by Red Buck (dead).... 2:28½

Mambrino Startle, blk s, 1884, by Mambrino Startle—Maggie, by Black Flying Cloud 2:26¼

Mambrino Swift, ch m, 1890, by Elyria—Schaible Girl, by Bobby.... 2:26¼

Mambrino Swigert, blk s, 1876, by Swigert—Jenny Hamilton, by Lakeland Abdallah 2:30

Mambrino Thorn, br s, 1885, by Gen Washington—Cuba, by Mambrino Pilot 2:25½

Mambrino Wilkes, gr s, 1875, by George Wilkes — Hattie Fitch, by Williams' Mambrino 2:28¾

Mambritonian, b s, 1883, by Belmont—Sonnet, by Bourbon Chief 2:20½

Mamet, b s, 188—.... 2:27½

Mamie, b m, 1885, by Mercury—Mambrino Rose, by Mambrino Joker 2:28¼

Mamie, b m, 1878, by Blue Bull—Silverella 2:21¼

Mamie A., b m, 1884, by Landmark, dam by Clear Grit.... 2:25

Mamie Allen, b m, 188—, by Wilkerson 2:30

Mamie C., gr m, 1886, by Backus—Flora, by Bacon's Ethan Allen 2:28¼

Mamie Case, b m 1886, by Jalisco—Bird, by Fetter Horse 2:28

Mamie Comet, ch m, 1880, by Nutwood—Black Betty by Sportsman.. 2:23¼

Mamie D., b m, 1887, by Woful—Belle, by Oysterman 2:26¼

Mamie Griffin, b m, 188—, by Reavis' Blackbird 2:20¾

Mamie Haywood, b m, 188—, by Marquette 2:29½

Mamie J., ch m, 188—, by Ben Wright 2:28½

Mamie M., br m, 1877, by Crittenden—Lucy Marshall, by Clark's Daniel Boone 2:22½

Mamie Phillips, ch m, 1885, by Hambletonian Downing—Mattie, by Redwood 2:28

Mamie Strike, blk m, 188—, by Strike 2:26¼

Mamie Tyler, b m, 1884, by Squire Talmage—Belle Maxwell, by Clark's Mohawk Jr.... 2:27¼

Mamie W., b m, 1882, by Pickpocket—Hattie 2:27½

Mamie W., ch m, 188— by Hannis . 2:30

Mamie Woods, ro m, 1884, by Wood's Hambletonian—Mary Ann, by Magnolia.... 2:29

Manawa, br s, 1888, by Mambrino Yorick—Adele Tyler, by Chester 2:20

Manchester C., b s, 1887, by Madison Smith—Toney, by Hamdallah 2:28¼

Mandame, ch m 1884, by Mambrino King — Sally Griffin, by Crosby's son of Field's Royal George.... 2:29¼

Mandolin ch g, 188— 2:24¼

Manille, ch m, 1887, by Whips—McCa, by Almont 2:29½

Manipulator, b s, 1886 by Nutwood—Gladys, by Hetzel's Hambletonian 2:29¼

Manning, b s, 188— by Elial G. ... 2:24½

Manning (Col. Bradshaw), b g 1883 by Messenger Clay—Jewell, by Gill's Vermont 2:18¼

Manon, b m 1877, by Nutwood—Addie, by Hasbrouck's Hambletonian Chief.... 2:21

Mansfield, ch s, 1876 by Messenger Duroc — Green Mountain Maid, by Harry Clay 2:26

Manville, b s 1886 by Meander—Norma by Scutari 2:25

Manzanita, b m 1882, by Electioneer—Mayflower, by St Clair 2:16

Marsy, b m, 185—, by George M. Patchen, dam by Saladin (dead) .. 2:28

Mary, b m, 1890, by MacCullummore, dam by Aladdin 2:20¼

Mary, b m, 1888, by St. Just—Dolly, by Hamlet 2:24¼

Mary A., b m, 1886, by Altamont—Daisy A., by Kisbar 2:30

Mary Anderson, b m, 188—, by Hamlin's Almont Jr.—Elmo, by Wood's Hambletonian 2:27¼

Mary Anderson, ch m,1884, by Lightwood—Molly Hal, by Moore's Tom Hal 2:26

Mary Ann, b m, 1879, by Bay State—Grand Duchess, by Handley's Hiatoga 2:28½

Mary A. Whitney, b m, 1867, by Volunteer—Peggy Slender (dead) 2:28

Mary B., br m, 1878, by Alcalde—Mary Weaver, by Black Hawk Vermont 2:29

Mary B., b m, 188—, ... 2:29½

Mary Best, ch m, 1890, by Guy Wilkes—Montrose, by Sultan 2:12¼

Mary Brown, b m, 1885, by Egbert—Annie Brown, by Ashland Chief .. 2:29½

Mary C., br m, 1884, by Wagner Bashaw—Puss Cunningham, by Green's Bashaw 2:30

Mary C., br m, 1880, by Wilson Horse—Maggie Day 2:24½

Mary Caldwell, b m, 1888, by Wilkes Boy—Lulu Patchen, by Tom Patchen 2:20

Mary Cecil, b m, 1884, by Thomas K.—Fanny, by Thornton's Abdallah .. 2:22½

Mary Crit, blk m, 188—, by Rohmer (pacing record 2:19) 2:23¾

Mary Davis, b m, 186—, by Werner's Rattler—Mary Rotan 2:26¼

Mary Ferguson, b m, 1888, by Granby 2:29½

Mary Hanford, b m, 1887, by Chosroes—Mary Long, by Bashaw 2:28¾

Mary G., b m, 188—, by Almonarch, dam by Stephen A. Douglas 2:27¼

Mary Karr, br m, 1884, by Gov. Sprague—Maddie Karr, by Administrator 2.24

Mary Kent, br m, 1881, by Kent—Burbank Mare, by Gen. Grant.... 2:28½

Mary Lee, blk m, 1887, by George O.—Roxie Belle, by Squire Talmage (dead) 2:29½

Mary Lou, ch m, 1885, by Tom Benton—Brown Jenny, by McCracken's David Hill Jr. 2:17

Mary Maderia, ch m 1889, by Strathroy—Mattie Lake, by Pacing Abdallah 2:27¼

Mary Magdalene, ch m, 1890, by Du Bois' Superior — Magdalene, by Magnet 2:27¾

Mary Marshall, b m, 1885, by Billy Wilkes—Bennie Sydner, by Mambrino Abdallah 2:12¾

Mary Mc, b m, 188—, by Lumps, dam by Lexington Chief 2:18½

Mary O., ch m, 1885, by Brown Jug—Betsey, by Budd Doble 2:29¼

Mary Powell, blk m, 1880, by De Witt Clay, dam by Young Cardinal 2:22¾

Mary R., ch m, 1885, by McCurdy's Hambletonian—Maggie 2:24½

Mary Russell, gr m, 1871, by Joe Brown—Kate Odell, by Burt's Young Bellfounder 2:23½

Mary S., br m, 1882, by Barney Wilkes—Gin Burner, by Frank Allen 2:28

Mary S., ch m, 1881, by Alcantara—Lady Carr, by American Clay ... 2:28

Mary Spillman, b m, 1883, by Rolling Wave 2:30

Mary Sprague, br m, 1879, by Gov. Sprague—Little Ellen, by Goldsmith's Abdallah 2 21

Mary W., br m, 1883, by Gov. Sprague—Dora Dunton, by Smuggler 2:29¾

Mary Wilkes, b m, 1885 by Tennessee Wilkes—Modjeska, by Enfield 2:19

Mascot, ch m, 1884, by Triceps—Kit 2:24¼

Mascot, b s, 1887, by Stamboul—Minnehaha, by Steven's Bald Chief (dead) 2:25¾

Mascot Bob, ro g, 1882, by Col. Howe—Pet, by Pacing Joe 2:29¼

Mason, b s, 1885, by Greenbacks—Frazel, by Trophy 2:27½

Mason Nutwood, b s, 1891, by Ira Nutwood 2:22

Massasoit, ch s, 1885, by Phallamont—Theresa Lambert, by Daniel Lambert 2:25¾

Master, b s, 1886 by Masterlode—Maggie Hubbard, by Magna Charta (dead) 2:27½

Master Dudley, br s, 1884, by Mambrino Dudley—Octavio, by Rysdyk's Hambletonian 2:20¼

Master Medium, b s, 1885, by Happy Medium—Venture, by Volunteer ... 2:29½

Matanzas, b m, 1885, by Lord Russell—Malmaison, by Alexander's Abdallah 2:27½

Matchless, b g, 187—, by Nil Desperadum—Mattie Lyle, by Young Morrill 2 24¾

Matchless, br s, 1886, by Dauntless—Jenny, by Iowa 2.25½

Matchwood, b s, 1887, by Woodbrino Smuggle, by Hampton 2:27

Matilda, b m, 1884, by Nutwood—Luallaba, by Berkley's Edwin Forrest 2:30

Mathewson Sprague, b s, 1888, by Sprague—Daisy May, by John Bright 2:29¼

Matrimony, b m, 1889 by Aberdeen—Happy Choice, by Happy Medium 2:23¾

Matt, b m, 1877, by Louis Napoleon—Magg .... 2·30

Matt Fisher, b g, 1876, by Ripon Boy—Daisy, by North Star 2:29¼

Matthew Smith, b g, 186—, pedigree not traced (dead) 2;26½

Matthew W., gr g, 1887, by Neighbor Ups—Lady Lom 2:30

Mattie, b m, 1867, by Rysdyk's Hambletonian—Lucy Almack, by Young Engineer 2:22½

Mattie B., b m, 188—, by Louis Napoleon 2:28¼

Mattie B., b m, 1877, by Phil Sheridan Jr.—Flint, by McIntyre Horse 2:27¾

Mattie B., b m, 187—, pedigree not traced 2:25¼

Mattie Bassett, b m, 188—, by Hermes—Lida Brigand, by Brigand 2:26½

Mattie C., gr m, 1883, by American Ethan—Jessie, by Highland Grey.. 2:25¾

Mattie C., ch m, 1881, by Seneca Chief—Bay Dolly, by Ingersoll's Young Trustee 2.28¼

Mattie D., ch m 1880, by Bay Middleton—Kit, by Hero Jr 2.25¾

Mattie G., b m, 188—, by Pan 2:22¼
Mattie Graham, b m, 1874, by Harold —Vic, by Mambrino Chief 2:21½
Mattie H., b m, 1886, by Abdallah Mambrino—Ella Hopkins, by Octoroon 2:11¼
Mattie H., gr m, 1874, by Blue Bull —Nelly Miller, by Coulter's Davy Crocket 2.27½
Mattie Hunter, b m, 1884, by Strideaway Jr.—Clara Benton, by Robinson's Benton 2:21¼
Mattie Hunter, b m, 1877, by Glendale—Flora, b y Jim Crow (dead) . 2:30
Mattie K., b m, 187—, by Hinsdale Horse, dam by Harris' Mambrino Chief Jr. 2:24¼
Mattie Lyle, br m, 186—, by Young Morrill 2:28
Mattie Marco, b m, 1885, by Monaco —Mattie Hunter, by Prince Pulaski 2:25
Mattie Merrill, b m, 188—, by Wilkes, dam by Mayhew 2:27¼
Mattie Mosier, b m, 1890, by Wilkeswood 2:27¼
Mattie P, b m, 1884, by Jackson Temple, dam by Tom Hyer 2:26¼
Mattie Price, br m, 1873, by Woodford Mambrino—Miss Taylor, by Aker's Idol 2:29¼
Mattie Scott, blk m, 188—, by Estill Eric 2:25
Mattie Solomon, blk m, 1885, by Director—Martha Solomon, by Reavis' Blackbird 2:30
Mattie S. Wilkes, ch m, by Simmons —Celeste, by Alcyone 2:26½
Mattie Swope, ro m, 1884, by Young Jim—Roan Fanny, by Mambrino King 2:30
Mattie Wilkes, br m, 1881, by Lyle Wilkes—Molly Lumber, by Lumber 2:30
Mattie Wilkes, b m, 1885, by Barney Wilkes—Maggie Underwood, by Titus 2:24¾
Matt Kirkwood, b g, 1870, by Kirkwood—Maggie Davis 2:29¼
Maud, b m, 1882, by Clay Cadmus—Jenny Lynn 2.29½
Maud, b m, 1866, by Rysdyk's Hambletonian—Starlight, by Seely's American Star .... 2·29¾
Maud, b m, 1881, by Young Napoleon —Minnie Rifel, by Arbuckle's Rattler 2:18½
Maud, b m, 188—, by C. V. B. 2:29¼
Maud, br m, 1883, by Othello—Betsy 2:29½
Maud, ch m, 1882, by Aurora—Lady Sherman, by Milliman's Bellfounder 2:27
Maud, blk m, 1884, by McDonald Chief—Puss, by Gen Taylor 2:29¾
Maud, ch m, 188—, by Hiram 2:30
Maud, ch m, 188—, by Hotspur Jr.... 2:29¼
Maud, ch m, 1882, by Abdallah Duroc —Nancy 2:29¼
Maud, b m, 188— by George Sprague 2 28¼
Maud A., b m, 188—, by Embassador, dam by Billy Green (pacing record 2·28½) 2:29¼
Maud A., b m, 1877, by Rysdyk—Jessie, by Roebuck 2:26¼
Maud A., br m, 1886, by Pyramid—Judith B., by Lord Almont 2:19½
Maud A., 188—, ... 2:28¼
Maud Almeda, gr m, 188— by Gaviota 2:24
Maud Archibald, br m, 1881, by Glenwood 2.27¼
Maud B., ch m, 188—, by Dow S. 2:28½
Maud B., ch m, 1884, by Charley B.—Doll 2.23¼
Maud B., b m, 188—, by Barkis....... 2:29¼
Maud Banks, ch m, 188—, by Dictator Chief—Empress, by Sterling 2:27½
Maud C., blk m, 1889, by Binderton—Nita, by Atlantic........................ 2:15¾
Maud C., ch m, 1886, by California Nutwood—Zola, by Steinway 2:15
Maud C., b m, 1882, by Sir Charles—Bessie, by Southerner.... .... 2:27½
Maud C., b m, 1883, by Alexander Button—Gipsy, by Woodward's Don. 2:28½
Maud C., b m, 188—, by Landmark... 2:28¼
Maud Clay, gr m, 1889, by Fire Clay —Lou, by Pilot Duroc.............. 2 24
Maud Cook, b m, 187—, by Iron Duke. 2 30
Maud Cooper, rn.m, 188—........... 2.28¼
Maud D., b m, 1881, by Burns, dam by Tippoo Saib........................ 2:20½
Maud D., ch m, 188—, by Clarion Chief—Nelly, by States Rattler.... 2:29¼
Maud D. N., b m, 1889, by Hamdallah—Esther, by Silas Wright....... 2 25
Maud E., b m, 1885, by Clifford...... 2:22¼
Maudee, b m, 1887, by Anteeo—Maud, by Nutwood 2:24¼
Maud F., b m, 1882, by Troy—Maud Carlin, by Hugo........................ 2.25¼
Maud F., b m, 1882, by Oneida Chief —Babe 2:30
Maud Fowler, b m, 1888, by Anteeo—Eveline, by Nutwood 2.21¾
Maud G, b m, 188—, by Woodman, dam by Atlantic........................ 2:28¼
Maud Greenwood, br m, 188—, by Gen Knox 2:26¼
Maud H., b m, 188—, by Jay Bird.... 2:26
Maud H, br m, 1883, by Duroc Volunteer—Lady Hamilton 2:29¼
Maud H., ch m, 1883, by Carr's Mambrino—Flora, by Dan Voorhees...... 2 24
Maud H., ch m, 188—, by Landmark, dam not traced........................ 2:29¼
Maud Halbert, b m, 188—, by Halbert 2:30
Maud Haywood, b m, 1890, by Gambetta Wilkes, dam by Almont....... 2:24¼
Maud Howe, ch m, 1883, by Bashaw Hambletonian—Kate P.... .... 2:27¼
Maudie Belle, b m, 1882, by Wood's Hambletonian—Helen V., by Enfield. 2.29¼
Maud J., b m, 1886, by Winfield Scott. 2:25¼
Maud J........................ 2:25¼
Maud Knox, ch m, 1882, by Winthrop Knox 2:27
Maud L., b m, 188—, by Seaside...... 2 29¾
Maud L., br m, 1880, by Grey Dan, dam by a son of Hiram Drew...... 2:30
Maudlen b m, 1883, by Harold—Nutula, by Belmont........................ 2:25¾
Maud Lightfoot, ch m, 188—, by Prince Almont........................ 2 25½
Maud M., ro m, 1884, by Crazy Nick Jr.—Dolly Elder, by Young Prince Albert 2:28
Maud M., b m, 188—, by Abdallah Hambletonian 2:20¼
Maud M., br m, 1888, by Janus—Frolic, by Dick........................ 2:28
Maud M., b m, 1881, by Little Hamilton 2:28¼
Maud M........................ 2:25
Maud M., br m, 187—, pedigree not traced 2:30
Maud M, br m, 188—, by Anteeo.... 2 20¼
Maud M., ch m, 188—, by Gift Jr..... 2·30
Maud Mace, br m, 1885, by Dan Mace —Maud, by Quaker General........ 2 27¼
Maud Macey, ch m, 1871, by Joe

Hooker—Jenny Martin, by Star Denmark 2:27¾
Maud Medium, br m, 188—, by Chief Medium 2:28
Maud Medium, b m, 188—.... 2:26¼
Maud Merrill, blk m, 1888, by Antevolo—Belle A., by Tilton Almont.. 2:18
Maud Messenger, b m, 1877, by Messenger Chief—Eliza Jane, by Gentle Breeze.... 2.16¼
Maud Muller, gr m, 1873, by Coupon—Chesley, by John Robinson.... 2:29¾
Maud Muller, ch m, 1882, by Lockerbie — Bessie Turner, by Kentucky Traveler 2:20¼
Maud P., b m, 1891, by Idaho Patchen 2:26½
Maud N., br m, 188—, by Col. Crockett.... 2:26¼
Maud Patchen, b m, 1887, by Idaho Patchen—Maud W. W. W., by Gen. Reno.... 2:19¼
Maud R., ro m, 1879, by Cunard..... 2:27
Maud S., br m, 188—, by Capt. Jinks. 2:30
Maud S., ch m, 1874, by Harold—Miss Russell, by Pilot Jr.... 2:08¾
Maud Singleton, b m, 1885, by Singleton—Lettie, by Wayland Forrest .. 2.28½
Maud S. M., b m, 1887, by Pedo—Fanny M., by Louder's Printer..... 2.22
Maud Stillson, ch m, 1880, by Stillson.... 2:29¼
Maud T., b m, 1877, by Hamlin's Almont Jr.—Fanny Fern, by Sovereign Jr 2:19¼
Maud V., ch m, 1887, by Nutmeg—Maggie W., by Richmond Boy...... 2:29¾
Maud W., ch m, 1891, by Epicure, dam by Hotspur Jr.... 2:26¼
Maud White, ch m, 1886, by Little Ben—Nelly, by a son of Cub...... 2.22
Maud Wright, b m, 1889, by Silas Wright — Fanny Newton, by Allie Gaines.... 2:15¼
Maud W. W. W., blk m, 1875, by Gen. Reno, dam by Bidwell's Rattler... 2:23¼
Maud Y., b m, 1889, by Dexter Prince—Nelly Nelson, by John Nelson..... 2:29½
Maud Z., rn m, 188—.... 2:29¾
Maumejan, b g, 1885, by Messenger Chief—Edna D., by Dr. Almont ... 2:26½
Maurice S., b g, 188—, by Coupon, dam by Col. Heywood.... 2:23½
Mauston, b s, 1886, by Rysdyk—Helen McGregor, by Robert McGregor.... 2:25¼
Max, b g, 188—, by Black Ben, dam by Don Juan.... 2.24¾
Max, gr g, 1887, by Pilot Medium—Kit Reese, by Billy D.... 2:20½
Max, ch g, 188—, by Young America . 2:28½
Maxey, ch s, 1885, by Ben Franklin—Kitty Cook, by General Sherman... 2.30
Maxie, b s, 188—, by Joe Hooper..... 2:27¾
Maxie B., b s, 188—, by Ashland Wilkes.... 2.28½
Maxie Cobb, b g, 1881, by Donnybrook, dam by Rocket.... 2:25¼
Maxie Cobb, b s, 1875, by Happy Medium—Lady Jenkins, by Black Jack (dead) 2:13¼
Maxie Cobb Jr., b s, 1881, by Maxie Cobb — Wheeler Mare, by Brown Dick 2:28½
Maxie McGregor, blk g, 1886, by Ben McGregor — Jessie Grant, by Gen. Grant.... 2:28¾
Max O'Rell, b g, 1884, by Altitude—Jule, by Slasher.... 2:24½
Max T., blk g, 1891, by Piloton, dam by Neptune.... 2:29½
Maxwell, gr s, 1882, by William Tell 2:28¼
May, ch m, 1873, by Jordan's Young Moscow — Belle Windflower, by Windflower 2.25
May B., blk m, 188—, by Altoona, dam by Wapsie.... 2:30
May B., br m, 188—, by Sir Knight... 2:30
May Be, b m, 1883, by Ben Franklin—Pedunk, by Vermont Volunteer..... 2.24
May Bee, br m, 1889, by Happy Russell—Beeswing, by Kent.... 2.25
May Belle, b m, 1892, by Phallamont—Daisy Maid, by Hickory 2:29½
May Bird, blk m, 1868, by George Wilkes, dam by John C. Fremont.. 2.21
May Bird, b m, 1867, by Jimmie—Kate Smith, by Cady's Champion.... 2.21¼
May Bird, b m, 1877, by Blue Bull—Finley, by Bourbon Chief.... 2:23
May Bird, b m, 1886, by Jay Bird—Maud B., by Seneca Chief.... 2.21½
May Boy, b s, 1878, by Whipple's Hambletonian — Harvest Queen, by Rysdyk's Hambletonian 2:23¾
May Breaker, ch m, 1889, by Nutbreaker—May H., by Chicago Volunteer.... 2:17½
May Brino, ch m, 1887, by Dall Brino—Mayflower 2:26½
May Clark, ch m, 1873, pedigree not traced.... 2.29¾
May Conkling, b m, 1885, by Roscoe Conkling — Sally Mills, by Moore's Orange Chief.... 2:28
May Day, br m, 1877, by Dread—Kitty Whalen, by Fenian Chief 2:23¾
May Day, b m, 1870, by Ballard's Cassius M. Clay Jr.—Kate, by Hiram Drew 2:30
May Day, b m, 1890, by Abdallah Mambrino—Mignon, by Messenger Chief 2:24¼
May Day, b m, 1888, by Dominion—Idol Belle, by Aker's Idol.... 2:27
May Douglass, gr m, 1885, by Fred Douglass — Badger Girl, by Black Flying Cloud.... 2.15½
May Eddy, b m, 1887, by Jerome Eddy—Flora Hebel, by Young Dick Taylor (pacing record 2:22½) (dead).... 2:25½
May F., b m, 188—, by Gen. Stanton, dam by Young Cadmus.... 2.30
May F., gr m, 187—, by Adirondack 2:30
Mayflower, b m, 187—, by Mambrino Pilot 2:27¼
Mayflower, br m, 1881, by Walkill—Mayflower, by Victor Bismarck..... 2:21¼
Mayflower, b m, 1891, by Young Jim, dam by Robt McGregor.... 2:29¼
Mayflower, b m, 1889, by Israel—Lucy, by All Right.... 2.28
May Gould, b m, 1874, by Jay Gould—Columbia, by Draco 2:24¼
May H., ch m, 1876, by Chicago Volunteer, dam by Plow Boy.... 2:26¼
Mayhill, br m, 1887, by Edge Hill—Maywood, by Blackwood (pacing 2:17¼).... 2:19
May Homer, b m, 1889, by Homer—Hannie, by Jerome Eddy.... 2:18¾
May Howard, gr m, 1865, by Capt. Hanford—McCormick Mare.... 2:24
May King, b s, 1886, by Electioneer—May Queen, by Alexander's Norman 2:20
May McGregor, ch m, 188—, by Bonnie McGregor 2:30
May Mitchel, gr m, 1884, by Pasacas—Maid of the Mist, by Conklin's American Star 2:22¼

Claus—Easter Medium, by Happy Medium ... 2:27
Merry Thought, b m, 1879, by Happy Medium—Four Lines, by Blackwood ... 2 22¼
Mertis Wilkes, ch m, 1888, by Ashland Wilkes—Daisy ... 2:29¼
Mertzy, b m, 1891, by C. F. Clay, dam by Red Wilkes ... 2:24¼
Merula, b s, 1887, by Frank Noble—Manila, by Joe Gavin ... 2.29¾
Merva K., gr m, 1880, by Mambrino Boy—Grey Fan, by Grey Hawk Jr. 2.27½
Merzalia, b m, 188—, by W. H. Maxwell—Lady Annie, by Cazenovia Star ... 2.29¼
Mesquite, br m, 1892, by Lancelot—Malvasia, by Lord Russell ... 2.29½
Messenger Knox, gr s, 1866, by Gen. Knox, dam by Prince ... 2:30
Messenger Wilkes, b s, 1883, by Red Wilkes—Rena C., by Messenger Chief ... 2 23
Metal, b m, 1886, by Referee—Silverfoil, by Jackson's Flying Cloud ... 2:27¼
Metamora, b s, 1886, by Jerome Eddy—Madeleine, by Rysdyk's Hambletonian ... 2:19¾
Meteor, blk s, 188—, by Commodore Belmont ... 2·28½
Meteora, ch m, 1888, by Tennessee Wilkes—Aline, by Allie West ... 2:20½
Metropolis, br g, 188—, pedigree not traced (dead) ... 2:30
Metzger, gr g, 1889, by Moody, dam by Peacock ... 2:21
Metta, b m, ... 2:24¼
Miami Chief, b s, 1885 by Squire Talmage—Lena, by Clay Cadmus (Joe Hooker) ... 2 28
Michael, b g, 1883, by Herod—Queen West, by Ware Colt ... 2:28½
Michael O'Harra, b g, 188—, pedigree not traced ... 2:25½
Michael, b g, 188—, by Lexington Chief Jr. ... 2.29¼
Michigan Jim, br s, 1888, by Dictator Almont—Jess, by Hambletonian George ... 2 29¼
Michigan Prince, blk s, 1884, by Young Wilkes—Fanny Essler, by Nighthawk ... 2·26¾
Middlesex, ch g, 1872, by Seneca Chief—Nelly Litchfield, by Greyhound ... 2:24
Middletown Jr., ch s, 1875, by Middletown—Nelly Warner, by Andrew Jackson ... 2:27¼
Middleway, b g, 1884, by Bay Middleton—Ida Mills, by Fisk's Mambrino Chief Jr. (dead) ... 2:22¼
Midge, b m, 187—, by Wilkie Collins—May Thorne ... 2 27¾
Midget Wilkes, b m, 188—, by Wilkes 2.29¾
Midnight, blk s, 188—, by Adrian Wilkes ... 2 23¼
Midnight, blk g, 1872, by Peacemaker, dam by Drew Horse ... 2:18¼
Midnight Chimes, b m, 1889, by Chimes—Jennie Jackson, by Mambrino King (dead) ... 2·16¼
Midvale Prince, b s, 1885, by Red Wilkes—Belle Brino, by Hambrino 2 25
Midway, b m, 1886, by Middlesex ... 2:29¾
Mignon, b m, 1873, by Sentinel—Sally Warfield, by Toronto ... 2·27¼
Mikado, b g, 1881, by Highland Chief—Nelly Grey ... 2:20¾
Mikagan, b s, 1884, by Onward—Aldine, by Woodford Mambrino ... 2 19¾
Mike, br g, 1877, by Beecher—Kate Bradley, by Clifton Pilot ... 2·28
Mike Bowerman, b g, 188—, by Wilton—Ella, by Cripple ... 2 29¼
Mike Jefferson, ch g, 1868, by Thomas Jefferson—Mizema ... 2·29½
Mike Knight, b s, 1887, by Sir Knight—Polly, by Morgan Star ... 2 28¼
Mike Scott, gr s, 188—, by Winfield Scott ... 2·23¼
Mike Wilkes, b g, 1875, by George Wilkes—Nelly B., by Harry B. Patchen (pacing record 2·15¾ dead) 2 26½
Mila C., ch m, 1866, by Blue Bull—Cutaway ... 2:26½
Mild Cloud, ch s, 1888, by Black Cloud, dam by Hambletonian Hunter ... 2.28
Mildred, ch m, 1888, by Egotist—Ray, by Pilot Mambrino ... 2:29¾
Milkmaid, b m, 1880, by Forbes—Miss Soules, by King's Champion ... 2:22½
Milkshake, sp g, 1885, by Strathmore—Birthmark by Kentucky Prince.. 2:28
Millard, ro g, 1884, by Gen. Benton—Daisy Miller, by Electioneer ... 2·23
Mill Boy, b g, 187—, by Jay Gould—Dolsey, by Shaffer Pony ... 2:26
Miller's Damsel, ch m, 184—, by Jackson, dam by Little Duroc (dead) ... 2:28¼
Mill Girl, br m, 1878, by Jay Gould—Dolsey, by Shaffer Pony ... 2 22¼
Millie Wilkes, br m, 1887 by Guy Wilkes—Rosetta, by The Moor ... 2·26
Millionaire, b s, 1887, by Happy Medium—Young Winnie, by Woodford Mambrino ... 2.24½
Mill Lady, b m, 1891, by Count Wilkes—Mill Girl, by Jay Gould (pacing record 2.30) ... 2.26¼
Milo, b s, 1874, by Milwaukee—Minnie B., by Bay Mambrino ... 2 21
Milton, b s, 1879, by Smuggler—Lizzie, by imp. The Knight of St. George 2 30
Milton, b g, 1884 by Hickory Jr.—Kitty Glyde, by Abdallah Hambletonian ... 2·16
Milton Blackwood, blk g, 1879, by Blackwood—Irene, by Enchanter ... 2:26¼
Milton Medium, b s, 1871, by Happy Medium—Fan, by Sackett's Hambletonian ... 2.25½
Mimic, b s 1884, by Messenger Chief—Rose Chief, by Brown Chief ... 2:21
Miner, b s, 1890, by Nutwood—Velvet, by Volunteer ... 2:19¾
Minerva, gr m, 1884, by Pilot Medium—Silky Lambert, by Daniel Lambert 2 18
Minet, b m, 1885, by Electioneer—Minx, by Don Victor ... 2.27½
Mink, blk s 1877, by Michie—Abbie, by Onderdonk ... 2 29¼
Mink, blk m, 188—, by Alcantara—Souvenir, by Administrator ... 2:22¼
Mink Wilkes, blk s, 1886, by Young Wilkes—Doll Thayer, by North Hawk Jr ... 2·28½
Minneola, ch s, 1883, by Young Jim—Jessica by Hamlet ... 2:20½
Minnesota, b m, 1878, by Portion—Lorena, by Mambrino Patchen... 2.27¼
Minnie, br m, 1883, by Sweep—Lady Julian, by Toronto Chief... 2.29½
Minnie A., b m, 1884, by Hamdallah—Topsey, by DeGraff's Alexander... 2 29¼
Minnie B., br m, 1889, by Billy Thorn-

E. BITHER, Pittsfield, Mass.

Bither placed the world's record for trotters at 2:10 with Jay-Eye-See,
the world's record for stallions at 2:13¾ with Phallas,
and at 2:07¾ with Kremlin.

FRED KEYES, RANDALL, O.
Keyes was for a number of years identified with the Elyria
family. He is now at the Forest City Farm and
was out last year with Hyannis 2:11¼.

hill—Laura R, by Electioneer...... 2:29¾
Minnie B., ch m, 1881, by Charley B. —Belle, by Seneca Chief........... 2:20¼
Minnie B., b m, 1887, by John Wilkes. 2:30
Minnie Brown, b m, 1889, by Pilot Medium—Sunbeam, by Grand Sentinel.... .... 2:29¼
Minnie C., b m, 1877, by Jack Sheppard—Lady Cummings, by Taggart's Abdallah 2:25¼
Minnie Clay, b m, 1886, by King Ashland—Beck, by McDowning.......... 2:27½
Minnie D., b m, 1875, by Nonpareil—Black Kit..... .... 2:23½
Minnie Dale, b m, 1883, by Hero of Thorndale—Maggie Fred, by Raven. 2:29½
Minnie G., rn m, 1888, by Jay Bird—Betsey Higgins, by Strathmore..... 2:19¼
Minnie Grey, gr m, 1881, by Harry Morgan—Bloss, by Jacques Cartier.. 2:30
Minnie Keene, gr m, 1881, by Young Jim—Miss Weeks, by Joe Downing.. 2:21¾
Minnie L., ch m, 1884, by Emery Fearnaught—Molly Lunt, by Victor. 2:20¼
Minnie L., gr m, 188—............. 2:27
Minnie Lee, b m, 188—, breeding not traced....... .... 2:29¾
Minnie May, b m, 188—, by Mark Twain........ .... 2.29¾
Minnie Maxfield, b m, 1865, by Charley...... .... 2.28¼
Minnie Moak, b m, 1885, by Mohawk Hambletonian — Flora, by Baskins Horse...... .... 2:28½
Minnie Monroe, b m, 1888, by Mark Monroe—Minnie, by Whirlwind Chief 2 25¼
Minnie Moore, b m, 188—, by Toronto Chief Jr., dam by Clarion Chief.... 2:27¼
Minnie Moulton, blk m, 1875, by Lambert Chief—Jenny, by Drew Horse.. 2:27¼
Minnie O., b m, 1884, by Young Volunteer 2:21¼
Minnie P., b m, 188—, by Port Leonard........ .... 2:19¼
Minnie R., b m, 1872, by John C. Breckinridge (pacing record 2:16½).. 2.19
Minnie R., dn m, 188—, by Rescue (pacing record 2:20¼).... .... 2:25
Minnie Shaffer, b m, 188—, by Hambletonian Bashaw.... .... 2:30
Minnie's Almont, br s, 188—, by Almont Sentinel.... .... 2:28¼
Minnie Warren, ch m, 1875, by Night Hawk...... .... 2·27¼
Minnie Whitestone, blk m, 1885, by Little Rock—Nancy.... .... 2:24¼
Minnie Wilkes, b m, 188—, by Invader....... .... 2:30
Minnie Wilkes, b m, 1886, by King Wilkes—Ida, by Little Ben........ 2:17
Minnola, b m, 1890, by Earl—Lady Wedgewood, by Wedgewood.... ... 2·24¼
Minot, b g, 1880, by Rochester—Estelle Eastin, by Mambrino Patchen. 2·26¼
Minting, b s, 1891, by Ellerslie Wilkes, dam by Aberdeen........... 2:29¼
Minnetto, br s, 1889, by Epaulet, dam by Administrator.... .... 2 27¼
Mira, b m, 1883, by Roy Executor—Adeline, by Antar.... .... 2·28¼
Minta Linder, blk m, 1890, by Jersey Wilkes...... .. .. 2.22¾
Mintur Wilkes 2:30
Mira Startle, b m, 1885, by Mambrino Startle—Fleetwood, by Lyle Wilkes. 2:21¼
Mischief, b m, 1885, by Mambrino Wilkes—Kitty Coram, by Col Cross. 2:17¾
Mischief, br m, 1889, by Brown Jug —Flora, by Ford's Belmont 2:22¼
Misdeal, b s, 1888, by Midas—Mishap, by Cashman.... .... 2:20½
Misfortune, gr m, 187—, by Chancellor Black Hawk.................. 2:21½
Miss Albert, b m, 1889, by Albert W. —Young Woodbine, by Electioneer.. 2·25¼
Miss Alice, b m, 1884, by Alcantara—Thorndale Maid, by Thorndale..... 2:13½
Miss Carroll, b m, 1890, by Santa Claus, dam by Mambrino Pilot..... 2.23¾
Miss Cawley, br m, 1879, by Jack Lambert — Madam Cawley, by Broughton Horse.... .... 2:23½
Miss Cecil, b m, 1890, by Gambetta Wilkes—Jeannie C., by Nutwood... 2·21½
Miss Clay, g m, 1890, by Clay....... 2·29¾
Miss Cleveland, b m, 1887, by Aytoun —Ole Mammy.... .... 2·17¼
Miss Edith, b m, 1888, by Midas—Maggie V., by Revenue Jr.. .... 2:19
Miss Egbert, b m, 1885, by Egbert—Miss Patchen, by Mambrino Patchen 2·29¾
Miss Fanny Jackson, b m, 1880, by Bay Lambert — Fanny Jackson, by Stonewall Jackson.... .... 2:30
Miss Foxie, b m, 1887, by Inca—Lady Foxie, by Daniel Lambert.......... 2·22
Miss Fullerton, b m, 188—, by Young Fullerton.... .... 2:19¾
Miss Grace, b m, 1888, by Ambassador—Grace Darling, by Grand Sentinel...... .... 2·20¾
Miss Grant, br m, 1891, by Round's Sprague...... .... 2:27¼
Miss Harper, b m, 188—, by Harper.. 2:29¾
Miss Hoke, b m, 1888, by Osrick—Kate Hoke, by Ned Patchen . .... 2·29¾
Miss Hunter, br m, 188—, by Intrigue —Ida, by Dutchman 2:21¼
Miss Huon, b m, 1886, by Huon—Dolly Dutton, by McClellan......... 2:24¼
Miss Ida, b m, 1887, by Linkwood Chief—Sunbeam, by Backman's Idol 2:27¼
Miss Kent, b m, 1887, by Alcamont —Rowena, by Black Hawk Traveler. 2:25
Miss Kate, b m, 1892, by Direct—Fannie K., by Redwood 2:24¼
Miss Kirkman, b m, 1888, by Wedgewood—Queenie, by Enfield Jr 2:17
Miss Ledo, br m, 1885, by Ledo—Nell, by Black Sultan...... .... 2:29
Miss Legacy, b m, 1872, by Legacy—Mary A., by Dusty Miller......... 2:24½
Miss Leland, b m, 1879, by Leland—Rosema, by Young America.. ..... 2·25¼
Miss Lida, b m, 1889, by King Clay—Molly C., by Contractor.... ..... 2:10¾
Miss McCurdy, b m, 1884, by McCurdy's Hambletonian—Dot, by Blackwood Jr....... .... 2:28¾
Miss McGregor, b m, 1889, by Robert McGregor — Morgan Belle, by Administrator 2:19¼
Miss McLain, b m, 1889 by Gregor McGregor — Hattie Woodruff, by Hiram Woodruff.... .... 2:28½
Miss Majolica, b m, 1884, by Startle—Jessie Kirk, by Clark Chief . ..... 2·24½
Miss Maud............... .... 2·28
Miss May, b m, 1887 by Hidalgo—Edith Beloit, by Beloit.. .... 2.27¼
Miss Miller b m, 187—, by Monogram—Berkshire Girl ..... 2·29¼
Miss Monroe, b m, 1885, by Monroe Chief—Aloha, by A. W. Richmond. 2·27½
Miss Murray, gr m, 1878, by Doty's Union—Grey Kate, by Lent's Messenger 2:28½
Miss Naude, b m, 1886, by Electioneer

Nadine, by Wildidle 2:29½
Miss Nelson, b m, 1889, by Norfolk—Lassiter. 2:12¾
Miss Patchen, b m, 1888, by Linkwood Chief—Lady Patchen 2:25
Miss Olive, ch m, 188—, by Mambrino King.......... 2:27½
Miss Pilot, blk m, 188—, by Sealskin Wilkes—Sally J., by Administrator.. 2:30
Miss O'Neil, b m, 188—, by Brignoli W.......... 2:28¾
Miss Q., b m, 1886, by Wilkesonian—Nell, by Abdallah Mambrino (dead). 2:29¾
Miss Rachel (Skylark), blk m, 1890, by Bourbon Wilkes—Lark, by Abdallah Mambrino.......... 2:20
Miss Redmon, b m, 1881, by Bourbon Wilkes — Becky Bird 2d, by Westwood.......... 2:23¾
Miss Simmons, ch m, 1885, by Simmons — Alberta, by Red Norman (dead).......... 2:29¼
Miss Sontag, ch m, 1879, by Victor Mohawk—Sontag Dixie, by Toronto Sontag.......... 2:28
Miss Strathmore, b m, 1888, by Strathmore—Miss Kirksey, by Mambrino Legrand 2:29¾
Miss Superior, gr m, 1890, by James' Superior, dam by Winfield Scott. . 2:23
Miss Thompson, br m, 1885, by Toodles Jr — Primrose, by Hetzel's Hambletonian.......... 2:20½
Miss Van S., ch m, 1887, by Simmons —Lizzie Martin 2:27½
Miss Vida, b m, 188—, by Red Jacket 2:28¾
Miss Wilkes, br m, 1885, by Kaiser—Nonparell, by Morrill Champion.... 2:29½
Miss Wilkes, b m, 1876, by George Wilkes — Gilbert Mare, by Clifton Pilot.......... 2:29
Miss Wilton, br m, 1889, by Wilton—Miss Lane, by Mambrino Patchen... 2:25
Miss Woodford, b m, 1882, by Blackwood Jr.—Lizzie Anderson, by Clark Chief 2:23½
Miss Woodford, b m, 188—, by Boulder.......... 2:27½
Miss Zura Belle, br m, 1891, by St Bel—Zura, by Osman 2:26½
Miss Woolsey, b m, 1889, by Queechy —Dolly Pomeroy, by Highland Gray. 2:22½
Mist, b m, 1879, by King Rene—Snowbird, by Steele's Snowstorm.......... 2:29½
Mista, b m, 1887, by Alcazar—Lady Dey, by California Dexter. 2:29
Mistake, b m, 1883, by Marshal Kleber —Lady Yelser, by Garrard Chief ... 2:29¼
Mistletoe, blk m, 1875, by Mambrino Patchen — Josie Ralley, by Gen. George H. Thomas 2:30
Misty Morning, b m, 1880, by Marksman—Morning Mist, by Aker's Idol 2:21
Mitchell, blk s, 188—.......... 2:28¾
Mite, b m, 1891, by Delmarch—Brightlight 2:27¼
Mizie Douglass, b m, 188—, by Douglass—Lady Hooker, by Ericsson..... 2:23¼
M J Henderson, b g, 1887, by Landmark—Kit, by Lysander.......... 2:20¼
Mocking Bird, ch m, 1884, by Mambrino King—Mabel A., by Toronto Chief Jr.......... 2:16¾
Model, br s, 1880 by Lexington Chief Jr.—Fanny Buck, by Flushing Boy.. 2:30
Modesty, b m, 1869, by Tom Wonder —Wells' Star, by Seely's American Star.......... 2:26½
Modesty, blk m, 1886, by Pascarel—Fancy H 2:30
Modesty, b m, 1891, by Count Folsio. 2:29¼
Modie H., ch g, 1874, by Bayard—Colle, by Foote's Clay.......... 2:29¼
Modjeska, b m, 1876, by Advance—Gipsy, by Clark's Black Hawk.... 2:29¼
Modoc, ch g, 1866, by Tornado, dam by Powers' Morgan Rattler......... 2:25
Modoc, gr g, 187—, by Morgan Hunter 2:25
Modoc, ch g, 187—, by Aberdeen 2:19½
Modred, b s, 188—, by Lumps—Isabella, by Wedgewood.......... 2:29¼
Mogul, b g, 1884, by Middletown—Lady Shamrock, by Shamrock..... 2:19¼
Mogul, b g, 1888, by Baymont—Maud, by Black Ranger 2:16¼
Mohawk Blondi, b s, 1884, by Hall's Mohawk Jr.—Lady Washington, by J. H. Welsh.......... 2:24¾
Mogul, b g, 1888, by Baymont—Maud, by Black Ranger 2:22½
Mohawk Chief, ch s, 1869, by Hall's Mohawk Jr.—Mary Bostwick 2:30
Mohawk (McCue's), ch s, 1881, by Mohawk Island—Lady Richardson .. 2:29½
Mohawk Gift, ch s, 1874, by Hall's Mohawk Jr.—Sis James, by Campbell's Hiatoga 2:21¼
Mohawk Jr (Clark's), b s, 1866, by Mohawk — Moselle, by Robinson's Bellfounder 2:25
Mohawk Jr., (Hall's) b s, 1865, by Mohawk—Lady Weaver 2:26
Mohawk Kate, b m, 1875, by Hall's Mohawk Jr.—Lady Wheeler, by Flying Hiatoga 2:26¾
Mohawk McGregor, ch s, 1884 by Robert McGregor—Minerva, by Fisher's Mohawk 2:29
Mohawk Prince, b g, 187—, by The Commodore 2:28
Molde, b m, 1891, ... 2:28½
Molino, ch g, 188—, by Belmont ... 2:27¼
Molly, b m, 1859 by Dolphus (dead) 2:27½
Molly, b m, 1863, by Magna Charta—Fox Cline, by Young Florizel (dead) 2:27
Molly, blk m, 1867, by Monro Champion, dam by Way Horse (dead) 2:27¼
Molly B., b m, 1873, by Duke of Saratoga—Jenny 2:28
Molly B., b m, 1883, by Hamdallah—Maud by Altitude 2:26½
Molly B., b m, 1877 by Fearnaught Gift, dam by Charles' Royal George 2:29¾
Molly B., b m, 1885, by Sovereign—Katy P 2:25¼
Molly B., br m, 1885 by Willie Schepper—Black Suse, by Lovelace's Black Hawk 2:29½
Molly Bell, b m, by Consternation.. 2:30
Molly C., b m, 1884, by Mammont—Nelly, by Prince Billett 2:29¼
Molly C., ch m, 1887, by Young Dirigo —Daisy, by Daniel Boone 2:23½
Dolly D., b m, 188—, by Goldenbow 2:26
Molly Drew, ch m, 1874, by Winthrop —Fanny Fern, by Jack Hawkins .. 2:27
Molly G., blk m, 188—, by Charles Caffrey 2:28
Molly G., b m, 188—, by Pickett, dam by St. Charles 2:20¼
Molly G., gr m, 1881 by Eclipse Clay —Grey Dolly, by Ranger 2:29¼
Molly Green, br m, 188—, by Pontiac 2:26¼
Molly H., ch m, 188—, by Young Detective 2:29¼
Molly Harris, blk m, 187—, by Couch's Bashaw 2:25½

Molly J., b m, 188–, by Hambletonian
Tranby 2:19¾
Molly K., b m, 188–, breeding not
traced 2:20½
Molly K., ch m, 1884, by Bashaw
Hambletonian—Katie P. 2 29½
Molly Kistler, b m, 1875, by Blue Bull
—Moss Rose, by Man Eater 2:27½
Molly Long, br m, 1876, by Mambrino
Champion—Kate Beamer, by Beam-
er's Hiatoga 2:20¼
Molly Mc, b m, 1885, by Long Branch
Fan, by Steer's Indian Chief ... 2:13¾
Molly Middleton, b m, 1872, by Bay
Middleton—Betsey Allen, by King's
Champion 2.25¼
Molly Mitchell, gr m, 1881, by Ken-
nebec, dam by British Hunter... 2:26½
Molly Morrill, b m, 1872 by Walker
Morrill—Molly 2:28¼
Molly Morris, ch m, 186–, pedigree
not traced 2:22
Molly Morton, gr m, 1883, by Banker
Rothschild—Lady Forrester, by
Field's Royal George 2.30
Molly O'Connor, br m, 1880, by Swi-
gert 2.25¼
Molly Patten, blk m, 1886, by Whip-
pleton—Napa, by Naubuc 2:20½
Molly S., g m, 188–, by Daniel Lam-
bert 2:24¾
Molly S. Lightfoot, b m, 1886, by
Richmond—Crane Mare 2:21¼
Molly Sprague, ch m, 1888, by George
Sprague—Perlie Cardinal, by Wilkes
Booth 2.16½
Molly Stanton, b m, 1882, by Gen.
Stanton..................... 2:20¼
Molly T, b m, 1887, by Dr. Talmage
—Blanche, by Cardinal 2:20¼
Molly Talbert, ch m, 1878, by Mam-
brino Gift—Kitty Talbert 2:29¼
Molly Wilkes, b m, 1882, by Young
Jim—Augusta, by Allie West 2:22¼
Molly Work, blk m, 1888, by Combina-
tion—Patch Work, by Haw Patch.. 2:24¾
Moloch, br g, 1892, by Warlock, dam
by Strathmore 2:26¼
Moloch, blk s, 1888, by Stranger—
Mystery, by Socrates 2:17
Molsey, b m, 1863, by Whiteside's
Black Hawk—Moll by Dallas ... 2:21¾
Mona, b m, 1886, by Jay Gould—Mol-
ly B............................ 2.29
Mona Lisa, blk m, 1888, by Monroe
Chief, dam by Reavis' Blackbird.. 2:21
Monadock, b s, 188–, by Allandorf—
Mosella 2:29¾
Mona B., b m, 1888, by Monon—
Princess Annie, by Kentucky Prince 2:28¼
Monaco, b s, 1889, by Electioneer—
Mano, by Piedmont 2:19½
Monarch, br g, 188–, by Brown
Frank 2:25¼
Monarch, b g, 1869, by Woodburn—
Victress, by Belmont 2:28¼
Monarch, b s, 188–, by Mambrino
Jackson 2:25¼
Monarch Jr., ro s, 1866, pedigree not
traced 2:24¼
Monarch Rule, b m, 1869, by Monarch
—Young Bob Rule, by St. Lawrence 2:24¼
Monbars, br s, 1889, by Eagle Bird—
Lady Maud, by Gen. Knox (pacing
record 2:16¾) 2:11¾
Mondace, b g, 1882, by Ringgold—
Fanny Whetstone, by Tobe Drum 2:27¼
Monette, blk m, 1887, by Monon—

Doska, by Woodford Mambrino 2:14¼
Money Hunter, b s, 1883, by Fleeting
Ray 2:25¼
Money Maid b m, 1888, by Money-
maker—Lady C., by Canada Black
Hawk 2:21½
Moneymaker, br s, 187–, by a son of
Young Columbus (dead) 2:29
Monie, b m, 188–, by Baird's Ham-
bletonian Prince, dam by Victor ... 2:29¼
Monitor, gr g, 1876, by Strathmore—
Martha Myers, by Benton's Diomed 2:29¼
Monitor Chipple, b m, 1886, by Moni-
tor—Bay Dixie, by Coleman's Abdal-
lah 2:27
Monk, ch g, 1888, by Gift Jr.—Miss
Stanley, by Snap Dragon 2:30
Monk, blk s, 1888, by Seneca Patchen
—The Nun, by Gatlin 2:26¼
Monocacy, b s, 1887, by King Wilkes
—Vivandier, by Volunteer 2:19½
Monocrat, b s, 1887, by Monitor
Prince—Bay Dixie, by Coleman's
Abdallah Jr. (dead) 2:27¾
Monogram, blk m, 1878, pedigree not
traced 2:20¾
Monologue, b m, 1888, by Monroe
Chief—Susie, by Ayers' Mambrino
Wilkes 2:20½
Monopolist, b s, 1878, by Jupiter
Abdallah—Undine, by Rysdyk's
Hambletonian 2.29½
Morning Glory, b m, 188–, by Rich-
ard's Elector 2.27
Monroe, ch s, 1867, by Iron Duke—
Young Saline, by Guy Miller 2:27½
Monroe, b s, 188–, by Monroe Chief
—Lady Tiffany by Gibraltar 2:29¼
Monroe Chief, br s, 1870, by Jim
Monroe—Madam Powell, by Bay
Chief 2:18¼
Monroe Prince, br s, 1886, by Monroe
Chief, dam by Buccaneer 2:29
Monroe Wilkes, b g, 1883, by Barthol-
omew Wilkes—Nelly R., by Jim
Monroe 2:17¼
Montague, b g, 188–, by Russel's
Hambletonian 2:29¼
Mont, b s, 188–, ... 2:24
Monta Lee, b m, 1888, by Montaigne
—Nancy Lee, by Almont Chief 2:30
Montana, blk s, 188–, by Montana
Wilkes—Alberta 2:27½
Montana, b s, 1890, by Sidney—Hat-
tie, by Commodore Belmont 2:10
Montclair, b s, 1884, by Montello,
dam by James Bludso 2:27½
Monte Carlo, b s, 1881, by Monaco—
Bicara, by Harold 2:20¾
Monte Christo, gr g, 1882, by Malta—
Kate Prasch, by Grey Eagle (Blind
Eagle) 2.29
Monte Christo, b s, 1887, by Baymont
—Kate, by Capt. Thompson 2:29¾
Monte Christo, ch g, 188–, by Jubilee
—Kit, by Monogram 2:18½
Monte K., ch g, 188–, by John W.
Norton—Nigger 2:20½
Monteo, b s, 1887, by Montgomery—
Minnie S., by Pasacas 2:24½
Monte Phister, b g, 1884, by Jot O.,—
Belle B., by Hero of Thorndale ... 2:29
Monterey, b s, 1886, by Electioneer—
Minx, by Don Victor 2:25¼
Monto Vista, ch s, 1885, by Nutwood
—Totsey, by Mambrino Transport. 2.28¼
Monte West, br g, 1882, by West-

mont .... 2·25¾
Montgomery, b s, 1878, by Inheritor
—Bazarr, by Kentucky Chief (dead) 2·21¼
Montgomery Boy, ch g, 1875, by
Sweepstakes—Mag, by Smith's
Henry Clay .... 2·28¼
Montreal Girl, b m, 1871, by Tiger . 2·30
Mont Rose, b m, 1888, by Electioneer
—Rosemont, by Piedmont 2.18
Montrose, b s, 1882, by Dartmouth,
dam by McAllister Horse 2.26½
Moody, gr s 1874, by Swigert—Moll,
by Ward Horse 2.18½
Moody, b g, 1881, by Moody—Fanny
Bond, by McCommon's Magna
Charta .... 2·18
Moonlight, b m, 1879, by Richmond,
dam by Toledo .... 2·25½
Moonstone, b m, 1888, by Sultan—
Montana Maid, by George Wilkes .. 2:28½
Moorzouk, b s, 1890, by Sidney—Sul-
tan Queen, by Sultan 2:26
Moose, b g, 187—, by Washburn Horse-
—Morrisey Mare .... 2·19½
Moquette, br m, 1889, by Wilton—
Spirea, by Stillson .... 2·30
Moquette, ch m, 1889, by Belmont—
Mosa, by Woodford Mambrino 2:27¼
Moquette, b s, 1888, by Wilton—Betsy
and I, by Ericsson 2:10
Morea, b m, 1882, by Electioneer—
Maria Pilot, by Mambrino Pilot .. 2·24¼
Morefield, b s, 1881, by Richwood—
Fanny Cox, by Kossuth .... 2·29¼
Morelein, b s, 1886, by Monte Carlo
—Nora Wilkes, by Lyle Wilkes .... 2·25½
Morelight, b g, 1883, by Starlight—
Violet, by Volunteer (dead) 2:28
Morelight, b s, 1885, by Twilight—
Lady Carr, by American Clay .... 2·30
Morgan Ethan, b s, 1880, by Ameri-
can Ethan—Dolly Perry, by Orange
County Morgan 2:29½
Morgan Wheeler, br g, 188—, by Pal-
adine 2:29¾
Morgan Wilkes, blk s, 1889, by Bour-
bon Wilkes—Fern by Rebel 2:27
Morgwood, b s, 188—, by Atwood..... 2·29½
Morning, gr m, 1869, by Mambrino
Pilot—Granite, by John Plowman. 2·30
Morning Glory, b s, 188—, by Harry
B. .... 2·30
Morning Star, b s, 188—, by Valde-
meer 2.27
Moro, blk m, 1883, by Pasha—Adele,
by Messenger Duroc 2.25
Morocco, b g, 1875, by James R
Reese—Patchen Maid, by Henry B.
Patchen .... 2·30
Morris, br g, 186—, by Ed Sherman 2:29
Morris H, br s, 188—, by Hero ...... 2·26½
Morris H., br s, 1882, by Lowell
Chief—Myrtle, by Wood's Hamble-
tonian 2:22½
Morrisey, ch g, 1857, by Black War-
rior 2:26½
Mortimer, br s, 1884, by Electioneer
—Marti, by Whipple's Hamble-
tonian 2:27
Morton, ch g, 188—, by Wilkes Spirit
—Nelly Brown, by Kentucky .... 2·29½
Moscova, ch m 1883, by Belmont—
Mosa, by Woodford Mambrino 2:28½
Moscow, b g. 183—, pedigree not
traced (dead) 2:28¾
Moscow, br g, 188—, ... 2:28½
Moscow, gr g, 1881, by Privateer—
Goldie, by Hendric Hudson .. ... 2·26¼

Moscow, blk g, 186—, pedigree not
traced (dead) 2.28¾
Moses, gr g, 1880. by Nutbreaker—
Maid of Windsor, by Peavine ... 2.24¾
Moses S, b s, 1885, by Hawthorne—
Ryan Mare, by McCracken's Black
Hawk 2:19½
Moss Rose, ch m, 1880, by Vitalis 2.30
Motion, ch s, 1873, by Daniel Lam-
bert—Never Mind, by a son of
Young Moscow (dead) 2.29
Motion Golddust, b g, 1884, by Gold-
dust Jr—Ella Leonard, by Judge
Leonard 2.28½
Motor, b s, 1884, by Onward—Griselda,
by William Rysdyk .... 2·29½
Motor, b s, 1882, by Colonna—Emma,
by Tippoo Sultan Jr .... 2·27¼
Mott, b g, 188—, by Ulster Prince,
dam by Edsall's Hambletonian 2:25½
Mott Medium, b g 187—, by Happy
Medium—Belle Vernon, by Gen.
Mott .... 2·29½
Motto, b g, 188—, by Col Bruce 2.28
Monche Guise, gr m, 188—, ... 2·28½
Mountain Boy, b g, 1860, by Edward
Everett, dam by Gridley's Roe-
buck (dead) 2.20¾
Mountaineer, b s, 1884, by Young
Rolfe—Ink, by Louis Napoleon . . 2·23¾
Mountain Girl, b m, 1877, pedigree
not traced 2:27¼
Mountain Maid, br m, 1858, by Morrill
(dead) 2:27¾
Mountain Maid, b m, 188—, by An-
teeo, dam by Nutwood .... 2·22¼
Mountain Quail, b m 1871, by Weige 2:25½
Mount Airy, b s, 1887, by Walsing-
ham—Belle, by Volunteer 2.19¼
Mount Hood, br s, 1885, by Eros—
Alice, by Almont 2:22¾
Mount Morris, ro s, 1882, by Smug-
gler—Christine, by Wood's Hamble-
tonian .... 2·19½
Mount Vernon, b s, 1881, by Nutwood
—Daisy, by Chieftain 2.15¼
Mount Vernon, ch s, 1878, by Cham-
pion Knox .... 2·26
Moxie, b g, 1887, by Opal.......... 2:24¼
M R, br g, 188—, by Raven Gold-
dust—Nelly Dean, by Major Buck 2:19¾
M. R., b g, 1871, by Jupiter—Molly
B., by Mambrino Black Hawk..... 2.28
Muchado, b s, 1889, by Judge Salis-
bury—Lady Simmons, by Simmons 2:20½
Mudrona, br m, 1888, by Baron
Wilkes—Mudra, by Sentinel 2:26
Muggins, ch m, 1887, by Elyria—May
Lady, by Alexander's Norman ... 2·28½
Muggins, b m, 188—, by Embassador 2.25
Muggins, b m, 188—, by Haro 2.20¼
Mulatto, bl s. 1883, by Aberdeen—
Nig, by Mambrino Patchen 2:22
Multiform, br s, 1887, by Pero—Maria,
by Guide .. .. 2·28
Murtha, b m, 1887, by Stamboul—
Posey, by Flextail 2.18
Muscovite, ch s, 1885, by Nutwood—
Reina Victoria, by Rysdyk's Ham-
bletonian 2:18
Musette, gr m, 1886, by Lew Scott—
Linda, by Star Mambrino 2.17½
Musette. b m, 187—, by Almont—Mag
Cooper, by Ashland .... 2·29¼
Music, ch m, 1867, by Middletown,
dam by Roe's Fiddler 2.21¼
Music, b m, 187—, pedigree not traced 2:29½
Mustache, br s, 1883, by Sweepstakes

—Mag, by Smith's Henry Clay 2:30
Mustapha, ch s, 1889, by Guy Wilkes—Lalla Rookh, by Grand Moor ... 2:23
Musty, ch g, 188—, by Hambletonian Prince 2:26½
Muta Wilkes, b m, 1888, by Guy Wilkes—Montrose, by Sultan 2:11
M. W., ch g, 1884, by Billy Hensly—Bat 2:20¼
M. Y. D. Colt, ch m, 1877, by Daniel Lambert—Fanny Jackson, by Stonewall Jackson 2:28¾
My Charley, ch s, 188—, by Motor.. 2:21
My My, b m, 1885, by Eros—Nettie Walker, by Mohawk Chief 2:25¾
Myra Simmons, b m, 1890, by Simmons—Nelly West, by Allie West 2.20¼
Myriad, b m, 1885, by Stranger—Myra, by Gen. Knox 2:28½
Myritte Thorne, br m, 1890, by Grandissimo—Belle Thorne, by Hawthorne 2:20¾
Myron McHenry, ch s, 1888, by Ashland Wilkes—Dame Wood, by Wedgewood 2:18¼
Myron Perry, b g, 1860, by Young Columbus, dam by Hopkin's Abdallah (dead) 2:24½
Myrtella G., ch m, 1879, by Blue Bull—Myra Shaw, by Tom Lang ... 2 28
Myrtle, b m, 1876, by Louis Napoleon—Nelly Hulick, by Fisk's Mambrino Chief Jr. 2:22¼
Myrtle B., b m, 1884, by George Chief—Lady Wonder 2:22½
Myrtle Peak, b m, 1887, by Wilkesonian—Kitty Kimbrough, by Kimbrough's Abdallah 2:29¼
Myrtle, b m, 187—, by King's Champion—Old Jane, by Magnum Bonum 2:25½
Myrtle, ro m, 1872, by Flying Cloud—Little Moon 2.26½
Myrtle, gr m, 1882, by Warwick Boy—Kit, by Kilpatrick 2:28½
Myrtle, br m, 1888, by Anteeo—Luella, by Nutwood, ... 2:19½
Myrtle, ro m, 1886, by Oxford Boy . 2 30
Myrtle Boy, blk s, 1891, by Myrtleton—Bertha James, by Dictator 2:25½
Myrtle N., b m, 1890, by Alburn—Kitty E., by Honest Irishman ... 2:20½
Myrtle R., b m, 1886, by Monaco—Lucy, by Trascan 2:15¼
Myrtle S., b m, 1886, by Charley Wicker, dam by William M. Rysdyk's 2:28¼
Myrtle T., blk m, 1888, by Grand Moor—Gyp, by Devoy's Vermont .. 2.27¼
Myrtle Twig, b m, 1890, by Myrtleton—Vado, by Cyclops 2:28½
Myrtlewood, b s, 1883, by Wedgewood—Myrtle, by King's Champion 2:25¼
Mystery, b s, 1876, by Magic—Ned .. 2·25¼
Mystery, b m, 1888, by Phallas—Mystic, by Nutwood 2 21¼
Mystery, b s, 188—, by Milwaukee Jr.—Nelly B., by Stockholm .... 2·26½
Mystic, b g, 186—, by Reliance 2:22
Nabby G., br m, 1876, by Hambletonian Bashaw 2:30
Nabocklish, blk g, 1853, by Rising Sun (dead) 2:29½
Nabob, b g, 1887, by Willet—Adele Tyler, by Chester 2:30
Naboth, b s, 1888, by Walsingham—Tinsel Maid, by Messenger Duroc.. 2:19¼
Nadji, br m, 1886, by Earl—Frankie, by McAfee's Drennon 2:28
Nadjy, b m, 1887, by Stamboul—Lady Graves, by Nutwood 2:26
Nadjy, ch m, 188—, by Declaration.. 2:28
Naiad King, b s, 1888, by Recorder—Naiad Queen, by Gooding's Champion 2:23
Naiad Queen, b m, 1875, by Gooding's Champion—Tackey, by Pilot Jr. 2:20¼
Nailor, b s, 1886, by Sultan—Nelly, by Rysdyk's Hambletonian........ 2:29
Namouna, b m, 1873, by Pelham Tartar—Kit Jackson 2:28¼
Nana, b m, 1891, Rockefeller—Modena, by Messenger Wilkes 2:29½
Nana, b m, 188—, pedigree not traced 2.24¼
Nancy, ch m, 1872, by Daniel Lambert—May Day, by Miles Standish.. 2:23½
Nancy B., br m, 188—, by Wade Hampton 2 29¼
Nancy Carr, br m, 1888, by Kenny Wilkes—Eliza Jane, by Girrard Chief 2:25
Nancy H., br m, 188—, by Japan ... 2:24¼
Nancy Hackett, rn m, 187—, by Wood's Hambletonian—Hackett Mare ...... 2·20
Nancy Hackett, rn m, 1886, by Allegheny Boy—Quibble, by Solicitor ... 2:29
Nat Howe, b g, 188—, by Ben Franklin 2:28½
Nancy Haas, b m, 188—, by Jim Swigert 2:29¾
Nancy Hanks, br m, 1886, by Happy Medium—Nancy Lee, by Dictator.. 2:04
Nancy K., br m, 188—, by King William.............................. 2:29¼
Nancy Rice, b m, 1891, by Alcantara—Belle Medium, by Happy Medium . 2:25
Nancy S., b m, 188—, by Wood's Hambletonian........................ 2:27
Nancy Time, b m, 188—, by Phillip's Blue Bull.......................... 2:29¼
Nancy V., br m, 1887, by Mambrino Bashaw—Nelly Elmo, by St. Elmo... 2.24¼
Nancy W., b m, 1889, by Patron—Locrine, by Duke of Brunswick....... 2·26¼
Nankeen, ch s, 1888, by Mambritonian—Nancy, by Jones' Independence 2:28
Nannie K., b m, 1880, by Deucalion—Emblem, by Minchin's Tom Moore.. 2·27¼
Nanny B., b m, 1878, by Daubigne—Miss Christian, by Darnaby's Bay Messenger.......................... 2·27
Nanny Talbott, ch m, 1877, by Strathmore—Kitty Morgan, by Joe Downing Jr............................ 2:29¼
Nannie Wilson, blk m, 1890, by Simmons—Alga, by Indianapolis........ 2.28½
Nantilla J., blk m, 1883, by Rockwood—Old Fly, by Fly-by-Night......... 2 30
Natila, b m, 188—, by Goldmine, dam by Arnold.......................... 2.25¼
Naomi, b m, 1888, by Indian Hill—Juno, by Rysdyk's Hambletonian... 2 25
Napoleon Belle, br m, 1881, by Ambassador.......................... 2·27½
Narcus, b g, 1890, by Messenger Wilkes, dam by Hampton.......... 2:25½
Narka, b m, 1888, by Messenger Wilkes—Tribon Mare, by Hampton. 2·29
Narka, b m, 1885, by Young Jim—Lucille Golddust, by Golddust........ 2·27¼
Narragansett, br g, 188—, by Narragansett.......................... 2:23½
Nashville, gr g, 1885, by Chesterfield—Jenny, by Carlisle................ 2.28
Nat Bruen, ch s, 188—, by Egmont... 2 21¼
Natchez, b g, 186—, pedigree not traced (dead)..................... 2:30

Nathalie, ch m, 1888, by Jersey Wilkes
—Nemea, by Nutwood............ 2.17
Nathalie, ch m, 1890, by Simmons—
Katy Eastman, by Enfield......... 2:28¼
Nathan, blk g, 1877, by Empire—
Frisky, by Mahew............... 2:29¼
Nathan Wilkes, b m, 188—, by Red
Wilkes, dam by Monroe Chief...... 2:25¾
Natila, b m, 188—, by Goldemar..... 2:23½
National, b s, 1887, by Wellington—
Agnes, by Aberdeen............. 2:20¼
Native Son, br s, 1889, by Sable
Wilkes—Blanche, by Arthurton.... 2·26½
Native Son, br s, 1890, by Waldstein—
Gertrude, by The Moor........... 2:29½
Native State, b s, 188—, by a son of
Electioneer.................... 2:27¼
Naughty Clara, b m, 1890, by Young
Jim—Miss Mamie, by Contractor.... 2 28¼
Naumkeag, br s, 188—, by Lexington. 2:28
Navarro, b s, 1887, by Nutmont—
Nelly G., by Electioneer.......... 2:22
Navidad, b g, 1886, by Whips—Lady
Thorne Jr., by Williams' Mambrino. 2:22½
Navy Wilkes, blk s, 1886, by Black
Ambassador—Black Hawk Beauty,
by Champlain John.............. 2:27
Neal Whitbeck, blk g, 1883, by Black
Bashaw—Dot, by Gen. Knox...... 2:22½
Ned, b g, 187—, by Overland........ 2 29¾
Ned Biddle, b g, 187—............. 2:25
Ned Allen, ch g, 188—, by Rex Patch-
en........................... 2·29½
Neddie D., b g, 188—, by R. F. Gallo-
way.......................... 2:26
Ned Forrest, blk g, 1864, by Keene's
Brandywine (dead)............. 2:28½
Ned Forrest, ch g, 187—, by Reavis
Blackbird..................... 2:25¾
Ned Hastings, b s, 187—, by Taggart's
Abdallah...................... 2:28½
Ned Lock, ch s, 188—, pedigree not
traced........................ 2·24½
Ned Wallace, b s, 1868, by Taggart's
Abdallah...................... 2:25
Needham's Whipple, blk s, 1891, by
Steve Whipple—Young Flora Hill, by
Chieftain..................... 2:27¾
Neernut, b s, 1892, by Albert W.—
Clyte 2d, by Nutwood........... 2:26
Nehushta, b m, 1885, by Stamboul—
Neluska, by Sultan.............. 2:30
Nekima, dn g, 188—, by Hailstorm.. 2:23
Nell, b m, 1872, by Thomas Jefferson
—Rose Terry, by Rysdyk's Hamble-
tonian........................ 2.27
Nelia, b m, 1871, by Camden Denmark 2:24¼
Nell, blk m, 187—, pedigree not traced 2:29¼
Nellette, br m, 1887, by Grand Senti-
nel—Nellie G., by Brentham....... 2:26½
Nelly, b m, 1886, by Oberon—Nelly,
by Glencoe.................... 2:23¼
Nelly, blk m, 188—, by Little Hamil-
ton.......................... 2:28
Nelly, b m, 1871, by Green's Hamble-
tonian — Holcomb Mare, by Young
Morrill....................... 2:30
Nelly, b m, 1879, by Baird's Hamble-
tonian Prince—Kit, by Victor...... 2:29¼
Nelly, b m, 188—, by Oberon........ 2:27½
Nelly A., b m, 1891, by Wilkes Boy—
Wilksie G, by Robert McGregor.... 2:16¼
Nelly Aldine, blk m, 1889, by Wilkes
Boy—Josie King, by The King..... 2:21¼
Nelly Alfred, b m, 188—, by Alfred G 2:27½
Nelly Allison, br m, 1883, by Forest
Hiatoga—Black Polly............ 2:19½
Nelly B., br m, 1876, by Gooding's
Champion—Nelly, by Henry Clay Jr. 2:29¼

Nelly Bar.ett, blk m, 1882, by John
Sherman—Cloud, by Black Ranger. 2 29½
Nelly Benton, b m, 1880, by Gen. Ben-
ton—Norma, by Alexander's Norman 2:30
Nelly Blackwing, blk m, 188—, by Al-
mont M....................... 2:29½
Nelly Bly, b m, 1889, by Advance—
Molly C., by Gov Scott.......... 2 30
Nelly Bly, b m, 1886, by Middletown
Jr.—Black Kate, by Andrew Jackson 2:23¼
Nelly Bryant, b m, 1872, by Palmer's
Norman—Lady Bryant, by Robinson
Horse........................ 2.25¼
Nelly Burns, b m, 187—, by Milli-
man's Bellfounder—Lucy Foster, by
James W. Foster............... 2:25
Nelly C., br m, 1881, by Daniel Web-
ster—Nettie, by Fearnaught Gift.. 2 26¾
Nelly C., blk m, 1879, by Peter Jef-
ferson—Ida Shepper, by Mott's In-
dependent.................... 2 27½
Nelly C., br m, 188—, by Grimalkin
—Molly H, by Rothschild....... 2 30
Nelly C, b m, 1883, by Wattle's
Little Grant—Bay Ann.......... 2:29½
Nelly C., ch m, 1883, by Ben Butler
—Duster, by a son of Cassius M.
Clay......................... 2.25¼
Nelly Chatterton, b m, 1890, by Chat-
terton—Modjeska, by Harold..... 2.29¼
Nelly Cobb, b m, 188—, by Charles
Caffrey...................... 2:20¼
Nelly D, br m, 1882, by Taylor, dam
by Allen C. Patchen............ 2:27¾
Nelly D., b m, 188—, by Toodles Jr.
—Romany.................... 2.19¼
Nelly D, blk m, 188—, by Robinson
D., dam by Dow Rysdyk......... 2:27
Nelly Earl, b m, 188—, by Earl..... 2:29¼
Nelly F., rn m, 188—, by Rex Patchen 2:23¾
Nelly F., ch m, 1888, by Alroy—Pet.. 2:28¾
Nelly F., b m, 1888, by Anteros—
Sharlie, by Roger Hanson (pacing
2·13¼)....................... 2:25
Nelly G., br m, 1874, by Brentham
(dead)....................... 2.20
Nelly G., ch m, 1883, by St. Almo—
Kate McCann................. 2:29½
Nelly G., b m, 188—, by Kearsarge.. 2:28¼
Nelly G, blk m, 1885, by Ira Wilkes
—Molly by Esple's St. Lawrence.. 2.24
Nelly Gamwell, b m, 188—, by
Elial G....................... 2 30
Nelly Grant, ch m, 1874, by Major
Grant—Madam Mank, by Frank
Pierce Jr..................... 2:28¼
Nelly Gray, gr m, 188—, pedigree not
traced....................... 2:29¾
Nelly Gray, gr m, 1883, by Ned
Patchen—Dolly, by Patrick Henry. 2:20
Nelly Gray, gr m, 187—, by Young
Cassius...................... 2.26¼
Nelly H., b m, 1882, by Raven Gold-
dust......................... 2:24½
Nelly H, blk m, 1884, by Ambassador
—Lady Greer, by Joe Curry...... 2:28¼
Nelly Hardwood, b m, 1885, by Hard-
wood—Lucy.................. 2:18¾
Nelly Holcomb, gr m, 1853, by Adams'
American, dam by Harris' Hamble-
tonian (dead)................. 2:28
Nelly Howard, br m, 1886, by Gen
Stanton—Nelly T., by Fulton..... 2:18¾
Nelly Irwin, b m, 186—, by Middle-
town, dam by Bay Abdallah (dead). 2:25
Nelly J., b m, 1890, by George J.—
Black Rose, by Revolution ...... 2·29¾
Nelly K., b m, 1879, by Young Wash-

tenaw Chief 2:29¾
Nelly L., b m, 1878, by George Wilkes—Lady Oaks, by Gill's Vermont.... 2:23¼
Nelly Loyd, b m, 1885, by Elgin Boy—Jenny Roberson, by Pilot Duroc. 2:22½
Nelly M., b m, 1877, by Daniel Boone—Page Mare, by Page's Gen. Sherman 2:28¼
Nelly M., gr m, 188—, by Barkis—Maggie Colburn, by Coeur De Lion Jr. 2:27¼
Nelly M., b m, ... 2:28¼
Nelly McGee, b m, 188—, by Springbrook 2:30
Nelly McGregor, b m, 1882, by McGregor Chief—Nelly Weeks Jr., by Captain 2:26¼
Nelly McGregor, ch m, 1887, by Robert McGregor—Minnie Brown, by Dictator 2:14
Nelly Mason, b m, 1887, by Onward—Rachel Russell, by Woodford Abdallah 2:14
Nelly N., blk m, 188—, by Alcyonium—Topsy Knox 2:25¼
Nelly O'Neill, b m, 1884, by Petoskey—Fanny, by Iron's Cadmus 2:22½
Nelly Orloff, b m, 1886, by Prince Orloff—Fanny Bashaw, by Bashaw Jr. 2:26¼
Nelly P., b m, 1883, by Meeker Hambletonian—Sprague Mare, by American Eagle 2:28½
Nelly Patchen, b m, 187—, by Alexander—Jenny Shepherd, by Williamson's Belmont 2:27¼
Nelly R., ch m, 1881, by Red Cloud—Nell by Cole's Black Hawk 2:28
Nelly R., b m, 188—, by Santa Claus—Helena, by Lancewood 2:21½
Nelly R., b m, 187—, by Gen. McClellan Jr.—Susie Rose, by Sam McClelland 2:17½
Nellie R., b m, 1876, by Stephen A. Douglas........................ 2:22¼
Nellie R., blk m, 1891, by Don Felix, dam by St. Elmo 2:26¾
Nelly Rose, b m, 1872, by Henry B. Patchen 2:30
Nelly Rose, ch m, 1878, by Sacramento—Nelly Walworth, by Toronto Patchen 2:25¼
Nelly S., b m, 188—, by Jersey Wilkes 2:28½
Nelly S., blk m, 1867, by Commander, dam by Ross' Tom Crowder 2:23¾
Nelly S., b m, 1889, by Jim Wilson—Maud, by New Jersey Volunteer. 2:23¼
Nelly S., b m, 1884, by Pickett (pacing 2:16¼)........................ 2:21¼
Nellie Shank, b m, 1890 by Dr. Talmage—Annie Penn, by Simmons .. 2:29¼
Nelly Sherman, blk m, 1881, by John Sherman—Nichols Mare 2:29¾
Nelly Stillson, b m, 1882, by Stillson—Nelly, by Hiatoga Chief 2:24
Nelly T., b m, 188—, by Mambrino Morgan 2:29½
Nelly T., b m, 188—, by Hambrino.. 2:20¼
Nelly V., b m, 187—, pedigree not traced 2:20¾
Nelly W., gr m, 1884, by Rolla Golddust—Belle, by Norman Temple.... 2:14¼
Nelly W., b m, 1886, by Sweepstakes 2:23¼
Nelly W., blk m 2:29¾
Nelly W., ch m, 188—, by Woolsey—Nelly Reynolds, by Inca 2:17¼
Nelly Walton, b m, 1865, by Jules Jurgensen—Nelly, by Defiance (dead) 2:26½
Nelly Webster, br m, 1865, by American Ethan—Colonel's dam, by Biggart's Rattler (dead)........ 2:28¾
Nelly Wilkes, b m, 188—, by Red Wilkes 2:18½
Wilkes—Belle, by Kimbrough's Abdallah 2:28½
Nelly Wilson, b m, 1885, by Baird's Hambletonian Prince—Nelly, by Victor 2:30
Nelly Woodruff, gr m, 1871, by Rooker 2:30
Nelly Woods, ch m, 188—, by Emerson Golddust—Topsy 2:28½
Nelson, b s, 1882, by Young Rolfe—Gretchen, by Gideon 2:09
Nelson, ch g, 1883, by Sir Walkill—Floretta, by Messenger Duroc 2:24¼
Nelson D., b g, 188—, by Lord Nelson 2:26½
Nelson Jr., b s, 188—, by Nelson.... 2:26¾
Nemesis, b m, 1883, by Nutwood—Four Lines, by Blackwood 2:28
Nemo, br g, 1884, by Ed Barton—Uarda, by Buckeye Chief........ 2:21¼
Nemo, b g, 186—, by John Nelson (dead) 2:30
Nemo, br s, 1884 by Clay—Nettie Benton, by Gen. Benton 2:26¾
Nemoline, blk m, 1890, by Jersey Wilkes—Nemesis, by Nutwood 2:13¼
Nenox, br g, 1888, by Nephew—Miss Knox, by Knox 2:27¾
Neome, b g, 186— by Post Boy Frank—Fanny Snyder, by Dave (dead) .. 2:24
Neponset, b s, 1887, by Nutwood—Maud S. T., by Gov. Sprague 2:24¼
Neponset, b s, 188—, by Alcyone—Betsey Bump, by Stockholm 2:24¼
Nerea, ch m, 1867, by John Nelson—Sally Taylor, by Gen. Taylor (dead) 2:23½
Neri Newcome, b s, 1883, by Starmont—Gipsy, by Young Belshazzar. 2:28¾
Nerissa, b m, 1886, by Pennant—Allet, by Almont 2:21¾
Nero, b s, 1888, by Valley Chief, dam by Darkey 2:25½
Nest Egg, ch s, 1881, by Amboy—Molly Merrell, by Kentucky Chief. 2:29¾
Nestor, ch s, 1880, by Pasacas—Celia, by Knowles' Stranger 2:26¼
Nestor, b s, 1880, by Alden Goldsmith—Harriet, by Swigert 2:30
Nestor, b g, 188— 2:29¼
Nestwood, b g, 1886, by Nestor—Jesmont, by McAlmont 2:23¾
Neta Medium, b m, 1874, by Happy Medium—Sally, by Yankee Tricks.. 2:22½
Neta Pine, br m, 1881, by American Ethan—Dolly Perry, by Orange County Morgan 2:29½
Nettie, ch m, 1882, by Blue Bull Jr.—Kate, by Col. Ellsworth 2:19
Nettie, b m, 1866, by Rysdyk's Hambletonian—County House Mare, by Seely's American Star (dead) 2:18
Nettie, blk m, 188—, by Atlantic Chief 2:29½
Nettie, b m, 1885, by The King—Nelly, by Kirkwood 2:19¼
Nettie, dn m, 188—, by Ben Harrison 2:29½
Nettie B., br m 1887, by Ansel—Nettie Benton, by Gen Benton 2:20½
Nettie B., b m, 1883, by Jim Ervin—Kate, by Pilot Duroc 2:25½
Nettie B., br m, 1884, by Keystone—Blanche C. Arthurs, by Kentucky Burr 2:27½
Nettie Burlew, b m, 1869, by King's Champion—Nipper, by George M.

Briton .... 2·26¼
Nobby, br g, 1876, by Nobby—Fanny Rawlings, by May's Sir Wallace... 2:18¾
Noble Harold, b s, 1883, by Harold—Wilna, by Belmont 2:29¾
Noblement, b s, 1887, by Frank Noble—Tremona, by Tremont 2.29½
Noblesse, b s, 1887, by Dictator—Fuga, by George Wilkes 2:24
Nobody's Claim, blk s, 1884, by Almont Pilot—Pet, by Erie 2:26
N. O D., b g, 1884, by Ben Franklin—Trinket Girl, by Jubilee Lambert 2:30
Nogero, b g, 1886, by Kingston—Betty 2·28½
No Hurry, b g, 188—, by Harry Clay 2:30
Nomad, b g, 1883, by Smuggler—Mary A. Whitney, by Volunteer 2.29½
Nominator, b s, 1887, by Stranger—Sapphire, by Jay Gould ... 2:17¼
Nominee, b g, 1888, by Rescue—Molly Wilson, by Sirrocco 2:25
Nominee, b s, 1885, by Stranger—Sapphire, by Jay Gould 2:17¼
Nona Downing, b m, 1887, by Patterson's Joe Downing Jr.—Flora L., by Sandy 2 26¾
Nona Y., b m, 1881, by Admiral—Black Flora, by Black Prince ... 2·25
None Better, b m, 1886, by Allandorf—Bashaw Belle, by Green's Bashaw 2:23¾
Nonesuch, b g, 1879, by Netherland—Lady Shire, by Comus 2.30
Nonesuch, ch m, 1862, by Daniel Lambert—Jenny, by Bigelow Horse.... 2 25½
Noonday, br s, 1883, by Wedgewood—Noontide, by Harold 2.30
Noontide, gr m, 1874, by Harold—Midnight, by Pilot Jr. .... 2·20½
No·a, ch m, 188—, by Walkill—Nelly.. 2:27¾
Nora, ch m, 1873, by Springville Chief—McAleese Mare, by Parker's Black Hawk 2 28½
Nora B., ch m, 1889, by Betterton—Sunnyside, by Richelieu 2:17½
Nora, ch m, 188—, by Del Sur ... 2 22
Nora G., b m, 1878, by Ahue—Beatrice 2 25¾
Nora Lee, b m, 1874, by Woodford Mambrino—Young Portia, by Mambrino Chief 2.29¼
No·a Lee, br m, 188— by Penny Pack 2 29½
Nora Temple, b m, 1877, by Belmont—Bland Temple, by Lexington 2:27¼
Norhawk, br m, 1888, by Norval—Sontag Mohawk, by Mohawk Chief.... 2:15½
Norman, gr g, by Whipple's Hambletonian—Lady Suffolk, by Harry Belmont 2 28¾
Norman Medium, gr s, 1881, by Happy Medium—Alice Drake, by Alexander's Norman 2 20
Nornette, ch m, 1888, by Norway—Katana, by Rochester 2 30
Norrick, b g, 188—, by Richwood..... 2 29½
Norris, ch s, 1887, by Ansel—Norma, by Alexander's Norman 2 22¼
Norris N., br g, 1884, by Gilt Edge—Coleta, by Odin Bell 2:20¼
Norseman, br s, 1884, by Dean Sage—Bertha Duroc, by Messenger Duroc. 2:30
North Ann, ch m, 1881, by Antar—Bel'e Sande son, by Brigand 2.25¼
Norther, b s, 1889, by Onward—Ellen Prewitt, by Ashland Chief 2 15¼
Northlight, b s, 1886, by Twilight—Sally Western, by Empire........ 2·28
North Star Mambrino, b s, 1860, by Mambrino Chief, dam by Davy Crocket (dead) .... 2·26½

Northwest, b s, 1885, by Egmont—Tot, by Dictator (pacing 2:15) 2:22½
Norval, b s, 1882, by Electioneer—Norma, by Alexander's Norman.... 2:14¾
Norvalson, br s, 1889, by Norval—Trustie, by Messenger Duroc...... 2:28½
Novia, ch m, 1887, by Robert McGregor—Duenna, by Woodford Mambrino 2:27¼
Norvadine, b s, 1891, by Norval, dam by Onward 2.25½
Norvin G., br s, 1891, by Norval—Congo, by Blackwood 2 20½
Norway, ch g, 1885, by Gen. Grant—Columbia Maid, by Columbia Chief 2:20¼
Norway Knox, blk s, 1879, by Phil Sheridan Jr. 2 29½
Norwood Hambletonian, b s, 1884, by McCurdy's Hambletonian—Lula Golddust, by Messenger Golddust...... 2:22¼
Nosegay, b m, 1886, by Gen. Washington—Naomi, by Socrates 2.16¼
Notre Dame, b m, 1890, by Robert McGregor—Christine, by Hambrino.... 2.23¾
No Trouble, b g, 1886, by Waterloo—Nell, by Star of Catskill 2:21¼
Novelett, b m, 1890, by Norval—Norilla, by Tennessee Wilkes 2:29¼
Novelist, b m, 1889, by Norval—Elsie, by Gen. Benton 2:27
Novelty, b s, 1878, by Graphic—Maid of Mount View, by Woodward's Ethan Allen Jr. 2.20
Novelty, ch m, 1875, by Gooding's Champion—Minnie, by King's Champion 2:23½
Novelty, br m, 1881, by New York—Polly, by Clark's Tom Hal 2:28¾
Novi, b g, 1880, by Highland Golddust 2.29¼
Novice, b s, 1888, by Walsingham—Silica, by Princeps 2:26¼
Noya, b m, 1885, by Kentucky Prince—Prolific, by Electioneer 2:24
N. T. H., b g, 1885, by Pilot Mambrino—Molly, by Shelby Chief ... 2:17½
Nubbin, b g, 1884, by Herod Jr.—Maud, by Princeps 2:17½
Nubia, b g, 1889, by Soudan—Emma Anderson, by Wapsie 2:24¼
Nubbin W., blk s, 188—, by Simmonette—Mulatto Girl. 2:26¼
Nuggett, ch s, 1878, by Wedgewood—Minerva, by Pilot Jr. 2 26¾
Nugetta, ch m, 1889, by Nugget—Belle Lambert, by Godfrey Patchen. 2:24¼
Nugget Jr., ch s, 1886, by Nugget—Marchesa, by Woodford Mamb·ino. 2·28
Number Seven, b g, 1885, by Favorite Wilkes—Bettie, by Joe Downing.... 2:20½
Numero, ch s, 1884, by Nugget—Vesper Bell, by Belmont 2.27
Numidian, b s, 1881, by Almont or Happy Medium—Susan Brady, by Strader's Cassius M. Clay Jr....... 2.25½
Nuncio, b s, 1883, by Nutwood—Starling, by Cuyle............... 2:23¾
Nutallee, ch m, 1886, by Nutwood—Dot, by Bird 2 29
Nutant, b s, 1888, by Nutmeg—Juno, by Administrator............. 2:26½
Nutbreaker, b s, 1883, by Nutwood—Bonny Doon, by Aberdeen .... 2·21½
Nutbrown Maid, br m, 1888, by C. F. Clay—Margarita by Lightheart.... 2:28¾
Nutcoast, b s, 1886, by Nutwood—Augustine, by Pancoast......... 2:19
Nutgall, b g, 1877, by Nutwood—Wild Rose, by Rysdyk's Hambletonian . 2·20

Nuthunter, b s, 1884, by Nutwood—Fanny, by Scott's Thomas 2:30
Nutland, b s, 1883, by Nutwood—Nelly Locke, by Kremer's Rainbow 2:29
Nutling, b s, 1885, by Nutwood—Queen West, by Ware Colt 2:29¼
Nut Maid, ch m, 1888, by Nutbreaker—Annie Sprague, by George Sprague 2:29¾
Nutmeg, ch s, 1883, by Nutwood—Coquette, by American Clay 2:16
Nutmont, b s, 1882, by Nutbourne—Strabo, by Knickerbocker 2:22¼
Nutmont, ch s, 1884, by Almont—Nutshell, by Nutwood 2:22½
Nutpick, b s, 1888, by Nutbreaker—Lady W., by Tramp 2:25¾
Nutrition, blk s, 1885, by Nutwood—Beckey, by Edwin Forrest 2:24¼
Nutshell, b m, 1889, by Bayonne Prince—Nutmeg, by Nutbourne 2:27¼
Nuttalite, b m, 1887, by Nutbourne, dam by Backman's Idol 2:26¾
Nutting King, ch s, 1883, by Mambrino King—Nutting Mare 2:19½
Nutwith, b s, 1887, by Nutwood—Virginia Maid, by Sam Purdy 2:19¼
Nutwood, ch s, 1870, by Belmont—Miss Russell, by Pilot Jr 2:18¾
Nutwood Chieftain, ch s, 1886, by Nutwood—Bettie G., by Red Chief.. 2:29¼
Nutwood Jr., ch g, 187—, by Nutwood 2:29½
Nutwood Prince, b s, 1886, by Nutwood—Sister Ruth, by Jim Monroe .. 2:23¾
Nutwood Wilkes, ch s, 1888, by Guy Wilkes—Lida W., by Nutwood 2:19
Nyanza, b m, 1889, by Quartermaster—Kitty Lambert, by Daniel Lambert 2:30
Nyanza, b m, 1889, by Robert McGregor—Telos, by Almont 2:15¾
Nymphia, blk m, 1879, by Mambrino Patchen — Fairy Belle, by Belmont (dead) 2:26¼
O. A. Hickok, b g, 186—, pedigree not traced 2:30
Oakbourne, ch s, 1889, by Gold Leaf—Chloe, by New York 2:27½
Oakdale Dot, blk g, 188—, by Wanderer 2:23¼
Oakhurst, b s, 1884, by Victor Bismarck—Abby, by Bassett's Abdallah 2:26
Oakland Baron, b s, 1892, by Baron Wilkes — Lady Mackey, by Silverthreads 2:14½
Oakland Maid, gr m, 1868, by Speculation—Lady Vernon 2:22
Oakleaf, ch s, 1887, by Gold Leaf—Chloe, by New York 2:28
Oak Leaf, b g, 1887, by Bolton Sprague—Fanny Belle 2:17¼
Oakley Maid, ch m, 1889, by Russia—Jenny, by Ajax 2:24
Oaknut, ch s 1885, by Dawn—Miss Brown, by Brown's Volunteer....... 2:24¼
Oakville Maid, blk m, 188—, by Whippleton 2:26
Oakwood, b s, 1889, by Cadmus Hambletonian — Queen Mab, by Blackwood Jr. 2:24¼
Oakwood, b s, 188— by Twilight.... 2:29
Oasis, b m, 1885, by Onward—Mistress, by Hamlin's Almont Jr. 2:29½
Obediah, br s, 1888, by Oberlin—Mambrino Betty, by Mambrino Chorister 2:25
Oberlin Boy, ch s, 1887, by Elyria—Gyp, by Star of the West 2:27½
O'Blennis, b g, 1841, by Abdallah (dead) 2:30
Observer, ch g, 1868, by Revenge 2:21¼
Ocala, b m, 1885, by Guyle—Nora Norman, by Blackwood 2:23
Occident, br g, 1863, by Doc—Mater Occidentis (dead) 2:16¾
Oceana Chief, ch s, 1863, by Aldrich Colt 2:28
Octavia, blk m, 1877, by Goldenbow—Allie Davis, by Joe Davis......... 2:29¼
Octavius, b s, 1881, by Oxmoor—Octavia, by Rysdyk's Hambletonian .. 2:26¼
Octo, b g, 1888, by Jerome Eddy—Miss Koch, by Homer 2:19½
Ogle Boy, b s, 188—, by Lord Harold. 2:30
Odessa, blk m, 1886, by Adrian Wilkes—Nelly, by Dewey Horse 2:29½
Oddity, b m, 1889, by Princeps—Jeza Belle, by Pilot Mambrino 2:30
Odin, blk g, 1890, by Out-Cross....... 2:29¼
Ofellus, b s, 1889, by Ellerslie Wilkes—Victor Maid, by Sir Walkill....... 2:23
Ogdensburg, ch s, 1885, by Mambrino Patchen—Variety, by Orange Blossom 2:28½
Ohio Boy, b g, 186—, pedigree not traced 2:27¾
Ohio Maid, br m, 1877, by Orr's Flying Cloud—Maggie 2:29¾
Oima, b g, 1885, by Onward—Clio, by Christian's Edwin Forrest......... 2:25¼
O. K., b s, 1887, by Walkill Prince—Gussie G., by Blue Bull............ 2:26¼
O. K., b s, 1891, by Walsingham..... 2:29¾
O. K., b g, 188—, by Brownmont..... 2:29¼
Okalona, blk m, 1881, by Warwick Boy—Brown Kate, by Virginia...... 2:27¾
Olaf, blk g, 1878, by Waveland Chief—Jenny Bryan, by John Dillard.... 2:22
Olaf, b g, 1885, by Mambrino King 2:21¼
Old Crow, ch s, 1885, by Onward—Meta, by Idol Patchen (dead) 2:22
Old Judge, ch g, 1874, by Mambrino Pilot Jr.—Nannie Hedges, by Ned Hawkins........................ 2:20¼
Old Nick, b g, 1878, by Electioneer—Stockton Maid, by Chieftain 2:23
Old Put, br g, 1859, by Clarion—Kate Fay, by Mambrino Messenger (dead) 2:30
Old Sport, dn g, 188—, pedigree not traced........................ 2:26½
Olga, b m, 1887, by Alcantara...... 2:28¼
Olive, b m, 188—, pedigree not traced. 2:27¼
Olive Branch, br m, 1882, by Bonnie Bay—Musette, by Ohio Volunteer .. 2:27¾
Olive K., br m, 188—, by McFarland's Hambletonian 2:29¼
Oliver, br g, 188—, by Adrian Wilkes 2:29½
Oliver, ro g, 187—, pedigree not traced 2:28
Oliver C., b g, 1887, by Dexter Prince—Lady 2:27
Oliver K., b g, 1880, by King Wilkes—Bessie Turner, by Virginius 2:16¼
Oliver Twist, b g, 188— by Graduate 2:29½
Oliver Ross, br s, 1885, by Charley Ross 2:30
Oliver W., b s, 1884, by Wagner Bashaw—Puss Cunningham, by Green's Bashaw 2:24
Oliver West, br s, 1885, by Great Western—Snip, by Magna Charta... 2:25¾
Olivette, b m, 1885, by Rescue—May Queen, by Dr Herr.............. 2:18½
Olivette, b m, 1877, by Black Sultan Jr., dam by Cobb's Brandywine..... 2:28¼
Olivette, b m....... 2:24¼
Olivette, ch m, 1883, by Leon—Gilkey

Boy.................................. 2:27½
Orphina, b m, 1889, by Norval—Orphan Girl, by Piedmont............. 2:17¼
Orrville, b s, 1884, by Redwood—Maggie Lambert, by Daniel Lambert 2:27¾
Ortine, b s, 1891, by Elyria—Schaible Girl, by Bobby..................... 2:22¼
Ortolan, blk m, 1891, by Wilton...... 2:28½
Orwell, blk s, 1883, by Ben Franklin—Dolly Richards, by Blackstone..... 2:24
O. S. B., ch s, 188—, by Sir John Franklin.............................. 2:27
Oscar, br g, 1868, by Reserve, dam by Hector................................ 2:30
Oscar J., b s, 1884, by Thomas K—Dixie, by Mambrunella............. 2:28¾
Oscar Jr., br g, 188—, by Oscar...... 2:28¼
Oscar W., ch g, 188—, by Mambrino Duncan.............................. 2:25¼
Oscar King, b s, 1886, by Mambrino King — Lady Barnes, by Hamlin Patchen.................................. 2:26½
Oscar William, b s, 1890, by Simmons—Lottie Thorne, by Mambrino Patchen.................................... 2:18½
Osito, b s, 1892, by McKinney, dam by Othello.............................. 2:30
Osman, ch s, 188—, by Ossidine, dam by Gen. Benton.......................... 2:27
Ossian Pet, b g, 1871, by Josh Billings, dam by imp. Lapidist....... 2:29¼
Otalgie, br s, 1889, by Greenlander—Amal, by Clay........................ 2:24½
Otard, b g, 1880, by Jay Gould—Martense, by Gen. Knox................. 2:26¼
Othello, br s, 1883, by Sultan—Atlanta, by The Moor...................... 2:28
Otho, blk g, 1877, by Green's Bashaw—Nell, by Prophet.................... 2:22½
Otis Shaw, b s, 1886, by Don Carlos—Nelly Otis, by Winthrop Morrill.... 2:19¼
Otis N., b g, 188—, by Triceps....... 2:26¾
Ottawa Chief, b s, 1878, by Byron—by Morgan............................ 2:25
Ottawa Maid, b m, 188—, by Climax. 2:28¼
Ottinger, b g, 188—, by Dorsey's Nephew................................ 2:11½
Otto, b s, 1889, by Landmark—Nelly Day, by Tower Colt.................. 2:25
Otto J., b g, 1886, by Adjuster—Ola Gurney, by Gurney..................... 2:19¼
Otto K., b g, 1874, by Blue Bull—Queen Guffin, by Pete Guffin......... 2:24¼
Ottumwa Maid, ch m, 1874, by Williams' Mambrino Chief Jr.—Lucy, by Honesty............................... 2:27¾
Ouida, b m, 1885, by Smuggler, dam by Charles Dickens.................... 2:25¼
Ouray, b s, 188—, by Onward—Bonita, by Idol Patchen....................... 2:28¾
Outcross, ch s, 1885, by Jeb Stuart—Happy Sis, by Scott's Hiatoga ... 2:30
Oudan, br s, 1890, by Epaulet—Ella Nutwood, by Nutwood........... 2:20
Outlaw, br g, 1873, by Draco—Iodine, by Gill's Vermont....................... 2:28¼
Overholt, b s, 1889, by Pilot Medium—Silky Lambert, by Daniel Lambert 2:19
Overman, ch g, 1876, by Elmo—Fern Leaf, by McCracken's Black Hawk (dead)...................................... 2:19¼
Ovid, b s, 1883, by Capoul—Mary, by Woodford Mambrino.................. 2:18¾
Owolssa, blk s, 1884, by Onawa—Lady Carney............................. 2:29¼
Ox Eye, b s, 1885, by Gen. Washington—Daisy, by Socrates 2:28½
Oxford, b g, 188—, by Cerokee Chief 2:25¼
Oxford, b g, 1878, by Deucalion—Alice, by Vroom's Toronto Chief Jr. 2:29¼
Oxford Boy, b s, 1883, by Backman's Idol—Lucy Tramp, by Tramp 2:29½
Oxford Chief, b s, 1884, by Chester Chief—Kit, by Wild Irishman....... 2:22½
Oxide, blk s, 1887, by Rumor—Ode, by Gen. Knox.............................. 2:29½
Pabst, b g, 1889, by Pilot Medium, dam by Cady's Champion............. 2:21
Packer, b s, 1879, by Sweepstakes—Lady Rockafellow, by Harry Clay.. 2:23¼
Packet, ch g, 1890, by Pactolus...... 2:27
Pacifica, b m, 1889, by Electioneer—Bicara, by Harold........................ 2:30
Pacolet, b s, 1889, by Phallas—Lady Rolfe, by Tom Rolfe..................... 2:29¼
Pactolus, b s, 1887, by Patronage—Buda, by Tramp.............................. 2:12¾
Paddy Collins, blk g, 187—, by Capt. Bogardus................................ 2:29¼
Paeony, b m, 1884, by Happy Medium—Kentucky Central, by Balsora 2:22
Pagan, blk s, 1880, by Wedgewood—Primrose, by Alexander's Abdallah 2:30
Paladin, ch s, 188—, by Hawthorne—March Fourth, by Whipple's Hambletonian.................................. 2:29½
Palatina, sp m, 1883, by Milton Medium—Snowflake, by Snowstorm .. 2:22¼
Palatine, blk m, 1891, by Palo Alto—Elaine, by Messenger Duroc 2:18
Pallas, b m, 1885, by Gen. Stanton—Roxy, by Caledonia Chief 2:26¼
Palermo 2:24¼
Pall Mall, br s, 188—, by Pancoast... 2:22¼
Palm, b g, 1887, by Messenger Wilkes—Jenny Allen 2:28¼
Palma, ch g, 1869, by Matchless, dam by Beal's Horse........................ 2:22¾
Palo Alto, blk s, 188—, by Barks—Maggie Colburn, by Coeur De Lion Jr.. 2:25¼
Palo Alto, b s, 1882, by Electioneer—Dame Winnie, by Planet (dead).. 2:08¾
Palo Alto Belle, b s, 1886, by Electioneer—Beautiful Bells, by The Moor... 2:22½
Palo Chief, b s, 1890, by Benefit.... 2:30
Pama, b s, 188—, by Woodford Pilot 2:30
Paloma Prince, b s, 188—, by Dexter Prince—Bessie Miller, by Gen. McClellan.. 2:17½
Panama, b s, 1885, by Jay Gould—Pandora, by Clark Chief 2:24½
Pamlico, b s, 1885, by Meander—Birthday, by Daniel Lambert (dead) 2:10
Pan, ch s, 1885, by Pancoast—Midge, by Belmont 2:28½
Pancoast, b s, 1877, by Woodford Mambrino—Bicara, by Harold (dead) 2:21¾
Panclare, b s, 1888, by Pancoast—Lady Clara, by Young Morrill 2:23¼
Pandetta, b m, 1891, by Pandect—Wanatah, by Wedgewood 2:29¾
Pandora, br m, 188—, by Ichi Ban .. 2:30
Pandora, b m, 1887, by Planter—Sally Burrell, by Autocrat 2:27
Pangold, ch s, 1887, by Pancoast—Anthem, by Cuyler 2:24¼
Panic, b g, 1853, by Sherman Black Hawk, dam by Harris' Hambletonian (dead) 2:28
Panic, b m, 188—, by Hannis 2:21½
Pankey John, ch s, 1881, by Capt. Pankey—Suse 2:28¼
Panstone, b s, 1889, by Plumstone—Bessie, by Pancoast 2:19½

Pansy, b m, 1887, by Hamlin's Almont Jr.—Barbara, by Kentucky Prince 2:17¾

Pansy, blk m, 1881,, by Berlin—Lady Hubbard by Benicia Boy 2:24¼

Pansy, br m, 188—, by Mink—Chloe, by New York 2:28¼

Pansy Blossom, b m, 1887, by Glencoe Wilkes—Jessie, by Cilley Horse 2:23

Pansy Blossom, br m, 1890, by Albert W.—Pansy, by Berlin 2:28½

Pansy McGregor, ch m, 1892, by Fergus McGregor—Cora, by Coriander.. 2:17¼

Pantomime, b m, 1890, by Arthurton —Iota, by Princeps 2:21¼

Paola, b s, 1887, by Electioneer—Dame Winnie, by Planet 2:25½

Paragon, b g, 1887, by Storm King—Canace, by Lord Coke 2:13¼

Paragon, b s, 1884, by Deceive—Waldo Mare, by Gray's Hambletonian 2:27½

Parana, b m, 1874, by Mambrino Hambletonian—Belle of Cayuga, by Post's Hambletonian Prince (dead) 2:19¼

Parapet, b s, 1888, by Harold—Mary Belle, by Belmont 2:21

Parker Jr., b g, 188—, pedigree not traced 2:29¼

Paris, b s, 1881, by Mohican—Merry Lass, by Rysdyk's Hambletonian . 2.29¼

Parkside b s, 1888, by Clay—Uinta, by Gen. Benton 2.22¾

Parkwood, ch s, 1888, by Nutwood—Irene Wood, by Combat 2:26½

Parnell, ch s, 1885, by Enfield—Ida Elliot, by Allie West 2.23

Parnell, b s, 1885, by Aberdeen—Betty Brown, by Mambrino Patchen 2:29

Parole, b s, 1889, by Patron—Rachel Ray, by Overstreet Wilkes 2:16

Parone, br s, 1883, by Almont Rattler —Pavonia, by Peacock 2:25¼

Parrott, b g 1873, by Vermont—Clough, by Lumox 2:26

Parthenia, b m, 188—, by Dexter Prince 2:27¼

Parthenia Pedro, b m, 188—, by Dom Pedro 2:29½

Parthenon, b s, 1884, by Aberdeen—Maggie Dunn, by Bourbon Chief.. 2:27¼

Pasadena Belle, br m, 188—, by Navigator 2.18

Pascal, blk g, 188—, by Pascolett 2:27½

Pasha, b s, 1882, by Echo—Young Fashion, by Correct 2:27½

Passenger, b s, 1887, by Red Wilkes —Susie Patchen by Mambrino Patchen 2:30

Pastime, gr s, 1888, by Lord Russell—Noonday, by St. Elmo (dead) 2 27¼

Pastoral, br m, 1888, by Acolyte—Cathedral, by George Wilkes 2:30

Pat, br g, 1882, by Thomas A. Scott —Betts, by Legal Tender 2:26¾

Pat, b g, 1885, by Fortunotus 2:29¼

Patch, b g, 1873, by Detective Patchen, dam by Draco Prince 2:29¼

Patchen, ch g, 1869, by King's Patchen—Old Jane by Wigwam (dead) 2:18¾

Patchen (Gidding's), ch s, 1884, by Seneca Patchen—Fanny G., by Mambrino Hambletonian 2:27¼

Patchen, b s, 187—, pedigree not traced 2:28½

Patchen Maid, ch m, 1875, by Henry B. Patchen—Maggie 2:30

Patchen Medium, b s, 1884, by Happy Medium—Mambrino Maid, by Mambrino Patchen 2:29½

Patchen Wilkes, blk s, 1882, by George Wilkes—Kitty Patchen, by Mambrino Patchen 2:29½

Patchen Wilkes Maid, br m, 1888, by Patchen Wilkes—Daisy B., by Administrator 2:22½

Patchmore, b s, 1886, by Byerly Abdallah—Colon, by Strathmore...... 2:24

Pat Dempsey, blk g, 1878, by Roman Chief, dam by Benedict's Pathfinder 2:29¼

Pat Donoven, b s, 1888, by Newton's Allie Wilkes—Kit, by Yankee Dan.. 2:27¾

Pat Downing, b s, 1885, by Abe Downing—Dagmar, by Mambrino Abdallah 2:13

Patenter, br s, 1887, by Pancoast—Tot, by Dictator 2:27½

Pat Farrel, b g, 188—, pedigree not traced 2:29¾

Pathfinder Jr., br s, 1877, by Buell's Pathfinder—Maggie, by Golddust.. 2:27¾

Pat Hunt, ch g, 186—, by Tecumseh, dam by Doc (dead) 2:25

Patience, blk m, 1879, by Gen. Knox —Sappho, by Jay Gould 2:28¼

Patience, b m, 1880, by Strathmore—Grey Fan, by Selim 2:26¼

Patience, b m, 1886, by Alcyone—Constance, by Aurora 2:27½

Patience, ch m, 1885, by Hull—Welcome, by Iron Duke 2:18¾

Pat L., b s, 1892, by Republican 2:27¼

Pat McCann, blk g, 1871, by Sir George 2:28¼

Pat McGinty, br s, 188—, by Indianap 2:28¼

Pat My Boy, ro g, 1887, by Hinder Wilkes—Bird, by Black Prince Jr... 2:18¼

Patoka Boy, b g, 1891, by Patoka..... 2:30

Patola, blk m, 1886, by Altitude—Julia, by Star of the West 2:19¼

Pat Quinn, br g, 1879, by Modoc Chief—Flora 2:25½

Patrician, b s, 1873, by Thomas Jefferson—Sylph, by Dunbarton 2:26¼

Patrick H, ... 2:27½

Pat Ring, b g, 186—, pedigree not traced (dead) 2:28

Patriot, b s, 1888, by Phallas—Clarinda, by Nutwood 2:24

Patron, br s, 1882, by Pancoast—Beatrice, by Cuyler 2:14¼

Patroness, b m, 1887, by Patronage —Flirt, by Gen. Hatch 2:26½

Patroness, b m, 1888, by Patron—Abbess, by Wedgewood 2.27½

Patroon, b s, 1889, by Patron—Souvenir, by Harold 2 23½

Patsy Curtis, br s, 1888, by Evermond—Bessie Curtis, by Mambrino St. Lawrence 2:16½

Patti, b m, 1879, by Jay Gould—Thornetta, by Gen. Knox 2:24

Patti, gr m, 1886, by Director, dam by Bayswater 2:29¼

Pattie, b m, 188—, by Clay Chief 2:29½

Pattie Cooper, blk m, 1881, by Black Doc—Lucy Marshall, by Clark's Daniel Boone 2:30

Pattie Moore, b m, 188—, by The King 2:30

Pattie P., b m, 1878, by Richmont... 2:27

Pattie R., ch m, 188—, by Bronze.... 2:29½

Paul, gr g, 1883, by Messenger Duroc —Titania, by Golddust Jr.......... 2:23½

Paul B., b g, 188—.......... 2:23¾

Paul Hacke, gr g, 187—, by Strath-
more—Ingoma, by Aker's Idol...... 2:24¼
Pauline, ro m, 1883, by Gov. Sprague
—Lida Lewis, by Sentinel.......... 2:27¼
Pauline, gr m, 1888, by Electrotype—
Kitty Earl, by Earl.................. 2:26
Pauline, ch m, 1890, by Planter, dam
by Rockwood...... .... 2:29¼
Pauline C., blk m, 1888, by Rolla
Golddust..... .... 2:29
Pauline H., b m, 1888, by Kidnapper
Nickel Mare (pacing 2:17¼)......... 2.24
Pauline Lambert, b m, 1880, by Dan-
iel Lambert — Pauline, by Lily's
Shakespeare..... .... 2·29
Paul Pinkham, b s, 1887, by L. P.
Thompson—Lydia Pinkham, by St.
Regis.... .... 2.24
Pawling, ch s, 1891, by Colonel Kip—
Merriment, by Happy Thought..... 2.21¼
Pawnee, b s, 1889, by Stamboul—
Minnehaha, by Stevens' Bald Chief.. 2:26½
Pawnee, b g, 1882, by Jim Wilson—
Legal, by Legal Tender 2.21¾
Peaceful, blk m, 187—, by Gen Knox
(dead)....................... 2:26
Peach, b g, 1878, by Bismarck—Lizzie
Mott, by Gen Mott................. 2:27¼
Peace Blow, br g, 1878, by South Jer-
sey Patchen..., ... 2.29¼
Pearl, b m, 187—, by Gentle Breeze—
Jane, by Gill's Vermont........... 2:30
Pearl, b m, 187—, by Regulus—Cora
F., by Brown Harry............. 2.23½
Pearl, b m, 1880, by Coleman's Abdal-
lah Jr. — Missouri Girl, by Dr.
Morey's Lath 2 30
Pearl, gr m, 188—, by Star Ethan.... 2:25¼
Pearl Belle, b m, 1892, by Bermuda—
Pearl Pinkerton, by Thomas K..... 2.26
Pearl C., rn m, 188—, by Alexander
Dumas............................ 2:30
Pearl Fisher, b m, 1886, by Altamont,
dam by Kisbar.... .... 2:18¼
Pearl McGregor, ch m, 1888, by Rob-
ert McGregor—Maud B., by Seneca
Chief...... .... 2:23¾
Pearl Medium, b m, 1883, by Happy
Medium—Pearl, by Gentle Breeze... 2:24
Pearl P., br m, 188—, by Aladdin..... 2.29½
Pearl Wilkes, br m, 188—, by Wilkes
Spirit Jr.—Giddy Ann............. 2·22¼
Pearl Winship, b m, 1886, by Legal
Tender Jr.—Nelly Mc., by Blue Vein 2 23¼
Pearwood, b s, 1888, by Patronage—
Zora, by Backman's Idol........... 2:25
Pedlar, br s, 1887, by Electioneer—
Penelope, by Mohawk Chief........ 2 23¾
Pedro, gr g, 1870, by Grey Jim, dam
by Paddock's Black Hawk.......... 2:25¼
Pedro L., gr g, 1884, by Bassett M.—
Suse, by Tom Hunter.............. 2:18
Peek-a-Boo, ro g, 1882, by Blue Boy—
Sully, by Green's Bashaw.......... 2:27
Peeler, b s, 1890, by Patron, dam by
Swigert........................ 2 27
Peep O'Day, ch g, 1887, by Dawn—
Emma Steltz, by Mountain Boy.... 2·21
Peerless Ben, ch s, 1886, by Ben
Franklin—Dolly Spooner, by Hola-
bird's Ethan Allen................ 2 26¼
Pegasus, br s, 1881, by Harold—Pera,
by Belmont....................... 2:30
Peko, b m, 1889, by Electioneer—Pen-
elope, by Mohawk Chief........... 2.24
Peleg, b s, 1890, by Reno Defiance—
Lucy Q., by McKinney Horse (pacing
2:16¼)...... .... 2:23¼
Pelerine, b m, 1889, by Madrid —

Blythesome, by Onward.......... 2:19
Pelham, b g, 1837, pedigree not traced
(dead)........................ 2:28
Pemberton, br g, 1872, by Fearnaught
Jr.—Fanny, by Dirigo 2:20½
Pembroke, ro s, 1887, by Sherman's
Hambletonian — Nancy Dillard, by
John Dillard.... .... 2:27¼
Pembroke, b s, 188—, by Jay Bird.... 2.28¼
Pence, br s, 1885, by Rienzi—Lady
Pence, by Almont Forrest.......... 2:24¼
Penelope, dn m, 1871, by Kleckner's
Kemble Jackson.... .... 2:27
Penelope, b m, 188—, by Hinder
Wilkes......................... 2:27½
Penelope, b m, 1890, by Quartermas-
ter—Bohemia, by Rumor.......... 2:29¼
Penelope, b m, 1891, by McEwen—
Elnora, by Tennessee Wilkes....... 2:20¼
Fendelum, b g, 1892, by Panclare..... 2:30
Penhorn, b s, 1887, by Stranger—Bes-
sie, by Shelby Chief............... 2:24¼
Penistan, b g, 1880, by Administrator
—Princess Medium, by Happy Med-
ium............................. 2:28½
Pennant, b s, 1880, by Abe Downing
—Louisa Duvall, by Harold........ 2:15
Penryn, br s, 1889, by Kentucky
Wilkes—Felice, by Mambrino Dud-
ley............................. 2.18½
Pequa Princess, ch m, 188—, by Pequa
Prince......................... 2.27½
Pequot, br s, 1880, by Piedmont—Lady
Duval, by Strader's Cassius M. Clay
Jr............................ 2:26
Peralto, ch g, 187—, by Baird's Ham-
bletonian Prince—Logan Maid, by
Page's Logan.................. 2.26½
Perlette, ch m, 188—, by Juror...... 2.22¼
Perduro, blk s, 1881, by Durango—
Maggie Wells, by Wadsworth Tuch-
ahoe.......................... 2:29¼
Perduro K., b g, 1887, by Perduro—
Fan Stark..................... 2:19¼
Perhaps, b s, 1883, by Hambletonian
Tranby—Easter, by Gen. Geo. H.
Thomas....................... 2:30
Pericles, ch s, 1881, by Mambrino
Patchen—Fancy, by Curtis Clay.... 2·30
Perihelion, b s, 1880, by Admiral—
Black Flora, by Black Prince....... 2:25
Periwinkle, b m, 1891, by Ponce de
Leon — Rowena, by Black Hawk
Traveler....................... 2:28¾
Perkins, ch s, 188—, by C. F. Clay.... 2:20¼
Pero, b s, 1883, by Backman's Idol—
Cora Jackson, by Stonewall Jackson 2:25
Perplexed, ch m, 1879, by Locksmith
—Early Rose, by Godfrey Patchen.. 2:24¼
Persica, b m, 1883, by Belmont—Nec-
tarine, by William Welch.......... 2:18½
Persimmons, br s, 1885, by Simmons
—Nona B., by Administrator....... 2:29¾
Peru, gr s, 1889, by Sphinx—Pilot
Belle, by Pilot Medium........... 2:29½
Pet, b g, 188—, by Black Ethan 2:19½
Pet, gr m, 188—, by Orphan Boy..... 2:25
Pet Davis, gr m, 1888, by Crit Davis
—Maud T., by Tuckahoe.......... 2:19½
Pete, b g, 187—, pedigree not traced. 2:28
Pete Curran, b g, 188—, by Chicago
Volunteer..................... 2:28½
Pete Lindley, ch g, 1881, by Royal
Fearnaught — Lindley Mare, by
Fisk's Mambrino Chief Jr .... 2·27¼
Peter Cooper, br g................. 2·21¼
Peter Hardwood, br s, 1886, by Hard-
wood—Eugenia, by Louis Napoleon. 2:20
Peter K., ch g, 1880, by Royal Fear-

naught—Kitty, by Magna Charta.... 2:29¼
Peter R., gr g, 188—, pedigree not traced.... 2:28½
Peter W., b g, 1887, by Roscoe—Hattie Barnum, by son of Gladiator... 2:24½
Peter Whetstone, b g, 1884, by McQuaid's Sprague—Fashion, by Norme 2:29¼
Petitioner, b s, 1887, by Sherman's Hambletonian—Nannie Dillard, by John Dillard.... 2:26¼
Petrolia, b s, 1886, by Red Wilkes—Belle Newman, by Long Boy.... 2:27½
Pet Thorne, b m, 1887, by Hawthorne—Lady Pet, by Reuben.... 2:29
Peveril, ch s, 1889, by Elyria—Jenny D., by Tom Hunter.... 2:14½
Pew House, ch g, 1889, by Mohawk Gift—Lady, by Star Hambletonian.. 2:30
Phalen, blk g, 188—, by Montello, dam by Billy Ring.... 2:22½
Plain Dick, b g, 188—, by South Side, dam by Duke.... 2:29
Phallamiss, b m, 1888, by Phallamont—Athena, by Mack Almont.... 2:29½
Phallamont Boy, b s, 1887, by Phallamont—Pocahontas Girl, by Pocahontas Boy.... 2:18
Phallamont Chief, b s, 1887, by Phallamont—Athena, by Mack Almont... 2:30
Phallamont Girl, b m, 1885, by Phallamont—Pocahontas Girl, by Pocahontas Boy.... 2:27¾
Phallamont Sprague, b s, 1890, by Phallamont—Carrie Dexter, by Billy Sprague.... 2:27¼
Phallamont Swigert, b s, 1889, by Phallamont—Mattie, by Dave Bonner.... 2:28
Phallas, b s, 1877, by Dictator—Betsy Trotwood, by Clark Chief.... 2:13¾
Phallene, b m, 1885, by Phallamont—Maud McK., by Richard.... 2:30
Phantom, b m, 1889, by Alcazar—Apparition, by Sir Walkill.... 2.24¼
Phantom, b s, 1886, by Strathmore—Princess Ethel, by Volunteer.... 2:29¼
Phay, b s, 1888, by Burdette—Margery D., by Broken Leg.... 2:27¾
P. H. Chapin, b s, 1885, by Chapin Egmont—Fanny Parvin, by Green's Bashaw.... 2:29¼
Pheon, gr m, 1882, by Jim Ervin—Oropea, by Pilot Duroc.... 2:24
Phil, b g, 186—, pedigree not traced.. 2:23¼
Phil Caswell, ch g, 188—, by Whalebone.... 2:28
Phil Dougherty, ch g, 186—, by Frank Pierce Jr. (dead).... 2:26
Phil Dwyer, b g, 1871, by Island Chief—Peerless, by Defiance.... 2:29¼
Philip H., b s, 188—, by Red Bird.... 2:27½
Phillis, b s, 1888, by Masterlode—Comet, by Lexington Chief Jr.... 2:30
Phil Mack, b g, 188—, by Phil Sheridan Jr.... 2:29¾
Phillis, b g, 188—, by Pickering.... 2:25¼
Phil O., b g, 188—, by Jim Swigert... 2:25¾
Philosee, b m, 1881, by Polonius—Philosee, by Warlock.... 2:22¼
Phil Sheridan, br s, 1862, by Young Columbus—Black Fly, by a son of Tippoo (dead).... 2:26½
Phil Sheridan, gr g, 1866, by Creeper—Lady Alice (dead).... 2:26½
Phil Sheridan Jr., blk s, 1877, by Phil Sheridan—Estelle B.... 2:28½
Phil Thompson, gr g, 1878, by Red Wilkes—Grey Nelly, by John Dillard.... 2:16½
Phil W., ch g, 1885, by Great Western—Nettie H.... 2.21
Phoebe Wilkes, br m, 1885, by Hambletonian Wilkes—Dolly Smith, by Fisk's Mambrino Chief Jr.... 2:08¼
Phurah, b s, 1884, by St. Gothard—Jessie D., by Niagara Chief.... 2:30
Phyllis, br m, 1874, by Phil Sheridan—Nelly Wagner, by Tom Sayers (dead).... 2:15½
Phyllis Tee, b m, 1890, by Ashland Wilkes—Nelly Carson, by Peavine... 2:23¼
Pickard, b g, 1874, by Abdallah Pilot—Lady Bowman, by Bourbon Chief 2:18¼
Pickering, b s, 1872, by Rysdyk's Hambletonian—Lady Fallis, by Seely's American Star.... 2:30
Pickett, ch g, 1887, by Pickett—Amanda, by Goldsmith Chief.... 2:16¼
Pickpania, b m, 1884, by Pickpocket—Lady, by Panic.... 2:14¼
Pickwick, br g, 1869, by Backman's Idol—Lady Brown, by Seely's American Star.... 2:29½
Pickwick, b g, 1876, by Hatch Horse, dam by Young Ethan Allen.... 2:27½
Piedmont, ch s, 1871, by Almont—Mag Ferguson, by Mambrino Chief (dead).... 2:17¼
Piletta, gr m, 1889, by Pilot Medium—Maggie, by Hambletonian-Charta 2:14½
Pilgrim, br s, 1885, by Coriander—Abdallah Duchess, by Silver Duke 2:24¼
Pilgrim, br s, 1889, by Acolyte—Cathedral, by George Wilkes.... 2:20¾
Pilgrimage, b s, 1882, by Egbert—April Fool, by Norwood.... 2:30
Pilot, blk g, 1850, by Pilot Jr. (dead) 2:28¾
Pilot, b g, 1886, by Middletown Jr.—Jessie, by David Bonner.... 2:22¾
Pilot, (Lee's) gr s, 1887, by Pilot Medium—Mady L., by Honest Dick.... 2:12½
Pilot Boy, b g, 187—, by Kilmore.... 2:27¾
Pilot Boy gr g, 1878, by Edward H.—Tackey, by Pilot Jr.... 2:20
Pilot Claus, blk s, 188—, by Santa Claus.... 2:26¼
Piloteen, b m, 1892, by Pilot Medium—Midget, by Orion.... 2:28½
Pilot H., gr g, 1886, by Pilot Medium—Gypsy, by Tom Hunter Jr.... 2:29½
Pilot Knox, b s, 1875, by Black Pilot—Nancy Knox, by Col. Ellsworth (pacing 2:20½).... 2:19¾
Pilot Lemont, ch s, 1887, by Lemont—Mellia Mack, by Deadshot.... 2:21¾
Pilot Maid, b m, 1887, by Black Pilot—Alice, by Harry W. Genet.. 2:21¼
Pilot Middleton, gr s, 1884, by Pilot Medium—Topsy, by Bay Middleton.... 2:26½
Pilot Jr., blk s, 1888, by Black Pilot, dam by Constellation.... 2:21
Piloton, br s, 1878, by Middletown—Forest Queen, by Mambrino Pilot.. 2:30
Pilot R., b g, 187—, by Black Knight, dam by Grey Wallace.... 2:21¾
Pilot R. Jr., b g, 187—, pedigree not traced.... 2:30
Pilot Temple, b s, 1859, by Pilot Jr.—Madam Temple (dead).... 2:24½
Pilot W., gr s, 1884, by Pilot Duroc—Kitty Wilson, by Blue Bull.... 2:24¼
Pilot W., gr g, 1885, by Pilot Medium—Maggie.... 2:24
Pink, ch m, 1882, by Inca—Fairy Queen, by Echo.... 2:23½
Pip, blk s, 1890, by Durango—Pyro-

JOHN E. TURNER. Ambler, Pa,

(THE GENERAL.)

"Give me races and few records, as I want the money and
have no craving for honors," has been the motto
of John E. Turner through life.

C. THOMPSON, INDEPENDENCE, IOWA.

One of the cleverest of Western drivers. He brought out
Manager 2:06¾ and Keno F. 2:17.

by Phil Sheridan 2:27

Prescott, ch g, 1882, by Knox—Annetta, by Messenger Duroc 2:27½

Present, b g, 1882, by Young Rolfe, dam by Whalebone Knox 2:23½

Presquile, b s, 1889, by Norfolk, dam by Mambrino King 2:29¼

Presto, b s, 1887, by Gen. Washington—Gilda, by Jay Gould (dead) ... 2:19½

Preston, dn g, 186—, by George Washington (dead) 2:28½

Preston, b s, 1888, by Wilkes Boy—Katherine, by Shelby Chief 2:27¾

Preston Wilkes, blk g, 1876, by Wilkes Spirit—Glencoe Maid 2:29½

Pretty Belle, b m, 1884, by Messenger Chief—Sorrel Belle, by Bay Dick (dead) 2:22½

Pretty Boy, br s, 1880, by Mambrino Patchen—Dixie, by Mokhladi 2:20½

Pricemont, b s, 1885, by Altamont—Belle Price, by Doble 2:26

Pride, b m, 1888, by Aquarius—Aggie G., by Trampaway 2:18

Pride of Idaho, br s, 1884, by Harper—Brown Jug, by Green's Bashaw 2:29¾

Prime, br m, 1888, by Primo—Dolly Smith, by Fisk's Mambrino Chief Jr. 2:21¼

Primmont, b s, 1884, by Belmont—Electric, by Princeps 2:21¼

Primrose, b s, 188—, by Melrose—May Day 2:29¼

Primus, ch g, 1888, by Wilkie Russell 2:29

Prince, blk g, 1885, by Appleby—Ann M., by Nimrod Tom 2:18½

Prince b g, 1882, by Swanbrough's Hambletonian Prince—Kate 2:26¼

Prince, b g, 1846, by Long Island Black Hawk (dead) 2:24½

Prince, ch g, 1860, by Jupiter Abdallah—Van Wyck Mare (dead)........ 2:27

Prince, b g, 188—, pedigree not traced. 2:28¼

Prince, ro g, 186—, pedigree not traced (dead)...... .... 2:27¾

Prince, b g, 1875, by Baird's Hambletonian Prince—Baird, by Superb.... 2:23

Prince, blk g, 187—, by Royal Revenge—Lady, by McKerson's Grey Eagle...... .... 2:21¼

Prince, b g, 188—, by Waxford....... 2:28¾

Prince, ch g, 1882, by Lysander—Harry's Daughter, by Harry Clay Jr. 2:20¼

Prince, b s, 188—, by Beaufort, dam by Black Ralph...... .... 2:27¼

Prince, b g, 188—, pedigree not traced........ .... 2:30

Prince, blk g, 188—, by Belmont Prince...... .... 2:30

Prince A., b g, 1886, by Swanbrough's Hambletonian Prince.... ... . 2:26¼

Prince A., br g, 1880, by Major Miller—Jenny........ .... 2:22¼

Prince A., b g, 1884, by Backman's Idol, dam by Orange Duroc........ 2:19¼

Prince A. G., ch s, 1887, by Princepter—Byron Girl, by Byron.......... 2:29½

Prince Albert, b g, 1888, by Hamilton 2:28¼

Prince Albert, b g, 1882, by Golden Bow, dam by Western Fearnaught.. 2:25¼

Prince Albert, b s, 1885, by Strathmore — Patchienie, by Mambrino Patchen...... .... 2:26

Prince Allen, ch s, 1859, by Honest Allen, dam by Green Mountain Eagle (dead)...... .... 2:26½

Prince Allen, b g, 1865, by Vick's Ethan Allen—Jenny Lind (dead).... 2:27

Prince Allerton, b s, 1891, by Allerton 2:28¾

Prince Almont, gr g, 1885, by Hamlin's Almont Jr..... .... 2:27

Prince Arthur, b g, 1873, by Volunteer...... .... 2:20

Prince Arthur, b g, 187—, by Western Fearnaught 2:18

Prince Axtell, b s, 1891, by Axtell—Athmald, by Athlete.... .... 2:28¼

Prince B., ch g, 188—, by Senator.... 2:26¼

Prince B., b g, 1880, by Brilliant—Maud, by son of George M. Patchen Jr...... .... 2:24½

Prince Belmont, b s, 1886, by Principe—Jenny Belle, by Belmont...... 2:29½

Prince Boy, b g, 1883, by Black Tom—Bay Nell, by Clarion Chief........ 2:27¼

Prince Brino, ch s, 1884, by Mambrino Barker — Polly Hopkins, by Mambrino Star....... .... 2:29¼

Prince Daniels, b g, 1887, by Dexter Prince, dam by Joe Daniels........ 2:22½

Prince Dexter, blk g, 1887, by Dexter Prince—Cole Mare, by Western Boy 2:19

Prince Dudley, b s, 1887, by Princeps—Belle Dudley, by Belmont (dead) . 2:29¾

Prince Eddy, b s, 188—, by Jerome Eddy...... .... 2:29¾

Prince Edsall, blk s, 1888, by Princeton—Lady Edsall, by Westwood.... 2:18¼

Prince Edward, b s, 188—, by King Rene—Smyrna, by Japhet........... 2:20

Prince Egbert, b s, 1886, by Egbert—Ella, by Clark Chief............... 2:29½

Prince Eugene, b s, 1887, by Bayonne Prince — Dolly Star, by Rysdyk's Hambletonian...... .... 2:27½

Prince Eugene, b g, 1884, by Bourbon Wilkes, dam by Edwin Forrest Jr.. 2:28¼

Prince Fearnaught, blk s, by Fearnaught Jr., dam by Col King....... 2:23¼

Prince G., b g, 188—, pedigree not traced........ .... 2:28

Prince Gould...... .... 2:24½

Prince H., b g, 1885, by Haw Patch—Mag, by Tom Hunter..... .... 2:17¾

Prince H., b g, 188—, by Marsh Young—Bird....... .... 2:29

Prince H., b g, 188—, by Sweepstakes 2:26½

Prince Harbinger, b g, 188—, by Harbinger, dam by Von Moltke......... 2:30

Prince Henry, blk g, 1883, by Lothair Chief—Maestro, by Rifleman 2:23¼

Prince Herschel, b s, 1889, by Herschel—Hibernia, by Princeps 2:13

Prince Hogarth, blk s, 1885, by Kentucky Prince — Hattie Hogan, by Harry Clay...... .... 2:27½

Prince Imperial, b s, 1879, by Gen. Stanton—Dolly, by Prince of Wales. 2:27½

Prince Karl, b s, 1886, by Commander—Katie, by Regalia.... .... 2:26½

Prince Karl, gr s, 1888, by Gambetta Wilkes—Lady Haseltine, by Mambrino Startle..... .... 2:30

Prince L., b s, 1882, by Bourbon Wilkes—Daisy Monroe, by Monroe Chief...... .... 2:21¼

Prince Lavalard, gr s, 188—, by Lavalard—Young Daisy, by Strideaway... 2:29¼

Prince M., b g, 1884, by Lucas Brodhead, dam by Coldwater Chief..... 2:16¾

Prince M., b g, 1884, by Swanbrough's Hambletonian Prince...... 2:29¼

Prince McMahon, blk g, 1883, by McMahon...... .... 2:21

Prince Medium, br s, 1882, by Happy Medium—Pensora, by Strader's Cassius M. Clay Jr....... .... 2:26

Prince Medium, b s, 1886, by Paris Medium — Lady Patchen, by Bully King.... 2:29½
Prince Middleton, b g, 1877, by Bay Middleton — Crosley, by Prince Charles 2d.... 2:20¼
Prince Miller, br s, 1887, by Maj. Miller—Starine, by Deucalion 2:20½
Prince N., b g, 188—, by Princeton... 2.30
Princeno, br g, 1890, by Princeps—Olympia, by Oxmoor.... 2:30
Prince Nero.... 2:29¼
Prince Nutwood, b s, 1885, by Nutwood—Empress, by Draco.... 2.26
Princionia, b m, 188—, by Prince Edward.... 2:28¼
Princeppa Belmont, b m, 1890, by Belmont—Hesione, by Princeps.... 2:30
Prince R., b g, 188—.... 2:28
Prince Regent, ch s, 1885, by Mambrino King—Estabella, by Alcantara (dead).... 2 16½
Prince S., b g, 1885, by Volunteer Swigert — Kit, by Gray Eagle (Blind Eagle.... 2:20¼
Prince S., br g, 188—, by Jumping Prince.... 2:22¼
Prince S., br g.... 2 25¼
Princeps Jr., blk s, 188—, by Princeps 2:26¼
Princess, blk m, 1870, by Dictator—Flora.... 2 29
Princess, b m, 1846, by Andrus' Hambletonian—Isaiah Wilcox Mare, by Burdick's Engineer (dead).... 2:30
Princess, b m, 188—, by Black Morgan 2:28
Princess, gr m, 1888, by Woolsey—Oakland Maid, by Speculation 2:19¾
Princess, b m, 1881, by Baird's Hambletonian Prince—Kitty B., by Edward Everett 2:27½
Princess, b m, 1878, by Hemlock—Queen of Trumps, by Continental.. 2·30
Princess, ch m, 1875, by Tramp—Barnford Mare, by Green's Bashaw 2 29½
Princess, ch m, 1878, by Masterlode—Kate Hunter, by Pierce Horse... 2:29½
Princess Belle, br m, 1890, by Bell Boy—Musetta, by King Rene.... 2:24¾
Princess Clara, b m, 1892, by Prince George—Reality, by Princeps.... 2 26½
Princess Eboli, ch m, 1889, by Don Carlos—Lizzie Thomas, by Wedgewood 2 24½
Princess M., ch m, 188—, by Merriworth, dam by Ethan Allen 2.26¼
Princess M., b m, 187—, pedigree not traced 2:30
Princess Maid b m, 1890, by Dresden Price—Maid Righter, by Victor Bismarck 2 22¼
Prince Rene b g, 1889, by King Rene—Amy 2 23¼
Princess Orloff, b m, 1887, by Prince Orloff—Lucy, by Frank Pierce Jr.. 2:29¼
Princess Royal, br m, 1890, by Chimes—Estabella, by Alcantara 2:20
Princeton, b g 1876, by Honest Abe—Lady Johnson, by Tornado .... 2·27
Princeton, br s, 1881, by Princeps—Reina Victoria, by Rysdyk's Hambletonian 2 19¾
Princeton, b g, 1880, by Alcazar—Echo Belle, by Echo 2 29¾
Prince T., ch s, 188—, by George O—Boscabel .... 2·29½
Princeton Boy, ch g, 188—, by Vermont Hero (dead) 2 28
Prince Wilkes, ch g, 1881, by Red Wilkes—Rose Chief, by Brown Chief 2:14¾
Prince Wilkes, b g, 1887, by Red Wilkes 2:20¼
Princewood, b g, 188—, by Lakewood Prince 2:21¼
Princewood, blk s, 1888, by Princeps—Jet, by Ravenswood 2:18¼
Princewood, blk g, 1889, by Dexter Prince—Hattie B., by Hawthorne. (dead) 2:16
Principe, b s, 1880, by Princeps—Nannie Dixon, by Velox .... 2·24½
Prinsonian, ch s, 1888, by Mambritonian—Ellen M., by Baird's Hambletonian Prince 2:20½
Prior, b s, 1888, by Primmont—Emma Clay, by American Clay 2:29½
Priscilla, blk m, 1888, by William Rysdyk—Jessie Downs, by Holmes' Wandering Jew 2:29¼
Pritchard, ch g, 187—, pedigree not traced .... 2·24½
Private Joe, ch g, 188—, by Golddust Lambert 2.29¼
Prize, b s, 1882, by Piloteer—Glasseye 2.22¼
Problem, b g, 1881, by Kentucky Prince—Mary A., by Messenger Duroc 2.18
Procrastination, br s, 1884, by Challenger—Belle, by Woodford Abdallah 2·29¼
Proctor, b g, 186—, by Harris' Mambrino Chief Jr. (dead).... 2:23
Proctor W., b s, 1889, by Jim Wilkes—Alice Hook, by Goldsmith Star.. 2.26½
Prodigal, b s, 1886, by Pancoast—Beatrice, by Cuyler .... 2·16
Proem, b m, 1884, by Dictator—Lady Holloway, by Holloway's Denmark 2 28¼
Professor, b g, 186—, pedigree not traced (dead) .... 2·27¾
Prohibit, br s, 1885, by Woodford Pilot—Van, by Baker's Hambletonian 2.25½
Prohibition, b s, 1885, by Petoskey—Lulu Parrish, by Almoore 2:27¼
Promoter, b s, 1888, by Acolyte—Musette, by Ohio Volunteer 2:19
Prose, b s, 1888, by Gen Washington—Sonnet, by Jay Gould 2:27¼
Prospect, br s, 1886, by Reno Defiance, dam by Sir Denton 2:18¾
Prospect, ch s, 1886, by Dominion—Penelope, by Album .... 2·27¼
Prospect Maid, br m, 1874, by George Wilkes—Neilsson, by Mambrino Pilot 2 23¼
Prospect Simmons, ch g, 1890, by Simmons—Maud A., by Almont Boy.... 2:23¾
Prosperity, blk s, 1887, by Leland—Integrity, by Belmont 2:23
Prosper Merimee, b s 1877, by Fritz—Anticipation, by Clay Pilot .... 2·24¼
Prospero, blk g, 1869, by Messenger Duroc—Green Mountain Maid, by Harry Clay (dead) 2 20
Prosperous, b s, 1887, by Vacher—Ida Charta, by Magna Charta.... 2·29¾
Protection, b g, 1880, by Ernest—Molly, by Gray Eagle 2.19¾
Protien, b m 1888, by Glenwold—Portia, by Startle 2:15½
Proteine, br m, 1871, by Blackwood—Sally Chorister, by Mambrino Chorister (dead) 2.18
Proth, b m, 188—, by Onward—Lady Allen 2:29½
P. R. T., br g 188— 2:28½
Prue, b m, 1889, by Pure Wilkes—

Lilly Clay, by Kensington......... 2 21½
Psyche, ch m, 1888, by Declaration—
Bessie Clay, by Strader's Cassuis
M. Clay Jr. 2.24½
Psyche, ch m, 1889, by Wilkes Gold-
dust—Beauty, by Lowell's Gold-
dust .... 2·15¼
Puck, blk g, 188—, by Tacoma—Har-
mony, by Middletown 2:17¼
Puella, b m, 1887, by Post Boy—Ella,
by Cripple 2:29
Puella, ch m,.1878, by Harold—Mary
Bell, by Belmont 2:29
Punchellino, br g, 1887, by Kentucky
Prince, dam by Sweepstakes 2 28
Pure Wilkes, b s, 1886, by Red Wilkes
—Purity, by Brignoli 2 17½
Puritan, b g, 1886, by Steele—Har-
mony, by Smuggler 2:18¼
Puritan, b g, 1878, by Champion
Drew—Belle Knox, by Gilbreth
Knox 2.30
Puritan, blk g, 1889, by Sable Wilkes
—Jane E. by Milliman's Bellfounder. 2:29½
Purity, ch m, 1864, by Blue Bull—
Susan Loder, by Daniel Boone ... 2·30
Purity, br m, 1884, by Royal Almont
—Kate 2 28
Purity Wilkes, b m, 1887, by King
Wilkes—Purity, by Middletown.... 2.15¾
Puzzle, br s, 1889, by Phallas—
Lizzie W., by Swigert 2.30
Pygmalion, b s, 188—, by Jay Gould . 2 25½
Pythias, ch s, 1883, by King Rene—
Romona, by Harold 2.28¾
Qu Allan, b s, 188—, by Champion
Medium 2 20
Quaker Boy, b s, 1888, by Ohio Knick-
erbocker—Lady B., by Bayard . . 2 24
Quaker Boy, b g, 185—, pedigree not
traced (dead) 2 28¼
Quaker Boy, ch g, 1887, by Cashier—
Minnehaha, by Star of the West 2:30
Quaker Girl, br m, 1870, by Hail-
storm—Fanny H., by Independence . 2 30
Quality, b m, 1889, by Electioneer—
McCa, by Almont 2 25½
Quarryville Boy, br g, 188—, by Mes-
senger Chief, dam by Red Wilkes . 2.26
Quartermain, b s, 1888, by Quarter-
maste—Patchen Maid, by Mam-
brino Patchen 2.27¾
Quartermarch, b s, 188—, by Quarter-
master, dam by Sir Walter 2.19¼
Quartermain, b s, 1888, by Quarte-
master—Patchen Maid, by Mam-
brino Patchen 2.27½
Quartermaster, br s, 1883, by Alcyone
—Qui Vive, by Sentinel 2.21¼
Quarterstretch, br s, 1888, by Quarter-
master—Lady Schofield, by Tippoo
Saib 2:15
Quartette, b g, 1880, by Richwood—
Coronet, by Almont 2 22¾
Quay, b s, 1887, by Beaumont—Nelly
Green, by Billy Green 2.28½
Queechee Maid, br m, 186—, by Bal-
lard's Cassius M. Clay, dam by
Morse Horse 2 25
Queechy, b s, 1886, by Alcyone—Myra
B., by Joe Brown............... 2 14¼
Queen, b m, 188—, by Nelson, dam
by Old Abe 2 19¼
Queen Alfred, b m, 1891, by Alfred
G —Alla Star, by Jay Bird 2 18¼
Queen Allah, ch m, 1891, by Almon-
arch—Flirt, by Leader Jr..... 2 21¼
Queen Almont, b m, 188—, by King
Almont 2 27½

Queen Ann, b m, 188—, by State of
Maine...................... 2:28
Queen Anne, gr m, 1885, by Totoway
—Queen 2.25
Queen Anne, ch m, 1885, by Alcantara
—Princess 2:30
Queen Clay, br m, 1886, by King
Clay—Irene, by Dusty Miller 2.28
Queen Esther, b m, 1888, by Viking—
Ada W., by Gideon 2:29¾
Queen Fearnaught, b m, 1886, by Al-
cantara—Modjeska, by Royal Fear-
naught 2 25½
Queen H., b m, 1880, by Hanover,
dam by Atlantic 2:29½
Queen Garrett, b m, 1891, by Garrett. 2:30
Queen Mab, gr m, 1877, by Daniel
Lambert 2 29¼
Queen Mab, b m, 188— 2.24½
Queen Mark, b m, 1889, by Victor
Bismarck—Big Six, by Hambrino... 2.27
Queen Nutwood, b m, 1889, by King
Nutwood—Mattie Windsor, by Wind-
sor 2:27¼
Queen of Cedars, b m, 1889, by Epau-
let—Princess Medium, by Happy
Medium 2 20¾
Queen of Scotts, ch m, 1889, by Scott
Chief—Minnie Wilson, by Spring-
field 2.28
Queen of the West, gr m, 1860, by
Pilot Jr.,—Nelly, by Young Turk
(dead) 2 26¼
Queen of Upland, b m, 1887, by
Epaulet—Audacity, by Happy Med-
ium 2:22¼
Queen Susie, b m, 1889, by King
Wilkes—Vinette, by Belmont 2:29¾
Queensware, blk m, 1888, by Wedge-
wood—Elvira, by Cuyler........ 2.25
Queen T., b m, 1885, by Monitor—
Katie Belle, by Peacemaker Jr... 2.26¼
Queen Tempo, gr m, 1890, by Poco
Tempo—Jenny A., by Lepanto...... 2.28¼
Queen Wilkes, blk m, 1879, by George
Wilkes—Lady Ethan, by Ethan Allen 2.23¼
Queen Wilkes, br m, 1886 by Jay
Bird—Jessica, by George Wilkes ... 2 26½
Quickstep, b m, 1889, by Pilot Med-
ium—Trixey, by Louis Napoleon... 2.27
Quillsine, b g, 188—, by Judge Bald-
win 2 22½
Quilp, b s, 188—, by Boston Wilkes. 2.27½
Quinine S., b s, 1884, by Abdallh
Mambrino—Ella Hopkins, by Octo-
roon 2.28¼
Quiver, b g, 188—, by Indus......... 2:29¼
Quiz, b m, 1890, by Wilkiemont—
Corida, by Bona Fide 2.23¼
Rabb Wilkes, b s, 1889, by Memento
Wilkes—Golden Rule, by Golden
Bow 2 26
Rabe, ch g, 1883, by Strader—Susie,
by Green's Bashaw 2.24
Rachel, br m, 187—, by Woodford
Mambrino—Princess Ann, by Alex-
ander's Abdallah 2 26¾
Rachel, ch m, 1891, by Warlock...... 2:25¼
Rachel B., b m, 1884, by Chester Chief
—Mattie H by Deucalion .... 2·18¼
Rachel B., blk m, 1876, by Allie West
—Molly, by Williams' Mambrino... 2.28½
Racer, b g, 1888, by Reveille—Nanny
Talbot, by Strathmore 2:19¼
Racine, gr g, 1886, by Pilot Medium,
dam by Mambrino Bruce 2.14
Racine, b s. 1884, by Swigert—Lady
Belle, by Richard's Bellfounder.... 2 30
Racket, br g, 1883, by Cylburn—Meta,

by Mambrino Pilot 2:30
Radius, g g, 188—, by Tangent 2:28½
Rag Baby, b g, 188—, by Hambletonian Downing.................. 2:22¼
Rainbow, b s, 1891, by Silver Bow, dam by Reliance 2:24¼
Rajah, br s, 1883, by Sultan—Kitty Wilkes, by George Wilkes 2:29¼
Ralph Wilkes, ch s, 1889, by Red Wilkes—Mary Mays, by Mambrino Patchen 2:06¾
Ramon, b g 2:23
Ramona, blk m, 188—, by Elevator... 2:29¼
Ramona, br m, 1886, by Pilot Wilkes—Neat, by New York 2:26¼
Ramona, b m, 1886, by Alcyone—Rachel, by Woodford Mambrino.... 2:16
Ramona, b m, 1884, by Cortland Wilkes—Wingate, by Blackwood.... 2:28¼
Ramona, br m, 1888, by Whitney—Empress, by Kensett 2:16¾
Ramona Wilkes, b m, 1886, by Brown Wilkes—Lady Whitelaw, by Mambrino Clay 2:29¼
Rampart Jr., b s, 188—, by Rampart, dam by Constellation 2:27½
Ranchero, ch s, 1877, by Clark Chief Jr.—Mary Eagle, by American Clay. 2:21¼
Randall, ch g, 186—, by Chauncey Goodrich (dead) 2:24½
Ranger, b g, 1886, by Nil Desperandum—Eugenia, by Thorndale....... 2:23¼
Ranger H., br g, 1886, by Typhoon—Fan, by Richmond Boy 2:27
Raola, br m, 1889, by Greenlander—Brilliant, by Electioneer 2:28¼
Rapid Ann, sp m, 187—, pedigree not traced 2:30
Rapid Transit, b g, 1889, by Autograph—Miss McGree, by C. W. Mitchell 2:29¼
Rapid Transit, b s, 1889, by Onward—Monette, by Bonnie Bay 2:18½
Rare Ben, b s, 1883, by Ben Franklin—Dolly Spooner, by Holadird's Ethan Allen 2:26
Rare John, blk g, 1889, by Rare Ben, dam by Wheeler Horse 2:18½
Rarely, gr g, 1875, by Ericsson—Miss Weeks, by Joe Downing 2:24½
Rare Ripe, b g, 1877, by Autocrat—Turner Mare 2:19¼
Rarus, b g, 1867, by Conklin's Abdallah—Nancy Awful, by Telegraph (dead) 2:13¼
Rashleigh, ch s, 1887, by Inglewood—Pat 2:28¼
Rattle Bones, b g, 1885, by Sterling—May D., by Joe David 2:28
Rattler, ro s, 188—, pedigree not traced 2:30
Rattler (Rowley's), ch s, 1877, by Allard Horse 2:25¼
Raven, blk s, 1883, by Ogden's Hambletonian Mambrino—Melissa, by Cuyler 2:26¾
Raven, blk s, 1886, by Cyclone—Kate Westwood, by Westwood 2:29¼
Raven, blk m, 1884, by Almont Raven—Queen 2:27¾
Raven Boy, blk s, 1888, by Mambrino Duke—Polly, by Ajax Jr. 2:29¾
Raven Sprague, blk g, 1883, by Rounds' Sprague—Betsy King, by Menelaus Jr. 2:19½
Raven Wilkes, blk s, 188—, by Lyle Wilkes 2:29½
Raven Wilkes, blk s, 1888, by Guy Wilkes—Lady Maud, by Rockwood.. 2:15½
Ray, b g, 188—, by Epicure.......... 2:28
Ray C., b g, 188—, by Antar 2:29
Ray Gould, b m, 1875, by Jay Gould—Emeline, by Henry B. Patchen.... 2:29½
Ray Jackson, b s, 1883, by Whirlwind Chief—Lady Austin, by Envoy 2:29¼
Raymon, b s, 1885, by Simmons—Lady Raymond, by Carlisle 2:27¼
Raymond, b s, 188—, by Rex Patchen. 2:27¼
Raymond Wilkes, ch s, 1888, by Raymond—Kitty Clover, by Captain.... 2:26
Rayometta, b m, 188—, by Anteeo—Debonaire 2:27
Razor B., b g, 187—, by Robert Whaley 2:25
R. B., b g, 1877, by Wood's Hambletonian—Fanny S., by Watkins Horse 2:29¼
R. C., ch g, 188—, by Black Bonner.. 2:28¼
R. D. F., b g, 1884, by Aristos—Empress, by Bay Lester 2:21¼
Readington Prince, b s, 1886, by Bayonne Prince—Belle Medium, by Happy Medium 2:22½
Ready Boy, gr s, 1884, by Arnold—Pearly Rothschild, by Rothschild... 2:23¼
Reality, b m, 1881, by Reliance—Ernestine, by Mambrino Rattler.... 2:19¼
Reality, ch s, 1885, by Pretender—Etta Mambrino, by Henry Mambrino 2:26
Realization, b s, 1884, by Great Hopes—Speedy Fanny, by Black's Hambletonian 2:26¾
Reaume, br g, 188—, by Chandler..... 2:29½
Rebel Medium, gr s, 1885, by Happy Medium—Bonny Belle, by Almont... 2:23¼
Reciprocity, b s, 188—, by Strait's Superior 2:26¾
Rectitude, b s, 1884, by King Rene—Virgie Wilkes, by George Wilkes.. 2:28
Redalia, b m, 1890, by Red Wilkes—Ethel, by Commodore Belmont... 2:26¼
Red Baron, br s, 1887, by Baron Wilkes—Lady Wilkes, by Red Wilkes 2:29½
Red Belle, ch m, 188—, by Red Cloud 2:29¾
Red Bells, ch s, 188—, by Redmond C. 2:26¼
Red Bird, ch m, 1883, by Weisbaden—Bay 2:25¼
Red Bird, b g, 1851, by Red Bird (dead) 2:30
Red Bird, b g, 1875, by Chenery's Gray Eagle—Dolly 2:27¼
Red Bird, ch m, 1890, by Red Fern—Laura, by McCurdy's Hambletonian 2:17
Red Brook, b s, 1886, by Meadow Brook—Fanny, by Col. Hambrick (dead) 2:22
Red Buck, br g, 1879, by Dr. Herr—Rhoda Red Buck, by Red Buck.. 2:29¼
Red Bud, ch s, 1891, by Red Fern, dam by Brown Dick Jr. 2:14½
Red Cedar, ch g, 1887, by McCurdy's Hambletonian 2:28¼
Red Cherry, b m, 1889, by Red Wilkes—Madam Herr, by Mambrino Patchen 2:22½
Red Cloud, b g, 1860, by Legal Tender (dead) 2:18
Red Clover, b s, 1886, by Principe—Maria, by Marabout 2:26¾
Red Cross, b g, 186—, by Night Hawk (dead) 2:26¾
Red Cross, ch s, 1873, by Brigand—Fanny, by Dole's Young Magna Charta 2:21½

Red Davis, ch g, 188—... 2:24¼

Red Dick, ch g, 1866, by Gen. Morgan—Sally, by Hiatoga (Old Togue) (dead) ... 2.28

Reddie Clay, b m, 1892, by Red Wilkes—Jennie Clay, by Harry Clay 2:28¼

Red Duke, ch s, 1882, by Duke of Brunswick—Whirlcloud, by Jay Gould ... 2:30

Reddy, b s, 1890, by Prairie Star—Ione, by Wapsie ... 2:29¾

Red Express, b s, 1892, by Right Onward ... 2:22½

Red Fern, ch s, 1885, by McCurdy's Hambletonian—Fernvale, by Enfield 2:27¾

Red Flame, ch g, 188—, by Red Buck dam by Davy Crockett ... 2:25¼

Red Flame Jr., ch s, 188—, by Red Flame, dam by Blue Bull ... 2:24¼

Red Girl, b m, 188—, by Red Wilkes 2:23¾

Red Hawk, b s, 1884, by Red Wilkes—Judy, by Plato ... 2:28½

Red Heart, b s, 1889, by Red Wilkes—Sweetheart, by Sultan... 2:19

Red Hot, ch s, 1888, by Red Wilkes—Clayola, by Strader's Cassius M Clay Jr. ... 2:26¼

Red Ink, ch g, 1889, by Col. Lillard—Nelly Smith, by Almont Pilot ... 2:22¼

Red Knight, ch s, 1886, by Sir Knight—Lady Hatch, by Gen. Hatch ... 2:28

Red Lake, b s, 1890, by Red King, dam by Sweepstakes ... 2:24½

Red Lambert, b s, 1886, by Red Wilkes—Lady Lambert, by Daniel Lambert ... 2:28½

Red Lassie, b m, 1886, by Red Wilkes—Lady Willis, by Squire Talmage.. 2:20

Red Leaf, b s, 1889, by C. F. Clay—Lady Heart, by Red Wilkes ... 2:28

Red Leaf, b s, 1887, by Reveille—Maple Leaf, by New York ... 2:29½

Red Light, b g, 1883, by Signal ... 2:27¼

Red Line, b s, 1886, by Red Wilkes—Molly Bawn, by Smuggler ... 2:15

Red Line, b g, 187—, pedigree not traced ... 2:25¼

Red Line, ch g, 188—, by Hidalgo... 2:24½

Red Line, b g, 188—, by Bourbon Wilkes ... 2:27

Red Mack, ch s, 1886, by Red Wilkes—Lizzie, by Harrodsburg Boy... 2:27¾

Red Mark, b s, 1888, by Victor Bismarck—Lucille Miller, by Miller's Hambletonian ... 2:26¾

Redmont, b s, 1884, by Atlantic—Redbird, by Blue Bull ... 2:21

Red Nutwood, ch s, 1885, by Nutwood—Bessie, by Temptation ... 2:27¾

Red Oak, b g, 187—, pedigree not traced ... 2:28¼

Red Oak, b s, 1890, by Redwood—Victress, by Victor Patchen ... 2:21

Red of Waranoke, b s, 1890, by Hornell Wilkes—Fifine, by Aberdeen .. 2:22¾

Redondo, b s, 1888, by Stamboul—Dido, by Scott's Hiatoga ... 2:23

Red Queen, b m, 1886, by Red Wilkes—Arnica by Almont ... 2:27¾

Red Rover, ch s, 1886, by Bourbon Wilkes—Mary Turner by Westwood 2:28½

Red Shawmut, b s, 1889, by Shawmut—Kate Mitchell, by Red Wilkes.. 2:25¾

Red Star, b s, 1887, by Red Wilkes Fanny Clay, by Union Clay ... 2:23

Redstone, b s, 1886, by Red Wilkes—Kate M., by Prince Albert... 2:26¾

Red Tom, ch g, 188—, ... 2:27½

Redwald, b s, 1885, by Lord Russell—Primrose, by Alexander's Abdallah ... 2:23½

Red Wedge, b s, 1889, by Red Wilkes—Ulva, by Wedgewood ... 2:29½

Redweed, ch g, 1888, by John O'Rourke—Fanny, by Dr. Syntax ... 2:29½

Red Wilkes (Kitchel's), b s, 1889, by Red Wilkes—Mambrino June, by Mambrino Patchen ... 2:19¼

Red Wilton, b s, 188—, by Wilton... 2:29¼

Red Wing, b s, 1885, by Red Wilkes—Elenora, by American Clay ... 2:29¼

Red Wing Maid, b m, 188—, by a son of Gen. Knox ... 2:29¼

Redwood, b s, 1885, by Anteeo—Lou Milton, by Milton Medium ... 2:21½

Redwood, ch s, 1880, by Nutwood—Alice R., by Naubuc ... 2:27

Redwood Wilkes, ch s, 1886, by France's Allie Wilkes—Jenny Redwood, by Redwood ... 2:28¼

Reed Wilkes, b s, 1889, by Red Wilkes—Nelly Crow, by Mambrino Eagle.. 2:25¼

Re-Elect, b s, 1886, by Elect—Lizzie, by Nephew ... 2:28

Re-Election, gr s, 1888, by Electioneer—Lady Russell, by Harold ... 2:27¼

Reference, br g, 1881, by Referee—Modjeska, by Enfield ... 2:18

Regal Wilkes, b s, 1887, by Guy Wilkes—Margaret, by Sultan... 2:11¾

Regie, b s, 188—, by King Rene—Cap, by Ward's Flying Cloud ... 2:26¼

Regina, br m, 1880, by Electioneer—Accident, by Elmo ... 2:18½

Reginald, b s, 1887, by Mambrino Dix—Dot, by Mambrino Jet... 2:30

Regret, ch m, 188—, by Lord Wellington ... 2:15¼

Regmont, b m, 1887, by Tremont—Dolly D., by Regulator ... 2:29¼

Rego, blk s, 188—, by Durango, dam by Regalia ... 2:23

Regulator, ch g, 1881, by Rooker—Jet ... 2:27½

Reina, blk m, 1885, by St. Arnaud—Mabel L., by Victor ... 2:12¼

Reina B., b m, 1884, by Abdallah Mambrino—Jane, by Frank Wolford... 2:28½

Reindeer, blk g, 1848, pedigree not traced (dead) ... 2:29

Reita U., b m, 1890 by Senator Updegraff—Molly U., by Almont Pilot. 2:25¾

Reliance, b s, 1874, by Alexander—Maud, by Mambrino Rattler ... 2:22½

Remsen, b s, 1885, by Mansfield—Velvet, by Volunteer ... 2:24¼

Rena, b m, 1883, by Alhambra—Helen De Long ... 2:26¼

Rena, ch m, 1884, by Ralston—Bally, by Bashaw Drury ... 2:25

Rena N., gr m, 1886, by Hamdallah—Nelly Gray, by De Graff's Alexander ... 2:22

Rena Rolfe, b m, 1888, by Revenue—Daisy Rolfe, by Blackwood Jr ... 2:19¾

Rene, b s, 1880, by King Rene—Effie, by Regular ... 2:26

Renie Silver, br s, 1886, by King Rene—Mary Blackwood, by Blackwood Jr ... 2:24½

Renne, gr m, 188—, by King Rene... 2:29¾

Reno, b g, 1887, by Boniface—Crazy Jane, by Crazy Jack ... 2:23¾

Reno, ch s, 188—, by Captain ... 2:27

Reno Defiance, br s, 1877, by Louis Napoleon—Mambrino Princess, by

' Fisk's Mambrino Chief Jr. 2.29¼
Reno's Baby, br s, 1887, by Reno De-
fiance—Lucy Q, by McKinney Horse 2.25½
Rensselaer Wilkes, b s, 1889, by Al-
cantara—Nena, by Nutwood....... 2.18¼
Repetition, b s, 1885, by Red Wilkes
—Nannie Dillard, by John Dillard. 2.19¼
Repetition Jr, b s, 188—, by Repeti-
tion 2.26
Reporter, ch g, 188—, by Richwood.. 2.29¾
Republican, b s, 1887, by Almont
Wilkes, dam by Coaster 2.19¾
Resemble, b m, 1887, by Earl—Wan-
nie Minor, by Pilot Mambrino.... 2.29½
Resolute, b g, 1870, by Swigert—Bay
Fanny, by Richards' Bellfounder.. 2.27¾
Resolute, ch g, 188—, by Aristos—
Fanny D., by De Long's Ethan Allen 2.26¼
Resolute, rn s, 1885, by Lothair Jr.—
Kitty Lambert 2.26¾
Resolution, b s, 1887, by Rampart—
—Kate 2.28¼
Result, b s, 1868, by Jupiter Abdallah
—Compromise, by Rysdyk's Hamble-
tonian 2.25
Retta, br m, 1880, by Whipple—Betty,
by Clark Chief 2.28¾
Rettie, b m, 188—, by Envoy 2.27½
Reveille, b s, 1875, by New York-
Fleet, by Kearsarge 2.21¾
Reveille, b g, 1888, by Quartermaster
—Roll Call, by High Private 2.27½
Revel, b s, 1888, by Reveille—Folle
Farine, by Strathmore 2.29½
Revenge, blk g, 1878, by Patchen
Chief Jr.—Wilsonia 2.24¼
Revenue, b s, 1876, by Smuggler—May
Morning, by Daniel Lambert....... 2.22¼
Reve So, b m, 1886, by Revenue—So
So, by George Wilkes, ... 2.28¾
Review. blk g, 1884, by Adjutant,
dam by Saracen Chief 2.29¼
Review, b m, 1879, by Joe Elmo 2.28¼
Revolver, ch g, 188—, by Don Carlos—
Devotee, by Pancoast 2.29½
Revolt, b s, 1880. by Reveille—Iva
Dee, by Clark Chief Jr........... 2.19
Reward J, ch s, 1887, by Bourbon
Wilkes—Lark, by Abdallah Mam-
brino (pacing 2:10¼) 2:29
Rex, b g, 1880, by Sweepstakes—Nelly,
by Volunteer 2.24¼
Rex, b g, 1884, by Anteeo—Accident,
by Elmo 2.22½
Rex, b g, 1879. by Orion—Mary Belle,
by Breckinridge 2:22¼
Rex, br g, 1877, by Earthquake—Kit
O'Nell. by Sumner Hazen 2.22½
Rex, blk g, 1877, by Rex Patchen,
dam by Hiram Drew 2:28½
Rex Americus, b s, 1890, by Onward
—Gleam, by Dictator 2.11¼
Rexford, b s, 1883, by Electioneer—
Rebecca, by Gen Benton 2.24
Rexford, br g, 188—, by Starlight... 2·30
Rex M, b g, 1884, by Somonauk—
Bird M, by Stoneman 2.26¼
Rex Patchen, b s, 1866, by Godfrey
Patchen 2:30
Rex Patchen, b s, 1882, by Seneca
Patchen—Maggie, by Seneca Chief. 2.29¼
R F. C., b g, 187—, by Darlbay—
Calmes, by John Dillard 2:23½
Rhahemes, b m 188—, by Earl—Helen
Walker by Pilot Mambrino 2:30
Rhode Island, br s, 1857, by White-
hall—Mag Taylor, by Davy Crockett
(dead) .... 2·23½

Rhoderick Dhu, blk s, 1886, by Mam-
brino Boy—Cricket, by Cuyler ..... 2·20
Rialto, b g, 188—, ... 2:30
Ricetta, b m, 1885, by Odd Fellow—
Buttercup 2:22½
Richard, ch g, 187—, by Red Wilkes,
dam by Rattler 2 30
Richard, ch g, 1867, by Blue Bull,
dam by Pete Guffin 2 21
Richard Almont, b s, 1890, by Almont
Medium—Lady Onyx, by Onyx.... 2 28½
Richard E., b g, 188—, pedigree not
traced 2:27¾
Richard E, b g, 1874, by Swigert—
Fanny, by Rhodes' Blood Royal Jr. 2:28¾
Richard H., b g, 1883, by Hayner's
Pathfinder—Jenny, by Gray Fear-
naught 2 30
Richard Lambert, ch s, 188—, by Ben
Franklin .... 2·25¾
Richard Wilkes, b g, 1876, by George
Wilkes—Miss Montague, by Wilson's
Snowstorm .... 2·26¼
Richbrown, br s, 1886, by Defiance—
Brown Kate, by Brown Chief 2.22¼
Richelieu, b g, 188—, by Reno De-
fiance 2 23½
Richelieu, gr g, 1886, by A W Rich-
mond—Ventura Belle, by Ventura.. 2 29¼
Richmond, blk g, 1871, by Gen. Lyons
—Smith Mare 2 26
Richmond Jr, b g, 1885, by A W.
Richmond 2 15
Richwood, b s, 1883, by Mambrino
Patchen—Sally Fox, by Seniour's
Davy Crockett 2 27
Richwood, b s, 1880, by Squire Tal-
mage—Lady Clay, by Strader's Cas-
sius M Clay Jr., ... 2.24¼
Richwood, b g, 187—, pedigree not
traced 2.27
Richwood Boy, b g, 188—, by Billy
Hinsley 2:29¼
Rideau Belle, b m, 1886, by George
Wood—Belle, by Glenell 2 23½
Rickreal, ch g, 188—, by Rockwood . 2.29
Rienzi, b g, 1872, by Erie Abdallah 2 25¼
Rienza Almont, br g, 1886, by Almont
Pilot—Kit 2 28
Rifle, blk g, 1890, by Elyria, dam by
Star Wilkes 2.18¼
Rifleman, br g, 1878, by Rifleman,
dam by son of George M. Patchen 2 27¼
Rigmarole, b g, 188—, by Prince Or-
loff .... 2 29 ¡
Rigolette. b m, 1874, by Exchequer—
Belle Gentry 2 22
Riley, b g, 1872, by Enoch 2.30
Riley S, br s, 1891, by Riley Med-
ium .... 2·21½
Rinaldo, b s, 1883, by Mambrino Dud-
ley—Wanatah, by Wedgewood .... 2·27¼
Rinaldo, blk s, 1884, by Reveille—
Lady Tennis, by Mambrino Patchen 2.27
Rinconada, b g, 1886, by Eros—Ac-
cident, by Elmo .... 2·17
Rintoul, br s, 1884, by Mambrino
Dudley—Alicia, by Messenger Du-
roc 2 24¼
Ripple P, blk g, 188—, by Simmons Jr. 2·26¼
Rio Alto, b s, 1891, by Palo Alto—
Elsie by Gen. Benton 2:16½
Ripon Boy. br s, 1863, by Ira Allen,
dam by Wiley's Blucher (dead).... 2:25
Ripple, br m, 1881, by Hill's Duroc—
Onoto, by Volunteer 2 17½
Ripple, ch m, 1886, by Crit Davis—
Lady Claire, by Risdon 2 20½

Ripplet, b m, 1889, by Phallas—Ripple, by Hill's Duroc 2:29¼
Rip Rap, br g, 1869, by Mambrino Brave, dam by a Copperbottom horse 2:26
Ripton, b s, 1889, by Ben Harrison—Betsey, by Sycamore.............. 2:30
Ripton, b g, 1870, by American Boy, dam by Seely's American Star...... 2:26
Ripsee, b s, 1889, by J. R. Shedd—Miss Logan, by Gage's Logan....... 2:30
Rival, gr s, 186—, by Whiteside's Black Hawk, dam by Black Hawk (Consternation).................... 2:30
Riverbend, b s, 1885, by Belmont—Sea Gull, by Strathmore................ 2:24½
River Side, b s, 1887, by Cadmus Hambletonian — Daisy Dayton, by Rysdyk's Bellfounder............... 2:29½
Riverside, b s, 188—, by Red Wilkes.. 2:20¾
Rizpah, b m, 1889, by Haroldmont—Lily Bowers, by Louis Napoleon.... 2:24¼
R. M. Lewis, b g, 1880, by Brown Harry, dam by Black Pilot......... 2.29
R. M. Wilkes, gr g, 1882, by Mambrino Wilkes—Lady Davis, by Kearsarge................................. 2:25¼
Roachmane, ch g, 1878, by the Scotia Horse, dam by Tebo Horse......... 2:27½
Roadster, b s, 1886, by Rex Patchen —Novelette, by George Wilkes Jr... 2:30
Roan Boy, rn g, 188—, by Eastlight—Strathanna, by Strathmore......... 2:25¼
Roanoke, b s, 1880, by Lysander Chief —Hammil Mare, by Riley's Consternation............................ 2:30
Roanoke Maid, br m, 1882, by Roanoke 2:22¼
Roanoke Maid, b m, 185—, pedigree not traced (dead).................. 2:30
Robbie P., b s, 1886, by Charles Caffrey—Nanny, by Long Island Chief. 2.12¼
Robbins, ro s, 188—, by Black Walnut 2:21½
Robbins, br g, 188—, by Swigert...... 2:29¼
Robert, b g, 1880, by Antar—Dark Dale, by Bale........................ 2 25¼
Robert A., b g, 188—, by Tasco...... 2:29¼
Robert A., b g, 1889, by Hartford—Regardless, by William M. Rysdyk.... 2:29¼
Robert B., ch s, 1884, by Squire Talmage—Lida J.......................... 2:29½
Robert Baso, blk s, 188—, by Diatonic 2:29¼
Robert Bell, b s, 1892, by St. Bel—Neocile, by Robert McGregor........ 2:30
Robert Bonner Jr., b s, 1881, by Vandergrift.............................. 2:29¼
Robert B. Thomas, ch g, 186—, by Prince Allen (dead)................. 2:25
Robert Burns, ch s, 1873, by Green's Bashaw—Dolly Weed, by Lamson's Iowa Chief.............................. 2:30
Robert H., b g, 187—, pedigree not traced.................................. 2:29¼
Robert H., br g, 188—, by Robert Fulton....................................... 2:17
Robert L., b g, 1885, by Sierra Boy, dam by Tom Atchinson............ 2:21
Robert L., b g, 188—, by Wellington.. 2:28
Robert L., blk s, 1884, by Haw Patch —Nora Shy, by Mambrino Patchen.. 2.26¼
Robert L., b s, 1880, by Artemas..... 2:29¾
Robert Lee, blk g, 187—, by Ridley Horse—Molly Stone, by Root Horse. 2:23¼
Robert Lee, blk s, 1890, by Alcantara —Meg Merillies, by Electioneer..... 2:18¾
Robert McGregor, ch s, 1871, by Maj. Edsall—Nancy Whitman, by Seely's American Star........................ 2 17½
Robert McGregor Jr., ch s, 1888, by Robert McGregor—Dayton, by Dictator................................... 2:30
Robert Medium, b s, 1878, by Happy Medium—Sally, by Yankee Tricks... 2.29
Robert M. Taylor, blk s, 1884, by Alcantara—Cora M., by Air Line...... 2:23½
Robert R., b g............................ 2.30
Robert Ransom, br s, 1887, by Gambetta—Black Maria, by Strader's C. M. Clay Jr.......................... 2:29¼
Robert Ryan, b s, 1886, by Goldsmith Pilot—Lassie, by Aladdin........... 2:21
Robert Rysdyk, br s, 1881, by William Rysdyk—Queen B., by Kearsarge.... 2:13¼
Robert S., b s, 1887, by Pero—Bird, by Guide.............................. 2:28
Robert T. McGregor, b s, 1886, by Silver King—Kit, by Young Tuckahoe.. 2:29¼
Robert Wilkes, blk s, 1885, by Bourbon Wilkes, dam by Trojan......... 2.24¼
Robin, gr g, 1874, by Enfield—Mary Weaver, by Black Hawk Vermont.. 2:24½
Robin, b s, 1891, by Axtell—Ozone, by Rysdyk's Hambletonian.............. 2:28
Robinson D., b s, 1881, by Daniel Boone—Gurney Mare................ 2:17¾
Rob Roy, b g, 1886, by Aubrey—Doctor...................................... 2:29¾
Rob Roy, b g, 188—, by Crawford Prince.................................... 2:26¼
Rockbridge, b s, 1884, by Nutwood—Rapidan, by Dictator................ 2:20
Rockburn, ch g, 188—, by Woodburn Pilot.. 2:19¼
Rockefeller, b s, 1884, by Electioneer —Edith Carr, by Clark Chief....... 2:29½
Rocket, blk g, 1879, by Knox Boy.... 2:29¼
Rocket, br g, 188—, by Capt Webb... 2:30
Rocket, b s, 1878, by Blue Bull—Kitty Patterson, by Dick Consternation... 2:28
Rocket, gr g, 1876, by Clematis...... 2:26¼
Rockingham, gr g, 1845, pedigree not traced (dead).......................... 2:25½
Rock Island Maid, b m, 187—, pedigree not traced...................... 2:30
Rocknight, ch s, 1885, by Beaumont—Girl.. 2:29½
Rocko, b s, 1891, by Sphinx—Nora D., by Louis Napoleon.................. 2:29¼
Rockton, b g, 187—, by Highland Beauty.................................... 2:25½
Rockwell Boy, b g, 188—, pedigree not traced.................................. 2 24¾
Rockwood, b g, 1886, by Treewood—Lady Hustler, by La Rock's Ben Franklin.................................... 2 25½
Rocky Mountain Tom, gr g, 187—, pedigree not traced..................... 2.25¼
Rodney J., b g, 188—, by Auctioneer.. 2:21¼
Roger, b g, 1885, by Gordon Windsor, dam by Will's Patchen............. 2.28¼
Roger, b g, 188—, by Black's Harry Clay.. 2:24¼
Roger Hanson, gr s, 1873, by Alta—Lualaba, by Berkley's Edwin Forrest.. 2:28½
Roger K., b s, 1886, by Attorney—Roxy, by Brougham.................. 2:26¼
Roland, br s, 1872, by Crown Chief—Dolly.. 2:28
Roleo, b s, 1890, by Nephew—Camma, by Norway............................ 2:23
Rolfe K., blk g, 188—, by Black Rolfe. 2:29½
Rolla, ch g, 1879, by Shelby Chief—Kate.. 2:24½
Rolla, b g, 1879, by Clark Chief Jr.... 2:21
Rolla Golddust, br g, 1860, by Golddust, dam by Bartlett's Mohawk

Royal, ch g, 1879, by Royal Fearnaught—Fanny Harris, by Kidder's Morgan 2:20¾

Royal Ambassador, b s, 1888, by Ambassador—Belle M., by Empire 2:26¾

Royal Bounce, b g, 187—, by Blue Bull—Clarionette, by Volunteer Jr. 2:19

Royal David, ch s, 188—, by Kankakee 2:26½

Royal Duke, b s, 188—, by Florida, dam by Night Hawk 2:29½

Royal George, gr g, 186—, by William H. Ripley (dead) 2:26½

Royal Guard, b s, 1890, by Beecher—Fanny Crowder 2:30

Royal John, gr g, 186—, by Woodstock, dam by Putnam Morgan..... 2:26¼

Royal King, ch g, 1883, by Mambrino King—Polly, by Hamlin Patchen.... 2:25¼

Royal Kisbar, b s, 1882, by Kisbar, dam by Garrison's Pathfinder 2:28½

Royalmont, ch s, 1880, by Bostick's Almont Jr.—Louisiana 2:20¼

Royal Phallas, blk s, 1886, by Prince Phallas—Blonde, by Woodward's Ethan Allen 2:30

Royal Prince, ch s, 188—, by Dexter Prince—Ida W., by Abbottsford ... 2:19¼

Royal Red, b s, 1886, by Red Wilkes—Christine, by Strathmore 2:21½

Royal Rysdyk, br s, 1884, by Rysdyk—Gypsy Maid, by Crown Imperial.. 2:28¼

Royalty, b s, 1876, by Swigert—Bay Fanny, by Richard's Bellfounder.. 2:25

Royal Wilton, blk s, 188—, by Wilton—Mary Sprague, by Gov. Sprague.. 2:21½

Royal Wilkes, br s, 1887, by Lumps—Lucy, by Royal George 2:25¼

Roy B., blk g, 1886, by Gilroy—Lady Loomis, by Claybrino 2:24¾

Roy K., b g, 1889, by Ethan Wilkes, dam by Grand Sentinel 2:29¾

Roy McGregor, ch s, 1887, by Ben McGregor—Belle Farwell 2:26

Roy Rex, b g, 1887, by Atto Rex, dam by Wapsie 2:28¾

Roy Princeton, b s, 1892, by Princeton, dam by Westwood 2:29¼

Roywood, ch s, 1889, by Neatwood—Aldina, by Alroy 2:21½

R. P., b g, 1874, by Happy Medium—Sunflower, by Bartholomew's American Star Jr. 2:22¼

R. R. H., ro g, 1871, by Emulus—Nelly Gray, by Gov. Banks 2:23¼

Rubinstein, b s, 188—, by Durango—Belle Bowen, by Richelieu 2:29

Ruberta, b m, 1889, by Bermuda—Rena C., by Messenger Chief 2:29¼

Ruby, b m, 188—, pedigree not traced 2:29¼

Ruby, b m, 188—, by Clinton 2:18¼

Ruby, b m, 1889, by Independence—Minnie 2:17¼

Ruby, b m, 1880, by Sultan—Fleetwing, by Rysdyk's Hambletonian .. 2:19¾

Ruby, b s, 1886, by Red Wilkes—Docia Payne, by Almont 2:22½

Ruby, b m, 1881, by Masterlode—Gypsy, by Resolute 2:25¼

Ruby, b m, 1887, by St. Arnaud—Mabel L., by Victor 2:28½

Ruby Macklin, ch m, 1885, by Pretender—Queen B., by Kearsarge.... 2:22¼

Ruby Wilkes, b s, 1885, by Young Jim—Jenny Daniel, by Rysdyk 2:25½

Ruby Wilkes, b m, 1889, by Memento Wilkes—Ruby Queen 2:25

Rufus, br g, 1872, by Bacon's Ethan Allen—Lady Fulton, by Stubtail 2:29

Rufus, b s, 1877, by Sir Henry 2:24¼

Rumor, blk s, 1879, by Tattler—Martense Maid, by Jackson's Flying Cloud 2:29

Rupert Gillig, b s, 1889, by Gillig—Cecil, by Waltham 2:21¾

Ruprecht, b s, 1891, by Favorite Wilkes—Kate Sprague, by Gov. Sprague 2:24½

Rurik, br s, 1888, by Lord Russell—Primrose, by Alexander's Abdallah 2:23

Rusenole, b m, 1888, by Electioneer—Rebecca, by Gen. Benton 2:30

Russell, b g, 188—, pedigree not traced 2:25¾

Russell, gr g, 1867, by Blue Bull (dead) 2:26

Russ Ellis, b g, 1873, by Bacon's Ethan Allen 2:27¼

Russellmont, b s, 1888, by Lord Russell—Yolande, by Belmont 2:14¼

Russell R., b g, 188—, by Thomas K.—Molly 2:29½

Russia, gr m, 1883, by Harold—Miss Russell, by Pilot Jr. 2:28

Russia, ch s, 1883, by Nutwood—Reina Victoria, by Rysdyk's Hambletonian 2:29¼

Russian Spy, b g, 1871, by Murphy's Royal George (dead) 2:26½

Russia White, ch g, 1889, by Russia, dam by Blue Bull 2:29¾

Rustic, gr s, 186—, by Whipple's Hambletonian—Lady Suffolk, by Harry Belmont.................... 2:30

Rustic, blk s, 1885, by Wildair—Lydia, by Aristos 2:27

Rustic Lady, b m, 188—, by Mambrino Rule 2:30

Rustic Maid, b m, 1888, by Mambrino Russell—Maud Righter, by Victor Bismarck 2:27½

Rustique, b m, 1888, by Electioneer—Miss Russell, by Pilot Jr. 2:18½

Rusty, b m, 188—, by Aristos 2:24¼

Ruth, b m, 188—, by President Garfield (?) 2:28¼

Ruth H., b m, 1889, by Laclede—Durango Queen, by Durango (pacing 2:22) 2:24½

Ruth M., g m, 1891, by Alastor—Kit Harris, by Young American 2:29¼

Ruth Nutwood, b m, 1885, by Nutwood—Sister Ruth, by Jim Monroe.. 2:24¾

Ruth S., b m, 1877, by Jim Fisk, dam by Grey Eagle 2:29¼

Ruth Wilkes, ch m, 1888, by Victor Wilkes—Nelly Lambert, by Daniel Lambert 2:17½

Rutledge, b g, 1867, by Conqueror, dam by Cassius M. Clay (dead) ... 2:30

Rutledge, gr g, 1883, by Onward—Estelle, by Clark Chief 2:27¼

R. W. S., blk g, 188—, by Ben Franklin—Fleda, by Ridler 2:29¼

Ryland T., b g, 1886, by Ledger Jr.—May, by Ulverston 2:07¾

Rysdyk Maid, b m, 1872, by Rysdyk's Hambletonian—Flora, by Benedict's Pathfinder 2:24¼

Ryswood, b s, 1884, by Bellwood—Lucy Plumb, by Rysdyk 2:16

Sabina, br m, 1889, by Sable Wilkes—Eva, by LeGrand 2:15½

Sabledale, b m, 1890, by Sable Wilkes—Viven, by Nutwood 2:18½

Sablehurst, blk s, 1890, by Sable

Wilkes—Gina Wilkes, by Guy Wilkes 2:25

Sablenut, br s, 1892, by Sable Wilkes—Auntie, by Dawn ... 2:22¼

Sable Wilkes, blk s, 1884, by Guy Wilkes—Sable, by The Moor ... 2.18

Sacaza, b s, 188—, by Robert McGregor, dam by Banker ... 2:29¾

Sacramento, br s, 188—, by Monroe Chief, dam by Gen. Reno ... 2:20¾

Sacramento Girl, b m, 1888, by Alcazar—Viola, by Flaxtail ... 2:30

Sadie, br m, 1885, by Mambrino Boy—West Union Girl ... 2:29½

Sadie Allen, b m, 1888, by Kentucky Jewel—Lady Jane, by American Ethan ... 2:29½

Sadie B., blk m, 188—, by Ashtabula 2:24¼

Sadie Belle, ch m, 1872, by Odin Bell—Molly, by Sebastapol ... 2:24

Sadie G., blk m, 188—, pedigree not traced ... 2:27¼

Sadie H., b m, 1865, by Price's St Lawrence (dead) ... 2:30

Sadie Hasson, ch m, 1889, by Newton's Allie Wilkes—Mabel, by Mambrino Howard ... 2.26¼

Sadie Howe, b m, 1869, by Mambrunello ... 2:26

Sadie L., b m, 1883, by Young Rolfe—Gretchen, by Gideon ... 2:26¼

Sadie M., b m, 1886, by Prince Orloff—Fossil, by Princeps ... 2:16¼

Sadie Moor, blk m, 1890, by Grand Moor, dam by Poscora Hayward .. 2:29½

Sadie S., gr m, by Pequawket—Kate Dudley, by Bayard ... 2:28½

Sagasta, ch s, 1885, by Nutwood—Verbena, by Princeps ... 2:29½

Sagwa, ch m 1884, by Ben Atwood—Chestnut Girl, by Alroy ... 2:27¾

St Albans, blk g, 1876, by Monmouth Patchen—Black Lady, by Daniel Boone ... 2:20¼

St Arnaud, b s, 1876, by Cuyler—Emma Arteburn, by Mambrino Patchen ... 2:29¼

St Aubin, br s 1890, by St Bel—Chantilly, by Nephew ... 2:28½

St Bel, blk s, 1882, by Electioneer—Beautiful Bells, by The Moor (dead) 2:24½

St Charles, sp g, 1868, by Grey Eagle (Blind Eye), dam by Dandy Jim . 2:26

St. Cloud, b g, 1873, by Conklin's American Star, dam by Bay Richmond ... 2:21

St Cloud, b s, 1876, by Swigert—Flora Lambert, by Spaulding's Abdallah ... 2:23¾

St. Cloud Jr., b s, 1887, by St. Cloud—Susie T., by Trumpeter Golddust 2:26¾

St Croix, b g, 1888, by Wilkes—Zulah, by Gideon ... 2:14¾

St Croix, b m, 1891, by St Bel—Topsy, by Will Crocker ... 2:28½

St. Croix Jr., b s, 1891, by St. Croix, dam by Fred Boone ... 2:30

St Denis, b g, 1877, by Blue Bull—Little Marg, by Gray's Tom Hal. 2:23¼

St Elmo, br s, 1860, by Alexander's Abdallah (dead) ... 2:30

St. Elmo, gr g, 1865, by Brown Harry—Jackson Mare, by French Tiger (dead) ... 2:29¼

St Elmo, br g, 1878, by Royal Fearnaught—Lucy Lincoln, by Masterlode ... 2:16¼

St Elmo, br g, 1879, by Frank Tuckahoe ... 2:22¼

St. Elmo, br s, 1879, by Duke Alexis—Nelly ... 2:25½

St. Felix, br s, 1891, by St. Bel—Beulah West, by Abdallah West.. 2:25½

St. Gothard, b s, 1876, by George Wilkes—Zora, by American Clay.. 2:27

St Helena, b m, 186—, by Gen. McClellan (dead) ... 2:27½

St. Ives, b s, 1886, by Harbinger—Red Rose, by Gideon ... 2:29¼

St Jacob, b g, 1878, by Hiram Drew 2:27

St. James, b g, 1866, by Gooding's Champion (dead) ... 2:23¼

St James, b g, 188—, by son of Gooding's Champion ... 2:26¼

St. James, b g, 188—, ... 2:26½

St Joe, br g, 188—, by Winthrop Knox ... 2:18

St. Joe, b g, 1886, by Junio—Emma, by Luceonia ... 2:26

St. Jonathan, br s, 1889, by Kentucky Dictator—Fanny Goldsmith, by Edward Everett (pacing 2:22½. 2:22¼

St. Julien, b s, 188—, by Gen. Wilkes 2.29¾

St Julien, b g, 1869, by Volunteer—Flora, by Harry Clay ... 2:11¼

St. Lambert, ch s, 1879, by Bay Star—Lady Douglas, by Bourban Chief 2:29¼

St Lawrence, b g, 1881, by Grey Dan 2:23¼

St. Lewis, b s, 1888, by St. Nicholas—Trinket G., by Harry Glenn... 2:19

St. Lookout, b s, 1889, by Sultan—Kitty Wilkes, by Red Wilkes ... 2:26

St Louis, b g, 187—, by Colossus Mambrino ... 2:27

St Louis Maid, br m, 1885, by Rysdyk Chief—Jenny Crews, by Aleck Douglas ... 2:24½

St Michael Boy, b g, 188—, ... 2:28

St. Minx, blk s, 1892, by St Bel—Minx, by Mambrino Patchen ... 2.26½

St. Patrick Jr., b s, 1888, by St. Patrick—Young Mountain Maid, by Long Island Patchen ... 2:28¾

St Regis, b s, 1886, by St. Arnaud—Mabel L., by Victor ... 2:29½

St Remo, b g, 1870, by Volunteer—Flora, by Harry Clay ... 2:28½

St Simon, br s, 1889, by Winfield Scott—Raven, by Highland ... 2:24¼

St Valentine, br s, 1881, by Westwood—Laura Logan, by American Clay ... 2.16¾

St Vincent, b s, 1884, by Wilkes Boy—Alleen, by Mambrino Boy ... 2:13½

Salando, b g, 188—, by Hernando ... 2:26¼

Salinas Maid, b m, 188—, by Junio—Mamie V., by Carr's Mambrino ... 2:30

Sallie, br m, 188—, by Jim Lambert 2:30

Sallie Cossack, b m, 1884, by Don Cossack—Almonia, by Almont ... 2:22½

Sallie Simmons, blk m, 1890, by Simmons—Sally Adams, by John Burdine ... 2:13½

Sally B., dn m, 1883, by Young Jim—Lady Dun, by Million's Copperbottom (dead) ... 2:20

Sally Benton, gr m, 1880, by Gen. Benton—Sontag Mohawk, by Mohawk Chief ... 2:17¾

Sally C., ch m, 188—, by McCurdy's Hambletonian ... 2:18¾

Sally G., ch m, 188—, by Dan G. ... 2:29¼

Sally Graham, b m, 1886, by Nutwood—Mattie Graham, by Harold ... 2:29¼

Sallie K., b m, 188—, by Jim Brister 2:28

Sally Ranger, blk m, 1887, by John Sherman—Cloud, by Black Ranger.. 2:24¾

Sally Scott, b m, 187—, by Magna Charta—Molly Pitcher, by Rysdyk's Hambletonian 2 28¼

Sally Vajan, b m. 1884, by Danville Wilkes—Carrie, by May's Sir Wallace 2.28

Salute, b s, 1891, by Overstreet Wilkes 2.26¼

Sam, gr g, 188—, by Sherman Morgan Jr. 2 25¼

Sam B, br g. 1880, by Pompey Smash—Shield's Mare, by King's Cadmus 2.26¾

Sam Bassett, ch s, 1887, by Elyria—Shoo Fly, by Young Tippoo Sultan 2.22½

Sam Browne, ch g, 188—, by Hawthorne 2 29

Sam Curtis, b g, 1866, by Winthrop Morrill, dam by Eaton Horse ..... 2·28

Same Kind, b m, 1887, by Virgo Hambletonian—Clochette, by Jubilee Lambert ...... 2·25½

Sam Estes, b g, 1891, by Aberdeen . 2.27½

Sam F., ro g, 187—, by Wood's Hambletonian 2 26¼

Sam Harris, b s, 1881, by Bostick's Almont Jr—Louisiana 2 29¼

Sam Hickson, br g, 1886, by Sam Purdy—Black Kate 2.30

Sam Hill, b s, 188—, by Wilkes Spirit Jr.—Lady Hill, by Rysdyk's Hambletonian 2 20¼

Sam Hill, ch s, 1886, by Invader—Minnehaha, by Abdallah Hambletonian 2 30

Sam Lakeland, b g. 188—, by Lakeland Abdallah—Judea, by Mambrino Archy 2 26½

Sam Medium, b s, 1892, by Prince Medium 2 30

Samovar, b m, 1886, by King Rene—Carrie, by Volunteer 2 28¾

Sam P., ch g, 188—, pedigree not traced 2 29¾

Sam Purdy, b s, 1866, by George M. Patchen Jr.—Whisky Jane (dead) 2·20½

Samuel A , b s, 1885, by Grand Sentinel—Evelyn, by Egbert ...... 2·27½

Samuel G., b s, 1888, by Simcoe Wilkes—Carrie G , by Almont Pilot 2 29

Sam Webber, b g, 188—, by Warwick Boy, dam by Chenery's Grey Eagle 2·25¼

Sam Weller, b s, 1888, by Charley B.—Princess Clay, by Baird's Hambletonian Prince 2.26½

Sam West, b g, 186—, by Davy Crocket (dead) 2 29

Sam Wilkes ,b s, 1884, by Barney Wilkes—Gin Burner, by Frank Allen 2 29½

Sanborn, b s, 1883, by Gen. Washington—Scotland Maid, by Rysdyk's Hambletonian 2 26½

Sun Bruno, b g, 186—, by George M M Patchen Jr. (dead) ...... 2·25½

San Carlos, ch g, 188—, by Brown Jug ...... 2·27½

Sancho. b s, 1875, by Knox Boy, dam by Gen. Knox ...... 2·29

S & E blk s, 1887, by Lumps—Bessie D , by Justin Morgan (dead) .. 2 26½

Sanders, ch g, 1888, by Sidney—Ellen Roy 2 26¼

San Diego, ch g, 188—, pedigree not traced 2 23¾

San Gabriel, b s. 1884, by Sultan—Minnehaha, by Stevens' Bald Chief 2·29¾

San Malo, b s, 1886, by Nugget—

Zelinda Wilkes, by George Wilkes.. 2.26¼

San Mateo, b m, 1881, by Santa Claus—Dolly Patchen, by George M. Patchen Jr ...... 2·28¼

San Pedro, blk g, 1885, by Del Sur, dam by Keating Horse (pacing 2 10¾) 2 14½

Samlle G , gr m, 1872, by Almont-Wiltona, by Mokhladi 2 27

Sans Souci, ch m, 1891, by Sidney—Miss Roy, by Buccaneer 2.28¼

Santa Belle, b m, 1890, by St. Belsis Nutwood, by Nutwood ...... 2·23

Santa Clara, b m. 1887, by Robb Wilkes—Gypsy M , by Eclair 2.29

Santa Claus, b s, 1874, by Strathmore—Lady Thorne Jr , by Williams' Mambrino 2.17½

Santa Gertrudes, br s, 1890, by C. F Clay—Winnie Wilkes, by Red Wilkes 2·29¾

Santie, br s, 1887, by Santa Claus—Gettie Greatman, by Othello 2.25

Sappho, ch m, 1883, by Aberdeen—Sally M , by Almont 2.30

Sappho, ch m, 1887, by Robert McGregor—Pauline, by Ashland Chief. 2.15¾

Sarah Ann, gr m, 188—, by Johnny Wonder (pacing 2 23¾) 2 27

Sarah B , b m, 187—, by Little Jack.. 2·29¾

Sarah B., b m, 1880, by Almonarch—Charlotte Jones, by Kester's Royal George 2 20¼

Sarah B., gr m, 1881, by Planet—Miss Jackson 2:30

Sarah O, b m. 188—, by Pistachio.. 2 22¼

Sarah Coln, b m, 188—, by Wilkes Spirit 2:29¼

Sarah G , b m, 1888, by C. F. Clay—Sophie D , by Lyle Wilkes 2.18½

Saran Gilbirds, blk m, 1885, by Gilbirds Sprague—Jule O., by Blue Dick 2.23½

Sarah Jane, b m, 188—, by Edgar Wilkes 2.24¾

Sarah L., b m, 1880, by Index—Rose Bud, by Young Wilkes 2.26

Sarah Shelton, ch m, 1890, by Bedford—Princess Clay, by American Clay 2 28¼

Saranac, blk s, 1885, by Gen Washington—Sappho, by Jay Gould ..... 2·25¼

Saratoga, b g, 187—, pedigree not traced 2:30

Sarcanett, b s, 1883, by King Rene—Gossamer, by Princeps 2:16¼

Sardis Ensign, br s, 1887, by Ensign—Lucy L, by I J ...... 2·30

Sargeant, b s, 188—, by Stamford Belmont 2:29¾

Sargent, gr g, 1884, pedigree not traced 2:28

Sargent, b s, 188—, by Almont Eclipse. 2:26¼

Sargent, b g, 187—, by Tariff 2 29¼

Sargent, gr g, 188—, pedigree not traced 2:29

Sargent, b s, 1889, by Alcantara—Volante, by Messenger Duroc 2 27½

Sartwell, b g, 1889, by Sensation—Lady Yeomans, by Rochester 2.23¾

Satilla, br m, 1885, by Almont Rattler—Lady Warfield, by Green's Bashaw 2:24

Satin Slippers, blk m, 1891, by Delancy—Satin, by Mambrino Alahambra 2 24½

Saturn L., b g, 188—, by Echo 2:28¼

Sauveur, b g, 1878, by Happy Medium Lydia Montague, by Tippoo Bashaw 2 29¼

Savoyard, b s, 1888, by King Rene—

Annulet, by Cuyler...... .... 2:23
Saxon, ch g, 1883, by Abdallah Wilkes
　—Snowflake, by Kentucky Prince... 2:22½
Scandinavian, blk g, 187—, by Ver-
　mont Black Hawk Jr............... 2:27
School Boy, b g, 188—, by Cassady—
　Dolly, by Bay Fisherman.......... 2:26¼
School Marm, ch m, 1885, by Olympus
　—Princess, by Cobbler............. 2:20
Schuyball, b g, 1874, by Gooding's
　Champion — Belle, by Thompson's
　Flying Cloud..................... 2:26½
Schuyler, b s, 1872, by Seneca Chief—
　Highland Maid, by Coleman's Amer-
　ican Star........................ 2:26
Sciola, b m, 186—, by Hanshaw Horse
　(dead)........................... 2:23½
Sciota Belle, br m, 186—, pedigree not
　traced (dead).................... 2:28
Scipio, b s, 1882, by Redwood—Nell,
　by Coupon....................... 2:26½
Scotia, b m, 1882, by Sacramento—
　Nelly Walworth, by Toronto Patch-
　en.............................. 2:21¼
Scotland, blk g, 1869, by imp. Bonnie
　Scotland—Waterwitch, by Pilot Jr.
　(dead).......................... 2:22½
Scotland Maid, b m, 1866, by Rysdyk's
　Hambletonian—Trusty, by Marlbor-
　ough........................... 2:28½
Scotsman, ch s, 1886, by Milo—Alfret-
　ta, by Mambrino Gift............. 2:27½
Scott, b g, 188—, by Gen. Sherman... 2:24¾
Scott, ch s, 1884, by Egbert—Birdie
　Tramp, by Tramp................ 2:26¾
Scott Ashton, b g, 1885, by Hampton
　—Flora Elmo, by St. Elmo........ 2:26¾
Scott B., b g, 1881, by Jim Scott—
　Belle, by Flying Hiatoga.......... 2:20½
Scott Chief, b s, 1879, by Egmont—
　Lou Scott, by Dey's Woodford..... 2:28
Scott Newman, ch g, 187—, by Henry
　Bell Colt, dam by Whirlwind...... 2:27½
Scott's Chief, b g, 186—, by Edwin
　Forrest—Lady Rice, by Whitehall.. 2:23
Scott's Thomas, b s, 187—, by Gen.
　George H. Thomas—Lady Rice, by
　Whitehall....................... 2:21
Scourine, br m, 1892, by Wilton—
　Mamie, by Star Almont........... 2:23½
Scramble, br g, 1883, by Antenor Jr.
　—Columbia, by Kenyon's Columbus. 2:22½
Scranton Belle, br m, 188—, by Bis-
　muth........................... 2:18¼
Screwdriver, ro g, 1875, by Tibbett's
　Patchen—Stockbridge Mare, by Mack 2.24½
S. D. C., b g, 1879, by Almont Eclipse
　—Punchard Mare................. 2:25¾
Sea Foam, gr m, 1863, by Young Co-
　lumbus, dam by Harris' Hamble-
　tonian.......................... 2:24½
Sea Girl, br m, 1888, by Wilton—
　Julia Patchen, by Mambrino Patchen 2·18¾
Sea King, ch s, 1886, by Melbourne
　King—Bertha, by Daniel Lambert.. 2:18¼
Sealskin Wilkes, br s, 1881, by George
　Wilkes—Woburn Maid, by Woburn. 2:20½
Seaside, b m, 1888, by Hector Wilkes
　—Alice, by Jacinto.............. 2:16½
Seamstress, br m 1885, by Alcantara
　—Senorita, by Sentinel........... 2:26
Secret, gr g, 188—, by Blackwood Jr.. 2:30
Secret, gr m, 1890, by Secretary—Pas-
　time, by Rustic................. 2:26½
Secret, b m, 1877, by Strathmore—
　Amanda, by Waxy............... 2:20½
Secure, b s, 1891, by Pelletier........ 2:29¼
Secure, br s, 1885, by Mambrino Patch-
　en — Bashaw Belle, by Green's Ba-

shaw........ .... 2:30
Sedina, ch m, 1887, by Sidney—Star,
　by George M. Patchen Jr.......... 2:28½
See, ch s, 1887, by Claimant—Fannie
　C., by Roscoe Jr................. 2:29¼
Seersucker, b m, 1888, by The Seer—
　Reglin, by Redwood.............. 2:30
Selah Chesterwood, b m, 188—, by
　Chesterwood.................... 2:27½
Selene, b m, 1878, by Grand Sentinel
　—Shadow, by Octoroon............ 2·29¾
Selim Mambrino, b s, 1888, by Dau-
　bigne — Peggy Murry, by Cayuga
　Chief.......................... 2·28½
Seline, b g, 188—, by Leon........... 2:29½
Selkirk, br s, 1867 (dead)........... 2:29¼
Sellita, br m, 188—, by Artillery..... 2:23½
Senator, dn g, 188—, by St. Cloud.... 2:30
Senator, b s, 1883, by Echo—Senator
　Jones Mare, by Winthrop Morrill... 2:21½
Senator, b g, 188—, by Porter Stanton 2:26¼
Senator, b g, 1876, by Robert R. Mor-
　ris—Wisely Mare, by Napper...... 2:26¼
Senator A., gr s, 1888, by Tramp
　Panic—Dolly Wonder............. 2:13¼
Senator Boy, ch s, 188—, by Senator
　Rose........................... 2:24¼
Senator Conkling, b s, 1885, by Roscoe
　Conkling—May Queen............ 2·12¾
Senator K., gr g, 188—, by Spink's
　Clark Chief.................... 2:23¼
Senator L., b s, 1888, by Dexter Prince
　—Fanny Bayswater, by Bayswater.. 2:23½
Senator L., ch s, 188—, by Renshaw.. 2:25½
Senator Maid, ch m, 1878, by Hi
　Miller — Hattie Brown, by Dan
　Brown......................... 2:30
Senator N., b s, 1881, by Wapsie—
　Bradshaw Mare, by Mambrino
　Patchen........................ 2:25
Senator Rose, b s, 1887, by Sultan—
　Georgiana, by Overland........... 2:18
Senator Updegraff, b s, 1884, by Sim-
　mons—Madam Updegraff, by Flying
　Hiatoga........................ 2·27½
Seamstress, b m, 1887, by Mambrito-
　nian — Flora Temple, by Bettsinger
　Horse.......................... 2:22
Seneca Bismarck, b s, 1884, by Victor
　Bismarck—Patchen Maid, by Patch-
　en Chief....................... 2·22¼
Seneca Maid, ch m, 188—, by John
　Adams......................... 2:22¾
Seneca Prince, blk s, 1888, by Bay-
　onne Prince—Pond Lily, by Seneca
　Chief.......................... 2:25¼
Sensation, gr g, 1881, by Peacock—
　Morey Mare.................... 2:22
Sensation, b g, 1865, by Dixon's Ethan
　Allen, dam by Indian Chief (dead).. 2:22¼
Sensation, b s, 1882, by Rochester—
　Estelle Eastin, by Mambrino Patch-
　en.............................. 2:29½
Sentinel, b s, 1863, by Rysdyk's Ham-
　bletonian—Lady Patriot, by Young
　Patriot (dead).................. 2·29¾
Sentinel, b s, 1885, by Almont Senti-
　nel—Mattie by Banta's Shakespeare 2:29½
Sentinel Wilkes, b s, 1883, by Red
　Wilkes—Sentinette, by Sentinel.... 2:20¾
Sentry, b g, 1880, by Grand Sentinel—
　Jenny, by Night Hawk........... 2.25
Serena, ch m, 1887, by Sidney—Blonde,
　by Elmo....................... 2:29½
Serpolet, b m, 1887, by King Rene—
　Belle Hewett, by Belmont........ 2:30
Seth Thomas, b g, 1880, by Hamdallah
　—Belle S., by Star of the West...... 2·25¼
Setting Sun, ch g, 1889, by Billy Har-

ward.......... 2:29¼

Seylax, b g, 188—, by Alban—Woodflower, by Ansel.......... 2:24¼

Seymour Belle, b m, 1878, by Commodore—Lucy, by Curtis' Sam Hazzard 2:19¾

Shadeland Acme, b m, 1888, by Wilkes Nutwood—Annabel Lee, by Satellite 2:28¾

Shadeland Almeda, b m, 1887, by Wilkes Nutwood—Criteria, by Criterion.......... 2:27½

Shadeland Baron, ch s, 1887, by Onward—Mattie Whitney, by Beecher.. 2:27¾

Shadeland Bellewood, ch m, 1886, by Nutwood—Shadeland Leona, by Satellite.......... 2:25¼

Shadeland Delmonia, b m, 1883, by Young Jim—Sue, by Ericsson ... 2:15

Shadeland Lamont, b s, 1889, by Wilkes Nutwood — Heroine, by Shadeland Hero.......... 2:29¼

Shadeland Leona, b m, 1882, by Satellite—Julia Patchen, by Mambrino Patchen.......... 2:28¾

Shadeland Onward, br s, 1883, by Onward—Nettie Time, by Mambrino Time.......... 2:18½

Shadow, b g, 188—, by Addison Lambert.......... 2:25

Shadow, b g, 1868, by Gen Lightfoot.. 2:28

Shadows, b m, 1892, by Nighthawk—Little Princess, by Kentucky Prince 2:28

Shakespeare, br s, 186—, by Honest Allen (dead).......... 2:30

Shemdallah, b s, 188—, by Hamdallah 2:25¾

Shamrock, gr g, 1872, by Samson—Bessie Maitland, by Tom Wonder.. 2:28

Shamrock, br g, 187—, by Gayo—Lady Emma, by Potter's Clay.......... 2:26½

Shamrock, blk g 1884, by Buccaneer—Fern Leaf, by Flaxtail.......... 2:25

Shandon Belle, gr m, 188—, by Black Republican.......... 2:21¼

Sharper, ch s, 1882, by Bourbon Wilkes—Lucy Sharp, by Joe Downing.......... 2:19¼

Sharpness, b m, 188—, by Hatto 2:27¼

Shaw Jehan, b g, 1890, by Aegon—Betsy Allen, by Thompson's Ethan Allen.......... 2:29

Shawmut, b s, 1877, by Harry Clay—Heroine, by Rysdyk's Hambletonian 2:26

She, b m, 188—, by Abbottsford 2:14½

Shea Wilkes, b s, 1889, by Alcyone—Maggie Shea, by Jefferson Prince.. 2:24¼

Sheba's Queen, b m, 188—, by Epaulet 2:26¼

Sheeny, b g, 1886, by Arthurton—Vixen, by Nutwood 2:29¾

Sheik, b g, 1884, by The King—Sheila, by Kimbrough's Abdallah ..2:29½

Shelby Maid, gr m, 1880, by Shelby Chief—Gray Bird 2:29

Shellbark, blk g, 1884, by Royal Fearnaught, dam by Tom Hunter 2:29¾

Shellmont, b s, 1888, by Egmont—Zula Maid, by Zula Hambletonian.. 2:24¼

Sheperd Boy, gr g, 1868, by Woodward's Ethan Allen 2:23½

Shepherd Knapp Jr., b g, 1861, by Shepherd F. Knapp, dam by Royal Oak (dead) 2:27¾

Sheraldine, b s, 1888, by Alex. H. Sherman—Kephart Mare, by Shakespeare Jr. 2:29¼

Sherbet, br s, 1888, by Sherman, dam by Ercole 2:20

Sheridan, b g, 187—, by Edward Everett, dam by Eureka 2:20¼

Sheridan Girl, b m, 188—, by Marlborough 2:29½

Sherman, b g, 188—, by George K... 2:27¼

Sherman, br s, 1875, by George Wilkes—Lady Belmont, by Belmont (dead) 2:23½

Sherman Bashaw, b g, 1880, by Billy Sherman—Lady Blanca, by Green's Bashaw 2:28

Sherman Morgan Jr., b s, 1869, by Sherman Morgan, dam by Stonewall 2:29

Sherwood, gr s, 1886, by Barkis—Flip, by Glencoe Golddust 2:25¼

Shillaly, blk g, 1886, by Bona Fide, dam by Young St. Lawrence.......... 2:21¼

Shilo, gr g, 188—, by White Cap 2:29

Shiloh, ch s, 1881, by Gen. Grant—Julia Logan, by Gage's Logan 2:23¾

Shiloh, b s, 1883, by Ensign—Alice West, by Allie West 2:30

Shipman, b s, 1883, by Kentucky Prince—Katie Clark, by Rysdyk's Hambletonian 2:24¼

Shooting Star, ch m, 1880, by Jefferson Prince—Sib, by Harris' Mambrino Chief Jr. 2:25½

Showeress, br m, 1888, by Comac—Madeline, by Goldsmith's Abdallah 2:27¼

Shuck Wilson, ro g, 188—, by Jay Bird 2:26¼

Shylock, ch g, 1886, by Tom Benton—Brown Jenny, by David Hill Jr ... 2:15½

Shylock, b g, 1886, by Charley B.—Ella J. 2:29¼

Siam, br g, 1890, by America—Sun Maid, by Belmont 2:26¼

Sibyl, br m, 1889, by Sphinx—Josie H., by Masterlode 2:29¼

Sibyl, br m, 188—, by Sidney—Maud K., by Whipple's Hambletonian.... 2:27½

Sickle Hambletonian, br s, 1874, by Masterlode — Ester, by Fisk's Belmont.......... 2:29¼

Sid, blk g, 1884, by John Goldsmith—Maud 2:23½

Sid Fleet, br s, 1889, by Sidney—Flight, by Buccaneer 2:26½

Sidlette, gr m, 188—, by Sidney 2:22

Sidney Boy, b s, 1891, by Sidney—Flirt, by Buccaneer 2:29

Sidney C., b g, 188—, by Acolyte 2:30

Sidner McGregor, b s, 1890, by Robert McGregor—Etta B., by Young Jim 2:18½

Sidney J., b g, 1886, by Dudley's Revolution—Nelly J., by Friday McCracken 2:26¼

Sidney Smith, b s, 188—, by Sidney 2:24½

Sidney Maid, b m, 1891, by Sidney.. 2:27

Sidnut, ch s, 188—, by Sidney, dam by Nutwood 2:25¼

Sidwood, b s, 188—, by Sidney, dam by Nutwood 2:18

Sierra La Salle, ch m, 1882, by Masterlode—Molly Nixon, by Post Boy—Frank 2:28

Siglight, b g, 188—, by Signal 2:22¼

Sigma Nu, b s, 1884, by Bourbon Wilkes—Lark, by Abdallah Mambrino (pacing 2:17¾) 2:29¼

Signet, ch s, 1877, by Hambletonian Pilot—Linda, by Soult 2:26¼

Signo Vinces, br s, 1885, by Grand Sentinel—Shadow, by Octoroon..... 2:27¼

Si Huntley 2:29¼

Silas F., b s, 1883, by Billy Sprague—Nelly Lefler 2:29¾

Silas Rich, ch g, 1855, by Young

Sir Vaughn, ch s, 1887, by Captain—Darline, by Romulus.............. 2:29¾
Sir Walter, b g, 1848, by Abdallah—Jen, by King's Bellfounder (dead).. 2:27
Sir Walter, ch s, 1873, by Aberdeen—Lady Winfield, by Edward Everett 2:24¼
Sir Walter Jr., ch s, 1882, by Sir Walter—Kate Clark, by American Clay 2:18¼
Sir Wilkes, b s, 188—, by Sable Wilkes 2:29
Sir William Wallace, b s, 1864, by Robinson Horse (dead) 2:27½
Sisal, b m, 1880, by Harold—Sapan, by Socrates 2:23¼
Sisson Girl, blk m, 186—, by McCracken's Black Hawk—Muggins, by Kelty Messenger 2:28½
Sister, br m, 1879, by Admiral—Black Flora, by Black Prince (dead) 2:19¼
Sister, b m, 1880, by Holabird's Ethan Allen—Brownell Mare, by Browney's Ethan Allen 2:25¾
Sister Barefoot, b m, 1883, by Kent—Dolly Lambert, by Daniel Lambert 2:25
Sister Ethel, b m, 1890, by Jay Bird, dam by Young Jim 2:19¼
Sister Lou, blk m, 1891, by Durango—Venie, by Haw Patch 2:29¼
Sister V., b m, 1885, by Sidney—Nettie Lambert, by John Nelson ... 2:18½
Silver Wilkes, ro m, 1876, by George Wilkes—Cherokee Girl 2:22¾
Sitra Wilkes, b m, 188—, by Knight Wilkes......................... 2:28
Siva, ch m, 1889, by Guy Wilkes—Sable Hayward, by Poscora Hayward........................... 2:13¾
Sixty-Six, b g, 1888, by Chimes—Jersey Lily, by Hambletonian Downing 2:15¼
S. J., ch g, 188—, pedigree not traced 2:16¼
S. J. B., ch g, 188—, pedigree not traced........................... 2:27½
S. J. Fletcher, b s, 1877, by Hambletonian Tranby—Pierce Mare, by Joslyn Horse........................ 2:23½
Skinkle Hambletonian, b s, 1861, by Gage's Logan...................... 2:28¾
Skipaway, br m, 1886, by Conductor—Louis Kellogg, by Pinole Patchen... 2:29¼
Skipper, b m, 188—, by Thorndale Idol, dam by Gaberlunzie......... 2:28¼
Skylight Pilot, b m, 188—, by Strathmore—Twilight, by Mambrino Pilot (dead)........................... 2:19
Slander, br s, 1879, by Tattler—Daisy Burns, by Skenandoah........... 2:28½
Sleepy Bill, br g, 186—, pedigree not traced (dead)................... 2:26
Sleepy Chief, b g, 1879, by Confederate Chief......................... 2:27½
Sleepy Dan, ch g, 1880, by Grand Duke—Winch Mare.................. 2:29¼
Sleepy George, b g, 188—, by George Sprague Jr......................... 2:19¼
Sleepy Jim, b g, 188—, by Duke Patchen............................ 2:30
Sleepy Joe, br g, 1873, by Joe Johnson—Obscurity....................... 2:19¼
Sleepy John, b g, 1860, pedigree not traced (dead)...................... 2:24½
Sleepy Ned, blk g, 1885, by Hamlin Patchen, dam by Fred Pierson..... 2:26¼
Sleepy Ned, b g, 1886, by Hannibal—Jessie.......................... 2:22¼
Sleepy Tom, b g, 1870, by Blazing Star, dam by imp. Champion....... 2:28½
Slick Nelson, b s, 188—, by Nelson.... 2:27¼
Sligo, b g, 1870, by Honest Dan...... 2:30
Slight, b m, 1886, by Electioneer—Sprite, by Belmont.................. 2:28½
Slippery Ben, b g, 188—, by Fieldmont................................ 2:29¼
Slippery Dick, b g, 1871, by Mazeppa. 2:30
Slippery Tom, blk s, 188—, by Island Chief.............................. 2:25½
Slow Go, gr g, 1865, by Sharatack Jr. (dead).......................... 2:18½
Sly Chubby, b g, 188—, by Jim Wilson.............................. 2:21¾
Small Hopes, br g, 1866, by Rysdyk's Hambletonian (dead)............ 2.26¼
Smock W., b s, 188—, by Alburn...... 2:28
Smith O'Brien, b s, 1875, by Sweepstakes—House Mare, by Young Columbus.............................. 2:29¼
Smilax.................................. 2:26¼
S. Montgomery, ch g, 1881, by Mammont—Lady Montgomery, by Flint's Morgan............................. 2:25½
Smuggle, b g, 1880, by Smuggler—Nelly Stevens, by Curtis' Hambletonian.............................. 2:24
Smuggler, br s, 1866, by Blanco (dead) 2:15¼
Smuggler's Daughter, b m, 1876, by Smuggler—Molly D., by Mambrino Chief............................... 2:24¾
Smuggler Wilkes, gr s, 1889, by Allie Wilkes—Lady Hayes, by Lace Dealer..................................2.22¼
Snakes, blk g, 1885, by Ed Kimble—Dolly............................... 2.30
Snap, b m, 1877, by Strathmore—Madam K., by Marshal Ney Jr...... 2:30
Snip Clay, b g, 188—, by Alar Clay... 2:25¾
Snip Nose, b m, 1888, by Cyclone—Nancy Wilkes, by Favorite Wilkes.. 2:24¼
Snow Ball, g g, 186—, pedigree not traced (dead)...................... 2.27½
Snow Ball, b g, 188—, by Star Hambletonian, dam by Lightwood....... 2:19½
Snowden, b g, 1885, by Strathmore—Topsey, by Williams' Mambrino.... 2:16¼
Sobol, br s, 1883, by Caesar—Senday, by Lion of Canada............... 2:27¾
Socrates, ro g, 1874, by Socrates—Belle of Augusta, by Young Indian Chief................................ 2:27¼
Socratist, b s, 1884, by Socrates—Belle Clay, by Kentucky Clay...... 2:26
Sol, ch s, 1886, by Nutwood—Sunshine, by Golddust.................. 2:30
Solano Chief, ch g, 188—, by Carr's Mambrino Chief Jr............... 2:29¼
Soldie, b g, 188—, by Socrates—Lady Ethan, by Ethan Allen.......... 2:28¼
Solferino, br s, 1885, by Grand Sentinel—Patchen Girl, by Mambrino Patchen.............................. 2:26½
Solita, br m, 1887, by Eros—Accident, by Elmo........................... 2:27
Solo, b m, 1877, by Strathmore—Abbess, by Albion..................... 2:28¾
So Long, gr g, 1882, by Erelong—Dalphine, by Harold................ 2.13¼
Somerset, ch g, 1889, by Sorrento—Impression, by Mambrino Rattler..... 2.27¼
Sonnet, b m, 1883, by Bentonian—Sontag Dixie, by Toronto Sontag... 2:24½
Sonnet, ch s, 1886, by Grand Sentinel—Nelly Clark, by Black Flying Cloud 2.30
Sonoma, gr m, 1885, by Electioneer—Sontag Mohawk, by Mohawk Chief. 2.28
Sontag Clay, ch m, 1880, by Seth Warner—Jennie Pratt, by Strader's Cassius M. Clay Jr.................... 2:24
Sonticus, b s, 1887, by Belmont—Sonnet, by Bourbon Chief............. 2:27
Sooner, b g, 186—, by Hambletonian

Rattler, dam by Murry's Cayuga Chief........ 2:24
Sophia Temple, br m, 1869, by Rattler, dam by a son of Cannon's Whip........ 2:27
Sorceress, b m, 1889, by Witchcraft—Adele S., by Kentucky Prince...... 2:24¼
Sorrel Dan, ch g, 1879, by Diadem—Blackbird........ 2:22¼
Sorrel Dapper, ch g, 1858, by King's Champion (dead)........ 2:28½
Sorrel Kate, ch m, 188—, by Mambrino Time........ 2:29½
Sorrel Ned, ch g, 187—, by Flying Cloud........ 2:25¼
So So, b m, 1875, by George Wilkes—Little Ida, by Edwin Forrest....... 2:17¼
Soto, b m, 1885, by Abdallah Mambrino—Jane, by Frank Wolford.... 2:20¼
Scudan, b s, 1883, by Happy Medium—Maria Sturgess, by Almont........ 2:25
Soudan, br g, 1883, by Combat—Maudette, by Capoul........ 2:18¼
Soudan, blk s, 1884, by Sultan—Lady Babcock, by Whipple's Hambletonian........ 2:27½
Soupy, ch s, 1884, by Gen. Hatch—Belle Green, by Green's Bashaw.... 2:23¼
Sour Mash, b s, 1881, by Red Wilkes—Brown Mary, by Bourbon Chief... 2:24¾
South Jersey Patchen Jr., b s, 1879, by South Jersey Patchen—Lucy ... 2:14¼
Southward, b s, 1887, by Onward—Admiration, by Mambrino Patchen. 2:28½
Spanish Maiden, ro m, 1886, by Happy Medium—Maggie Keene, by Mambrino Hatcher........ 2:29¼
Spartan, b g, 1880, by Strathmore—Alla, by Almont........ 2:24¼
Sparx, b s, 1889, by Jersey Wilkes—Blanche, by Egbert........ 2:24¾
Spectator, b s, 1884, by Dictator—Hattie Hogan, by Administrator.... 2:28
Speculation, gr s, 1885, by Mambrino Messenger — Mambrino Belle, by Mambrino Charta........ 2:25
Speedaway, gr s, 1885, by Brook—Nanette, by Hambrino........ 2:24¼
Speedress, b m, 1877, by King Philip—Nell, by Tenbrook........ 2:25¼
Spencer Girl, rn g, 1889, by Ashman—Savona Girl, by Wood's Hambletonian........ 2:30
Speedwell, g g, 188—, by Steele, dam by Mambrino Wilkes........ 2:26¼
Spencer Wilkes, b s, 1887, by Idol Wilkes—Molly Walker, by Captain Walker........ 2:28½
Sphinx, b s, 1883, by Electioneer—Sprite, by Belmont........ 2:20½
Spider, ro g, 187—, pedigree not traced 2:30
Spinella, b m, 1875, by Louis Napoleon—Scotia, by Dennison (dead).... 2:21¾
Spinaway, blk m, 1891, by Clay—Myrtle Herr, by Dr. Herr........ 2:29½
Spirea, ch m, 1886, by Autograph—Princess........ 2:24¼
Split Second, b m, 1891, by Happy Heir—Bird, by Harry Thorndale.... 2:28
Split Ears, ch s, 1883, by Star Ethan—Marie, by Young Columbus........ 2:29¼
Spofford, blk g, 1880, by Kentucky Prince, dam by Dispatch........ 2:18¾
Spokane, b s, 1888, by Stranger—Speedaway, by Socrates........ 2:26
Sport, gr s, 1884, by Piedmont—Sontag Mohawk, by Mohawk Chief (dead)........ 2:22¾
Spotted Beauty, wh g, 187—, by Mazeppa........ 2:29¼
Spotted Colt, sp g, 1862, by Hough's Hambletonian—Spotted Mare (dead) 2:25½
Spotted Sam, sp s, 1878, by Wood's Hambletonian — Spotted Moll, by Wallace's Phenomenon (pacing 2:25¾)........ 2:29¾
Sprague (Round's), br s, 1879, by Gov. Sprague—Davis Maid, by Mambrino Prince........ 2:24½
Sprague Golddust, br s, 1883, by Gov. Sprague—Lucille Golddust, by Golddust........ 2:15¼
Sprague Pilot, blk s, 1878, by Gov. Sprague — Lady Temple, by Pilot Temple........ 2:24
Sprague Superb, b s, 1885, by Wilmar—Nelly, by Black Diamond........ 2:29¾
Sprague Winship, br s, 1885, by Wilmar—Stella, by H. B. Winship........ 2:29¼
Spray, b m, 1887, by Princeton—Lady Edsall, by Westwood........ 2:28½
Spray, ch m, 1888, by Simmons—Patterson Mare, by Patterson's Trustee 2:28¼
Spreckles, b s, 1889, by Epaulet—Charm, by Santa Claus........ 2:30
Springcroft, blk s, 1887, by Alcyone—Hebe, by Emulus........ 2:26¼
Springdale, ch g, 188—........ 2:24½
Spring Day, b m, 1888, by C. F. Clay—Saratoga, by New York........ 2:26½
Spry, b g, 1882, by Gen. Benton—Sprite, by Belmont........ 2:28¾
Spurgeon, br s, 1880, by Charley B.—Jenny, by Freehold Bashaw........ 2:21¾
Spurrier Boy, ch g, 1881, by Brussels—Sally Beaver, by Coulter's Davy Crocket........ 2:30
Spy, ch s, 1887, by Allandorf—Style, by Maxim........ 2:27½
Squeezer, b g, 188—, by McEwen........ 2:25½
S. S., br g, 1883, by Kentucky Volunteer—Matilda, by Springville Chief. 2:20½
S. S. Ellsworth, ch g, 187—, by Andy Johnson........ 2:20
Stamboul, b s, 1882, by Sultan—Fleetwing, by Rysdyk's Hambletonian... 2:07½
Stamina, br m, 1888, by Patron—Clеora B., by Elial G........ 2:26½
Stammont, b s, 1890, by Stamboul—Zoraya, by Guy Wilkes........ 2:29¾
Stammal, b s, 1888, by Stamboul—Young Signal, by Arthurton........ 2:25½
Stanford, b s, 1885, by Piedmont—Irene, by Mohawk Chief........ 2:26½
Stanford, b s, 1885, by Clay—Flora, by Whipple's Hambletonian........ 2:20¼
Stanhope, b s, 1889, by Red Wilkes—Venus Almont, by Star Almont..... 2:25½
Stanley, b g, 1884, by Dartmouth........ 2:29¼
Stanley, b g, 1885, by Venture Boone, dam by Matchless........ 2:17
Stanley, b g, 188—, pedigree not traced........ 2:30
Stanley, b s, 1883, by Valentine Swigert—Kewanna, by Trojan Jr........ 2:27
Stanley, b'k s, 1889, by Quartermaster — Belle Medium, by Fairview Chief........ 2:24¼
Stanton Chief, b s, 188—, by Gen. Stanton, dam by Henderson Horse.. 2:27¾
Stanza, blk s, 1887, by Stranger—Sonnet, by Jay Gould........ 2:22½
Star, blk s, 1876, by Pennypack—Lady Fashion, by Long Island Black Hawk........ 2:30
Star, b g, 1871, by Aberdeen—Stella, by Carpenter's American Star...... 2:25¼

A. McDOWELL, San Francisco, Cal.

In 1894 McDowell placed the world's record for trotters at 2:03¾ with Alix and the world's record for two-year-old pacers at 2:07¾ with Directly.

MILLARD SANDERS, Pleasanton, Cal.
Millard Sanders drove the following yearlings to world's records:
Frou Frou 2:25¼, Fausta (p) 2:22¾, Rosedale (p) 2:22.
He also marked the pacer W. Wood 2:07
and drove the trotter Guy in 2:10¾.

Star, ch g, 186—, by Conklin's American Star.......................... 2:30
Star A.cyone, b s, 1887, by Alcyone —Olivette......................... 2:24½
Star Allen, blk m, 1884, by Frank Allen—Goddess of Liberty, by Phil Sheridan.......................... 2:26½
Star B., b g, 1885, by Dom Pedro— Cora Collins, by Ned Forrest....... 2:26½
Star Bashaw, blk s, 1885, by Star of of the West—Bonnie Doon, by Bashaw Drury.......................... 2:24½
Star Bashaw, ch s, 1884, by Wapsie —Gass, by Abdallah Star........... 2:27
Star Chief, b g, 188—, pedigree not traced.............................. 2:30
Star Duroc, b. s, 1874, by Messenger Duroc—Lorillard Mare, by Seely's American Star................... 2:25¾
Star Gazer, b g, 1878, by Tom F. Patchen.......................... 2.26¼
Star Girl, b m, 188—, by Star Lambert.............................. 2:29½
Star Hambletonian, br s, 1875, by Felte.'s Hambletonian—Belle Pitts, by American Boy...................... 2:28¾
Star Hawk, ch s, 1887, by Star of the West—Betula, by Romulus......... 2:17¾
Starin Medium, b s, 1880, by Happy Medium—Lady Emma, by Niagara Champion.......................... 2.26¼
Star King, dn g, 187—, by George M. Patchen Jr....................... 2.22
Starletta, blk m, 1881, by Starlight— Highland Mary, by Seely's American Star......................... 2.21¼
Starlight, ch g, 1878, by Cyclone— Modesty.......................... 2:28¼
Starlight, br m, 1889, by Electionee· —Sallie Benton, by Gen. Benton ... 2 15¾
Star Lily, ch m, 1884, by President Garfield—Star Queen, by Star Hambletonian........................ 2:20
Star Line, gr s, 1886, by White Line —Belle Parsons, by Star Hambletonian............................... 2:27
Star Line, br s, 1885, by White Line —Lady Star, by Star Hambletonian 2:29½
Starling, ch s, 188—, by Banks...... 2.27¼
Star Medium, b s, 188—, by Rupert Medium........................... 2.28½
Star Medium, gr s, 188—, by Pilot Medium........................... 2.26¼
Star Medium, b m, 1889, by Union Medium—Alpha, by Atlantic........ 2.29¼
Star Moak, b s, 1888, by Mohawk Hambletonian—Peggy Corrigan, by Jackson........................... 2:20¾
Star Monarch, br s, 1879, by Almonarch—Charlotte Jones, by Kester's Royal George..................... 2:23½
Starmont, blk s, 188—, by Hamlin's Almont Jr........................ 2:28½
Star of the West, blk s, 1860, by Flying Cloud—Grey Fanny, by Eureka (dead)............................ 2.26½
Star of the West Jr., blk s, 1876, by Star of the West—Lady Douglas, by Black Douglas..................... 2:29¼
Star Princeps, b s, 1889, by Princeps —Maybird, by Abdallah Bird........ 2:16¾
Startle, b s, 1887 by Mambrino Startle—Hamlettie, by Ham'et.......... 2·25
Startle, blk s, 1870, by the Andrews Horse, dam by Witherell Messenger 2:26½
Star W., b m, 1879, by Concord—Fan. 2:27¾
State Senator, blk g, 188—, by Fleet's Hambletonian—Princess........... 2.26
Stathard, b m, 1886, by St. Gothard—

Stacy, by Strathmore.............. 2:27¼
Stealaway, b m, 188—, by Elial G.... 2:28½
Steineer, b s, 1887, by Steinway— Katy G., by F'ectioneer........... 2:20¼
Steinway, b s, 1876, by Strathmore— Abbess, by Albion................. 2:25¾
Stella, b m, 1879, by Electioneer— Lady Rhodes, by Gen. Taylor...... 2·30
Stella, gr m, 188—, by Abdallah Glencoe—Fanny Ramsey, by Hogan's Henry............................ 2.29
Stella, br m, 1892, by Geo Washington, dam by McDonald Chief...... 2·30
Stella, br m, 1885, by Shawmut—Lady Eleanor, by Walkill Chief.......... 2 21
Stella Belmont, b m, 1887, by Belmont—Lida Goldsmith, by Goldsmith's Abdallah................. 2:19
Stella Blake, br m, 1871, by Pequawket—Rosa B., by Morgan Trotter... 2 25¼
Stella C, ch m, 187—, by Aberdeen— Maud............................ 2:27¼
Stella C., br m, 1885, by Director— Speculation Maid, by Speculation... 2.26
Stella H, br m, 1885, by Hambletonian Mambrino—Stewart Mare....... 2:29¾
Stella Magnet, b m, 1884, by Magnet— Leadville Girl, by Pilot Duroc...... 2.24½
Stellaria, b m, 1891, by Lancaster— Sun Maid, by Belmont............. 2:26½
Stemwinder, b g, 1884, by Altamont— Amanda, by Scamperdown.......... 2:25¼
Stephanie, b m, 1882, by Meander— Ruby Duroc, by Messenger Duroc... 2:22¼
Stephanus, b s, 1871, by Bajardo— Nancy, by Morgan Hunter.......... 2:28¼
Stephen G, b g, 1874, by Knickerbocker—Sunbeam, by Volunteer.... 2:20½
Stephen M., b g, 1872, by American Sta· Jr.—Miss Cadmus, by Long Island............................. 2:28½
Stephen R., ch g, 1884, by Gen. Thomas—Dolly Russell, by Mazeppa 2:20¼
Sterling Wilkes, ch g, 188—, by Bourbon Wilkes—Lucy Moore, by Sterling............................. 2:23¼
Sternberg, blk s, 1888, by Wilkes Boy —Fanny Allen, by Black Allen..... 2:15¼
Stet Brino, ch s, 1888, by Hambrino-Jewess, by Woodford Mambrino.... 2:26½
Steve, br g, 188—, by Steve Whipple, dam by Nephew................... 2:10¼
Steve Maxwell, gr g, 1867, by Ole Bull Jr. (dead).................... 2:21½
Steve Whipple, br s, 1884, by Ham·b'etonian Ch·isman — Twist, by Whipple's Hambletonian.......... 2:12
Stevie, blk g, 1880, by Kentucky Prince—Camille, by Rysdyk's Hambletonian........................ 2:10
Stevie H., blk g, 188—, by Washington............................. 2:22¼
Stewart, gr s, 1888, by Pilot Medium— Mercedes, by Masterlode.......... 2:25
Stewart Mac, ch s, 1878, by Blue Bull —Fanny Mac, by Night Shade...... 2:29
Stewart Maloney, b g, 1866, by Charles E. Loew (dead)........... 2:27
Stickfast, b g, 1882, by Duke of Crawford—Dora Houston, by Sam Houston Jr.......................... 2:27
Stonecutter, b g, 1877, by Enfield— Grey Fanny, by Pilot Jr.......... 2:28¾
Stone· Boy, ch g, 188—, by Mambrino Russel—Vivette, by Strathmore.... 2:26¼
Stoneridge, br s, 188—, by Happy Thought.......................... 2:21¼
Stonewall, ch g, 187—, by Frank Pierce 3d, dam by Moscow......... 2:24½

Stonewall, br s, 1889, by Egotist—Dixie Sprague, by Gov Sprague. .. 2.27½
Stonewall, b s, 1881, by Jim Hill—Lena. 2.28¼
Storm, b m, 1867, by Middleton—Green Mountain Maid, by Harry Clay (dead). 2.26¾
Storm, b s, 1887, by Durango—Deborah, by Squire Talmage 2.24
Stormer, b s, 1872, by Surprise—Nelly. 2.29¼
Stormer, b g, 1890, by Storm King—Fanny W., by Meredith 2.26¼
Storm King, b s, 1882, by Happy Medium—Topsy Taylor, by Alexander's Norman 2.25¾
Stornaway, b s, 1884, by Chichester—Naiad, by Belmont. 2.19
Story Teller, b m, 188—, by Peter Story. 2.27¾
Story's Clay, b s, 188—, by Everett Clay, dam by Stillson. 2.18¼
Strader H., b s, 1886, by Squire Talmage—Lucy H., by Napoleon. 2:09½
Strangemore, blk s, 1879, by Columbia Chief—Topsy, by Black Donald. . . . 2:29¾
Stranger, b g, 187—, pedigree not traced. 2.30
Stranger, gr g, 1876, by Selim—Kitty McDonald, by McDonald's Mambrino Chief 2.28
Stranger, gr g, 187—, by Mambrino Hambletonian—Grey Mary, by Traveler. 2.23¾
Stranger, ch g, 1872, by Alta—Sally. . 2.29
Stranger, gr g, 1849, by Eaton Horse (dead). 2.30
Stranger, b s, 1885, by Tilton Almont—Jessie, by Whipple's Hambletonian. 2.17
Stranger, ch g, 188—, by Sir John Dean. 2.25¼
Stranger Boy, br s, 188—, by Stranger, dam by Squire Talmage 2.29¼
Strangler, b s, 1887, by Stranger—Kate, by Allen Book. 2.26¼
Strategist, ch s, 1883, by Grand Sentinel—Peru Belle, by Ranger. 2.22
Stratford, b s, 1883, by Strathmore—Young Winnie, by Woodford Mambrino. 2.28¼
Strathbridge, ch s, 1885, by Grand Sentinel — Soprano, by Strathmore (dead). 2:28¼
Strathalan, b s, 1887, by Strathmore—Lady Waxy, by Beal's Waxy. 2.24¼
Strathlan, b s, 1874, by Strathmore—Shackleford, by Aker's Idol. 2:21¼
Strathboy, b s, 1886, by Strathmore—Esmeralda, by Hambrino Star 2.22½
Strathmore, b g, 1855, pedigree not traced (dead). 2.30
Strathmore Abdallah, b s, 1885, by Strathmore — Kate Abdallah, by Goldsmith's Abdallah. 2.28
Strathway, ch s, 1885, by Steinway—Countess, by Whipple's Hambletonian. 2:19
Strathwood, b s, 1881, by Strathmore—Betty Blackwood, by Blackwood. . 2.25½
Strephon, b g, 1888, by Kentucky Wilkes—Melinda, by Oxmoor. 2.26½
Strideaway, br g, 1861, pedigree not traced 2:28½
Strogoff, b s, 1884, by Grand Sentinel—Molly, by Grey Fearnaught 2:24¼
Strontia, gr g, 188—, by Sam Purdy—Madge, by Zirkle's Engineer. 2:14¼
Stuart, b g, 1880, by Strathmore—Carrie Clay, by Coaster 2.25
Student, ch g, 188—, by Socrates—Hattie Woodward, by Aberdeen . . 2.21¼
Success, b s, 1888, by Onward—Minnie Walker, by Harry Wilkes. 2:26¾
Success, b g, 188—, pedigree not traced. 2.30
Sucker Maid, gr m, 1868, by Rockaway, dam by Rob Roy. 2.29¼
Sue Gillig, b m, 1888, by Gillig—Cecil, by Waltham. 2.25¼
Sue Grundy, br m, 187—, by Getaway—Old Kate. 2.25½
Sulsun, b m, 1884, by Electioneer—Susie, by George M. Patchen Jr. . . 2.18¼
Suito, br s, 1884, by Blackwood—Sue, by Thorndale. 2.21
Sulfonal, b s, 1887, by Nutwood—Fulton Maid, by Clay Pilot. 2.16¾
Sultan, br s, 1875, by The Moor—Sultana, by Delmonico (dead). 2.24
Sultan, blk g, 1887, by Administrator 2.28½
Sultana, b m, 1882, by Sir Walkill—Free Love, by Blackwood 2.29¾
Sultandin, ch s, 188—, by Sultan 2.29½
Sulwood, b s, 1885, by Sultan—Lady Graves, by Nutwood 2.20
Summer Queen, ch m, 188—, by Joe You See 2.29¼
Summit, br s, 1886, by Oberlin—Cora, by Cottril Morgan 2.29¾
Summit Chief, b s, 1888, by Elliott Wilkes—Toga, by Country Boy . . . 2.21¼
Sumpter, b g, 1881, by Grand Sentinel—Pet, by Chadwick 2.25¼
Sunalto, b s, 188—, by Sunolo, dam by Washtenaw Chief 2.26¼
Sunbeam, ch m, 1889, by Ambassador—Mambrino Maid, by Chief 2.28
Sunbeam, br m, 1890 by Quartermaster—Magnolia, by Middletown . . . 2.28
Sunbeam, b m, 186—, pedigree not traced (dead) 2.30
Sunflower, ch m, 1882, by Elmo—Ella Kellogg, by Chieftain 2.24
Sunlight, gr s, 1885, by Tasco—Julia, by White Cloud 2.27
Sunlight, b s, 1886, by Bartholomew Wilkes—Our Mary, by Roup's American Boy 2.29½
Sunnyside, blk m, 185—, pedigree not traced (dead) 2.30
Sunol, b m, 1886, by Electioneer—Waxana, by Gen. Benton 2:08¼
Sunrise, br g, 1882, by Abbottsford—Belle by Signal 2.24¾
Sunrise, br m, 1889, by Brazilian—Sunday, by Young Volunteer . . 2.28½
Sunrise Patchen, b s, 1883, by Seneca Patchen—Lady Monmouth, by Winthrop Morrill, Jr. 2.19¼
Sunrise Prince, b s, 1889, by Hillside Prince—Jessica by Monaco . . 2.13¼
Sunset b s, 1885, by Anteeo—Nelly, by King Philip 2.29¾
Sunset Patchen, br s, 1885, by Seneca Patchen—Lady Monmouth by Winthrop Morrill, Jr. (pacing 2.18¾). . . . 2.23½
Sunshade Patchen, b s, 1888, by Seneca Patchen—Lady Monmouth by Winthrop Morrill, Jr 2.28
Sunshine, ch s, 1872, by Curtis' Hambletonian—Kate, by Kentucky Clay 2.29¼
Sunshine, ch g, 1878 by Tramp—Flaxy, by Green's Bashaw 2.29¾
Superintendent b s, 1887, by Almont Wilkes—Dazzle, by Happy Medium 2.22
Superior, ch s, 1881, by Egbert—

Mary, by Woodford Mambrino ... 2.17¼

Superior, b s, 1880, by Warwick Boy—Brown Kate, by Virginia 2:18½

Superior Wilkes, ch s, 1888, by Hector Wilkes—Lady Trojan, by Trojan 2:24¾

Surah, b s, 1889, by Rochester—Lady Carmen, by Neely's Henry Clay .. 2:29½

Surprise, b m, 1889, by Aberdeen—Jenny W., by Almont 2:29¼

Surprise, blk m, 187—, by Tom Knox.. 2:29½

Surprise, gr g, 185—, by Harry Clay, dam by Boanerges (dead) 2:26

Surprise, ch s, 1884, by McGregor Chief—Dolly, by Sam Kirkwood 2:23¾

Surprise, gr m, 1876, by Grey Dan, dam by Black Sultan 2:28½

Surprise Franklin, ch s, 1887, by Ben Franklin—Lady May, by Blackstone 2:29¼

Susan B., br m, 1878, by Mark Anthony 2:29¼

Susan Nipper, b m, 187—, pedigree not traced 2:30

Susette, b m, 1883, by Electioneer—Susie, by George M. Patchen Jr. .. 2:23½

Susette, b m, 1886, by Onward—Josie Sellers, by Mambrino Time 2:26½

Susie, ch m, 1862, by Hampshire Boy, dam by Wildair (dead) 2:21

Susie, b m, 1883, by Addison Lambert, dam by DeLong's Ethan Allan .. 2:26

Susie, ch m, 1872, by George M. Patchen Jr.—Santa Claus, by Owen Dale (dead) 2:26½

Susie B., b m, 188—, by Clinker—Dolly, by Searcher 2:26¼

Susie Collins, br m, 1884, by Volunteer—Madeleine, by Goldsmith's Abdallah 2:23¼

Susie D., b m 1876, by Middletown—Nelly Holly, by Ed Holly (dead).... 2:29¼

Susie G., br m, 1884, by Alcalde Jr. 2:26¾

Susie H., ch m, 1885, by Macon—Blanche, by Harold Mambrino ... 2:29¼

Susie H., b m, 188—, by Duroc, dam dam by Kenyon Columbus 2:27¾

Susie Mac, br m, 1882, by Nicotine—Thorndale Princess, by Thorndale ... 2:29

Susie Owen, br m, 1877, by Daniel Boone—Gretchen, by Gideon 2:26

Susie Parker, b m, 1864, by Henry B. Patchen, dam by Abdallah (dead) 2:25¼

Susie S., ch m, 1881, by Hambletonian Mambrino—Bellfounder Maid, by Milliman's Bellfoun 2:18

Susie S., b m 1884, by Hylas—Lady Byron, by Byron 2:15½

Susie T., blk m, 188—, by Bostick's Almont Jr. 2:23¼

Susie T., ro m., 1881, by Gov Sprague—Morning Dawn, by Marengo 2:28¼

Susie W., blk m, 1878, by Comet—Doll Watters 2:26½

Sussex, blk g, 187—, by Star, dam by Rysdyk's Hambletonian 2:30

Sut, blk s. 1888 by Sut Lovingood—Peerless, by Fearnaught 2:28½

Sutherland, b s, 1887, by Grand Sentinel—Empress, by Abdallah Mambrino 2:24¼

Sutton, ch s 1888 by Epaulet—Daisy Maid, by Mambrino Boy 2:26¼

Suzerain, b s 1884, by Grand Sentinel—Shadow, by Octoroon 2:29½

S. V. White, b s, 1891, by Alexander (Dumas—Topsy White, by Little Ben 2:29½

Swanock, b s, 1887, by Advance—Johnetta, by Honest John 2:20

Swanton Boy, br g, 1886, by Jimmy Blaine—Bird, by McKesson's Grey Eagle 2:23¼

Swanton Boy, br s, 1886, by Star Ethan—Daisy Dean, by Young Rip 2:27¼

S. W. Bennett, b s, 1885, by Pilot Medium—Belle B., by Masterlode .. 2:19½

S. W. G., b g, 1879, by Artemas—Lady Bellfounder, by Powhattan . 2:27

Sweepstakes, b g, 1875, by Kentucky Prince—Juno, by Conklin's American Star 2:24¼

Sweetbriar, gr m, 1870, by Eugene Casserly—Peanuts, by George M. Patchen Jr 2:26¼

Sweetbriar, ch m, 188—, by Favorite Wilkes—Sally Wood, by Westwood 2:17½

Sweet Child, b m, 1891, by April Fool, dam a Texas mare 2:29¾

Sweetheart, br m, 1878, by Sultan—Minnehaha, by Stevens' Bald Chief 2:22½

Sweetheart, b m, 1884, by Masterlode—Irish Girl, by Tam O'Shanter .. 2:29¼

Sweet Home, ch m, 187—, by Milliman's Bellfounder 2:30

Sweetness, b m, 1878, by Pequawket 2:26½

Sweetness, b m, 1871, by Volunteer—Lady Merritt, by Edward Everett.. 2:21¼

Sweetness, b m, 1874, by Young Volunteer—Fustey, by John Shylock (dead) 2:22¾

Sweet Rose, b m, 1891, by Electioneer—Rosemont, by Piedmont 2:25¾

Sweetwater, b m, 1889, by Stamboul 2:26

S. W. G., b g, 188—, by William H. Vanderbilt 2:26¾

Swigert Bellfounder, b s, 188—, by Swigert—Lady, by Bay Dick 2:25¾

Swigert Jr., b s, 1875, by Swigert—Pauline, by Mambrino Rattler 2:22¾

Swigert K., br s, 1889, by Swigert—Lady Belle, by Richard's Bellfounder 2:25¼

Syenite, ro g, 187—, by Waveland Chief—Nancy Dillard, by John Dillard 2:29¼

Sylvanite, ch m, 1891, by Delmarch.. 2:26

Sylva C., b m, 1891, by Sphinx—Coast Girl, by Coaster 2:29¾

Sylvan, b m, 1885, by Petoskey—Sally, by Monroe Chief 2:28½

Sylvan, b s, 1884, by Nutwood—Nora Lee, by Woodford Mambrino ... 2:23¼

Sylvan Glen, b s, 1883, by Duke of Glenlake—Beatrice, by Moro .. 2:30

Sylvester K., b g, 1885, by Lambertus—Young Pocahontas, by Strideway.. 2:17¾

Sylvia, b m, 1887, by Stranger—Sybil, by Jay Gould 2:29¼

Sylvia, ch m, 1883, by Middletown Jr.—Black Kate by Andrew Jackson 2:27¼

Sylvia M., gr m, 1878, by Baird's Hambletonian Prince—Faith Derrick 2:25¼

Syndicate, b m, 1878, by Erin Chief 2:23¾

T. A., b g, 1868, by Sentinel 2:26

Tackey, gr m, 1859, by Pilot Jr.—Jenny Lind, by Bellfounder (dead).. 2:26

Tacks, blk s, 1885, by Egbert—Jenette, by Mambrino Howard 2:24¾

Tacony, ro g, 1844, by Sportsman (dead) 2:27

Tague O'Ragan, b g, 1887, by Black's

Hambletonian 2.27¾
Tainter, br g, 1878, by Eclair—Nelly Wildwood, by Matchless 2:26
T. A. K., b g, 1875, by Gilroy 2.28½
Takina, b m, 1881, by Strathmore—Belle 2.30
Talavera, b s, 1881, by Happy Medium—Kate, by Alhoit 2.30
Talisman, b s, 1885, by Princeps—Dolly, by Billy Booker 2.30
Tall Leon, b s, 1890, by Tallmage—Lady Leon, by Leon 2:29½
Tamarack, gr g, 187—, by Jim Hawkins 2:28½
Tamerlane, blk s, 1889, by Aristos—Empress .... 2·29
Tam O'Shanter, blk g, 188—, by Charley B .... 2·28¾
Tandy, b s, 1884, by Robber Boy—Sister, by Strathmore 2 28¼
Tanner Boy, gr g, 186—, by Edward Everett .... 2·22½
Tansy D, b m, 188—, by Stephen A. Douglas 2:29
Tansy G., ch m, 188—, by Ajax 2.30
Tanhauser, br g, 188—, by Billy R... 2:22¼
Tarantella, br m, 1890, by Axtell—Gladys, by McMahon 2:21½
Tariff, blk g, 1883, by Young Wilkes—Nelly, by Robert Whaley 2:20¾
Tariff, b s, 1874, by Clarion Chief—Lillian, by Favorite 2:20¾
Tariff J., br s, 1883, by Tariff, dam by Champion 2:26
Tartar, b g, 1884, by St. Louis—Mary, by Milwaukee 2:26½
Tartar, br g, 1849, by Wild Deer (dead) 2:28½
Tattler, b s, 1863, by Pilot Jr.—Telltale, by Telamon '(dead) 2 26
Taurus, br s, 1885, by Backman's Idol—Clifton Girl, by Stonewall Jackson 2:30
Tavernier, b s, 1887, by Pilot Wilkes—Sid Offutt Mare, by Almont 2:26½
Taylor, b g, 188—, by Tom Scott..... 2:28¼
Taylor, ro g, 1872, by Johnny B...... 2:26¼
Taylorson, gr g, 1885, by Sweepstakes—Snowball, by Potter's Clay 2:27¼
Teakwood, b s, 1890, by Nutwood—Lady Bashaw, by Mambrino Boy .. 2:30
Teaser, b g, 1883, by Johnny Repp ... 2:29
Tecoma, b s, 1884, by Alecto—Sally Jenkins, by General Knox 2:19¼
Tecumseh, ch s, 1876, by Mambrino Gift—Lady Night Hawk, by Night Hawk 2:28
Teddy Look, ch g, 188—, by Look.... 2:28¼
Ted McMahon, b g, 1882, by McMahon—Daisy, by Hambletonian Chief.... 2:28
Telegraph Girl, ch m, 1880, by Harry Arlington—Nelly, by Winchester... 2:29¼
Telephone, ro g, 1877, by Wood's Hambletonian—Miss Roberts, by Young Andrew Jackson .... 2·22½
Telephone, b s, 1882, by Empire—Lark, by Abdallah Mambrino...... 2:15½
Tellie, br g, 1883, by Abdallah Jr..... 2·25¼
Tempest, ch m, 1880, by Sunshine—Nelly 2:27¾
Tempest, b m, 1883, by Hawthorne—Brown Tempest, by Chieftain 2:19
Tempest, blk g, by Tempest Jr...... 2:22¼
Tempest, ch g, 1876, by Millman's Bellfounder—Firefly, by Walnut Bark 2.29
Tempest, gr m, 187—, by Ledger—Tillie Fee, by Cook's Bulrush Morgan 2:29¼
Temple, b s, 1874, by Harold—Bland Temple, by Lexington (dead) 2.30
Temple Bar, blk s, 1886, by Egbert—Nettie Time, by Mambrino Time.... 2:17¾
Templemore, ch s, 1887, by Theseus—Delancy Tramp, by Tramp 2:29¾
Templeton, b s, 1885, by Warlock—Princess Royal, by Happy Medium (dead) 2:25½
Tempter, b s, 1889, by St. Bel—Nora Temple, by Belmont 2:24¾
Templette, b g, 1889, by Epaulet—Kitty Temple, by Rysdyk 2:29¼
Tennessee, blk m, 1861, by Commodore—Dairy Maid, by Vermont Black Hawk .... 2·27
Tennessee Wilkes, b s, 1880, by George Wilkes—Lizzie Hayden, by Peavine 2:27
Tennie O., blk m, 1890, by Major H .. 2:26½
Tennyson, ch g, 188—, by Thompson's Golddust 2 23¾
Tennyson, b s, 1885, by Tremont—Lady Wilkes, by George Wilkes 2 27¼
Terragon, b g, 1886, by Tauton—Barker Mare, by Bald Chief....... 2:23
Tentabit, gr s, 1888, by Pilot Medium—Minnie Hoag, by Bay Middleton... 2:29¼
Texas Bill, gr g, 187—, pedigree not traced 2:26¼
Texas Jack, ch g, 187—, by Blue Bull. 2:29¼
Texas Joe, b s, 188—, by Texas Jack.. 2:29½
Texas Rooker, br s, 188—, by Texas Jack, dam by Rooker 2.29¼
T. G., ch g, 1878, by Young's Hambletonian Prince, dam by Bilow Horse 2:26
Thad, b g, 1879, by Hambletonian Tranby 2:29¼
Thalberg, b g, 1878, by Mambrino Excelsior—Georgia Mack, by Cady's Champion .... 2·20
Thalia, b m, 1885, by Col. Hambrick—Miss Watson, by Billy Lewis 2:24¾
Thapsin, blk g, 1880, by Berlin—Lady Hubbard, by Benicia Boy 2:21¼
The Banker, ch s, 1874, by Mambrino Patchen—Lute Boyd, by Joe Downing 2:29½
The Bull, b s, 1885, by Thomas Jefferson—Sheppardess, by Jack Sheppard 2:30
The Colonel, b g, 1884, by White's Pete—Nell .... 2·26¼
The Conqueror, ch s, 1890, by Egotist—Arlotta, by Harold .... 2·13½
The Corporal, b s, 188—, by Baird's Hambletonian Prince 2:28½
The Item, b g, 1881, by Gov. Sprague—Molly Walker, by Captain Walker 2:23¼
The Jewess, b m, 1871, by Mambrino Patchen—Lettia, by Joe Downing.. 2:26
The Judge, b s, 188—, by Round's Sprague .... 2·22¾
The King, blk s, 1874, by George Wilkes—Jewel, by Gill's Vermont.. 2·29¼
Thelma, b m, 1891, by Thorr—Helen, by Kentucky Prince 2:25
Theme, ch g, 1890, by Ben Harrison—Dolly Smith, by Fisk's Mambrino Chief Jr 2:29¼
Themis, b m, 1885, by Achilles—Young Sontag, by Volunteer... .... 2·25
Theodore, br s, 1885, by Reveille—Maple Leaf, by New York (pacing 2:18½) .... 2·26¼
The Raven, blk s, 1886, by Elial G.—Maud, by Victor 2:19½
The Raven, blk m, 1890, by Clay

King—Annabel Lee, by Aberdeen.. 2:26
Theresa, br m, 1887, by Nelson—Lady, by Gen. Knox ... 2:25¾
The Seer, b s, 1885, by Gen. Benton —Odette, by Electioneer ... 2:15¾
Thetis, b m, 1885, by Mambrino Wilkes—Serena, by Vedder's Cadmus ... 2:16¼
The Turk, b s, 1887, by Sultan—Ida Elliott, by Allie West ... 2:30
The·ese Phallamont, b m, 1887, by Phallamont—Mollie Bradley, by Milwaukee ... 2:29¼
Theresa Sprague, b m, 1878, by Gov. Sprague—Bohemian Girl, by Almont 2:25¼
The Wasser, b s, 1884, by Washington—Kate Taylor, by Aberdeen..... 2:30
Thomas A. Doyle, b g, 188—, pedigree not traced ... 2:25¼
Thomas C., b g, 1881, by Blind Tom. 2:26¼
Thomas H., br s, 1884, by Mohawk Jr. —Myrtle, by Bashaw Drury ... 2:30
Thomas Jefferson, blk s, 1863, by Toronto Chief—Gipsy Queen, by a son of Black Hawk (dead) ... 2:23
Thomas L. Young, ch g, 1865, by Wells' Yellow Jacket, dam by D·agon (dead) ... 2:19½
Thomas Rysdyk, b s, 1886, by Rysdyk —Largessi, by Scott's Thomas 2:29¼
Thomas R., ch s, 188—, by Montgomery ... 2:20¼
Thomas S. Harrison, br s, 1883, by Hermes—Lady Aline, by New Jersey 2:29½
Thompson, ch s, 1890, by Boodle, dam by Jim Mulvenna ... 2:21¼
Thompson, blk g, 188—, by Redwood Boone, dam by Howe's Bismarck... 2:27½
Thornburg, b g, 1877, by Judge Advocate—Lady Reno, by Gen. Grant.... 2:21½
Thorndale, b s, 1865, by Alexander's Abdallah—Dolly, by Mambrino Chief (dead) ... 2:22¼
Thorndale F., b g, 1881, by Thorndale Chief—Lady Durgin, by Walter Allen ... 2:30
Thorndale Jr., b s, 1885, by Hero of Thorndale—Wild Maid, by Young Matchless ... 2:30
Thorndale Maid, b m, 1877, by Thorndale—Country Maid, by Country Gentleman ... 2:30
Thorndella, gr m, 1881, by Thorndale Chief—Maggie Wayne... 2:27¼
Thornden, b s, 1887, by Crittenden—Mary K., by Hero of Thorndale..... 2:30
Thornless, b g, 1878, by Dauntless—Nannie Thorne, by Hamlet ... 2:15¾
Thornley, b s, 1889, by Rumor—Thornleaf, by Jay Gould ... 2:29¼
Thornton, b g, 1885, by Alcantara—Tho·ndale Maid by Thorndale ... 2:26¼
Thorntonian b s, 1888, by Egtho·ne—Kit F., by William M. ... 2:30
Thorn Rose, ch m, 1888, by Nil Desperandum—Rosy Thorne, by Thorndale ... 2:26¾
Thorn Wilkes, b s, 1887, by Hector Wilkes—Smuggler Belle, by Smuggler ... 2:28½
Thornwood, b g, 188—... 2:29¾
Thornwood, ch s, 1887, by Hawthorne —March Fourth, by Whipple's Hambletonian ... 2:19¼
Three Tips, ch s, 1887, by Sam Purdy —Vi·ginia Girl, by Hetzel's Hambletonian ... 2:25¼
Thursday, blk m, 188—, by Noonday.. 2:25
Thurston, b s, 1889, by Sir Archie.... 2:29¾
Tickle Me, blk s, 1889, by C. F. Clay, dam by Lyle Wilkes ... 2:28
Tietam, b s, 188—, by Anteeo—Evaline, by Nutwood ... 2:19
Ticonic, ch g, 1875, by Milwaukee—Lady Dexter, by Black Flying Cloud 2:26½
Tick O' Tanic, b m, 1890... 2:28½
Tid Jefferson, blk m, 1880, by Alexander Jefferson—Jenny, by Pilot.... 2:27½
Tilford, b s, 1883, by Bourbon Wilkes —Julia, by Gibson's John Dillard Jr. 2:17¾
Tillie B., b m... 2:24½
Tillie Green, ch m, 188—, by Mambrino King ... 2:27
Tillie Macey, b m, 188—, by Macey, dam by Hero of Thorndale ... 2:26¼
Tillie S., br m, 1886, by Pasacas—Hatch Mare, by Patchen... 2:27½
Tilton, br g, 188—, by Constellation... 2:24¼
Tilton Almont, b s, 1872, by Almont, dam by Clark Chief (dead)... 2:26
Tilton B., b g, 188—, by Tilton Almont, dam by John Nelson... 2:24¾
Tim C., b g, 188—, by Graham's Mambrino ... 2:23¼
Time Medium, b s, 1880, by Happy Medium—Decorah, by Mambrino Time ... 2 27½
Tim Kane, br s, 1890, by Judge Trumble—Brown Nell ... 2:21¼
Timothy, b g, 187—, by Hindoo... 2:26¼
Tina F., b m, 1888, by Tamarisk..... 2:25
Tinker, b g, 188—, by Bickford Forrest 2:25¾
Tinker, b s, 1880, by Geo·ge M. Patchen Jr., dam by Uncle Tom ... 2:28
Tinnie B., br m, 1875, by Black Pilot—Cooney, by Stewart Morgan ... 2:27¼
Tin Plate, br s, 1891, by Durango—Nickle Plate, by Belmont ... 2:26
Tiny, b g, 1880, by Solicitor—Red Bird, by Harold ... 2:29¼
Tiny, br m, 1889, by Electioneer—Telle, by Gen. Benton ... 2:28¼
Tiny B., b m, 1886, by Charley B.—Pauline, by Prince Imperial ... 2.21½
Tiny Moore, b m, 1891, by Judge Tranby—Minnie H., by Legal Tender Jr. ... 2:29¼
Tiny Rogers, b m, 1886, by Prairie Star—Ione, by Wapsie ... 2:30
Tioga Belle, b m, 188—, by Hiatoga Chief ... 2:20½
Tipple, b m, 1884, by Echo—Hathaway Mare, by Whipple's Hambletonian ... 2:16¼
Tippo Tib, b g, 1880, by Reliance, dam by Mambrino Rattler ... 2:26
Tipseco, b s, 1884, by Louis Napoleon, dam by Garibaldi ... 2:10½
Tipton Boy, b g, 1881, by Gypsy Chief—Whelan Mare, by George S. Patchen ... 2:24¼
Tip Tyler, blk s, 1888, by Wilton—Lady Simmons, by Honest Allen.... 2:22
Tirzah, b m, 1877, by Swige·t—Lady, by White Stockings ... 2·30
Tirzah, ch m, 1888, by Penrose—Dinah, by Little Crow ... 2·26
Title Clear, ch m, 188—, by Great Hopes ... 2:30
Titania, ch m, 1878, by Aberdeen—Bonnie Lassie, by O. J. Wells... 2:27
Tito, b s, 1887, by Egbert—Laura, by Billy Adams ... 2:27
T. J. Potter, gr g, 187—, pedigree not traced ... 2:29¼
Tocsin, ch s, 1879, by Almont—Jenny Martin, by Star Denma·k ... 2:22¾
Toinette, b m, 1884, by Onward—

Sally B., by Lever 2:30
Token, b m, 1888, by Onward—Alarm, by Almont 2:14½
Tola, gr m, 1873, by Shilton—Nelly Grey 2:29¼
Tolu, b s, 1889, by Vatican—Callie C., by Peavine 2:21¾
Tolu Maid, br m, 1871, by Red Bird.. 2:23¼
Tomah, ch g, 1890, by Edgardo, dam by Olympus 2:12¼
Tom Allen, blk g, 1874, by Honest Allen—Lucy Smith, by Brignoli..... 2:22
Tom Arden, b g, 1885, by Russ Denmark 2:16¼
Tom Bailey, b g, 188—, by Sam B., dam by Tom Crowder.............. 2:28¼
Tom Baird, b s, 188—, pedigree not traced 2:28
Tom Barry, b g, 187—, by Warwick Boy, dam by Tattler Jr. 2:26¼
Tom Bayard, b g, 187—, pedigree not traced 2:27½
Tom B. Patchen, br s, 1871, by Churchill Horse, dam by Benson Horse. 2:27¼
Tom Britton, br g, 1865, by Mambrunello (dead) 2:26
Tom Brown, ch g, 1870, by Adam's Bald Chief, dam by Sam Slick...... 2:27½
Tom Cameron, gr g, 1872, by Scott's Hiatoga—Old Pac, by Pacolet 2:23½
Tom Carpenter, b g, 1883, by Thomas Jefferson—Shepperdess, by Jack Shepperd 2:23½
Tom Corwin, b s, 1880, by Smuggler—Lily Shields, by King's Cadmus.. 2:25
Tom Covington, blk s, 1883, by Limber Jim—Old Kate 2:28¼
Tom Dixon, b s, 188—, by Princeps... 2:24¼
Tom Drew, b s, 188—, by Young Dirigo—Wild Bird, by Patchen Boy.... 2:27¼
Tom Edran 2:28½
Tom H., b s, 188—, by Tom Scott.... 2:27¼
Tom Hook, b s, 1889, by Cyclone—Nan Brown, by Col. Hambrick............ 2:27½
Tom H., b g, 188—, by Tom Scott.... 2:27¼
Tom Hull, b g, pedigree not traced . 2:28
Tom Jacobs, b g, 1885, by Clark's Hambletonian 2:21
Tom Judge, b g, 1888, by Melrose—Molly Clark, by Holabird's Ethan Allen 2:25¼
Tom Hamilton, b g, 1885, by Hamilton 2:21½
Tom Hendricks, gr g, 1873, by Tom Hunter 2:30
Tom Hendricks, b g, 1868, by Tom Rolfe—Black Sal, by Copperbottom. 2:25
Tom Keeler, b g, 186—, by Jersey Star—Betsy Baker (dead) 2:25
Tom King, b s, 1883, by Daniel Boone—Dolly Bidwell 2:28
Tom Kirkwood, bl s, 1874, by Green's Bashaw—Nancy Bell, by Gales' Morgan 2:29¼
Tom Knox, ch s, 1883, by Telephone—Topsy, by Currier Horse 2:28¼
Tom Mackey, br g, 1886, by Hotspur Chief—Belle Herman, by Hermes . 2:26
Tom Malloy, bl g, 187—, by Phil Sheridan 2:30
Tom Medium, b s, 188—, by Riley Medium—Queen, by Harris 2:20¼
Tom Medley, b g, 187—, pedigree not traced 2:27¾
Tom Miller, ch s. 1889, by Williams—Pearl K., by Egmont 2:23¼
Tom Moore, b s, 1868, by Jupiter Abdallah—Nelly Moore 2:28
Tom Murray, b g, 1883, by Chester Chief—Murray Mare, by Nanny Horse 2:24¼
Tom Scott, g g, 188—, by Nutwood..2:26
Tommy, b g, 1879, by Aberdeen—Jenny Baker 2:30
Tommy B., b g, 1875, by Caledonian Chief—Kitty, by James' Toronto Chief Jr 2:25
Tommy B., b g, 188—, by Hotspur Jr. 2:24¼
Tommy Dodd, ro g, by Alexander, dam by Mystery 2:24
Tommy G., b g, 1887. by Queen's Phallas—Clara G., by Brilliant Golddust 2:25
Tommy Gates, br g, 1871, by The Moor, dam by Little John 2d....... 2:24
Tommy Lee, b g, 1886, by Rescue, dam by Allison's Red Buck........ 2:25¾
Tommy Norwood, b g, 1873, by Norwood, dam by Gen. Knox 2:26½
Tommy R., b g, 188—, by Tom Jefferson 2:29¼
Tommy Root, gr g, 188—, by Teller—Nelly Elmo, by St. Elmo 2:25¼
Tommy Tosser, b g, 188—, by Busy Boy 2:30
Tommy Wilkes, br s, 1883, by Young Wilkes—Lady Gift 2:22
Tomoka, gr s, 1886, by St Leon—Columbia, by Knickerbocker 2:28¼
Tom Pugh, ch s, 1886, by Red Wilkes—Lottie Temple, by Mambrino Temple 2:30
Tom Rogers, b g, 188—, by Dartmouth 2:28
Tom Rogers, bl s, 1876, by George Wilkes—Nelly (dead) 2:20
Tom Rolfe, b g, 1877, by Tom Rolfe—Carlotta, by Fearnaught Jr 2:22¼
Tom Thorne, ch s, 1886, by Western Boy—Belle Cromwell, by Abdallah Mambrino 2:20½
Tom Tinker, bl g, 1881, by Hamblehawk—Gentle Anna, by Black Dan.. 2:30
Tom Tucker, b g, 1886, by Fieldmont—Flirt, by Forrest Golddust 2:29¾
Tom Walter, ch g, 186—, by Grey Messenger (dead) 2:29
Tom Wonder, br g, 186—, pedigree not traced (dead)........................ 2:27
Tono, ch g, 188—, by Judge Salisbury 2:26½
Tonquin, b s, 1888, by Lord Russell—Tricara, by Annapolis 2:28
Tony, ch s, 1887, by Kenmore—Aristina, by Aristos 2:27
Tony Boy, ch s, 1889. by C. F Clay—Lady Alexander, by France's Alexander 2:26
Tony D., cr g, 188—, by Goodfellow... 2:28
Tony Denton, ch s, 1887, by Sir Denton—Belle C., by Masterlode 2:22
Tony Hill, blk s, 188—, by Boston Wilkes 2:30
Tony Klock, ch s, 1887, by Mambritonian—Lady Klock 2:18¾
Tony Medium, b m, 188—, by Shennan Medium—Jessie B. 2:24¼
Tony Newell, b g, 1874, by Clark Chief Jr.—Collins Mare, by Embry's Lexington 2:19½
Tony V., b s, 1890, by Vatican, dam by Sales Horse 2:27¾
Topaz, bl s, 1888, by Culler's Ham—Motly, by Sam 2:18½
Top Royal, b s, 1888, by Nil Desperandum—Roeburn, by Thorndale 2:24¼
Topsy, b m, 1885, by Jim Swigert—Lady Erlington, by Erlington 2:28

Wilkes—Kate, by Stockdale's Dillard ... 2:21¼

Tuscarora, b s, 1890, by Antonio—Reality, by Princeps ... 2:22½

Twang, b g, 185—, by Handley's Hiatoga, dam by Young Eclipse ... 2:28½

Twang, b s, 1886, by Alcyone—Twinkle, by Knickerbocker ... 2.18½

Twiggs, b g, 1887, by Judge Rysdyk—Jess, by Beckwith Horse ... 2:24¼

Twilight, b m, 1883, by Pocohontas Boy—Champion Belle, by King's Champion ... 2:28¼

Twilight, gr g, 1884, by Arnold—Grey Mag, by Mike McCool ... 2:20½

Twilight, gr m, 186—, by Washington Jackson (dead) ... 2:27

Twinebinder, br g, 1880, by Panic ... 2:29¼

Twinkle, ch m, 1889, by Egmont—May Powell, by Major Powell ... 2:27¼

Twinkle, br m, 1887, by Dictator—Flora Wilkes, by George Wilkes ... 2.25¼

Twist, ro m, 1886, by Jay Bird—Tassell, by Rathlin (dead) ... 2 26

Tybalt, blk s, 1885, by Altamont—Nelly Kahler, by Mike ... 2:27¼

Tycho, b s, 1885, by Jerome Eddy—Clay Thorne, by Hiram ... 2:28¼

Tyler, ro g, 187—, pedigree not traced 2:28½

Tyler Wilkes, br s, 188—, by Wild Wilkes ... 2:29½

Typhoon, br s, 1879, by Narragansett—Ellen Swigert, by Swigert ... 2:28¼

Typhoon, b m, 1886, by Lord Russell—Storm, by Middletown ... 2:28

Tyranus, blk s, 1889, by Young Wilkes—Rosetta, by Pickering (pacing 2:22¼) ... 2:21¼

Tyrant Chief, b s, 1883, by Tyrant—Nelly, by Young Woful ... 2:26¾

Tyringham, b s, 1883, by Alcantara—Volante, by Messenger Duroc ... 2:29½

Tyrolean, gr s, 1884, by Pilot Medium—Mary Courts, by Bay Middleton ... 2:20½

Ulee Wilkes, blk m, 1888, by Guy Wilkes—Sable, by The Moor ... 2:23

Ulva, gr m, 1879, by Wedgewood—Tulip, by Alexander's Abdallah ... 2 27

Umber, br s, 1881, by William Rysdyk—Begum, by Alcalde ... 2:25¼

Umbria, b m, 1886, by Pennant—Mambrino Maud, by Mambrino Paris ... 2:25¼

Una, b m, 1874, by Almont—Mangostine, by imp. Mango ... 2:27¼

Una Wilkes, b m, 1886, by Guy Wilkes—Blanche, by Arthurton ... 2:15

Una Young, b m, 1885, by Gen. Stanton—Jenny, by Grantham Chief ... 2:29½

Uncas, b g, 188—, by Onsight ... 2:22¾

Uncle Dave, sp g, 187—, by Independent ... 2.26½

Uncle Henry, br s, 1889, by Bolton Sprague—Black Rose, by Swigert ... 2 29¾

Uncle Josh, ro s, 1890, by Arsaces—Nydia Sprague, by Governor Sprague 2:20½

Uncle Sam, b s, 1888, by Louis Napoleon—Seldom, by Durango ... 2:22

Uncle Tom, ro g, 1889, by Sphinx—May O., by Dunbarton ... 2:18¼

Union Medium, b s, 1885, by Happy Medium—Camilla, by Strader's Cassius M. Clay Jr. ... 2:18¾

Union Wilkes, gr s, 188—, by Mambrino Wilkes ... 2:20½

Unkamet, ch s, 1890, by Lancelot—Rusina, by Belmont ... 2:22¼

Unknown, ch g, 186—, pedigree not traced (dead) ... 2:23

U. N. O., ch g, 1877, by Carenaught. 2:24½

Unolala, b m, 1871, by Volunteer—Flora, by Harry Clay (dead) ... 2:22¼

Up-and-Up, b g, 187—, pedigree not traced ... 2:28

Upright Wilkes, blk s, 1888, by Honor—Miss Haydon, by Mambrino Foster 2:14¾

Urbana Belle, b m, 1878, by J. H. Welsh—Mary Belle, by Breckinridge 2:20¼

Useful, b g, 188—, by Gambetta ... 2:22¾

Ursula, b m, 1889, by Onward—Maud, by Mambrino Time ... 2:28½

Utell, b s, 1887, by Square Dealer—Romping Girl, by Mambrino Royal 2:24¾

U. Tell, br g, 1886, by Star Ethan ... 2 29½

Utella, blk m, 1888, by Charley B. Wilkes, dam by Miller Horse ... 2:26¼

Utility, b m, 1885, by Electioneer—Consolation, by Dictator ... 2:20¾

Vadel, b m, 1887, by Vasco—Delmonetto, by Delmonico ... 2:29¾

Val, b s, 188—, by Vasco—Lee, by Magic ... 2.18

Valcour, ch s, 1882, by King Rene—Marietta, by Mambrino Hedgeford. 2:28

Valdemeer, b s, 1880, by Harold—Vassar, by Belmont ... 2:28

Valensin, ch s, 1883, by Crown Point—Netty Lambert, by John Nelson .. 2:23

Valentine, br g, 1880, by Kentucky Clay Jr.—Queen ... 2:22

Valentine, gr m, 1883, by Georgia Wilkes ... 2:18½

Valentine Chief, blk s, 188—, by Valentine Swigert—Maggie, by Monroe Chief ... 2.29½

Valentine Sprague, blk s, 1884, by Gilbird's Sprague—Fleda, by Grant's Hambletonian ... 2 29¼

Valletta, br m, 1887, by Dresden—Nelly Wilson, by Onward ... 2:23

Valiant, b s, 1871, by Enchanter—Lorena, by Volunteer ... 2:28¼

Valissa, b m, 1887, by Vasco—Chess, by Magic ... 2.19

Valkyr, b m, 1882, by Volunteer Star—Susie, by Corbeau ... 2·19¾

Valley Boy, b g, 1876, by Aberdeen—Flora, by Plow Boy ... 2:24½

Valley Chief, gr s, 187—, by Phil Sheridan, dam by Ben Bolt ... 2:25

Valley Girl, b m, 1870, by Walkill Chief—Madam Swiveller, by Henry Clay Jr. ... 2.30

Valley Girl, ch m, 1889, by Valdameer—Ella Steele, by Dan Underwood ... 2.29½

Valley Queen, b m, 1891, by Sphinx—Mascot, by Red Wilkes ... 2·28½

Valse, b m, 1889, by Onward—Cachuca, by Almont ... 2:30

Vanadis, ch s, 1886, by Star of the West—Fringa, by Almont Rattler .. 2:26½

Van Buren Wilkes, blk s, 1885, by Young Wilkes—Fanny Essler, by Night Hawk ... 2:21½

Vancor, b g, 188— ... 2:23½

Vandeen, b s, 1889, by Clay Cuyler—Dolly Dean, by Forest Mambrino ... 2:26½

Vanderlynn, b g, 1874, by George M. Patchen Jr.—Lady Scully, by Joseph 2:21

Van Duke, b s, 1880, by Ryse Duke—Indian Maid, by Saturn ... 2 30

Vanessa, b m, 1888, by Aberdeen—Belle Donna, by Peavine ... 2:26

Van Helmont, blk s, 1884, by Harbinger—Lady, by Gen. Knox ... 2.19½

Vanity, b m, 1889, by Valdemeer—Addie Wilkes, by Idol Wilkes ... 2:22

Vanity Fair, b g, 1867, by Albion ... 2:24¼

Van Robin, ch g, 1891, by Vatican ... 2:19¼

Vanquish, blk s, 1889, by Hambletonian Mambrino—Natilla J., by Rockwood 2:19
Van Tassel, b s, 1884, by Crittenden—Princess Alice, by Ashland Chief. 2:28½
Van Tromp, b s, 1884, by Badger Boy—Springfield Maid, by Lakeland Abdallah 2:29
Vashto, b s, 1886, by Ambassador—Jenny, by Robert Fillingham J'.... 2.27½
Vassar, b s, 1889, by Vatican—Nell, by Estill Eric (pacing 2:07)........ 2:21¼
Vatican, b s, 1879, by Belmont—Vara, by Rysdyk's Hambletonian 2:29¼
Vatican, ch s, 1887, by Acolyte—Santa Claus, by Magic 2:18
Veda, b m, 1887, by Electioneer—Isma, by Gen. Benton 2:26¼
Vega, blk s, 1887, by Woodb·ino—Blackstone Belle, by Blackstone.... 2:15¾
Velmar, b s, 1887, by Robert McGregor,—Credulity, by Belmont.... 2:28¾
Velocity, b g 2.26
Velox, b m, 1875, by Knickerbocker, dam by Rysdyk's Hambletonian.... 2:30
Velvet, ch s, 1886, by Tramp—Bracket, by Peacock 2:28
Velvet, blk m, 1888, by Brown Wilkes—Helmet, by Nutwood 2:22¾
Vendetta, blk m, 1886, by Black Cloud—El-Pe-Nice, by Parisian 2:28¼
Vendetta, b s, 1888, by Reveille—Kitty Morgan, by Joe Downing Jr. 2:20½
Venita Wilkes, b m, 188—, by Guy Wilkes — San Mateo Maid, by Speculation 2:13
Venture, b s, 1887, by Jerome Eddy—Maggie Burns, by Green Mountain Chief 2:30
Venture, ch s, 1864, by California Belmont—Miss Mostyn, by American Boy Jr (dead) 2:27¼
Vera, b m, 1886, by Kentucky Volunteer—Lady Graves, by Smuggler. 2:25
Vera, b m, 1886, by George O.—Roxie Bee, by Squire Talmage 2:29½
Vera, b m, 1886, by Hamdallah—Dolly 2d, by Abdallah Bird........ 2:22¼
Vera, br m, 1889, by Stamboul—Garred, by Junius 2:18½
Vera, b m, 1889, by Viking—Marquette, by Bona Fide 2:25¼
Vera, b m, 188—, by Young Harry Clay 2:26¼
Verdi, b s, 1890, by Rumor—Cymbal, by Gen. Knox 2:25½
Verdict, b s, 188—, by Hamlin's Almont Jr. 2.27¾
Veritas, b g, 1884, by Mark Field—Bay Dell, by Advance 2:16½
Verlinda B, gr m, 188—, by Orion, dam by Mambrino Columbus 2:20
Vermont, ch g, 1887, by Beaumont—Verdant, by Billy Green .... 2·29¼
Vernet, b g, 188—, by Red Eagle, dam by Wright's Rattler 2:27¼
Vernette, b m, 1881, by Manchester—Ella Madden, by Rysdyk's Hambletonian .... 2·23¾
Vernmont, ch s, 1886, by Flaxmont—Fancy, by Bill 2:29
Vernon, gr s, 1885, by May Boy—Lucy Vernon, by Speculation 2 26¼
Vernwood, gr s, 1889, by Wilkeswood—Verney, by Haw Patch .... 2:26'
Verona, ro m, 1883, by Picket—Berks County Maid 2:21½
Verona Wilkes, b m, 1886, by Guy Wilkes—Glen Ellen, by Arthurton.. 2:27
Veronica, b m, 1884, by Alcona¹—Fontana, by Almont 2:20
Versailles Girl, b m, 1870, by Stephen A. Douglas, dam by Tippoo 2:25½
Vertex, b g 2:21¼
Vesolia, b m, 1886, by Stamboul—Inez, by The Moor................ 2:29½
Vespasian, b s, 1882, by Hull—Bonnie Bessie, by Backman's Abdallah Star 2:24¼
Vesta, bl m, 1885, by Monaco—Country Girl, by Blazing Star ... 2:27¼
Vesta, ch m, 188—, by Guy Wilkes—Annie G., by Dan Voorhis 2.30
Vestabula, b s, 1890, by Pilot Medium, dam by Olmedo Wilkes........ 2:25
Vesta Medium, gr m, 1886, by Pilot Medium—Vesta, by McFerran 2:29¼
Vic H., br m, 1884, by Reavis' Blackbird—Ellen Swigert, by Swigert 2:12¼
Vichmont, ch g, 188—, by Olympus... 2:30
Vic Hunter, b m, 188—, by Gen. Thomas 2:23¼
Victor, ro g, 1888, by Garnet Wilkes—Darkness, by Reconstruction 2:29¼
Victor, br s, 1871, by Gen. Knox—Kate 2:23
Victor b g, 188— 2:24¾
Victor, b g, 1877, by Rysdyk—Dolly by Phenomenon 2:21½
Victor, br s, 188—, by Echo........... 2:22
Victor, br s, 1870, by Young Darkey—Fanny Norton, by Vermont Morgan. 2:29½
Victor B., br s, 1883, by Alaric—Daisy, by Coon Horse 2:20
Victor Clay, b g, 1879, by Victor Mohawk—Lady Clay, by Clark's Paymaster 2:26¼
Victor Duroc, ch g, 1878, by Victor Mohawk—Annetta, by Messenger Duroc 2:28
Victor E., br g, 188—, by H. W. Beecher 2:28¼
Victor Hambrino, b s, 1885, by Victor Bismarck—Beauty, by Hambrino .. 2:20
Victor Hugo, ch s, 1889, by Seneca Patchen—Carrie P., by Spink 2:23¼
Victoria, ch m, 1878, pedigree not traced 2:30
Victoria McGregor, ch m, 1887, by Robert McGregor — Victoria, by Dictator 2:19¼
Victoria Wilkes, b m, 1885, by Onward—Victoria, by Dictator 2:19½
Victor M., b g, 188—, pedigree not traced .... 2·29¼
Victor Sprague, b s, 1881, by George Sprague—Sylvia, by Swigert 2:29½
Victor Sprague, ch s, 1890, by Sprague—Adelaide, by Tendoy 2:26½
Victor V., ch s, 1889, by Deacon—Pauline, by Darby 2:29¼
Victor Wilkes, b s, 188—, by Victor Bismarck 2:29½
Victor Wilkes, gr g, 188—, by Young Wilkes—Dolly, by Little Giant 2.26¾
Victory, b s, 1881, by Alden Goldsmith—Jannette, by Swigert 2:24¾
Victress, b m, 1888, by Brown—Victoria, by Dictator 2.28¼
Vidalia, br m, 1883, by Abdallah Wilkes—Visette, by Voltaire 2:23¼
Vida, b g, 188—, by Viking, dam by Ben Morrill 2:23½
Vida Wilkes, ch m, 1888, by Guy Wilkes—Vixen, by Nutwood 2:18¼
Vidette, b m, 1882, by Scott's Dave

Wells Fargo, ch g, 1880, by George M. Patchen Jr., dam by Gen. Taylor. . 2:18¾

Wentworth, b g, 1880, by Abdallah Pilot.... 2:29½

Werther, b s, 1886, by Red Wilkes—Belle Brino, by Hambrino.... 2:20½

Wesley Boy, ch g, 188—, by Charley B. 2:26¾

Wesley R., b g, 188—.... 2:26½

Westbrook, blk s, 1887, by Patchen Wilkes—La Belle, by Joe Young. .. 2:23

Westchester Girl, blk m, 187—, by Peter Story.... 2:26¼

West Egbert, b s, 1881, by Egbert—April Fool, by Smith's Norwood. .. 2:29¼

Western, b g, 186—, by Stephen A Douglas (dead).... 2:30

Western, ch g, 187—, by Tramp Dexter—Miss Ray, by Dalley Horse..... 2:25¼

Western Belle, b m, 1876, by Comet—Blackbird, by Simpson's Blackbird (dead).... 2:24½

Western Boy, b s, 1882, by Empire—Jose, by Joe Downing 2:29½

Western Girl, b m, 1859, by Richard's Bellfounder—Fanny, by Wild Harry 2:27

Western New York, b g, 1862, by Nonpareil—Kate, by Blucher (dead). 2.29

Western Pathfinder, b s, 1878, by Buell's Pathfinder—Flora, by Fisk's Mambrino Chief Jr.... 2:28

Western Wilkes, b s, 1886, by Sentinel Wilkes—Lilly, by Surprise..... 2:29¾

Westfall, ch s, 1888, by Pretender—Sport, by Onward.... 2:29¼

Westfall, dn s, 1887, by Adrian Wilkes—Orphia, by Orphan.... 2:29¾

Westfield, ch g, 186—, by Whipple's Hambletonian (dead).... 2:26½

Westland, br s, 1885, by Col. West—Knox Girl, by Gen Knox.... 2:29¾

West Liberty, ch s, 1869, by Wapsie (dead).... 2.28

Westmont, b s, 1877, by Col. West—Fanny, by Mambrino Sherman 2.24

Westover, b g, 1875, by Marshal Ney—Kate Lawrence, by Price's St. Lawrence.... 2:26¼

Westward, gr s, 1886, by Onward—Helen D., by Amber 2:29¼

West Wilkes, blk s, 1886, by Simmons—Nelly West, by Allie West... 2:22¼

West Wilkes, blk s, 188—, by Norman Wilkes.... 2·27

W H., blk s, 1888, by Fred Forest, dam by General Taylor.... 2:24¼

W. H Cassidy, b s, 1884, by Young Jim—Molly, by Rothschild.... 2:29¾

What Ho, gr g, 188—, by A W. Richmond.... 2 25½

Whalebone, b g, 186—, pedigree not traced (dead).... 2·29

Whalebone, b g, 1878, by Walkill—Dolly Hoyt, by Seely's American Star 2 23½

Whalebone, br s, 1892, by Sable Wilkes—Anita by La Grand.... 2:24

W. H. Bailey, b g, 1885, by Vidette Boy Jr, dam by Delmonico (dead) . 2·20¼

Wheatland Onward, ch s, 1887, by Onward—Third Lute, by Antar 2:16¼

Whips, b s, 1880, by Electioneer—Lizzie Whips, by Enquirer (dead) .. 2:27½

Whipsaw, b g, 187—, by Red Wilkes, dam by Corbeau (pacing 2:26¼) ... 2 27¾

Whirlwind, b g, 1876, by Zilcaadi Golddust—Molly Beale, by Cottonpicker .... 2·24

Whirlwind b s, 1888, by Glencoe Wilkes—Katie Morgan, by Robert Allen .... 2·20¾

Whist, b g, 1885, by Motion—Dr. Porter Mare, by Mambrino Patchen ... 2 18¾

White Cloud, gr g, 186—, by Joe Brown 2 25¾

White Flag, b m, 188—, pedigree not traced.... 2.28½

Whitefoot, b s, 1887, by Alcyone—Addie H., by Ashland Chief.... 2 22¾

White Line, gr s, 1869, by Strong Horse (dead).... 2.30

White Oak, ch g, 1875, by George M. Patchen Jr.—Flora, by Black Warrior.... 2:30

White Oak, b g, 1884, by Pasacas, dam by Napoleon Jr .... 2·24¼

Whitesboro Chief, br s, 1878, by Roman Chief, dam by Henderson's Pathfinder 2:28¼

White Socks, ch g, 1880, by Alcantara—Dixie, by Rattler.... 2.20½

White Stockings, b g, 1867, by Blackwell's Hambletonian — Seaserpent Laura, by Seaserpent.... 2:21

White Stockings, b g, 187—, pedigree not traced.... 2 16

Whitewater Chief, br s, 1884, by Allegro—Topsy.... 2:25

White Wings, ch g, 1887, by Montezuma—Flaxy, by Kentucky Clay.... 2.24½

Whizz Wilkes, b'k s, 188—, by Alcyone, dam by Dirego. 2:29¼

W. H. Kerr, b s. 1887, by Ethan Wilkes — Lucy Patchen, by Mambrino Patchen 2:28

W. H. Nichols, br s, 1882, by Blackwood Chief—Miranda, by Mambrino Patchen.... 2:23¼

W. H. P., br g, 1887, by Riddle's Hambletonian—Hettie C., by Draco (dead).... 2:27¼

W H Taylor, ch g, 1857, by Crawford Horse, dam by Witherell Messenger (dead) 2 29¼

Why Not, gr m, 1890, by Hambrino—Zephyr, by Mambrino Patchen..... 2:20¾

Wick, b g, 187—, by Justin Morgan—Moonbeam, by John Dillard.... 2 26½

Wick C., br s, 1885, by Egbert—Jane Carlisle, by Antar.... 2:24¼

Widow Bedott, ro m, 1875, by Bashaw Drury.... 2.29¾

Widow Machree, ch m, 1851, by Seely's American Star — Duryea Mare, by Pintler's Bolivar (dead... 2 29

Wilbur, b g, 1890, by Hurly Burly.. . 2.19½

Wilbur Chief, b s, 1886, by Ottawa Chief—Clay Queen, by Ensign.... 2:21

Wilbur F., blk g, 187—, by Hinsdale Horse—Tate Mare (dead).... 2:24½

Wildair, b g, 1869, by John Morgan—Pocahontas, by Portsmouth.... 2.23

Wild Bee, b m, 1888, by Piedmont—Wildflower, by Electioneer.... 2.20

Wild Bill, br g,.... 2 28½

Wilbooka, b m, 1890, by Wilkes Boy, dam by Allen Brook 2 19¼

Wildbrino, br s, 1885, by Hambrino—Molly, by Wildwood.... 2:19½

Wild Crocus, br m. 1891, by Wildbrino 2 25¾

Wilder Boy, b g, 188—, by Stranger.. 2 29¼

Wildey, br s, 188—, by Waveland Chief—Dolly H., by Royal Revenge . 2 29

Wildflower, b m, 1879, by Electioneer—Mayflower by St. Clair.... 2 21

Wild Idol, blk g, 1885, by Vero—Fly, by Gen Butler .... 2·28¼

Wild Lily, b m, 1872, by Daniel Lambert—Whalebone, by Carter's Colum-

Woodbrino, b s, 1883, by Nutwood—Malaga, by Woodford Mambrino.... 2:25½
Woodburn Boy, ch g, 1880, by Woodburn Pilot, dam by Smith's Morgan. 2:27¼
Woodbury Thorne, b g, 1889, by Harold Thorne—Lodi Maid, by William M. Rysdyk........ 2:25¼
Woodchuck, b g, 186—, by Fisk's Mambrino Chief Jr........ 2:30
Woodford Chief, b s, 1872, by Clark Chief—Virginia, by Billy Townes (dead)........ 2:22¼
Woodford Mambrino, br s, 1863, by Mambrino Chief—Woodbine, by Woodford (dead)........ 2:21½
Woodford Pilot, br s, 1873, by Woodford Mambrino—Bruna, by Pilot Jr.. 2:23¼
Woodford Pilot Jr., b s, 1886, by Woodford Pilot—Kate, by Star Denmark........ 2:27½
Woodlark, b m, 1887, by Woodcraft—Geraldina, by Glenview........ 2:20½
Woodlawn, ch s, 1888, by Pickett—Patchenette, by Edwin Booth...... 2:22½
Woodline, b s, 1888, by Nutwood—Four Lines, by Blackwood......... 2:19
Woodnote, b s, 1888, by Wedgewood—Minuet, by Harold........ 2:28
Woodnut, ch s, 1882, by Nutwood—Addie, by Hasbrouk's Hambletonian Chief........ 2:16½
Woodside Prince, br s, 1890, by Haw Patch—Jennie, by Jupiter.......... 2:24¾
Woodstock, ch s, 1889, by Robert McGregor—Kitty Golden, by Onward... 2:17½
Wood Talmage, b s, 1888, by Squire Talmage—Belle, by Westwood...... 2:30
Woodstock Belle, b m, 1886, by Chicago Volunteer 2:29½
Wood Wilkes, b g, 1886, by Lyle Wilkes—Flora, by Skedaddle........ 2:25
Woodwine, b m, 188—, by Quartermaster........ 2:28½
Woolly Jim, b g, 1877, by Blood Chief—Jenny Martin, by Canada Jack.... 2:29½
Wormwood, b g, 187—, by Nutwood—Nelly Parker, by Skenendoah....... 2:25
W. T. Allen, gr g, 186—, by Pearsall (dead)........ 2:29
W. Van, br g, 1881, by Bellwood—Flora, by Benedict's Pathfinder..... 2:24¼
W. W., blk s, 188—, by Tilton Almont........ 2:29¾
Wyandot, ch s, 1885, by Ambassador—Lilybloom, by Daniel Lambert (dead) 2:19½
Wyandotte, b s, 1885, by Artemas—Fanny, by Baker Boy (dead)........ 2:24¼
Wyatt, blk g, 1888, by Cuyler—Totsey, by Mambrino Transport......... 2:27
Wyoming, b s, 1887, by Egalite—Sally L., by Harry Wilkes............ 2:30
Wzmakh, gr s, 1887, by Wistrel—Sanika, by Zarez.......... 2:27¼
X. L., b s, 1890, by Emperor Wilkes—Molly Sprague, by Gov. Sprague... 2:20¼
X. Y. Z., ch g, 1879, by Bristow—Drucilla, by Prophet............ 2:29½
Yankee H., ch g, 1883, by Jim Schriber—Lilly H........ 2:19¼
Yankee Luck, b g, 1888, by Blackstone Jr.—Pike Mare, by Holabird's Ethan Allen........ 2:23
Yankee Sam, dn g, 1870, pedigree not traced 2:27
Yaqui, ch s, 1890, by Yataghan, dam by Kentucky Prince........ 2:28½
Yarmouth, b s, 1888, by Sandwich—Yuba, by Harold........ 2:25¾
Yazoo, ch s, 1881, by Harold—Yolande, by Belmont........ 2:27½
Yellow Duck, ch m, 1875, by Clark's Mohawk Jr., dam by Iowa Copperbottom 2:20¾
Yellow Jacket, dn g, 1887, by Brown Frank 2:20¼
Yellow Ochre, dn s, 1884, by Wapsie—Topsy, by Pasic 2:28½
Yellow Yam, b s 1889, by Parisian—Lou, by Mambrino 2:30
Yorker, b g, 1882, by Frank Ellis—Anna Hough, by Kentucky Prince.. 2:24¼
York State, b g, 186—, by Gooding's Champion (dead) 2:23¼
Yorktown Belle, b m, 1883, by Young Volunteer—Molly Patchen, by Arab 2:20½
Young Ambassador, b s, 1881, by Ambassador—Nelly, by Royal George.. 2:24¾
Young Bruno, br g, 1864, by Rysdyk's Hambletonian—Kate, by Bellaire (dead) 2:22¾
Young Buchanan, b s, 1868, by Buchanan 2d, dam by Hiram Drew 2:29½
Young Columbus Jr., br s. 1871, by Young Columbus—Dolly, by Morse Horse 2:30
Young Dauntless, b s. 1889, by Dauntless—Calamity, by Billy Whaley .. 2:26½
Young Frank, ch g, 1881, by Royal Fearnaught, dam by Fisk's Mambrino Chief Jr. 2:30
Young Fullerton, ch s, 1875, by Edward Everett—Flora, by Jupiter ... 2:20¾
Young Gypsy Boy, b s, 1885, by Gypsy Boy—Net, by Ripple 2:28½
Young Leland, b s, 1886, by Leland—Young Gypsy, by Mambrino Pilot .. 2:27¼
Young Magna, b g, 1865, by Magna Charta 2:29
Young Morrisey, blk g, 1874, by Morrison—Hepsey Jane, by Foreigner .. 2:28¼
Young Netherland, b s, 1886, by Netherland—Pineo, by Black Prince 2:29
Young Pilot, ch s, 1887, by Black Pilot—Nancy Knox, by Col. Ellsworth 2:22¼
Young Rattler, br g, 186—, by Oregon Pathfinder 2:30
Young Rolfe, b s, 1876, by Tom Rolfe—Judith, by Draco (dead) 2:21¼
Young Royal George, b g, 185—, pedigree not traced (dead) 2:30
Young Sentinel, b s, 186—, by Sentinel—Fanny, by Seely's American Star 2:26
Young Smuggler, b s, 1876, by Smuggler—Parepa Rosa, by Andrew Jackson 2:29¼
Young Stockbridge, b s, 1882, by Stockbridge Chief Jr.—Alice, by Manchester Tuckahoe 2:27
Young Sweepstakes, b s, 1880, by Sweepstakes—Lady Rockafellow, by Harry Clay (dead)........ 2:30
Young Vermonter, br g, 1879, by Walkill Chief 2d,—Black Fawn, by Ring Horse........ 2:30
Young Voltaire, b s, 1884, by Voltaire—Lotta, by Alburn 2:30
Young Watchmaker, blk s, 1885, by Watchmaker—Gypsy, by Constellation 2:30
Young Wildidle, ch g, 188—, by Electioneer, dam by Wildidle 2:25
Young Wilkes, blk s, 1868, by George Wilkes—Jane Brown, by Prince of Wales 2:28¼
Yuba, b m, 1882, by Harold—Yolande,

by Belmont 2.24½
Yuca Solis, blk s, 1889, by Swigert
   Petaluma, by Alhambra 2:20¼
Yucatan, b m, 188—, by Freshman.. 2·30
Yula, b m. 1887, by Rounds' Sprague—
   Hazel Belle, by John Bright ..... 2·27½
Yuletide, ch m, 1885, by Lord Russell
   —Yolande, by Belmont 2 28¼
Yulo, b s, 1891, by George Simmons . 2·30
Yum Yum, b m, 1884, by Ferguson—
   Lady McKenney, by Sweepstakes.. 2 29¼
Za Za, b s, 1888, by Jay Bird—Ida, by
   Little Ben 2.27½
Zahn, gr g, 187—, by Dauntless—Sally
   Hall, by Young America 2 23½
Zebidee, b g, 1891, by William M,
   dam by The Baron 2 29¼
Zebu, b s, 1887. by Regent—Zingera,
   by Almont Rattler .... 2·29½
Zeeland, b s, 188), by Ethan Wilkes
   —Topsy, by Kentucky Prince ... 2 24
Zembla, br m, 1887, by King Almont—
   Minnie Helm, by American Boy 2 15½
Zenas, br s, 188–. by Brown Wilkes,
   dam by Oberlin 2 27½
Zenith, b s. 1890, by Egotist—Nadir,
   by Dictator 2 28¾
Zeno, blk s, 1879, by Stillson—Molly,
   by Green's Bashaw 2.26½
Zenobia, b m, 1880, by Ohio Knicker-
   bocker—Nettie Windsor, by Panic . 2 29¼
Zenobia. b m, 1890, by Prince Regent
   —Eudora, by Hamlin's Almont Jr... 2 22
Zephyr, br m, 1865, by Frank Allen .. 2.30

Zephyr, ch s, 186—, pedigree not
   traced 2 29½
Zerbrino, b s, 1890, by Woodbino—
   Kitty Abbot, by Abbot 2 27¼
Zero, br m, 188—, by Aubrey 2 18½
Zero, ch s, 1891, by Danville Wilkes
   —Lucy, by John Boner 2 29¼
Zig, b g, 1877, by Guide—Lady Staples 2 25
Zigzag, ch s, 1886, by Rumor—Zoe,
   by Gen. Knox 2 30
Zillica, b m, 1891, by Recorder..... 2.20½
Zoda, b m, 1889. by Erelong—Maggie
   B, by Menelaus 2 29¾
Zoe B, b m, 1871, by Blue Bull—Cut-
   away ... . 2·17¼
Zoe Hammond, br m, 1884. by Nor-
   wood Star—Dot, by Daniel S, ... 2 26¼
Zoe K., b m. 1883, by Egmont—Flaxie,
   by Flaxtail 2 30
Zora Zar, br m, 1889, by Alcazar—
   Ledo, by Cohannet (pacing 2.24¼) .. 2·24¾
Zuleka, ch m, 1884, by Daubigne—
   Vidi, by Alhambra 2 29¼
Zuletta, b m 1891 by Onward—Ro-
   mana, by Harold 2 23½
Zulu b m, 1889, by Neno—B'ue Belle,
   by Hammall ... . 2·25
Zulu, br s, 1879, by Harold—Miss
   Duvall, by Duvall's Mambrino ... 2 29½
Zulu, b g 1879, by Capoul—Katie, by
   Como Chief 2 29¼
Zulu Girl, b m, 188—. by Western Boy 2 27¼
Zyco, b s. 1885, by Sherman—Argalia,
   by Rochester 2.26¼

W. J. ANDREWS, Buffalo, N. Y.

The graduate of the Village Farm school who cut the world's
record to 2:04 with Mascot.

T. J. DUNBAR, Milwaukee, Wis.

A clever horseman, skillful reinsman and able driver, who showed
his ability at Lexington in 1894 when he won
with Vera Capel 2:10¼.

THE 2:30 PACERS.

The following are all of the horses that have made records of 2:30 or better to harness to the close of 1894.

Aaron R., b g, 187—, by Morgan Messenger 2:20

Abbie H., ch m, 188—, by Abdallah Jr. 2:26½

Abbott Wilkes, b s, 1889, by Red Wilkes—Minnie Patchen, by Mambrino Patchen 2:12½

Abdallah, ch s, 188—, by Darling's Abdallah 2:26

Abdallah (Grant's), b s, 1886, by Abdallah Bruce—Martha, by Hoosier Jim 2:10½

Abdallah (Stiles'), b s, 1879, by Hamdallah—Leland Mare 2:23

Abdallah Boy, b g, 188—, by Erie Abdallah 2:22¼

Abdallah Girl, b m, 1890, by Abdallah Jr 2:19

Abdallah Wilkes, b s, 1884, by Bourbon Wilkes—Lulie, by Star Dixie 2:14

Abe, ch g, 188—, by Churchill, dam by Blanco 2:23¼

Abe Johnson, g g, 186—, (dead) 2:29

Abe Lincoln, b s, 188—, by Trouble 2:26

Aberdeen, wh g, 187— 2:23¼

Abeto, b m, 1887, by Woolsey—Abbess, by Mohawk Chief 2:21¾

Accident, ch m, 188— 2:26½

Ace of Clubs, ro g, 186— 2:24¼

Ace of Diamonds, b s, 1882, by Honest John—Fly 2:24¼

Ace of Diamonds, b g, 186—, (dead) 2:28¼

Acmon, ch s, 1887, by Nutwood—Iona, by Alcyone (dead) 2:29½

Acrobat, b s, 1886, by Sterling—Madam Buckner 2:18¼

Actor, b g, 1883, by Hamlin's Almont Jr.—Lady Clay, by Clay Trustee 2:22¾

Ada, blk m, 1886, by Legal Tender Jr—Warlusa, by Blue Bull 2:17¼

Ada, b m, 188—, by Gold Boy, dam by Traveler 2:13¼

Addie Belle, gr m, 1882, by Archie—Milly, by Stump the Dealer 2:17¼

Addie C., b m, 1883, by Gloster—Fanny, by Flying Dutchman 2:20

Addie C., b m, 1881, by Ryse Duke—Miss Wilson, by Blue Bull (trotting 2:30) 2:29

Addie H., ch m, 188—, by Pacing Abdallah 2:26½

Addie Stewart, b m, 188—, by Addison Lambert 2:20¼

Addie Wilkes, blk m, 188—, by Madison Wilkes—Molly Clark, by Holabird's Ethan Allen 2:23¼

Adella Wilkes, blk m, 188—, by Tom Rogers Jr. 2:26

Adlina, b m, 1889, by Jersey Wilkes—Lady Mac, by Mambrino King 2:29¾

Admore, b s, 1886, by Advent—Kentucky Girl, by Edward G. (trotting 2:26) 2:24

Adonis, b g, 1885, by Sidney—Venus, by Captain Webster 2:11½

Adonis, g s, 188—, by son of Almont 2:19¼

Afright, b s, 1891 2:27½

Agamemnon, br m, 188—, by Walferl 2:19½

Agate, ch g, 1883, by Opal 2:21

Aggie, br m, 187— 2:26

Aggie Downs, b m, 183—, (dead) 2:29

Agnes M., b m, 188—, by Vandergrift 2:24½

Aileen, b m, 1891, by Gazette—He nia, by Nuncio 2:19¼

Aimee, b m, 1885, by Del Sur, dam by Echo 2:24¼

A. K. Davis, b g, 1884, by Denmark Jr 2:21½

A. K. R., blk s, 188—, by Nuncio 2:22½

Alannah, b m, 1887, by Guy Wilkes—Molly Drew, by Winthrop 2:11½

Albany Boy, ch g, 186— 2:20

Albatross, ch s, 1884, by Floramour—Alice Golddust, by Highland Golddust 2:16¾

Albena, b m, 188—, by Albani 2:26

Albert D., b g, 188—, by Island Chief 2:26¼

Albert Darling, b g, 188—, by Nutpatch, dam by Whirlwind 2:21¼

Albert E., br g, 1889, by Penrose—Ringlett, by Ringwood Jr 2:10¾

Albert H., b s, 1886, by California Nutwood 2:27¾

Albertha, ch m, 188—, by Alroy 2:22½

Albrazia, blk s, 1887, by Absolute—Bessie Wilkes, by Red Wilkes 2:24

Albright, b s, 188—, by George Brick 2:21

Alcedo, b g, 1890, by Alcantara 2:23¼

Alcinta, b m, 188—, by Alcantara—Ballett, by Electioneer 2:16¾

Alcyo, b s, 1887, by Alcyone—Louise, by Sunshine 2:11

Alda, gr m 1887, by Solon—Topsy, by Mark Field 2:14¼

Aldaban, b s, 1888, by Alvan—Nina, by Tennessee Rock 2:21

Aldebaran B., ch s, 1889, by Maximus—Dolly by Magic 2:27¼

Alden G., br s, 1887, by Richard Alden—Belle Swigert, by Swigert 2:19¼

Al Donis, b g, 188—, by Pocahontas Boy 2:28

Alert, br g, 1885, by Hambletonian Downing—Nance, by Young Mohawk 2:22½

Alessandro, gr s, 1886, by George Sprague—Sally Brown, by Dan Brown 2:18

Alexander Boy, b g, 1881, by Adjuster—Ola Gurney, by Gurney 2:18¼

Alexander Dumas, b s, 1887, by Dumas—Jenny Martin, by Canada Jack 2:15¼

Alexis, b s, 1887, by William L.—Sue Stout, by Surplus 2.18

Alfred, b g, 1889, by Bayard Wilkes—Daylight, by Glenarm 2:23¾

Aigetta, rn m, 1891, by Clay 2:24¾

Alhambra, blk s, 1889, by Legal Tender Jr—Little Miss, by Blue Bull 2:14¼

Alice Crittenden, b m, 1887, by Crit-

Aral, g s, 1877, by Chenery's Gray Eagle—Katie, by Hampton 2:29½
Archie C., b g, 187—, by Hinsdale Horse, dam by Stephen A. Douglass 2:30
Architect, b s, 188—, by Bullet 2:23¾
Arch White, gr g, 188—, ... 2:19¾
Arctic, blk s, 1884, by Atlantic—Golden Girl, by Blue Bull 2:21¼
Arcturus, b m, 1891, by Artillery—Orange Girl, by Rysdyk's Hambletonian 2:25
Ardock, br g, 188—, ... 2:24¾
Argosy, b s, 188—, by Atlantic, dam by St. Omer 2:25
Argot Wilkes, b s, 1886, by Tennessee Wilkes—Sally Ward, by Bennett Chapman 2:14¼
Argyle, gr g, 187—, by Baker Horse—Mary Hal, by Tom Hal 2:14¾
Arkalon, ch s, 1890, by Kankakee—Susie Mac, by Lyle Wilkes 2:16
Arlington, b s, 1888, by France's Allie Wilkes—Maggie D., by Dave Hill Jr. 2:23¼
Arnold Boy, ch s, 188—, by Ajax 2:18¾
Arpansa, ch m, 1888, by Pancoast—Arabelle, by Aristos (trotting 2:30) 2:23¼
Arrow, b g, 1883, by A. W. Richmond—Crichton's First, by Crichton 2:13¼
Ashton, b g, 1887, by El Capitan—Grey Nell, by Dan Voorhees 2:17½
Ashton Boy, b s, 188—, by Hunter.. 2:26
Ashby, blk g, 188—, by Wagner Bashaw 2:26¾
Athlo, ch s, 1885, by Dunraven—Sunflower, by Alexander's Abdallah.... 2:25
Atlanta, br g, 1883, by Atlantic—Fanny 2:22½
Atlantic Gem, b s, 188—, by Atlantic 2:28¼
Atlantic Gift, br s, 188—, by Atlantic 2:17½
Atlantic King, blk s, 1887, by Atlantic—Carrie Blackwood, by Blue Bull 2:09¾
Atlas, ch s, 188—, by Alroy—Nelly M., by Joe Hooker 2:28½
Atmont, b s, 188—, by Atwood, dam by Starmont 2:28¼
Attas, b m, 1890, by Wildbrino... ... 2:23¾
Attorney Jr., ch s, 1885, by Attorney—Dolly, by Iowa 2:12
Attraction, b m, 1883, by Onward—Little Fortune, by Scott's Thomas 2:28¼
Attractive, b s, 1885, by Alcantara—Jane Loomer, by Dick Loomer 2:18¼
Augusta, ch m, 188—, ... 2:29¼
Aurelian, b g, 188—, by Riley Medium 2:29¼
Avon, b m, 188—, by Edgewood 2:24½
Axtell, b s, 188—, by Thompson's Golddust 2:16¼
A. W. Thorne, br s, 188—, by Hawthorne—Jenny, by Jim Fisk...... 2:29½
Babette, b m, 1890, by Sir John—Nettie Rose, by Winfield Scott (trotting 2:22¼) 2:14¼
Baby Boy, b g, 188—, by Finality.. 2:20½
Baby Girl, ch m, 188—, by Ringwood 2:26¼
Baby Wilkes, ch m, 1891, by Tommy Wilkes 2:24
Bacillus, ch g, 1887, by Star Hambletonian, dam by Printer Jr 2:23¾
Bacon, b g, 1885, by Ajax—Polka, by Pocahontas Boy.... .... 2:23
Bacon, b s, 1885, by Ajax—Polka, by Pocohontas Boy 2:23
Badge, br g, 188—, by Silas Wright 2:13¼
Bald Chief, b g, 188—, ... 2:26¼
Badger, b s, 186—, by Kerr's Bashaw 2:29

Bald Eagle, ch s, 1886, by Hoosier Tom, dam by Blue John 2:22¼
Bald Hornet, ch s, 187—, by Neaves' Old Bald Hornet 2:21
Ball R., b g, 188—, by Ball Reckless 2:23¼
Balsora Wilkes, ch g, 1881, by Wilkie Collins—Laura Bassett, by Balsora 2:17¼
Bandella, b s, 188—, by Maximus..... 2:24¼
Banner Boy, rn g, 187—, ... 2:29¾
Banner Wilkes, b s, 1889, by Brown Wilkes—Lizzie C., by Star Hambletonian 2:20¼
Barbara Riddle, br m, 1889, by Reno Defiance, dam by McKinney Horse 2:22½
Barb Wire, ch g, 188—, by Naaman.. 2:24¾
Barb Wire, b g, 188—, by Hartford, dam by Empire Bellfounder 2:24¾
Barney, b g, 187—, ... 2:27¾
Barney 2:23
Barney, b g, 188—, by Barney Wilkes 2:08¾
Barney A., ch g, 188—, by Chicago Volunteer—Carlotta, by Fearnaught Jr. 2.27
Barney C., b g, 188—, by Statesman 2:21¼
Barney Crossin, b g, 188—, by Jos. Broils, dam by Gibson's Tom Hal.. 2:29¾
Barney G., b g, 188—, by Capt Williamson, dam by Scott's Hiatogo.. 2:29½
Barney Horn, b g, 1883, by Nephew—Ritchelders, by Messenger Chief 2:23¼
Baron Bel, blk s, 1890, by St. Bel—Batrina, by Baron Wilkes 2:11½
Barondale, br s, 1890, by Baron Wilkes—Nathalie, by Nutwood 2:11¼
Baronial, b s, 1886, by Baron Wilkes—Sunset, by Strathmore (dead).. .. 2:29¼
Barrington Wilkes, br s, 1885, by Wilkes Spirit Jr—Mercer Mare.... 2:25
Bas-Bleu Wilkes, b m, 1885, by Georgia Wilkes—Mag Wood, by Blue Bull 2:18¾
Bashaw Fred, br g, 1881, by Bashaw Bolly—Bessie, by Selim 2:17
Bashford, b s, 1889, by Brown Wilkes—Edna Wilkes, by Ethan Wilkes ... 2:22¼
Bastion, b s, 188—, by Tennessee Wilkes 2:27½
Bawley, b g, 188—, by King Pharoah. 2:15
Bayard Wilkes, b s, 1885, by Alcantara—Barcena, by Bayard 2.13¾
Bay Baron, b s, 1887, by Baron Wilkes—Carrie Wilkes, by George Wilkes 2.24¼
Bay Billy, b g, 188—................ 2:29½
Bay Billy, b g, 187—................ 2:14
Bay Charley, b s, 1880, by Green Mountain Morgan—City Pet, by Copperbottom Horse 2:23¾
Bay Dan, b g, 1883, by Stanley, dam by Blue Bull 2:23½
Bay Diamond, b g, 1880, by Milo..... 2:23½
Bay Fly, b m, 188—, by Booth's Clear Grit 2:23¼
Bay George, b g, 188—............... 2:20¼
Bay Hal, b s, 1886, by Brown Hal—Yellow Mag, by Thompson's Slasher 2:20¼
Bay Henry, b s, 188—, by Brown Henry 2:23
Bay Jim, b g, 187—, ... 2:21¾
Bay Leaf, b m, 1884, by Quilna Chief—Bessie B., by Stillson 2:24¼
Bay Lucy, b m, 186—, ... 2:30
Bay Pilot, b s, 188—, by Red Pilot.... 2:21½
Bay Rob, b g, 18—, (dead) 2:25
Bay Sally, b m, 1866, by Tom Crowder—Jane 2:20
Bay Tom, b s, 1869 (dead) 2:23
Bay Tom, b g, 186—................. 2:26

Baywood b s, 188—, by Woodnut—Graves' Mare, by Echo 2:14¾

Baywood, b s, 188—, by Flying Cloud 2:28

Bay Tom Jr., b s, 1879, by Bay Tom. 2:30

B. B., ro g, 1883, by Hale's Veto Jr.—Fanny Covington, by John 2:12¼

Becker, b g, 1887, by Oohannet—Becca, by St. Elmo 2:24½

Beecher Boy, blk s, 188—, by Beecher 2:27¾

Beechnut, b s, 1885, by Louis Napoleon—Jenny Lewis, by Joe Gavin.... 2:23¼

Bee Line, b s, 1887, by Elevator—Lula Wilkes, by Red Wilkes 2:19¼

Be Jax, ch s, 1888, by Ajax—Goldie, by Miller's Blue Bull 2:14¼

Bell Boy, b g, 1884, by Rochester—Belle Clay, by American Clay...... 2:20½

Belle, ch m, 1891, by Melbourne King—Hattie, by All Right 2:15

Belle Acton, b m, 1891, by Shadeland Onward—Lottie P., by Blue Bull Jr. 2:16¼

Belle B., b m, 188—, by Richard Scobell 2:19¼

Belle Bayard, gr m, 1888, by Bayard, dam by Joe Larkin 2:26¼

Belle Burton, b m, 188—, by Edgar Wilkes—Belle Herr, by Dr. Herr.. . 2:19

Belle Button, br m, 1885, by Alexander Button—Flora, by Dietz's St. Clair. 2:18½

Belle Calley, b m, 1892, by Robert Ryan 2:27½

Belle Chase, br m, 188—, by Robinson D. 2:21¼

Belle D., b m, 188—, by De Long's Ethan Allen, dam by Rollin Burchard Horse 2:24¼

Belden Boy, b s, 1883, by Brownwood—Winona, by Blue Bull 2:29¼

Belle Durland, b m, 1886, by Mike Snyder—Gipsey A., by Frank Pilot. 2:10¼

Belle Girl, ch m, 1882, by Harold—Pena, by Belmont 2:24

Belle Hamill, b m, 188—, by Scott's Hiatoga 2:26¼

Belle J., br m, 1888, by Brook—Snapp 2:12½

Belle M., b m, 188—, by Willoughby. . 2:19¾

Belle Mahone, ro m, 1889, by Sea Foam—Bird 2:10¼

Belle McGee, b m, 188—, by Richard Scobell—Modock 2:24½

Belle Meade, b m, 1892, by Charleston 2:28½

Belle Moody, b m, 188—, by Moody.. 2:29

Belle Morse, gr m, 187—, by Caldwell's Grey Diamond—Jane Oliver, by Gen. Taylor 2:20¼

Belle N., ch m, 188—, by Red Dick.... 2:27¼

Belle Nira, b m, 188—, by Brick Wilkes, dam by Captain Jack...... 2:24¼

Belle Noble, b m, 1891, by Harry Noble 2:16

Belle of Kentucky, b m, 188— 2:27½

Belle Pedro, br m, 188—............... 2:29¼

Belle Potter, b m, 188—, by Chesterwood 2:29¾

Belle R., rn m, 188—................... 2:20¼

Belle Shackett, ch m, 1876, by Abraham—Clover Fed, by De Long's Ethan Allen (trotting 2:27½)........ 2:27¾

Belle Simmons, br m, 1887, by Betterton—Della, by Hero of Thorndale.. 2:17¾

Bellvue Maid, b m, by Jim Fisk..... 2:28

Bellevue Wilkes, ch s, 1887, by Red Wilkes—Lady Tassell, by Shelby Chief (trotting 2:27¾)............. 2:29¼

Belle W., blk m, 188—, by George H. D. 2:26

Belle West, b m, 188—, by Double Stroke 2:24¼

Belle Wilkes, b m, 188—, by Don Wilkes 2:29½

Belmont Boy, ch g, 1879, by Nutwood—Lilly Vernon, by Tom Vernon.... 2:15

Belmont Chief, b s, 188—, by Belmont Star 2:20½

Belmont Chief, b s, 188—, by Detractor 2:30

Belton, b s, 1882, by Belmont—Sally D., by Strathmore 2:17¼

Belva Lockwood, b m, 1880, by Bob Ridley Jr., dam by Shawhan's Hal. 2:17¼

Ben Adhem, b s, 188—, by Ben Franklin—Lady Rogers, by Len Rogers... 2:21¼

Ben Allie, b g, 1891, by Ben Harrison 2:21

Ben B., ch s, 188—, by Clipper 2:13¼

Ben Butler, blk g, 188—, by Nelson's Onward 2:29½

Ben Butler, b g, 1865, by St. Clair—Mary 2:19¾

Benefactor Jr., ch s, 1887, by Benefactor—Midway by Combat 2:18½

Ben F., ch g, 188—, by Quilna Chief.. 2:24½

Ben H., b s, 188—, by Smith's Mambrino (dead).............................. 2:20¼

Ben Hadad, b s, 1890, by Doc Vail—Lady Fergus, by Fergus McGregor.. 2:23¾

Ben Harrison, br g, 1887, by Kingston, dam by Bourbon Chief, Jr 2:18½

Ben Higdon, dn g, 184—, by Clark's (dead) 2:27

Ben Hur, bl g, 188—, by Jim Roberts 2:21¾

Ben Lambert, g, 188—, by Golddust Lambert 2:27¼

Ben Mitchell, gr, 188—.............. 2:22¼

Ben Morgan, br g, 188—, by Clark's Hambletonian 2:17¼

Benny, gr g, 1872, by Fearnaught, Jr.—Martha, by Gilbreath Knox...... 2:18½

Ben's Misfit, blk s, 1892 by Ben Easton, dam by Squire Talmage...... 2:19¼

Benson H., ro g, 1881, by Louis Napoleon 2:17¼

Ben Jack, b s, 188— ,by Butler's Bashaw 2:29

Ben S., b s, 188—, by Ben Morrill.. . 2:29¼

Ben Star, b g, 1876, by Tom Hazzard—Dolly Buxton, by John Richards, Jr., (trotting 2:21¾), (dead)........ 2:19¼

Ben Swigert, b g, 188—, by Vero ... 2:30

Benton Boy, b s, 1886, by Gen. Benton—Gazelle, by Rysdyk's Hambletonian 2:16¾

Benzine, b g, 188—, by Dunbarton, dam by Byerly Abdallah.............. 2:24¼

Bergletta, ch m, 188—, by Antar.... 2:28½

Berkshire Courier, b s, 188—, by Ira Wilkes—Kate Windsor, by Windsor 2:14¼

Bernecia, ch m, 188—, by Commander. 2:30

Bernica, ch m, 188—, by Commander Dolly Smith, by Flying Hiatoga 2:21¼

Bernice, ch m, 188—, by Game Onward 2:23

Berry Davis, b g, 188—,........... 2:22

Bertha W., g m, 188—, by Roderick. 2:25

Bertie W.............................. 2:30

Bessemer, b m, 188—, by Billy Brister 2:24¾

Bessemer, b s, 1884, by Voltaire—Cora, by Concord................. 2:13¼

Bess H., br m, 1885, by May Boy—Belle, by Signal Chief............ 2:21½

Bessie, bl m, 188—,.................. 2:25

Bessie Ann, gr m, 188—, by White Cloud 2:30

Bessie Braddock, ch m, 188—, by Mountain Boy—Maud.............. 2:26¼

Bessie B., b m, 188—, by Gold King—Dolly Smith, by Flying Hiatoga.. 2:21¼

Bessie B., b m, 188—, by Look, dam

by Baird's Hambletonian Prince 2:18¼
Bessie B., rn m, 188—, by Sea Foam 2:22
Bessie C., ... 2:24½
Bessie H., br m, 1888, by Newton's Allie Wilkes—Star Eye 2:22¾
Bessie H., br m, 188—, by Brook 2:19¼
Bessie M., gr m, by White Cloud—Fanny 2:14
Bessie M., br m, 188—, by Little Billy 2:23½
Bessie M., blk m, 1875, by Capt. Gay, Jr.—Buxom 2:16¼
Bessie Moore, b m, 187—, by Tom Moore 2:24¼
Bessie Polk, b m, 188—, by Jim Monroe, Jr 2:25
Bessie R., cr m, 1886, by Blue Bayard—Bessie, by Johnson's Copperbottom 2:21½
Bessie R., b m, 1887, by Redmond Wilkes 2:23¾
Bessie Shedd, b m, 188—, by J R. Shedd 2:23¼
Bessie Wilkes, b m, 1892, by Wilkes U. 2:23¼
Bessie Young, bl m, 188—, by Joe Young 2:24
Be Sure, b s, 1891, by Bessemer—Jessie R., by Smuggler 2:14
Betty Battle, b m, 188—, by Jesse James 2:24¼
Betty M., br m, 188—, by Cresco 2:20
Betty Walker, b m, 187—.... 2:30
Beulah, gr m, 1890, by Du Bois' Superior—Maggie H., by Iron Duke 2:14½
Beulah Boy, br g, 1889, by Robert C.—Lady M., by Billy Almont 2:23¼
Beulah C., ch m, 1891, by Badger's Clay, dam, by Gov. Wilkes (trotting 2:27), (dead) 2:28¼
B. H. D., br s, 188—, by Brown Hal, dam by Tempest, Jr. 2:20½
Bide A Wee, b s, 1887, by Ashland Wilkes—Lucy Glover, by Thalaba 2:25
Big Hopes, ch g, 188—, ... 2:20¼
Big Injun, ch g, 188—, by Brown Hal. 2:20½
Big John, br g, 188—, by Belmont Boy 2:28
Big Mike, br s, 1889, by Studer—Maria, by Burnside 2:19
Big Wonder, b g, 188—, by Ajax—Big Mary, by Blue Bull (dead) 2:25
Billy B., b g, 187—, by Mountain Boy 2:29¼
Billy Boyce, b g, 1861, by Corbeau—McGinnis Mare, by Tom Hale 2:10
Billy Breen, b g, 188—, by Mambrino Motor 2:26¼
Billy Briggs, 188—, by Trojan, Jr. 2:21
Billy Brister, rn g, 188—, ... 2:27
Billy Bunco, rn g, 188—, ... 2:24¼
Billy Bunker, bl g, 1879, by Harry Clay, Jr.—Larue 2:19¼
Billy Burns, ch g, 188—, by Billy Davis 2:24¾
Billy Button, g g, 185—, (dead) 2:20½
Billy C., br g, 186—, ... 2:25¾
Billy C., br g, 188—, by Middletown, Jr 2:26½
Billy C., blk g, 188—, by Rescue 2:27¼
Billy C., b g, 1887, by Billy Davis, dam, by Gloster 2:20
Billy Carr, b g, 188—, by Mambrino Smuggler 2:27
Billy Cleveland, ch g, 188—, by Don—Alice, by Indian Chief, Jr. 2:19½
Billy D., b g, 187—, by Henry Middleton 2:29½
Billy Dorhman, b g, 188—, by Messenger Golddust 2:24¼
Billy E., b g, 188—, by Egbert 2:29¼
Billy E., b g, 188—, by Red Joe 2:22
Billy E., b g, 188—, by Pocohontas Sam 2:29½
Billy F., br g, 187—, ... 2:28¼
Billy F., br g, 1881, by Land Pilot 2:20½
Billy Flemming, b g, 188—, by Copperbottom 2:25½
Billy Frazier, ch g, 188—, by Bourbon Wilkes—Daisy, by Kitchell's Telegraph 2:21¼
Billy G., bl g, 188—, by Tempest Jr. 2:24½
Billy Gault, b g, 1883, by Frank Noble—Olive Logan, by Mambrino Logan. 2:20
Billy Golden, ch s, 1887, by Headlight—Madam Golddust, by Brilliant Golddust 2:21
Billy Hayes, b g, 188—, by Tramp 2:29½
Billy Hopper, ch s, 186—, by Jack Fowler 2:24
Billy J., b g, 188—, by Johnson's Hambletonian 2:29½
Billy J., rn s, 188—, by Gen Hardee—Rosa Lee, by Newsboy 2:26¼
Billy Jay, b s, 1891, by Whalebone 2:17¼
Billy Kedron, b g, 187—, by Glencoe—Annie, by Wiley Thompson 2:29
Billy Larkin, b g, 186—, ... 2:27
Billy M., br g, 1881, by Bob Hunter—Miner Mare 2:19¼
Billy M., b g, 187—, by Clear Grit—Billet Doux, by St Lawrence 2:19¾
Billy Mack, br g, 188—, by Nathan Mills 2:24¼
Billy Mayo, gr g, 185—, ... 2:20
Billy McCracken, blk s, 1885, by Hambletonian Mambrino—Fanny Redding, by Tom Hal 2:24¾
Billy N., ch g, 187— 2:30
Billy Nye, blk g, 188—, ... 2:29
Billy Nye, b g, 188—, ... 2:29¼
Billy P., br s, 1891, by Edge Hill—Irene, by Wilkes' Nutwood 2:29¼
Billy Patchen, b s, 188—, by Henry B. Patchen 2:29¾
Billy Pierce, b s, 1892, by Pelletier 2:22¼
Billy R., b g, 188—, by Paul Jones, Jr.—Collie, by Solomon Hager 2:27¼
Billy Richbald, ch m, 188—, by King Mac 2:20½
Billy Russell, b g, 188—, by Alley Russell 2:19¼
Billy Russell, g g, 188—, by Grey Duke 2:16¼
Big Sam, ch g, 187—, ... 2:29½
Bill White, rn g, 184—, (dead) 2:30
Billy S., b g, 1873, by Corbeau—Pacing Kate, by Redmond's Boston 2:14¼
Billy Sample, b s, 1889, by Egmont—Kate Medium, by Time Medium 2:20
Billy Scott, ch g, 187—, by Billy Green Green—Lady Jones, by Heflin's Hiatoga 2:21¼
Billy Silk, b g, 187—, ... 2:29¼
Billy Steinman, b g, 188—, by Bronx Jr. 2:21½
Billy Sprague, br s, 1878, by Gov. Sprague—Lake Breeze, by Swigert 2:28
Billy Stewart, b g, 188—, by American Boy 2:18¾
Billy T., g g, 188—, ... 2:30
Billy T., b g, 1883, by Don Ozro, dam by Jamestown Horse 2:21¾
Billy T., gr g, 188—, by Aberdeen 2:30
Billy the Kid, ch s, 188—, by Bashaw Uwharie, dam, by Sandusky 2:21
Billy the Kid, ch s, 18—, by Boshaw Bill 2:28
Billy the Twister, ch g, 188—, by Gray Harry 2:18¼
Billy V., b g, 188—, by Ned Warfield 2:28

Billy V., b g, 187—, by Blue Bull . . . 2 25¼

Billy Warren, b g, 188—, by Billy Green 2:29¼

Billy Watters, b s, 1891, by Whalebone, dam, by Vick's Morgan..... 2:18¼

Billy Webb, ch g, 187—,.......... 2:27

Billy Wilkes, b g, 187—,. 2.30

Billy Wilson, b g, 188—, by Embassador 2 26¼

Binnie C., blk, 188—, by Wyandotte Chief . . . . 2·30

Birchwood, b s 1889, by Nutwood—Kate F, by Mambrino Boy 2:15

Birdie, br m, 1882, by Capt Sligart, Jr 2 24¾

Birdie L, ch m, 187—, by Lance, dam, by Smith Horse 2 28¼

Birdie L, g m, 188—, by Ingraham Horse 2:27

Bird Mont, br s, 188—, by Bird—Ada Mont, by Edmont.. .... 2:22¾

Birentha, br m, 1889, by Walsingham 2 25

Black Ambassador, bl s, 1880, by Ambassador—Quaker Girl, by Star Hambletonian 2:25

Black Bassinger, blk s, 1877, by Legal Tender, dam, by Bassinger.... 2·29¼

Black Bird, br g, 188—, by Blackhawk McGregor .... 2·28¾

Black Cat, blk m, 187— 2 29

Black Cloud, blk s, 185—, by Glen . 2 24¾

Black Cloud, blk s, 1888, by Brown Kimble .... 2·23½

Black Crook b g, 188—, by Adjutant 2:26

Black Diamond, gr g, 188—, by Grey Harry 2.16

Black Dick, blk s, 1886, by Black Dick, dam, by Dr Herr 2 11

Black Hawk blk s, 188—, ... 2·25

Black Hal, blk s, 188—, by Morrison's Clipper 2 30

Black Hawk Menelaus, b s, 1881, by Menelaus—Millie, by Black Hawk Chief 2 22¼

Black Nell, blk m, 18—, by Hard Tack 2·28

Black Prince, blk g, 188—, by Jefferson Prince .... 2·29¾

Black Eph, blk g, 187—,.......... 2:29

Black Henry, blk g, 187—,.......... 2 27½

Black Hunter, blk s, 188—, ... 2 29¼

Black Jack, blk g, 186—, ... 2·29½

Black Morgan, blk g, 187—, ... 2 27

B'ack Ne'l, b'k m, 188— by Hard Ta k 2 28

Black Rover, blk s, 188—, by Pretender, dam, by Bourbon Wilkes.. 2 21

Blacksie, blk m, 1886, by Patchen Wilkes—Betsey, by Draco 2:20

Black Shy, blk g, 185—, (dead)....... 2·30

Black Tom, blk g, 188—,............ 2:23¾

Black Vitulis, blk s, 1889, by Vitulis Jr........................... 2 25

Black Weasel, blk g, 187—, by Longfellow 2:27¾

Black Wilkes blk s, 1882. by Ambassador—Bird, by Hiatoga....... 2:24¼

Black York, blk g, 188—, by Tempest, Jr 2.18¼

Blairwood, b s 1889, by Wedgewood—Pink by Chieftain.............. 2:15¼

Blanche, b m, 1881 by Middletown, Jr—Lady Bailey, by Bacon's Ethan Allen Jr............................ 2 20½

Blanche, gr m, 188—, by Round's Sprague 2 24½

Blanche Louise, b m, 1888, by Red Wilkes—Missie, by Westwood 2:10

Blanche M, b m, 188—,...... .... 2·23¼

Binky Morgan, g g, 188—, by Pilot Wilkes 2:26¾

Blizzard, b s, 188—, by Sandy Short—Gipsey McGregor, by Robert McGregor 2 12¾

Blonde, ch g, 1884, by Brunswick Chief—Kit by Kansas Duke 2.14¼

Blonde Wilkes, ch s, 1888, by Guy Wilkes—Blonde, by Arthurton...... 2 22¼

Blue Wing, br m, 1883, by Pluto—Bay Fanny, by Richard's Bellfounder .... 2·27

Blondie, ch s, 1886, by Lemont—Molly, by Frank Chapman (trotting 2.24½) 2:15

Blue Bell, ro m, 188—, by Sea Foam. 2 19¾

Blue Bell, ro m, 1883, by Sea Foam.. 2.17

Blue Bell, br m, 188—, by Christie's Bull 2.29½

Blue Bob, gr g, 188—, by Blue Britton 2 23

Blue Dick, g g, 188—, by George Washington 2 30

Blue Hal, ro s, 1890, by Gibson's Tom Hal, Jr—Tiny, by Blue Ball 2:23

Blue Note, rn g, 1884, by Legal Note—Belle 2.22¼

Blue Ridge, rn s, 188—, by Gold Boy, dam by Pointer's Slasher........ 2.20

Blue Sign b g, 1887, by Ensign—Polly Hopkins.. .... 2 08¼

Bob, blk m, 188—, by Young Abner 2 23¼

Boadicea, ch m, 18—, by Good Luck. 2·28¼

Bob, blk g, 188—,.................. 2.15

Bobby Burns, b s, 1888, by Gen Wilkes—Dixie, by Dictator . 2 19¼

Bob Cotton, b g, 188—, by Little Grant 2 29¼

Bob Ingersoll, blk g, 188—, by Legal Tender Jr.—Bolly, by Capt Walker 2.26¼

Bob Ingersoll, ro g, 188—. by Frank M 2 23¼

Bob Taylor, ro g, 1885, by Gibson's Tom Hal, Jr—Jennie, by Enfield. 2 18½

Bob Volunteer, b g, 1888, by Sunrise Patchen—Beaitrace, by Rysdyke. 2 19¼

Bokara, b s, 1890, by Alcantara—Siren, by Nutwood 2 20

Bob R, b g 188—, by Woodburn Pilot 2 29¼

Bonair, Jr, b s, 188—, by Bonair . 2 26¼

Bonaventure b s, 1886, by Indianapolis—Susan Ann, by Balsora...... 2·18

Boncher, b s, 188—, by William L . . . 2 26

Bonnie B, b s 1887, by Orion—Nelly V, by Bonner..... ..... 2 18¾

Bonnie B, b g, 1887, by Happy Traveler—Merrimac, by Wilder. 2 19¾

Bonnie Bell, blk m, 1887, by Adirondack—Daisy James 2 24½

Bonnie Belle, b m, 1890, by Bonnie Boy—Ardelle, by Rochester. . 2 17¼

Bonnie Belle br m, 188—, by Blackhawk Paragon 2 20

Bonnie Boy, b g, 188—, by Brown Henry—Lady Shellbark, by Corbeau 2·29¼

Bonnie Wilkes Jr., blk m, 1886, by Adrian Wilkes—Princess, by Arabian Golddust 2 24½

Bonnie Wilson, b s, 188—, by Jim Wilson 2.26½

Boodler, br s, 1887, by Madrid—Sahara, by Challenger 2.26

Boone Wilson, gr s, 1887, by Jim Wilson—Nelly Boone, by Daniel Boone (trotting 2 20½) .... 2·13

Bonus, b s, 188—, by Morgan Ethan 2 29½

Bo Peep, b g, by Raven 2 16¼

Boswell Jr., ch s, 1883, by Boswell—

Maude, by Bertrand Black Hawk . 2.19
Bourbon Patchen, ch s, 1889, by Bourbon Wilkes—Carrie Patchen, by Mambrino Patchen 2.09
Bourbon Sneak, b m, 1891, by Bourbon Prince—Sneak, by Sam Hazzard 2:21¼
Bovee K., b s, 1890, by Royalton—Old Queen, by Jack 2:15¾
Boy B., b g, 188—.................. 2.28
Brac, gr m, 188—, by Tom Hal Jr., dam by John Dillard 2.25¼
Bracelet, b g, 1882, by Nephew—Ritchelders, by Messenger Chief ... 2.21
Bradburn, b g, 1886, by Mohican—Nantaska, by Hamlin's Almont Jr... 2:24
Branchwood, b g, 1885, by Woodburn Hambletonian—Belle 2.25
Brandywine, gr g, 188—, by Roscoe Boy 2.20¼
Branolia, b m, 1889, by Brown Wilkes—Julia H., by Monaco... ... 2.22
Brant Arnold, blk g, 188—, by Arnold 2.29¼
Breastplate, b g, 188—, by Rosedale, dam by Monroe Chief 2.20
Brennan, gr s, 1891, by Gambetta Wilkes, dam by Mambrino Startle... 2.16¼
Brent Wells, ch g, 188—, by Bedford.. 2.19¾
Brewery Boy, b g, 187—, ... 2.29
Bridget, b m, 188—, by Emery's Caffrey 2.27½
Bright Hope, blk s, 1887, by Hyperion, dam by Surplus 2.25
Bright Light, b s, 187—, ... 2.29
Bright Pat, b g, 188—, by Red Mark, dam by Pat Malone 2.23¼
Brighton Boy, b g, 1883, by Hambletonian Morgan 2.22¾
Brighton Girl, b m, 188—, by Victor Napoleon 2.21¼
Bright Regent, ch s, 1891, by Prince Regent—Bright Eyes, by Blackwood Chief.......................... 2.26¼
Brightwood, b g, 188—, by Abraham—Pritchard Mare, by Flying Morgan 2.19¼
Brilliantine, dn m, 1887, by Brilliant—Smut, by Prompter 2.17¼
Brinoda, b m, 1889, by Mambrino Davis—Molly, by son of Red Buck. 2.15¼
Brino Tricks, b s, 1888, by Mambrino Wilkes—Sally Tricks, by Patchen Vernon 2.18½
Broadwell, b s, 1890, by Splendor, dam by Young Wilkes 2.21½
Brookfield, b s, 1891, by Redfield, dam by Martin's Tom Brown 2.22
Brookside, gr s, 1891, by Martin's Tom Hal—Lucinda, by Henry Clay. 2.11½
Brooks, ch s, 1889, by Nettle Keenan—Minnie M., by Planeroid 2.15¼
Brother Geers, br g, 1882, by Old Hank 2.29¾
Brown Al, br g, 1889, by Aladdin—Mattie Logan, by Dick Turpin ... 2.24½
Brown Frank, br g, 1885, by Tom Hal Jr.—Nelly 2:16¼
Brown George, br g, 188—.......... 2.21¾
Brown Hal, br s, 1879, by Gibson's Tom Hal—Lizzie, by John Netherland 2:12½
Brown Hal Jr., blk s, 1888, by Brown Hal—Midnight, by Crim's Black Hawk 2.17¼
Brownie, br g, 1887, by Roulette—Blue, by Billy Hazzard 2:22¾
Brown Jim, br g, 188—, by Lace Dealer, dam by Atlantic 2.26¼
Brown Nell, br m, 1883, by Stockholm—Gray Nell, by Hercules. 2.23
Brown Sam, b g, 188—, by Whistle Jacket 2.29¼
Buck Dickerson, ch g, 188—, by Jack Fowler 2.25½
Buckeye Girl, b m, 188—, by Dill Green Horse, dam by Sam Patch.. 2.27
Buck Franklin, b s, 1891, by Ben Franklin—Echo, by Enfield 2.16½
Buckner, b m, 1887, by Earnheart's Brooks—Molly, by son of Stackpole . 2:15½
Buckshot, blk g, 188—, by Levi Aristos.................................. 2.28½
Buckskin, dn s, 187—, ... 2:27
Bud Crooke, b s, 1880, by George Wilkes—Lizzie Brinkner, by Brinkner's Drennon 2:15½
Bud Dille, br s, 188—, by Kinlock.... 2.22½
Budd Doble, b g, 1883, by Indianapolis—Kate, by Stocking Chief......... 2.13½
Budd Doble, b g, 188—, by Clay Abdallah—Dot, by Almore............ 2.19¼
Bud Onward, b g, 1885, by Onward—Maria.............................. 2.21¼
Bud Weiser, br g, 188—............. 2.28
Buffalo Girl, b m, 1873, by Pocahontas Boy—Kit Freeman, by Gray's Tom Hal 2.12½
Bugher, b g, 187—................. 2.30
Bunco Jr., b g, 188—, by Bunco—Delilah................................ 2.12½
Bullmont, gr g, 1887, by Blue Skin—Lady Almont, by Almont Pasha.... 2.16
Burback, b s, 1891, by Red Wilkes ... 2.29¼
Burdette, b s, 1886, by Alcantara—Minnie, by Broken Leg.......... 2.21½
Burkholder, b g, 188—............. 2.26½
Burley F., b g, 188—, by Legal Tender Jr. 2.18½
Buster, rn s, 188—, by Sam Purdy ... 2.27¾
Butcher Boy, ch s, 188—, by Pocahontas Boy........................ 2.26¼
Butler Chief, b s, 1888, by Reveille—Lady, by Kansas Wilkes—........ 2.25
Byrl C., br m, 1890, by Victor Patchen.................................. 2.23¼
Caesar, b g, 1885, by Steinway—Olita, by Nutwood 2.16½
Cairn, b s, 1890, by Anteros—Governess, by Gov. Sprague.......... 2.23¼
Calera, b m, 1890, by McEwen—Cuylera, by Cuyler.................... 2.18½
Callie S., br m, 1889, by Mambrino Logan—Delphine, by Wade Hampton 2.23¼
Calvin C., b g, 188—, by Hambletonian Down 2.28
Calyce, blk m, 1888, by Endymion—Opponent, by Madrid 2.29½
Cama K., gr m, 188—, by Bog Oak—Josie, by Mambrino Bruce (dead)... 2.23¼
Cambridge.......................... 2.25
Cambridge Boy, ch s, 188—, by American Boy 2.18
Cambridge Girl, ch m, 188—, by American Boy 2:11½
Camille, b m, 188—................ 2:28½
Candidate, ch s, 1884, by Pocahontas Boy................................ 2.29¾
Caneland Wilkes, b s, 1887, by Young Jim—Augusta, by Allie West 2.12
Cannon Ball, br s, 1886, by Red Jacket—Jip.............................. 2.19¼
Cantab, ch g, 188—, by Sphinx—Home Maid, by Royal Fearnaught 2.14¾
Can Tell, br m, 188—, by Grove's Blue Bull Jr......................... 2.25
Capital, b s, 188—, by Byron......... 2.26½
Capitola, ch m, 186—, ... 2.25½
Capsheaf, blk s, 188—, by Confederate Chief................................ 2.21¼
Capt. Dan, b g, 187—.............. 2.24½

Capt. Hunter, br s, 188—, by Clear Grit.... 2:19¼
Capt. Jack, b s, 187—, by Old Red Buck 2:24¾
Capt. John, b s, 1887, by Don Wilkes—Molly, by Dillard Dudley.... 2:21¼
Capt. Kinney, b g, 184—, (dead).... 2:24½
Capt. Mack, blk s, 188—, by Cuthbert 2:25¾
Capt. Payne, ch s, 188—, by Black Captain.... 2:20
Capt. Thorne, b s, 1888, by Hawthorne—June Second, by Ben Franklin.... 2:19½
Capt. Turney, b g, 188—, by a son of Dictator.... 2:27¼
Capt. Walker, ch s, 186—.... 2:27½
Capt. Wood, g s, 188—, by Wilkeswood 2:16¼
Carbonate, rn s, 1892, by Superior—Maggie H., by Iron Duke.... 2:09
Careless, b g, 1879, by Spring Hill—Victoria Almont, by Almont.... 2:23¼
Carmel, b s, 188—, by Bourbon Chief Jr.... 2:30
Carrie H., b m, 188—, by Edgewood.. 2:29¼
Carrie L., b m, 188—.... 2:29¼
Carrie M., b m, 1887, by Dispatch—Miss Herrington, by Star Hambletonian.... 2:21¼
Carrie Onward, b m, 1889, by Onward—Carrie B., by Blue Bull.... 2:18¼
Carrie Strathmore, b m, 188—, by Strathmore—Carrie Blackwood, by Blue Bull.... 2:17¼
Carrie T., b m, 188—, by Signal.... 2:20½
Carrie W., b m, 188—, by Royalty.... 2:20
Carro, b g, 1886, by Erie Wilkes—Celia, by Black Henry.... 2:24¾
Cash Boy, b g, 188—, by Wayne Wilkes.... 2:27¼
Cashier, gr s, 188—, by Nelson.... 2:25½
Cashier Jr., b g, 1886, by Cashier—Pattie Dodd.... 2:24¼
Cassie, b m, 1887, by Tennessee Wilkes—Jenny, by Enfield.... 2:12¾
Catherine H., r m, 188—, by Judge Advocate.... 2:27½
Cato, b g, 188—, by Guilford Boy.... 2:23½
Cayuga Maid, b m, 184—, (dead).... 2:28
C. C., blk s, 188—, by Butler.... 2:28
Ceb'on, b s, 1888, by Belvoir—Minnie Russell, by Mambrino Russell.... 2:17¼
Cecelia, b m, 1892, by Iris—Scratch, by Loppy.... 2:23½
Cedar Rapids, b s, 1892, by Mambrino Payne.... 2:24
Cedar Snag, b g, 188—, by Locomotive 2:25¾
Centerville Maid, b m, 185—, (dead).. 2:25½
Chamois, ch s, 1888, by Champlain—Royalty, by Almont.... 2:16¼
Champion, br g, 188—.... 2:30
Champy, br g, 188—.... 2:24½
Chan, b m, 1886, by Chandos—Midnight, by Red Cloud.... 2:17½
Change, b g, 187—.... 2:19½
Chapman, ch g, 1881, by St. Omer.... 2:19½
Chapman, b g, 188—, by Western.... 2:22½
Charland, b s, 188—.... 2:29½
Charles L., ch g, 1885, by Ashley's Ethan Allen, dam by Earthquake... 2:19¼
Charles P.... 2:27¾
Charles S., b g, by Red Joe.... 2:21½
Charley, blk g, 188—.... 2:27
Charley B., ch g, 188—, by Dan Brown 2:18¼
Charley B. Wilkes, br s, 188—, by Charley B.... 2:28
Charley Brown, gr g, 187—.... 2:22
Charley C., b g, 188—, by Brussels... 2:24
Charley C, ch s, 188—, by Piedmont—Bloomfield Maid, by Hambletonian Jr.... 2:18½
Charley D., b g, 188—, by Stride Wilkes.... 2:19¼
Charley D., ch g, 188—, by Dan Rice. 2:20¾
Charley D., ch g, 1882, by John A. Logan—Tabitha, by Black Ben.... 2:24¼
Charley Danforth, ro g, 188—, by Fred Lothair.... 2:23¾
Charles H. Hoyt, b s, 1889, by Newmont—Reel, by Blue Bull (trotting 2:21½).... 2:15¼
Charley E., dn g, 188—, by Old Sambo 2:25
Charley Evans, ro g, 186—, (dead).. 2:21¼
Charley F., b g, 187—, by Cloud Mambrino.... 2:28
Charley Ford, ch g, 1888, by Dexter Prince—Nellie, by Corsica.... 2:12½
Charley Foster, rn g, 187—, by Joe Brister.... 2:29¼
Charley Friel, ch g, 1877, by Allie West—Old Lady, by Capt. Walker.. 2:15¾
Charley H., b g, 187—.... 2:21
Charley G., b g, 188—, by Gen. Stanton 2:29½
Charley Hicks, b g, 188—, by Iowa Mambrino.... 2:28¼
Charley M., ch g, 188—.... 2:22¾
Charley M., gr s, 188—.... 2:20¼
Charley M., blk g, 188—.... 2:28¼
Charley M., ch g, 188—.... 2:25¼
Charley Miller, b g, 1888, by George Steck, dam, by Simm's Edwin Forrest.... 2:21¼
Charley Mozee, b g, 1886, by Woodmont—Lizzie, by Daniel Payne.... 2:20½
Charley P., gr g, 1882, by Gov Sprague—Martha, by Rothschild (trotting 2.25½).... 2:11¼
Charley P., g g, 188—, by Kilbuck Tom.... 2:19¼
Charley P., ch g, 188—.... 2:18½
Charley Pegg, b g, 188—.... 2:27½
Charley R., ch s, 188—, by Pilot Champion.... 2:25¾
Charley Stillson, b g, 1886, by Stillson—Nell, by Bob Ridley.... 2:20¼
Charley Wilkes, b s, 1889, by Redfield—Topsy, by Commander (dead) 2:18
Charm, ch s, 1882, by Leroy—Bessie 2:24½
Charton, ch s, 188—, by Charleston 2:16¾
Chase, b g, 188—, by Billy Green... 2:23¼
Chattie C., b g, 188—, by Hambletonian Chief.... 2:29¼
Chautauqua Prince, gr s, 188—, by Sinbad.... 2:28¾
Cheerful Alcy, ch g, 188—, by Clay Wilkes—May Wilkes, by Young Wilkes.... 2:15¼
Cheerful Charlie, b g, 188—, by Broadway, dam by Gen. Knox.... 2:28¾
Chehalis, blk s 1890, by Altamont—Tecora, by Strader's Cassius M Clay Jr.... 2:24½
Chepita, rn m, 188—, by Hambletonian Messenger.... 2:25¼
Cherokee Prince, ch s, 1887, by Dexter Prince—Brownie, by Capt. Lewis 2:22¼
Cherry, b g, 188—, by Hambletonian Mambrino.... 2:27¼
Chester Boy, gr s, 188—, by Joe Hall 2:30
Chestnut Bird, ch s, 188—, by Chestnut Wilkes.... 2:24½
Chestnut Day, ch g, 187—, by Tam O'Shanter—Meg Merriles, by Mambrino Eclipse.... 2:29¼
Chestnut Hal, ch s, 188—, by Tom Hal 2:27
Chestnut Star, ch s, 1876, by Arnold's Redbuck—Flora Voss, by Sleepy Abe.... 2:22
Chester C., b g, 188—, by Chester A 2:24¼

Brister.... .... 2.29¾

Dallgetty, b g, 188—, by Thorndale... 2 17¾

Damiana, ch g, 187—, by Gladiator. . 2·26¼

Dan, b g, 188—,.................... 2 28

Dan Conkling, b s, 188—, by Roscoe Conkling.... .... 2·18¼

Dan D., b g, 1878, by Diadem—Miss Woods, by Hollingshead's Sambo... 2 15

Dandy, b g, 188—, by Lord Cook (dead) 2.29¼

Dandy, b g, 188—, by Rocky Mountain 2 30

Dandy B., gr g, 188—,............ 2.23¼

Dandy Boy, ch g, 1876, by Blue Bull—Mary Baker, by Pocahontas Boy.... 2 22½

Dandy Boy, blk g, 188—, by Legal Tender Jr...... .... 2.23¼

Dandy Boy, blk s, 188—, ... 2 23¼

Dandy Brown, br g, 188—, by Tom Brown Jr. 2 23½

Dandy Eastmont, b g, 188—, by Allie Clay—Topsy, by Fearless.......... 2.26½

Dandy O., b s, 1888, by Dall Brino—Mayflower 2 11

Dandy R., b s, 188—, ... 2.27¼

Daniel Boone, dn g, 188—, by Hylas Jr...................... 2 20¾

Daniel C., b g, 188—, by Daniel Boone 2 30

Dan Mahoney, ro s, 185—, (dead)..... 2 21½

Daniel S., ch g, 187— 2 26½

Daniel Webster, ch g, 184—, (dead) .. 2 25¾

Dan Miller, ch g, 184—, (dead)........ 2.23

Dan Mitchell, b s, 1886, by Regulator—Dolly Fritts, by Marshal Chief.... 2 22¾

Dan Murphy, br s, 188—, by Young Jim, dam by George Wilkes......... 2 25

Danness, ch g, 188—, by Rockaway... 2 26¼

Dan R., ch s, 1882, by Smuggler—Fanny, by Brahan's Copperbottom..... 2 19½

Dan Rice, b g, 187—, by Signal...... 2.20½

Dan Rice, rn g, 184—, (dead)......... 2.28

Dan Ripley, b s, 188—, by William H. Ripley.... .... 2.24¾

Dan Robinson, ch g, 1890, by Nuthurst, dam by Abdallah Mambrino.. 2 25¼

Dan Tucker, b s, 1885, by George P Tucker—Belle..... .... 2:16¾

Danube, b g, 188—, by Chickamauga—Dart, by Trojan.... .... 2 25½

Dan Voorhees, gr g, 186—, (dead)..... 2 19½

Dan Webster, b g, 187—, . 2 29¼

Daphne, b m, 188—, by Aurora. . . 2 29½

Darklight, b m, 188—, by Twilight.... 2.23½

Darling, b m, 188—, ... 2 30

Dartford, b s, 1886, by Captain Lyons—Jenny Martin, by Star Denmark.. 2.22¼

Dartmouth, blk s, 1885, by Dictator—Almaid, by Almont.... .... 2 28¾

Daughter, b m, 1886, by Reliance.... 2.23½

Dauntless Bess, b m, 1882, by Dock. 2 21¾

Dave, b g, 186—, (dead)............ 2 27

Dave Boy, br s, 1891, by Gilley 2 29½

Dave R., gr g, 188—, by Lucy Horse. 2 29½

Dave R., gr g, 188—, by Leroy Horse. 2 26¼

David Copperfield, blk g, 1884, by Quilna Chief—Jennie Curtis, by Morgan Messenger.... .... 2.16

David S., b g, 188—, by Dr. Herr—Lady Benton, by Stockbridge Chief.. 2 29¼

David Wilkes, blk g, 1878, by Almont Eclipse—Lady Simmons, by George Wilkes . ... 2·22½

Davy B., gr g, 188—, by Davenant.... 2 23

Davy Crockett, blk s, 188—, by Illinois Chief.. .. .. 2.20

Davy Crockett, blk g, 187—, by Legal Tender Jr 2 24¼

Dawson Lake, ch m, 1891, by Nutbreaker...... .... 2·20¼

Day Star, b s, 1886, by Chestnut Star—Belle, by Frampton's Wood....... 2 17

Deacon, b g, 1886, by Ben Bolt—Bessie Lincoln, by Justin Morgan (dead) 2·20

Debrino, b g, 188—, by Detractor..... 2:17½

Deck Wright, ch s, 1887, by Quilna Chief—Kate O., by Blue Bull.... . 2:18¼

Decoy, b s, 1892, by Detective—Pet, by son of Dan Voorhees............ 2.30

Defiance, br g, 186—, by Chieftain (trotting 2.24)......... .... 2.17¾

De Jarnette, b s, 1883, by Indianapolis—Belle, by Litton's Warfield.... 2:17

De Kalb, b g, 188—, by Eisman 2 23½

Delaware Boy, b g, 188—, ... 2 19¼

Delgardo, b s, 1886, by Egbert—Illinois, by Contractor............. 2:28

Delight, b s, 188—, by Good Luck .. 2 29½

Delineator, b s, 1882, by Dictator—Maisie, by Shelby Chief.. .... 2:18

Della S., ch m, 1890, by Thistle.... 2 21

Della Sherman, ch m, 188—, by Ashland Wilkes 2 21½

Dell Wind, b s 188—, by Del Sur—Imogene, by Norwood.............. 2.25

Del Norte, blk s, 1888, by Altamont—Tecora, by Strader's Cassius M. Clay Jr.. .... 2 14½

Delph, b g, 1888, by King Almont—Beck, by Hutchison Chief (trotting 2·27½). 2.24¾

Delta, b s, 1890, by Patalka—Hattie, by Heptagon.... .... 2.21¼

Demand, b g, 188—, by Diplomat..... 2 29

Dempsey, b s, 188—, by Tribute..... 2 16½

Den Ledyard, ch s, 188—, by McCurdy's Hambletonian 2 20

Dennie B., b m, 188—, by Ethan Wilkes 2 24¼

Dennison Wilkes, b s, 188—, by Star Wilkes..... .... 2 26¼

Densmore, br s, 1889, by Bayonne Prince—Lillian C., by Warwick Boy. 2.23¾

De Soto Belle, b m, 188—, by Burns' De Soto.......................... 2 18¾

Despot, ro s, 1878, by Dictator—Spray, by Bay Munson (trotting 2 29).... 2 24½

Detractor, blk s, 1877, by Gossip—Evening Rose, by Black Dutchman. 2 26½

Dexter, b g, 1885, by George—Nichols Mare, by Louis Napoleon.......... 2 24

Dexter, ch g, 187—, by Woodard's Ethan Allen...... .... 2 29

Dexter Power, ch s, 1887, by Major Doke—Molly, by Champion. 2.24¼

Dexter Thorne, b s, 1888, by Dexter Prince—Clyde, by Hawthorne. 2 23

Diablo, ch s, 1889, by Charles Derby—Bertha, by Alcantara.... ... 2 09¼

Dial, rn g, 188—, by Barbarian 2 28¼

Diamond, blk s 188—, by Joe Pond. . 2 22

Dicer, ch s, 188—, by Hoosier Tom . 2 30

Dick, gr g, 188—, by Ira N ... 2 29¼

Dick B., b g, 1885, by Alhamar—Litta, by Bayard.. .... 2·18½

Dick B., b g, 188—, by Stonewall Jackson...... .... 2.21¼

Dick O., b g, 188—, by Glester ... 2:18¾

Dick Fitzgerald, br s, 188—, by Elial G., dam by Hercules..... ..... 2 24¼

Dick H., br s, 1887, by American Boy—Daisy, by Gen. Putnam 2.18

Dick Hal, b s, 188—, by Tom Hal... 2:23¼

Dick Kitchen, b g, 188—, by Wyoming Chief... .... 2 27½

Dick Mason, b g, 188—, by Nutnunter 2 14¼

Dick Pennell, ch g, 188—, by Baywood 2:14½

Dick R., b g, 188—, by William H Vanderbilt. 2 27½

Dick Smith, b g, 1885, by Prince Im-

perial—Maggie, by Charles Douglas. 2:19½
Dick Thorn, b g, 188—............... 2:20¾
Dick Trumpet, b g, 188—.............. 2.17
Dick Vail, blk g, 1888, by Detractor—Night, by Swigert.................... 2:14¼
Dick West, blk g, 188—, by Col. West. 2:29¼
Dick Wills, b g, 188—, by Wilkesonian, dam by Indian Chief (trotting 2:25¼) 2:16½
Dick Wilkes, b g, 188—, by Young Wilkes............................ 2:23½
Dido, b m, 1876, by Scott's Hiatoga—Columbia, by Young Columbus...... 2:23¼
Dinah, b m, 188—, by Flaco.......... 2:25¼
Direct, blk s, 1885, by Director—Echora, by Echo (trotting 2:18¼).... 2:05½
Direction, blk s, 1887, by Director—Lulu Wilkes, by George Wilkes..... 2:10¼
Directrix, blk m, 1890, by Director—Lady Wattles, by Abbottsford...... 2:20½
Directly, blk s, 1892, by Direct—Mabel, by Naubuc................. 2.07¾
Dirego Jim, b g, 188—............... 2:28¼
Dirigo Maid, b m, 188—, by Dirigo... 2:21¼
Divan, blk s, 1889, by Patchen Wilkes—Betsy, by Draco................. 2:15
Dixie, gr m, 187—, ... 2:29¼
Dixie Van, b s, 188—, by Paris....... 2:24¼
Doc, b g, 188—, by William Corbett... 2:27¼
Doc Christie, b s, 1888, by Anteros—Thornette, by Happy Medium...... 2:21
Doc H., br g, 1887, by Clarion Chief.. 2:19½
Doc Snyder, b g, 187—, by Wild Tom. 2:27¼
Doc Sperry, br g, 1889, by Altamont—Kitty Kisbar, by Young Kisbar..... 2:09
Dr. A., ch g, 188—, by Ahue, dam by Hunter's Lexington................ 2:24¼
Dr. Dix, br s, 188—, by Albrino, dam by Daniel Boone.................. 2:30
Dr. Elmo, b g, 188—, by St. Elmo.... 2:22
Dr. G., b g, 188—, by Pacing Abdallah............................. 2:25¼
Dr. H., gr g, 188—, by Hazel Bashaw. 2:22½
Dr. H., b g, 188—, by Tom Hal Jr.... 2:14½
Dr. Haile, b s, 1888, by Guy K—Lady Kahn, by Bushwhacker............. 2:15¼
Dr. J., b g, 1885, by Allie West, dam by Mambrino Forrest.............. 2:13¾
Dr. Keeley, b g, 1891, by Almont King—Nelly, by Whip Horse........ 2:24
Dr. Keely, blk s, 188—, by Mambrino Diamond........................ 2:13¾
Dr. L., gr g, 188—, by Blew's Hiatoga 2:29¼
Dr. M., br g, 1882, by King Mambrino—Jenny D........................ 2:13¼
Dr. Miller, rn g...................... 2:25
Dr. Miller, ch s, 188—, by McCurdy's Hambletonian, dam by Gibson's Tom Hal.......................... 2:21
Dr. M., br g, 188—, by Brown Prince 2:23½
Dr. Mac, b g, 188—, by Elberon...... 2:16
Dr. McClellan, b g, 188—, by Maitland........................... 2:28¼
Dr. Perkins, b s, 188—, by Louis Napoleon............................ 2:26¼
Dr. Snyder, b s, 1888, by Duquesne—Puss Patchen, by Patchen Chief.. 2:17¼
Dr. Swift, ch g, 1885, by Baywood—American Girl, by Young America.. 2:13
Dr. W., br g, 1876, by Robert Fillingham Jr.—Bolly Peters, by Crim's Sam Peters....................... 2:24½
Dr. West, br g, 1878, by Contractor—Sue, by Thorndale................ 2:17½
Dr. Wood, ch s, 188—, by Mambrino Wilkes........................... 2:29¼
Dr. Wood, ch s, 188—, by Chester .. 2:20½
Dodd Peet, gr s, 1886, by Pancoast—Belle Dudley, by Belmont.......... 2:18
Dolce, b m, 188—, by Diplomat—Nelly, by Mark Twain............ 2:20¼
Dolly Brown, br m, 188—, by Dan Brown............................ 2:16½
Dolly Franklin, ch m, 188—, by Gen. Franklin......................... 2:23¼
Dolly M., br m, 188—, ... 2:27½
Dolly Quinn, b m, 188—, by Landmark.............................. 2:29½
Dolly Spanker, b m, 184— (dead) . 2:27
Dolly Spanker, blk m, 1891, by Jim Wilkes—Lucy Douglass, by True Boy............................... 2:11½
Dolly T., ch m, 188—, ... 2:15¾
Dolly W., b m, 1888, by Reno Defiance—Molly W.................. 2:24¼
Domino, rn m, 188—, by Masker—Gipsey, by Gibson's Tom Hal 2:19½
Domino, g s, 188—, by Masker—Stella, by Sweepstakes 2.19¼
Donald, b g, 188—, by Embassador .. 2:30
Donald H., b g, 188—, by Darwin, dam by Golddust 2:18¼
Don Angus, b s, 1880, by Hughey Angus—Pauline, by Swigert 2.18½
Don C., b g, 188—, by Don Carlos, dam by Gen. Lee 2:23½
Don Cameron, gr g, 188—, ... 2:24¼
Don Carlos, b g, 187—, ... 2:29½
Don Donaldo, b g, 1887, by Hambletonian Chief—Ambea, by Skinkle Hambletonian...................... 2:24½
Donne, ch s, 1891, by Don Pizarro—Hallie B., by Hambrino 2:22
Don Lorenzo, b s, 1889, by Gambetta Wilkes—Lady Yeiser, by Garrard Chief 2:17¾
Don Payne, br s, 1886, by John F. Payne—Donna, by Orange Duroc.. 2:18
Don Pedre, br g, 1882, by Kirkwood Jr., dam by Autocrat 2:25
Don Pizarro, b s, 1886, by Gambetta Wilkes—Lady Yeiser, by Garrard Chief................................ 2:14¾
Don Q., ch g, 188—, by Prince Albert................................ 2:26
Don Richards, b s, 1887, by Belmont—Lulu, by Harold 2.21½
Don T., ... 2:25
Don W., ch g, 188—, ... 2:27½
Door Knob, b g, 188—, by Grantham Chief 2:21
Dora D., gr m 2:24¼
Dora Holmes, b m, 188—, by Miltonian—Kit, by Awaga Chief 2:29½
Dora Martin, b m, 188—, by Petoskey Charmer, by Contractor 2:19¼
Dorcas, b m, 188—, by Deceive 2:25½
Doris, b m, 188—, by Don Wilkes... 2:20
Douglass, b g, 188—, by Ingomar.... 2:27½
Drover, b g, 183—, (dead) 2:25
Dupignac, b s, 1889, by Meander—Mab, by Harry Vane 2:22¼
Doty, b g, 1885, by Tommy Wilkes, dam by Doty's Lexington 2:11½
Doubtful, b g, 188—, by Yellow Jacket 2:25¼
Drelincourt, b s, 1888, by Hambrino—Mabel, by Middletown 2:17¼
Duchess County Belle, rn m, 1890, by Favorite Wilkes—Ulster Belle, by Holabird's Ethan Allen 2:28¾
Dud Davis, b s, 188—, by Dumas 2:29¾
Dudley, b s, 188—, by Anteros—Lily Langtry, by Nephew 2:14¾
Dude, br g, 1887, by Jay Gould—Mary, by George M. Patchen (trotting 2:27½) 2:28
Du-ex, b s, 1889, by Duexmillion—

Rosa Da·tle, by Middleton 2.24¼
Fausta, b m, 1890, by Sidney—Faustina, by Crown Point 2:22¾
Fay, blk m, 188— .... ·· 2 28¼
Fearless, ch g, 188— 2:30
Fedalma, gr m, 1884, by Caliph-Nelly 2:20
Fedalma, ch m, 1880, by Greystone—Amorita, by Hambrino 2:22¼
Fedora, br m, 1885, by Tom Brown Jr., dam by Young Nigger Dick..... 2:15
Felipe, ch s, 1887, by Egbert—Rosa Monroe, by Jim Monroe 2 25
Felix, ro g, 1874, by Dictator—Lady Farlow, by Gray's Tom Hal........ 2·24¼
Female Pirate, blk m, 1884, by Archer's Almont—Polly Hopkins, by Prince Imperial 2:17½
Fenmore W., b g, 188—, by Don Ozro 2:24½
Ferd Keyt, b s, 188—, by Bismarck... 2.18¼
Fergustine, b s, 1886, by Fergus McGregor—Lady De Moss............ 2·20¾
Fern Cliff, gr m, 188—, by Elgin Boy 2:24
Ferndale, blk m, 1890, by Simmocolon—Fern Leaf, by Flaxtail...... 2 16½
Feura, br m, 1891, by Allerton ...... 2·28
Fidol, b s, 1887, by Backman's Idol—Molly Jackson, by Stonewall Jackson ....·...... 2:10
Fieldmont, blk s, 1887, by Young Alarm, dam by Saturn 2:19
Fife, br m, 188—, by Slander 2:17½
Findley, blk g, 188—, by Corbin Bashaw 2:20
Finnigan, gr g, 188—, by Joe Hooker. 2:20
Fisherman, b g, 186—, pedigree not traced (dead) 2:21
Flash, b g, 188—, ... 2:27
Flash, b s, 1889, by Rumor—Flageolet, by Gen. Knox 2:16
Flavilo, b s, 188—, ... 2·25
Flavorita, b m, 188—, by Elevator.. 2 24¾
Flax Hal, b m, 188—, by Duplex... 2:23½
Fleetfoot, ch m, 1886, by Booth's Clear Grit 2.12
Fleetfoot, br m, 186—, (dead) 2 25
Fleety H., ch m, 188—, by Bay Tom Jr. 2:25½
Flitterfoot, ch s, 186—, (dead) ... 2.24½
Flora, b m, 186—, by Chieftain (dead) 2:30
Flora A., gr m, 188—, by J. W. 2:23½
Flora B., b m, 188—, by Brussels..... 2.26¾
Flora B., b m, 188—, by Ayre's Mambrino Wilkes 2:22½
Flora Belle, blk m, 1876, by White Cloud 2:13¾
Flora Belle, b m, 188—, by Dick Taylor 2.22½
Floral Boy, b s, 1889, by American Boy—Fanny T., by Telegraph Jr... 2:17¼
Flora C., rn m., 1890, by Kirby's Cadmus Hambletonian 2:25
Flora C., b m, 188—, by Jumbo.... 2:26
Flora Hill, b m, 188—, by Capt. Walker 2:24¼
Flora Little, br m, 1883, by Gen. Lee—Dolly St. Lawrence, by Charter Oak 2:23
Flora M., b m, 188—, ... 2:30
Flora Mask, blk m, 1882, by John Cole 2.27¼
Flora Silver, ch m, 1889, by Pat Silver—Topsy Knox 2.25
Flora Temple, b m, 1880, by Longstrider—Lady 2:18½
Flora W., gr m. 1882, by Tom Wonder Jr.—Jennie, by Tom Wonder Jr. 2.24¾

Flora Wilkes, b m, 1875, by George Wilkes—Gray Fanny, by Conscript 2:19½
Florence, ch m, 188—, ... 2:25½
Florence G, br m, 188—, by Clear Gilt—Nelly .... 2·18
Florence J., gr m, 1885, by Gray Harry 2 24½
Florette, blk m, 1890, by Adrian Wilkes—Flora, by Sir Alfred.... 2.24½
Floss, blk m, 188—, by George M. Patchen Jr. 2:28¼
Flossy, rn m, 188—, by Smuggler... 2:25¾
Flossy L, blk m, 1885, by Regalla—Belle, by Danville Boy 2.23
Flossy Reed, b m, 188—, by Mambrino Abdallah—Bird, by Ansel 2:26¼
Flowing Tide, ch m, 1888, by Albert W.—Uarda, by Echo 2.14¾
Flying Hiatoga Jr., b s, 188—, by Flying Hiatoga, dam by Rodney 2.23¼
Flying Jib, b g, 1884, by Algona—Middletown Mare, by Middletown 2:04
Flying Morgan, ch g, 188—, by Star Ethan 2:28¼
Flying Prince, b g, 188—, by Prince Pulaski Jr. 2:24½
F. M. B. A., rn g, 188—, by Hazel Heel 2:22
Foggy, b g, 1884, by Alcantara—Thalimer Mare, by Hamlet (trotting 2:27½) 2:13¼
Forest Wilkes, b s, 1885, by Bourbon Wilkes—Florence C., by Forest Clay 2:15
Fortuna, b m, 1884, by Jay Gould—Pandora, by Clark Chief 2:19¾
Fortune, b g, 188—, by Acuff 2:29¾
Fox, b g, 188—, by Reavis' Blackbird 2:21¼
Foxglove, ch m, 1890, by Nutwood—Four Lines, by Blackwood 2:24½
Foxhound, b s, 1890, by Alfred G., dam by Hinder Wilkes 2:26¼
Frank, ch g, 188—, by Capt. Webster 2:20
Frank, blk g, 1881, by Dr. Herr—Topsy, by Idler 2.21¾
Frank A., gr g, 188—, by Rex Hiatoga 2.22
Frank Agan, b g, 1890, by Mikagan—Flora 2:10¼
Frank B., b g, 1887, by Clark's Hambletonian—Bird B., by Stockbridge Chief Jr. .... 2·18
Frank Bogash, b s, 1892, by Atlantic King, dam by Almont Patchen ... 2:26¾
Frank Burgess, b s, 1887, by Peacemaker—Clothesline, by Melrose ... 2:20½
Frank Champ, blk g, 187—, by Allie West—Molly Whitefoot, by Little Priam 2:16¼
Frank Dortch, gr g, 1884, by Locomotive—Molly Lumsden, by Gibson's John Dillard Jr 2.15¾
Frank E, b g, 1884, by Messenger Chief—Lucy Pope, by Telegraph .. 2:19¼
Frank F., b g, 188—, ... 2:19¼
Frank F., b g, 188—, by Red Buck.. 2:30
Frank F, b g, 188—, by Lexington Chief Jr. 2:21¼
Frank Finch, b g 188—, by Windsor, dam by Empire 2:21¼
Frank G., b g, 188—, ... 2:30
Frank H, b g, 188—, by Black Prince 2:26
Frank H., ch s, 1877, by Squire Talmage—Lucy Farris, by Tom Crowder 2:22½
Frank Hanson, g s, 188—, by Roger Hanson 2 23¼

Frankie C., br g, 188—, by Morgan . 2:20
Frankie D., b m, 188—, by Smith's Mambrino Chief Jr. 2:24¼
Frankie Folsom, b m, 188—, by Updegraff 2:28¼
Frank J., b g, 188— by Tom Allen. 2.19½
Frank Logan, b s, 1885, by Sprague—Belle Shandon, by Rothschild ... 2:25
Frank M., rn s, 188—, by Charlie Brister 2:27½
Frank Nevins, b g, 188—, by Hoosier Dick 2.30
Frank Oxman, blk g, 188—, by Scrugg's Eland 2.17
Frank P., b s, 1885, by Walkill Jr.. 2:17¾
Frank Pierce, ch g, 184—, (dead)... 2:23¼
Frank R., blk g, 188—, by Indianapolis 2.28
Frank Russell, b s, 1887, by Alley Russell—Eyerie, by Winchip 2:25
Frank S., ch g, 188—, by Silvertail. 2:22½
Frank Smith, ch s, 188—, by Hiatoga Chief .... 2·23¼
Frank T.,.................................. 2:29¼
Frank Taylor, b g, 188—, by Mohican 2:23¾
Frank W., b g, 188—, by Denver Wilkes 2.20¾
Frank W., dn g, 1877, by Bishop Berkley 2:21¼
Frank W., br g, 187—,.............. 2:24¼
Frank Wilson, gr s, 188—, by Jim Wilson 2:22½
Frank Wood, blk s, 188—, by Wedgewood—Lady Allen, by Frank Allen. 2:25½
Fraro, b s, 1885, by Jerome Eddy—Hiatoga Maid, by Scott's Hiatoga 2·28½
Fred, br g, 188—,.................... 2:26¼
Fred, b g, 1879, by Hambletonian Horse—Jenny, by Country Boy... 2:27
Fred Ackerman, b g, 187—, by Washington, dam by Signal 2:23
Fred Ager, ch s 1886, by Greenback—Tad, by Melnott 2:24½
Fred Arthur, b s, 1884, by Belmont—Gipsy, by Blue Bull 2:12¼
Fred Douglass, b s, 188—, by Phil.. 2:17¼
Frederick, gr g, 187—,............ 2·22¼
Fred Gibbs, b g, 188—, ... 2:26¾
Fred H., b g, by Stanway's Crowder 2:17¼
Fred Holcomb, b g, 1883, by Stockholm—Lady Patchen, by Bush's Patchen 2:23
Fred Hooper, rn g, 188—, by Monarch Jr 2:21¼
Fred Jams, b g, 187—, by Champion . 2:30
Fred Johnson, gr g, 184—, (dead) 2·27½
Fred K., blk g, 1888, by Shadeland Onward—Signet, by Satenite ... 2:09¾
Fred M., blk g, 188—, by Daniel Boone 2:26¼
Fred Mason, b g, 188—, by Bob Mason 2.13½
Fred Mills, rn g, 1879, by Nathan Mills—Babe, by Stonewall Jackson 2:21¾
Fred Ross, b g 187—,.............. 2.22
Fred S., b g, 1881 by Lexington Chief—Flora, by Gardner's Red Buck.... 2:16
Fred Smuggler, b g, 188—, by Gladiator—Merry 2:22
Fred V., ch g, 1879, by Clay Pilot—Miss Nancy 2:22½
Fred W., ch g, 188—, by Bay Chief . 2:17½
Fred Wilson, gr g, 188—, by Dan Wilson 2:21½
Fred Wormley, b g, 186— (dead) 2.29
Free Coinage, gr s, 1890, by Steinway—Nelly E., by Elmo 2:11¾
Free Trade, b g, 188—, by McMullen's Mohawk 2:25½
Freeland, b s 1887, by Bald Hornet—Cal Stebbins, by Rambler 2:19¾
Frenchy, br m, 1885, by Baron Wilkes—Weiss 2:22¼
Frenchy, ch m, 188—, by Bay Ethan 2:28¼
Frenchy, b g, 188—, by Royal George 2:20¾
Fresno Prince, blk s, 1889, by Bayonne Prince—Lizzie, by Blackwood .. 2:17¾
Friendly Dan, rn g, 188— 2:25
Fritz gr g, 187— 2:18
Fritz, ch g, 187— 2.30
Frolique, ch m, 1884, by Egbert—Rena Burdett, by Alexander's Norman 2:24½
Fuller, b g, 1876, by Clear Grit—Dolly, by Niagara Champion...... 2.13¾
Fullerton D., blk s, 1878, by Regalia—Kate F., by Bourbon Chief .... 2·19¾
Gaiters, b g, 188—, by Steele's Walkill 2:23¼
Galileo Rex br s, 1888, by Billy Sayre—Dewey Eve, by George Wilkes... 2:12¼
Gallietta, blk m, 1889, by Gambetta Wilkes—Nectar, by Nutwood 2:16¼
Gambier, blk s, 1887, by Gambetta Wilkes—Lady Palm, by Thomas Jefferson 2.18
Gambolier, b s, 1887, by Gambetta Wilkes—Attie Belle, by Messenger Chief 2:22½
Gambrel, b s, 1887, by Gambetta Wilkes—Bellfield, by Enfield 2:10½
Gammon, blk s, 188—, by Gambetta Wilkes—Fib, by Enfield 2:18
Gamrose, b s, 1890, by Gambetta Wilkes—Red Rose, by Red Wilkes 2:19¾
Ganymede, ch g, 188—, by Ajax. .. 2:25
Garrett, b s, 188—, by Maryland Volunteer 2:26½
Gaslight, br g, 1885, by Ajax—Fanny, by Baker Boy 2:23
Gasper, b s, 188—, by Egbert—Rose Monroe, by Jim Monroe (dead) 2:30
Gawain, gr s, 188—, by Gambetta Wilkes—Eye See, by Nutwood ... 2:18¼
Gay Widow, b m, 188—, by son of Denver Wilkes .... 2·28
Gazette, b s, 1887, by Onward—Siren, by Dictator (trotting 2:23¾) 2.09¾
G. D., gr m, 1890, by Frank Almont—Nettie 2:21
Gem, b m, 1875, by Tom Rolfe—Lady Gem, by Sam Hazzard 2:13¾
Gene Ayer, b g, 188—, by Rhomer.. 2·28¼
Gen Blackford, b s, 1885, by Gen. Wilkes—Molly Blackford, by Mambrino Boy 2:24¼
Gen Ewell, rn g, 188—, by Gold Boy 2:23¾
Gen Garfield ch s, 188—, by Centennial 2:24½
Gen Garfield, ch g, 188—, ... 2:24¼
Gen Stak, b g, 188—, ... 2·28½
Gen Stoughton, ch g, 187—, ... 2:29½
Gen Turner, b s, 1881, by Harold—Claytonia, by American Clay (trotting 2:26¼) 2:25¾
Genevieve, b m, 188—, by Startle.. 2:23½
Genius, b s, 188—, by Inventor.... 2·29½
George, b g, 188— 2:28
George A., gr g, 188—, by Rex Hiatoga 2:27
George B., b g, 188—, by American Boy 2.26¼
George Campbell, br s, 1890, by Reno Defiance—Possum Pie, by Octoroon 2:17
George Cloud, blk g, 1890, by Black Cloud—Dolly, by Don Roderick 2:19¼
George G., gr g, 188—, by Roscoe Jr 2:20¼
George G., dn g, 187—, by Fletcher's Duke of Kent .... 2·17

MATT LAIRD, Mansfield, Ohio.
The driver of Rubinstein 2:08.

WILLIS LAIRD, Mansfield, Ohio.
The driver of Magnolia 2:09¼.

Flying Dutchman—Lightning, by
George Gordon, ch s, 187—, by Gen.
Hardee, dam by Clark's Traveler... 2:27½
George Gould, b s, 1885, by Jay
Gould—Sophia, by George Wilkes. 2:25
George Hayes, ch s, 188—, by Pre-
tender 2:23¾
George Jones, b g, 188-, by Quick-
silver 2:24½
George K., b s, 1888, by Goldbeater.. 2:18¼
George M., b g, 188—, ... 2:24¾
George Mack, b g, 1888, by Harold
C., dam by Jim Brister 2:19¼
George N., gr g, 188—, by Dorsey's
Nephew 2:22½
George Russell, br g, 188—, by Alley
Russell 2:23½
George S., br s, 1887, by Hamble-
tonian George—Mina, by Lothair.. 2:19¼
George Sherman, b s, 1887, by Sher-
man—Clara B., by Chandler J
Wells 2:19¼
George St. Clair, b s, 1888, by Better-
ton—Ill Wind, by Young Jim (trot-
ting 2:15½) 2:22½
George Swift, b g, 1888, by Louis Na-
poleon 2:30
George Steese, ch s, 188—, by Rex
Hiatoga 2:28½
Georgetown, b g, 1877, by Blue Bull—
Sister, by Invincible 2:16½
George W., gr g, 188—, by Honest
Dick 2:22½
George Wapple, ch s, 1882, by Briga-
dier, dam by Copperhead 2:25
Georgie C., br m, 188—, ... 2:26
Georgie H., ch m, 188—, by William
Penn 2:29
Georgie M., ch m, 188—, by Ashland
Clay 2:16½
Georgie S., ch m, 188—, by Adjutant 2:16½
Georgie Wilkes, blk m, 188—, by Am-
bassador 2:29¼
Geraldine, b m, 1888, by Mt. Vernon
—Edith C., by Gen. McClellan 2:16¾
Gertie, gr m, 188—, by King William 2:26¾
Gertie B., b m, 1884, by Clinton—
Dolly Wilkes, by George Wilkes Jr. 2:15¼
Gertie J., b m, 1886, by Wonder—
Belle B., by Bayard 2:24¾
Gertie K., b m, 188-, by Harry Hon-
tas 2:25¾
Gertrude G., ch m, 1891, by Redwood
—Dolly, by Meek's St. Lawrence.. 2:22
Getty Grant, ch m, 1887, by Motion—
Dixie, by Vermont Boy 2:22
G. H. K., ch g, 188—, by Aristos 2:21
Gideon, br g, 187—, ... 2:26½
Gideon, b s, 188—, by Mountain Boy.. 2:28
Gil Curry, gr g, 1887, by Almont
Boy—Grey Jenny 2:11½
Giles Noyes, b g, 1891, by Charles
Caffrey—Vida 2:24¼
Gilman, ch s, 1891, by France's Allie
Wilkes—Daisy, by Atlantic 2:21¼
Gypsy, b g, 187—, by Scott's Hiatoga 2:28½
Gypsy B., b m, 188—, by H. Z Leon-
ard 2:30
Gypsy Boy, b s, 188—, by Hiatoga
Chief—Gypsy Kate 2:21¼
Gipsey Girl, blk m, 1888, by Pilot Al-
mont—Fanny 2:15
Gipsey Golddust, ro m, 188—, by
'Rounds' Sprague 2:24¾
Gipsey M., br m, 1887, by Baffle-
Kit, by Black Prince............ 2:25
Gipsey M., br m, 188—, by McBeth.. 2:13½
Gipsey P., ch s, 188—, ... 2:29

Gipsey Queen, blk m, 186—, (dead).. 2:24
Gipsey Roan, ro m, 186—, (dead) 2.25
Gladstone, blk g, 1886, by Harry
Hoyer 2.19½
Gladys, gr m, 188—, by Alonso Hay-
ward 2:20½
Glen, b g, 188—, by Sir Knight 2:26¼
Glen Athol, b s, 1888, by Gambetta
Wilkes—Hallie B., by Hambrino.... 2:29¼
Glendale, b s, 188—, by Glenarm.... 2:26¼
Glendennis, b s, 1886, by Hamlin's
Almont Jr.—Black Golddust, by
Hamlin Patchen (dead) 2:17¼
Glenora, b g, 186—, by Gen. Brock .. 2:22¼
Glenwood, b s, 1888, by Nutwood—
Jemima, by Scotland Boy, (trotting
2:29½) 2:13¼
Glide, b m, 1885, by Gibson's Tom
Hal—Hettie, by Dudley's Snow
Heels .... 2·19¼
Glidemont, ch m, 1890, by Pacing
Almont—Knatt Mare, by Gladstone 2:21½
Glidess, b m, 188—, by Goodluck ... 2:26¼
Gloster, gr g, 188—, by Sleepy Rock.. 2:23¼
Goethe, blk s, 1887, by Gambetta
Wilkes—Hallie B., by Hambrino... 2:19½
Gold Bar, g g, 188—, by Dartmouth.. 2:28¼
Gold Beater, ch s, 1883, by Alcantara
—Flora Belle, by Stevens' Uwharie 2:20½
Gold Bud, ch g, 1888, by R. E. Lee,
dam by Star Hambletonian 2:25½
Gold Coin, ch g, 188—, by Forest
Wilkes 2:25
Golddust, dn m, 1884, by Dr. Spauld-
ing—Molly, by Prince Albert 2:18¼
Golden Boy, ch s, 1887, by Plato—
Belle Ervin 2:13¼
Golden Girl, b m, 188—, by Happy
Union 2:25
Golden Prince, ch g, 1877, by Golden
Bow—Kit, by Erie Abdallah 2:18¾
Golden Slipper, b m, 188—, ... 2:28
Golden W., b m, 188—, by Hamble-
tonian Wilkes 2:29½
Gold Leaf, ch m, 1885, by Sidney—
Fern Leaf, by Flaxtail .... 2·11¼
Gold Medal, b g, 1884, by Nephew
Jr.—Peggy Danohoo 2:14½
Goldmine, b s, 1886, by Harry Gold-
dust—Baby Mine, by Stonewall Jack-
son 2:17
Goldmont, b s, 188—, by Westmont— 2:23¼
Gold Plate, b m, 1888, by Fairy Gift
—Nickel Plate, by Belmont 2:23½
Gossip, ch s, 1871, by Tattler—Molly
Golddust, by Golddust 2:18
Gossip Jr., b g, 1877, by Gossip—Nelly
M., by Pilgrim Patchen 2:13¼
G. O. Taylor, b s, 188—, by Ben
Franklin 2:15¼
Gov. Foraker, b g, 188—, by Ben
Bolt 2:24½
Gov. France, b s, 188—, by France.. 2.24¾
Gov. Lucas, b s, 1883, by Attorney—
Sally, by Tramp 2:24¾
Gowan, b s, 188—, by Gambetta
Wilkes—Effie Davis, by Red Wilkes 2:22½
Graceful George, ch s, 188—, by Al-
cona Jr., dam by Washington...... 2:23
Grace Wilkes, b m, 188—, by Repeti-
tion, dam by Ford's Hambletonian 2:20½
Gracie, g m, 188—, by Hamlin's Al-
mont Jr. 2:21¼
Gracie, g m, 188—, ... 2:26¼
Gracie L., b m, 1884, by American
Boy—Jessie K., by Rex Hiatoga .. 2:24¼
Grapevine, g g, 188—, by McCurdy.. 2:26½
Grand George, ch s, 1880, by Hamble-

Hamden, b g, 1890, by Aladdin—Polly Hopkins, by Amber............ 2:23¼
Hamilton, b s, 1888, by Dick Wilkes—Kate M., by Edgewater............ 2:23¼
Hamlet, b g, 188—, by Highland Boy.. 2.23½
Hamlin, gr s, 1884, by Alcantara—Jane Loomer, by Dick Loomer..... 2.26¼
Handalier, b s, 1891, by Ammath..... 2.25
Handy Andy, rn g, 186—, (dead)...... 2:29¼
Handy B., b s, 1882, by Artemas—Millie, by Crittenden Jr............ 2.16¾
Handy Pat, ch g, 188—, by De Soto.. 2:29½
Hanford Medium, b s, 1888, by Milton R.—Tave, by Signal............... 2:14
Hannis Jr., ch s, 1885, by Hannis—Queen Almont, by Almont.......... 2:17¼
Happiness, b m, 1891, by Judge Salisbury, dam by Bonnie Wilkes....... 2:17¼
Happy, ch s, 1892, by Happy Chief... 2:27½
Happy Girl, blk m, 1888, by Champlain—Durango Maid, by Durango.. 2:23¾
Happy Girl, b m, 188—, by Gen. Hancock.............................. 2:26¼
Happy Russell, br s, 1884, by Mambrino Russell—Odd Stocking, by Happy Medium........................... 2:21½
Happy Tom, b s, 1887, by Pegasus—Belle, by Mambrino Champion...... 2.23¼
Hard Cash, b g, 1889, by Cashier, dam by Cady's Champion.......... 2:15¼
Hargis H., rn g, 1884, by Clinker.... 2:29¼
Harleigh, ch s, 1886, by Mambrino King—Lady Weston, by Mohican.... 2:28
Harlow, ch s, 188—, by Anderson Wilkes............................ 2.27¾
Harpeth, b s, 1888, by Wedgewood—Hilda, by Cuyler.................. 2 21½
Harrison, b s, 1886, by Ottawa Chief—Mary Wood, by Richard Wheelock (trotting 2.18¼)................... 2.19½
Harrison Reed, ch g, 188—, by Hickory Jr............................ 2.23½
Harry, b g, 186—, by Niagara Champion—Lop Ear, by Montreal 2:19¾
Harry, b g, 188—, by Dauntless Jr., .. 2:17¾
Harry B., b s, 188—, by Col. Moore.. 2:19¾
Harry B., br g, 1882, by Waldensian 2 20¼
Harry B., b g, 1890, by Elgin Boy.. 2:27¼
Harry B., gr g, 1891, by Happy Day, dam by Messenger Chief 2:20¼
Harry Brooks, ch g, 188—, by Bland 2.24¼
Harry Brown, b g, 188—, by Durant 2:21¼
Harry C., b s, 1889, by Comus—Midget, by Egmont 2:15½
Harry Clay, b s, 1891, by Clay Thorne 2.26½
Harry D., b g, 187—, ... 2:28
Harry E., g g, 188—, by Davy Crocket 2:23½
Harry G., br g, 188—, by Gold King 2 25¼
Harry G., b g, 188—, by Green Mountain Morgan.......................... 2:28
Harry Golddust, ch s, 187—, by Messenger Golddust.... .... 2·27½
Harry Gold King, gr s, 188—, by Gold King 2 27¾
Harry H., b g, 188—, ... 2:28
Harry H., gr g, 1885, by Alroy.......... 2:23½
Harry H., b g, 188—, by Ashley's Ethan Allen 2.22¼
Harry Hall, ch s, 1881, by Ben Patchen—Cora, by Edward Everett 2 29½
Harry Hayes, ch s, 1880, by Pilot Champion—Gipsy Girl, by Steven A. Douglas.......................... 2:28
Harry Holton, br s, 188—, by Dictator Wilkes .... 2·24
Harry Hontas, ch s, 1883, by Pocahontas Boy—Ratty, by Major Edsall 2 24¼
Harry Hornet, blk s, 1886, by Dan G.—Phil, by Snoddy's Arabian 2:21½

Harry Hoyer, ch s, 188—, by Pilot Champion 2:28
Harry Jones, ch g, 1885, by Elgin Boy—Fanny, by Hudson's Eclipse .. 2·18¼
Harry K., b g, 188—, by Charley.... 2;16¼
Harry K., b g, 1890, by Harry Wilson, dam by Bourbon Chief Jr...... 2:23¼
Harry Lynn, b g, 188—, by Morris' Almont, dam by Cloud Mambrino... 2:19¼
Harry M., b g, 188—, by Ledger... 2:27½
Harry M., b g, 188—, by Priam.... 2.22¼
Harry Omer, gr g, 1890, by St. Omer. 2:20¾
Harry P., br g, 188—, by Denmark.. 2:21¼
Harry P., blk g, 188—, by Joe Blackburn, dam by Gibson's Tom Hal.... 2·21¼
Harry Phelps, b s, 188—, by Crumley Hiatoga (trotting 2 27½) 2 22¼
Harry S., gr s, 1884, by Backman's Idol—Seboyo, by Orange Duroc..... 2.29½
Harry Strathmore, b s, 1884, by Strathmore—Belle, by Belmont..... 2:26
Harry Strathmore, g s, 188—, by Morgan's Strathmore—Nancy Hazard, by Blaine's Tom Hazard........... 2:24¼
Harry T., br g, 188—, by Nutwood... 2.25¼
Harry Van, ch s, 1884, by George Washington, dam by Wilson's Clipper 2:22¼
Harry Victor, blk s, 1890, by Black Victor, dam by Baird's Hambletonian Prince 2 20
Harry W., gr g, 188—............... 2:27¾
Harry West, blk g, 188—, by Col. West—Thornless, by Kenney's Denmark.......................... 2:27¼
Harry Wilkes, b s, 1883, by Col. Wilkes—Lady 2:23
Harry Wood, b s, 1888, by Rusco—Kitty H. Wood, by Rader's Dexter 2 16
Harry Z., b g, 1881, by Little Logan 2.17
Harvey Mc, blk g, 1892, by McKinney, dam by Nephew 2.18
Hastings Boy, b s, 1886, by Abe Downing—Lady R., by Green's Bashaw 2.15
Hat Rack, b g, 188—, by Prince Jr. 2:29¼
Hattie F., gr m, 1887, by LeGrand—Silver, by Silverthreads 2:18
Hattie P., ch m, 188—, by Rex Hiatoga 2:28½
Hattie P., b m, 188—, by Alcantara .. 2 27½
Hattie Shawan, ch m, 186—, by Blue Bull 2:24½
Hattie T., b m, 188—, by Day Star.. 2:25
Haverly, ch g, 187—, by Kansas Central—Puss, by Skenandoah 2:25
Haviland, b g, 188—, by Sterling ... 2:27
Hayseed, b g, 188—, ... 2:27
Hazel Cossack, b m, 1888, by Don Cossack—Lady Rene, by King Rene 2:16½
Hazel H., b m, 1889, by Bismarck—Lady Hamilton, by Jack Roberts Jr. 2:12¼
Hazel Heel, br s, 188—, ... 2.22½
Hazel Kirk, blk m, 1884, by Red Cloud—Lady Rutherford, by Phil Sheridan.......................... 2.29¼
Head Center, b g, 188—, by Spartacus 2.25
Headlight, br g, 1884, by Warrior Jr—Kate, by Tom Hal Jr 2.22½
Headlight, b g, 188—, by son of Ben Patchen 2:29¼
Heffner's, blk g, 185—, (dead) 2.30
Hello, br m, 1885, by Sherman—Molly 2:20½
Helen, b m, 188—, by Melbourne King 2:16½
Henrietta, blk m, 188—, by Haywood 2.24¼
Henry Clay, blk g, 188—, by Prince

Wilkes—Nanette, by Brown Hal .. 2:14
Ida A., b m, 1879, by Cash—Nelly, by Shellbark 2:22
Ida K., b m, 1887, by Lothair Jr.,—Melvin Mare, by Monte Christo 2:25
Ida S., br m, 1887, by Burton's Hardee—Muggins, by Joe Rockdale ... 2:15¾
Idler, blk s, 188—, by Idol Wilkes.. 2:20
Idol Dude, b s, 188—, by Joe Young 2:16¾
Idolater, ch s, 1884, by Blackman's Idol—Nelly, by Brougham (trotting 2:28½) 2:23¾
Ilderim, b g, 188—, by Wade Hampton 2:19¾
Idlewild, b m, 187—, by Star of the West 2:25¼
Illusion, b g, 1880, by Constellation—Lady Emma, by Hiram Drew 2:24¼
Imperial Hal, br s, 188—, by Gibson's Tom Hal 2:26¼
Importer, blk g, 1889, by Wayward—Greymont, by Aladdin 2:22½
Independent Frank, ch g, 188—, ... 2:27¼
I. N., b s, 188—, by Ajax 2:17¼
In It, b s, 1892, by Davy Belmont.... 2:29¾
Indianapolis Boy, b s, 1886, by Indianapolis—Madam Golddust, by Brillant Golddust 2.13½
Inkle, br s, 188—, by Princeps 2:26½
Interest, br s, 1886, by Onward—Little Fortune, by Scott's Thomas.... 2:18
Intreped, b g, 1888, by Hamlin's Almont Jr.—Quadroon, by Sherman.. 2:26¼
Iola Wilkes, ch m, 1887, by Willie Wilkes—Lucy Index, by Index 2:22½
Inez, b m, 1891, ... 2:29¼
Innocent Sam, b g, 187—, ... 2:27¾
Iona, b m, 188—, by Black Pat 2:27½
I. R., b s, 188—, ... 2:26¼
Ira Band ,b g, 188—, by Jaywood.... 2:28¾
Ira C., b g, 188—, by Brussells 2:26¼
Ira King, b s, 1888, by Ira Wilkes, dam by Marshall Chief 2:24¼
Iras, b m, 188—, by Vere de Vere—Annie Bashaw 2:19½
Ira Wilkes, br s, 1876, by George Wilkes—Nelly B., by Harry B. Patchen (trotting 2:28) 2:22¾
Irene, blk m, 1886, by Dexter Prince—Black Dolly, by Morse's Longfellow 2:25
Irene, b m., 1886, by Star Wilkes—Irena 2:11¾
Irene B., b m, 188—, by Stillson 2:23½
Irene L., b m, 188—, by Equinox.... 2:24¼
Irish Boy, ch g, 1883, by Billy H., dam by Flying Morgan 2:20
Irish Moll, blk m, 186—, ... 2:28½
Irma, b m, 1885, by Nutwood—Maggie Medium, by Happy Medium... 2:18½
Irma C., gr m, 1884, by Jim Wilson—Fanny, by Pocahontas Boy 2:18
Iron Quill, b s, 1892, by Kankakee .. 2:22¼
Ironwood, b g, 188—, by Wedgewood 2:26¼
Isa B., b m, 1888, by Vasco—Sadie Roe, by Magic 2:23½
Isabelle, ch m, 188—, by Subscriber (dead) 2:27¼
Island Belle, ch m, 1884, by Volenvent 2:24¾
Islander, b s, 188—, by Legacy 2:22½
Ithuriel, b s, 1888, by Red Wilkes—Topsy, by Strathmore (trotting (2.29¾) 2:29¾
Ivolo, b m, 1891, by Antevolo—Salinas Belle, by Vermont 2:21½
Ivorine, blk m, 1884, by Black Charley 2:18
Jack, b g, 188— by Almont M.—Laura T., by Greenback 2:22
Jack, b g, 188—, by Harkaway—Calamity, by Mambrino Pilot (dead).. 2:10¼
Jack (Conlisk's), rn g, 185—, (dead).. 2:27
Jack, blk g, 187—, ... 2:24½
Jack Ayers, b g, 188—, by Jack Rapid 2:29¼
Jack Bowers, b g, 1885, by Kilbuck Tom—Flora, by Bethel 2:11¼
Jack Evans, br g, 186—, (dead) 2:29¼
Jack Curry, gr g, 188—, by Traveler, dam by Rainbow 2:21¼
Jack Hart, ch g, 1876, by American Boy—Shoo Fly, by Young Tippoo Sultan 2:23¼
Jack Jewett, b s, 1885, by Winnebago Chief—Lulu Belle, by Black Jack.. 2:13¼
Jack Rapid, gr s, 1871, by Jack Rapid—Bourbon Maid, by imp. Glencoe .. 2:25
Jack Rapid, Jr., gr g, 188—, by Jack Rapid 2:29¼
Jack Shiel, b s, 1887, by Ross Wilkes—Brown Sue 2:21¾
Jack the Ripper, b g, 188—; by Syler's Almont Pilot 2:26¼
Jack the Ripper, b g, 188—, by Pat 2:27½
Jack the Ripper, blk s, 1886, by Texas Jack Sr.—Kinney Rooker, by Kenney 2:18¼
Jack Thorne, blk g, 1887, by Edsall Thorne.................. 2:24½
Jack W., ch g, 188—, ... 2:28¼
Jacob M., b g, 188—, ... 2:29¼
James D., gr g, 188—, by Hamlin's Almont Jr. 2:26
James K. Polk, ch g, 183—, (dead).. 2:27
Janey, blk m, 1890, by Alcantara—Zoe, by Gen. Knox 2:16½
Janey Woody, ch m, 188—, by Red Buck 2:26½
Jap, br g, 188—, by Robert Rysdyk.. 2:25¾
Jarenta, b m, 1891, by Bonnie Boy.... 2:27¼
Jasey, b s, 188—, ... 2:17¾
Jay, g g, by Gen. Sprague 2:28½
Jay and See, blk g, 188—, by Black Oak 2:30
Jay Eye See, blk g, 1878, by Dictator—Midnight, by Pilot Jr. (trotting 2:10) 2:06¼
Jay Girl, ch m, 1888, by Ben Adhem—Pet 2:21¼
Jay Gould Jr., ch s, 188—, by Jay Gould 2:29¼
Jaywood, ch s, 1883, by Nutwood—Lady Blanche, by Privateer 2:29¼
J. B., b g, 188—, by Albert S. Patchen 2:26¼
J. C., sp g, 188—, ... 2:25
J. C. C., ch g, 188—, by Legal Tender Jr. 2:16
J. C. R., b g, 188—, by Harkaway.. 2:29
J. D. K., blk g, 188—, ... 2:29¼
Jeff Davis, gr g, 1882, sire unknown, —Jenny Harwell 2:23
Jeff Davis, br g, 186—, (dead) 2:25¾
Jeff Smith, b g, 1881, by Ohio—Doll, by Manchester Tuckahoe (trotting 2:27¼) 2:29¼
Jenny Brown, gr m, 1887, by Joe Brown 2d 2:25
Jenny Hall, b m, 188—, by George Hall 2:29¼
Jenny J., b m, 1881, by Daniel Boone—Dinah, by Monogram 2:18¼
Jenny K., b m, 187—, by Blue Bull.. 2:22¼
Jenny Lind, br m, 1881, by Longstrider—Lady 2:17
Jenny Lind, b m, 1886, by Capt. Jack, dam by Anglo Saxon 2:23¼
Jenny Lind, ch m, 186—, by Scott's Hiatoga (dead) 2:28

dallah.. 2.26½
Judge Mallory, dn g, 188—, by Butcher Boy—Lottie C., by Oceana Chief.. 2.30
Judge Sterling, rn g, 188—, by Detractor......................... 2:15½
Judge Swing, br s, 1887, by Wilkes Boy—Long Molly, by Nigger Jr.... 2.11¾
Judge T., b g, 188— by Roseberry. 2:20¼
Judge West, b s, 1888, by Bivouac—Verona, by Lord Wellington...... 2·22¾
Judge Woolsey, b s, 1887, by Louis Napoleon—Hattie Mapes, by Abdallah Star 2:27¾
Jud Nick, b g, 188—, by Horace Wilkes 2.20
Julia L., ch m, 188—, by Green's Bashaw 2:28
Julia R., b m, 188—, by Tasco 2.22½
Juliet, ch m, 1885, by Bonnie Clay—Minnie 2:14½
Juliet, b m, 187—, ... 2:21¼
Juliette, blk m, 188— by Kaiser..... 2:30
Juliette, b m, 188—, by Tybalt—Bird, by son of Vermont 2:22
Junetta, b m, 1892, by Jura........ 2:20
June Bug, ch g, 188— by Almonarch, dam by Prince of Wales 2:15½
Junior, blk g, 188—, ... 2:26¼
Juno, ch m, 188—, by Young Swindler 2:27
Jurist, b s, 188—. 2.30
Jurist, b g, 188—, by Baymont...... 2:26½
Jury Boy, b g, 188—, by Juryman... 2:23¼
J. W. C., br g, 188— by Wedgewood 2.24½
Kaiser Wilkes, b s, 188—, by Wayne Wilkes 2:27¼
Kansas, ch s, 1887, by Karatas—Shining Star, by Guiding Star 2:10½
Kansas Jack, ch g, 188—, by Alhambra 2.20
Kansas Boy, blk s, 188—, ... 2:29½
Kantoka, b m, 188—, by Bay State—Deceitful, by Garibaldi............. 2:27¼
Kaota, blk m, 1889, by Sir Knight—Alla C., by Alroy 2:15¾
Kasouls, blk m, 188—, by John A. Kasson 2:25
Kate Bender, b m, 1883, by Little Burl 2:20½
Kate C., b m, 188—, by Abdallah Wilkes 2:18½
Kate Collins, b m, 188—, by Brown Henry 2.26
Kate Craig, ch m, 188—, by Stephen A. Douglas 2:25¾
Kate Eaton, ch m, 1885, by Frank Eaton—Lady Emrich 2.16
Kate Ham, b m, 1888, by Glen Miller—Rilee, by Hotspur Jr...... 2:24½
Kate Lewis, ru m, 188—, by Plato.. 2:29¼
Kate Long, b m, 188—, by Gen. Grant 2:30
Kate Poverty, br m, 188—, by St. Cloud 2:24½
Katie F., dn m, 187—, ... 2:27½
Katie Howard, blk m, 187—, by Almont Smith 2.19½
Katie Q., b m, 188—, by Highland Gay 2:22½
Keno, br g, 187—, ... 2:26½
Keno, br g, 1886, by Jim Mulvenna—Hattie S., by Budd Doble...... 2:23¼
Kenoma, blk s, 1888, by Herod—Nancy, by Seth Warner 2d..... 2:23
Keno R., blk g, 188— by Magic—Daisy R., by Belding's Nutwood... 2.20½
Kenton George, b s, 188—, by Kenton Mambrino 2 20½
Kentucky Ruler, b s, 1881, by Eg-

bert—Lady Almont, by Almont (dead) 2:24
Kentucky Star, b g, 188—, by Robert McGregor 2.17¼
Kentucky Tom, ch g, 188—, by Alexander's Norman 2:26¾
Kessall, b s, 188—, by Dunton Wilkes 2:26½
Ketchum, b s, 1891, by Gossiper, dam by Echo 2:17
Kid, b g, 188—, by Sunshine....... 2:25¼
Kid Davis, rn s, 188—, by Davis..... 2:27¼
Killarney, b s, 1879, by Black Ralph 2:20½
Killarney Girl, b m, 188—, by Killarney 2:28¼
Kilbuck Tom, ch s, 1873, by White Cloud—Doty Mare (dead) 2:26
Kimball, b m, 187—, by Tom Hal..... 2:30
King, blk g, 188—, by Record's Black Hawk, dam by Daniel Lambert ... 2:30
King Brister, rn s, 188—, by Joe Brister 2:30
King Goldmar, b s, 1891, by Goldmar 2:25⅜
King Hiro, ch s, 188—, by Bob Buzzard 2:27½
King Jim, b g, 1879, by Belmont—Maud, by Alexander's Abdallah... 2.20½
King Medium, b s, 1886, by Happy Medium—Maria Sturgess, by Almont 2:20
King of Belair, b s, 1883, by King Rene—Alma, by Almont 2:24
King of Diamonds, b s, 1892, by Velocity, dam by Denmark 2:22
King of Salem, b s, 188—, by King of Belair, dam by Tip Cranston.... 2·21¾
King Priam, ch s, 1884, by Hambletonian Mambrino—Miss Hooker, by Joe Hooker 2:29
King Wagoner, b s, 188—, by King Wilkes 2:26½
King Wilson, rn g, 1891, by Wayne Wilson 2:25½
King's Protector, b s, 1889, by Mambrino King—Ada, by Hamlin's Almont Jr. .... 2·18¾
Kingtoska, b s, 1885, by Petoskey—Susie King, by Mambrino King... 2:17
Kinney, b g, 188—, by son of Walkill Boy 2:25½
Kinsman, ch g, 1880, by Stranger—Jenny, by Young Country Boy (trotting 2:23¼) .... 2·17¼
Kismet, blk g, 187—, by Capt Walker 2:24¾
Kismuth S., ch s, 188—, by St. Jacob.. 2:19½
Kit Carson, b g, 188—, by Gray Dick 2:21¾
Kit Cloud, b m, 188—, by Flying Cloud 2:26¼
Kit Clinker, gr m, by Merriworth.. 2:28
Kittitas Ranger, b g, 188—. 2:20½
Kitty B., blk m, 1889, by Messenger Clay, dam by Tom Wonder 2:11
Kitty C, b m, 1883, by Bruce 2:14
Kitty M., b m, 188—, by Charm..... 2:25
Kitty M., ch m, 188—, by Mimic.... 2:25¾
Kitty Gray, gr m, 188—, by Hero ... 2:24
Kitty R., ch m, 188—, by Mountain Boy—Pet 2:21¼
Kitty Redbuck, ch m, 188—, by Jackson 2:20¼
Klickitat Maid, b m, 188—, by Altamont, dam by Capt Sligart Jr.... 2.19
Kitty White, b m, 188—, by Rich Wilson 2:27¼
Klick Klock, br m, 1887, by Mambritonian—Jenny Klock, by Luce Horse 2:14¾
Knight I., b g, 1890, by Sir Knight.. 2:27¾
Kosciusko, rn s, 188—, by Sea Foam

—Tilly, by Sharp's Hambletonian... 2:27
La Belle, b m, 1889, by Lockheart—Rosewood, by Blackwood Jr. 2:09
Lackawanna, b s, 1885, by Hamlin's Almont Jr.—Nelly Mac 2:24¼
La Bessa, b m, 188—, by Wilkesmont 2:24¼
L. A. Dick, ch g, 188—, by Richard's Elector 2:25
Lady, b m, 188—, by Star Hambletonian 2:23½
Lady, rn m, 188—, by Kilbuck Tom... 2:26¼
Lady, b m, 188—, by Henry Ham, dam by Cloud 2:24¼
Lady A., b m, 188—, by Arthur Wilkes, dam by son of Reavis' Blackbird 2:23¼
Lady Alice, b m, 186—, (dead) 2:29
Lady Anderson, ro m, 1889, by Anderson Wilkes—Vic, by Frank 2:24½
Lady B., b m, 188—, by Moody 2:26½
Lady B., gr m, 188—, by Prince Hal—Lula 2:29¼
Lady B., br m, 188—, ... 2:28½
Lady B., b m, 188—.................. 2:27
Lady Belle, b m, 187—, ... 2:28¾
Lady Belle, b m, 188—, by Pasacas, dam by Sherry Cobbler 2:28¾
Lady Belle, ch m, 188—, by Red Wilkes.............................. 2:27¼
Lady Bevins, rn m, 184—, (dead)..... 2:26
Lady Clairmont, blk m, 1890, by Gold King 2:24¼
Lady Crawford, b m, 1888, by Crawford—Gypsy Girl, by Black Chief.. 2:27
Lady Cummings, b m, 188—, by William Wallace, dam by Kemball's Pelton 2:29¼
Lady Dafoe, b m, 187—, ... 2:29¼
Lady Drennon, b m, 188—, by Drennon 2:28½
Lady Duroc, ch m, 1880, by Iowa Duroc—Lady Green, by Green's Bashaw 2.21½
Lady Elgin, gr m, 186— (dead) 2:24½
Lady Gray, gr m, 185— (dead) 2.25
Lady H., b m, 1888, by Sidney—Sultana, by Del Sur 2.15
Lady H., b m, 188—, by Hidalgo 2.25
Lady Hamilton, ch m, 188—, by Alcantara 2:23¼
Lady Hamlet, b m, 1891, by Buckeye Bayard 2:24¼
Lady Harrison rn m, 1887, by Billy Hartshorn, dam by Jim Brister..... 2:28¼
Lady Head, b m, 1882 .... 2:24
Lady Helen, b m, 188—, by Montrose. 2:27¼
Lady Hill, ch m, 1881, by Messenger Duroc—Joan D'Arc, by Alexander's Abdallah 2:22
Lady Hornet, gr m, 1892, by Freeland 2.24
Lady J., b m, 188—, by Advance...... 2:26½
Lady J., b m, 1889, by Dark Night—Belle Oakwood, by Black's Hambletonian (trotting 2:30).... .... 2:20
Lady Jones, gr m, 188—, ... 2:27¾
Lady L., gr m, 188—, by White Line.. 2:26¼
Lady Lee, ch m, 188—, by Abdallah Wilkes—Daisy Maid, by Mambrino Boy 2:24½
Lady Lee, br m, 1889, by Alcantara—Lady Maud, by Thomas Jefferson.. 2:20
Lady Lightfoot, b m, 187—.......... 2:23
Lady Logan, ch m, 188—, by Gen. Logan 2:24¼
Lady Long, b m, 188—, by Petoskey.. 2:20¼
Lady M., ch m, 188—, by Pilot Wilkes 2:25½
Lady M., gr m, 188—, by Billy H 2 21¼
Lady M., br m, 188—, by Doubtful Boy 2:25½
Lady Mac, rn m, 184—, (dead) 2:25½
Lady Mac, br m, 187—, by Paddy Cork—Belle, by Mambrino Templar. 2:25¼
Lady Mac, b m, 188—, by Warwick Boy 2:25¼
Lady Markham, b m, 1886, by Bismark—Lapwing, by Western 2:17¾
Lady Oaks, b m, 1889, by Colonel Bruce—Maud, by Bay Bashaw...... 2:19¼
Lady Pearl, br m, 187—, by Abraham—Nellie B., by Gen. Washington.. 2:28¼
Lady Pendleton, ch m, 1884, by ..encoe Jr. 2:21¼
Lady Picco, br m, 1885, by Picco—Lassie, by Aladdin... .... 2.30
Lady Princeton, b m, 1889, by Princeton—Wait-a-Bit, by Basil Duke.... 2;15½
Lady Rolfe, b m, 1874, by Tom Rolfe—Nelly, by Montezuma (trotting 2:22¼) 2:23
Lady Rooker, b m, 1887, by Coaster, dam by Rooker 2:25½
Lady Ryan, b m, 186—, (dead) 2:28
Lady St. Clair, b m, 1862, by St. Clair Jule 2:20
Lady Sheridan, b m, 1880, by Confidence—Nelly Nelson, by Brother's Pride 2:15¼
Lady Spencer, b m, 188—, by Ignaro.. 2:27
Lady V. 2:26½
Lady Van, blk m, 1891, by Van Also.. 2.24¼
Lady Vice, b m. 1886, by Viceroy... 2:17
Lady Vivian, br m, 1888, by Aristos Jr.—Maud A., by Capt. Jack........ 2:17¼
Lady Wallace, b m, 1885, by William Wallace—Lucille, by Messenger Golddust 2:21½
Lady Westmont, b m, 188—, by Westmont 2.25¼
Lady Wilkes, b m, 1882, by Brown Wilkes—Kitty Ethan, by Drury's Ethan Allen 2:24½
Lady Wilkin, br m, 1880, by Ambassador—Sleepy Jane 2:15½
Lady Win, b m, 187—, ... 2:28¾
Lalla Rookh, br m, 1887, by Allie Gaines—May, by Star of the West.. 2:20
Lamplighter, ch m, 188—, ... 2:23¾
Land Lord, br g, 1886, by Land Pilot. 2:25¾
Lantana, b m, 1891, by Cohannet, dam by Steven's Bald Chief....... 2:25¼
Larchleigh, b s, 1886, by Hinsdale Chief—Fanny Ferguson, by McKesson's Grey Eagle 2:23
Laredo, br s, 1888, by Wedgewood—Ruby, by Dictator 2:19½
Larry C., b g, 1875, by Black Hawk Messenger—Maud 2:19¾
Late Rose, b m, 1877, by Happy Medium—Astoria, by George M. Patchen Jr. 2:23¼
Latimer, b g, 1891, by Latitude...... 2:27¼
Latimer Girl, blk m, 1889, by Pyramid 2:29¼
Laura, b m, 188—, ... 2:20¼
Laura Bell, b m, 188—, by Elevator.. 2:29¼
Laura Belle, ch m, 188—, by Commander 2:27¼
Laura Belle, b m, 188—, by St. Mark. 2:27
Laura J., blk m, 187—, by Legal Tender Jr. 2:27¼
Laura Lee, blk m, 188—, by Despot.. 2:29¼
Laura M., b m, 188—, by Almont Patchen—Lady Fay 2:13¼
Laura Nuttingham, ch m, 188—, by Nuttingham 2:21¾
Laura T., b m, 1886, by Al West—Lizzie 2:09¾
Laura W., b m, 1891, by Cyclone—Nancy Wilkes, by Favorite Wilkes.. 2:30
Laura Wilkes, b m, 1889, by Lexing-

ton Wilkes—Laura Swigert, by Swigert 2:30
Laurel, b m, 1883, by Brown Hal—Myrtle, by Enfield 2:10¾
Lauretta, b m, 1891, by Patchen Wilkes—Dinnie, by Rochester (trotting 2:30) 2:24¼
Laverne, b g, 1882, by Jim Monroe—Bally, by Cockspur 2:23¼
Lavoque, br s, 188—, by Anderson Wilkes 2:22½
Lawnwood, gr s, 188—, by Clinker.... 2:25½
Lazy Jim, b g, 188—, by Lothair Jr... 2:28
L. B. Curtis, ro g, 188—, by Hamenger 2:22¾
L. C. Lee, br s, 187—, by Elmo, dam by Kentucky Chief 2:15
Leah K., blk m, 188—, by Jefferson Prince 2:23½
Leander, ch s, 1886, by Strader Jr.—Lady Jane Sprague, by Gov. Sprague 2:22.
Lebbeas L., b s, 1887, by Hamdallah—Belle H., by Zeno 2:13¼
LeClede, b s, 1886, by Princeps—Fallacy, by George Wilkes 2:21¼
Lee Buoyant, br s, 188—, by Joe Elmo 2:27½
Leeward Wilkes, b s, 188?, by Onward, dam by Lyle Wilkes 2:19¼
Lee H., ch g, 1884, by Harding's Bay Tom—Fanny, by Lew Boyd 2:13
Legal Hontas, ch s, 1892, by Pocohontas Boy, dam by Legal Tender Jr. 2:24
Legal Tender, b s, 185—, by Legal Tender (dead) 2:28
Legal Vein, b g, 188—, by Legal Tender Jr. 2:24½
Leila C., b m, 1882, by James Madison—Rill, by Prompter 2:20½
Leila May, b m, 1889, by Recorder—Almonte, by Bostick's Almont Jr... 2:18¼
Lelah W., ch m, 188—, by Von Mark, dam by Old George 2:23¾
Lella B., b m, 188—, by Bedford Beauty 2:22¾
Lena F., ch m, 188—, by American Boy 2:27¼
Lena H., ro m, 1883, by Gen. Hardee—Pick, by Earnharts' Brooks...... 2:22
Lena Hill, blk m, 1891, by William M. Hill—Possum Pie, by Octoroon..... 2:12
Lenatur, b s, 188—, by Pelletier..... 2:16¾
Lena Willetts, br m, 1885, by Ferguson—Rosemond, by Abdallah Prince 2:14
Lennie Striker, b m, 188—, by Petoskey 2:20
Lenore K., b m, 1888, by Sweepstakes—Molly Strait, by Jerry Clark 2:23¼
Lenwood, b g, 188—, by Vandalia Wilkes 2:30
Leo, b s, 188—, by Kentucky Clay Jr.. 2:29½
Leo, ch g, 187—, by Argonaut 2:24¼
Leon, gr m, 1889, by Hiatt's Wild Wagner—Fanny H. 2:23¼
Leonard, br g, 188—, by Champion Knox 2:23¼
Leon Baker, b s, 188—, by Lakeland Abdallah Jr. 2:21¾
Leontine, b m, 188—, by Draco Medium 2:19½
Leo S., b s, 1885, by Allegro—Minnie, by Hickory 2:22
Leta May, br m, 188—, by Autevolo—Steinola, by Steinway 2:23½
Lettie Sprague, sp m, 188—, by Jim Schriber 2:23¼
Leverone, b s, 1888, by Gen. Hancock—Patience, by Blue Bull 2:16
Leviathan, ch g, 187—, ... 2:24
Lewis B., br s, 188—, by Drennon.. 2:17¼
Lew Wallace, ch s, 188—, by Pratt's Mohawk 2:28¼
Lex, blk s, 1883, by Legal Tender Jr.—Lucy, by Blue Bull 2:23½
Lexington Chief, sp g, 188—, by Aristos—Dolly Varden (trotting 2:30) . 2:20¼
Lida W., b m, 1880, by Nutwood—Belle, by George M. Patchen Jr... 2:18¼
Lieut. Wilkes, b s, 1886, by Gov. Wilkes—Kit, by Wells' Cockspur ... 2:28½
Like Like, br m, 188—, by Whippleton 2:25
Lila King, br m, 1886, by Gold King—Jennie Lind 2:22½
Lillian, b m, 1884, by Adrian Wilkes—Abdallah Lightfoot, by Mambrino Abdallah 2:14¼
Lillian, br m, 188—, by Daniel Lambert—Whalebone, by Carter's Columbus.......... 2:29¼
Lillian S., b m, 1880, by Morgan Messenger 2:17¾
Lilly, gr m, 188—, by Capt. Clay 2:19½
Lilly, b m, 188—, by Wedgewood..... 2:28¼
Lilly B., b m, 1890, by Elgin Boy.. 2:21½
Lilly Banks, gr m, 1886, by Ayer's Black Hawk Morgan—California Pet 2:22
Lilly Bush, ch m, 188—, by Ball R... 2:29½
Lilly C., gr m, 1884, by Steinway—Bloomfield Maid, by Hambletonian Jr. 2:20½
Lilly M., b m, 188—, by Hartford.... 2:21
Lily You, b m, 188—, by Adrian Wilkes 2:26¾
Limber Jack, b g, 187—, by Gray's Tom Hal 2:18½
Limber Jim, blk s, 188—, by Richmond Chief 2:30
Limber Jim, ch g, 185—, (dead) 2:26
Limber Jim, b s, 188—, by Adjutant 2:25¼
Lincoln, ch g, 187—, by Tempest Jr. 2:23¾
Linda, b m, 1892, by Frank Buford, dam by Denmark 2:22½
Linda Gale, b m, 1888, by Chastelard—Pallas, by Sheldon's Jupiter 2:19
Linden, b s, 188-, by Aristos 2:27
Linden, b s, 1886, by Madison Wilkes—Lady Maud, by Young Trustee ... 2:15
Linewood, ch m, 1890, by Nutalwood 2:21
Linkwood Patchen, b g, 1875, by Linkwood Chief—Lady Patchen..... 2:12½
Little Actor, b g, 188—, ... 2:28¼
Little Baby, b m, 188—, by Shaker Boy—Dolly Smith, by Flying Hiatoga 2:27¾
Little Barefoot, b m, 188—, by Repetition—Lady Barefoot, by Kent ... 2:27½
Little Black, gr m, 188—, ... 2:29¼
Little Brown Jug, br g, 1875, by Gibson's Tom Hal—Lizzie, by John Netherland 2:11¾
Little Chief, blk g, 188—, by Daniel Boone 2:21¼
Little Cyclone, gr g, 1884, ... 2:28½
Little Dick, b g, 188—, by Hayward Hazzard 2:23
Little Dan, ch g, 188—, by Elial G., dam by Red Cloud 2:21¼
Little Dan, blk g, 188—, by Whirlwind Jr. 2:28
Little Doc, b g, 188—, by Little Johnny—Jenny Wells, by Jack Hawkins 2:25
Little Doubtful, b m, 188—, by Nuthurst 2:29½
Little Ed, gr g 187—, ... 2:25¼
Little Em, b m, 1878, by Billy Green

—Old Wiley, by Rattler Tuckahoe.. 2:18½
Little Frank, br s, 188—, ... 2:30
Little Frank, br s, 1884, by Ashland Clay—Flora 2:19¼
Little Fred, ch g, 188—, by Phillips' Blue Bull 2:23¼
Little George, rn g, 188—, by Cephas 2:29¾
Little Hank, b s, 1888, by Colonna—Maid, by Brolley 2:24¼
Little Hope, br g, 188—, by Tempest Jr., dam by Blue Bull 2:21¼
Little Ida, b m, 1880, ... 2:19¼
Little Jay, rn s, 188—, by Jay Bird.. 2:26¾
Little Jack, b g, 188—, by Abdallah Mambrino 2:26¼
Little Jeff, b g, 188—, by H. W. Beecher 2:23¼
Little Jenny, blk m, 187—, ... 2:26¼
Little Joe, blk g, 188—, by Ira Wilkes, dam by Marshall Chief 2:15½
Little Joe, b g, 188—, by Schmidlap's Get-a-way—Lucy 2:23½
Little Joe, br s, 188—, by Red Buck 2:29½
Little John, b g, 188—, by Bassett M.. 2:30
Little John, blk g, 188—, ... 2:30
Little Johnny, b g, 188—, by Oshkosh 2:19½
Little Jimmy, ch g, 188—, by Graves' Mohawk Chief 2:30
Little Joker, b s, 1884, by Charley Foster—Dolly, by Bayswater 2:19¾
Little Joker, ch g, 188—, by Forest Hal 2:16¼
Little Lulu, ro m, 1882 by Sea Foam —Promise Lady 2:23¼
Little M., b m, 1890, by Wildbrino.. 2:22
Little Mac, b s, 188—, ... 2:28½
Little Mac, br g, 1877, by Kentucky Dan 2:13¾
Little Maid, b m, 188—, by Rockwood —Pocohontas 2:26
Little Pat, b g, 188—, by Captain Walker.......... 2:27¼
Little Pete, ch g, 188—, by Sutton's Dave Hill.......... 2:22¼
Little Pitt, b g, 188—, by Lapidist Chief.......... 2:13¼
Little Rhea, br g, 188—, by Jim Fisk.. 2:27½
Little Rich, b g, 188—.......... 2:26
Little Rocket, b g, 188—.......... 2:21¼
Little Rube, ch g, 188—, by Mohawk.. 2:25
Little Sam, b g, 1885.......... 2:29¼
Little Sam, b s, 188—, by Aristos Jr.. 2:22½
Little Sam, ch g, 1892, by Alcyone Jr., dam by Wilkes Spirit Jr.......... 2:29¼
Little Tony, ch g, 187—, by Blackbird —Gonier.......... 2:29¼
Little Willie, sp s, 1876, by King Pharoah—Dolly.......... 2:23¼
Little Wonder, ch g, by son of Blue Bull.......... 2:20¼
Little Wonder, ch s, 188—, by John F. Payne.......... 2:26¼
Livia, b m, 1885, by Orton—Helen, by Rysdyk's Hambletonian 2:22¾
Lizzie, b m, 188—, by Brown Hal..... 2:27
Lizzie H., b m, 188—, by Brown Hal Jr.......... 2:23½
Lizzie H., ch m, 1886, by Longstrider Dove, by Camden Denmark.......... 2:22
Lizzie Hunter, ch m, 1887, by Nantucket—Mattie, by Almont Smith... 2:22
Lizzie Mack, b m, 1890, by Warrior Jr.......... 2:14¼
Lizziemont, b m, 1884, by Jerome Eddy—Evemont, by Piedmont...... 2:16¾
Lizzie N., b m, 1878, by Wilkesmont.. 2:21¼
Lizzie Wonder, gr m, 187—, by Tom Wonder — Dolly Sawyer, by Black Prince.......... 2:29¾
Lloyd, gr s, 1887, by Conway—Sunshine, by Atlantic.......... 2:10¼
Loafer, gr g, 188—, by Typhoon...... 2:14½
Lochinvar, blk s, 188—, by Clipper, Brooks.......... 2:18¼
Lochinvar, b g, 188—, by Socrates.... 2:28
Lock Boy, blk g, 188—, by son of Old Darkey 2:30
Logan, gr g, 188—, by White Cloud... 2:26
Logan F., b g, 188—, by Woodford Boy 2:20¼
Logan K., blk g, 188—, by Logan Chief.......... 2:27½
Lolla B., blk m, 1890, by Jim Long—Maggie T.......... 2:24¼
Lone Jack, br g, 187—.......... 2:19
Lon G., b g, 188—, by Bald Hornet... 2:21¼
Longfellow, ch g, 186—, by Red Bill (dead).......... 2:19¼
Longitude, b s, 1886, by Osman—Galita, by Adirondack.......... 2:18
Long Shot, g s, 1886, by Walsingham —Dulce, by Belmont.......... 2:23½
Long Taw, gr g, 188—, by Newsboy... 2:23
Long Wilkes, b s, 1888, by Petoskey, dam by Vindex.......... 2:23
Longworth, br s, 1885, by Sidney—Gray Dale, by American Boy Jr.... 2:19
Lora, ch m, 1888, by Royal Fearnaught, dam by Manchester.......... 2:14¾
Lord Clayton, br s, 1890, by C. F. Clay—Lady Palm, by Thomas Jefferson.......... 2:24¾
Lord Egbert, ch s, 1890, by Lord Russell, dam by Egbert (dead).......... 2:30
Lord Ferguson, br s, 1887, by Ferguson—Lady Ethan, by Ethan Allen... 2:19¼
Lord Tennyson, ch g, 188—, by Onward King, dam by Daniel Lambert. 2:24¼
Lorene, blk m, 1878, by Col. West—Fancy Downing, by Joe Downing... 2:15¼
Lorine, ch m, 188—, by Tasco.......... 2:27
Lota, blk m, 1886, by Singleton—Evangeline, by Ophir.......... 2:29
Lothair Boy, b g, 1884, by Lothair Jr. 2:19
Lotta, blk m, 187—.......... 2:25¼
Lottie K., gr m, 1877, by Blue Bull Jr.......... 2:25
Lottie Loraine, b m, 1890, by Gambetta Wilkes—Lady Yelser, by Garrard Chief 2:10½
Lottie M., gr m, 1884, by Grey Harry —Lottie Stevens.......... 2:20¼
Lottie P., b m, 1876, by Blue Bull Jr. —Fanny, by Proud American Jr.... 2:17¼
Lottie Rocket, ch m, 1886, by Redmont—Blue Kitty, by St. Omer. ... 2:18¼
Lottie S., blk m, 1890, by Duroc Boy, dam by Arnold's Red Buck.......... 2:25
Lottie Wright, br m, 188—, by Silas Wright.......... 2:27½
Louisa, ro m, 186—, (dead).......... 2:20¼
Louis M., b g, 188—.......... 2:19½
Louis P., b g, 188—.......... 2:26¾
Loupe, blk s, 188—, by John Sevenoaks—Lallah Rouke, by Echo.......... 2:20¾
Lou Shaffer, ch m, 188—, by Chipper Brooks.......... 2:30
Lower Stoner, ro g, 188—, by Strathmore—Kate Dillard, by John Dillard 2:21
Lowmark, b s, 188—, by Waymart—Peggy, by Haywood.......... 2:10¾
Lucian W., b g, 188—, by Viceroy—Puss, by Frank.......... 2:28½
Lucille, ch m, 188—, by Elgin Boy, dam by Kentucky Chief.......... 2:24½
Lucille, b m, 1885, by Wedgewood—Pauline, by Shakespeare.......... 2:14½
Lucille H., b m, 1889, by Socrates—

Motto, by St. Mark................ 2 12
Lucille S., g m, 188—, by Duplex, dam
by King Hal........ .... 2.15¾
Lucky Boy, b s, 188—, by American
Boy...... .... 2.21
Lucra, b m, 188—, by William L...... 2:23¼
Lucy, gr m, 187— (dead)............. 2.14
Lucy B., br m, 1881, by Legacy....... 2:18¼
Lucy C., b m, 188—, by Robert B..... 2.20½
Lucy D., gr m, 1887.................. 2.18¾
Lucy Dumas, br m, 1888, by Dumas—
Vinewood, by Ironwood............. 2.16
Lucy J., dn m, 188—, by Hawpatch.. 2.27½
Lucy K., ch m, 1886, by Rattler
Brooks, dam by Roscoe............. 2.21¼
Lucy L., b m, 1889, by Gen. McClel-
lan Jr.—Mag, by Alexander........ 2.22½
Lucy M., ro m, 188—, by Appleby.... 2 23¼
Lucy Pan, ch m, 1889, by Pan—Lucy,
by Blue Bull..... .... 2:17
Lucy Smith, ch m, 188—, by Bay
Chief Jr...... ....;.. 2.28¾
Luella, b m, 1884, by Legal Tender Jr.
—Flaxy................... ...... 2:19¼
Luella Shawhan, blk m, 1892, by Ar-
rowwood, dam by Anteros.......... 2:23
Lula, b m, 188—.................... 2.21
Lula, b m, 188—, by Ellwood....... 2.29¼
Lulu G., ch m, 1886, by Consul—
Grace.................... .... 2.16¼
Lulu Mc., b m, 188—, by McCurdy's
Hambletonian.................... 2.25
Lulu McCurdy, b m, 1886, by Bay-
wood—Belle R., by Wonder........ 2:14¼
Lulu N. b m, 188—, by Reveille—Jenny
R., by Mohawk Chief............. 2.24¼
Lutie Strathmore, ch m, 188—, by
Strathmore, dam by Champ Fergu-
son..................... .... 2:15¼
Lydia Allen, b m, 188—, by Piatt Al-
len............................... 2:30
Lydia Wilkes, b m, 1886, by Red
Wilkes—Aileen, by Mambrino Boy.. 2:17¼
Lyle, br s, 188—, by Anoka, dam by
Swigert........................... 2 21½
Lyttleton, b g, 187—, by King Pharoah 2.20½
Mabel Flood, ch m, 1886, by Pocahon-
tas Abdallah—Jenny F., by Mercury. 2 19
Mabel P., b m, 188—, by Bou-bon
bon Wilkes....................... 2:17¼
Mabel Sharpe, ch m, 1888, by Sharper
—Lady Elliot, by Ryedyk.......... 2:23½
Mac, b g, 1887, breeding unknown. .. 2.18½
Macbeth, b s, 1891, by Alexander Du-
mas.............................. 2:30
Macleay, blk s, 1889, by Sable Wilkes
—Mamie Comet, by Nutwood (trot-
ting 2:22¼)....................... 2 29¼
Mack, b g, 188—, by Almont M...... 2:26¼
Macklin, b s, 1889, by Onward—Lottie
Wall, by Strathmore.............. 2.28½
McAmber, b g, 188—, by Fergus Mc-
Gregor........................... 2.22½
McBride, b s, 1889, by Rumor—Myra,
by Gen. Knox.................... 2:17¼
McCleery, b g, 188—, by Smith's Mam-
brino Chief Jr.................... 2:18½
McClintock, b g, 188—, by Bay Chief. 2:20¼
McCurdy Jr., b s, 188—, by McCurdy's
Hambletonian.................... 2:21½
McDorton, ch g, 188—,.............. 2 23¼
McDowell, b s, 1885, by Triton—Molly,
by St. Elmo...................... 2.25
McFadden, b g, 188—............... 2 20½
McGinty, b s, 1890, by Delineator 2:15¾
McGinty, blk s, 188—, by Woodford
Wilkes........................... 2.2b
McKinley, b s, 1889, by Alto—Day-
light, by Starlight... ... . 2 20½

McKinley, b g, 188—, by Wilkesmont. 2:24¼
Mac H., ch g, 188—................. 2:23
Macey, b s, 1880, by George Wilkes—
Belle Clay, by Kentucky Clay....... 2:29½
Machette, b m, 1889, by Brown Hal.. 2.21¾
Mack Noble, b s, 188—, by Frank No-
ble.............................. 2:28½
Madel, b s, 188—, by Medonius 2 18½
Madge D., ch m, 188—, by Tempest.. 2:23½
Madge Medium, b m, 188—, by Draco
Medium—Fanny, by Black Dutchman
(dead)........................... 2:21¾
Madge Miller, b m, 1883, by Young
Wilkes—Kit, by Creeper.......... 2:20¾
Madge W., br m, 188—, by Mamaluke. 2:25¼
Mage, b g, 188—.................... 2:30
Meggie, b m, 188—, by Niles 2.28
Maggie A., b m, 1887, by Attorney—
Mattie, by Carenot............... 2·25
Maggie Almont, b m, 1884, by Almont
Pilot—Maggie, by Magna Charta.... 2:18
Maggie H., b m, 188—.............. 2:28
Maggie H., blk m, 1885, by Legal Ten-
der Jr.—Miss Davidson, by Pocahon-
tas Boy.......................... 2·25
Maggie H., b m, 188—, by Irish George 2:22¾
Maggie H., g m, 188—, by son of Bay
Billy............................. 2 30
Maggie H., b m, 188—, by Schuyler
Colfax. ...·...... .... 2·27½
Maggie J, blk m, 188—, by Hylas.... 2.14½
Maggie May, ro m, 1879, by Sea Foam 2:24¾
Maggie McDowell, b m, 1887, by Sid-
ney—Lady Hannah, by Arthurton... 2:21¼
Maggie Mitchell, gr m, 188—, by Blue
Hal.............................. 2.24¼
Maggie Mitchell, gr m, 188—, by Blue
Duster........................... 2.27½
Maggie N., b m, 188—, by Colfax.... 2:24½
Maggie R., b m, 188—, by Tom Scott.. 2.27½
Maggie R., b m, 1884, by Kilbuck Tom
—Topsy, by Bethel............... 2:14¼
Maggie T., b m, 1887, by Nihilist—
Fanny........................... 2:18¼
Magna Monte, b s, 1886, by Douglas
Almont, dam by Sovereign......... 2:14½
Magnet, b g, 188— by Smuggler 2:27½
Magoozler, gr g, 185—, (dead)....... 2:20½
Magoth, b m, 188—, by St. Gothard.. 2:29¼
Magown, blk g, 188—, by Brown
Wilkes........................... 2:27¼
Maid of Rocky Run, b m, 188—, by
George Forrest................... 2:25
Major Clelland, ch s, 188—, by Artist
Wilkes........................... 2 20½
Major Hal, br s, 188—, by Brown Hal 2:29¼
Major Ham, b s, 1886, by Hambrino.. 2.25
Major Kyle, b g, 188—.............. 2:30
Major Lambert, br s, 1889, by Cali-
fornia Lambert — Fifty, by Haw-
thorne........................... 2:19¼
Major P., b g, 188—, by Bay Tom.... 2.30
Major Wilkes, b s, 1883, by Young Jim
—Catharine, by Blue Bull........ 2:16¼
Major Wolfe, b s, 1889, by Bourbon
Wilkes—Late Rose, by Happy Med-
ium............................. 2:14¼
Major Wonder, b g, 1885, by Major
Edsall Jr.—Brigham.............. 2.09¾
Mallrine (Walling's)................ 2·26¾
Mambrino Hannis, b g, 1883, by Han-
nis — Dolly, by Preston's Patrick
Henry........................... 2:16¼
Mambrino Prince, br g, 188—, by Mam-
brino Abdallah—Lena Bolton, by An-
sel............................... 2·23¼
Mamie Gift, ch m, 188—, by Pilot Gift 2 29¼
Mamie Golddust, b m, 1891, by
Sprague Golddust—Mamie, by Blue

Bull 2:26¼
Mamie L., b m, 188—, by Bay Tom... 2:24
Mamie Wilkes, b m, 188—, by Sir Wilkes.... .... 2:29¼
Manager, gr s, 1888, by Nutwood—Carrie Wilkes, by George Wilkes.... 2:00¾
Mandan, b g, 188—, by Patchen Volunteer........................ 2:25
Mando, b g, 188—........................ 2:29¼
Mandolin, ch g, 188—, by Tramp..... 2:15¼
Manette, b m, 188—, by Guelph—Daisy, by Steven's Uwharie 2:24
Manilla Girl, b m, 188—, by Artemas 2:24¼
Manson E., b g, 1888, by Tattler Jr. 2:24¼
Mapeline, b m, 188—, ... 2:29¼
Maplewood, ch s, 1884, by Ajax—Belle, by High Jack 2:25
Marchioness, b m, 188—, by California, dam by Pilot Medium 2:27¼
Marendes, gr s, 188—, by Walker Morrill—Henry Mare, by Sherman Morgan Jr. 2:17¼
Margaret M., ch m, 188—, by Oneida 2:25½
Margery H., b m, 1891, by Warfare—Sally Adams, by John Burdine.... 2:26½
Maria Theresa, b m, 188—, by Hambletonian Gem 2:23¼
Marie Scott, b m, 186—, by Scott's Hiatoga—Jenny Lind, by John Stanley 2:24
Marietta Wilkes, ch m, 1892, by Don Pizarro, dam by Nutwood 2:17¼
Marion, b g, 1887, by Gen. Marion—Kit, by Flying Cloud 2:21¼
Marion Mills, b m, 188—, by Harry Mills 2:21¼
Maritana, b g, 1886, by Kentucky Volunteer—Marie, by Long Island Patchen 2:20¼
Marjie C., ch m, 1887, by Albatross— 2:20
Markland, b s, 1884, by Victor Bismarck—Sally Dudley, by Standard Bearer 2:18½
Marksmaid, b m, 1891, by Marksman 2:21
Mark Wakefield, b g, 188—, by Joe Elmo 2:29¼
Marlowe, b g, 1878, by Standard Bearer—Puss Kenny, by Kenny's Eclipse 2:15
Marr, b s, 1891, by Roy Wilkes 2:26
Mars Pointer, b g, 188—, by Masker.. 2:27¾
Martha H., b m, 1889, by Gambetta Wilkes—Kitty Kimbrough, by Kimbrough's Abdallah 2:18¼
Martin Box, b g, 188—, by Clipper.. 2:17½
Martin M., b g, 188—, ... 2:28¼
Marvin, ch g, 1885, by Scriba Boy—Maggie, by Jefferson Prince 2:20½
Mary Anderson, b m, 188— 2:29
Mary B., g m, 188—, by Frank Almont 2:23
Mary Centlivre, b m, 188—, by R C. Brown—Carrie Blackwood, by Blue Bull 2:12
Mary Crit, blk m, by Rohmer (trotting 2:23¾) 2:19
Mary J., ch m, 1889, by Bay Tom Jr. —Forestola, by Bostick's Almont Jr. 2:18¾
Mary Lou, b m, 1886, by Petoskey—Susie King, by Mambrino King.... 2:19½
Mary West, blk m, 1887, by Patchen Wilkes—Jenny West, by Allie West 2:21½
Mascot, b g, 1885, by Deceive—Miss Delmore 2:04
Mascot, b s, 188—, by Jot C. 2:28¼
Mason B., blk g, 188—, ... 2:30
Matt T., b g, 188—, by Twilight ... 2:20¾
Matt Wall, b g, 1891, by Hazel Heel 2:27½
Matterhorn, b s, 1883, by Nutwood—Malmaison, by Alexander's Abdallah 2:16¼
Mattie B., br m, 188—, by Alexander Button 2:26¾
Mattie Bond, br m, 187—, by Tom Hal 2:27¼
Mattie G., b m, 188—, ... 2:22¼
Mattie Graham, br m, 188—, by Pilot Almont—Madeline, by Tom Crowder (dead) 2:21
Mattie Harle, g m, 187—, ... 2:25¼
Mattie Hunter, ch m, 1872, by Prince Pulaski—Lettie, by Driver (dead) . 2:12¾
Mattie J., ro m, 188—, by Ultimus.. 2:19
Mattie K., b m, 188—, by Sir Charles 2:25½
Mattie Warren, ch m, 1890, by Jaywood—Ruth, by Bald Hornet 2:19¼
Maud A., b m, 188—, by Embassador, dam by Billy Green (trotting 2:29¼) 2:28½
Maud A., b m, 187—, by St. Nicholas, dam by son of Royal George....... 2:26¼
Maud Adair, b m, 1884, by Floramour —Bello 2:18
Maud B., b m, 188—, by Capt. Davis 2:29¼
Maud B., ch m. 1886, by King Legacy—Zephyr 2:20
Maud C., b m, 188—, by Architect.. 2:26½
Maud Clay, ch m, 188—, by Charley Clay, dam by Satellite 2:23¼
Maude, b m, 1877, by Bertrand Black Hawk—Selby Mare, by Hamilton Chief 2:20
Maud Elenah, ch m, 188—, by Harry Knox 2:19¼
Maud F., b m, 188—, by Critic 2:24¼
Maud H., br m, 1885, by Harold—Lady Faulkner, by Hoffman's Mountain Boy 2:20½
Maud K., br m, 188—, ... 2:29¼
Maud L., gr m, 188—, by Lapadist Chief 2:24½
Maud M., b m, 1888, by Adrian Wilkes Wilkes—Flash, by Alfred........... 2:15½
Maud M., b m, 188—, ... 2:26½
Maud M., gr m, 188—, by Cheatham 2:21
Maud Mac, br m, 188—, by Mount Morris 2:30
Maud McGregor, b m, 1886, by Capt. McGregor 2:20½
Maud Muller, ro m, 188—, by Atlantic 2:25
Maud Neff, ro m, 1880, by Sea Foam 2:19
Maud P., ch m, 1885, by Pepper's Pharaoh—Birdie Clay, by Little Arthur 2:15¼
Maud P., gr m, 1885, by Frank A.—Finney Mare 2:14¼
Maud Z., rn m, 188—, ... 2:29¾
Maumee, b m, 188—, by The Baron.. 2:28¾
Mauprat, blk s, 1887, by Egbert—Jessie Blackwood, by Blackwood ... 2:20
Maurice Mullens, b g, 188—, by Volunteer Duroc 2:26½
Max, b g, 188—, by Agitator 2:27
Maxey B., b s, 1890, by Ashland Wilkes—Carrie B, by Burger (trotting 2:28½) 2:23½
Maxie B., b g, 188—, by Billy Cobb, dam by Magna Charta............ 2:29¼
Maxie B., b g, 188—, ... 2:22
Maxwell Star, blk g, 1886, by Reynold's John Morgan—Florence, by Tom Gregory 2:24½
May Be, br m, 188—, by Elector—Maggie Mitchell, by Hero Hamble-

tonian 2:23¼
May D., br m, 188—, ... 2:21¾
May Eddy, b m, 1887, by Jerome Eddy—Flora Hebel, by Young Dick Taylor (trotting 2:25½) (dead)...... 2:22½
Mayflower, b m, 188—, by Dave Bonner 2.23½
Mayflower, b m, 188—, by Allen Stonay 2:25½
Mayhill, b m, 1887, by Edgehill—Maywood, by Blackwood (trotting 2:19) 2.17¼
May Marshall, b m, 1887, by Billy Wilkes—Bennie Sydner, by Mambrino Abdallah 2:08¼
May Murphy, b m, 188—, by Hibbard Wilkes 2:29¾
May Temple, blk m, 1882, by Prince Imperial—Star of Birmingham, by Magnolia 2:30
Maywood, b m, 187—, by Limber Bill—Molly White, by Sadding Buck 2:27¼
Mc O'dell, ch g, 188—, by Silver Heel 2:28½
Mecca, b s, 1884, by Nutwood—Hyacinthe, by Volunteer 2.19¼
M. Compton, b g, 188—, by Baker Bashaw 2:20½
Meacham, b g, 188—, by Lexington Chief Jr. 2:20
Mechanic Girl, gr m, 188—, by Le Blanc Horse (dead) 2:24½
Medeoyone, b s, 188—, by Alcyone—Rose Medium, by Happy Medium.. 2:25
Mediator, blk s, 1888, by Grand Regent—Ailsie, by Happy Medium.... 2:30
Medley, b s, 188—, by Claimant.... 2:23½
Melson, b s, 1891, by Token P., ... 2:28½
Melwood, rn g, 188—, ... 2:29¼
Menegain, ch m, 188—, by Menelaus Jr. 2:15
Mentor Maid, ch m, 1890, by St. Omer 2:27¼
Mephisto, ch s, 1890, by Sidney, dam by Guy Wilkes 2.21¼
Mercurius, b s, 1886, by Olmedo Wilkes—Belladonna, by Woodlawn 2:22¼
Mercury, ch s, 1880, by Summit—Bird, by Bashaw Webb 2:24¾
Mercury, b s, 188—, by Sidney—Juno, by Buccaneer 2:21
Merit, b g, 188—, by Regalia. 2:23
Merit, blk m, 1887, by Dictator Jr.—Lady Turner, by Harry Turner 2:18½
Merrill, br g, 1882, by Dakota—Flora 2:21¼
Merrill, ch s, 188—, by Nelson, dam by Watchmaker 2:24½
Merrimark, b m, 1890, by Prince Bismarck—Maggie Shrader, by Shrader 2.18¾
Merry Boy, b g, 188—, by Sutton D. 2:24¼
Merry Chimes, b s, 1888, by Chimes—Hypatia, by Blackwood Chief.... 2:08½
Merry Legs, b m, 188—, by Strideaway 2:15¼
Mertie, ch m, 1882, by Flying Indian 2:25½
Messina Boy, b g, 188—, by Walkill—Gypsy 2:16¼
Michigan Mattie, b m, 1883, by Pilot Medium—Prairie Girl, by Landseer 2:26¾
Midget, b m, 188—, by Emmet Clay.. 2:24½
Midland Maid, br m, 188—, by Carlton—Dolly 2.21½
Midnight, blk g, 188—, by Warwick Boy 2.20¼
Midnight, blk s, 1885, by Nigger Boy—Starlight 2:17¼
Midnight Bell, b m, 188—, by Harry Green 2:26¼
Mikado, b g, 1886, by Maxim—Cicada, by Clermont 2:13

Mike, b g, 188—, ... 2:28½
Mike, ch g, 188—, by Frenchman 2:15
Mike Logan Jr., b s, 188—, by Mike Logan 2:23
Mike Wilkes, b g, 1875, by George Wilkes—Nelly B., by Harry B. Patchen (trotting 2 26½) (dead) 2:15¾
Milan, b s, 188—, by Victor Bismarck 2:29
Milk Shake, gr g, 188—, ... 2:22½
Milkmaid, ch m, 188—, by Gen Turner 2:27¼
Mill Lady, b m, 1891, by Count Wilkes—Mill Girl, by Jay Gould (trotting 2:26¼) 2:30
Miller Boy, b g, 188—, by Hoosier Tom 2.18
Miller Ward, b s, 1888, by Bourbon Wilkes—Daisy K., by Kitchen's Telegraph 2:16½
Millie A., b m, 188—, by Goldbar 2.23
Milo, gr g, 188—, by George Milo . 2:27½
Mink, b g, 188—, ... 2 22
Minnehaha, b m, 1892, by Mark Sirius, dam by Blue Bull 2.27¼
Minnie, b m, 1889, by Edgehill—Niles, by Ledger 2.29¼
Minnie, b m, 188—, by Sweep 2.29½
Minnie A., blk m, 1886, by Clinker—Bally 2.19¼
Minnieator, b m, 1887, by Delineator—Lucy, by Estell Eric 2 25½
Minnie Barb, b m, 188—, by Mambrino Logan 2.26
Minnie Bell, blk m, 188—, by Mambrino Davis 2:24¼
Minnie C., b m, 188—, by Wilksonian 2.20¼
Minnie C., b m, 1886, by Indiana Boy—Lucy 2:20
Minnie Cassell, b m, 1884, by Dictator—Creta, by Sam Broadus ... 2:16¼
Minnie F., b m, 1887, by Bob Patterson—Grey Molly, by George Gordon 2:23¼
Minnie G., g m, 188—, by Stillson Jr. 2:27¼
Minnie H., br m, 1887, by Legal Tender Jr.—Minnie F., by Joe Jefferson 2:24¾
Minnie Hanks, b m, 188—, by Dr. Herr 2:29
Minnie Higgins, b m, 188—, by Billy 2:10½
Minnie Holden, b m, 188—, by Rattler Brooks, dam by Locomotive 2:15½
Minnie Irene, ch m, 1891, by Tecumseh 2:25
Minnie K., b m, 1880, by Billy Cone—Bird 2.18¾
Minnie L., blk m, 188—, by Gen. Lee 2:24
Minnie L., gr m, 188—, by Rex Hiatoga 2.29¼
Minnie M., b m, 1884, by Wapsie—Fanny, by Panic 2:24¼
Minnie May, b m, 188—, by Aristocrat 2:27½
Minnie Martin, b m, 188—, by Jim Wilson 2:24¾
Minnie P., b m, 188—, ... 2:16¼
Minnie Palmer, rn m, 187—, by Tempest Jr. 2:30
Minnie R., br m, 187—, by J. C. Breckinridge (trotting 2:19) 2:16½
Minnie R., dn m, 188—, by Rescue (trotting 2:25) 2 20¼
Minnie R., br m, 1887, by George Gift—Nell 2:24¼
Minnie Roberts, b m, 1889, by Wagner Bashaw 2.22¼
Minnie T., b m, 188—, by Tramp Panic 2:30
Minnie Taylor, b m, 188—, by Clipper 2:30
Minnie V., b m, 188—.............. 2:24¼

Minnie Wilkes, br m, 1884, by Ira Wilkes, dam by Mambrino Excelsior 2.20½

Minnie Young, b m, 188—, by Almont Chief.......... 2·28

Min Young, ch g, 1886, by Harry Green—Fanny E., by Scott's Hiatoga.......... 2 16½

Miss Annie, blk m, 1886, by Mambrino Hipple.......... 2:24¼

Miss Bruce, ch m, 1882, by Ben Bruce—Old Queen, by Black Harry Clay.. 2:20

Miss Charley Jo John, ch m, 188—, by Tramp—Belle, by Granite State.... 2:29¼

Miss Copeland, gr m, 188—, by Almont Star.......... 2.25¼

Miss Crull, b m, 188—, by Gooding's Champion.......... 2.26

Miss Cumskey, b m, 188—, by Embassador, dam by Harry Scott.......... 2:22¼

Miss Garfield, b m, 1888, by Garfield—Nell, by Whalebone.......... 2 21¾

Miss Mamie, b m, 188—.......... 2.29¼

Miss Maybee, br m, 188—, by Miner's Pilot.......... 2:29¼

Miss McGinty, dn m, 188—, by Maplewood Chief.......... 2.24

Miss Mouser, b m, 187—.......... 2:25

Miss Pawley, ro m, 188—, by Bay Hawk.......... 2.21¼

Miss Quickly, ch m, 1892, by Fergus McGregor.......... 2.24¼

Miss Ridgeway, ro m, 188—, by Lochinvar.......... 2.29½

Miss Williams, b m, 1891, by Williams, dam by Capoul.......... 2.16¼

Miss Woodford, b m, 1889, by Sam Purdy, dam by Orange Bud.......... 2:19¼

Mistake, rn m, 187—.......... 2:29¼

Mistrea, br m, 188—, by Stratford.... 2:23¼

Misty Morning, b m, 1887, by Accidental—Fanny.......... 2 24¼

Misty Morning, ch g, 188—, by George Hall.......... 2 25¼

Mite, b m, 1891, by Prinmont.......... 2:26¼

M. K., dn g, 188—, by Grey Eagle.... 2 19¾

M. L. Hare, b s, 188—, by Hambrino. 2.19

Modern Belle, b m, 1890, by Elyria—Pollywog, by PilotWilkes.......... 2.26¼

Molly Allen, blk m, 1889, by Mambrino Wilkes—Lady Allen, by Vick's Ethan Allen Jr.......... 2 20½

Molly B., b m, 188—.......... 2 25

Molly B., b m, 188—, by Beecher..... 2.29¼

Molly Brown, b m, 188—.......... 2:28½

Molly Clark, b m, 188—, by Bacon's Ethan Allen.......... 2 26¾

Molly Cooper, ch m, 188—.......... 2:24

Molly F., ro m, 1886, by Monarch Jr.—Rosa F., by Don J. Robinson...... 2.25

Molly Gibson, b m, 188—, by Stratagem.......... 2:23½

Molly Hayden, rn m, 188—, by Blue Duster.......... 2 27¼

Molly Hooper, b m, 1887, by Carver—Lady Peck, by Black Bashaw....... 2:24½

Molly L., br m, 187—, by Ballard's C. M. Clay Jr., dam by Morse Horse... 2:26½

Molly Malloy, b m, 1886, by Red Wilkes—Hugueley, by John Dillard. 2:20

Molly McCaully, b m, 188—, by Elector.......... 2:16¾

Molly Pitcher, b m, 188—, by Thorndale Chief.......... 2 23¼

Molly S., ch m, 188—, by Oxford Boy. 2.27¼

Molly Slimmer, b m, 1891, by Pilot Medium.......... 2 23½

Mona, b m, 1887, by Jay Gould Jr.—Louise H., by Hamlin's Almont Jr.. 2:24¼

Monabel, br s, 1891, by St. Bel—Almona, by Almont.......... 2:18

Monadel, br s, 1889, by Monon—Adele, by Rysdyk's Hambletonian (dead).. 2 18¾

Monbars, blk s, 1889, by Eagle Bird—Lady Maud, by Gen. Knox (trotting 2.11¾).......... 2:16¾

Monita, blk m, 1887, by Patchen Wilkes—Honda, by Wedgewood..... 2.19¼

Monk, b s, 188—.......... 2.23½

Monkey Rolla, b g, 188—, by Tempest Jr.......... 2:15½

Monkey Wonder, ch s, 1888, by Major Wonder.......... 2.29¼

Monogram, b s, 1886, by Red Pilot—Willie, by Gibson's John Dillard Jr. 2 20¼

Monreo, b s, 188—, by Tennessee Wilkes.......... 2.26¼

Monreve, b g, 188—, pedigree not traced.......... 2:19¼

Monroe Brister, b s, 1883, by Red Dick—Jane, by Curtis Horse....... 2 20

Monroe S., b s, 1885, by Monroe Chief—Lurline, by Belle Alta.......... 2:20

Monset, blk s, 188—.......... 2:29

Montaigne, ch s, 1883, by Bourbon Wilkes—Mary Thomas, by Abdallah Mambrino (dead).......... 2 27¼

Montana Wilkes, br s, 1883, by Red Wilkes—Eva, by Lumber.......... 2.17

Mont Blanc, b m, 188—, by Matterhorn.......... 2:30

Monte, blk g, 188—, by Abdallah Prince — Lady Stow, by Putnam Horse.......... 2 26¼

Monte, b s, 188—, by Monte Christo, dam by George Wilkes.......... 2:23¼

Monte Christo, b g, 188—, by Little Wonder—Orphan Lass.......... 2.18½

Monteg, br s, 188—, by Almont Raven—Topsey, by Brougham.......... 2:29½

Montezuma, br s, 1880, by Alcantara—Winona, by Curtis' Hambletonian.. 2.29¾

Montgomery Wilson, gr g, 188—, by Jim Wilson.......... 2:27

Montrose, ch g, 188—, by McCurdy's Hambletonian—Ellen.......... 2:24¼

Moonstone, blk m, 1889, by Mambrino King—Clarice, by Hamlin's Almont Jr.......... 2.09¾

Mordica, b m, 188—, by Messenger Wilkes—Mojeska, by Enfield........ 2.20¾

Morena, b m, 1888, by Tennessee Wilkes — Lizzie Moore, by Gibson's Tom Hal.......... 2:24

Morganthaler, rn g, 188—, by Van Morgan.......... 2.29¾

Moscow, gr m, 1886, by Red Oak—Shoo Fly, by Legal Tender......... 2:20

Motion Jr., ch s, 188—, by Motion.... 2.24¾

Motto, b s, 1883, by Maxim — Miss Herr, by Mambrino Patchen........ 2:20

Mountain Boy, b g, 188—, by Blazing Star.......... 2·27

Mountain Maid, br m, 188—, by Hannis.......... 2:27¼

Mountain Pink, b m, 1888, by Ellerslie Wilkes—Kit, by Edgewater.......... 2:15¼

Mountain Queen, b m, 188—, by Belvoir.......... 2:24½

Moxie, b g, 188—, by Warwick Boy.. 2:27¼

Moxie, b s, 188—, by Barnes' Dictator Chief.......... 2:25

Moxie Hiatoga, b s, 1885, by Proclamation—Kitty Foster, by Old Gurney.......... 2:21¼

Moyer, ch g, 188—, by El Mahdi...... 2.23

Mozanetta, b m, 188—.......... 2:28

Muggins, b g, 188—.......... 2·26¾

Muggins, b s, 1884, by Strathmore,

dam by Norman Jr.................... 2:25
Mugwump, b g, 188—, by Ensign..... 2:21¼
Mugwump, br g, 1885, by Pilot Chief. 2:20¼
Mutual, b m, 188—, by American Boy. 2:29¼
Myra Wilkes, g m, 188—, by Mambrino Wilkes.................. 2:24¾
Myronet, b m, 188—, by Diplomat.... 2:29¼
Myrtle S., b m, 1882, by Billy Cone—Lulu, by Green Mountain Morgan... 2:21¼
Nada, b m, 1890, by King Medium—Weta.............................. 2:25
Nana, b m, 188—.................... 2:25
Nancy Harkaway, b m, 188—, by Harkaway 2.25¾
Nancy Time, ch m, 188—, by Phillip's Blue Bull........................ 2:29¼
Nannie E., b m, 1889, by Reno Defiance—Lucy Q., by McKinney Horse 2:17¼
Nannie W., b m, 188—, by Red Wilkes, dam by Venture............ 2:22
Nannie Ward, b m, 1888, by McCurdy's Hambletonian—Daisy, by Lookout................................ 2:16
Natalie Wilkes, b m, 1889, by Red Wilkes—Rosalie Wilkes, by George Wilkes.............................. 2.26¼
Nate O., b g, 1884, by Nathan Mills—Lady Ellis, by Bucklin's Champion Black Hawk.......................... 2:24¼
Nathan P., b g, 188—, by Theron..... 2:28
Natie, ch g, 188—, by Job C.......... 2:27¼
Naughty Girl, b m, 1889, by Connaught—Fannie Stranger, by Chestnut Tom.......................... 2:23½
Neatbud, b s, 1887, by Neatwood—Rosebud, by Sweepstakes........... 2:26
Ned, b g, 188—..................... 2:23¼
Ned, gr s, 186—, (dead).............. 2:25
Ned, b g, 186—, (dead).............. 2:28
Ned B., b g, 188—, by Ned Warfield—Hattie, by Simm's Clark Chief Jr.. 2:18¼
Neddie H., b g, 1884, by Messenger Chief, dam by Gill's Vermont....... 2:17¼
Ned Forrester, ch g, 187—, by Young Forrester............................ 2:23½
Ned H., b g, 188—, by Gen. Grant.... 2:24¼
Ned Hanlon, blk g, 188—, by Kimball Morgan.......................... 2:26½
Ned Hull, gr g, 188—, by Hull........ 2:30
Ned M., ch g, 1882, by Billy Hibbard—Polly, by Richner's Hambletonian............................. 2:24¼
Ned Rawlin, b g, 188—, by Greenback 2:30
Ned V., b s, 1884, by Detractor—Silkey, by Rushville................ 2:19¼
Ned Winslow, blk g, 1881, by Tom Benton—Brown Jenny, by David Hill Jr.................................. 2:12¾
Neernut, b s, 1891 .... 2:27¼
Nelly, b m, 188—, by Abdamed Allen. 2:24¾
Nelly B., gr m, 1878, by Pocahontas Boy—Lady McGee, by Blue Bull.... 2:21
Nelly B., ro m, 188—, by Old John.... 2:23
Nelly B., b m, 1884, by Notable—Jenny.............................. 2:14¾
Nelly B., ch m, 188—................ 2:20
Nelly B., b m, 188—, by Ernest....... 2:16¾
Nelly B., b m, 188—, by William Rysdyk Jr.............................. 2:29¾
Nelly C., b m, 188—, by Garret Wilkes 2:24¼
Nelly Davis, b m, 1868, by Kremer's Rainbow............................ 2 24¼
Nelly F., b m, 1888, by Anteros—Sharlie, by Roger Hanson (trotting 2:25) 2:13¼
Nelly G., ch m, 188—, by McCurdy .. 2:27¼
Nelly G., b m, 188—, by Montgomery.. 2:26¼
Nelly Gray, gr m, 186—, by Gray Eagle (dead) 2:24
Nelly Gray, g m, 188—, by Conway.. 2:25½
Nelly Green, ch m, 188—, by Wilkie Collins 2:29
Nelly H., b m, 188—................. 2:22
Nelly Hastings, b m, 188—, by Ned Hastings 2:27¾
Nelly I., br m, 188—, by Booth 2:15
Nelly June, gr m, 1880, by Highland Gray,—Belle Hammond, by Honest Dan 2:24¼
Nelly M., ch m, 188—, by Butler's Bashaw 2:15½
Nelly M., br m, 188—, by Mohawk Chief 2:29½
Nelly Mayo, b m, 1885, by Pocahontas Abdallah—Jenny F., by Mercury 2:30
Nelly Mambrino, b m, 1887, by Meredith—Mambrinette, by Kentucky Prince Jr. 2:18¼
Nelly McCrory, b m, 1889, by Legal Tender Jr.—Lucy, by Tobe Jr..... 2:18¼
Nelly Neal, b m, 1890, by Agricola... 2.26½
Nelly O., br m, 188—, by Henry Mambrino 2:23¼
Nelly O., ch m, 1884, by Bald Chief Jr.—Bernice, by Hailstorm........ 2:13¼
Nelly R., b m, 188—.................. 2:22½
Nelly R., br m, 187—................ 2:17¾
Nellie R., blk m, 188—, by Walkill Jr.. 2:25½
Nelly S., g m, 188—, by Bayonne Prince—Mary C., by Harry Wood... 2:22¼
Nelly S., b m, 1884, by Pickett (trotting 2:21¼) 2:16¼
Nelly Seal, blk m, 188— 2:26½
Nelly Shaw, dn m, 187—.............. 2:26¾
Nelly Sprague, b m, 188—, by Alexander Sprague 2:22½
Nelly Tasco, rn m, 188—, by Tasco.. 2.23½
Nelly Turner, b m, 1887, by Hunt's Blue Bull—Molly, by High Jack.... 2:23¾
Nelly W., b m, 188—, by Raven Wilkes 2:27¼
Nelly Y., b m, 188—, by Hamlin's Almont Jr. 2:25½
Nelson Allen, blk s, 1891, by Nelson, dam by Hugenot.................... 2:29¼
Nels Randall, ch s, 188—, by Pocahontas Sam.......................... 2:29¾
Nettie, b m, 188—, by Bright Light. 2:22¼
Nettie C., b m, 188—, by Moonstone—Maggie, by Fields' Royal George.. 2:23½
Nettie D., b m, 188—, by Patchen Volunteer 2:24¼
Nettie E. Hontas, ch m, 188—, by Harry Hontas—Flora E., by Scott's Hiatoga 2:29½
Nettie Field, b m, 1887, by Fairy Gift—Nettie, by Volunteer 2:23
Nettie Green, cr m, 188—, by Billy Green—Kitty Scott, by Scott's Hiatoga 2.25
Nettie Hoppin, ch m, 187—, by Longstrider, dam by Smoke Boy 2:20
Nettie Swan, b m, 188—, by Accidental 2.29
Nettie Wilkes, ch m, 188—, by Adrian Wilkes 2.19¼
Nettie Keenan, b s, 188—, by George Gordon—Old Crow 2:26½
Nettlewood, b s, 1890, by Merchant —Gloria, by Almont Pilot 2:23
Nevada, b s, 1877, by Gen. Reno—Marysville Queen, by Signal 2:24¼
Nevins' First, b s, 1884, by Nevins—Polka, by Pocahontas Boy 2:19
Newcastle, ch g, 1888, by Kentucky Prince—Dolly by Niagara Cham-

G. BOWERMAN, Lexington, Ky.

When Silicon placed the race record for two-year-olds at 2:15¾
George Bowerman was up behind the winner.

M. BOWERMAN, LEXINGTON, KY.
M. Bowerman cut the four-year-old trotting record
to 2:10 with Mcquette.

pion (dead) 2:29¼
New Dominion, ch s, 188—, by Do-
    minion 2:24¼
New Era, ch g, 1890, by Hamble-
    tonian Wilkes.... .... 2·13
New Hope, blk g, 187— 2:16
Newkirk, b g, by Clinker............ 2:25½
New Medium, b s, 188—, by Happy
    Medium, dam by Strader's Cassius
    M. Clay Jr. 2:30
Newsboy, dn g 1886, by Brentwood
    —Lemons, by Dan Allen 2:12¾
News Boy, b s, 1885, by Oscar, or
    Byerly Abdallah—Nettie, by Gray's
    Tom Hal 2:22¼
Nicoll, gr g, 188—, by John Bell, dam
    by Gibson's Tom Hal 2:19¼
Nicholas B., gr s, 188—, by Ohio
    Knickerbocker.... .... 2:19½
Nicolette, blk s, 1887, by Adrian
    Wilkes—Edwina, by Blackwood .. 2:20¼
Nidia, b m, 1890, by Wayne Wilkes—
    Carrie F., by Almont Pilot 2:13¼
Nigger, b g, 187—.................... 2:30
Nigger Baby, blk g, 188— 2:21¼
Nigger Boy, blk g, 1887, by Black
    Prince Jr., dam by L. C. Lee...... 2:19¼
Nigger Boy, blk g, 186— (dead) 2:25¾
Nightingale, ch m, 1883, by Alcan-
    tara—Neoscaletta, by Daniel Lam-
    bert 2:13½
Nimrod, ch g, 186—, by Missouri Chief,
    dam by Williamson's Belmont ..... 2·19¾
Nina, br m, 1880, by Eclaire 2:22¼
Nina W., ch m, 1886, by J. W Bailey
    —Maud W., by George Miller.... 2:25
Nodine, b g, 1884, by Peacemaker—
    Lady Burgett 2:19¾
Non Parole, gr m, 1888, by American
    Boy—Maud L., by Gray Charley.. 2:18¼
Noonday, b g, 187— 2.27
No Other Kid, b g, 188—, by Illinois
    Chief 2:28¼
N. Q Lancewood, ch m, 188—, by
    Fleetwood 2:25¼
Nora L, b m, 188—, by Norwood Sta · 2·20¼
Nora Marks, b m, 1886, by Rounds'
    Sprague—Vellin Danville, by Dan-
    ville Boy 2:23¼
Nora T., gr m, 188—,............... 2:25¼
Nordeck, b g, 188—, by Bassett M... 2·30
Norristown, b g, 188—................ 2·24¼
Northwest, b s, 1885, by Egmont—Tot,
    by Dictator (trotting 2:22½)...... 2:15
Notion, b s, 1889, by St Bel — Rit-
    chelders, by Messenger Chief 2:16
No Trouble, b m, 1884, by Dick Tur-
    pin 2.21¼
Novice, ch m 1890, by Tennessee
    Wilkes—Ida Elliott, by Harold 2:24¼
Nox, b m, 1887, by Nutwood—Four
    Lines, by Blackwood .... 2·25¼
Noxall, b s, 188—, by Roseberry 2:18
Nutcoal, ch s, 1886, by Nutwood —
    Bessie, by Temptation 2:24
Nutford, ch s, 1886, by Abbottsford
    —Annie Nutwood, by Nutwood 2:15
Nuthurst, ch s, 1886, by Nutwood—
    Enterprise, by Onward 2:12
Nutmage, b g, 188—, by Blind Bashaw 2:20¼
Nutmeg, b m, 1886, by Richwood—
    Sheila, by Dauntless 2:27¼
Nutpan, br s, 1887, by Nutwood—Issa-
    quena, by Pancoast 2:19¼
Nutpine, ch s, 1887, by Nutwood—
    Maggie Wilkes, by George Wilkes 2:15¼
Nutrose, b s 1887, by Nutwood—
    Moss Rose, by Woodford Mambrino 2:22

Nutwood Wilkes, b s, 188—, by Nut-
    wood 2.25¼
Nydia, Wilkes, b m, 1887, by Baron
    Wilkes—Anne Belle, by Nutwood . 2.12¾
Oklahoma, b m, 188—, by Cham-
    pion Wilkes .... 2·28
Oakland, blk s, 1887, by Detractor—
    Jule, by Mambrino Sotham 2:16
Oceana Prince, b g, 188—, by Oceana
    Chief 2:25
O'Connell, b g 188—, by Woodland,
    dam by Olympus 2:30
Oddfellow, ch g, 186—, (dead) .... 2·28½
Odessa Clipper, b g, 188—, by Al
    West Jr. 2:23¾
Odilla, b m, 890, by Onward—Rachael
    Russell, by Woodford Abdallah .. 2:24½
O B., ch g, 188—, by Strathmore.... 2:26¼
Ohio Boy, b s, 188—, by Cardinal.... 2.24¼
Ohio Maid, rn m, 187—,............. 2:28
Old Hunter, ch s, 187—,............. 2:29¼
Ole Bull, b g, 188—, by Denmark.... 2·26½
Ollie Belle, b m, 187—, by Tempest
    Jr. 2:23½
Oliver C., b g, 188—, by Marlborough 2:26¼
Oliver E., gr g, 188—,............... 2:29
Olivette, br m, 188—, by Director .. 2:28½
Olivette, ch m, 188—, by Johnny Mac. 2.20
Omega, rn m, 188—, by Walker Mor-
    rill 2:22½
Ome D., b m, 1881, by Warwick Boy
    Tackey, by Happy Medium 2.20
Ouline, b s, 1890, by Shadeland On-
    ward—Angelina, by Chester Chief 2·04
Ontario, blk g, 188—................ 2:29½
Ontonian, b s, 1889, by Shadeland
    Onward—Angelina, by Chester Chief
    (dead) 2:07½
Onward, blk g, 186—, by Chieftain
    (dead) 2:24¾
Onward Boy, b s, 1887, by Prodigal
    —Bessie B., by Blanco Abdallah.... 2:24¼
Onyx, blk s, 188—, by Valentine
    Swigert 2.20¾
Ophelia, gr m, 188—, by Alfred.... 2:16¼
Opulence, blk s, 188—, by Ferguson
    —Lady McKinney, by Sweepstakes 2·29½
Oran C., gr g, 1887, by Orion—Jenny
    Ross, by Crook's Corbeau 2:22¾
Original Package, b g, 188— 2:28
Orland, ro g, 1888, by Upright—Top-
    sy, by Nephew Jr. 2:23¼
Orley Wilkes, br s, 188—, by Seal-
    skin Wilkes 2:27
Orphan Alice, b m, 188—, by Mam-
    brino Rescue .... 2·27¼
Orienta, b m, 188—, by Aberdeen.... 2:28
Orlinda Richmond, b m, 188—, by A.
    W. Richmond, dam by Ulster Chief. 2:15
Orphan Boy, b g, 188—, by Walker
    Morrill 2.24¼
Orphan Boy, b s, 1888, by George
    Steck—Doska, by Bald Stockings... 2:18
Oscar, b s, 188—, by De Soto. 2:26¼
Osceola, bl g, 1880, by Blue Vein—Pol-
    ly, by Cadmus 2:18
Otta Neely, b m, 188—, by Ottawa
    Chief............................. 2:28
Otis M., b s, 188—, by Triceps........ 2:26¼
Otto, b g, 188—, by Onawa.......... 2·23¼
Otto W., b s, 1887, by Dall Brino—
    Bessie B., by Teeter's Horse 2:13¼
Ouida, b m, 188—,.................... 2:24
Our Boy, b g, 188—, by Vernon Boy—
    Black Bess, by Wapsie 2:17½
Our Dick, b g, 188—, by Gibraltar ... 2:10¼
Our Dick, b g, 188—, by Redwood.... 2:23¼
Our Nora, bl m, 188—, by Alamosa—

Trevena mare .... 2·17
Out of Sight, b g, 188—, ... 2.19¼
Overbrook, b g, 188—, ... 2 24¼
Ovid, b s, 188—, by Hamlin's Almont Jr.—Silk, by Alcantara 2.15½
Oxygen, ch g, 187—, by Simpson's Capt. Walker 2:30
Pacing Phallas, blk g, 188—, by Sha·k 2·2.
Palmetto, br s, 1886, by Brown Hal—Maggie, by Enterprise 2 12¾
Palo Alto Chimes, b s, 1888, by Chimes—Velvet, by Mambrino King 2:17½
Panic, b s, 188—, by Algiers 2 28¼
Panama Maid, ch m, 1890, by Panama—Red Girl 2 20
Pansy Blossom, gr m, 1889, by Gen. Wilkes, dam by Harrodsburg Boy.. 2:12
Pansy L., gr m, 1888, by Pan—Nelly Conner, by Legal Tender, Jr 2 23½
Paola, ch m, 1888, by Frank Logan—Fanny Logan, by Little Logan. ... 2.20
Pappoose, b m, 1886, by Ultimus, dam by Gill's Vermont 2.18¼
Parker, b s, 1883, by Alcantara—Marie, by Blackstone 2:28½
Parker, ch g, 188—, by Wilson, dam by Daniel Lambert 2.19½
Passmont, br s, 1885, by Pasacas—Piccola, by Harvester 2 18¼
Pascal, b g, 188—, by Victor, dam by California Brock 2:21¾
Pat, b g, 188—, ... 2 24½
Patasco, br s, 1887, by Brown Hal—Yellow Mag, by Pointer's Slasher.. 2:24¾
Pat Bruen, ch g, 1880, by Ajax—Fashion, by Millett Horse.......... 2.24
Patchen T., b g, 1877, by Shadow—Nelly Bell, by Hole-in-the-Day..... 2.24¼
Pat Delaney, b g, 1890, by Anderson Wilkes—Steinlet, by Steinway (dead). 2:18½
Pat Harold, b s, 1884, by De Soto—Maggie Patton, by Masteriode.. ... 2:21
Pat Heron, b g, 188—, by Pharon, dam dam by Honest John 2.17¼
Pat Legg, bl g, 1886, by Mambrino Redmon.......... 2·25
Pat Murphy, br g, 188—, by Palmetto—Molly Murphy, by Dodson's Davy Crockett 2 20
Pat O'Brien, br s, 188—, by Billy Davis 2 21¼
Patoche, b m, 1890, by Princeps, dam by George Wilkes 2.27¼
Patrick Henry, br s, 188—, by Ajax, dam by Harold 2.26¾
Patrick's Pacer, b g, 188—, by Sharon Benton 2 21¾
Patrol, b g, 188—, by Constellation.. 2.14½
Patsey Clinker, gr g, 1877, by Charley—Nellie 2 20
Patsey K., b g, 1885, by Highlander Boy—Sue, by Red Eye.......... 2:22¼
Patti, b s, 188—, ... 2.22
Pattie Belle, b m, 1891, by Don Pizarro, dam by Messenger Chief ... 2 23
Pattie D., ch m., 188—, by Ultimus.. 2·12¼
Pattie West, b m, 1884, by Al West—Patti Dodd .... 2·17
Paul, ch g, 188—, by Bald Hornet—Lucy .... 2·09½
Paul Clifford, b s, 188—, by Tennessee Wilkes 2 20½
Pauline H., b m, 1888, by Kidnapper—Nicol Mare (trotting 2·24) 2:17½
Paul M., b g, 1884, by Manchester—Mary, by Louis Napoleon 2 24¼
Payne Stone, b g, 188—, by Judge Salisbury 2 25¼
Payrock, b g, 188—, by Diplomat, dam by St Nicholas 2.28½
Peacock, gr s, 1878, by Whipple's Hambletonian—Jane McLane, by Budd Doble 2 23¼
Pearl, wh m, 187—, ... 2 27½
Pearl, b m, 188—, by Pomeroy—Nell Morgan, by Judge Advocate 2 19¼
Pearl L., ch m, 188—, by Elgin Boy... 2 23
Pearl Logan, b m, 188—, by Mambrino Logan 2 26¼
Pearl R., b m, 1883, by Lucas Brodhead—Maud Medium, by Happy Medium 2.17½
Pedro, b g, 188—, ... 2.26¾
Peerless, b m, 188—, by Equity Wilkes 2:13¼
Peleg, b s, 1890, by Reno Defiance—Lucy, by McKenney Horse (trotting 2.23¼) 2 12¼
Pendleton, b g, 188—, by Hambletonian Downing.......... 2·29¼
Perine, b m, 1890, by Paul Jones Jr.. 2.24¼
Perkins, ch s, 188—, by C. F. Clay—Miss Brewer, by Red Wilkes 2.29¼
Peruvian Bitters, b g, 1879, by Electioneer—Nellie Walker, by Thorndale or son of Edwin Forrest 2 23½
Pet, ro g, 184—, (dead).......... 2 18½
Peter Cooper, br g, 188—, by Steele's Walkill, dam by Golddrop 2:21¼
Peter Piper, b g, 1886, by Nantucket—Puss Miller, by Sir Walter 2.14¼
Peter T., b g, 188—, by Fisk's Mambrino Chief Jr 2:29
Peter V., b s, 188—, by Longstride.. 2 16½
Phantom, b m, 188—, by Steele's Walkill, dam by Billy Bowlegs.......... 2:26½
Pharon, b s, 1887, by Pharos, dam by Antenor 2 16¾
Pharos, b s, 1883, by Phallas—Hoosier Girl, by Blue Bull 2.21½
Phenom, rn s, 1892, by Director—Maud B., by Red Wilkes.......... 2 21½
Phenol, g·m, 188—, by Jersey Wilkes—Adelina, by Egbert 2:16¾
Phil Fowler, ro g, 188—, by Copperbottom 2:26¼
Phillis, b s, 1888, by Masteriode—Comet, by Lexington Chief Jr 2.17½
Phillis Wilkes, b m, 1889, by Balmont Wilkes—Jessie H., by Stephen A Douglass 2 20¼
Phillios, b g, 188—, by Pickering, dam by Nelson's Onward 2.27½
Phylle, b s, 1889, by Patron—Bessie Turner, by Virginius.......... 2 19¼
Pickaway, ch g, 188—, by Red Joe .. 2 16¾
Pierpont Girl, blk m, 188—, by Atlantic 2 24¾
Pierron, ch g, 1890, by Iliad, dam by Onward 2 15
Pilatoga, ch s, 1886, by Bayard—Jenny, by Scott's Hiatoga.......... 2.20¼
Pilot Bird, b m, 1886, by Pilot Knox—Lil Williams, by Kohinoor 2.22¾
Pilot Gift, br s, 1883, by Fairy Gift—Pussy .... 2·13½
Pilot Knox, br s, 1875, by Black Pilot—Nancy Knox, by Col. Ellsworth (trotting 2.19¾) 2.20½
Pilot Wilkes, b s, 1880, by George Wilkes—Grace, by Pilot Jr. 2 23
Pine Level, gr g, 188—, ... 2.22¼
Pinewood, b s, 1890, by Artemas—Mamie F., by Joe Jefferson 2 20
Piquant, b g, 188—, by Sea Bird .. 2 29¼
Pistachio, ch s, 1886, by Belmont—Miss Russell, by Pilot Jr 2:29¼
Pixley Boy, br s, 1884, by Pocahontas

Sam—Bird, by George Bell 2:12
P. J., b g, 1892, by President Wilkes. 2:23¾
Play Fair, b s, 188—, by Olmedo Wilkes 2:24½
Plaza, gr s, 1887, by Tennessee Dictator—Claire, by Bayard 2:22¾
Plow Girl, blk m, 188—, by Black Sam 2:26¼
Plunger, b g, 188—, by Gibson's Tom Hal 2:27
Plunkett, b g, 1887, by Strathearn—Fly, by Bulger 2:13¼
Plus, b s, 1886, by Happy Heir—Lady West, by Col. West 2:20½
Plush, ch m, 1880, by Don J. Robinson—Stella P., by Magna Charta....... 2:23½
Pluto, ch g, 188—, by Bob Patterson.. 2:26½
Plutowood, b s, 1890, by Pluto—Mollie R., by Recorder 2:20¾
Poca Eagle, b s, 1885, by Pocahontas Sam—Molly Coshow 2:21½
Pocahontas, ch m, 1847, by Iron's Cadmus, dam by Big Shakespeare (dead) 2:17½
Pocahontas, ch m, 187—, by Little Washington, dam by St. Clair...... 2:22½
Pocahontas Prince, blk s, 1884, by Pocahontas Boy—Faro Queen (trotting 2:20½) 2:19¼
Pocahontas Sam, ch s, 1879, by Pocahontas Boy—Fanny, by Blue Bull 2:27¾
Pointer (Kissel's), b g, 1886, by Ravenswood—Molly, by Mohawk.... 2:16½
Polka Hot, b s, 188—, by Elgin Boy... 2:28½
Polly Ann, rn m, 186—, (dead) 2:26½
Polly T., br m, 188—, by Red Bird.. 2:21¼
Pomona, b s, 1887, by Albion—Pansy, by Re-Echo 2:15
Pomp, ch g, 1881, by Dick—Pearl, by Platte Allen 2:17½
Pomp A., br g, 1881, by Mohawk.... 2:24¼
Pompey Jones, gr g, 186—, (dead)..... 2:28½
Po Po Lo, br s, 188—, by Albert Lea, dam by Florida 2:20
Posey Golden, br g, 188—, by son of Golddust (dead) 2:19¼
Prairie Bird, b m, 1867, by Flaxtail—Fashion, by John Baptiste (dead). 2:28¼
Prairie Girl, b m, 1891, by Grey Harry 2:20
Prairie Lily, b m, 1891, by Adrian Wilkes, dam by Hamdallah 2:19¼
Prairie Maid, b m, 1884, by Mammonteer—Prairie Girl, by Brougham 2:30
President, blk s, 1880, by Swigert—Patsey Lee, by Rock 2:23¼
President Wilkes, b s, 1885, by Ashland Wilkes—Caltha Robertson, by Al West (dead) 2:19½
Pressley M., gr g, 188—, by Benson... 2:21¼
Prestoria Wilkes, ch m, 188—, by Anderson Wilkes.......................... 2:22½
Pretension, b s, 1888, by Pretender—Meg Rodman 2:24½
Priest, br g, 188—, ... 2:29¼
Prima Donna, ch m, 1887, by Betterton—Dame Tansey, by Daniel Lambert 2:09¼
Prim Wallace, b m, 1890, by William Wallace—Rachel........................ 2:27½
Prince S., b g, 188—, ... 2:22¼
Prince, rn g, 188—, ... 2:28
Prince, b s, 188—, by Fremont.......... 2:23¼
Prince, br g, 187—, by Missouri Chief dam by Williamson's Belmont 2:23¾
Prince, blk g, 188—, ... 2:30
Prince Albert, b g, 188—, by Hamilton 2:28¼
Prince Alcander, ch s, 1889, by Alcander—Rhea, by Winooski......... 2:17¼
Prince Alcyone, b g, 188—, by Alcyone 2:15½
Prince Almont, b s, 1889, by Almont Medium—Queen of the West, by George M. Patchen Jr. 2:13½
Prince B., blk g, 188—, by Black Republican 2:29½
Prince Brennan, b g, 188—,.......... 2:23
Prince C., b s, 188—, by Cutler.... 2:27½
Prince Columbia, br s, 1881, by Prince Pulaski, dam by Granberry's Slasher 2:20
Prince Edict Jr., ch s, 1886, by Edict—Bell, by High Jack 2:22
Prince Echo, ch s, 1882, by Cloud Mambrino—Lucy, by Pacing Togue. 2:14½
Prince Elwood, ch s, 1890, by Greystone—Juno, by Hambrino......... 2:22¾
Prince Erie, b s, 1886, by Erie Wilkes—Katie C., by Mambrino Patchen.. 2:29½
Prince Farlie, b s, 1886, by Kentucky Prince—Maggie Duroc, by Messenger Duroc 2:30
Prince Frederick, b s, 1883, by Langley's Valentine—Nancy Wise 2:24¼
Prince Gift, b g, 188—, by Hambletonian Gift 2:27¼
Prince Gould, ch g, 188—,........... 2:26½
Prince Hal, br s, 1883, by Brown Hal—Jenny, by Prince Pulaski 2:16¼
Prince Hal, b s, 188—, by King Hal. 2:29¼
Prince M., b g, 188—, by Hotspur Jr., dam by Scott's Hiatoga 2:21¼
Prince Mac, ch g, 188—, by Logan Hambletonian—Jessie Mac.......... 2:19¾
Prince Nutwood, blk s, 1891, by Dexter Prince—Luella, by Nutwood..... 2:21¾
Prince Orange, b s, 1884, by Orange Blossom—Queen Bess, by Backman's Idol 2.25
Prince Pilot, b s, 188—, by Prince Pulaski 2:22½
Prince S., b g, 188—, ... 2:29¼
Princess, b m, 187—,................. 2:27
Princess, ch m, 1892, by Prince, dam by son of Mambrino Howard 2:17¼
Princess, b m, 1874, by Pocahontas Boy—Lady McGee, by Blue Bull .. 2:19¾
Princess Alice, blk m, 1886, by Dexter Prince, dam by Gen. McClellan. 2:16
Princess Alice, gr m, 1890, by Evan Lewis—Frances, by Merit 2:23
Princess Eulalia, b m, 1892, by Emperor Wilkes 2.18¼
Princess H., br m, 188—, by Fleet's Hambletonian 2:23¼
Prince T., rn g, 188—, by Climont... 2:13¾
Princeton R., b s, 1890, by Sphinx.. 2:25¼
Printer Boy, b g, 188—, by Independence 2:29½
Proctor, b s, 1887, by Pancoast—Silence, by Alexander's Abdallah.. 2:17
Procul, blk s, 1889, by Embassador—Kit, by Black Ambassador........ 2:30
Promise, b g, 188—, by Black Wilkes 2:25¼
Pronto, blk s, 1887, by Pancoast—Mercedita, by Cuyler 2:24
Pronto, br g, 187—, by George Fletcher—Snow, by Canadian Lion 2:17¼
Prophet Wilkes, b s, 1882, by George Wilkes—Mollie, by Kentucky Clay.. 2:21¼
Prussian Boy, b g, 1889, by Gen. Benton—Prussian Maid, by Signal 2:26½
Prussian Maid, b m, 186—, by Signal—Lady Jasper 2:19
Psyche, sp m, 1884, by Bayard—Arabian Girl, by Carnac 2:19¼
P. T. Barnum, b g, 188—, by Jim Wilson.................................... 2:22

Pull Back, b g, 188—, by Uncle Ned—Topsey, by Bethel 2:26¼
Puritan, br g, 187—, by Almont 2:16
Quaker Boy, b s, 188—, by Whalebone, dam by Kelly Horse 2:14¼
Quaker K., ch g, 188—, by Wayne Wilson—Nettie, by Col. Howe...... 2:22½
Queen, b m, 188—, by Commander.... 2:19¼
Queen Esther, b m, 1886, by Ajax,—Miss Frost, by Bedford.......... 2:27
Queen Gothard, b m, 1886, by St. Gothard—Mignon Medium, by Happy Medium 2:14½
Queen McGregor, ch m, 188—, by Don McGregor 2:13
Queen of the West, dn m, 186—, (dead) 2:28¾
Queen Stanton, b m, 188—, by Gen. Stanton 2.18
Quicksilver, ch s, 188—, by Silvermine, dam by Hotspur Jr......... 2:26½
Quiz, br m, 1891, by Robin Hood......... 2:17¼
Q. R. Z., ch s, 188—, by Ed Sutherland 2:22¼
Racquet, blk g, 188—, ... 2:20¾
Rahleta, blk m, 1888, by Gambetta Wilkes—Bellfield, by Enfield 2:21¼
Rally Wilkes, b s, 1887, by Allie Wilkes—Bessie Davis.......... 2:20½
Ralph D., b s, 188—, by Allen Sontag 2:26¾
Rambling Dick, b g, 188—, by Joe Coleman 2:27¾
Raritana Boy, g g, 188—, ... 2:28½
Rat, b g, 188—, ... 2:27¼
Rattler, b g, 188—, by Al West...... 2:22½
Rattler, b g, 1886, by St Mark 2:19¼
Rattler Brooks, ch s, 1878, by Earnheart's Brooks, dam by Pat Malone 2:23¼
Rattling Dan, b g, 187—, ... 2:25¼
Rattling Jim, b g, 187—, by Yellow Jacket 2.28
Rattling Jim, b g, 186—, by Flying Hiatoga, (dead) 2:23¾
Ravelli, br s, 1883, by Hermes—Jessie Morrill, by Winthrop Morrill 2:20¾
Raven, blk m, 1877, by Alcantara—Rachel B., by Allie West.......... 2:11¼
Raven Boy, blk g, 1878, by Pocahontas Boy—Tina Wilson, by Legal Tender. 2:15¾
Raven T., blk s, 1877, by Bay Tom Jr.—Kate McCrory, by Coleman's Traveler 2:22¼
Raymond, b g, 188—, by George B.. . 2:19¼
Razor Blade, b g, 188—, by Henry B.. 2:22¼
Razzle Dazzle, b g, 1889, by Prince Medium—Worm Mare 2:22
Reality, b g, 1886, by Polonious, dam by Middletown 2:20½
Reavis, b s, 1888, by Monroe Chief—Belle S. 2:20½
Rebellion, b g, 1875, by Locomotive—Ruby, by Gen Hardee 2:25
Red Bell, ch s, 1885, by Red Wilkes—Heatherbelle, by Anthony Wayne.. 2:11¼
Rebus, b g, 1886, by Chesterwood—Roxy, by Miller's Hambletonian.... 2:12¾
Recall, rn s, 188—, by Reveille........ 2:26½
Red Bandana, b s, 1888, by Almont Wilkes—Dazzle, by Happy Medium.. 2:14½
Red Bud, b s, 1883, by Red Wilkes—Kate Blackwood, by Blackwood Jr.. 2:24½
Red Cloud, ch g, 188—, by Rainbow... 2:19¼
Red Cloud, b g, 188—, by Golddust.. 2:25¼
Red Davis, ch g, 188—, ... 2:18
Redfield, b s, 1884, by Red Wilkes—Loretta, by Enfield 2:19¾
Red Grant, ch s, 1890, by Red Blossom—Nelly Grant, by Pacing Abdallah 2:27¼
Red Hal, b s, 1887, by Martin's Tom Hal—Lucinda, by Henry Clay 2:13¾
Red Hawk, b g, 188—, ... 2:20¼
Red Hornet, ch s, 188—, by Bald Hornet 2:23¼
Red Lady, b m, 1889, by Red Wilkes—Severn, by Grand Sentinel 2:16¾
Redleaf, ch m, 188—, by Charm 2:28¾
Red Leaf, b m, 188—, by Elgin Boy... 2:26½
Redmon C., ch s, 1887, by Joe Thorndale, dam by Highlander 2:30
Red Rock, b s, 188—, by Kilbuck Tom 2:25½
Red Rover, b g, 188—, by Al West... 2:25½
Red Rover, b g, 188—, by Redfield ... 2:24¼
Redskin, ch g, 1887, by Royal Jim—Fanny, by Kirkpatrick's Buck...... 2:17¾
Red Star, ch s, 188—, by Chestnut Star 2:20
Red Star, b m, 188—, by Hale's Red Buck 2:23½
Red Thorn, b g, 188—, by Rescue.... 2:15½
Red Wing, ch s, 1889, by Music—Kitty, by Flying Mohawk 2:13¼
Redwood, ch g, 188—, by Red Buck.. 2:22¼
Redwood, ch g, 188—, by Ringwood... 2:28½
Reflector, b s, 1887, by Duplex, dam by Norfolk 2:07¾
Reform, rn g, 188—, by Prince Columbia 2:26
Regardless, b g, by Dewitt's Norman 2:16¼
Regulator, b s, 188—, by Indianapolis—Lady Forrest 2:25
Reil Rooker, gr s, 188—, by Rooker.. 2:28½
Reno Clipper, b s, 1890, by Reno Defiance—Lady Clipper, by Clipper Jr. 2:20½
Reno M., blk g, 1891, by Reno's Baby 2:20
Reno's Baby, br s, 1887, by Reno Defiance—Lucy Q., by McKinney Horse (trotting 2:25½) 2:14
Renvoi, br s, 1892, by Game Onward. 2:21½
Reserve Fund, ch s, 1885, by Nutwood—Lizzie Wilkes, by George Wilkes.. 2:26
Retainer, b g, 188—, ... 2:24¼
Retla Boy, ch s, 1888, by Kimo—Molly, by Blue Vein.......... 2:19¼
Reuben, b g, 188—, by Barnes' Dictator Chief, dam by Reuben........ 2:26½
Reuben W., b g, 188—, by Clark Chieftain 2:16¼
Revenue, br g, 1885, by Reveille 2:29¼
Reward J., ch s, 1887, by Bourbon Wilkes—Lark, by Abdallah Mambrino (trotting 2:29) 2:10¼
Rex King, gr s, 1887, by Rex Hiatoga—Maud L., by Gold King 2:25
Rex Princeton, b s, 188—, by Princeton 2:23½
Rhea, gr m, 188—, by Judge Advocate 2.17¾
Rhinehart, gr s, 188—, by Monroe S.. 2:24¾
Rhinestone, b s, 1890, by Dunton Wilkes 2:25
R. H. W., ch g, 188—, by Almont.... 2:25¼
Richard, b g, 188—, by Major Ringgold 2:16¾
Richard B., b g, 188—, by Black John 2:25¾
Richard Jay, b s, 1888, by Dictator Wilkes—Jean Wilkes, by Adrian Wilkes 2:17¼
Richard Wilkes, br s, 1886, by Clay Wilkes—Kate, by Palm's Kennebeck 2:25
Rich Ball, gr g, 188—, ... 2:23½
Richball, b g, 1876, by King Pharaoh—Genevra 2:12½
Richmond, b s, 188—, by Richwood... 2:27½
Rifle Ball, b g, 188—, by Bullet 2:14
Riley, br g, 188—, by Howard's Copperbottom 2:19¼
Riley Medium, br s, 1881, by Happy Medium—Maud R., by Mambrino

Wilkes—Ollitipa, by Aristos .... 2·08
Ruby Mac, ch m, 1885, by George M. Patchen Jr.—Lady Goldsmith, by Volunteer 2:21½
Ruby Messenger, b m, 188—, by Messenger Chief 2:23
Rufe Wilkes, b g, 188—, by Star Wilkes 2:28¼
Rufe Wilson, blk g, 188—, by Brown Golddust 2:24½
Rupee, br s, 1887, by Guy Wilkes—Sable Hayward, by Poscora Hayward 2:11
Rupert, ch s, 188—, by Corbin Bashaw—Psyche, by George Miller 2:23½
Rushmont, ch s, 188—, by Almont M.. 2:23¾
Ruskin Wilkes, br s, 1884, by Sherman Wilkes—Lady Clay, by Black Harry Clay 2:17
Russell (Miller's), b s, 1881, by Col. H. S. Russell—Molly Vestal, by Dragon 2.24
Russell B., br s, 1890, by Alley Russell—Bessie B., by Teeter's Horse. 2:15
Russell Chief, ch s, 1885, by Mambrino Russell—Bessie, by Strathmore 2:22¾
Russell T., blk g, 188—, by Russell.. 2:19¼
Ruth H., b m, 1889, by Laclede—Durango Queen, by Durango (trotting 2:24½) 2:22
Sabatia, b m, 1884, by Taunton—Barker Mare, by Bay Chief 2:18¼
Sable Gift, b s, 1890, by Gift Jr.—Illian, by Stansifer's Woful .... 2·13¼
Saboya, b s, 1886, by Nugget—Ida, by Little Harry Clay 2:19½
Sadie Burns, b m, 187—, by Billy Green .... 2·29½
Sadie Gray, gr m, 1890, by Simmons.. 2:29½
Sadie H., b m, 1885, by Bourbon Wilkes 2:20¼
Sagwa, g g, by Montgomery 2:29¼
Sagwa, br g, 188— 2.29¾
Sagwa, ch g, 188—, by Rattler 2 24
Sailor Boy, rn g, 1876, by Smuggler Jr.—Laura, by Rowe Horse .... 2·17¼
Sailor Boy 2 30
Sailor Wilkes, b g, 188—, by Star Wilkes—Lizzie C., by Star Hambletonian 2.25¼
St Catharine, gr m, 1885, by Sir Peter—Sunflower, by Prince Elmo. 2.22¼
St. Cloud, b g, 188—, by Kentucky Prince 2 27
St Croix, b s, 188—, by Guelph 2:18¾
St. Francis, blk s, 1888, by Sigma Nu—Francis, by Admiral 2:23¼
St. John, gr g, 188— 2 26
St. Jonathan, br s, 1888, by Kentucky Dictator—Fanny Goldsmith, by Edward Everett (trotting 2:22¼) 2:22½
St. Nick, b s, 188—, by St. Nicholas.. 2:27¼
St. Omer, gr s, 1873, by Blue Bull—Black Snake, by Legal Tender 2:28¾
St. Patrick, gr g, by Dall Brino 2:29¾
St. Patrick, b s, 1884, by Volunteer—Young Saline, by Guy Miller .... 2·14¼
Saladin, br s, 1886, by Sultan—Ella Lewis, by Vermont 2:05¾
Salisbury 2 20¼
Sally B., blk m, 1873, by Dow's Green Mountain Morgan 2 23
Sallie Bronston, blk m, 1891, by Gambetta Wilkes—Weston, by Marshal Kleber 2 17½
Sally C., gr m, 187—, by Senator 2 17¼
Sally Clinker, b m, 1885, by Clinker—Dolly, by Searcher .... 2·13
Sally Ranger, blk m, 1887, by John Sherman, dam by Black Ranger 2:29¼
Sally Walker, b m, 188—, by Hylas 2:28¼
Salol, br g, 1887, by Winnebago Chief 2:21½
Sam, b g, 188— 2.28½
Sam, gr g, 188— 2:27½
Sam Hall, b s, 188—, by George Hall. 2:28½
Sam Jones, b g, 187—, by Thompson's Traveler, dam by Cato's Washington 2:18¾
Sam Keith, b s, 1884, by Egbert—Molly Lynch, by Blind Morrill 2:24¾
Sam Lewis, b s, 187—, by Echo—Bessie Taylor, by St. Clair .... 2·25
Sam N., b g, 188—, by Dauntless 2:28¼
Sample, b g, 188— 2:30
Sam Sharp, b g, 187—, by Gloster—Kate, by Pocahontas Boy 2.26
Sam Slick, b g, 185—, (dead) 2:28
Sam Weller, ch g, 188—, by Advance.. 2:27¼
Sancho, rn g, 188— 2:20½
Sancho, b s, 1886, by Pocahontas Boy—Matlock, by Grey Diomed 2:20
Sand Boy, ch g, 188—, by Strathmore—Aline, by Almont 2:21
San Diego, b g, 188—, by Victor 2:21
Sandy, ch g, 188—, by Sperry's Westmont 2 23¼
Sandy Mack, b s, 188—, by Captain Moshier .... 2·28
Sandy Morris Jr., ch s, 188—, by Sandy Morris 2:28¼
Sandy Wilkes b s, 1890, by Crawford.. 2:29¼
Sanford L., ch g, 188—, by Dick Gilder 2:19¼
Sanger, b g, 188—, by King Sprague.. 2:20¾
Sangefield, b s, 1889, by Roman Chief 2·30
San Jose, b g, 188—, by Santa Claus.. 2.30
Sankey, gr g, 1884, by Sandy Lake, dam by St. Omer 2.25
Sankey, ch g, 188— 2:19½
San Pedro, blk g, 1885, by Del Sur, dam by Keating Horse (trotting 2·14¼) 2.10¾
Santa Rita, br m, 1885, by Sidney—Titania, by Buccaneer 2:24¼
Sarah Ann, gr m, 188—, by Johnny Wonder (trotting 2·27) 2:23¾
Sarah Jane, b m, 188—, by Edgar Wilkes 2:24¾
Sateen, b m, 1886, by Alroy—Kit, by Virgil 2:28
Saturn, rn g, 188— 2 30
Saturday Night, ch g, 188— 2:29¼
Sawtelle, ch g, 1886, by Baywood—Daisy Y., by Captain Jack 2:17½
S. B., b g, 188—, by Knight Errant. 2:24¾
Scarlet Wilkes, b s, 1884, by Red Wilkes—Tipsey, by Alcalde .... 2·27½
School Boy, ch s, 188—, by Meander. 2:22¼
School Boy, gr g, 188— 2:26½
Sciota Girl, br m, 188—, by Ambassador—Hattie Thomas, by Hiatoga Jim 2:15¼
Sclavonic, gr s, 1891, by King Wilkes—Miss Russell, by Pilot Jr. 2:23¼
Scott Smith, b s, 1888, by Gen. Hancock, dam by Blue Bull 2:28¼
Scratch, b g, 188—, by Glencoe Jr. 2:28¾
Sea Bird, ch s, 1887, by Lord Russell—Naiad, by Belmont 2:18¼
Seafoam Jr., ro s, 188—, by Major Doke 2:17¼
Seal, b g, 1888, by Notary—Hiatoga Maid, by Patterson Horse 2:08¾
Sealskin, blk s, 186—, (dead) 2:20½
Sea Shell, ch m, 1889, by Lord Russell—Wavelet, by Belmont .... 2·20
Second, b m, 188— 2.22½
Secret, b m, 1888, by Sigma Nu 2:22½

Susie G., b m, 188—, by Little Henry —Lucy ... 2:11¼
Susie K., b m, 188—, by Brown Jug—Lady Benton, by Gen. Benton ... 2:24½
Susie Wonder, b m, 1886, by Wonder —Susie Thorn, by North Star Mambrino ... 2:19½
Sutton Boy, g s, 188—, by Sutton D. 2:24½
Sweet Violet, b m, 1890, by Wildbrino ... 2:21¼
Sweetzer, gr g, 1868, by Tom Crowder —Lady Farlow, by Gray's Tom Hal 2:15
Swift Bird, br s, 1885, by Billy Sprague—Pocohontas Girl, by Pocohontas Boy ... 2:26¼
S. X. Boy, b g, 188—, by Charles M.—Fanny Everett, by Bonney Knox . 2:19¾
Sybil, b m, 188—, by Ready Money.. 2:29¾
Sylvester, b g, 187—, ... 2:26¾
Symboleer, b s, 1892, by Campbell's Electioneer—Symbol, by Onward ... 2:11
Syndicate, br g, 188—, by Black Ambassador ... 2:19¾
Syrena, b m, 1889, by Sphinx—Maud T., by Jefferson Prince ... 2:14¼
Tade Jefferson, gr m, 188—, by Joe Jefferson ... 2:16¼
T. A. Hendricks, b g, 186—, (dead).. 2:29
Takamah, b g, 188—, ... 2:25
Tammany Wilkes, ch s, 1890, by Hambletonian Wilkes ... 2:24¼
Tanny Bug, b m, 1891, by Chimes—Lady Bug, by Hamlin's Almont Jr. 2:17½
Tangent, b s, 1885, by Onward—Fanchon, by Hamlin's Almont Jr. ... 2:18½
Tartar Chief, ch g, 188—, by Caledonia Chief ... 2:25½
Tasco, ch s, 1882, by American Boy—Neil, by Midland ... 2:21¾
Tasco Jr., b s, 188—, by Tasco ... 2:23½
Tascot, b g, 188—, by Brightlight 2:26¼
T. B., ch g, 188—, by Juanita... 2:27
T. C. B., b s, 188—, by St. Gothard 2:27¼
Teazer D., b g, 187—, by Haw Patch 2:30
Tecumseh, ro g, 184—, (dead) ... 2:20½
Ted, blk g, 1890, by Bessemer—Kittie M., by Amboy ... 2:24½
Teddie Collins, ch s, 188—, by Wilkie Collins ... 2:24¼
Tekla, b m, 188—, by Hambrino, dam by Middletown ... 2:26¼
Telegram, ch g, 1884, by Telegraph 2:12½
Tempest, blk g, 1883, by Rounds' Sprague—Bess, by Columbia Chief 2:17
Tempest N., b g, 1886, by Harry F.—Daisy Springstead, by Newton's Hotspur ... 2:19¼
Temple H., b g, 188—, ... 2:24½
Temple O., br s, 188—, by Distingue, dam by Mambrino Yorkshire ... 2:21¼
Templeton, ch s, 188—, by Hambletonian Tranby ... 2:29¼
Testator, br s, 188—, by Dictator Chief ... 2:23½
Texas Jack, Jr., b s, 188—, by Texas Jack ... 2:27¼
Texas Jack Sr., br s, 188—, by Judge Durell ... 2:19¾
Texas Mike, br s, 188—, by Texas Jack ... 2:27¼
Texas Rooker, b s, 188—, by Texas Jack, dam by Rooker ... 2:24½
Tezuca, b m, 1889, by Reserve Fund —Rococo, by Onward ... 2:15
Thad, blk g, 188—, by Keeler ... 2:26¼
The Dude, b g, 1886, by Elevator—Sally Surplus, by Surplus ... 2:13½
The Duke, ch g, 1891, by Scarlet Wilkes ... 2:24¾
The Parson, ch s, 188—, by Madison Smith ... 2:19
The Princess, b m, 188—, by Nutbreaker—Queen Sprague, by George Sprague ... 2:19
Theodore, br s, 1885, by Reveille—Maple Leaf, by New York (trotting 2:26¼) ... 2:18½
Theresa Scott, gr m, 1876, by Winfield Scott ... 2:25
Thistle, blk s, 1887, by Sidney—Fern Leaf, by Flaxtail ... 2:13½
Thistle Dew, b m, 1889, by Sentinel Wilkes—Belle H., by Clark Chief Jr 2:17¼
Tho, b s, 1890, by Sidney ... 2:23
Thomas L., ch g, 187—, by Tempest Jr. ... 2:27¾
Thomas Ryder, b s, 188—, by Alexander Button, dam by Black Ralph.. 2:13¼
Thorndale Prince, blk s, 1889, by Hambletonian's Last—Molly, by Blood Chief ... 2:21
Thornton Girl, b m, 1890, by Whalebone, dam by Hambletonian Tranby 2:26¾
Thunder, ch g, 187—, by Gen. Hardee —Puss ... 2:22¾
Tillie B., b m, 188—, by Alcantara.... 2:21½
Tillie Herr, b m, 1886, by Dr. Herr, dam by Dyke ... 2:21¼
Tilman, ch s, 1889, by Bourbon Wilkes —Julia, by John Dillard Jr. ... 2:29¼
Timbuctoo, b s, 188—, by Majesty . 2:28
Tim Cawley, gr g, 188—, by Highland Gray—Madam Cawley, by Broughton Horse ... 2:27¼
Tip O'Tip, b g, 188—, by Peacock—Julia, by a son of Campbell's Ned Forrest ... 2:12¼
Tippecanoe, ch g, 183—, (dead) ... 2:29
Tip Top, b s, 1887, by Petoskey—Nelly Monroe, by Jim Monroe ... 2:19
T. L. D., ch g, 1880, by Hercules... 2:22¼
T. N. B., gr g, 1888, by White Cloud 2:10½
Toboggan, b s, 188—, by Clipper.... 2:23½
Toby, b g, 188—, by George Hall—Peggy, by Top Gallant ... 2:29¼
Tod Crook, b g, 1889, by Frederick's Hambletonian ... 2:14½
Tod Mohawk, rn g, 188—, by Mohawk King ... 2:25
Toledo Girl, ro m, 187—, by Monarch Jr. ... 2:15
Tom, b g, 188—, ... 2:19¼
Tom, b g, 188—, ... 2:26½
Tom Cooper, b g, 188—, by Blazing Star ... 2:25½
Tom D., b g, 188—, ... 2:29½
Tom Edison, b s, 1887, by Artemus—Grace, by Ensley's Blue Bull..... 2:21½
Tom Ellis, ch g, 188—, by Bayard's Hambletonian Prince ... 2:26¼
Tom Exum, b s, 1888, by Onward—Vision, by Administrator ... 2:19¼
Tom F., b g, 186—, by Black Boy.... 2:30
Tom G., ch s, 188—, by Col. Walker . 2:29¼
Tom Hal Jr., rn s, 187—, by Gibson's Tom Hal—Nellie Slasher, by Mountain Slasher ... 2:30
Tom Harold, ch s, 188—, by De Soto 2:28¼
Tom Howard, b s, 188—, by Bay Tom 2:29¼
Tom Hughes, ch s, 188—, by Brown Trigham ... 2:27½
Tom Johnson, blk g, 1888, by Sigma Nu. ... 2:28¼
Tom Linderman, b g, 188—, ... 2:19
Tom McCarthy, br g, 188— ... 2:29¼
Tom McGregor, ch s, 1888, by Robert

McGregor—Rebecca, by Rysdyk's Hambletonian 2:12

Tom Miller, rn g, 1884, by Harkaway, dam by Stonewall Jackson 2:25¼

Tommy, wh g, 1885, by Kilbuck Tom —Topsy, by Marksman 2:17½

Tommy B., b g, 188—, by Kilbuck Tom 2:25½

Tommy Brown, b g, 188—, by Scott's Hambrino 2:11½

Tommy H., gr g, 188—, by Harry Goldberg 2:21¼

Tommy J., br g, 188—, ... 2:30

Tommy L., b g, 188—, ... 2:29½

Tommy Lynn, b g, 188—, by son of Addison Jr. 2:15¼

Tommy M., b g, 188—, ... 2:27¾

Tommy P., b s, 188—, by Roscoe C... 2:23

Tommy R., ch g, 188—, by Pocohontas Chief 2:26¼

Tommy Thompson, gr g, 188—, by Slasher 2:29½

Tommy Wilkes, b s, 188—, by Dumas 2:28½

Tom Ogden, b g, 1890, by Bacon.... 2:12¼

Tom Parker, br g, 185—, (dead) 2:30

Tompat, b g, 188—, ... 2:24¼

Tom Porter, b g, 1885, by Lumps—Kitty Kimbrough, by Kimbrough's Abdallah 2:24

Tom Rogers, ch g, 188—, by Ned Forrest 2:29¾

Tom Shirley, b g, 1890, by Maximus —Myrtle, by Nutwood 2:20½

Tom Smelzy, gr g, 188—, by Grey Harry 2:18½

Tom Smiley, ch g, 184—, (dead).... 2:30

Tom Webster, b s, 1889, by Bay Tom —Lucy by Granberry Slasher....... 2:11¼

Tom West, b s, 1885, by Kilbuck Tom—Jenny M., by Frank Forrester 2:23¼

Toney, ro g, 188—, by Richard Scobell—Modoc 2:24¼

Tonsorial, b m, 1888—, by Penrose—Belle Payton, by Panic 2:23¾

Tontine, b g, 188—, ... 2:26

Tony Boy, b s, 1886, by Judge Craven Fanny, by Limber Bill 2:20½

Tony H., b g, 188—, by Swigert..... 2:26¾

Tony H., b s, 188—, by Kimball...... 2:15¾

Tony Monarch, ch g, 188—, by Hi Monarch 2:26¼

Tony R., b s, 188—, by Hambletonian Downing 2:26½

Tony Wilcox, ch g, 188—, by Betterton, dam by Black Damon 2:13¾

Toomey, b s, 1890, by Balmont Wilkes —Empress, by Panic........ 2:26¼

To Order, blk s, 1890, by Thistle—Maude, by Bertrand Black Hawk .. 2:12¾

Tootsie D., ch m, 188—, by Jubilee, dam by Young St. Lawrence 2:21

Topsey, blk m, 187—, ... 2:25½

Topsey D., ch m, 188—, by Locust Tempest 2:24¾

Topsey F., b m, 188—, by Frederick 2:22

Tot Macey, b m, 1889, by Macey—Onetonto, by Pocohontas Boy 2:26¼

Touchet, b m, 1891, by Almont, dam by Strader's C. M. Clay Jr. 2:15

Touch Me Not, ch m, 188—, by Pocohoutas Sam 2:13¾

Touchstone, b g, 1890, by Forest Wilkes—Della, by Roscoe 2:19¼

Tough End, b g, 188—, by Daniel Boone 2:20¾

Toxie R., b s, 188—, by Ignaro...... 2:16

Track Wilkes, b s, 188—, by Ira Wilkes 2:27

Trader, b s, 1892, by Trade Wind—Jennie J., by McCurdy's Hambletonian Jr. 2:25

Trafford, ch s, 1887, by Red Wilkes—Missie, by Westwood (trotting 2:27½) 2:23½

Transfer, b g, 188—, by Enfield—Fanny Blackwood, by Blackwood.. 2:27½

Travilla, ch m, 1877, by Tramp—Black Sally, by Barnard's Muscatine........ 2:24¾

Treasure, b s, 1884, by Aberdeen—Ladora, by Strader's Cassius M. Clay Jr........ 2:18¼

Treet, ch s, 188—........ 2:27

Trego, ch s, 1883, by Egmont—Ribbon, by Black Hawk Jr........ 2:16½

Trenton Girl, ch m, 188—, by Kilbuck Tom........ 2:26¼

Trevor, ch s, 1888, by Gogebic—Rose Shipman, by Blue Bull 2:25

T. R. Fox, ch g, 188—, ... 2:16

Trixie P., br m, 1883, by Bajardo Jr.. 2:27¼

Trixy, b m, 188—, by Judge Trumbull. 2:25

Trixy Hal, ch m, 188—, by Tom Hal.. 2:19¼

True, b g, 1883, by Rocket—Fanny 2d, by Magna Charta Boy........ 2:23¾

Trump, b s, 1887, by Adrian Wilkes—Colletta, by King Cole........ 2:21

Truro, b g, 188—, by Hamlet, dam by Red Squirrel........ 2:22¾

Try Me, gr m, 188—, by Try Me On, dam by Gen. Jackson........ 2:27

Tucker B., b g, 187—, ... 2:30

Turco, b s, 1889, by Erie Wilkes—Celia, by Black Henry........ 2:12

Turk, gr g, 1886, by Johnson's Sam—Mayday........ 2:18½

Turk, b g, 188—, by Tennessee Wilkes. 2:19½

Turk Franklin, b g, 1879, by Prospect —Daisy........ 2:16¼

Twilight, blk s, 188—, by Conn's Harry Wilkes........ 2:28

Twister, blk g, 187—, by Bull Pup.... 2:20¼

Two Strike, gr g, 188—, by Ferguson.. 2:10¾

Tyrannus, blk g, 1889, by Young Wilkes —Rosetta, by Pickering (trotting 2:21¼)........ 2:22¼

Tyrone, ch g, 188—, ... 2:20

Uca Wan, ch g, 188—, by Chestnut Fearnaught........ 2:26¼

Ulster Belle, ro m, 1878, by Holabird's Ethan Allen—Molly, by Roe's Abdallah Chief........ 2:17¼

Una Forrest, ch m, 1887, by Rockwall Success—Kit Malone, by Helmstutter's Morgan........ 2:20

Uncle Eb, gr g, 187—, ... 2:24¼

Uncle George, ch s, 188—, by Bald Hornet........ 2:30

Uncle Jack, b g, 1880, by Glencoe Jr. —Kate Willcoxson........ 2:16¼

Uncle Jack, b g, 188—, ... 2:17¼

Uncle Ned, ro g, 187—, by John Hadley—Fanner........ 2:23¾

Uncle Sile, ch g, 1880, by Star Harold —Black Belle, by Aroostook Boy... 2:25

Uncle Tom, gr s, 188—, by Brown Chief........ 2:25¾

Unknown, ch g, 183—, (dead) 2:23

Uranus, br s, 1889, by Herschel—Lady Dingman, by Favorite Wilkes...... 2:17¾

Valid, b s, 1890, by Pelletier—Lady Goldsmith, by Alden Goldsmith..... 2:17½

Valley, gr m, 1889, by Pilot Medium —Allie Thornton, by Shelby Chief.. 2:19¾

Valley Chief Jr., gr g, 188—, by Valley Chief........ 2:24¼

Van Cott, b g, 188—, by Polonius..... 2:20¼

Vandal Wilkes, br s, 1882, by Gov. Sprague—Vandalia Wilkes, by Geo. Wilkes........ 2:24
Vanzant, blk g, 188—, by Red Buck.. 2:29
Vanzant, b g, 187—, ... 2:29
Vasco, b g, 187—, ... 2:26¾
Vassar, rn s, 1889, by Vatican—Nell, by Estill Eric (trotting 2:21¾)...... 2:07
Vasto, b s, 188—, by Vasco—Chess, by Magic.......... 2:10½
Velocipede, b g, 186—, (dead)........ 2:27¼
Velox, ch g, 188—, ... 2:27
Veni, b g, 188—, by Valentine, dam by Idol Wilkes.......... 2:24½
Venture, ch s, 1887, by Bald Hornet—Peggy G., by Haywood.......... 2:09½
Venture, ch s, 188—, by Cunard Jr.... 2:23½
Venturer, br g, 188—, by McRobert's Venture.......... 2:26½
Vera Capel, blk m, 1889, by Wilton—Cricket, by Mambrino Abdallah..... 2:10¼
Vernie V., ch m, 1889, by De Leon—Snap, by Colonna.......... 2:18¼
Vestigie, b s, 1891, by Valentine...... 2:15¾
Veta, b m, 1891, by Dunton Wilkes, dam by Blue Bull.......... 2:17½
Viceroy (Snider's), b s, 1885, by Viceroy—Molly, by Legal Tender...... 2:20
Victor, gr g, 188—, ... 2:20¼
Victor, gr g, 187—, ... 2:28
Victor, gr g, 1888, by Pilot Medium, dam by Greenback.......... 2:23¼
Victorine, b m, 1886, by Ferguson—May Hudson, by Gen George H. Thomas.......... 2:20
Victor Mazzone, br s, 1891, by Gen. Hancock—Lorena, by Strathmore... 2:21½
Victory, b g, 188—, ... 2:23¼
Vidette, b m, 188—, by Alexander Button—Viola, by Flaxtail.......... 2:16
Vigor, br s, 1887, by Sterling—Olive, by Prompter.......... 2:28
Vinette, b m, 1886, by Ethan Wilkes—Kate, by Peavine.......... 2:09¼
Vinnie, b m, 1886, by Oshkosh Boy... 2:23¼
Viola, b m, 188—, by San Gabriel..... 2:25¼
Violet, blk m, 188—, by Legal Tender Jr—Susan, by Nigger Dick......... 2:30
Virgie K., b g, 188—, by Herschel.... 2:25
Virginia, ch m, 1880, by Young Frenchman—Dexter, by Tom Crowder.......... 2:18½
Vitello, br s, 1885, by Legal Tender Jr—Rushville Maid, by Blue Bull... 2:11¼
Vixen, b m, 188—, by Idol Boy....... 2:13
Vogeine, dn g, 187—, ... 2:29¾
Volk, b g, 188—, by Vanzant—Laura, by Jack Shephard.......... 2:28
Vollula, b m, 1888, by Kentucky Volunteer — Marie Wilkes, by George Wilkes.......... 2:15
Voneta, br m, 188—, by Bona Fide.... 2:24½
Vonmore, b s, 188—, by Ashmore..... 2:30
Waif, b m, 1887, by Nutwood—Conquest, by Princeps.......... 2:27¼
Wait-a-Little, b g, 188—, ... 2:17½
Wait-a-While, blk g, 1888, by Black Ed.......... 2:17½
Wake-Up-Jake, br g, 187—, ... 2:30
Waldo J., b g, 1890, by Bob Mason, dam by A. W. Richmond.......... 2:13¼
Walker, b s, 1885, by Prompter—Flash, by Egmont.......... 2:23½
Walnut Boy, br s, 1887, by Ferguson—May Hudson, by Gen. George H. Thomas.......... 2:11½
Walnut Bud, b m, 1888, by Brod Walnut—Topsy, by Bethel Horse........ 2:16¾
Walter Roberts, gr g, 188—, ... 2:16½
Walter D., b g, 188—, ... 2:19¼
Walter D., dn g, 188—, by Jim Wilson 2:30
Walter D., b g, 188—, by Sir Walter Jr.......... 2:24¼
Walter Wilkes, b s, 188—, by Wilkes. 2:14½
Walter Wilton, b s, 1885, by Wilton—Samara, by Strathmore.......... 2:19½
Wanderer, br g, 188—, ... 2:22¼
Wanita Proctor, b m, 1891, by Fortunatus—Ida Advent, by Advent.... 2:24
Wapple, ch g, 188—, by Brigadier.... 2:27
Wapsie Boy, b s, 188—, ... 2:25
Wapsie L., dn s, 188—, by Wapsie... 2:29
Warburton, b s, 188—, by Wilkes Boy—Annie Almont, by Bostick's Almont Jr.......... 2:18½
Wardwell, b g, 1883, by Hamlin's Almont Jr.—Grace, by Hailstorm (trotting 2:14¼).......... 2:16¼
Warren Daily, ch s, 187—, ... 2:28½
Warren H., b g, 188—, by Hinkston Boy.......... 2:26½
Warrina, b m, 1885, by Algona—Middletown Mare, by Middletown...... 2:25
Warrior, b g, 1870, by Warrior...... 2:22¼
Warwick Girl, ch m, 188—, by Warwick Boy.......... 2:26¼
Warwitch, b m, 1889, by Warlock—Badinage, by Madrid (trotting 2:18¼).......... 2:25¼
Wasatch, ch s, 1887, by Woodnut—Flora Peacemaker, by Peacemaker.. 2:26¼
Washington, b g, 187—, ... 2:20
Washington, blk s, 187—, by Bucephalus, dam by Red Fox.......... 2:21¾
Washington Maid, ch m, 186—, ... 2:20
Waste Ferris, b g, 188—, by Valentine 2:28¼
Watcheye, br g, 1888, by Bright Light—Dixie, by Black Dick.......... 2:19
Water Bird, b m, 188—, by Waterloo. 2:29¼
Waterloo Boy, b g, 1883, by Adrian Wilkes — Abdallah Lightfoot, by Mambrino Abdallah.......... 2:14¾
Watco, br s, 188—, by Abdallah Wilkes — Mamie Marders, by Clark Chief.......... 2:14¾
Waupaca, b s, 188—, by Mohican..... 2:25
Waveland, b s, 188—, by Westland... 2:26¼
Waverly King, blk s, 188—, ... 2:27½
Waymark, b s, 188—, by Waymart, dam by Mambrino Davis.......... 2:10¼
Wayne Wilkes, b s, 1881, by Red Wilkes—Ida Smith, by Gage's Logan 2:16
W. C. B., ch s, 188—, by Jim Medium 2:17¼
W. D., b g, 188—, ... 2:24¼
Wealthy, b m, 188—, by Adrian Wilkes 2:27¼
Weber Wilkes, b s, 1888, by Penrose—Fanny Garrett, by Panic.......... 2:13¼
Weed Wilkes, b s, 1891, by Gambetta Wilkes, dam by Mambrino Startle.. 2:14¼
Well Ahead, br s, 1888, by Wedgewood—Kate Isler, by Munsey....... 2:19¼
Welter, b g, 1885, by Orange County—Nelly, by Malcolm.......... 2:20¼
Wesley R., b g, 188—, by Strathboy.. 2:19½
West Liberty, ro g, 188—, ... 2:16¼
Westmont, ch g, 1875, by Almont—Annie, by Cottrill Morgan.......... 2:13¾
Westmont (Sperry's), ch s, 1883, by Westmont—Hattie, by Billy Cozad.. 2:27¼
W. H., sp g, 188—, by Red Cloud..... 2:25
Whalebone, b s, 1884, by Hambletonian Tranby—Lady W.......... 2:18½
What's Wanted, g s, 188—, by Clinker 2:30
Wheeler F., ch s, 1889, by Charleston Addie, by Alroy.......... 2:12½
Whipsaw, b g, 187—, by Red Wilkes, dam by Corbeau (trotting 2:27¾).... 2:20¼
Whirley, blk s, 188—, by Calamity

York Wilkes, b s, 188—, by New York
Dictator 2 25
Young America, br g, 184—, by Ver-
mont Black Hawk (dead) 2 23
Young Bonair, b s, 1886, by Bonair—
Molly bon 2 21
Younger Bull, b g, 188—, by Bob Pat-
terson 2 20¼
You Tell, ch g, 1888, by Opal ... 2 19¼
Zadia blk m, 1886, by Clay Wilkes
—Nellie Grant, by Pacing Abdallah. 2 20¼
Zaida K., ch m, 188—, by Alamo—
Blonde, by Live Oak 2.30
Zaney Wilkes, blk s, 1887, by Clay
Wilkes—Nellie Grant, by Pacing Ab-

dallah (dead) 2 23½
Zandora, ch m, 188—, by Steele's
Walkill 2 22½
Zeliah H , b m, 188—, by Gift Jr , dam
by Schuyler Colfax 2:26
Ze'lete, b s, 188—, by Epaulet 2:25½
Zelpha Burns, b m, 188—, by Penrose 2:15¾
Zero, blk m, 1887, by Alcantara—
Gertie Cook, by Gray Eagle . .. 2:20
Ziglar, ch s 1888, by Pocahontas Sam
—Molly Kiger 2 13¾
Zingerelli, b m, 188—, by Greenlander 2 27
Zip M , b m, 188—, by Meriton ... 2·26¼
Zora Zar, br m, 1889, by Alcazar—
Ledo, by Cohannet (trotting 2 24¾) 2 24¼

THE MONEY WINNERS.

The following are the Trotters and Pacers that have won $5,000 or over in 1892, 1893 and 1894.

1892.
TROTTERS.

Nancy Hanks, by Happy Medium	$33,000 00
Muta Wilkes, by Guy Wilkes	14,925 00
Nightingale, by Osgood's Patchen	14,750 00
Directum, by Director	12,657 50
Silicon, by Wilton	12,270 00
Nightingale, by Mambrino King	9,500 00
Martha Wilkes, by Alcyone	8,800 00
Belleflower, by Electioneer	8,315 00
Belle Vara, by Vatican	7,250 00
Alvin, by Orpheus	7,050 00
Trevillian, by Young Jim	6,850 00
Kentucky Union, by Aberdeen	6,600 00
Geneva, by Leland	6,000 00
Kremlin, by Lord Russell	5,750 00
Grace Napoleon, by Louis Napoleon	5,375 00
Greenleaf, by Simmons	5,350 00
Oro Wilkes, by Sable Wilkes	5,200 00

1892.
PACERS.

Guy, by Shiloh	$16,250 00
Flying Jib, by Algona	14,875 00
Hal Pointer, by Tom Hal	9,500 00
Robert J, by Hartford	5,300 00
Direct, by Director	5,000 00

1893.
TROTTERS.

Nancy Hanks, by Happy Medium	$17,552 00
Walter E, by Patchen Mambrino	15,100 00
Oro Wilkes, by Sable Wilkes	13,900 00
Harrietta, by Alcyone	13,875 00
Pixley, by Jay Gould	10,950 00
Directum, by Director	10,000 00
Nellie A., by Wilkes Boy	9,580 00
Alix, by Patronage	9,450 00
Courier, by Crittenden	9,341 66
Nightingale, by Mambrino King	9,150 00
Margrave, by Baron Wilkes	9,000 00
Director's Flower, by Director	8,650 00
Double Cross, by Sable Wilkes	7,950 00
Phoebe Wilkes, by Hambletonian Wilkes	6,900 00
Bellini, by Artillery	6,825 00
Fantasy, by Chimes	6,450 00
Ellard, by Charlie Wilkes	6,375 00
Miss Lida, by King Clay	6,160 00
Ryland T, by Ledger Jr.	6,000 00
Pamlico, by Meander	5,775 00

Muta Wilkes, by Guy Wilkes	5,750 00
Arion, by Electioneer	5,500 00
Peveril, by Elyria	5,100 00
Hulda, by Guy Wilkes	5,000 00
Corinne, by Robert McGregor	5,000 00
Fannie Wilcox, by Jerome Eddy	5,000 00

1893.
PACERS.

May Marshall, by Billy Wilkes	$7,450 00
Hal Pointer, by Tom Hal	7,150 00
Hal Dillard, by Brown Hal	5,775 00
Mascot, by Deceive	5,375 00
Hal Braden, by Brown Hal	5,055 00

1894.
TROTTERS.

Beuzetta, by Onward	$22,880 00
Mary Best, by Guy Wilkes	21,050 00
Nellie A., by Wilkes Boy	17,390 00
B B P., by Pilot Medium	13,762 50
Silicon, by Wilton	12,225 00
Directum, by Director	11,500 00
Alar, by Alcantara	11,250 00
Alix, by Patronage	10,500 00
Azote, by Whips	10,225 00
Dancourt, by Ambassador	9,800 00
Sallie Simmons, by Simmons	9,300 00
Ballona, by Stranger	8,645 00
Cobwebs, by Whips	7,900 00
Red Bud, by Red Fern	7,600 00
Wistful, by Wedgewood	7,163 75
Expressive, by Electioneer	7,100 00
Nightingale, by Mambrino King	6,950 00
Trevillian, by Young Jim	6,900 00
J. M. D., by Handsome Harry	6,800 00
Onoqua, by Keeler	6,775 00
Newcastle, by Cornelian	6,750 00
Rex Americus, by Onward	6,475 00
Altivo, by Electioneer	5,232 50
Phoebe Wilkes, by Hambletonian Wilkes	5,050 00
Ralph Wilkes, by Red Wilkes	5,000 00
Boreal, by Bow Bells	5,000 00

1894.
PACERS.

Robert J, by Hartford	$29,875 00
Joe Patchen, by Patchen Wilkes	17,350 00
Rubinstein, by Baron Wilkes	6,800 00
Clayhontas, by Pocahontas Boy	6,530 00
Hal Braden, by Brown Hal	5,750 00
Online, by Shadeland Onward	5,025 00

THE WINNING SIRES.

The following are the stallions whose get won $10,000 or over in 1892, 1893 and 1894.

1892.

WINNING SIRES.

Happy Medium	$44,487 50
Guy Wilkes	32,685 50
Director	23,590 00
Alcyone	23,433 50
Wilton	19,689 75
Mambrino King	19,450 25
Electioneer	18,941 50
Young Jim	17,406 25
Pilot Medium	17,209 00
Simmons	16,584 50
Shiloh	16,250 00
Alcantara	16,082 25
Onward	16,031 25
Nutwood	15,315 50
Robert McGregor	15,117 00
Algona	14,875 00
Osgood's Patchen	14,750 00
Aberdeen	14,367 50
Tom Hal	13,595 25
Baron Wilkes	13,207 50
Dexter Prince	12,910 25
Red Wilkes	12,717 82
Hamlin's Almont Jr.	12,617 50
Louis Napoleon	11,542 50
Chimes	10,937 50
Cyclone	10,805 00
Egbert	10,380 00
Sable Wilkes	10,280 62

1893.

Director	$35,047 50
Sable Wilkes	32,555 00
Alcyone	27,045 00
Happy Medium	23,231 75
Guy Wilkes	22,362 50
Robert McGregor	20,694 00
Wilkes Boy	20,082 50
Alcantara	19,587 00
Mambrino King	18,185 25
Nutwood	18,069 25
Pilot Medium	17,704 43
Baron Wilkes	16,816 50
Patchen Mambrino	15,100 00
Jay Bird	14,755 05
Young Jim	14,407 50
Electioneer	13,912 50
Elyria	13,627 39
Red Wilkes	13,536 15
Brown Hal	13,495 00
Hamlin's Almont Jr.	13,393 75
Bourbon Wilkes	13,023 75
Simmons	13,013 00
Gen. Stanton	12,887 00
Dexter Prince	12,490 00
Tom Hal	12,065 00
Jay Gould	11,925 00
Onward	11,805 50
Atlantic	11,359 75
Chimes	11,300 00
Hambletonian Wilkes	10,892 50
Gambetta Wilkes	10,090 50

1894.

Onward	$52,521 91
Alcantara	36,070 40
Hartford	30,050 00
Guy Wilkes	29,552 50
Pilot Medium	28,198 25
Wilton	28,198 75
Baron Wilkes	26,733 75
Electioneer	24,372 50
Simmons	24,343 75
Wilkes Boy	23,453 75
Director	22,180 00
Young Jim	19,432 50
Sidney	18,778 25
Whips	18,592 50
Altamont	18,512 59
Patchen Wilkes	18,287 50
Mambrino King	17,021 75
Red Wilkes	16,196 00
Bourbon Wilkes	16,193 50
Sable Wilkes	16,117 50
Favorite Wilkes	14,977 50
Ambassador	13,852 50
Stranger	13,740 00
Brown Hal	12,270 00
Robert McGregor	11,994 75
Chimes	11,782 25
Jay Bird	11,655 00
Adrian Wilkes	11,505 00
Gambetta Wilkes	10,902 50
Nutwood	10,940 00
Patronage	10,618 75
Dexter Prince	10,420 00
Wedgewood	10,258 75

JOE THAYER, LEXINGTON, KY.
The popular Kentucky reinsman who was up behind Trevillian when
he trotted in 2:10¾, 2:08¼, 2:09¾, the three fastest consecu-
tive heats ever placed to the credit of a stallion.

JOHN DICKERSON, San Mateo, Cal.

Indiana's crack reinsman. He marked Arion 2:07¾, Pixley 2:08¼, Ellard 2:09¾, etc.

PART 2

SIRES OF 2:30 PERFORMERS.

The following are the sires of 2:30 trotters and pacers up to the close of 1894.

Aaron Pennington by Tipperary
Bee 2 24¼
Gypsy Girl 2.22

Aaron Pennington, Jr., by Aaron Pennington.
Harry Pennington 2 15½

Abbott by Tattler.
Kitty Abbott 2 26¾

Abbottsford by Woodford Mambrino.
Abbottsford, Jr. 2:27
Conde 2:19¼
C. W. S. 2:26¼
Dohrman 2:27
Free Coinage 2:18¼
Jim Crow 2:23¾
Lucy Abbott 2:23¾
She 2:14½
Sunrise 2:24¾
Waterford 2:27
Nutford, p 2 15

Abby by Abbottsford.
Genevra 2 20

Abdalbrino by Woodford Mambrino.
Altar 2:16¼
Barney Clay 2:28
Green B 2 29¼

Abdallah by Mambrino.
Frank Forrester 2:30
O'Blennis 2 30
Sir Walter 2 27
Ben Higdon, p 2:27

Abdallah (Alexander's), by Rysdyk's Hambletonian.
Goldsmith Maid 2 14
Major Edsall 2.29
Rosalind 2.21¾
St. Elmo 2:30
Thorndale 2:22¼

Abdallah (Hurst and Thornton's) by Alexander's Abdallah.
Little George 2:25½

Abdallah (Taggart's), by Farmer's Beauty.
Dauntless 2:26¾
Ned Hastings 2:28½
Ned Wallace 2:25

Abdallah (Goldsmith's), by Volunteer.
Alexander 2:28¾
Dictator 2:27
Hickory 2 27¾
Little Miss 2:26½

Abdallah (Darling's).
Abdallah, p 2:26

Abdallah (Conklin's), untraced
Rarus 2:13¼

Abdallah, Jr. (Truesdale's), by Erie Abdallah.
George A 2:21¾

Abdallah, Jr. (Coleman's), by Alexander's Abdallah.
Forsee 2:27
Pearl 2:30
Abbie H., p 2:26½

Abdallah, Jr.
Abdallah Girl. p 2:19

Abdallah Jr., by Abdallah Messenger.
Tellie 2 25¼

Abdallah Boy by Goldsmith's Abdallah.
Dutch Girl 2:27¾

Abdallah Bruce by Bruceton
Abdallah (Grant's), p 2:10½

Abdallah Duroc by Messenger Duroc.
Maud 2:29¼

Abdallah Glencoe by Joe Abdallah.
Stella 2 29

Abdallah Hambletonian by Hickory.
Dolly H 2 20¼
Frank E 2:29½
Granny 2:28
Maud M 2:20¼

Abdallah Mambrino by Almont.
Aeleta 2 29½
Annie B. 2:29½
Betty Jones 2 19½
Betty Mac 2:29
Effie Thornton 2:30
Elkin 2 22¼
Geneva S 2.19¼
Keller V 2 21¾
Mattie H 2:11¼
May Day 2:24¼
Quinine S 2:28¼
Rena B 2.28½
Soto, b m. 2:20¼
Hickory B., p 2:30
Little Jack, p 2:26¼

Abdallah Messenger by Alexander's Abdallah.
Abdallah Boy 2:24¼

Abdallah Messenger by Jupiter Abdallah.
Bijou 2.24½

Abdallah Pilot by Alexander's Abdallah.
Frank S 2:25½
Pickard 2:18¼
Wentworth 2:29½

Abdallah Prince by Young America.
Monte, p 2.26¼

Abdallah Thorne by Mambrino Patchen.
Easter Boy 2:30

Abdallah Tranby by Strader's Cassius M. Clay, Jr
Flora C. 2 29½

Abdallah West by Allie West.
Wilkin 2:27½

Abdallah Wilkes by Geo. Wilk's
Allen Wilkes 2:29
Nixon 2:28½
Saxon 2:22½
Vidalia 2:23¼
Voleta 2 23
Wauco 2:25
Kate C., p 2:18½
Lady Lee, p 2 24½
Wauco, p 2:14¾

Abdallah Woodford by Woodford Mambrino.
Dennis P 2:29¼

Abdamed Allen by Woodward's Ethan Allen.
Abdamed Allen, Jr. 2:26½
Dexter L 2 25
Dot L 2 21
Fanny A 2:26¼
Nellie, p 2:24¼

Abe Downing by Joe Downing.
Pat Downing 2 13
Pennant 2:15
Chronometer, p 2:15¾
Hastings Boy. p 2:15

Abe Lincoln by Young Columbus.
Flora Belle 2:27¼

Aberdeen by Rysdyk's Hambletonian.
Abbiedeen 2:29¼
Abbie V 2.16¾
Alabaster 2:15
Almont Aberdeen 2:22½
Annabel Lee 2 26
Augusta Schuyler 2:26
Bannockburn 2:29¾
Bay Tom 2:29¼
Bessie D 2:20
Bonny Deen 2:30
Corena 2.24¼
Daisy Hartshorn 2:24½
Dolly Withers 2 29½
Edgewood 2 25¼
Godelia 2:19½
Hattie Woodward 2 15½
Hugh McLaughlin 2 23
Irish Lad 2:23¼
Kate Taylor 2.23¾
Kentucky Union 2:11¾
Knighthood 2.29½
Leda 2:25½
Lewellyn 2:19¼
Lycurgus 2 15½
Matrimony 2:23¾
Memona 2 24¼
Modoc 2:19½
Mulatto 2:22

Parnell 2:29
Parthenon 2:27¼
Sam Estes 2:27½
Sappho 2:30
Sir Walter 2:24¼
Star 2:25¼
Stella C 2:27¼
Surprise 2:29¼
Titania 2:27
Tommy 2:30
Valley Boy 2:24½
Vanessa 2:26
Wanita 2:20½
Billy T., p 2:30
Jim Jewell, p 2:19¼
Orienta, p 2:28
Treasure, p 2:18¼
Abraham by Daniel Lambert.
Alice 2:28
Belle of Albany 2:29¼
Belle Shacket 2:27½
Bessie H 2:25¾
Frank 2:19½
Jennie 2:27¼
Kitty Cook 2:26½
Belle Shacket, p 2:27¾
Brightwood, p 2:19¾
Lady Pearl, p 2:28¼
Absolute by Dictator.
Albrazia, p 2:24
Accidental, untraced.
Charley C 2:29¾
A. P., p 2:17¼
Misty Morning, p 2:24¼
Nettie Sloan, p 2:29
Sunlight, p 2:24¾
Achilles by Mambrino Patchen.
Barney F 2:29¼
Achilles by Carenought.
Blanche R 2:28½
Themis 2:25
Acolyte by Onward.
Amberlyte 2:30
Classic 2:27½
Crissolyte 2:27¼
Faubourg 2:25¼
Pastoral 2:30
Pilgrim 2:20¾
Position 2:22¼
Promoter 2:19
Sidney C. 2:30
Vatican 2:18
Addison Jr by Addison.
Clementine 2:21
Addison Lambert by Daniel Lambert.
Shadow 2:25
Susie 2:26
Addie Stuart, p 2:20¼
Adirondack by Bona Fide.
Bonnie Belle, p 2:24½
Adjuster by Administrator.
Marvel 2:18¾
Otto J 2:19¾
Alexander Boy, p 2:18¾
Limber Jim, p 2:25¾
Max, p 2:27
Adjutant by Administrator.
George L 2:24½
Review 2:29¼
Black Crook, p 2:26
George S., p 2:17¾
Henry S., p 2:17¾
Admar by Admiral.
Lenmar 2:16¼
Administrator by Rysdyk's Hambletonian.
Adjuster 2:26
Arbiter 2:22¾
Catchfly 2:18½
Clarkia 2:27
Col. Stevens 2:28½
Dot 2:22¾
Executor 2:24¾
Langtrey 2:26½
McMahon 2:21
Marcus 2:29¼
Mars 2:28½
Penistan 2:28½
Sultan 2:28½
Viscount 2:28
Administrator (Riley's) by Administrator.
Colonel 2:29½
Administrator Jr by Administrator.
Grace Medium 2:29½
Admiral by Volunteer.
Huntress 2:28
Nona Y 2:25
Perihelion 2:25
Sister 2:19¼
Admiral Patchen Jr. by Admiral Patchen.
Brandy Boy 2:20¼
Adonis.
C. W. G., p 2:18¾
Adrian by Whipple's Hambletonian.
Rosita, p 2:14¾
Adrian Wilkes by George Wilkes.
Babe Wilkes 2:30
Bonnie Wilkes 2:15¾
Ebony Wilkes 2:19¾
Focus R 2:27¼
Grace Wilkes 2:17¾
May Verden 2:26¼
Midnight 2:23¼
Odessa 2:29½
Oliver 2:29¼
Omnia 2:29¾
Silver Wilkes 2:25
Waterloo Girl 2:19½
Westfall 2:29¾
Wilkes Maid 2:27½
Bonnie Wilkes Jr., p 2:24½
Ethel A., p 2:10
Emma Wilkes, p 2:19¾
Florette, p 2:24½
Lillian, p 2:14¼
Lil Yon, p 2:26¾
Maud M., p 2:15½
Nettie Wilkes, p 2:19¼
Necollite, p 2:26¼
Prairie Lily, p 2:19¾
Roy Wilkes, p 2:06½
Trump, p 2:21
Waterloo Boy, p 2:14¾
Wealthy, p 2:27¾
Wilkesota, p 2:25¼
Adrola.
Effie M 2:29¾
Advance by Volunteer.
Mahaska 2:25
Modjeska 2:29¼
Advance by Onward.
Advance Jr 2:28
Nelly Bly 2:30
Swanock 2:20
Cyrus V., p 2:22½
Lady J., p 2:26¼
Sam Weller, p 2:27¼
Advent by Strathmore.
Admore 2:26
Admore, p 2:24
Advertiser by Electioneer.
Adbell 2:23
Aegon by Nutwood.
Shaw Jenan 2:29
Æmulus by Mambrino Pilot.
Boss H 2:25¼
R. R. H 2:23¼
Agile by Dictator.
Elector H 2:25
Agricola by Gambetta Wilkes.
Nelly Neal, p 2:26½
Ahue by Rodford's Ahue.
Nora G 2:25¾
Dr. A., p 2:24¼
William M. Singerly, p 2:16½
Ajax by Rysdyk's Hambletonian.
Belle Unrne 2:29¼
Clarence H 2:24¼
Columbus Hambl'ian 2:26
Duke of Kent 2:29½
Jeffersonian 2:27
Florence C 2:29
Fred 2:29½
Tansy G 2:30
Apple Jack, p 2:18
Bacon, p 2:23
Anetta C., p 2:23¾
Arnold Boy, p 2:18¾
Be Jax, p 2:14¼
Big Wonder, p 2:25
Clay Jax, p 2:25
Ganymede, p 2:25
Gaslight, p 2:23
I. N., p 2:17¼
Maplewood, p 2:25
Pat Bruen, p 2:24
Patrick Henry, p 2:26¾
Queen Esther, p 2:27
Ajax by Slocumb Horse.
Jessie Wales 2:30
Aladdin by Rysdyk's Hambletonian.
Joker 2:24
Pearl P 2:29½
Brown Al, p 2:24¼
Hamden, p 2:23¼
John Kenny, p 2:23
Alamode by Daniel Webster.
Adele Maloney 2:24
Alamo by Almont.
Zaida K 2:30
Alamosa by Alamo.
Our Nora, p 2:17
Alar Clay by Almont.
Alar Clay Jr 2:29½
Almambro 2:28½
Snip Clay 2:25¾
Alar Clay Jr by Alar Clay.
Hattie S 2:16¾
Alaric by Cuyler.
Emma Hayes 2:24
Alaric by Richwood.
Victor B 2:20
Alaric by Arcturus.
Elwood 2:30
Alaric by Almont.
Jim Golden 2:30
Alaric Almont by Almont.
Jim Corbett, p 2:19¼
Alarm by Walkill Chief.
Dancer 2:25½
Alaska by Electioneer.
Lena H 2:29¾
Alastor by Almont.
Ruth N 2:29¼
Alban by Gen. Benton.

Hilarita 2:29¼
Seylax.................2:24¼
Albani.
Albena, p... ......2:26
Albatross by Floramour.
Marjie C., p 2:20
Albert by Pilot Duroc.
Honest George 2:14½
Albert by Algiers.
Billy Warren 2:24½
Albert Lee by Florida. |
Po Po Lo, p. 2:20
Albert W. by Electioneer,
Albert T........ ...... 2:19¼
Arthur Dodge........2:20¼
Dudley Olcott 2:18¼
Little Albert..........2:10
Miss Albert..........2:25¼
Neernut............2·26
Pansy Blossom......2:28¼
William Albert 2:20¼
Amelia, p..... .... 2 21½
Flowing Tide, p.......2:14¼
High Tide.... ...... 2:17½
Albert Mack by McGregor Chief.
Henry G........ ....2:28
Albert S. Patchen
J. B., p........ .. 2:26¼
Albion by Peters' Halcorn.
Vanity Fair. 2:24½
Albion by Gen. Benton.
Pomona, p.... ....2:15
Albion by Highland Boy.
Capt. Hamner...... 2:30
Gen. Smith........2.20
Albrino by Almont.
Albrina. 2:27
Fauntleroy...... .. 2:23¼
Iona S..............2:17¼
Dr. Dix, p.. ......2:30
Elsmere. p..........2:29¼
Alburn by Almont.
Almont..............2:17¼
Grace Darling....... 2:26¼
Myrtle N 2:20¼
Smock W..... ..... 2:28
Alcalde by Mambrino Chief.
Enigma 2:26
Fancy Day...........2:30
Hylas 2:24½
Mary B..............2:29
Alcalde Jr by Alcalde.
Adelaide............ 2:30
Susie G............2:26¼
Alcamont by Bostick'sAlmont Jr.
Miss Kent...........2:25
Alcander by Alcantara.
Annacander........2:28¾
Col. Crombie. 2:26¼
Prince Alcander, p...2:17¼
Whistle, p 2:11¼
Whisper, p 2:26¼
Alcandre by Alcyone.
Solarion, p.......... 2:23¼
Alcantara by George Wilkes.
Ada.......... ....2:28¼
Addie L..............2:24¼
Alar.................2:11
Alcagetta..... ....2:25
Alcander.............2:20½
Alcantarus...........2:20¼
Alcantine............2:29¼
Alcavala 2:29
Alcazar..............2:24½
Alhambra....... ...2:20
Alicante............2:20¼

Alice Wilkes 2:17¼
Alpha 2:23½
Altus................2:25¼
Apollo Wilkes........2:28¾
Arena................2:15½
Arguile..............2:25
Autograph 2:16½
Black Victor....,...2:26½
Callisto..............2:26½
Curio................2.25
Daun R.............2:22¾
Estabrook.. ....2:29¾
Etta.................2:28
Etiquette...... ..:...2:28¼
Fillmore............2:29¾
Foggy...............2:27½
Georgia H..........2:17¼
Irene 2:23¼
Joe Wilkes 2:30
Lady Emma.........2:23½
Lady Tessa 2:27¼
Lavender.. ....2·28¼
Lightning 2:11
Mahlon 2.13¾
Mary S............ 2 28
Mink...............2:22¼
Miss Alice 2:13¼
Nancy Rice 2:25
Olga... .. ..2:26¼
Porcelain.. .. ..2:23¾
Queen Anne 2:30
Queen Fearnaught...2:25½
Rensselær Wilkes ...2:18¼
Robert Lee. 2:18½
Robert M. Taylor....2:23½
Sargent.......... .....2:27½
Seamstress..........2 26
Thornton............2:26¼
Tryingham. 2:29½
White Socks.........2:20½
·Willis A.............2:24¾
Wilkimont... ....2:27¾
Wilkes Bee.........2:27¼
Wilkesdale.......... 2:29
Alcedo, p 2:23¼
Alcinta, p..... ...2.16¼
Allegro, p 2:19¼
Allen Lowe, p........2:12
Attractive, p 2.18¼
Bayard Wilkes, p....2:13¼
Burdette, p...........2:21½
Bokhara, p...........2.20
Chronos, p 2:12½
Clara C. p...........2 24
El Capitan, p........2:20½
Eugenie, p 2:19¼
Foggy, p............2:13¼
Gold Beater, p 2:20½
Hamlin, p...........2:26¼
Hattie P. p..........2:27¼
Janey, p 2:16¼
Jed Davis, p.... ... 2:16
Lady Hamilton, p...2:23¼
Lady Lee, p 2 20
Montezuma, p......2:29¾
Nightingale, p 2:13¼
Parker, p............2:28¼
Raven. p............2:11¼
Tillie B. p..........2:21½
Zero, p..............2:29
Alcantara Jr. by Alcantara.
Eliza S.............2:16½
Alcantara Prince by Alcantara.
Chet Wilkes.........2:25
Alcazar by Sultan.
Ardent..............2:30
Bric-A-Brac.........2:28¼

Kaffir.................2:29¾
Kebir................2:28¼
Mista................2:29
Princeton 2:29¾
Sacramento Girl......2:30
Alcazar by Alcantara.
Alcazar Belle 2:24¼
Lobelia. 2:24½
Phantom.............2:24¼
Zora Zar, p..........2:24¾
Almary, p...........2:23¼
Zora Zar, p 2:24¼
Alcona by Almont.
Alcona Jr............2:19
Almonition 2:24¾
Clay Duke.... ......2:29
Flora Belle 2:25
Lulu C............. ..2:29¾
Veronica 2:29
Alcona Clay by Alcona.
King Orry. 2:21½
Alcona Jr. by Alcona.
Silas Skinner........2:17
Graceful George, p..2.23
Alcone by Alcyone.
Benton Wilkes.... ..2:22
Jefferson Wilkes. ...2:26
Shea Wilkes 2:24¼
Alcryon by Alcyone.
Albert 2:29¼
Alcyo by Alcyone.
Lady Alcy 2:19
Alcyone by George Wilkes.
Adventurer 2:27½
Alaska 2:27¼
Alcandre.............2:26¼
Alcryon 2:15
Alcyona.............2:29
Alcyone Belle 2:29¾
Alcyonium 2:24¼
Alcyone Jr......... ..2:18¾
Alcy Wilkes 2:16
Alcyrene 2:27¾
Alcyrene 2:28¾
Berkshire Belle......2:22¼
Bush 2:14¼
Carrie Wilkes 2:28
Don Wilkes... ......2:24¾
Eastview 2:23¾
El Banecia...........2:20¼
Erena. 2:19¾
Florence Palmer.....2:29¼
Geraldine...........2:21
Golden Rod 2:19¼
Guardsman.... ....2:23½
Hallie B.............2:26¾
Harrietta 2:09¾
Iona... ....2:17¼
Ione... ....2:27
J. J. Audubon 2:19
L'Empereur 2:25
McKinney...........2:11¼
Martha Wilkes...... 2:08
Neponset 2:24¼
Patience 2:27½
Quartermaster 2:21¼
Queechy 2:14¼
Ramona.............2:16
Silverone... ....2:19¾
Springcroft..........2:26¼
Star Alcyone.........2:24¾
Turner...... ....2:23¾
Twang...............2:18¼
Whitefoot............2:22¾
Whizz Wilkes 2:29¾
Alcyo, p.............2:11
Allmyown, p........2:24¼
Jones Ordway, p.. ..2:16¾

Medeoyone, p.......2:25
Prince Alcyone, p....2:15½
Alcyone Jr. by Alcyone.
Little Sim, p....... 2:29¼
Alcy Wilkes by Alcyone.
Cheerful Alcy, p..... 2:
Alcrayon by Alcyone.
Florence S............2:23¼
Alcryon by Alcyone.
Albert................ 2:29¼
Al Carroll............ 2:24¼
Alcyonium by Alcyone.
Nelly N.............2:25¼
Alden Goldsmith by Volunteer.
Alden...............2:26
Jane R.............2:26¼
King Rock 2:30
Lilly Dale 2:25¼
Nestor 2:30
Victory.........2:24¾
Aldrich Colt by Nero.
Oceana Chief 2:23
Alecto by Almont.
Australia 2:30
Tecoma 2:19¼
Alert by Rysdyk's Hambletonian.
Alex C 2:21
Freddy 2:24¼
Edwin H 2:27½
Alexander by George M. Patchen Jr.
Alex 2:26
Alexander Button......2:26½
Nelly Patchen....... 2:27¼
Reliance 2:22½
Tommy Dodd 2:24
Alexander (De Graff's) by Goldsmith's Abdallah.
Ivica................2:24¼
Silas Wright . . . 2:23¼
Alexander (France's) by Ben Patchen.
Dillard Alexander 2:30
France........... 2:28
Alexander Button by Alexander.
Alexander Button Jr 2:26¾
Billy Button..........2:27
Gen. Logan 2:23¼
Bird Button..........2:29¾
Hattie B 2:20¾
Laura Z............2:18¼
Lucy B..............2:17½
Mabel H 2:17¼
Margaret Worth 2:17¼
Maud C 2:28½
Rosie Mac.........2:20¾
Belle Button, p 2:18½
Mattie B., p.......... 2:26¾
Thomas Ryder, p.....2:13¼
Vidette, p.............2:16
Yolo Maid, p 2:12
Alexander Dumas by Dumas.
Pearl C...............2:30
S. V. White......... 2:29¾
Jubilo, p.............2:28¼
Mac Beth, p 2:30
Alexander H. Sherman by Backman's Idol.
Accident 2:26½
Harry Sherman.. . 2:25
Maggie Sherman 2:16¼
Sheraldine............2:29¼
Alexander Jefferson by Thos. Jefferson.
Belle Jefferson....... 2:30
Tid Jefferson 2:27½
Alexander Norman.
Kentucky Tom, p . . 2:26¼
Alfonso by Baron Wilkes.
Freeland 2:17¾
Alfred by Gen. Benton.
Langton 2:21¾
Alfred by Charles Backman.
Ophelia, p........... 2:16¼
Alfred G. by Anteeo.
Nellie Alfred . . . 2:27½
Queen Alfred.......2:18¼
Foxhound, p..........2:26¼
Algardia
Black Bess........... 2:26¼
Algeria Wilkes by Alcyone.
Algeria Belle....... 2:28½
Jessie Wilkes. 2:19¼
Hugar, p 2:21
Algiers by Atlantic.
Panic, p............... 2:28¼
Algona by Almont.
Addie E...............2:19
Flying Jib, p 2:04
Warrina, p . 2:25
Alhamar by Almont Chief.
Clifton Boy, p 2:21½
Dick B., p..........2:18½
Alhambra by Middletown.
Limber Jim. . 2:30
Lottie 2:26¼
Rena..................2:26¼
Alhambra by Legal Tender Jr.
Kansas Jack, p..... 2:20
Alhambra Chief by Almont Chief.
Magnoma...........2:30
Allahoe.
Joe Fifer, p 2:27¼
Allandorf by Onward.
Celaya 2:17½
Cudahy 2:21
Dorfmark............2:21¼
Goldman 2:29½
Monadock 2:29¾
None Better 2:23¾
Silverthorne 2:19½
Spy...................2:27½
Virgin................2:29½
Strong Boy, p 2:12
Allan Stonay.
Mayflower, p. 2:25½
Allard Horse, pedigree unknown.
Rattler (Rowley's) 2:25¼
Alleghany Boy by Wood's Hambletonian.
Harry McNair..... 2:18
Hattie H 2:26½
Nancy Hacket. . . 2:29
Rosewater, p 2:13¼
Alleghany Chief by Sir Solomon.
Jilt 2:28½
Allegro by Swigert.
Whitelaw Chief......2:25
Leo S., p...........2:22
Allen Sontag by Ethan Allen.
Ralph D., p............2:26¾
Allerton by Jay Bird.
Bird Allerton....... 2:29½
Falfa............... 2:20
Prince Allerton.......2:28¾
Feura, p...........2:28
Allegro by Ethan Allen.
Dixie................. 2:26¾
Monald McKay...... 2:22½
Alley Russell by Mambrino Russell.
Alice Russell.........2:26¼
Dandy R............2:27¼
George Russell.......2:23½
Billy Russell, p 2:19¼
Frank Russell, p . 2:25
Robert Russell, p .. 2:13¼
Russell B., p 2:15
Allie Clay by Almont.
Clayola 2:21¼
Clayson, p.........2:25
Dandy Eastmont, p. 2:26½
Allie Gaines by Almont.
Alice 2:26½
Allie Gee 2:22¼
Allie Graham 2:29¼
Alta 2:17½
Ben Gaines....... . 2:27¼
Billy Gaines '....... 2:23
Douglas Almont.... .2:29
Ira Gaines 2:13¼
J. B. S.................2:19¼
Jessie Gaines....... 2:15½
Joe Gaines 2:25
Lalla Rookh, p.... 2:20¾
Star Gaines, p 2:20¼
Allie West by Col. West.
Dr. J., p. 2:13¾
Allie West by Almont.
Charley West........ 2:27
Holden Davis........2:24½
Jewett 2:20
Rachel B 2:28½
Charley Friel, p.......2:15¾
Frank Champ, p.... 2:16¼
Jewett, p. 2:14
Allie Wilkes (France's) by Red Wilkes.
Allie Gee 2:29¼
Ben Downs......... 2:29¼
Capt. Wilkes 2:25¾
Mad Eye.......... 2:29½
Redwood Wilkes ... 2:28¼
Smuggler Wilkes. ...2:22¼
Allie A., p.......... 2:20
Arlington, p..........2:23¼
Gilman, p. 2:21¼
Jenny W., p 2:26½
Allie Wilkes (Newton's) by Geo. Wilkes.
Biddy Donovan. . 2:27
Grover Wilkes 2:30
Loughran W......... 2:17¾
Pat Donovan....... 2:27¾
Sadie Hasson....... 2:26¼
Bessie H., p....... 2:22¾
Joe Wilkes, p 2:19¾
Rally Wilkes, p 2:20½
All Right by Taggert's Abdallah
All Right Jr.......... 2:29½
C. P. R................2:26½
Charley Mitchell.....2:28¼
George Lee............2:23¼
Folly.................2:27¼
Rowdy, p.............2:28
Almanace Tattler by Almanace.
Sir Rae, p............2:24½
Almonarch by Almont.
Almarch 2:30
Allmonarch 2:19½
Darbee................2:23¾
Frederica 2:20¼
Harry B...............2:29½
Mary G...............2:27¼
Queen Allah.......... 2:21¼

Sarah B 2:20¾
Star Monarch..........2:23½
Daisy Webb, p........2:28¼
June Bug, p...........2:15¼
Edith D., p...........2:26
Elmonarch, p..........2:15¼
S. R., p..............2:13¼
Almoneer by Young Jim.
Golden Link 2:30
Lady Lightfoot....   2:28½
Almont by Alexander's Abdallah.
Alchemist.............2:30
Aldine................2:19¼
Alice Addison.........2:28½
Alice West............2:26
Allie West............2:25
Almonarch 2:24¾
Almont Eagle 2:27
Almont Jr. (Bostick's)2:29
Almont Jr. (Hamlin's)2:26
Almont Star 2:28¾
Alta..................2:23¼
Altamont..............2:26¾
Altitude..............2:28
Annie S...............2:26¾
Atlantic..............2:21
Clermont..............2:29¼
Dolly Davis. 2:29
Early Rose 2:20¼
Effie.................2:27¼
Ella Earl.............2:25
Fanny Witherspoon..2:16¼
Grandmont.............2:25½
Jack Splan............2:26¾
John F. Phelps Jr. ..2:26
Katie Jackson 2:25¾
King Almont...........2:21¼
Lillian 2:23
Lister 2:25¼
Musette...............2:29¼
Nutmont 2:22½
Piedmont..............2:17¼
Sannie G..............2:27
Tilton Almont.........2:26
Tocsin................2:22¾
Una 2:27¼
Puritan, p............2:16
R. H. W., p...........2:25½
Westmont, p 2:13¾
Almont (Archer's) by Almont.
Female Pirate, p..... 2.17½
Almont (Wirt's) by Almont.
Allie Ambassador. . 2:27
Almont (Connor's) by Bostick's Almont Jr.
Col. Dorsey...........2:25
Almont (Morris') by Almont.
Almont................2:25
Daisy M 2:25
Almont, p.............2:29
Grover C., p..........2:20
Harry Lynn, p.........2:19¼
Almont Jr. (Bostick's) by Almont.
Adfield...............2:22½
Albion................2:25¼
Almont M..............2:30
Alvan.................2:25½
Andante...............2:20½
Annie W...............2:20
B. B. Custer..........2:22½
Beaumont..............2:28½
Col. Lamont 2:26¼
Elkmont 2:30
Frank Buford 2:20
Ianthe 2:16
Judge Lindsey 2:21¼
Laura F...............2:19½
Lightfoot.............2:30
Louisa Almont. . .. 2:25
Royalmont.............2:29¼
Sam Harris............2:29¼
Susie T............. 2:23¼
Almont Jr. (Hamlin's) by Almont.
Aileen Almont.........2:25¼
Albany................2:30
Algonquin.............2:18¼
Almont General........2:24½
Almont Patchen. 2:29¼
Altogether............2:19¼
Belle Hamlin..........2:12¾
Blaine................2:27½
Clarice...............2:29½
Colden Belle..........2:20¼
Cora..................2:26
Delegate 2 21¼
Etelka 2:21¼
Gilmore...............2:21¼
Globe.................2 14¾
Grandee...............2:27½
Hollander 2:30
Hollister.............2:21
Huon..................2:28¼
Justina...............2:20
Lucretia..............2:20
Mary Anderson 2:27¼
Maud T................2:19¼
Pansy.................2:17¾
Play Boy..............2:18½
Prince Almont.........2:27
Starmont..............2:28½
Touchstone 2:30
Verdict 2:27¾
Wardwell..............2:14¼
Actor, p 2:22¼
Dustmont, p...........2:26½
Glendennis, p 2:17¼
Gracie, p.............2:21¼
Grandmother, p........2:20¾
J. S. U., p...........2:22
Lackawanna, p 2.24¼
Intrepid, p.......... 2:26¼
James D., p...........2:26
Nelly Y., p...........2:25½
Ovid, p.............. 2:15½
Wardwell, p...........2:16¼
Willink, p............2:30
Woodmont, p 2:23½
Almont (Ramer's).
Judge A., p...........2:20
Almont Aberdeen by Aberdeen.
A. A..................2:26
Alleen, p.............2:21
Almont Boy (Jenkin's) by Almont.
Bessie G..............2:25½
Grafton...............2 20½
Almont Boy (Paschall's) by Bostick's Almont Jr.
Adra Belle............2:17½
Aline 2:14½
Dr. Almont............2:21¾
Dallas, p.............2:11½
Gil Curry, p..........2:11½
Hal Clay, p.. ..   2 24¼
Robin Boy, p 2:26¾
Almont Chief by Almont.
Almont Brunswick....2:25¼
Almont Gift...........2:27¼
Almont Wagoner......2:29½
Dandy C...............2:21¾
Gold Leaf Maid........2:24¼
Minnie Young, p.. ...2:28
Almont Eagle.
Fred O 2:29½
Almont Eclipse by Almont.
C. C. K 2:24
F. H..................2:29½
Fremont...............2:30
Harry Almont..........2:24¼
Sargent...............2:26¼
S. D. C...............2:25¾
David Wilkes, p.......2:22½
Almont Ford by Hamlin's Almont Jr.
Acme Girl.............2·29¼
Hideaway..............2:23¾
Almont Gift by Almont Chief
Earlmont..............2:21
Almont King by Al West.
Dr. Keely, p. 2:24
Almont Ledo by Gen. Withers
Belle B...............2:25½
Don 2:19¾
Almont Lightning by Almont
Lightning Maid 2:27½
Almont M. by Bostick's Almont Jr.
Allen Boy.............2:27¼
Alma..................2:28½
Nelly Blackwing ......2·29¼
Jack, p...............2:22
Mack, p 2:26¼
Rushmont, p...........2:22¾
Almont Mambrino by Almont
Gracie Almont.. ......2:30
Almont Medium by Happy Medium.
Eva T.................2:26½
Lynmont 2:23½
Mark Medium...........2:16½
Richard Almont........2:28½
Warwick Medium........2:21¼
Prince Almont, p......2:13½
Almont Patchen by Juanito.
Laura M., p...........2:13½
Almontonian by Almont.
Jerry Almont..........2:26¼
Almont Pilot by Almont.
Billy Bolton 2:15¼
Clairmont.............2:28¾
Eli Almont............2:22½
Nobody's Claim........2:26
Rienzi Almont.........2:28
Rosemont..............2·23½
Maggie Almont, p....2:18
Almont Pilot by Almont.
Almont Star.... .... 2:25
Almont Pilot (Sayler's).
Jack the Ripper. p...2·26¼
Almont Prince by Almont.
Harrop's Tom..........2:26¼
Almont Prince by Almont.
Josie Bates......... 2:27¼
Almont Rattler by Almont.
Dandy Boy 2:29¾
Orphia............... 2:27½
Parone................2:25¼
Precocious............2:29
Satilla 2:24
Almont Raven by Almont.
Raven 2:27¾
Almont Bashaw, p...2 12
Altana, p.............2:27¼
Monteg, p 2:29½
Almont Revenge.
David P...............2:24½
Almont Sentinel by Sentinel.
Sentinel 2:29¼
Almont Smith by Almont.
Katie Howard, p.....2:19¾

Almont Star by Almont.
Altamont............2:29¾
Fremont...........2:29¾
H. L. J....2:27¼
Louise Kellogg....2:27½
Miss Copeland, p....2:25¼
Rose Almont........2:30
Almont Wilkes by Almont.
Republican........2:19¼
Superintendent....2:22
Red Bandana, p....2:14½
Almont Wilkes by Wilkie Collins.
Allegro........2:18¼
Dahlia Wilkes....2:24½
Almoon by Algona.
Delmas.........2:25¾
Leona..........2:28
Almoor by New York.
Goldie May.....2:30
Almore by Almont.
Belle Mora....2:28
Alonzo Hayward by Billy Hayward.
Gladys, p....2:29½
Alpine by Almont.
Algoma....2:19¾
Alpine by Edward Everett.
Louise N....2:20¼
Alpington by Pilot Medium.
Dandy L....2:29¾
Alroy by Almont.
Alcaide........2:28¼
Albertha....2:22½
Alzippa....2:14¼
Nelly F....2:28¾
Alois, p....2:25
Atlas, p....2:28½
Harry H., p....2:23½
Sateen, p....2:28
Also by Blackwood Jr.
Also Jr....2:30
Alta by American Clay.
Roger Hanson....2:28¼
Stranger....2:29
Altamont by Almont.
Almonette........2:29¼
Alta....2:23½
Alta A....2:29¼
Altao....2:16
Altena....2:26¼
Althaia....2:27½
Canemah....2:19¾
Coqueta....2:30
Georgie Woodthorpe.2:19¾
Lady Beach....2:26½
Lady Daphne....2:21¼
Malheur....2:27
McMinnville Maid....2:22
Mary A....2:30
Oneco....2:29¾
Pearl Fisher....2:18½
Pricemont....2:26
Stemwinder....2:25¼
Truemont....2:21½
Tybalt....2:27¼
Vinmont....2:29
Wallula....2:29¼
Altawood, p....2:24½
Chehalis, p....2:24½
Del Norte, p....2:14½
Doc Sperry, p....2:09
Ella T., p....2:12
Klickitat Maid, p....2:19
Touchet, p....2:15
Altamore.
Allmore....2:29¾
Altar by Abdalbrino.

Grover C....2:30
Altimont by Almont.
Jasper....2:25¼
Altitude by Almont.
Black Joe....2:27¼
Doctor S....2:29¼
Greystone....2:28½
Max O'Rell....2:24½
Patola....2:19¼
Sir Archy, p....2:16¼
Altheus by Onward.
Amboies....2.26½
Alto by Indianapolis.
McKinley, p....2:20¼
Altoona by Almont.
Allo....2:22¼
Allorita....2:16¾
May B....2:30
Flora G....2:25
Almo Jay, p....2:19
Altorf by Almont.
Boniface....2:26½
Alturas by Harold.
Altaree....2:30
Altus by Alcantara.
Alrich....2.30
Alvan by Bostick's Almont Jr
Ellemac....2:27
Alvan Swift, p....2:11¾
Aldeban, p....2:21
Alvarado by Knickerbocker.
Alvary....2:30
Martin B....2:30
Al West by Almont.
Almont King....2:29¼
John L....2:29¼
Lou Gates....2:29¼
Dr. J....2:28
Cleveland, p....2:29¼
Laura T., p....2:09¾
Pattie West, p....2:17
Red Rover, p....2:25¼
Rattler, p....2:22½
Al West Jr. by Al West.
Odessa Clipper, p....2:23¾
Alwood by Almont.
Joe Kinney....2:26½
Ciatawa, p....2:23¾
Ambassador by George Wilkes.
Abercrombie....2:21½
Abnet....2:29¼
Amaranth....2:27¼
Amazon....2:29¾
Amoskeag....2:23
Bandoline....2:23
Belle of Navarre....2:28¼
Bridal Gift....2:28¼
Corinne....2:24½
Dandy Wilkes....2:23¾
Dancourt....2:16½
Ebony Wilkes....2:29¾
Election....2:26¼
Embassador....2:25
Embassy....2:21¾
Emblem....2:27¼
Exarch....2:23¾
Gen. Alger....2:24
Keokee....2:20¾
King Nasir....2:21¼
Lady Houk....2:29½
Lulawah....2:29¼
Lucy W....2:25¼
Miss Grace....2:29¼
Napoleon Belle....2:27½
Nelly H....2:28¼
Pontoosuc....2:29¾
Royal Ambassador....2:26¾

Roxiana....2:25½
Sunbeam....2:28
Vashto....2:27¼
Wyandot....2:19½
Young Embassador....2:24¾
Ambulator, p....2:21½
Black Ambassador, p.2:25
Black Wilkes, p....2:24¾
Cuckoo, p....2:16½
Georgia Wilkes, p....2:29¼
Hy Wilkes, p....2:20
Lady Wilkins, p....2:15½
Sciota Girl, p....2:15½
Amber by Clear Grit.
Amber F....2:30
Ivanhoe....2:27¼
John Duncan, p....2:25
Amboy by Green's Bashaw.
Atlas....2:29½
Clara Cleveland....2:23
Corbin Bashaw....2:26¾
Gov. St. John....2:27½
Gov. Wood....2:29
James H....2:21¼
Lady Kerns....2:29½
Liberty Boy....2:27
Nest Egg....2:29¾
Wade Hampton....2:29½
Amboy (Hazlett's) by Amboy.
Biddle B....2:26½
Eva....2:26¾
Jessie McCorkle....2:15
Amender by Meander.
Cameo....2:28¼
Golden Gem....2:24
America by Kentucky Prince.
Siam....2:26¼
American by Whitehall.
Nelly Holcomb....2.28
American Boy by JohnGilpin
Ripton....2:26
American Boy by Star Hambletonian.
Lucy C....2.30
William G....2:25¼
Gracie L., p....2:24½
Jack Hart, p....2:23¾
American Boy by Pocahontas Boy.
American Boy Jr., p.2:20
American Girl, p....2:20¾
American Lady, p....2:24¾
Billy Stewart, p....2:18¾
Cambridge Boy, p....2:18
Cambridge Girl, p....2:11¼
Daisy Mack, p....2:25
Dick H., p....2:18
Euchre Boy, p....2:29¼
Floral Boy, p....2:17¾
George B., p....2:26½
Lena F., p....2:27¼
Non Parole, p....2:18¼
Lucky Boy, p....2:21
Mutual, p....2:21¼
Tasco, p....2:21¾
William V., p....2:21
American Clay by Strader's Cassius M. Clay Jr.
Ella Clay....2:27½
Granville....2:26
Maggie Briggs....2:27
American Emperor by Bridges' Emperor.
Dot....2:29¾
American Emperor Jr. by American Emperor.
Lottie K....2:27

American Ethan by Ethan Allen.
Daniel Webster 2:29¼
Fanny Raymond.. ...2:30
George H. Mitchell...2 26
Mattie C. 2:25¾
Morgan Ethan 2:29½
Nelly Webster........2:28¾
Neta Pine.............2:29½
American Star (Conklin's) by Seely's American Star.
Lowland Mary........2:25
St. Cloud 2:21
Star....................2:30
American Star Jr. by Seely's American Star.
Stephen M 2:28½
American Star (Seely's) by American Star.
Bolly Lewis 2:29½
Lady Whitman 2:30
Newburg..... . .. ..2:30
Widow Machree......2:29
Amurath by Sultan.
Handalier, p..........2:25
Andante by Bostick's Almont Jr.
Andrew Allison.......2:22½
Camlet.. ....2:20½
Anderson Wilkes by Onward.
Jack Sheppard 2:14½
Lacova................2:22¾
Lady Anderson.......2:28¼
Laomi 2:24¼
Waltz,,...... . .....2:29¼
Effie Powers, p........2:10½
Harlow, p. 2:27¾
Lady Anderson, p ...2:24½
Lavogue, p 2:23
Pat Delaney 2:18½
Prestoria Wilkes p...2:22½
Robert B., p 2:20
Andes by Clay Cuyler.
O'Neill...... .. ..2:29
Andrew Jackson, untraced.
Elmore Everett.......2:30
Andrew Jackson Jr. by Long Island Black Hawk.
California Damsel...2:24½
Happy Jack 2:30
Andrew Jackson (Sheffield's), untraced.
Brutus Girl.. ....2:21¼
Andrews Horse by Crawford Horse (Canadian).
Startle... ....2:26½
Andy Johnson by Henry Clay.
Belle S.......... ....2:28½
Joe Hooker...........2:30
S. S. Ellsworth 2:29
Sir Henry, p..........2:22¾
Star Henry, p.. ......2:28½
Annapolis by Woodford Mambrino.
Jack D.................2:28½
Anoka by Egmont.
Lyle, p 2:21½
Ansel by Electioneer.
Anselma..............2:29½
Answer.................2:14¼
Antella.................2:26½
Ariana 2:26
Clarion. 2:25¾
Maria Ansel..........2:25
Nettie B...............2:20½
Norris..................2:22¼
Ansonia by Jay Gould.
Cremonia 2:28

W. B.....................2:29¼
Antar by Almont.
Alto 2:26½
Billy W.. ... .2:25¾
Flossie G 2:18¼
Jack Clark...........2:27¼
Little Billy 2:21½
North Ann 2:25½
Ray C..................2:29
Robert 2:25¼
Volusia.. ....2:20½
Bergletta, p...........2:28½
Antar Jr. by Antar.
Dandy L., p...........2:29¼
Anteeo by Electioneer.
Abanteeo..............2:17½
Alfred G...............2:19¾
Antarees...............2:27½
Anteeo Jr 2:25¼
Anteeo Richmond....2:24¼
Anteeoyne. 2:23
Anthelia 2:18
Dan Brown 2:24¾
Electeo.................2:29½
Eoline...................2:14¾
Ethel Mack.. ....2:24½
Fanny D................2:26
G. and M......... ....2:29½
Gray Belle............2:27
James Madison 2:17¾
Maudee 2:28¼
Maud Fowler.... ....2:21¾
Maud M................2:20½
Myrtle..................2:19½
Mountain Maid.......2:22¼
Rayonetta 2:27
Redwood.... ....2:21½
Rex............ ....2:22½
Sunset...... . ....2:29¾
-Tietam..................2:19
Anteeo Jr. by Anteeo.
Hailstorm............ 2:30
Antenor by Messenger Duroc.
Lyra........ ....2:28¾
McKenzie 2:25¼
Antenor Jr. by Antenor.
Scramble 2:22½
Antioch by Daniel Boone.
Emmaetta............2:29
Antonio by Messenger Duroc.
Antonina......... ....2:26¾
Comanche 2:27¾
Tuscarora 2:22½
Anteros by Electioneer.
Anterose 2:25
Don Anteros 2:30
Major Ross...........2:24¼
Nellie F........ .....2:25
Antidote, p...........2:27
Cairn, p...............2:23¼
Doc Christie, p 2:21
Dudley, p.............2:14¾
Nelly F. p.............2:13¼
Antevolo by Electioneer.
Antioch..................2:21¼
Berceto.............. .2:29
Maud Merrill.........2:18
Consolation, p........2:17
Ivolo, p.............. 2:25½
Leta May, p..........2:23½
Anthony Wayne by Andy Johnon.
Brown Dick...........2:29¼
Antinous by Electioneer.
Hillsdale............. 2:17¾
John Bury.............2:22
Antonilli by Cardinal.
Lady G................2:29¼

Appleby by Antar.
John W 2:29¼
Prince 2:18½
Lucy M. p.. ....2:23¼
April Fool by Administrator.
Sweet Child.... .....2:29¾
Aquarius by Pancoast.
Pride 2:18
Arabesque by King Rene.
Arabelle................2:26½
Aarasene...............2:28¼
Aravant... .... 2:24¼
Aragon by Madrid.
Alice Eddy............2:25
Arcadian by Egbert.
Forest King..........2:29¾
Genie L................2:25¾
Arbiter by Administrator.
Artamesa 2:29¾
Archie Hambletonian by Sentinel.
Jessie Ballard........2:25
Archie Mambrino, pedigree not traced.
Billy Dayton......... 2:27½
Architect by Princeps.
Maud C., p............2:26½
Argamont.
Argamont.............2:29¾
Argonaut Woodburn by Pilot.
Clotilda................2:28¼
Indiana Boy.........2:29¾
Leo....... ....2:24¼
Argyle by Cuyler.
Fiction..................2:24¼
Lady of Lyons...... .2:21½
Aristocrat by Dictator.
Eager...... ..... .2:28
Minnie May, p 2:22½
Aristos by Daniel Lambert.
Arctic...................2:24
Aristomont........... 2:27¾
Aristotle................2:22½
Aristos Chief..........2:30
Carlotta. 2:26
Clegg Wright 2:29
Col. Kip,...............2:24¼
Essex....................2:29
Frank Dana.......... 2:29¾
Gillig....................2:23½
H. B. Winship........2:20¼
Jack........ ....2:29¼
John I. 2:26½
Levi Aristos 2:26½
Lexington Chief......2:30
R. D. F 2:21¼
Tamerlane...... .....2:29
Rusty...... ....2:24¼
Warren..... ....2:20¾
G. H. K. p..............2:21
Lexington Chief, p...2:20¼
Linden, p...............2:26½
Sherman Aristos, p...2:29
Aristos Jr. by Aristos.
Don Aristos...........2:29¾
Treadway..............2:24½
Lady Vivian, p.......2:17¼
Lady Sam, p..........2:22½
Arkansaw Traveler.
Yankee Girl, p........2:22¼
Arlington by Aberdeen.
Lady Douglas........2:24¼
Arminius by Reveler.
Dodger.................2:18
Armagh by Aberdeen.
Adelaide...............2:29¾
Alpha 2:21¾
Roman..................2:29

Arnold by Goldsmith's Abdallah.
McCready.................2:29¾
Ready Boy...............2:23¼
Twilight.....................2:20½
Brant Arnold, p.........2:29¼
Arostook Boy.
Cleopatra, p..............2:29½
Arrowwood by Nutwood.
Luella Shawhan, p....2:23
Arsaces by Alcyone.
Capt. Walbridge........2:18¼
E. W. L.....................2:25½
Uncle Josh................2:20½
Artemas by Rysdyk's Hambletonian.
Allie Swift.................2:27
Abe Smith..................2:24¾
Artemas B.................2:25¾
Belva B......................2:20¼
Billy B.......................2:23¼
Blanalco.....................2:29¼
Belle Girl..................2:25½
Charley Burch............2:23½
Claudius....................2:29¾
Green Girl.................2:21¼
Robert L....................2:29¾
S. W. C......................2:27
Wyandotte.................2:24¼
Eylight, p...................2:19¼
Handy B.....................2:16¾
Manilla Girl, p............2:24¼
Pinewood, p...............2:20
Tom Edison, p............2:21½
Arthur S. by Oceana Chief.
Turk...........................2:27
Arthur Wilkes by Gov. Wilkes.
Annie Wilkes.............2:24½
Lady A., p..................2.23¼
Arthur Wilkes by Guy Wilkes.
Lucy W.......................2:28½
Wayland W.................2:12½
Welcome....................2:27½
Arthurton by Rysdyk's Hambletonian.
Arab...........................2:15
Bonanza....................2:29½
Joe Arthurton.............2:20½
Lady Escott...............2:26½
Pantomime................2:21¼
Sheeny......................2:29¾
Artillery by Rysdyk's Hambletonian.
Armory.......................2:29¾
Artilla.........................2:20
Bellini.........................2:13¼
Item...........................2:26¼
Selleta.......................2:23½
Arcturus, p................2:25
Artist Wilkes by Red Wilkes.
Maj. Clelland..............2:20½
Ashland by Mambrino Chief.
Fanny Burroughs.......2:27¼
Highland Win.............2:26
Joe Pettit...................2:30
Ashland Almont by Almont.
Belle A.......................2:30
Ashland Boy by Fergus McGregor.
Ashland Girl...............2:22¼
Ashland Chief by Mambrino Chief.
Ashland Kate.............2:29¾
Black Cloud...............2:17¼
Blue Cloud.................2.27
Ashland Clay by Curtis' Clay.
Georgie M., p.............2:16¼
Little Frank, p............2:19¼

Ashland Sprague by Gov. Sprague.
Dandy Sprague..........2:25
Ashland Wilkes by Red Wilkes.
Bert Oliver.................2.19¼
Carroll Wilkes............2:25¼
Laudema Wilkes........2 26½
Maxie B.....................2:28½
Mertis Wilkes.............2:29¼
Myron McHenry..........2.18¼
Phyllis Tee.................2:23¼
Wilkecho....................2:30
Bide-a-Wee, p...........2:25
Della Sherman, p.......2:21½
John R. Gentry, p.......2:03¾
Maxey B, p................2:23½
President Wilkes, p...2:19½
Ashman by Sherman.
Spencer Girl..............2:30
Ashtabula by Atlantic.
Sadie B......................2:24¼
Ashwood by Wedgewood.
Cora Ashwood............2:21¾
Athlete by Almont.
Athlete Jr..................2:29¼
Athlete Rex...............2:28¼
Athlot........................2:?4¼
Aubrey......................2:27
Bessie F...................2·29½
First Call...................2:20¼
Isaac G.....................2:26¾
Mabel M....................2:30
Craighead, p..............2:27
Atlantic by Almont.
Atlanta Meleager......2:26½
Algiers.......................2:29¾
Atlantic General........2:25
Atlantic Jr..................2:21¼
Betsy Trotwood.........2:26½
Dandy.......................2:14¾
Gypsy Belle..............2:25½
Jeff Davis..................2:17¼
Lulo...........................2:27½
Redmont....................2:21
Alton L., p..................2:23½
Arctic, p.....................2:21¼
Argosy, p...................2:25
Atlantic Gem, p.........2:28¼
Atlantic Gift, p...........2:28½
Atlantic King, p..........2:09¾
Maud Muller, p...........2:25
Pierpont Girl, p..........2:24¾
W. L., p......................2:19½
Atlantic (Bard's) by Almont
Atlanta, p...................2:22½
Atlantic Chief by Stevens' Bald Chief.
Boston Davis.............2:26½
Nettle.........................2:29½
Atlantic King by Atlantic.
Frank Bogash, p........2:26¾
Atto Rex by Attorney.
Alta Reina..................2:27
Roy Rex.....................2:28¾
Attorney by Harold.
Atto Rex.....................2:21¾
Chadron....................2:27
Dandy Dan.................2:24¼
Kitty C.......................2·30
Mabel A.....................2 23¼
Roger K.....................2:26¼
Attorney Jr., p...........2:12
Gov. Lucas, p............2·24¾
Maggie A., p..............2:25
Atwood by Green's Bashaw.
Sagwa........................2:27¾

Atwood by Nutwood.
Estella Atwood..........2:29¼
Hazelwood................2:29½
Marwood....................2:30
Morgwood..................2 29½
Weden K....................2:?6¼
Almont, p...................2 28½
Aubrey by Athlete.
Rob Roy.....................2:29¾
Zero...........................2:18½
Auctioneer by Alcantara.
Alta May....................2.28½
Auctioneer.
Rodney J...................2:21¼
Auctioneer Johnnie by George M. Patchen.
Lilly Mack..................2:24¼
Auditor by Rysdyk's Hambletonian.
Bracelet.....................2:25
Burglar......................2.24¼
Epaulet......................2·19
August Bel· ont by Rysdyk's Hambletonian.
Astral.........................2:18
Don Cossack.............2:28
Aurora by Daniel Lambert.
Constance.................2 21¼
Daniel Lambert..........2.28
Maud.........................2 27
Daphne, p..................2:29½
Austerlitz by August Belmont
Australia....................2·26¾
Dolly B......................2:27½
Lady Lannon..............2:25½
Autocrat by Volunteer.
Rare Ripe..................2 19¼
Autocrat by George M. Patchen.
Little Frank................2:24¾
Autocrat by Havoc.
Alarmist.....................2:21¼
Autograph by Alcantara.
Fraulein.....................2:29½
Jacksonian................2:19¾
Rapid Transit.............2 29¼
Spirea.......................2:24¼
Autumn by Time Medium.
Agatha.......................2:24½
Avalon by Marlborough.
Mattie........................2:29½
A. W. Richmond by Simpson's Blackbird.
Dick Richmond...........2·20
Jack...........................2:26
Larco.........................2:28
Leon..........................2:22¼
Richelieu....................2:29¼
Richmond Jr..............2:15
Romero......................2·19½
Rosewald...................2:29½
What Ho....................2:25¼
Arrow p......................2.13¼
Ellwood, p..................2:17¾
Orlinda Richmond, p.2:15
Axtell by William L.
Axinite.......................2:17½
Axle...........................2:15¾
Axtella.......................2:29¼
Axtellite.....................2:27¼
Axtelloid....................2:29¼
Axworthy...................2:28¾
Elloree.......................2:18
Go Tell.......................2:29¼
Kate Bradley.............2:30
Leetell........................2:29¼
Maytell.......................2:24
Praytell......................2:29¼

Prince Axtell. 2:28¼
Robin 2:28
Tarantelle... .... 2:21¼
Aytoun by King Rene.
　Miss Cleveland ..-.. .2.17¼
Azim by Almont Pasha.
　Ella D................2:28¼
Azmoor by Electioneer.
　A. A. A 2:25
　Azmon................ 2:23¼
　Bonnibel............2:17¾
　Rowena..... ....2:17

Bacon by Ajax.
　Tom Ogden, p........2:12¼
Badger by Kerr's Bashaw.
　Cleo.. ....2:21
Badger Boy by Hambletonian
　Mambrino.
　Van Tromp 2:29
BadgerBoy by RossmanHorse
　Gen. Howard 2:26½
Badger Clay by Charles Hel-
　burn.
　Beulah C............. 2:27
　Beulah C., p 2:28½
Badger Sprague by Gov.
　Sprague
　Allie K 2:26½
　Gladys' Sprague 2:19¼
Baffle by Alar Clay.
　Gipsey M., p.. .....2:25
Bajardo by Stephen A. Doug-
　las.
　Stephanus 2:28¼
Bajardo Jr. by Bajardo.
　Trixie P., p 2:27¼
Baker Pilot by Pilot Mam-
　brino.
　Lamar.... .... 2:24¼
Balaklava by Onward.
　Highland Wilkes. ...2:25
　Leta Howe............2:27¾
Bald Chief by Alexander's
　Bay Chief.
　Tom Brown.... ...2:27¾
Bald Chief Jr. by Adams'
　Bald Chief.
　Nelly O., p.... ......2:13½
Bald Hornet (Nave's) by Sul-
　tan.
　Bald Hornet. p 2:21
Bald Hornet by Robinson's
　Bald Hornet.
　Clint Kiff, p 2:16¾
　Freeland, p 2:19¼
　Hornet Girl, p....... 2:30
　Guy C., p.............2:14½
　Lon G., p.............2:21¼
　Paul, p 2 09½
　Red Hornet, p........2:23¼
　Uncle George, p......2:26¼
　Venture, p 2:09½
Balmont Wilkes by Wilkie
　Collins.
　Phillis Wilkes, p.... 2:20¼
　Toomey, p............2:26¼
Ball R.
　Lilly Bush, p....2:29½
Balsora by Alexander's Ab-
　dallah.
　Kentuckian 2:27¼
　Rosita................2:26¼
Banker by Rysdyk's Hamble-
　tonian.
　Bermuda...............2:20¼
　Bradstreet.. .... 2:27½

Hornpipe............ 2:22¾
Banker Messenger by Rys-
　dyk's Hambletonian.
　Dexter H 2:29¼
　Duroc.. ... .2:26¼
Banner Boy by De Long's
　Ethan Allen.
　Robert R., p 2:30
Banker Rothschild by Roths-
　child.
　Dayball 2:30
　Hunter...............2:23¾
　Molly Morton 2:30
Banquo by Daniel Boone.
　Hampton Girl, p......2:27¼
Banks by Ambassador.
　Starling, p.............2:27¼
Barbarian.
　Guide, p. 2:28½
Barkis by Rysdyk's Hamble-
　tonian
　Athlete............ 2:21
　Andy K.. . ...2:25
　Banknola 2:26¾
　Clematis 2:21¼
　Conundrum...........2:25¼
　Florence S..... .. 2:'5¾
　Mamie C...............2 28¼
　Nelly M................2:27¼
　Palo Alto.............2 25¼
　Sherwood 2:22¼
　Sorosis, p........... 2:27½
Barney Monroe by Jim Mon-
　roe
　Joe Barney 2 26
Barney Wilkes by Red Wilkes
　Wilkie Knox, p . ..2:10¼
Barney Wilkes by Geo.Wilkes
　Ba ney Wilkes Jr... 2:26¼
　Champion Wilkes....2:22¼
　Conley.... ....2:25
　Dan Cupid 2:09¼
　Henry Grady.........2:28
　Lena Wilkes...........2·29¼
　Maggie H.......... ..2:28¼
　Mary S................2:28
　Mattie Wilkes.........2:21¼
　Sam Wilkes............2:29¼
　Barney, p 2:08¾
Baronial by Baron Wilkes.
　Bellronial 2:29¼
　Fielder... ....2·25¾
Baron West by Col. West.
　Anderson...... .....2:29¼
Barnhart by Jay Bird.
　Barnetta 2:27¼
Baron Wilkes by Geo. Wilkes
　Alice Leyburn 2:21¼
　Alfonso...............2:29¾
　Anita.............. 2 29¾
　Baron Brown.........2:26¼
　Baron Crisp..........2:24
　Baron Posey..........2:21¼
　Baron Jean 2:30
　Barolite.......... . 2:21½
　Baronmore............2:17½
　Baron Rodgers........2:17½
　Baron Russell.... ....2:24½
　Baronet...............2:11½
　Blue Blood.. ....2:22¼
　Bon Mot.............2·25¼
　Boniface 2:29¼
　Brava 2:14½
　Brown Silk 2:22¼
　Earl Baltic............2 25¼
　Enfin 2:28¼
　Euroclydon 2:25
　Jingles 2:28¾

Lady Ethel............2:24¾
Margrave 2:15½
Madrona 2:26
Oakland Baron. 2:14½
Red Baron.............2:29½
Baronial, p 2:29¼
Barondale, p 2:11½
Bay Baron, p.........2:19¾
Frenchy, p............2:22¼
Nydia Wilkes, p.....2:12¾
Rubinstein, p.........2:08
Barony by Simmons.
　Cantella Wilkes......2:25½
Bartholomew Wilkes by Geo.
　Wilkes.
　Ben Buxton 2:26¾
　Besor 2:28¾
　Dryden...............2:20
　Ed Wilkes. 2:28½
　Geneva Wilkes. 2:22¼
　Jolly Wilkes. 2 20
　Monroe Wilkes.......2:17¼
　Sunlight..............2:29½
　Whitcomb Riley, p ..2:14½
Bashaw by Vernol's Black
　Hawk.
　Amboy 2:26
　Bashaw (Butler's)...2:28¼
　Bashaw Jr ....2·24¾
　Fred Douglas.... ...2:20¾
　Gen. Lee 2:26½
　Governor.............2·24
　Green Charley.... .. 2 26¼
　Hambleto'an Bashaw.2:21¼
　Josephine..... .... 2:30
　Josephus 2:19¾
　Kirkwood 2:24
　Otho.... ....2:22½
　Robert Burns 2:20
　Rose of Washington..2:21¾
　Tom Kirkwood......2:29¼
　Wagner Bashaw.....2:25¾
　Wild Oats 2:29¼
　Julia L , p...........2:28
Bashaw (Johnson's).
　Daisy M., p............2:20
Bashaw.
　Lord Nelson......... 2:29½
Bashaw by Green's Bashaw.
　Benny B..............2:24
　Buddinger 2:24
　Gardner H...........2:25½
　Ben Jack, p..........2:29
　Nelly M.. p 2:15½
Bashaw (Springsteen's) by
　Green's Bashaw.
　Elsie B...............2:29¼
Bashaw (Couch's), untraced.
　Molly Harris.........2:25½
Bashaw (French's) by Black
　Bashaw.
　Carl G 2:27¾
　Little Daisy. 2:20¾
Bashaw Bill.
　Billy the Kid, p 2:28
Bashaw Bolly by Chester.
　Bashaw Fred 2:17
Bashaw Chief by Paystreak.
　Rose. 2:18¾
Bashaw Drury by Green's
　Bashaw.
　Widow Bedott........2:29¾
Bashaw Hambletonian by
　Romulus.
　Maud Howe...........2:27¼
　Molly K..............2:29½
Bashaw, Jr.
　Henry H., p........ .2·23¼

Bashaw Pilot by Pilot Temple.
Louis S..................2:26¼
Bashaw Prince.
Favorite..................2:30
Bashtine by Bashaw, Jr.
A. W. Fawcett..........2:26¼
Cabash....................2:27¼
Bassett M. by Masterlode.
Pedro L...................2:18
Lulu B.....................2:24
Little John, p..........2:30
Nordeck, p...............2:30
Bayard by Pilot, Jr.
Aimee.....................2:30
Billy Q....................2:29½
Bliss.......................2:21½
Eagle Plume............2:29¼
Emma B...................2:22
Kitty Bayard............2:12¼
Lilly J......................2:25½
Modie H...................2:29½
Belle Bayard, p........2:26¼
Em Pierce, p............2:23¼
Fanny C, p...............2:24¼
Gray Bayard, p........2:24¾
Pilatoga, p...............2:20¼
Psyche, p.................2:19¼
Bayard Wilkes by Alcantara.
Alfred, p..................2:24¾
Bay Billy, untraced.
Dan.........................2:25¼
Bay Billy by Rysdyk's Hambletonian.
Dandy R...................2:27¼
John McDougall.......2:29
Bay Bird by Jay Bird.
Dr. Puff...................2:29
Baybrino by Swigert.
Edgecliff..................2:27
Bay Chief by Louis Napoleon.
Lyman......................2:25½
Bay Chief by Richelieu.
Fred W....................2:17½
McClintock...............2:20¼
Bay Chief Jr. by Bay Chief.
Lucy Smith, p..........2:28¾
Bay Dick by Addison.
Dick Hartford..........2:25
Bay Ethan by Ethan Wilkes.
Frenzie L.................2:20¼
Frenchy, p...............2:28¼
Bay Henry.
Harry Admire...........2:26
Bay Lambert by Daniel Lambert.
Miss Fanny Jackson..2:30
Bay Middleton by Middletown.
Belle Middleton.......2:27½
Charles B................2:24¼
Frank Middleton.......2:20¾
Harry P...................2:29¾
Henry Middleton......2:26¼
H. M. Strong............2:25¼
Maggie G. Middleton 2:20¾
Mattie D.................2:25¾
Middleway...............2:22¼
Molly Middleton.......2:25¼
Prince Middleton......2:20¼
Baymont by Alden Goldsmith
Justina....................2:25
Monte Christo..........2:29¾
Mogul......................2:16¼
Jordan, p.................2:11½
Jurist, p...................2:26½

Bayonne Brince by Kentucky Prince.
Annie Bennett...........2:26¼
Black Prince.............2:26¼
Cad..........................2:27¾
Grace Hastings.........2:24
Lulu.........................2:26¼
Mahogany.................2:12¼
Nutshell....................2:27¼
Readington Prince.....2:22½
Seneca Prince...........2:25¼
Densmore, p..............2:23¾
Ella A., p..................2:24¼
Fresno Prince, p........2:17¾
Nellie S., p................2:22¼
Bay Richmond by Rysdyk's Hambletonian.
Fritz.........................2:27½
Bay Rolfe by Young Rolfe.
Charley Rolfe............2:29¼
Bay Rose by Sultan.
Col. K. R...................2:22¼
Lyda C......................2:27
Bay Star by Daniel Lambert.
Amy Lee....................2:14
Roxie Lee..................2:26¾
St. Lambert...............2:29¼
Bay State by Jay Gould.
Mary Ann.................2:28½
Cohannet, p...............2:17½
Kantoka, p................2:27¼
Bay Tom (Harding's), by Knight's Snow Heels.
Lee H., p...................2:13
Bay Tom.
Fred Neil...................2:24¼
Bay Tom, Jr., p..........2:30
Major P., p................2:30
Mamie L., p...............2:24
Tom Howard, p..........2:29¼
Tom Webster, p..........2:11¼
Bay Tom, Jr. by Bay Tom.
Billy A......................2:13¼
Nickel Plate...............2:22
Duplex, p..................2:17¼
Elk Tom, p................2:19
Fleety H., p...............2:25½
Grand View, p...........2:21¾
Johnny Woods, p........2:21
Mary J., p.................2:18¾
Raven T., p...............2:22¼
Smuggler, p..............2:29¾
Bay Wilkes by George Wilkes.
Black Wilkes.............2:29¼
Baywood by Blackwood.
Lulu McCurdy, p.......2:14¼
Baywood by Nutwood.
Dr. Swift, p...............2:13
Baywood (Barnes') by Phillip's Blackwood.
Bewilder...................2:28½
Dick Pennell, p..........2:14½
Sawtelle, p................2:17½
Beaconsfield by Fayette Denmark.
Clopton, p.................2:24½
Bearce Horse by Horner Horse
Belle Smith..............2:29
Beauclerc by Princeps.
Bethel.......................2:16¼
Beaufort by Woodward's Ethan Allen Jr.
Beaufort Girl............2:27¼
Frank L....................2:27¼
Larry........................2:23¼
Prince......................2:27½
Beaumont by Belmont.
A. J..........................2:30

Ethel H....................2:20
Plympton..................2:29
Quay........................2:28½
Vermont...................2:29¼
Rocknight................2:29½
Beaver by Hermes.
Laura.......................2:28¼
Beecher by Blue Grass.
Mike........................2:28
Royal Guard.............2:30
Beecher Boy, p..........2:27¾
Molly B., p...............2:29¼
Beechnut by Louis Napoleon.
Woodberry, p............2:26
Bee Line.
Grasshopper, p.........2:21
Bedford by Strathmore.
Sarah Shelton...........2:28½
Brent Wells, p...........2:19¾
Belden Boy by Brownwood.
Bellton......................2:24¾
Belladonna by Ambassador.
H. B. M....................2:29¾
Simmons, p...............2:14¼
Bell Boy by Electioneer.
Beauty Bells.............2:29½
Bridal Bells..............2:22½
Corner Bell..............2:23
Liberty Bell..............2:24
Princess Belle...........2:23¾
Anderson Bell...........2:20¼
Bellfounder (Milliman's) by American Bellfounder.
B. B.........................2:21½
Bellflower..................2:28¼
Dexter......................2:27
Gus..........................2:26¾
Kitty Lynch..............2:26¼
Nelly Burns..............2:25
Sweet Home.............2:30
Tempest...................2:29
Wonder....................2:27½
Bellfounder (Richard's) by Hungerford's Blucher.
Western Girl.............2:27
Belgium by Onward.
Belgia.......................2:26¼
Bellman by Indiaman.
Baltimore.................2:30
Belfry.......................2:24½
Belltone....................2:30
Bellette.....................2:24¼
Bell Morgan by Cottrill Morgan.
Lady Turpin.............2:23
Bellwood by Belmont.
Ryswood..................2:16
W. Van.....................2:24¼
Belmont by Alexander's Abdallah.
Belmont...................2:28½
Betsey Belle.............2:28¼
Blitzen.....................2:27½
Buttercup.................2:28
Clara D....................2:14¾
Christine..................2:25¼
Cora Belmont...........2:24½
Crescent...................2:25½
Currer Bell...............2:29¾
Davenant..................2:26¼
Dick Moore...............2:22½
Don Ricardo..............2:21½
Ecru.........................2:27½
Earl Belmont.............2:25½
Ella Belmont.............2:26¾
Erin.........................2:24¾
Fanny Belmont..........2:25¼
Flossie......................2:30

George Willis........ 2:29¼
Globard...............2:19¼
Gondola...............2:25¼
Grosjean..............2:24¾
Ichi Ban..............2:29¼
Ida...................2:29½
Lady Kelso............2:29
Laurabel..............2:27¾
Mambritonian 2:20½
Meander...............2:26½
Molino................2:27¼
Moquette..............2:27¼
Moscova...............2:28½
Newmont...............2:29¾
Nil Desperandum... 2:24
Nora Temple...........2:27¼
Nutwood...............2:18¾
Persica...............2:18½
Primmont..............2:21¼
Princippie Belmont..2:30
Riverbend.............2:24½
Stella Belmont........2:19
Sonticus..............2:27
Tremont...............2:28½
Vatican...............2:29¼
Viking................2:19¼
Warder................2:29¼
Waterloo..............2:19¼
Wavelet...............2:24½
Wedgewood.............2:19
Wimbledon.............2:29¾
Belton, p.............2:17¼
Don Ricardo, p........2:21
Fred Arthur, p........2:12¼
King Jim, p...........2:20½
Roseman, p............2:18¾
Pistachio, p.......... 2:29¼
Belmont (Williamson's) by American Boy.
Venture...............2:27¼
Belmont (Fisk's) by Irish Foxhunter.
Belle H............ 2:24½
Belle of Shelby.......2:28¾
Belmont Boy.
Big John, p...........2:28
Belmont Chief by Belmont.
Alex. C...............2:28¼
Jim Burns.............2:24½
Belton by Belmont.
Romola................2:20¼
Belvidere by Belmont.
Bartholdi.............2:30
Belvoir by Belmont.
Corrie................2:28½
Cebron, p.............2:17¼
Mountain Queen, p. .2:24½
Wickopee, p...........2:17½
Ben Adhem by Ben Franklin.
Jay Girl..............2:21¼
Ben Atwood by Green's Bashaw,
Sagwa.................2:27¾
Ben Bolt by Phillips.
Deacon, p 2:20
Gov. Foraker, p.......2:24¾
Ben Bruce by Corbeau.
Miss Bruce, p.........2:20
Ben Butler by Knickerbocker.
Nelly C...............2:25¼
Ben Easton by Louis Napoleon.
Ben's Misfit, p.......2:19¼
Benefactor by Egbert.
Benediction...........2:27¼
Benefactor Jr. (p)....2:18¼
Benefit by Gen. Benton.
Palo Chief............2:20

Ben Franklin by Daniel Lambert.
Althea................2:24½
Belle Franklin........2:28¼
Belle Girl............2:28¾
Bessie................2:29¾
Cambridge Girl........2:28½
California Lambert ..2:27
Cassie B..............2:29¾
Charley Ray...........2:29
Dennis H..............2:28
Dynamite..............2:20¾
Frank H...............2:27½
George C.......... 2:28¼
Helena................2:26¼
Huldy B...............2:21¾
Katisha...............2:26¾
Little Witch..........2:29
Maxey.................2:30
May Be................2:24
May Queen.............2:29½
McMyatt...............2:25½
Nat Howe..............2:28½
Nimbus................2:26¼
N. O. D...............2:30
Orwell................2:24
Peerless Ben..........2:26¼
Rare Ben..............2:26
Richard Lambert,......2:25¾
R. W. S...............2:29¼
Surprise Franklin....2:26¼
Ben Adhem, p...... 2:21¼
Buck Franklin, p......2:16½
Henry C., p...........2:22¼
G. O. Taylor, p.......2:15¼
Sherman Franklin, p.2:28
Ben Harrison by Squire Talmage.
Ripton................2:30
Theme.................2:29¼
Ben Harrison by Allie Gaines.
Ben Allie, p..........2:21
Ben Lomond by Trojan.
Ben Lomond Jr.........2:27
Ben Lomond Jr. by Fanning's Ben Lomond.
Blue Jay..............2:29½
Johnny A.............. 2:22¾
Ben Lomond Jr. by Ben Lomond.
Ben Cole..............2:23¾
W. W. P., p...........2:10¾
Ben McGregor by Robert McGregor.
Maxie McGregor........2:28¾
Roy McGregor..........2:26
Ben Morrill by Winthrop Morrill.
Black Morrill.........2:23
Blacksmith Boy........2:28¼
La Prairie Girl.......2:29¼
Little Ben............2:28¼
Ben S., p.............2:29¼
Ben Patchen by Burlington.
Alexander.............2:19
Harry Hall, p.........2:29½
Ben Snatcher, Jr. by Ben Snatcher.
Rowdy Boy.............2:13¾
Ben Wicks by Hinsdale Horse
Donovan............... 2:27¼
Benson Horse by Crawford Horse
Lew Pettee............2:29
Benton by Gen. Benton.
Volta.................2:19
Bentonian by Gen. Benton.
Sonnet................2:24½

Benson.
Pressley M., p........2:21¼
Ben Wright by Royal Fearnaught.
Coon Hallow...........2:23½
Locomotive............2:29¼
Mamie J............... 2:28½
Berbrino by Mambrino Patchen.
Castianira............2:29¾
Berlin by Reavis' Blackbird.
Denis Ryan............ 2:29
Kate Ewing............2:21¼
Pansy.................2:24¼
Thapsin...............2:21¼
Bermuda by Banker.
Baron Brown...........2:24½
Bermuda Boy...........2:20¾
Bermuda Girl..........2:21¼
Boabdil...............2:23¼
Magdalene.............2:20
Pearl Belle...........2:26
Ruberta...............2:29¼
Rosemary, p...........2:20¾
Bernal by Electioneer.
Aria..................2:16¾
Bertrand by Jupiter Star.
Silverton.............2:27¼
Bertrand Black Hawk by Champlain.
Frank Fisk............2:29
Maude, p..............2:20
Bessemer by Thomas Jefferson.
Ted, p................2:24½
Bessemer by Voltaire.
Be Sure, p........... 2:14
Betterton by George Wilkes.
Betterman............. 2:27¼
Bettie King...........2:26¼
George St. Clair......2:15¼
Lulu B................2:20
Mabelle...............2:25½
Nora B................2:17½
Belle Simmons.........2:17¾
George St, Clair, p.. 2:22½
Prima Donna...........2:09¼
Tony Wilcox, p........ 2:13¾
Beverly Wilkes by George Wilkes.
Billy Thornhill.......2:24½
Bomba.................2:29¾
Bezant by Chichester.
Azant.................2:27½
Bayzant...............2:26¼
Belinda...............2:21½
Bezent Rule...........2:30
Bifty Duck............2:25
Biwabic...............2:28½
Flossie Bezant........2:25¼
Vysant................2:27¼
Billy by Gentry's Denmark.
Minnie Higgins........2:16½
Billy Bacchus by Aldrich's Bacchus.
Jennie Holton.........2:22¼
Billy Bashaw by John Bull.
Factory Boy...........2:20¼
Billy Bowlegs by Young Columbus.
Kitty.................2:30
Billy Cone by Flying Morgan.
Minnie K., p..........2:18¾
Myrtie S., p..........2:25
Billy Davis by Blue Bull.
Billy C., p...........2:20
Henry Dexter, p.......2:24¼
Pat O'Brien, p........2:21¼

Sunset, p............2:15¾
Billy Denton by Rysdyk's Hambletonian.
Captain..............2:28
John Love..........2:28½
Billy Denton, Jr., by Billy Denton.
Lady Jerauld 2:24¾
Billy Glenn, p, by John C. Breckinridge.
Frank Ferguson..... 2:26
Billy Green, by Scott's Hiatoga.
Billy Burns, p.........2:24¾
Billy Scott, p 2:21¼
Billy Warren, p.......2:29¾
Chase, p..............2:23¼
Judge Kail, p..........2:24
Little Em, p..........2:18½
Nettie Green, p 2:25
Sadie Burns, p...... 2:29½
Billy H. by Charley Brister.
Lady M..............2:21¼
Billy H. by Scott's Hiatoga.
Irish Boy.............2:20
Billy Hartshorn.
Lady Harrison, p 2:28¾
Billy Hayward by George M. Patchen, Jr.
Alonzo Hayward......2:30
Poscora Hayward....2:23½
Setting Sun.........2:29¾
Billy Hinsley by Blue Bull.
M. W...............2:20¾
Richwood Boy........2:29¾
Billy Hibbard by Marshall Chief.
Ned M., p...........2:24¾
Billy Kitchen.
Flora Mack 2 29¾
Billy Knox by Wood's Hambletonian.
Gypsy K.............. 2:25¼
Humbug..............2:21¾
Billy Mont by Gifford.
M. C. S...............2:30
Billy Mustapha.
Little Mary 2:25
Billy Norfolk by Norfolk.
Jim...................2:22½
Lady I................2:29
Billy Patterson by King's Champion.
Col Wood, p.........2.21¼
Billy Sayre by Young Jim.
Galileo Rex, p.........2.12¾
Billy Sherman by Jesse Stowe.
Sherman Bashaw.....2 28
Billy Sprague by Gov. Sprague.
Badger State....... 2:30
Silas F 2:29¾
Swift Bird, p........ 2:26½
Billy Stranger.
Billy R...............2:29¼
Billy Stanton by Gen. Stanton.
Epitaph..............2:30
Gee Whiz..............2:30
Billy Thornhill by Beverly Wilkes.
Great Stakes ....2·24¼
Minnie B...............2:29¾
Billy Toronto
Eddie B. p 2:17½
Sleepy Rover..........2:30

Billy Wilkes by Harry Wilkes.
Alta Boy.............2:26½
Bertnot...............2:25¾
Bloomfield 2:27½
Darkey Wilkes........2:28½
Judge Rider..........2:20
Jura...................2:22½
Mary Marshall........2:12¾
Prelude 2:25¾
Jo Jett, p............2:14½
May Marshall, p......2:08¾
Billy Wilson by Blue Bull.
Sir Gay..............2:26½
Binderton by Belmont.
Maud C..............2:15¾
Bird
Birdmont.............2:22¾
Bishop by Tom Allen.
Capt. Douds..........2:27¾
Bishop by Princeps.
Belle H 2:26¼
Bishop Hero..........2:26
Gregory..............2:30
McGlynn 2:25
Bishop Berkely by Lance.
Frank W. p 2:21¼
Bismark by John B. Stockton.
Peach................2:27¼
Bismark by Index.
Chancellor. 2:16
Hazel H. p 2:12¾
Bismark by David Hill.
Lady Markam, p.....2:17¾
Bismuth by Rysdyk's Hambletonian.
Scranton Belle........2:18¾
Bivouac by Onward.
Judge West, p........2:23¾
Black Ambassador by Ambassador.
Bad Actor 2:21¼
Navy Wilkes.........2:27
Syndicate, p.........2:19¾
Black Arthur by Altitude.
Hawthorne 2:29¼
Black Bashaw by Young Sleepy Davy.
Cozette 2:19
John H 2:20
Neal Whitbeck.......2:22¼
Black Bassinger by Legal Tender.
Bassinger Boy........2:23
Black Ben by Ben Franklin.
Wax...................2:24¾
Blackbird by Camden.
Blackbird............2:22
Blackbird (Reavis') by Simpson's Blackbird.
Mamie Griffin........2:20¾
Ned Forrest........2 25¼
Vic H 2:12¼
Fox, p 2:21¾
Blackbird, (Atherton's) by Cassius.
Frank Allison.........2:28¾
Black Bonner by David Bonner.
A. G...................2:27¼
R. C...................2:28¾
Black Chief by Copperbottom.
Bickford 2:29¾
Black Cloud by Ashland Chief.
Black Cloud Jr.......2:25
Fredonia..............2:21½

Harry D..............2.27
Mild Cloud 2:28
Vendetta............ 2:28¼
George Cloud, p......2 19¾
Black Cloud (Bemis') by Mambrino Patchen.
Charmer.............2:27
Jingo Jim 2 26½
Black Dan.
Comet, p..............2:24¼
Black Diamond by Clermont
Kentucky Jim 2:28
Black Diamond.
Clara J...............2:28
Black Dick.
Black Dick, p.........2:11
Black Doc by Dr. Herr.
Pattie Cooper.........2·30
Black Douglas by Clay Cadmus.
Barney Clay.........2:29½
Billy Holmes......... 2:27
Black Dutchman by Doble's Black Bashaw.
Eve....................2 27
Flora D 2:29¼
Frank R 2:23¾
Hunter.................2:29
Lady Independence 2 29¼
Lady Kildeer........ 2:28
Black Ed
Wait-a-While, p........2:17½
Black Ethan.
Pet 2 19½
Black Flying Cloud by Hill's Black Hawk.
Badger Girl........... 2·22½
Black Frank by Bull Pup.
Fred Douglas .... 2·24½
Black Frank by Mitchell's Black Hawk Morgan.
Black Joe..........2:29½
Dan Voorhees 2:30
Black Harp by Peavine.
Frank P 2:19¼
Black Harry Clay by Doty's Harry Clay.
Bateman 2:22½
Roger 2:24¼
Black Hawk (Vermont) by Sherman Morgan.
Belle of Saratoga ......2·29
Ethan Allen 2:25½
Lancet 2 27½
Young America, p 2 23
Black Hawk (Long Island) by Andrew Jackson.
Prince. 2:24½
Black Hawk by Vermont Black Hawk.
Sisson Girl............ 2 28½
Black Hawk (Whitesides') by Canada Black Hawk.
Molsey.................. 2·21¾
Rival 2:30
Black Hawk (Canadian).
Fearnaught...........2 28
Village Girl...........2:28
Black Hawk (Record's) by Champion Black Hawk.
Flossie R 2:27¼
King, (p)..............2:30
Black Hawk (Vernol's) by Long Island Black Hawk.
Jessie................2:21

Black Hawk (Tyler's) by Gen. Stark.
- Fred B. 2 28½

Black Hawk.
- Howell, p 2 18¼

Black Hawk Hero by Vermont Black Hawk.
- Grey Mack 2 25½

Black Hawk Harry by Lightfoot.
- Eli 2 29¼

Black Hawk McGregor by Robert McGregor
- Amberlou 2 27¼
- Gen Wiles 2 15
- Black Bird, p 2 28¾

Black Hawk Messenger by Morgan Messenger.
- Larry C., p 2:19¾

Black Hawk Morgan.
- Lilly Banks, p 2 22

Black John
- Richard B., p 2 25½

Black Knight, p by Dave Highlander.
- Pilot R 2 21¾

Black Mack by Mansfield
- Chick Bills .... 2·26¼

Black Milo by Cornish Morrill
- Judgment 2 26¼

Black Morgan.
- Princess 2 28

Black Morrill by Vermont Ranger.
- Lyndon Boy 2 26¼

Black Oak
- Jay and See, p 2 30

Black Pat.
- Iona, p 2 27½

Black Pilot by All Right.
- Pilot Jr 2:21

Black Pilot by Roscoe.
- Centurion 2 27¼
- Pilot Knox 2:19¾
- Pilot Maid 2 21¼
- Pixie 2:29½
- Tinnie B 2 27¾
- Young Pilot 2:22¼
- Pilot Knox, p 2:20½

Black Prince by Dictator
- Dan Velox 2:16½
- Frank H., (p) 2 26

Black Prince Jr. by Black Prince.
- Nigger Boy, p 2:19¼

Black Ralph by Wicker's Flying Cloud.
- George D. Sherman 2 29¼

Black Ralph, by David Hill.
- Belle Spencer 2 26¼
- Keepsake .... 2·29¼
- Killarney, p 2.20½

Black Ranger.
- Edgewood 2:27¼
- Elmwood Chief 2:18¾

Black Republican.
- John A. Logan 2 30
- John A. Logan, p 2 26¼
- Prince B., p 2 28½

Black Rolfe.
- Janet .... 2·24¾
- Rolfe K 2:29½

Blackstone by Rysdyk's Hambletonian.
- Daisy Hamilton 2 28½
- Walter O 2.30
- Hiram H; p 2 23¾

Blackstone Jr. by Blackstone.
- Yankee Luck 2 23

Blackstone Prince by Blackstone.
- Jack Raleigh 2:23½

Black Sam
- Plow Girl, p 2 26¼

Black Sultan Jr. by Black Sultan.
- Olivette 2 28¼

Black Tom
- Prince Boy 2:27¼

Black Victor by Alcantara.
- Bay Victor 2:30
- Arabian Wilkes, p 2 28¼
- Harry Victor, p 2 20

Black Walnut by Administrator
- Robbins 2 21½
- Secret 2 30

Black Wilkes by George Wilkes
- Bay Wilkes 2:25½
- New Fashion 2:25
- Angelina p .... 2·16¼
- Promise, p 2 25¼
- Winslow Wilkes, p 2 09¾

Blackwood by Alexander's Norman
- Alice Blackwood 2 27
- Blackwood Jr 2 22½
- Blackwood Prince 2 23¼
- Edgerton 2 26½
- Leda Wood 2 30
- Milton Blackwood 2.26¼
- Proteine 2:18
- Rosewood 2 27
- Suitor 2 21
- Wildwood 2 30
- Seraph, p .... 2·29

Blackwood (Phillips') by Blackwood
- Blackwood Belle .... 2·30

Blackwood Chief by Blackwood.
- Little Dan 2:21¾
- Toy 2 27½
- W. H. Nichols 2:23¼

Blackwood Jr. by Blackwood.
- All So 2 20¼
- Gracie B 2:22¾
- Hardwood 2 24¾
- Little Tommy 2:27¾
- Miss Woodford 2:23½
- Secret 2 30
- Rolfewood, p 2:20¾

Blackwood Mambrino by Protos
- Baywood 2 29½
- Grace W 2 21¼
- Silkwood, p 2 07

Blanco by Iron's Cadmus.
- Smuggler 2 15¼

Blanco Abdallah by Erie Abdallah.
- Judge M., p 2 26½

Bland by Auditor
- Harry Brooks, p 2 24½

Blazing Star by Henry Clay.
- Sleepy Tom 2 28½
- Mountain Boy, p 2 27
- Tom Cooper, p 2 26½

Blind Bashaw.
- Nutmace, p 2 29¼

Blind Tom, untraced.
- Friday 2:27¼
- Friday Jr. 2:29¼
- Thomas C 2:26¼

Blind Tom.
- Lottie E 2:29½

Blitzen by Belmont.
- Charley Wheeler 2 19½
- Jim Savory 2:29¼

Blondin by Clark's Mohawk Jr.
- Billy Ford 2 26¼

Blood Chief by Blood's Black Hawk
- Fanny Robinson 2 20¼
- Woolly Jim 2:29½
- Chief, p .... 2·24½

Blood Chief Jr by Blood Chief.
- Joe Hal 2 30

Bloodmont by Olympus
- Ada P 2 25½

Bloomfield by Billy Wilkes
- Joe Fifer 2 18

Blucher by Ball's Black Eagle.
- Martha Washington 2 20¾
- Blackstone 2:21¼

Blue Bayard by Bayard
- Bessie R., p 2 21½

Blue Boy, by Blue Buck.
- Peek-a-Boo 2 27

Blue Blood by Kentucky Prince.
- Blue Prince 2 26
- True Blue 2 30
- Blue Queen .... 2·29¼

Blue Britton
- Blue Bob, p 2.23

Blue Bull (Wilson's) by Pruden's Blue Bull.
- Alice Peyton 2 27½
- Beauty 2 28
- Belle Wilson 2:23½
- Bertha 2 23¼
- Bertie 2 27
- Bessie 2:17½
- Blanche H .... 2·26¼
- Blue Bell 2:26¼
- Blue Bull (Grove's) 2:26¼
- Boy 2:29¾
- Bullion 2 28
- Bulwer .... 2·23
- Chance .... 2·20½
- Commander 2 26¼
- Daisy Blackwood 2 29¼
- Dayton Belle 2.29¾
- Dick Stauffer 2 20¼
- Dr Sheppard 2 29¼
- Dom Pedro 2:27
- Edward B 2 26½
- Ella Wilson 2.30
- Elsie Good 2.22½
- Ethel 2 23
- Florence M 2:22¼
- Gen. Russ 2.29¼
- Gladiator 2.22¼
- Hoosier Girl 2 25¾
- Ina G 2:24½
- Ira M 2 30
- James Halfpenny 2 29¼
- Joseph 2.29¼
- Kate Bennett 2 29¼
- Kate Hall 2:24½
- Kate McCall 2 23
- Lena Swallow 2 19
- Little Wonder 2:30
- Lona Guffin 2:23½
- Lucy Fry 2:20¾
- Mamie 2 21¼
- Mattie H 2:27½
- May Bird .... 2·23
- Mila C 2 26½
- Molly Kistler 2:27½
- Myrtella G 2:28
- Otto K 2:24¼
- Purity .... 2·30
- Richard 2 21

Sharper 2:19¼
Sigma Nu 2:29¼
Sterling Wilkes 2:23½
Tilford 2:17¾
Wawona 2:19½
Wilkiemont 2:28
Willamore 2:25
Abdallah Wilkes, p 2:14
Billy Frazier, p 2:21¼
Bourbon Patchen, p 2:09
Coast Boy, p 2:10½
Coastman, p 2:08½
Elmer E., p 2:28¾
Forest Wilkes, p 2:15
Mabel P., p 2:17¼
Major Wolf, p 2:14½
Miller Ward, p 2:16½
Montaigne, p 2:27¼
Reward J., p 2:10¼
Sadie H., p 2:20¼
Sigma Nu, p 2:17¾
Tilman, p 2:29¼
Bow Bells by Electioneer.
Alarm Bells 2:29¾
Boreal 2:17¼
Bowery Boy.
J. R. L., p 2:21¼
Boxer by Jefferson Prince.
Emma W 2:25½
Brandywine (Keene's) by Cobb's Brandywine.
Ned Forrest 2:28½
Brandywine by Brandywine.
Careless Boy 2:28
Grey Bill 2:30
Brazilian by Skeptic.
Sunrise 2:28¼
Brentham by Lex Loci
Nelly G 2:20
Brentwood by Blue Grass.
Kitewood 2:23
Newsboy, p 2:12¼
Brewer.
Roscoe, p 2:24½
Brewster by Hotspur Chief.
Brewster F 2:24¾
Brick Wilkes by Alcantara.
Belle Nira, p 2:24¼
H. J. Rockwell, p 2:12¼
Bretwood by Nutwood.
Albert Bretwood 2:26¾
Brigadier by Happy Medium.
Balance All 2:29¾
Brignolia 2:29¼
Brigadier (Doty's) 2:29¼
Cyclone 2:26¾
Ed Biggs 2:28½
Hazel Kirke 2:24
George Wapple, p 2:25
Brigand by Mambrino Chief.
Red Cross 2:21½
Bright Clay by John Bright.
Jerry M 2:30
Bright Light
Gyp, p 2:26¼
Nettie D., p 2:27¼
Tascott, p 2:26½
Watcheye, p 2:19
Brignoli W.
Miss Cecil 2:28¾
Brignoli Wilkes by Geo. Wilkes.
Blue Brig 2:21¾
Brilliant by Sterling.
Brilliantine, p 2:17¼
Brilliant by Young Morrill.
Prince B. 2:24½
Brilliant Golddust by Golddust.
Billy G 2:17¼
Lida D 2:24½
Brinker Sprague by Governor Sprague.
Gen. Sprague 2:26¼
Bristow by Mambrino Patchen.
X. Y. Z. 2:29½
Broadway by Robert Smith.
Cheerful Charley, p 2:28¼
Broadway.
Fascination, p 2:20¾
Brod Walnut by Lucas Brodhead.
Dan H 2:25¾
Fanny Rush, p 2:19
Walnut Bud, p 2:16¼
Broken-Leg by Rysdyk's Hambletonian.
Anna Knowlton 2:27¼
Big F 2:16½
Bronze
Pattie R 2:29½
Brook by Bayard
Speedaway 2:24¼
Belle J., p 2:12½
Bessie H., p 2:19½
Brookie Forest.
Jo He, p 2:12½
Brookmont by Belmont.
William R 2:28¼
Brooks, p, by Stone's Pilot.
Bonesetter 2:19
Brooks (Earnhart's)
Buckner, p 2:15½
Rattler Brooks, p 2:23¼
Bronx Jr. by Bronx
Billy Steinman 2:21½
Brougham by Rysdyk's Hambletonian.
Bromo 2:26
Brighton 2:28½
Clarence Girl 2:26¼
Edna W 2:29
Genevieve 2:26¾
Brown by Combat.
Judge Brown 2:29¼
Victress 2:28¼
Judge Case, p 2:17¼
Brown Chief by Mambrino Chief.
Maggie K. 2:29¼
Uncle Tom, p 2:25¾
Brown Douglas by Pelham Tartar.
Charley Gibson 2:21½
Brown Frank by Marshal Ney.
Dr. Cronin 2:27½
Monarch 2:25¼
Yellow Jacket 2:29¼
Brown Hal, by Gibson's Tom Hal.
Bay Hal, p 2:20¼
B. H. D., p 2:20½
Brown Hal Jr., p 2:17¼
Grapeshot, p 2:18
Hal Braden, p 2:07¼
Hal Carter, p 2:22¼
Hal Dillard, p 2:04¾
Hal Parker, p 2:13¾
Hal Pulaski, p 2:13½
Jim Mears, p 2:23¼
Laurel, p 2:10¾
Lizzie, p 2:27
Machette, p 2:21¾
Major Hal, p 2:29¼
Palmetto, p 2:12¾
Patasco, p 2:24¾
Prince Hal, p 2:16¼
Roxie, p 2:20
Soda Water, p 2:21½
Star Pointer, p 2:11¾
Storm, p 2:08½
Susie Brown, p 2:20¼
Brown Harry by Thurston's Black Hawk.
Cora F 2:28
Jenny W 2:30
St Elmo 2:29¼
Brown Henry by Corbeau.
R. M. Lewis 2:29
Bay Henry, p 2:23
Bonnie Boy, p 2:29¼
J. K., p 2:16½
Kate Collins, p 2:26
Brown Horse.
Grateful 2:28½
Brown Golddust.
Rufe Wilson, p 2:24½
Brown Jug by Nutwood.
Alviso 2:20
Charley C 2:14¼
Mary O 2:29¼
Mischief 2:22¼
Susie Carlos 2:27½
Susie K., p 2:27½
Brown Kimble by Ed Kimble
Black Cloud 2:23½
Brownmark by Victor Brownmark.
Diddie 2:25¼
Brownmont by Almont.
O. K. 2:29¼
Brown Tingham.
Tom Hughes, p 2:27½
Brown Wilkes by George Wilkes.
Aroon 2:27¾
Barderah 2:26¾
Bellona 2:29¼
Blanca 2:19¼
Brandoline 2:28½
Brazilian 2:24¼
Brown Donna 2:29½
Hattie Belle 2:25½
Keewaydin 2:28¼
Leo Wilkes 2:24¼
Ramona Wilkes 2:29¼
Rostoko 2:24¼
Velvet 2:23¾
Wintergreen 2:24½
Winterset 2:24½
Witch Hazel 2:21½
Zenas 2:27½
Banner Wilkes, p 2:20¼
Bashford, p 2:22¼
Branolia, p 2:22
Lady Wilkes, p 2:24½
Magown, p 2:27¼
Roland Wilkes, p 2:28½
Rosencrantz, p 2:27¼
Brownwood by Swigert.
Belden Boy, p 2:29¼
Bruce.
Kitty C., p 2:14
Brunswick Chief by Duke of Brunswick.
Fanny Brunswick 2:29¼
Blonde 2:14½
Brussells by Blue Bull.
Allen B 2:20¼
Frazee 2:29½
Spurrier Boy 2:30
Charley C., p 2:24
Ira C., p 2:26¾
Buccaneer by Iowa Chief.
Bulwer 2:26½
Flight 2:29

J. GOLDEN, MEDFORD, MASS.

The popular New England reinsman who marked Ralph
Wilkes 2:06¾ at Nashville.

A. C. PENNOCK, GLENVILLE, OHIO.

In 1893 Pennock drove Ortine to a two-year-old race record of 2:22¼
at Nashville, and in 1894 he gave Mambrino Queen
a race record of 2:13½.

Carleton by Gen. Geo. H. Thomas
Midland Maid p.. ... 2:21½
Carleton Colt by Don Fulano
Helen Wilkes 2 25¼
Carlos by Crittenden
Roy. 2.30
Carver by Onward.
Molly Hooper, p 2:24¼
Cash by Lance.
Ida A , p... .. 2 22
Cashier by Banker.
Quaker Boy 2 30
Cashier Jr , p 2:24¼
Cashier by Capoul.
Hard Cash, p 2:15¼
Cassady by Overton's Chieftain.
School Boy 2:26¼
Cassius M. Clay by Henry Clay.
George M. Patchen 2 23½
Cassius M. Clay Jr (Neave's) by Cassius M. Clay.
George Cooley 2 27
Harry Clay 2:29
Lady Lockwood.. ... 2:25
Lew Sayres 2:28¾
Cassius M. Clay Jr (Amos') by Cassius M Clay.
American Girl 2 16½
Cassius M. Clay Jr. (Strader's) by Cassius M Clay.
Annie C... ... .. . 2 23¼
Durango ... 2:23¾
Equinox......... . 2 27½
Harry Clay 2:23¾
Sinbad 2:29¾
Molly L , p 2:26½
Cassius M. Clay Jr (Ballard's) by Cassius M. Clay.
Cassius Prince . 2:29
May Day... . ... 2:30
Queechee Maid 2 25
Queechee Maid, p 2:26½
Castelar by Ajax
Katie Drew 2:28
Castilian by Gov. Sprague.
Josephine 2:19¼
Catawba.
Josie B., p 2:14½
Cazique by Aker's Idol.
Cazique 2 27¼
Cedarwood by Nutwood.
Lumpwood 2 21¾
Celadon by Triton
Colored Man 2:23
Centennial by Saturn.
Gen. Garfield, p 2:24½
Cephas.
Little George, p 2:2¾
C. F. Clay by Caliban
Allen Kinney . . . 2:24¼
Bermuda Chief 2:29¼
Carmencita 2 27½
Cecilian Prince . .. 2 30
Clayton Lee...... .... 2:24¾
Claret.. .. ..2:29½
Clementine . 2:29¼
Clorine 2:18¼
Clover Leaf 2:21¾
Coleridge 2:23½
Connor...... .... 2:13¼
C cel 2:29¾
Flare 2:26½
Honest Clay 2:29¾
J. D Creighton 2:25½
Josephine.... .. ...2:29¼

Margaret W .. 2:25½
Mertz 2:24¼
Nut Brown Maid . 2:28¾
Perkins... . ...2:29¼
Red Leaf.. . . 2 28
Rosa S 2:21½
Santa Gertrudes . .. 2:29¾
Sarah C. 2:18½
Spring Day 2.26½
Tickle Me 2 28
Tony Boy 2:26
Wanetah 2 21¼
Winks. 2.20¼
Choral, p 2 15
Claybourne, p 2:11¼
Coleridge, p 2:08¾
Lord Clayton, p 2:24¾
Chadwick by Robert Bonner.
Marshal B . 2:26½
Challenge by Sherman Black Hawk
Doty. ... 2:21
Challenger by Almont
Challenger Chief 2:16
Procrastination . .. 2:29¼
Trumpeter 2:20¼
Champion (King's) by Champion.
Charley B 2 25
Col. Barnes 2 28½
George B. Daniels .. 2 24
Golden Girl 2:25¼
Myrtle ....2·25½
Nettie Burlew ....2·24
Newsboy. 2:27
Sorrel Dapper .. 2:28½
Champion (Gooding's) by King's Champion
·Castle Boy 2 21
·Champion ..... 2·26¼
Champion Girl . . 2 28
Chauncy M Bedle 2:30
Clarence E .... 2·30
Edwin... ... . .2 29¼
Edwin A.. . ...2·24¾
Elmer 2:22¼
Eva 2.25¼
Hornet 2:29¼
Lady Sargent 2:27¼
Naiad Queen . . 2:20¼
Nelly B 2.29¼
Novelty. 2 23½
St James 2 23¼
Schuyball 2 26½
York State 2:23¼
Miss Kruett, p 2 26
Champion (Fitzsimmons') by King's Champion
Jim Early .. .. 2·22¼
Champion (Canadian).
Joe H., p.... ..... 2 21¼
Champion Drew by Gen. Burnside.
Puritan 2:30
Champion (Howard's) by Gooding's Champion
Ben Hur......... ....2:24¼
Champion King by King's Champion.
Flirt.. . .. .2 28¼
Champion Knox by Bismarck.
Blacksmith 2 30
Mount Vernon.... ...2.26
Leonard, p 2:23¼
Champion Medium by Happy Medium.
Qu Allan. 2 20

Champion Prince by King's Champion.
Little Mike 2:23½
May Williams.. ......2.26¼
Champion Wilkes.
Oklahoma, p 2:28
Champlain by Daniel Lambert.
Happy Girl 2:23¾
Chamois, p............2 16¼
Chance by Strathmore.
Col. Matson. 2:27
Chance by Rockwood.
Pluto 2:29¼
Chancellor Black Hawk by Mitchell's Black Hawk.
Misfortune... .... 2:21½
Chandler J. Wells by Royal George.
Filbert 2.28
Chandos by Strathmore
Chan, p . . 2.17¼
Chapin Egmont by Egmont.
P. H. Chapin 2 29¼
Charles Backman by Rysdyk's Hambletonian
Backman Maid 2:25¼
Dan Backman 2:22½
Charles Caffrey by Gen. Knox.
Billy Hustler . . 2:27
Eddy Hayes 2:23½
Guy Sheridan . .. 2·22½
Kate Caffrey.. ......2 18½
Lord Caffrey. 2:21¼
Louis P. 2:29¼
McFarland 2·29¼
Major Buford .... 2·28½
Molly G 2 28
Nelly Cobb . 2:20¼
Robbie P . . 2:12¼
Rose Copeland.. 2·29¼
Wanamaker 2:29¼
Giles Noyes, p ... . 2·24¼
Gumbo, p 2 29¼
Charles Derby by Steinway
Derby Princess . 2:25
Cebolo, p 2 13¼
Diablo, p 2:09¼
J. F. B., p 2.26½
Charles Dickens by Superb.
Bub McLaughlin ....2·29
Charles Douglas by Royal George
Cora . 2:29¼
Charles E. Loew by George M. Patchen
Stewart Maloney 2:27
Charles G Hayes by Tramp.
Haidee B 2:26
Hazel Maid.... . .. 2:29¼
Henry Colby 2.27½
Elsie B , p.. ... .2:28
Charles M. by Prescott
S. X. Boy, p... . 2·19¼
Yellow Ash, p 2.24½
Charleston by Bourbon Wilkes.
Belle Meade, p 2:28½
Charton, p 2:16¾
Wheeler F., p 2:12½
Charley by Washtenaw Chief.
Minnie Maxfield . 2:28½
Charley
Patsey Clinker, p . 2:20
Charley
Harry K , p 2:16¼
Charley B. by King's Champion.
Addie Fitz B. 2 26¼
Alice Burlew 2.22¼
Bonnie L . ...2·27¼

Consolation 2:29
Electra 2:25½
Douglass 2:27¼
Gold Boy 2:23¼
Gus Fellows 2:29¼
Honey B. 2:25¼
Maggie Morrill 2:29¼
Maud B 2:24¼
May R 2:29¼
Minnie B 2:29¼
Rosa B 2:26¼
Roseberry 2:26¼
Shylock 2:29½
Spurgeon 2:21¾
Tam O'Shanter 2:28¾
Tiny B 2:21½
Topsey 2:29¼
Wesley Boy 2:26¾
Charley B. Wilkes, p ... 2:28
Charley Bashaw.
Gray Bashaw 2:30
Charley Brister.
Dallas H., p 2:29¾
Frank M. p 2:27½
Charley B. Wilkes by Charley B.
Utella 2:26¼
Charley Clay.
Maud Clay, p 2:23¼
Charley Foster by Billy Green.
Little Joker, p 2:19¾
Charley Ross by Smuggler.
Emma Carroll 2:27
Oliver Ross 2:30
Charley West by Allie West.
Fleta West 2:30
Charley Wicker by Daniel Lambert.
Josie D 2:30
Myrtle S 2:28¼
Charley Wilkes by Red Wilkes.
Arrival 2:24½
Ellard 2:09¾
Farnum's Wilkes, p 2:22½
Charm.
Kitty M., p 2:25
Redleaf, p 2:28¼
Chastelard by King Rene.
Ella Rene 2:25
Linda Gale, p 2:19
Chatham by Cuyler.
Chattel 2:29½
Chatterbox by Victor Bismarck.
Josie B., p 2:13¼
Chatterton by Crittenden.
Nelly Chatterton 2:29¼
Chauncey Goodrich by Marshall Chief.
Randall 2:24½
Chazey Patchen.
Chazey Maid 2:28
Cheatham.
Maud M., p 2:21
Cheltenham by Oxmoor.
Hildeburn 2:18
Chelton by Princeps.
Burleigh 2:28½
Cherokee Chief by Almont Eagle.
Oxford 2:25¼
Chesbrough.
Castleton 2:21
Chester.
Dr. Wood, p 2:20½
Chester Chief by Rysdyk's Hambletonian.
Clochette 2:17¼
Oxford Chief 2:22½
Pitt Kellogg 2:27¼
Prairie King 2:23½
Rachel B 2:18¼
Tom Murray 2:24¼
Chesterfield by Enfield.
Nashville 2:28
Chesterfield by Hetzel's Hambletonian.
Lillis H 2:23¾
Chester Lion.
Silversides 2:22
Chesterwood by Nutwood.
Brooklawn 2:28¼
Selah Chesterwood 2:27½
Belle Potter, p 2:29¾
Chromette, p 2:24
Rebus, p 2:12¾
Chestnut Fearnaught.
Yuca Wan, p 2:26¼
Chestnut Hill by Strathmore.
Roy Hill, p 2:29½
Chestnut Hill Jr. by Chestnut Hill.
Little Bell 2:22½
Chestnut Joe by Murphy's Royal George.
Baby 2:29½
Deleware 2:29¼
Lizzette 2:25
Chestnut Star by Arnold's Red Buck.
Day Star, p 2:17
Grey Star, p 2:29½
Red Star, p 2:20
Chestnut Wilkes by Red Wilkes.
Konvalinka 2:25
Chestnut Bird, p 2:24½
Chevalier by Kearsarge.
Chevalier 2:27
Chevron by Banker Messenger.
Carl 2:30
Chicago Volunteer by Volunteer.
Edwin Q 2:23¼
Ella E 2:25
Gypsy Maid 2:23¼
May H. 2:26¼
Volatile 2:27¼
Woodstock Belle 2:29½
Pete Curran p. 2:28½
Barney A., p 2:25½
Chichester by Harold.
Bezant 2:21½
Chetwood 2:27
Marchester 2:29
Stornaway 2:19
Chickamauga by Vermont Boy.
Charley B 2:30
Luella 2:21½
Danube p 2:25½
Chief by Fisk's Mambrino Chief Jr.
Indiana Belle 2:24¼
Mambrino Maid 2:29¾
Chief by Atlantic Chief.
A. B. C 2:28
Chief Justice by Satellite.
Ego 2:24¾
Chief Medium by Happy Medium.
Cresco 2:29½
Lucy W 2:27¼
Magna Medium 2:24¾
Maud Medium 2:28
Chief of Echo by Echo.
Daylight 2:21½
Chieftain by Hiatoga.
Cairo 2:26
Defiance 2:24
Defiance, p 2:17¾
Flora, p 2:30
Onward, p 2:24¾
Chieftain.
Shamrock, p 2:21¼
Chimes by Swigert.
Chimes E 2:28¼
Chimes E., p 2:15
Chimes by Electioneer.
Beautiful Chimes 2:22½
Bessie Chimes 2:27½
Blue Bell 2:22¾
Boy Blue 2:25¼
Carillon 2:27¼
Charming Chimes 2:18½
Chide 2:26¼
Chimes Boy 2:17¼
Chimesbrino 2:28½
Chimes Girl 2:26
Curfew 2:24¼
Electmont 2:22¼
Fantasy 2:06
June Bug 2:29¼
Josie Chimes 2:29¼
Midnight Chimes 2:16¼
Princess Royal 2:20
Sixty-Six 2:15¼
Ed Easton, p 2:09¾
Era Chimes, p 2:19¾
Merry Chimes, p 2:08½
Palo Alto Chimes, p 2:17½
Tanny Bug, p 2:17½
Chismore by Administrator.
Beauty 2:29½
Lady Mack 2:25½
Chosroes by Rysdyk's Hambletonian.
C. H. H 2:27¼
Lady Mills 2:24¾
Longford 2:20½
Mary Hanford 2:28¾
W. K 2:21¼
Chrisman Patchen.
Ed Fay 2:28¾
Churchill by Favorite Wilkes.
A. B. C., p 2:23¼
Churchill Horse by Young Black Hawk.
Tom B. Patchen 2:27¼
Circulator by Forrest Golddust.
Bobby Howard 2:30
Civilization by J. H. Welch.
Cavalier 2:27¾
Civilian 2:21
Civiltine 2:17½
Jessie C 2:24¾
Claimant by Red Wilkes.
Diana 2:29¼
See 2:29¼
Medley, p 2:23½
Clarion by Naugatuck.
Old Put 2:30
Clarion Chief by Tippoo Chief.
Clara K 2:17½
Hastings 2:28½
Little Walter 2:29¼
Maud D 2:29¼
Tariff 2:20¾
Doc H., p 2:19½
Grover S., p 2:27½
Clark Chief by Mambrino Chief.
Blanche Amory 2:26
Croxie 2:19¼
Governor 2:30
John E 2:28¾
Lady Prewitt 2:30
Woodford Chief 2:22¼

Clark Chief (Spink's) by Confederate Chief.
Col Owen 2:15½
Confederate Star. ... 2 28
Fleety L 2 30
Senator K 2 24¼
Clark Chief (Sim's) by Clark Chief
Elevator 2 22¾
Lady B. 2 22¼
Clark Chief Jr. by Clark Chief
Cottonwood Chief . 2 29
Ranchero...... . . 2:21½
Rolla . . 2:24
Tony Newell... ...2:19½
Clark Chieftain by Clark Chief.
Lottie W 2:21
Reuben W 2.16¼
Chief Justice, p 2 22¼
Clay by Electioneer
Clatina . . . 2:18¼
Clayone . . 2 27¼
Hazel 2 28
Knotty Boy ... . 2·24¼
Miss Clay 2 29¾
Nemo 2:26¾
Parkside . 2.22¾
Spinaway . . 2 29½
Stanford 2 29¼
Algetta, p 2 24¾
Claytina, p .. . 2·19½
Count Clay, p . .. 2:27¼
Wire Nail, p. . 2 29½
Clay Abdallah by Strader's Cassius M Clay Jr.
James D 2 30
Marquis . . . 2·26¾
Budd Doble, p.. .. 2 19¼
Clay Abdallah Jr. by Clay Abdallah.
Rocky P, p . 2 12½
Clay Cadmus by Neave's Cassius M. Clay Jr.
Maud .. 2 29½
Clay Cuyler by Cuyler.
Andes .. .. 2·27½
Vandeen .. . 2·30
Clay Davis by Strader's Cassius M Clay Jr.
Clay Forest 2 24¼
Kid Davis, p ... 2:27¼
Clay Duke by Alcona.
Dell Ray ... . .. .2·24¾
Lillian Smith ...2:29
Clayford by Harry Clay.
Belle A . . .... 2·29¼
Bessie S ... 2·26
Dr C 2 26¾
Clay Hambletonian by Mapes Horse
Lady Ulster . . 2 20
Clay King by King Clay.
Durado ... . 2·27½
Guard . ..2 28½
The Raven .2.26
Clay Pilot by Neave's Cassius M. Clay Jr
Billy R 2:25¼
Fulton Maid . . . 2 29¼
Fred V., p 2 22½
Claythorne
Harry Clay, p. . 2·26½
Clayton Edsall by Maj. Edsall
Jewel 2 27¼
Kitty Edsall .. 2.28½
Lady Douglass .. . .2·29½
Clay Wilkes by George Wilkes.
Cambria Wilkes . .....2·29¼

Richard Wilkes, p . 2 25
Zadia p . 2 29¼
Zaney Wilkes p.. . 2.23½
Clear Grit by imp Lapidist
Amber . 2 25¼
Flora F . 2 24¼
Gold King . 2·29½
Little Billy. ... 2 23¾
Billy M, p . .. 2 19¾
Capt Hunter, p . 2·19¼
Florence G., p . 2 18
Fuller, p 2:13¾
Sir John, p . . . 2·26
Clear Grit (Booth's) by Clear Grit
Bay Fly, p 2.23¼
Fleetfoot, p 2.12
Clematis by Robert Bonner
Rocket . . 2 26¼
Clifford by Bay Eagle.
Famous Girl 2 26½
Maud E . 2.22¼
Clifton Boy by Squire Talmage.
Johnny Smoker, p 2:29¾
Clifton Pilot by Old Pilot
Jack Lewis 2 28½
Climate by Contractor
Climatize . . . 2 24¾
Client 2:24
Climax by Almont.
Fanny Cope 2:28½
March 2:25¾
Ottawa Maid 2.28¼
Clmont.
Prince T., p............2.13¼
Clinton by Fulton.
Gertie B., p 2.15¼
Clinker.
Clinker Jr 2 24
Lynwood 2.20½
Susie B 2 26¼
Hargus H., p....... . 2 29¼
He's-a-Seed, p 2:25½
Jim Clinker, p . 2.21¾
Lawnwood, p . ..2 25½
Minnie A., p........2 19¼
Newkirk, p. 2:25½
Sally Clinker, p .. 2 13
Susie B., p... . .. 2.20¾
What's Wanted, p . 2 30
Clipper.
John Murphy 2 28¼
Clipper by Red Buck Jr
Ben B., p 2.13¼
Martin Box, p . . 2 17½
Minnie Taylor, p. 2 30
Clipper (Moore's) by Clipper Brooks
Rube Burrows, p . 2 22½
Clipper Jr.
Silver Heel, p ... 2 27½
Clipper Brooks by Brooks
Annie Rhea, (p)... . . 2:14¾
Lochinvar, p 2 20½
Lou Shaffer, p .2 30
C L Martin by Wilkesonian.
Frank McDonald . . 2 26½
Cloud Mambrino by Dan Underhill
Alfred 2 26½
Billy Lamberson . . 2 28¼
Cloud Mambrino by Cloud Mambrino
Charley F. p.. . . ... 2 28
Prince Echo, p. .. . 2:14½
Coaster by Caliban.
Cruiser 2 28¼
Lady Rooker, p 2:25½

Cobden by Daniel Lambert.
Helen M . . . 2·27
Cobden 2d 2 24
Cobdella, (p) 2 26½
Cobden Boy, p 2 28¼
Cobden Jr. p.. 2:15
Ellen M, p 2 17
Coeur D'Alene by Dexter Bradford.
Ad Alene . 2.26
An A'Lene, p 2.29½
Cognac by Raymond
Robin p .. 2 29¼
Cohannet (p) by Bay State.
Becker p 2 24½
Lantana p . 2 25¼
Coke Chief by Wilton.
J M C., p ... . 2·24¼
Colby Swigert by Swigert
Wirt Dexter .. . 2 30
Col Fisman.
DeKalb, p ... . 2·23½
Coligne by Echo
Jenny Wren . 2 25¼
Frank B .. 2 30
Col Bonner by Independent
Cornelia 2:21¼
Col Bruce by Mambrino Bruce.
Motto . 2 28
Lady Oaks, p . 2:19½
Col Crockett by Ripple
Maud N ... . . 2·26¼
Col Cross by Draco.
Hopemont . 2·28
Col Ellsworth by Gen. Knox
Arthur T . 2 27
Col Hambrick by Dictator.
Cigarette . 2 23¼
Daphne . . 2:16¼
Gallilee 2.26¼
Gov. Powell . .. 2·25
Gentile . .. 2.30
Thalia . . 2 24¾
Colonel Hare by Attorney.
Captain Hare .. 2 25
Lady Hare . 2 16¾
Col Harry Lambert by Daniel Lambert.
Ethel Lambert 2 29¾
Col. Howe by Blue Bull
Mascot Bob 2 29¼
Col H. S. Russell by Blanco
Russell, (Miller's) p 2·24
Colonel Kip by Kenwood.
Pawling . . . . 2·21¼
Col Lillard by Jay Bird.
Red Ink . . . 2 22¼
Colonel M.
Jimmy C . . . 2 23½
Col. Moore by Rocky Mountain Chief.
Dr. Norman 2:19¾
Harry B., p 2 19¾
Col Tom by Lumps.
Captain Tom . . 2 26½
Don L 2:23¾
Col Walker.
Tom G, p 2:29¼
Col West by Almont.
Mabel H. . . . ...2·26
Westmont. 2 24
Lorene, p 2.15¼
Sol Miller, p..... . 2:19
Col. West by Egbert.
Westland 2 29¾
Dick West, p. .... 2·29¼
Col Wilkes by George Wilkes
Coon Hollow, p . . .2 23¾

Harry Wilkes, p........2:23
Col. Winfield by Edw. Everett.
Edgar........2:30
Colonna by Belmont.
Alice........2.26½
Capitola........2 24¼
Edelweiss........2:30
Motor........2:27¼
Colossus, p........2:27¾
Little Hank p........2:24¼
S. G A., p........2:17¾
Colossus Mambrino by Colossus.
St. Louis........2:25
Columbia Chief by Mambrino Black Hawk.
Strangemore........2:29¾
Columbus.
Confidence........2 28
Columbus (Young) by Columbus.
Arthur........2 27½
Ben Smith........2:27
Com Vanderbilt........2:25
Farmer Boy........2:28
Fitzgerald........2:30
Harry Harley........2 25¾
Jim Ward........2:28½
Myron Perry........2 24½
Phil Sheridan........2:26½
Sea Foam........2:24½
Young Columbus Jr........2:30
Columbus (McKimmin's) by Brown's Bellfounder.
Little Mac........2:28½
Comac by Kentucky Prince.
Showeress........2.27¼
Combat by Hero of Thorndale.
Brown........2.18¾
Iona........2 27
Medah........2 27¼
Soudan........2:18¼
Warrant........2 21¼
Williams........2:20½
Combination by Dictator.
Molly Work........2.24¾
Combination by Egmont.
Hallie Harris........2:23½
Comet by Williams Horse.
Maid of Monti........2 28
Susie W........2:26½
Western Belle........2:24½
Comet.
Dictator........2 22¼
Commander by Blue Bull.
Nellie S........2:23¾
Bernica, p........2.30
Henry F. p........2 20¼
Sorrel Dan, p........2:18¼
Commander by Dictator.
Annie C........2:28¾
M'liss........2.21½
Prince Karl........2:26½
Anna, p........2 21¼
Laura Belle, p........2:27¼
Queen, p........2:19¼
Commodore by Boston.
Tennessee........2:27
Commodore by Botts' Commodore.
Dick Organ........2.24¼
Seymour Belle........2 19¾
Commodore Belmont by Belmont.
Carrie Belle........2:23½
Doncaster........2:28¼
Evening Star........2:29
Gale........2:27¾
Geranium........2:28½

Meteor........2:28½
Commodore Wilkes by Geo. Wilkes.
Coalburgh........2:30
Hardshell........2:28
Commonwealth by Phil Sheridan.
Eddie Wilkes........2:23¼
Como by Ballard's C. M. Clay Jr.
Margaret J........2 24½
Como Chief by Appleby's Chieftain.
Webber........2:28
Companion by Gen. Knox.
Cimarron........2:27¼
Lasis........2:20¾
Compeer by Rysdyk's Hambletonian.
Compwood........2:29
Competitor by Onward.
Checkmate........2:29
Comus by Lucas Brodhead.
Harry C., p........2:15½
Con by Corsair.
Brown Jim........2:22½
Concord by Lexington.
Star W........2:27¾
Conductor by Gen. Knox.
Skipaway........2:29¾
Lilydale........2:27½
Confederate Chief by Clark Chief.
Big Ben........2:28¾
Confederate Maid........2:29½
Lady Love........2 23½
Sleepy Chief........2:27¾
William Arthur........2:19¾
Cap Sheaf, p........2:21¼
Confidence by Sewall's Phil Sheridan.
Lady Sheridan, p........2:15¼
Conflict by Madrid.
Contest, p........2:21
Confusion by Electioneer.
Conaslee, p........2:26¼
Connaught by Wedgewood.
Clonmore........2 21
Grand Turk........2:29¼
Lady Connaught........2:30
Alice L., p........2:25¾
Naughty Girl, p........2:23½
Wickcliffe, p........2:20
Conqueror by Ed. Holly.
Ru ledge........2:30
Constellation by Almont.
Glenarm........2 23½
Kalula........2:28¼
Mahomet........2 28½
Tilton........2:24¼
Illusion, p........2:24¼
Patrol, p........2:14½
Consternation.
Molly Bell........2:30
Consul by Saturn.
Consul Chief........2:26
Harry K........2:22
Lulu G., p........2:16¼
Continental by Bacon's Ethan Allen.
Capt. Emmons........2:19¾
Contraband.
Gold Note........2:25
Contractor by Ajax.
Dr. West........2:17¼
Conundrum by Barkis.
Daisy........2:28

Conway by Wedgewood.
Judge Conway........2:28¼
Lloyd, p........2:19¼
Nell Gray, p........2:25½
Cope Chief by Wilton.
J. M. C. p........2:24¼
Copperbottom.
Billy Fleming, p........2:25½
Copperbottom (Comb's).
Dupe F., p........2:14¼
Copper Duke by Monroe.
Dolly M........2:23¼
Coralloid by Simmons.
Coraline........2:26¼
Coral Queen........2:28½
Don O'Loid........2:26
Corbeau by Black Corbeau.
Brown Billy........2:29
Rose Standish........2.29
Billy Boyce, p........2:19
Billy S., p........2:14¼
John Maloney, p........2:24¼
Corbeau (Walker's) by Corbeau Chief.
Libby S........2:19¼
Corbeau Chief by Corbeau.
Dora........2:26¼
Corbin Bashaw by Amboy.
Belle Corbin........2:23¾
Harry Reid........2:24
Lady Reid........2:28¼
Findley, p........2 20
Rita S, p........2:24¾
Rupert, p........2:23½
Cornell by Gen. Washington.
J. M........2:22¼
Coriander by Iron Duke.
Bicky Sharp........2 23½
Comrade........2:27
Coriander Maid........2:29½
Cora C........2:28¾
Jack Cade........2:26½
L. R........2:27¼
Nigger Baby........2:22½
Pilgrim........2:24¼
Turk........2:17¼
Cora, p........2:25
Cornwall by Florida.
Lady Woodhull........2:29¼
Coronet by George Wilkes.
George K........2:29½
Jenny Wilkes........2:25½
Sirock........2.19¾
Corneto, p........2:18¼
Fanny Wilkes, p........2.19¾
Cornelius by Nutwood.
Jim Nutwood........2:21¼
William Tell........2:18
Cornelian by Princeps.
Cornelius M........2:30
Magnetta........2:21½
Newcastle........2:14¾
Corsair by Rysdyk's Hambletonian.
Ada M........2:29½
Competine........2:29½
Cortland Wilkes by George Wilkes.
Ramona........2:28½
Wilkie Wonder........2.28½
Cosmopolitan by Landseer.
Will D........2:26½
Counsellor by Onward.
Ed Davis........2:24¼
Endeavor........2:29¾
Counsellor (Sabin's).2:26½
Majella........2:29

Count Folsio by Onward.
- Hazel 2:30
- Modesty 2:29¼

Count Louis by Louis Napoleon.
- Arthur T 2:29

Count Princeps by Princeps.
- King Princeps 2:23¼

Country Boy by Prince Charles.
- Denmark 2:30

Country Medium by Happy Medium
- Allie Medium 2:30

Count Waldemar by King Rene.
- Countess 2:27

Count Wilkes by George Wilkes.
- Dr. Kidd 2:24½
- Georgette 2:27
- Mill Lady 2:26¼
- Mill Lady, p. 2:30

Coupon by Gen. Knox.
- Maud Muller 2:29¾
- Maurice S. 2:23½

Crawford by Favorite Wilkes
- Lady Crawford, p 2:27
- Sandy Wilkes, p 2:29¼

Crawford Horse.
- W. H. Taylor 2:29¼

Crawford Prince.
- Rob Roy 2:26¼

Crazy Nick by Kremer's Rainbow.
- Charles W. Wooley 2:22½

Crazy Nick Jr. by Crazy Nick
- Cora R 2:25¾
- Maud M. 2:28
- William E 2:19½

Creeper by Peck Horse.
- Phil Sheridan 2:26½

Creole by John Randolph
- Joe S 2:30
- Rosewood 2:28½

Cresco by Strathmore.
- Allie Cresco, p 2:19¼
- Betty M., p 2:20
- Crescent, p 2:23¼

Cripple (Viley's) by Ward's Flying Cloud.
- Belle Brasfield 2:20

Crit Davis by Crittenden.
- Pet Davis 2:19¼
- Ripple 2:20½

Crittenden by Strader's Cassius M. Clay.
- Chatterton 2:18
- Clendon 2:26
- Courier 2:15
- Criterion 2:29¾
- Ed Turner 2:17¼
- Gracie V. 2:30
- Jean Valjean 2:14
- Mamie M 2:2[illegible]½
- Thornden 2:30
- Van Tassel 2:28½
- Alice Crittenden, p. 2:16½
- Critmore, p. 2:21½

Cromwell by Landseer.
- Auction 2:29¼
- Baby S. 2:24½
- Brightwood 2:29½
- Copeland 2:30
- Col. B., p 2:30
- Cromwell Jr., p 2:25
- Jimmy B., p. 2:16

Crowder (Stanway's).
- Fred H., p. 2:17¼

Crown Chief by Milford Mambrino.
- Roland 2:28

Crown Point by Speculation.
- Valensin 2:22

Crown Prince by Mambrino Patchen.
- Belleflower 2:21½

Crozier.
- Eva 2:29¼

Crumley Hiatoga.
- Harry Phelps 2:27½
- Harry Phelps, p. 2:22¼

Culpepper Allen.
- Brown Bess 2:25½

Cunard by Von Moltke
- Cunard Jr. 2:28¼
- Maud R 2:27

Cunard Jr. by Cunard.
- Cuckoo 2:19¾
- Duster 2:27
- Venture, p. 2:23½

Cupid by King Herod.
- Maggie N. 2:16¾

Cuthbert by Cuyler.
- Cuthbert H. 2:21¼
- Capt. Mack, p 2:25¾

Cutler
- Prince C. p 2:27½

Cuyler by Rysdyk's Hambletonian.
- Algath 2:23
- Belle Isle 2:28¼
- Borden 2:24¾
- Chanter 2:20¾
- Crayon 2:29¼
- Cuthbert 2:23¾
- Day Dream 2:21¾
- Edwin C. 2:21¼
- Elvira 2:18½
- Kate C 2:27½
- Kate Cuyler 2:26
- Ocala 2:23
- Orient 2:30
- St. Arnaud 2:29¼
- Wyatt 2:27

Cuyler Clay by Cuyler.
- Don Carlos 2:23

C. V. B. by Ensign.
- Maud 2:29¼

C. W. Mitchell
- Billy Mitchell 2:28¾
- John Mitchell 2:26¼
- Maggie Mitchell 2:21¼

Cyclone by Young America
- Starlight 2:28¼

Cyclone by Caliban
- Andy Cutter 2:19¼
- Annorean 2:26½
- Black Ide 2:17
- Cecile 2:28¾
- Cicerone 2:12½
- Cocoon 2:15
- Cyclone Wilkes 2:23¼
- Dr. Sparks 2:12¼
- Gillette 2:11¼
- Hurricane 2:25¼
- Kratz 2:21½
- Mahala 2:19¾
- Raven 2:29¾
- Snip Nose 2:24¼
- Tom Hook 2:27½
- Hessville, p 2:28¼
- Laura W., p 2:30

Cyclops by Marshal Ney.
- Cypress 2:30

Cylburn by Aberdeen.
- Racket 2:30

Cypress by Kentucky Prince.
- Orlando 2:23½

Cyril by Glenarm.
- Cephas 2:14¼

Dakota by Swigert
- Merrill, p 2:21¼

Dall Brino by Halbrino.
- May Brino 2:26½
- Dandy O p 2:11
- Otto W. p 2:13¼
- St. Patrick, p 2:29¾

Daly by General Benton
- Bonner N. B 2:17
- Clatawa 2:27½
- Julia D 2:23¼

Damo by Jerome Eddy.
- Blue Stem 2:28
- Eddy 2:22½

Dan B.
- Dan N 2:28¼

Dan Brown.
- Bert B 2:29½
- Jenny B 2:24
- Charley B. p 2:18¼
- Dolly Brown, p. 2:16½

Dandy by Long Island Black Hawk.
- Jenny 2:29¼

Dandy Boy by Almont Rattler.
- Billy F. 2:24½

Dandy Time by Mark Time.
- Dandy Time Jr 2:25

Dan G.
- Harry Hornet, p 2:21½

Dan G. by Pratt's Mohawk.
- Sally B. 2:29¼
- Gray Ben, p. 2:15¾
- Lillie B., p 2:29¼

Daniel Boone by Rysdyk's Hambletonian.
- Annie Boone 2:25¼
- Echo 2:27¼
- Fred M 2:28¼
- Nelly M 2:28¼
- Robinson D. 2:17¾
- Susie Owen 2:26
- Tom King 2:28
- Annie Boone, p 2:25¼
- Daniel C. p. 2:30
- Fred M. p 2:26¼
- Jenny J p 2:18¼
- Little Wing, p. 2:21¼
- Tough End, p. 2:29¼

Daniel Boone by Tom Crowder.
- Cooley 2:26

Daniel Boone by Kremer's Rainbow.
- Chimes C. p. 2:23

Daniel Lambert by Ethan Allen.
- Addison Lambert 2:27
- Annie Lou 2:30
- Annie Laurie 2:27¾
- Annie Page 2:27¼
- Aristos 2:27¾
- Baby Lambert 2:27¼
- Ben Franklin 2:29
- Ben Lambert 2:27
- Billy D 2:26
- Blanchard 2:25½
- Boston 2:27¾
- Clara Morris 2:29¼

Cobden.... 2:28¾
Col. Moulton 2:28½
Comee 2:19¾
Dan Miller 2:23¾
Dickard 2:25¼
Ella Doc 2:23½
Flora Huff 2:29¼
George A 2:24½
George R 2:24
Jim 2:23½
Jimmy Stewart 2:24¼
Joe S 2:30
John Hall 2:24½
Jubilee Lambert 2:25
Lady Foxie 2:24¼
Lambert B 2:22¾
Maggie Lambert 2:25¼
May Morning 2:30
Molly S 2:24¼
Motion 2:29
M. Y. D Colt 2:28¾
Nancy 2:23½
Nonesuch 2:25¼
Pauline Lambert 2:29
Queen Mab 2:29¾
Wild Lilly 2:24
Lillian, p 2:29¾
Daniel Lambert Jr. by Daniel Lambert.
Foxie Lambert 2:29¾
Dan Mace by Beacon Horse.
Maud Mace 2:27¼
Fanny K., p 2:28¾
Dan Mitchell by Regulator.
Darling 2:24½
Dan Rice by General McClellan.
Flora 2:20¾
Lompoc 2:24½
Charley D., p 2:26¾
Daniel Webster by Cassius M. Clay.
Nelly C 2:26¾
Danville by Provincial Chief.
Elsie Groff 2:15
Danville Wilkes by Lyle Wilkes
Sally Vajan 2:28
Zero 2:29¼
Dan Voorhees by General McClellan.
Jim L 2:20
Dan Wilson by Clark Chief.
Fred Wilson, p 2:21½
Darkey by Rounds' Horse.
Highland Grey 2:28
Dark Night by Alcyone.
Break O' Day 2:11½
Cleopatra 2:29½
Lady J 2:30
Silent Brook 2:16½
Lady J., p 2:20
Daribay by Mambrino Patchen.
Lady Thorne 2:25
R. F. C 2:23½
Roxie C., p 2:30
Darlington by Wellington.
Bloom Boy 2:28¾
Darmouth by Volunteer.
Montrose 2:26½
Stanley 2:17
Tom Rogers 2:28
Gold Bar, p 2:28¾
Darwin by Green's Bashaw.
Frank P 2:25
Darwin by Abdallah Jr.
Donald H., p 2:18¾

Dashwood by Legal Tender.
Lady Sutton 2:29½
Leonor 2:24
Andy, p 2:20
Daubigne by Mambrino Patchen.
Chief 2:27¾
Nannie B 2:27
Selim Mambrino 2:28½
Zuleka 2:29½
Dauntless by Rysdyk's Hambletonian.
Belle 2:27¾
Belle J 2:28
Billy Parks 2:26¼
Crusader 2:29½
Dan Voorhees 2:30
Danforth 2:27
Dauntless 2:28½
Dawnland 2:30
Deyo 2:24
Ephriam 2:29¾
Fearless 2:30
Gen. Cass 2:18½
Gen. Don 2:27½
Gene Smith 2:15½
Crusader 2:29½
Hendryx 2:17¾
Ida T 2:25
Inventor 2:25¾
Jim Lane 2:29¾
Kitty C 2:30
Lady Hendryx 2:30
Little Thorne 2:23¾
Matchless 2:25¼
Rollaway 2:29½
Rosa C 2:22
Thornless 2:15¾
Young Dauntless 2:26½
Zahn 2:23¾
Ed Annan, p 2:16¼
Rognab, p 2:27¾
Sam N., p 2:28¾
Senator Mills, p 2:25
Dauntless Jr. by Dauntless.
Dauntless L 2:20½
Harry, p 2:17¾
Dave Bonner by Swigert.
Mayflower, p 2:23½
Dave Hill (Sutton's) by Case's Dave Hill.
Little Pete, p 2:22½
Dave Hill (Case's).
Barney Lee 2:25
David C 2:25
Kinsman Boy 2:28½
Madge D 2:30
Davenant by Belmont.
Davie B 2:27¾
David Bonner by Robert Bonner.
Mark B 2:28¾
David Hill by Black Lion.
Black Swan 2:28½
David Hill Jr. by David Hill.
George Treat 2:25¼
Vidette 2:23¾
Davy Belmont.
In It, p 2:29¾
Davy Crocket.
Sam West 2:29
Davy Crocket (Parish's) by Blind Davy Crocket.
Etta Jones 2:20
Davy Crocket (Coulter's) by Davy Crocket (Moody's).
Rostrever, p 2:23

Davy Crocket.
Harry E, p 2:23½
Dawn by Nutwood.
Annabelle 2:27½
Dot 2:29½
Oaknut 2:24¼
Peep o' Day 2:21
Silkey, p 2:26
Day Star by Kearsarge.
Hettie T., p 2:25
Deacon by Robert Bonner.
Victor V 2:29½
Deadwood.
Live Oak Maid 2:22¾
Deamer by Ashland Wilkes.
Lunar 2:29¾
Dean (Riley's) by Dean Swift.
Onward 2:29¾
Dean Sage by Rysdyk's Hambletonian.
Beaconsfield 2:25¼
Norseman 2:30
Dean Swift by Bush Messenger, untraced.
Will o' the Wisp 2:29½
Decatur Chief by Durango.
Hazel N 2:26
Deceive by Rysdyk's Hambletonian.
George M 2:25¼
Mable R 2:27¾
Maggie K 2:26
M. C 2:27
Paragon 2:27½
Dorcas, p 2:25½
Mascot, p 2.04
Declaration by Young Jim.
Ella O 2:24
Nadjy 2:28
Psyche 2:24½
Decorate by Masterlode.
Delegate 2:29¾
Defender by George Wilkes.
Ben Wilkes 2:26½
Dottell 2:25½
Defiance by Com. Belmont.
Bronco 2:26¼
Frank Quirk 2:18¼
Defiance by William Rysdyk.
Mab 2:21
Rich Brown 2:22¾
Delancey by Director.
Satin Slippers 2:24½
De Leon by Pretender.
Vernie V., p 2:18¼
Delineator by Dictator.
Concilio, p 2:21¾
McGinty, p 2:15¾
Imitator, p 2:23½
Minneator, p 2:25½
Delmarch by Hambrino.
Berry 2:26¼
Delmont 2:18¾
Image 2:19
Mite 2:27¼
Sylvanite 2:26
Delmonico by Guy Miller.
Darby 2:16½
Delmonico Sprague by Gov. Sprague.
Anna May 2:27¾
Del Sur by The Moor.
Don Thomas 2:20
Nora D 2:22
San Pedro 2:14½
Aimee, p 2:24¾
Cousin Joe, p 2:21¾
Dell Wind, p 2:25

San Pedro, p . . . 2:10¾
Democrat by Columbus.
Fred. . . . 2:30
Denmark (Collins') by Denmark (Price's).
Edgar A . . . 2:23¼
Denmark by Gen. Withers.
Harry P., p . . . 2:21¼
Denmark by Denmark.
Winder, p . . . 2:24¾
Denmark.
Ole Bull, p . . . 2:26½
Denmark Jr. by Denmark.
Kenton Belle . . . 2:30
Denmark Jr. by Kinney's Denmark.
A. K. Davis, p. . . 2:21½
Denning Allen by Honest Allen.
Lord Clinton . . . 2:08¾
Denver Wilkes.
Frank H., p . . 2:26¾
Dennis Ryan by Berlin.
Dennis . . . 2:27¾
Dentist.
Dude . . . 2:27½
De Soto by Harold.
Dakoma . . . 2:27½
Georgia . . . 2:24½
Willow . . . 2:22¼
Handy Pat, p . . . 2:29½
Oscar, p . . . 2:26¼
Pat Harold p. . . 2:21
Tom Harold, p . . . 2:28¼
Despot by Dictator.
Edward B. . . . 2:21¼
Laura Lee . . . 2:29¼
Detective by Attorney.
Decoy, p. . . . 2:30
Detective Patchen by Star Patchen.
Patch . . . 2:29¼
Detractor by Gossip.
Arden . . . 2:29¾
Grace B. . . . 2:26
Decider . . . 2:29¼
Annie E., p . . . 2:16½
Belmont Chief, p. . . 2:30
Debrino, p. . . 2:27½
Dick Vail, p. . . 2:14¼
Judge Sterling, p . . . 2:15¼
Ned V., p. . . 2:19¼
Oakland, p . . . 2:16
Deucalion by Rysdyk's Hambletonian.
Alley K . . . 2:29½
Blauvelt . . . 2:29¼
Deuxmillion . . . 2:29½
Duane . . . 2:26¼
Duellion . . . 2:28
Edith H . . . 2:12½
Hot Shot . . . 2:21¾
Jesse . . . 2:21
Leicester . . . 2:17¼
Lizzie K . . . 2:26½
Nannie K . . . 2:27¼
Nino . . . 2:30
Oxford . . . 2:29¼
Deuxmillion by Deucalion.
Du-ex, p . . . 2:24¼
De Witt Clay by Harry Clay.
Mary Powell . . . 2:22¾
Dexter Bradford by Rysdyk's Hambletonian.
Amelia C . . . 2:19¼
Coeur d'Alene . . . 2:19¾
Dexter Prince by Kentucky Prince.
Alijandri . . . 2:15¾
Aster . . . 2:12
Chloe . . . 2:24
Crown Prince . . . 2:17½
Del Paso . . . 2:24½
Dexter Princess . . . 2:24¼
Erin . . . 2:25½
Erwin . . . 2:29¾
Fitzsimmons . . . 2:20
Flora S . . . 2:18¼
George Dexter . . 2:18¼
Index . . . 2:27¼
Inez . . . 2:30
James L . . . 2:16¼
Jessie . . . 2:22
Lottery Ticket . . . 2:19¼
Lucille . . . 2:26
Lurline . . . 2:23½
Maggie . . . 2:20
Maud Y . . . 2:29½
Oliver C . . . 2:27
Paloma Prince . . . 2:17½
Parthenia . . . 2:27¼
Prince Daniels . . . 2:22½
Prince Dexter . . . 2:19
Princewood . . . 2:16
Archie, p . . . 2:29¼
Charley Ford, p . . 2:12½
Cherokee Prince, p. . 2:22¼
Dexter Thorne, p. . . 2:23
Edith, p. . . 2:10
Irene, p . . . 2:25
Prince Nutwood, p . . 2:21¾
Princess Alice . . . 2:16
Diadem by Satellite.
Diadem . . . 2:25¼
Sorrel Dan . . . 2:22¾
Dan D., p. . . 2:15
Roxie L., p . . . 2:25½
Diamond Volunteer by Volunteer.
Beeswax . . . 2:23
Don Miff . . . 2:23
Diatonic by Fairy Gift.
Georgia . . . 2:24¾
Robert Bass . . . 2:29¼
Dick.
Pomp, p . . . 2:17½
Dick Benton.
Rodman, p . . . 2:26¾
Dick by Buckskin
Ingomar . . . 2:29¼
Dick Edwards by Clark Chief Jr.
Capt. Edwards . . . 2:25¾
Dexter C . . . 2:24½
Dick Executor.
Billy H . . 2:28
Dick Flaherty by Flaherty's Fearnaught.
Lilly McCarthy . . . 2:30
Dick Jones.
George . . . 2:26¼
Dick Loomer by Dictator.
Elastic Starch . . . 2:24
Dick Preble by Daniel Lam-
Lady M . . . 2:24
Dick Slider by Paul Jones.
Sanford L. p . . . 2:19½
Dick Taylor.
Flora Belle, p . . . 2:22½
Dick Turpin by Swinburn's Hambletonian.
J. B . . . 2:24½
John L., p. . . 2:29¼
No Trouble, p . . . 2:21¾
Dick Wilkes by Petoskey.
Turner Boy . . . 2:21¼
Hamilton, p . . . 2:23¼
Dictator by Rysdyk's Hambletonian.
Absolute . . . 2:30
Annie G . . . 2: 8
Ashby . . . 2:27¼
Betsy Baker . . . 2:30
Black Diamond . . . 2:29¾
Blue Grass Maid . . . 2:30
Bon Accord . . . 2:26
Charley K . . . 2:30
Charles Dickens . . . 2:29¼
Charles M . . . 2:26¼
Chatsworth . . . 2:24¾
Code . . . 2:22¼
Dainty . . . 2:26¾
D. C. . . . 2:23
Delectus . . . 2:18½
Delegate . . . 2:27¾
Delegate . . . 2:19½
Despot . . . 2:29
Dictator Chief . . . 2:21¼
Dictator Prince . . . 2:29¾
Dictionary . . . 2:30
Diligent . . . 2:28½
Director . . . 2:17
Donald . . . 2:27
Edgehill . . . 2:25¼
Edmonita . . . 2:30
Effie Rene . . . 2:26¾
Endymion . . . 2:23¼
Impetuous . . . 2:15¾
Isabella . . . 2:25¾
Jay-Eye-See . . . 2:10
Junius . . . 2:27¼
Keeler . . . 2:29
Kentucky Dictator . . 2:19½
Lady Majolica . . . 2:25
La Oscaletta . . . 2:29¾
Noblesse . . . 2:24
Orator . . . 2:23
Phallas . . . 2:13¾
Princess . . . 2:29
Proem . . . 2:28¼
Spectator . . . 2:28
Trombone Rex . . . 2:15¾
Twinkle . . . 2:25¼
Dartmouth, p . . . 2:28¾
Delineator, p. . . 2:18
Despot, p. . . 2:24½
Felix, p. . . 2:24¼
Jay-Eye-See, p . . . 2:06¼
Minnie Cassell . . . 2:16¼
Satrap . . . 2:20½
Dictator Jr. by Commander.
Hill Boy, p . . . 2:27¼
Merit, p . . . 2:28½
Dictator Almont by Dictator.
Dictum . . . 2:20½
Michigan Jim . . . 2:29¼
Dictator Chief (Barnes') by Dictator.
Moxie, p . . . 2:25
Reuben, p . . . 2:26½
Testator, p . . . 2:28½
Dictator Chief by Dictator.
Artist . . . 2:29
Betty . . . 2:28¼
Crete . . . 2:27¾
Dora May . . . 2:27¾
Faith . . . 2:27½
Maud Banks . . . 2:27¼
Edna, p . . . 2:24
Ellsworth, p . . . 2:19¼
Dictator Wilkes by Red Wilkes.
Don Donnan . . . 2:29¼
Gus Tupper, p . . . 2:23

  Harry Holton, p. 2:24
  Richard Jay, p 2:17¼
Dictatum by Dictator.
  Gothatum 2:29¼
Dille Horse.
  Bud Dille, p. 2:22½
Dillingham by Volunteer Star.
  Hasdrubel 2:27½
Diplomat by Nutwood.
  Dwyer 2:23¼
  Volunteer D 2:30
  Demand, p 2:29
  Dolce, p. 2:20¼
  Myronet, p 2:29¼
  Pay Rock, p. 2:23½
  White Wings, p 2:29¼
Direct by Director.
  Miss Kate 2:24¼
  Directly, p 2:07¾
Director by Dictator.
  Bonny Bon 2:29¾
  Direct. 2:18¼
  Directa 2:28
  Direct Line 2:29
  Director's Flower 2:20
  Directress 2:28¾
  Directum 2:05¼
  Director's Jug 2:29½
  Ellen Mayhew 2:22
  Erector 2:25
  Erma 2:25¼
  Evangeline 2:11¾
  Guide 2:16¼
  Katie S 2:19¼
  Jack Dawson 2:30
  Lena Holly 2:18¾
  Letcher 2:18¾
  Little Witch 2:27
  Margaret S 2:12½
  McClelland Stewart 2:29¼
  Mattie Solomon 2:30
  Patti 2:29¼
  Stella C. 2:26
  Waldstein 2:22½
  Alice Director, p 2:19¼
  Direct, p 2:05½
  Olivette, p 2:28½
  Direction, p 2:10¼
  Directrix, p 2:20½
  Phenom, p 2:21½
  Rokeby, p 2:13¾
Director Chief by Director.
  Coupon 2:26¼
Dirigo by Drew Horse.
  Bully Brooks 2:28
  Camors 2:25¼
  John Virgin 2:29
  Little Fred 2:26¾
  Dirigo Maid, p 2:21¼
  Skylark, p 2:22
Dirkee V. by Dictator.
  Anna B 2:27
Dispatch by Onward.
  Carrie M 2:26
  Patoka Boy 2:30
  Carrie M. p 2:21¼
Dispntant by Harold.
  Walton Boy 2:27¾
Distinguie by Blackwood Jr.
  Temple O., p 2:21¼
Dixie by Swigert.
  Dixie V. 2:25¼
Dixon by Happy Medium.
  Columbia 2:30
  Hattie 2:29¾
Doc by St. Clair.
  Occident 2:16¾
Dock.
  Dauntless Belle, p 2:21¾
Dr. Downing by Miller's Joe Downing.
  John D 2:30
Dr. Franklin by Gen. Knox.
  Dr. Franklin, Jr 2:26
  Frank S 2:29¼
  Harold M 2:27¼
  Lawrence 2:25½
Dr. Henry by Grandson
  Walter R 2:25½
Dr. Herr by Mambrino Patchen
  Clay Herr 2:16¾
  Joe Davis 2:17¾
  Lady Preston 2:30
  Lilly C 2:21¾
  Mella G 2:22½
  Merrilies 2:28¼
  Oriole 2:29¼
  Red Buck 2:29¼
  David S., p 2:29¼
  Farmer Miles, p 2:22
  Frank, p 2:21¾
  Minnie Hanks, p 2:29
  Tillie Herr, p. 2:21¼
Dr. Maxwell by Little Arthur.
  Abner F 2:24¼
Dr. Spaulding by Sandon.
  Golddust 2:18¾
Dr. Speers by Boxer.
  Speers, p 2:14¼
Dr. Spurr by Young Jim.
  Jim Deen 2:29¾
Dr. Strong by Athlete.
  Governor Strong 2:21
Dr. Tallmage by Onward.
  Molly T 2:29¼
  Nelly Shank 2:29¼
Doc. Vail by Swigert.
  Ben Hadad, p 2:23¾
Dolan.
  Kitty Ives 2:28¼
Dolphus by Nimrod.
  Lady Sampson 2:28¾
  Molly 2:27½
Dominion by Red Wilkes.
  May Day 2:27
  Prospect 2:27¼
  New Dominion, p 2:24¼
Dom Pedro by Tom Patchen.
  Carrie T 2:26¼
  Josie Campbell 2:29¼
Dom Pedro by Mambrino Champion.
  Billy H 2:27¼
  G. B 2:20¼
  Marshall Maid 2:23½
  Star B 2:26½
Don by Hermit.
  Billy Cleveland, p 2:19½
Don A. by Fayette Mambrino-
  Lady Don 2:29½
Doncaster by Happy Medium.
  DeWitt C 2:29¼
Don Carlos by Cuyler Clay.
  Alspur 2:21
  Carldon 2:10¼
  Carlos 2:27
  Combination 2:28¾
  Don C 2:18¼
  Lady Blanche 2:26¼
  Otis Shaw 2:19¼
  Princess Ebolt 2:24½
  Revolver 2:29½
  Don C., p 2:23½
Don Clay by Kentucky Clay
  Blanche Brown 2:30
Don Cossack by August Belmont.
  Dina Cossack 2:25¼
  Diplomacy 2:27
  Don Cossack Jr 2:30
  Dora Cossack 2:23
  Elect Cossack 2:29¼
  Ilma Cossack 2:24¾
  Jeannette 2:26¼
  Sally Cossack 2:22½
  Hazel Cossack p. 2:16½
Don Felix by Electioneer.
  Nelly K. 2:26¾
Don J. Robinson by Marshall Chief.
  Daisy Kelly 2:29¼
  Jessie B 2:24¼
  Jesse James 2:29½
  Lizzie H 2:27¼
  Plush, p 2:23½
Don Juan by Donathan.
  Shamrock, p 2:21¼
Don L. by Fieldmont.
  Bud D 2:29¾
Don McGregor by Robert McGregor.
  Bud Ewing 2:25
  Col. H 2:22¾
  Jack Riley 2:23½
  Major 2:11
  Queen McGregor, p. 2:13
Don Marvin by Fallis.
  Boneset 2:27½
  Don Lowell 2:14½
Don Pedro by Knickerbocker.
  Belle Pedro 2:29¼
Don Pizzaro by Gambetta Wilkes.
  Donne, p 2:22
  Marietta Wilkes, p. 2:17¼
  Pattie Belle, p 2:23
Donnybrook by Autocrat.
  Frank L. 2:28
  Maxie Cobb 2:25¼
  Skip, p 2:18¾
Don Ozro by Major Edsall.
  Billy T. p 2:21¾
  Fenmore W p 2:24½
Don Wilkes by Alcyone.
  Boston 2:26¼
  Allabreve, p. 2:20¼
  Belle Wilkes, p 2:29½
  Captain John, p 2:21¼
  Doris, p 2:29
Dorsey Golddust by Golddust.
  Arthur 2:28¾
  D. A. T 2:23¼
  Lock Boy 2:22½
Double Stroke by Monte Christo.
  Belle Wise, p 2:24¼
Doubtful Boy.
  Lady M., p 2:25½
Doug'as by Blackstone.
  Etta K 2:21¾
  Judge McCue 2:25½
Downing Abdallah by Joe Downing.
  Lady Martin 2:23
Douglas Almont by Allie Gaines.
  Magna Monte, p 2:14½
Douglass Wonder by Stephen A. Douglass.
  Mizie Douglass 2:23¼

Dow S. by Cyclone.
Lady Weeks 2:25¼
Maud B 2:28½
Draco by Young Morrill.
Blanche............ 2 25¼
Draco Prince..........2:24¾
Outlaw............ 2:28¾
Draco Medium by Happy Medium.
Dora Thorne... ......2:23
Elva Medium, p......2:18¾
Leontine, p........ 2:19½
Madge Medium, p ...2 21¾
Dread by Commonwealth.
Commonwealth..... .2:23¼
Ida P J 2 29¼
May Day 2:23¾
Common Pleas, p ... 2:24¼
Commonwealth, p 2:18¾
Dresden by Administrator.
Bessie Allen 2:26½
Valita 2:23
John C...... ....2:22½
Dresden Prince by Kentuky Prince.
Princess Maid........2·22¼
Drew Horse.
Gen. McClellan 2:29
Dirigo.............2:29
Dubuque by Nutwood.
Idea 2:30
Dudley Buck by Winthrop Morrill.
Honest Tommy 2:26¾
Duke Alexis.
St. Elmo...........2:25½
Duke of Brunswick by Rysdyk's Hambletonian.
Gov. Hendee 2.23
Red Duke 2:30
William Wallace .. 2:29¾
Duke of Crawford by Satellite.
Stickfast............2:27
Duke of Glen Lake by Mambrino Abdallah.
Charles H...........2:21¼
Flashy 2:21¾
Sylvan Glen 2:30
Duke McClellan by Gen. McClellan.
Maid of Oaks 2:23
Duke of Saratoga by Young Woful.
Molly B. 2:28
Duke of York by Duke of York.
Duke..............2:26½
Duke Patchen by Duke of Brunswick.
Sleepy Tom.......... 2:30
Dumas by Onward.
Alexander Dumas, p .2:15¼
Dud Davis p....... .2:29½
Eva Wilkes, p 2:19½
Lucy Dumas, p 2:16
Tommy Wilkes, p.....2:28½
Dunbarton by Rysdyk's Hambletonian.
Benzine, p... ......2:24¾
Dundee by Jay Gould.
Hokeland. 2:19
Jim Blaine..........2:30
Dunham Abdallah by Erie Abdallah.
Dan Mace........ ...2·23

Dunraven by Cuyler.
Athlo, p 2:25
Dunton Wilkes by Geo. Wilkes.
Joco, p 2:18½
Kiesal, p... ....2 26½
Rhinestone, p........2:25
Veta, p 2:17½
Duplex by Bay Tom Jr.
Combination, p.......2:23¾
Complex, p. 2:14½
Flax Hal, p..........2:23¼
Lucille S., p. 2:15¾
Reflector, p 2:07¾
Rosa Lee, p 2:23¾
Star Plex, p 2:12¼
Duquesne by Tippoo Bashaw.
Dr. T 2:27½
May Quesne..........2:21
Dr. Snyder, p 2:17¼
Durango by Strader's Cassius M. Clay Jr.
Bertha D........ 2 22½
Billy...............2.23¾
Durango Belle........2:22¾
Durango Maid.........2:28¼
Edith N 2:27¼
Garfield.............2:29¾
Jalisco.............2:19¼
Ophelia.............2 30
Perduro..............2:29½
Pipp..............2:28
Rubinstein .... 2·29
Rego ....2·23
Sir Albin 2 29½
Sister Lou 2:29¾
Storm 2:24
Tin Plate......... 2:26
Durango Chief by Durango.
Mark P...............2:25¾
Durant by Janson.
Harry Brown, p.......2:21¾
Duroc by Banker Messenger.
Ben Duroc 2:26¼
Frank T............ 2:23¾
May Queen 2:28¼
Ripple.............. 2 17½
Susie H.............2·27¾
Duroc Boy by Duroc.
Lottie S., p........ .2:25
Duroc Prince by Messenger Duroc.
Rosie C., p ....2·16
Duroc Volunteer by Messenger Duroc.
Maud H... ...... 2:29¼
Duster.
Hood, p...............2:17
Dusty Miller by Canada Grey Eagle.
Dutch Girl..........2:29½
Irene........ ....2:20½

Eagle Bird by Jay Bird.
Allan Line.. ....2:27¼
Alamito .... 2·13¾
Dave Cox 2:29¾
American Jay 2:24¾
Dr. Barch............2:30
Monbars 2:11¾
Eagle Pass 2:23½
Eagle Princess, p 2:17¾
Monbars, p 2:16¾
Earl by Princeps.
Earline..............2:24½
Earlite..............2:29¾
Earl's Lad. 2:25½

Earl's Laddy..........2:24¼
Earl's Lassie.. ....2:30
Florence D 2:28¾
Gypsy Earl ....2·19¾
Havilla 2:29¼
Helen H. 2 30
Idavan.............2:19½
J. O. D 2:30
Katie Earl..........2:16½
Minnola..............2:24¾
Nadji. 2:28
Nelly Earl...........2:29½
Resemble 2:29½
Rhademes........ 2:30
Earl Van Dorn by Thompson's Traveller.
Cora Mack, p.......2:22¾
Earnest by Volunteer.
Protection 2:19¾
Nelly B............2:16¾
Earthquake by North Star.
Rex...............2.22½
Eastlight by Mambrino Patchen.
Roan Boy.. ....2:25¼
Eastman Morgan by Green Mountain Morgan (Hale's)
Little Fred. 2:20
Eastwood by Eastlight.
Jim Blaine 2:30
Eaton Horse by Avery Horse.
Stranger 2:30
Ebony by Green's Bashaw.
Baby Bashaw 2:30
Echo by Rysdyk's Hambletonian.
Annie Laurie....... 2:30
Belle Echo...........2:20
Bob Mason 2:27¼
Col. Hawkins.........2:29¾
Deputy..............2:19½
Echora. 2:23½
Economy.............2:30
El Monte 2:29
Gibraltar 2:22½
Lohengrin 2:27¼
Bashaw.. ....2:27½
Senator 2:21½
Tippie............. 2:16¾
Victor 2:22
Costello, p.......... 2:24¼
Sam Lewis, p.........2.25
Eclair by Gen. Knox.
Tainter............ 2·26
Eclair Jr, p..........2:19
Nina, p 2 22¼
Eclipse Clay by Strader's Cassius M. Clay Jr
Molly G.. ....2:29¾
Ecorse.
Rouge Boy, p........ 2:30
Ed. Barton by Shelden Messenger.
Nemo............ 2:29¼
Ed. Ellis.
Kingston 2:18¾
Eden Golddust by Golddust.
Goldie.. ....2:29¼
Gold Ring............2:12¼
Edgardo by Rumor.
Tomah.......... 2:12¼
Edgar Wilkes by Ethan Wilkes
Charles R.............2:29¾
Edgar Herr..........2:29¾
Sarah Jane 2:24¾
Belle Barton, p......2.19¾
Dennie B., p 2:24¼

Edgehill by Dictator.
Frank Hill............2:18¾
Harry Hill. 2 25¼
Hilldale.............2:29¼
Josie J.............2:21¾
Mayhill.. ....2:19
Billy P., p..........2:29¾
Mayhill, p..........2:17¼
Minnie, p 2:29¼
Edgemark by Victor Bismarck
Lifemark 2:26¼
Silvia....... ....2:28
Romulus, p 2 28¼
Edgewater by Curtis' Hambletonian.
Harry W 2 27¼
Highland Boy 2:28¼
Edgewood by Nutwood.
Wild Olive... ...... 2:27¾
Romulus..... ...... 2:28¼
Avan, p 2:24¼
Carrie H., p 2:19¼
Edict by Dictator.
Black Bess 2:30
Prince Edict Jr., p. .2:22
Editor by Princeps.
Ignis Fatuus 2:20¼
Ed Kimble by Almont.
Grover 2 28½
Snakes....... ....2:30
Ed R. Be by Tramp.
Farmer Boy........2.27¼
Edsall Clay by Harry Clay.
Vision........... 2 26¼
Edsall Star by Major Edsall.
Lou Edsall........ 2:26
Silver Star 2.16¼
Ed Sutherland by Egbert.
Q. R. Z., p..........2:22¼
Edward Everett by Rysdyk's Hambletonian.
Big Fellow.........2 23¼
Clark S 2;27¼
Eclipse...........2:24¼
Electric............2:20
Everett Ray. 2 25
Hambrino........2 21¼
Independence........ 2:19¼
Judge Fullerton......2:18
Lady Scudd.........2:29¼
Maj. Lord 2:23¾
Mountain Boy.......2:20¼
Sheridan 2:20¼
Tanner Boy 2:22½
Young Fullerton.... 2 20¼
Edward Everett Jr. by Edward Everett.
John A., p..........2:29¼
Edward G. by John Dillard.
Kentucky Girl... ...2:29¼
Edward H. by Gooding's Champion.
Pilot Boy.........2:20
Edwin Forrest by Young Bay Kentucky Hunter.
Billy Hoskins 2:26¼
Champagne.... 2:30
Edwin Forrest (Fisher's) by Edwin Forrest.
Scott's Chief.. . 2:23
Edwin Forrest (Hughes') by Edwin Forrest,
Cleveland 2:28¼
Edwin Forrest (Lee's) by Edwin Forrest.
Kate Owen 2:26¼
Edwin Forrest (Gratz's) by Edwin Forrest.

Little Belmont........2.30
Ed Sherman by Gen. Sherman
Morris.......... . .2·29
Egalite by Egbert.
Gertrude 2:26
Wyoming 2:30
Egbert by Rysdyk's Hambletonian.
Appanoose 2 26½
Arcadian........ .2:23½
Armand 2:23
Barney Egbert 2:27½
Benefactor.........2:28
Betina..............2:29¾
Clayberta..... 2 30
Col. Egbert....... 2:30
Congress..........2 21
Constantine.........2:28½
Czarina 2:21
Douglas 2 18¾
Edgar.... ....2.30
Ed Sutherland..... 2:29¼
Edna M 2:26
Egalite.......... 2.20½
Egbertime 2:18½
Egdale...........2:27½
Egg Hot. 2:27¾
Egg Nog...........2:25½
Eggrog............2:24½
Eglantine 2:25
Egmont............2:27½
Egthorne..........2:12½
Egwood...........2:18½
Elbert............2:26½
Elbertie 2:27¼
Ethelbert..........2:27½
Eventime 2:29½
Frank P. Porter.....2.27½
Goodbye 2:19¼
Guinea............2:29
Hilbert........... 2 28¾
Illinois Egbert........2:16½
Kentucky Ruler......2.29
Kitty Hooker 2:29¼
Knight Templar... 2:27
Lamartine.. . ....2.27½
Lanark............2:29¼
Lexington Boy......2:23
Linnie............2:25
Lyndon.... . .....2:29½
McAllister..........2:27
McGuire 2:29¼
Mary Brown 2:29½
Miss Egbert 2 29¾
Pilgrimage........2:30
Prince Egbert........2:29¼
Scott............2:26¾
Superior 2:17¼
Tacks............2:24¾
Temple Bar.... .. ..2:17¾
Tito..............2:27
West Egbert........2 29¼
Wick C............2:24½
Winsome..........2:28¾
Billy Egbert, p... ...2:29¼
Count Kilrush, p....2:27
Delgardo, p..........2:28
Edwin, p..........2:22½
Egberta, p..........2:29¼
Egbertime 2:16½
Eglon, p..........2:14¾
Egroe, p..........2:18¼
Emma, p..........2:16½
Eskbert, p..........2:21½
Expert Prince, p.....2:13½
Felipe, p...........2:25
Frolique, p 2:24½

Gasper, p 2:30
Guesswork, p 2:14¼
Kentucky Ruler, p.. 2 24
Mauprat, p 2:20
Sam Keith, p. .. . 2:24¼
Egmont by Belmont.
Bashawmont.... ...2:22½
Bertha.............2:29¼
Billy Cramer. .. 2:26¼
Birdie Egmont... ..2:29
Combination .2:18½
Coppermont.... . 2 30
Egmont Chief.......2:24¼
Flaxmont 2:26¾
Flaxseed.. ....2:29
Foxmont...........2:27¼
Johnny R.......... 2:25¼
John Thomas.......2:28¾
Joseph See........ 2.27¾
Lew Wann 2 26¾
Lobasco...........2 10¾
Martha H 2 25¼
Nat Bruen ... 2 21¼
Northwest.........2 22½
Pneumatic.........2:29¾
Scott Chief.. . .. 2:2,
Shellmont.........2 24¼
Sir Lancelot........2:27
Twinkle 2 27½
Wildmont. 2.27
Zoe K....... ......2:30
Billy Sample, p.......2:20
Clear Grit, p 2:19¼
Chief Scott, p......2 28¼
Northwest, p. 2:15
Trego, p..........2:16½
Egmont Chief by Egmont.
Lady Egmont.. . 2 30
Egotist by Electioneer.
Betsey Britton........2·20¾
Birdie 2 27¾
Bishop Dudley......2 27
Dramatist..........2:29¼
Elton.. ....2 21
Genevieve. 2 29¾
Guilford Dudley ... 2 30
Lovelace 2 20
Mildred...........2:29¾
Stonewall 2 27½
The Conqueror 2 15½
Zenith... .... 2 28¾
Egthorne by Egbert.
Grace Thorne 2 28¾
Thorntonian. 2 30
Jenny Hill.........2 29¼
El Capitan by Nutwood.
Ashton, p 2:17½
Dorrance, p 2:13¾
Eldridge by Edward Everett.
Cartridge..........2:14½
Elect by Electioneer.
Elect Moores... . 2·27
Re-Elect..........2.28
Electioneer by Rysdyk's Hambletonian.
Adair.... ....2:17¼
Addie Lee..........2 23¾
Advance...........2:22½
Advertiser 2:15¼
Ah There 2:18¼
Albert W. ....2·20
Aldeana...........2.25
Alaska 2 29
Aleck B.............2 24¾
Alma 2:28¼
Altivo............2 18¼
Amigo.............. 2:16¾

Ansel ... 2:20
Anteeo ... 2:16½
Antevolo ... 2:19½
Antinous ... 2:28½
Arbutus ... 2:26½
Arion ... 2:07¾
Arol ... 2.24
Azmoor ... 2:20½
Athena ... 2:25¼
Bell Bird ... 2:22
Bell Boy ... 2 19¼
Belle Electro ... 2:30
Belle Electric ... 2:29½
Belleflower ... 2:12¾
Belle Monte ... 2:22¼
Bernal ... 2:17
Bonita ... 2:18½
Bow Bells ... 2:19¼
Brilliant ... 2·23
Candidate ... 2:26½
Cara Mia ... 2:29½
Carrie C ... 2:24
Caution ... 2:25½
Cecilian ... 2:22
Clay ... 2;25
Clinton Bell ... 2:24½
Colma ... 2:25¼
Commotion ... 2:30
Conductor ... 2:18¾
Coquette ... 2:29½
Coral ... 2:18½
Cubic ... 2·28½
Dan ... 2:26¾
Del Mar ... 2:16¾
Don Felix ... 2:27¼
Don Monteith ... 2:29¾
Egotist ... 2:22½
Electant ... 2:27
Electioneer ... 2·28½
Electioneer(C'mpb'ls) 2·17¾
Elector ... 2:21¼
Elector ... 2:25
Electrician ... 2:23¼
Electricity ... 2.17¾
El Benton ... 2:28¾
Electress ... 2:30
Electric Coin ... 2.18¼
Electric King ... 2:24
Electrobenton ... 2:24½
Electrix ... 2:28½
Electwood ... 2:30
Electryon ... 2:24¾
Ella ... 2:29
Electuary ... 2·27
Elleneer ... 2.21½
Elma Sontag ... 2:29
Elwina ... 2:27¼
Emaline ... 2:27½
Emma R ... 2:28¾
Eros ... 2:29½
Expedition ... 2:15¾
Express ... 2:21
Expressive ... 2:12½
Fallis ... 2:23
Fay ... 2:25
Fowler Boy ... 2:26
Fred Crocker ... 2:25¼
Gen Wellington ... 2:30
Gertrude Russell ... 2 23½
Golden Slippers ... 2 30
Gov. Stanford ... 2:21
Grace Lee ... 2·29¼
Grover Clay ... 2:23¼
Hattie D ... 2:26¾
Helena ... 2:21
Hernani ... 2:29¾
Hinda Rose ... 2:19½
Hugo ... 2:27½

Idelia ... 2:30
Idle May ... 2 27½
Ivo ... 2 26
Ivy E ... 2:29½
Junio ... 2·22
Jim ... 2:27¼
Kerner ... 2:23¾
Ladywell ... 2:16½
Laura C ... 2:29¼
Laura R ... 2:21¼
Legal Test ... 2:29¾
Lent ... 2:26½
Linnet ... 2:29½
Liska ... 2:28¼
Loraneer ... 2·26½
Lot Slocum ... 2:17¼
Lucyneer ... 2:27
Maiden ... 2:23
Manzanita ... 2;16
Marvin ... 2:23½
May King ... 2:20
Memento ... 2:25¼
Minet ... 2:27½
Miss Naude ... 2:29½
Monterey ... 2:25½
Monaco ... 2:19½
Mont Rose ... 2:18
Morea ... 2:24¼
Mortimer ... 2:27
Norval ... 2:14¾
Old Nick ... 2:23
Pacifica ... 2:30
Palo Alto ... 2:08¾
Palo Alto Belle ... 2:22½
Paola ... 2:25½
Pedlar ... 2:23¾
Peko ... 2:22
Pomona ... 2:28¼
Quality ... 2·25½
Re Election ... 2.27¼
Rexford ... 2:24
Regina ... 2:18½
Rustique ... 2:18½
Rockefeller ... 2:29½
Rusanole ... 2:23
St. Bel ... 2:24½
Sir Outcross ... 2:28
Slight ... 2:28½
Sonoma ... 2:28
Sphinx ... 2:20½
Starlight ... 2:15¾
Stella ... 2:30
Suisun ... 2:18½
Sunol ... 2:08¼
Susette ... 2:23½
Sweet Rose ... 2:25¾
Tiny ... 2:28¼
Truman ... 2:12
Utility ... 2:20¾
Veda ... 2:26¼
Whips ... 2:27½
Wildflower ... 2:21
Wild May ... 2:30
Young Wildidle ... 2:25
Peruvian Bitters, p ... 2:29½

Electioneer (Campbell's) by Electioneer.
Electioneer(B'wm'n's) 2:26½
Symboleer, p ... 2:11

Elector (Richard's) by Electioneer.
Acclamation ... 2:24¾
Allie Sloper ... 2:28
Cora S ... 2:19¼
Despardo ... 2:29¼
Elect ... 2:26
Elector Jr ... 2:29¾

Electress ... 2:27¼
Electra ... 2:18¾
Electrina ... 2:20
Ella M ... 2:28¾
Flora M ... 2:16
J. R ... 2:20
Leck ... 2:29
Lizzie F ... 2:16¼
Nettie C ... 2:28
Pleasanton ... 2:29½
Eric, p ... 2:17
L. A. Dick, p ... 2:25
May Be, p ... 2:26¼

Elector (Morrow's) by Electioneer.
Molly McCaulley, p ... 2:16¾
Edwin C. p ... 2:15

Electricity by Electioneer.
Fly ... 2:29¼
Welbeck ... 2:24½

Electrotype by Electioneer.
Electro Bell ... 2:27¾
Pauline ... 2.26

Elevator.
Ella McGee ... 2:29¼
Ramona ... 2:29¾
Wild Rose ... 2:28
Bee Line, p ... 2:19¼
Flavorita, p ... 2 24¾
Laura Bell, p ... 2:29¼
The Dude ... 2:13½

Elgin Boy by Pocahontas Boy
Nelly Lloyd ... 2:22½
Easter Girl, p ... 2:25¾
Edwin O. p ... 2:20
Ferncliff, p ... 2:24
Harry B. p ... 2:27¼
Harry Jones, p ... 2:18¼
Lily B. p ... 2.21½
Lucille, p ... 2.24½
Pearl L. p ... 2:23
Polka Hot, p ... 2:27½
Redleaf, p ... 2:26½
William J. p ... 2:26¼

Elial G. by Aberdeen.
Ada D ... 2:21½
Ben Hur ... 2:29¾
Bunnie G ... 2:23¾
Dick Wood ... 2:27½
Hannah Dustin ... 2:29¾
Harrie ... 2:28¼
Joe ... 2:29¼
Kitty Can ... 2 30
Malacca ... 2: 24½
Manning ... 2:24½
Nelly Gamwell ... 2:30
Nixon ... 2:26¾
Stealaway ... 2:28¼
The Raven ... 2:19½
Dick Fitzgerald, p ... 2:24½
Emerson, p ... 2:22½
Little Dan, p ... 2:21¼

Elial G. Jr. by Elial G.
Jessie Sheridan ... 2:21¾

Ellerslie Wilkes by George Wilkes.
Bismuth ... 2:23¼
Emmet B ... 2·28½
Lady Wilkes ... 2 16½
Minting ... 2:29¼
Ofellus ... 2:23
Mountain Pink, p ... 2.15¼

Ellington Boy by Amboy.
Ellington D ... 2.26¾

Elliott Wilkes by Forward.
Summit Chief ... 2:21¼

Ellwood.
Lula, p 2:29¾
El Mahdi by Onward.
Fulano. 2:22½
Onward Fewell.......2:27½
Moyer, p 2 18¾
Elmo by Mohawk
Alfred S . . . 2·16¼
Como. . . .. . . 2·26¾
Emma G....... ....2:27¼
Overman .. 2 19¼
Sunflower 2 24
Elma, p . .. 2:24
L C. Lee, p 2.15
Elmo by St. Elmo.
Bess ..... 2·29¼
Gold Charm. 2:25¼
Elsmere by Albrino.
Eldora 2 23
Elwood Medium by Happy Medium.
Conte Rosso ....2·22
Elyria by Mambrino King
Amherst Boy.. .....2:24¼
Ben H.. .. .. 2.25¼
Elixir. .. ..2·22½
Elyrina 2 20¼
Gertrude 2:12
Henrietta G.... ... 2:19¼
Jessie D 2 19¼
Joe Gales.... .... 2:29¼
Lady Clare..... ..2 18¾
Marion Messenger . 2·30
Muggins. 2 20¼
Mambrino Queen .2.13¼
Mambrino Swift... .2·26¼
Nickle D 2 29¼
Oberlin Boy. 2:27½
Ortine .. 2·22¼
Peveril 2 14¼
Rifle. ...... 2·18¼
Sam Bassett .. . 2 22½
Modern Belle, p. ... 2·26¼
Emerson Golddust by Golddust.
Nelly Woods 2:28½
Embassador by Ambassador.
Maud A. 2.29¼
Trixey........ .2.30
Annie Embassador, p 2.25
Billy Wilson, p. .....2·26¼
Donald, p 2.30
Green Wilkes, p...2:22¼
Maud A., p..........2:28½
Miss Cumskey, p. 2.22¼
Procul, p 2.30
Embassador by Satelite.
Herman H 2 21¾
Muggins 2:25
Emery Fearnaught by Paul's Fearnaught Jr.
F D.. .. ..2.24¼
Minnie L 2:20¼
Emperor Wilkes by William L.
X. L .. ?:20¼
Princess Eulatia, p 2 18¼
Emperor William by Gen Knox.
Frank F .... 2·26¼
Empire by Mambrino Patchen.
Eminence 2 18¾
Telephone 2:15¼
Western Boy. 2:29½
Empire by Gen. Knox.
Nathan.......... 2:29¾
Enchanter by Administrator.
Ensign 2:28½

Valiant 2 23¼
Endymion by Dictator.
Comal 2:26
Edenia . . 2 13¼
Kingmoor 2 28¾
Calyce. 2:29¼
Energy by Onward.
Aristall 2:25¾
Enfield by Rysdyk's Hambletonian.
Parnell.............2:23
Robin 2 24½
Stonecutter 2 28¾
Tosa. 2:19¼
Ed Geers, p... .. 2 26½
Transfer, p 2.27½
Enfield Jr. by Enfield.
Betty B. . 2·29¼
Engineer
Roy H.. p 2.18¾
Engineer 2d by Engineer.
Lady Suffolk.... ...2:29½
Enoch by Ethan Allen,
Riley............ 2·30
Enright by Nutwood.
Elata... ... 2 24¼
Ensign by Enchanter.
Alert .... .. 2·24
Alice Ensign . 2·23
Andy Ensign. ...2:26½
Belle M.. ....2:30
Bertie Ensign ...2·25½
Bob Burdette 2:30
Capitola 2.24¼
Chevalier Ensign . 2·29¾
C. V. B 2:15¼
Ensign 2:25½
Guido.... ....2·21½
Harry Ensign . . 2:19¾
Helen G 2:28¼
J. W. Tedford 2.19¾
Sardis Ensign ... 2 30
Shiloh ..... . 2·30
Alice Ensign, p. . 2.25
Blue Sign, p........ 2 08¼
Empress, p 2 28¾
Mugwump, p 2·21¼
Envoy by Gen. Hatch.
Environ 2:26½
Rettie 2 27½
Eolus.
Jim Alone 2 29¼
Epaulet by Auditor.
Comedy 2 23¼
Ella Vertner . 2 19¼
Edwardo.... ..2:26½
E. L. Robinson . 2:17¾
Flutter. 2:26¾
Gold Lace 2 30
Guardian.... ...... 2 24½
Minuetto 2:27¼
Oudan 2 20
Queen of Cedars 2 20¾
Queen of Upland ..2:22¼
Shebas Queen.... ..2 26¼
Spreckles.............2·30
Sultan.... ..... .2 26¼
Templette.... ... 2:29¼
Zilette, p 2 25½
Epicure by Princeps.
Maud W 2 26¼
Nicollet...... ... 2:30
Ray ... 2 28
Equinox by Strader's Cassius M. Clay Jr.
Irene L. p .. . 2 24¼

Equity Wilkes by George Wilkes.
Peerless. p........ ... 2 13¼
Erelong by Belmont.
Fannette... ....2:29¾
So Long.. ... ...2 13¼
Waco 2:16¼
Zoda 2 29¼
Ericsson by Mambrino Chief
Belle.............2:28¼
Doble 2 28
Eric 2:28¼
Lulu F 2.29
Nightingale . . 2 28¾
Rarely. .....-2:24½
Erie Abdallah by Rose's Abdallah Chief
Rienzi 2:25¼
Abdallah Boy, p . 2 22¾
Erie Chief by Erie Abdallah.
Hideaway. 2 28¼
Erie Wilkes by George Wilkes.
Carro, p........ .. 2 24¾
Prince Erie, p. . . . 2:29½
Turco, p 2 12
Erin Chief by Howe's Royal George.
Syndicate.... .... 2 25¾
Ernest by Volunteer.
Protection 2 19¼
Erratta, p 2:29½
Nelly B p... ... 2:16¾
Eros by Electioneer.
Daylight ..... . 2·27¾
Don Zella 2:29¾
Eclectroid 2 30
Heros 2:26¼
Maraquita 2 30
Mount Mood 2 23¾
My My 2:25¾
Oro Fino 2.18
Rinconada... . . 2·17
Solita.... . 2·27
Wanda 2 14¾
Willema 2:26
Erwin Davis by Shenandoah
Carrie F...... ... .2·27¾
Ed............... 2:26
Estill Eric by Ericson.
Mattie Scott. 2:25
Ethan Allen by Vermont Black Hawk.
Billy Barr 2:23¾
Fanny Allen 2 28¼
Fanny Lee . . 2:29¼
Hotspur 2.24
Pocahontas . . 2 26¾
Warwick..... . 2 29¼
Parnell, p 2 29¼
Ethan Allen by Bacon's Ethan Allen.
Baldwin..... ..2 24¼
Billy Allen . 2 27
George R 2:27½
Lew Ives . . 2 28
Rufus 2 29
Russ Ellis. 2:27¼
Molly Clark. p . 2:26¾
Ethan Allen (Dixon's) by Ethan Allen.
Sensation 2:22¼
Ethan Allen (Woodward's) by Ethan Allen.
Archbishop 2 18¼
Aulinda... .. .2:25
Charles Reade . 2 24¼

Charle C.............2:28½
Duplex.............2:25¼
Falka.............2:29½
Shepherd Boy.............2:23½
Tuna.............2:18½
Dexter, p.............2:29
Eckford.............2:25¼

Ethan Allan (Holabird's) by Ethan Allen.
Charley Mac.............2:25
Laura Williams.............2:24½
Little Dick.............2:24½
Sister.............2:25¾
Edson Allen, p.............2:17¼
Ulster Belle, p.............2:17¼

Ethan Allen (Drury's), by Black Hawk.
Fady Fox.............2:30

Ethan Allen (DeLong's) by Ethan Allen.
Arthur.............2:26½
Headlight.............2:29¼
Lucca.............2:30
Belle D., p.............2:24¼

Ethan Allen (Ashley's), by Holabird's Ethan Allen.
Little Ethan.............2:24½
Allen Maid, p.............2:16½
Charles L., p.............2:19½
Harry H., p.............2:29¼

Ethan Allen (White's), by Holabird's Ethan Allen.
J. B. S.............2:29¾

Ethan Allen (Kelley's), by Vick's Ethan Allen, Jr.
Kate Castleton.............2:26½

Ethan Allen, Jr., (Vick's), by Ethan Allen.
Prince Allen.............2:27

Ethan Allen, Jr. (Holland's), by Ethan Allen.
Barney Kelley.............2:25

Ethan Allen 2d.
Deceiver.............2:29¼

Ethan Wilkes by George Wilkes.
American Lad.............2:26½
Edgar Wilkes.............2:24¼
Emory.............2:30
Ethan K.............2:27¾
Eva Wilkes.............2:28½
Kate Ethan.............2:25
Roy K.............2:29¾
W. H. Kerr.............2:28
Zeeland.............2:24
American Lad, p.............2:17¼
Edna Wilkes, p.............2:29¾
Roy K., p.............2:28
Vinette, p.............2:09¼
Willett Wilkes, p.............2:22¼
Will Kerr, p.............2:07½

Euclid by Glenview.
Euchre.............2:30
Euclare.............2:29½
Lady Euclid.............2:25

Eugene Casserly by Gen. Taylor.
Sweetbriar.............2:26¼

Everett Clay by Harry Clay.
Story's Clay.............2:18½
Kitty Story.............2:22½

Evan Lewis by Geo. Sprague.
Princess Alice, p.............2:23

Evermond by Harold.
C. C.............2:30
Evergood.............2:24¼
Patsy Curtis.............2:16½
Everway, p.............2:14¾

Exchequer by Revenue.
Lucille.............2:21
Rigolette.............2:22

Executor by Administrator.
Trixter.............2:25½

Extra by Lockwood.
Chevalita.............2:25½

Fairholm by Aberdeen.
Dennis.............2:24¼

Fairlawn Medium by Happy Medium.
Ethelyn Fairlawn.............2:29¼
Lady Fairlawn.............2:28¼
Leland Medium.............2:23¼

Fairy Gift by Hero of Thorndale.
Ada.............2:29½
Cephas.............2:25
Claudius.............2:29¾
Diatonic.............2:27¼
Dora.............2:30
George Gift.............2:29¼
Good Gift.............2:28
Hazel Thorne.............2:29¼
Kenwood.............2:17
Little Gift.............2:29¼
Rosamond.............2:27¾
Gold Plate, p.............2:23½
Hoodoo, p.............2:18¼
Nettie Field, p.............2:23
Pilot Gift, p.............2:15½
Sigma Chi, p.............2:25

Fairview by Glenview.
William M. Purdy, p.............2:26½

Falcon by Young Hambletonian.
Falcon, Jr.............2:21¾
Wayland.............2:25½

Falcon by Messenger Duroc.
G. H. F.............2:25½

Fallis.
Bradtmoor.............2:26¼
Don Marvin.............2:22½
Fallacy.............2:17½
Falmon.............2:23¾
Lustre.............2:23½
Menlo Fallis.............2:27¾
Falrose, p.............2:19

Fancy Golddust by Dorsey's Golddust.
Fred Golddust.............2:27½

Fashion by Stranger.
Fashion Maid.............2:24¼

Fast Mail by Nutwood.
Kate Weber.............2:30

Favorite Wilkes by George Wilkes.
Albert M.............2:29¼
Areida.............2:26
Chestnut Wilkes.............2:29½
Crescent.............2:25
Duchess Wilkes.............2:27
Ella Wilkes.............2:26¾
Elmer Wilkes.............2:28
Favorite Girl.............2:28¼
Favor Wilkes.............2:29¼
Hippia.............2:21½
Lucy Cooper.............2:30
Nelly Wilkes.............2:28¼
Number Seven.............2:20½
Ollie Wilkes.............2:16¼
Ruprecht.............2:24½
Sweetbriar.............2:17½
Wilkerson.............2:29¾
Crawford, p.............2:07¾
Ulster County Belle, p.............2:21¾
Winola, p.............2:22

Fayette Chief by Mambrino King.
King Herod.............2:16½

Fayette Wilkes by George Wilkes.
Silver Wilkes.............2:26¼

Fearnaught by Young Morrill.
Argonaut.............2:23¾
Fearnaught Jr.............2:26
Galatea.............2:24¾

Fearnaught by Black Hawk (Canadian)
Lady Shepherd.............2:28½

Fearnaught (Whitcomb's) by Fearnaught.
Lady Brooks.............2:29¼

Fearnaught (Flaherty's).
Colonia.............2:24¼
Dick Flaherty.............2:29¼
H. M. Stanley.............2:19½

Fearnaught Gift by Western Fearnaught.
Molly B.............2:29¾

Fearnaught Jr. by Fearnaught.
Pemberton.............2:29½
Prince Fearnaught.............2:23¼
Benny, p.............2:18½

Fearnaught Spy by Robinson's Black Spy.
Malvina.............2:21¼

Feegee by Harold.
Feather Edge.............2:18

Fenian Chief by Canadian Grey Eagle.
Capt. Smith.............2:28½

Ferdinand C. by Conductor.
Lah-de-Dah.............2:26

Fergus McGregor by Robert McGregor.
Ashland Boy.............2:28¾
Billy McGregor.............2:28½
Carlisle McGregor.............2:29¾
Cora McGregor.............2:23¼
Greenwood.............2:29
Lady Wonder.............2:23½
McDuff.............2:23
Pansy McGregor.............2:17¼
Fergustine, p.............2:20¾
McAnder, p.............2:22½
Miss Quickley, p.............2:24¼

Ferguson by George Wilkes.
Belle Ferguson.............2:28½
Freddy C.............2:26½
Indo Wilkes.............2:29
Yum Yum.............2:29¼
Lena Willetts, p.............2:14
Lord Ferguson, p.............2:19¼
Opulence, p.............2:29½
Two Strike, p.............2:10¾
Victorine, p.............2:20
Walnut Boy, p.............2:11½

Fessenden by Andrew Jackson
Fred Casey.............2:23¼

Fieldmont by Almont.
Dark Night.............2:25½
Bon Bon.............2:29¾
Don L.............2:28¾
Julietta.............2:21¾
Tom Tucker.............2:29¼
William Gill.............2:29

Finality.
Baby Boy, p.............2:20½

Fitzgerald's Enterprise by Red Wilkes.
Harry Wilkes.............2:29¼

Mazz ntine 2:29¼
Fire Clay by Shawmut.
Eva Clay . . . . . 2·24
Maud Clay 2.24
Fine Cut by John C. Fremont
Jackson 2 27¾
Firefly by Daniel Lambert.
Del Monte. 2:21¼
Fisher Patchen.
Capt. Jack 2:26
Flasco
Dinah, p 2:25½
Flatbush Abdallah by Jupiter Abdallh.
Fascination. 2:16¼
Flaxmont by Egmont.
Budd Flax... . . . . 2.24½
Vernmont 2 29
Flaxtail.
Dan 2:30
Empress. 2.29¾
Prairie Bird, p 2 28¾
Fleance by Marmaduke.
Arlington. 2 24½
Fleeting Ray by North Morrill.
Money Hunter . . . 2 25¼
Fleetwood.
N. Q. Lancewood, p 2:25¼
Floramour by Florida.
Albatross, p . . . . . . 2·16¾
Maud Adair, p. 2:18
Florida by Rysdyk's Hambletonian
Eva M . . . . 2·25¼
Fanny Swope... . . . 2:19¼
Faust.. . . . . 2 18¼
Florida Monarch. 2:17¼
Fortuna. . . . . 2·22
Frenzy 2:27¼
Hambleton 2:26¼
Lotta. 2 24½
Oneida 2 17
Orphan Lass 2:24¾
Royal Duke 2:29½
Walnut. 2 19¼
William V. 2:30
Florida M. by Florida
Aurora Prince. . . . . 2·16¾
Flying Banner by Black Banner.
Fanny 2 29
Flying Cloud by Vermont Black Hawk.
Star of the West . 2.26½
Flying Cloud.
Kit Cloud, p. 2:26¼
Flying Cloud (Orr's) by Vermont Black Hawk.
Ohio Maid.. .. . . 2:29¾
Flying Cloud (Corben's) by Black Flying Cloud.
Baywood, p. 2:28
Judge Lynch, p. 2:22
Flying Cloud by Flying Cloud
Myrtle. 2:26½
Flying Cloud.
Sorrell Ned 2.25¼
Frank Nelson .. 2:28½
Flying Dutchman.
George G., p. 2:17
Flying Hiatoga by Handley's Hiatoga.
Kathrina 2.30
Flying Hiatoga Jr., p. 2:23¼
Rattling Jim, p. 2:23¼
Flying Hiatoga Jr. by Flying Hiatoga.
McDuff 2:22¾
Flying Morgan.
Little Longfellow .. 2 29¼
Flying Morgan by Laflin Morse.
Traveler. 2:27½
Forbes by Iron Duke.
Milkmaid. 2:22½
Fordstan by Electioneer.
Melvar 2 22
Forest Duke by Dictator Chief.
Dora H. 2:20¼
Forest Hal by Looney's Tom Hal,
Col. Forest, p.. .. 2:18
Little Joker, p. 2 16¼
Forest Hiatoga by Flying Hiatoga.
Nellie Allison 2.19¼
Forest King by Mambrino Patchen.
Forest Queen.... 2 29¼
Lida Bassett 2:20½
Forest Mambrino by Mambrino Patchen.
Dr. Forest. . . 2·22¼
Forest Boy... .. . . . 2 16¼
Heward H... . . . 2.29¼
John Ferguson. . 2 25¼
King Forest 2.21½
Forest Prince by Baird's Hambletonian Prince.
David B 2:28
Emmons. . . . . 2·29¼
Forrest Bismarck by Victor Bismarck.
Diamond 2:24¼
Forrest Glencoe by Edwin Forrest.
Wildbriar, p. . . . . . . 2·22¾
Forrest Golddust by Dorsey's Golddust.
Circulator 2 27¼
Forest Wilkes by Bourbon Wilkes.
Gold Coin, p. 2 25
Touchstone, p . 2 19½
Fortunatus by Almont
Pat. 2 29¼
Winnie W. 2.22
Wanita Proctor, p. 2 24
Forsee by Coleman's Abdallah, Jr.
William L. 2 29¼
Fortune by Superb.
Weaver Boy 2:28¾
Forward by George Wilkes.
Tristan 2:22½
Foster Palmer by Gideon.
Lilly B. 2:28¼
Foxhunter.
Dirigo. 2.27
Foxhunter (Potter's), by Foxhunter.
Lottie 2:29½
Foxwood by Nutwood.
Fox Hunter. 2 30
France by France's Alexander.
Bessie R. 2:25¼
Clay France 2 26½
Franceps 2.24½
June France. 2:29½
La France. 2:26¼
Gov. France, p 2 24¾
Jay Jay, p. 2 28¼
Frank by Prendergast's St. Lawrence.
Black Frank 2 28¼
Dolly... .. .. 2 30
Frank A. by Rex Hiatoga.
Maud P., p 2:14¼
Frank Allen by Ethan Allen.
Major Allen 2 24¼
Zephyr 2:30
Frank Allen by Ethan Allen
Star Allen... . . . . 2·26½
Frank Almont by Bostick's Almont, Jr.
G. D., p. 2.21
Mary B., p 2 23
Frank Box.
Roy S., p .. .. 2·23½
Frank Buford by Bostick's Almont, Jr.
Linda, p 2 22½
Frank Cheatham by Andrews' Horse.
William R., p 2 15
Frank Eaton by Robert Whaley.
Kate Eaton, p 2:16
Frank Dunn by Winnebago.
Amy B 2:24¼
Frank Ellis by Happy Medium.
Dukes 2.25
Ellis Medinm. 2:24
Yorker 2.24¼
Frank Hampton by Volunteer
Judge Hampton . . . 2:27¾
Frank Logan by Little Logan
Paola, p . . . . 2·20
Franklin by Ben Franklin.
Lady Franklin 2 25½
Frank M.
Bob Ingersoll, p . . . 2 23¼
Frank Moscow by Fisk's Moscow
Frank Moscow . . . 2 27½
Frank Nichols by Night Hawk.
Al R 2:27½
Frank Noble by Louis Napoleon.
Corisco 2 21
Harry Noble 2 17½
Melton . . . . 2·30
Merula 2.29¾
Noblemont 2 29½
Billy Gault, p. 2:20
Mack Noble, p 2.28½
Frank Pierce, Jr. by Frank Pierce.
Phil Daugherty .. 2.26
Frank Pierce 3d by Frank Pierce Jr.
Stonewall 2 24½
Frank Tuckahoe by Tuckahoe.
St. Elmo 2 22¼
Frank Wilkes by George Wilkes, Jr.
Irene Wilkes 2 27¼
Frank Wolford by Telegraph.
Cuckoo 2:28
Fred by Highland Chief.
McDoel. 2:15½
Fred.
Birdseye 2.29½

Fred Boone by Daniel Boone.
- Honest Joe 2:24¼

Fred Douglas by Green's Bashaw.
- May Douglas 2:15½

Frederick by Satellite.
- Topsey F., p 2:22

Fred Drennon by Drennon.
- Lady Drennon, p ... 2:26½

Fred Forest by Forest King.
- Gypsy Patchen 2:30
- W. H. 2:24¼

Fred S. Wilkes by Hector Wilkes.
- Dr. French 2:23¼

Freeland by Bald Hornet.
- Lady Hornet, p 2:24

Freeman by Woodford Abdallah.
- Belle Freeman 2:18¼

Freestone by Gatling.
- Brownstone 2:28½

French Bashaw by Black Bashaw.
- Little Daisy 2:20¼

Frenchman (McDonald's) by Flying Frenchman.
- Frenchman 2:24¾

Fritz by Harold.
- Prosper Merimee 2:24¼

Fugleman by Princeps.
- Bradford 2:17¾
- Kate F 2:16¼

Fuller Wilkes by George Wilkes.
- David L. 2:19½

Fullerton D.
- Jess, p. 2:30

Gamaleon by Gambetta Wilkes.
- Charles P. 2:18¼
- Delbert 2:21
- Crimrose 2:29½
- Gambert 2:27¾

Gambetta by Volunteer.
- Bessie Jordan. 2:25¼
- Comfort 2:27½
- Cleo 2:19½
- Gentry 2:30
- Idol 2:27½
- Robert Ransom. 2:29¾
- Useful 2:22¼
- Volmer 2:24¼

Gambetta Wilkes by George Wilkes.
- Cecelian 2:19¼
- Cecil Wilkes 2:25
- Charlemagne 2:27½
- Galena 2:28½
- De Long 2:30
- Ethel T. 2:29½
- Gamaleon 2:25¼
- Gamarza 2:27½
- Gambonito 2:19¼
- Gambruno 2:29½
- Gambryon 2:19¼
- Gammer 2:23¼
- Gam Byron. 2:26¼
- Gascoigne. 2:24¾
- Gen. Boyle 2:24¼
- Genteel 2:29¾
- George Condit 2:29¼
- Georgie Lee 2:12¾
- Gill Boyle 2:27¼
- Grandley 2:23¾
- Gilfillan 2:26½
- Greenbriar 2:22½
- Grex 2:28
- Griselda 2:29¼
- Linda Fister 2:27½
- Miss Cecil. 2:21½
- Medora 2:19¼
- Prince Karl 2:30
- Wilkes Worthington. 2:23¼
- Alice Wilkes, p 2:19
- Alietta, p. 2:30
- Brennan, p 2:16¼
- Don Lorenzo, p 2:17¾
- Don Pizarro, p 2:14¾
- Gallietta, p 2:16¼
- Gambier, p 2:19
- Gambolier, p 2:21½
- Glen Athol, p. 2:29¼
- Goethe, p. 2:19½
- Gamrose, p. 2:19¾
- Gannon, p. 2:18
- Gambrel, p 2:10½
- Gawain, p. 2:18¼
- Gowan, p 2:22½
- Guerita, p. 2:13
- Guinette, p. 2:10
- Gusto, p. 2:19¼
- Lottie Loraine, p. 2:10½
- Martha H., p 2:18¼
- Rahleta, p. 2:21¼
- Sally Bronston, p 2:17½
- Weed Wilkes, p 2:14¼

Gambonito by Gambetta Wilkes.
- Gilbert. 2:28½

Game Onward by Onward.
- Lady Onward. 2:28
- Bernice, p. 2:23
- Edramon, p 2:21½
- Benvoi, p. 2:21½

Ganymede by Princeps.
- Dr. Caton. 2:18½

Garfield by Clear Grit.
- Miss Garfield, p. 2:21¾

Garfield by Durango.
- Daisy Garfield 2:27

Garibaldi by Rysdyk's Hambletonian.
- Birdie C. 2:28¼

Garibaldi by Duroc Messenger.
- Archie 2:24¼
- Belle Oakley 2:24¼

Garland by Twilight.
- Garland M 2:29¼

Garnet Wilkes by Onward.
- Duroc Wilkes. 2:18¾
- Jerry 2:27¼
- La Ferme 2:23½
- Marion Wilkes 2:17¼
- Sirius 2:19¼
- Victor 2:29½
- Combination, p 2:25

Garnet Wilkes by Ambassador
- Dr. Fritts 2:25

Garrard Chief by Mambrino Chief.
- Basil Duke. 2:28¼

Garrett by Maryland Volunteer.
- Queen Garrett 2:30

Garrett Wilkes.
- Nettie C., p 2:24¼

Gatling by Rysdyk.
- Freestone 2:25½

Gat Van Wagner by Jehu.
- Frank Kober 2:28

Gaviota by Electioneer.
- Dynamite 2:29½
- Maud Elmeda 2:24

Gayo.
- Shamrock 2:26½

Gazette by Onward.
- Aileen, p 2:19¼

G. C. by Onward.
- Kate Thomas. 2:24½

Gen. Benton by Jim Scott.
- Alban 2 24
- Albion 2:26½
- Alfred 2:25
- Benefactor 2:29¾
- Benton 2:20¾
- Benton Boy 2:17¼
- Bentoneer 2:28½
- Big Jim 2:23½
- Bonnie. 2:25
- Daly 2:15
- Daylight 2:26¾
- George H. 2:26¼
- Gypsy Queen 2:26¼
- Lord Byron 2:17
- Maralia 2:24¼
- Millard 2:28
- Nelly Benton. 2:30
- Ninette. 2:28
- Sally Benton 2:17¾
- Spry 2:28¾
- The Seer 2:15¾
- Benton Boy, p. 2:16¾
- Prussian Boy, p. 2:26¼

Gen. Beverly by Benefit.
- Bion 2:24¾

Gen. Brock by Rooker.
- Fin Fan. 2:25¼
- Gen. Banks. 2:29½
- Glenara, p. 2:22¼

Gen. Dana by Wood's Hambletonian.
- Volunteer 2:27

Gen. Franklin by Ben Franklin.
- Dolly Franklin, p. .. 2:29¼

Gen. George H. Thomas by Mambrino Messenger.
- Annie H. 2:20
- Billy Thompkins 2:29¼
- Ed Graham. 2:24¼
- Eulu Lee 2:29½
- George 2:29½
- Lady K 2:29½
- Scott's Thomas 2:21

Gen. Garfield.
- H. P. E. 2:25¼
- E. P. O. p 2:24¼

Gen. Grant by Gen. Withers.
- Ned H. p 2:24¼

Gen. Grant by Wapsie.
- Blanche Grant 2:25¾
- Golden Belle 2:30
- Jessie B 2:24
- Logan Grant 2:29
- Norway 2:29¾
- Shiloh 2:23¾
- Kate Long, p 2:30

Gen Grant by Draco.
- Eureka 2:23

Gen. Grant (Canadian).
- Lady Upton 2:29

Gen. Hancock by George Wilkes.
- Dunbar 2:26¾
- Gettysburg 2:29
- Mazone 2:29¾
- Cullen, p 2:25
- Halo, p 2:18½
- Happy Girl, p. 2:26¼
- Joe Rowell, p 2:23½

- Leverone, p. 2:16
- Scott Smith, p 2:28¼
- Victor Mazzone, p ... 2:21¼
- Wolverton, p 2:26¼

Gen. Hardee by George Washington

- Gen. Hardee 2:27¼
- Billy J. p 2:26¼
- George Gordon, p 2:27½
- Lena H. p 2:22
- Steel Nail, p 2:25
- Thunder, p 2:22¼

Gen. Hatch by Strader's Cassius M Clay Jr.

- Envoy 2:28
- Fleta 2:28
- Soupy 2:23¼

Gen. Howard by Badger Boy.

- John Hall 2:25

Gen. Knox by Vermont Hero.

- Beulah 2:19¼
- Camors 2:19¾
- Eastern Boy 2:29½
- Edison 2:27¾
- Emperor William 2:27½
- Gilbreth Knox 2:26¾
- Harry Spanker 2:30
- Independence 2:21¼
- Knox 2:29½
- Knox Boy 2:23¼
- Lady Maud 2:18¼
- Maud Greenwood 2:26¼
- Messenger Knox 2:30
- Patience 2:28¾
- Peaceful 2:26
- Victor 2:23

Gen. Knox Jr. by Gen. Knox.

- Wallace 2:29¼

Gen. Lee by Black Sultan.

- Black Diamond 2:29¾
- Flora Little, p 2:23

General Lee.

- Minnie L. p 2:24

Gen. Lee by George M. Patchen Jr.

- Lee 2:17¼

General Lee by Lee.

- Pomp 2:30

Gen. Lee Jr. (Johnson's).

- Joker 2:20

Gen. Lightfoot by Gen. Knox.

- Lookout 2:28½
- Shadow 2:28

Gen. Logan by Crompton Lambert.

- Lady Logan, p 2:24¼

Gen. Lyons by Morrill.

- Belle Dean 2:30
- Honest Lyon 2:30
- Richmond 2:26

Gen. McClellan by North Star.

- Dan Voorhees 2:23¼
- Flora Shepherd 2:30
- St. Helena 2:27½

Gen. McClellan Jr. by Gen. McClellan.

- Dick Jay 2:30
- Nelly R 2:17¼
- Lucy L p 2:22½

Gen. Magee by Andy Johnson.

- Henry Magee 2:17¼

Gen. Marion by New Jersey Volunteer.

- Marion, p 2:21¼

Gen. Morgan by Paul Jones.

- Ancient Order Boy 2:27
- Mazomanie 2:20¼
- Red Dick .... 2:?8

Green Oats by Tramp.

- Blanche B 2:20

Gen. Putnam by Rolla.

- Major 2:24¾

Gen. Reno by Tyler's Black Hawk

- Franklin 2:19½
- Maud W. W. W 2:23¼
- Nevada, p 2:24½

Gen Sherman by Young Columbus.

- Dio 2:30
- Lady Sherman 2:25½
- Mars 2:27¼
- Scott 2:24¾

Gen. Smith by Albion.

- Capt Crouch 2:25

Gen. Sprague by Gov. Sprague

- Jay, p 2:28½

Gen. Stanton by Rysdyk's Hambletonian.

- Alice K 2:30
- Belle Stanton 2:24½
- Comet 2:24¼
- Dolly C 2:19
- Fides 2:22¼
- Fides Stanton 2:15
- Geraldine 2:28½
- Henry R 2:25½
- Lulu Stanton 2:19¼
- Lizzie Gibson 2:29¼
- Maggie C 2:29½
- May F 2:30
- Molly Stanton 2:29¼
- Nelly Howard 2:18¾
- Nettie T. 2:22¼
- Pallas 2:26¼
- Polly Stanton 2:23¼
- Pogis Stanton 2:23¾
- Prairie Beile 2:23¼
- Prince Imperial 2:27½
- Stanton Chief 2:27¾
- Una Young 2:29½
- Charley P., p 2:29½
- Queen Stanton, p 2:18
- Stanton Maid, p 2:23

Gen. Thomas by Fisk's Mambrino Chief Jr.

- I. York 2:29¾
- Stephen R 2:29¼
- Vic Hunter 2:23¼

Gen. Turner by Harold.

- Annie Turner, p 2:30
- Milkmaid, p 2:27¼

Gen. Washington by Gen. Knox.

- Carlton Chief 2:21¼
- Erminie 2:30
- Gen. Benham 2:28¼
- Luzerne 2:27½
- Mambrino Thorn 2:25½
- Nose Gay 2:16½
- Ox Eye 2:28½
- Poem 2:13½
- Presto 2:19
- Prose 2:27¼
- Sanborn 2:26½
- Saranac 2:23
- Stella 2:30
- The Wasser 2:30

Gen Washington by Peck Horse.

- Bill Ed 2:28

Gen. Wilkes by George Wilkes

- Charley R 2:27¾
- Grateful 2:30
- Jenny Q 2:30
- St. Julien 2:29¾
- Willabald 2:29½
- Bobby Burns, p 2:19¼
- Gen. Blackford, p 2:24¼
- Pansy Blossom, p 2:12

Gen. Withers by Almont.

- Almont Maid 2:26
- C. T. L 2:23¼

Gentle Breeze by Whirlwind.

- Pearl 2:30

George.

- Lady Rowena 2:29½

George

- Dexter, p 2:24

George B.

- Raymond, p 2:19¼

George Brick.

- Albright, p 2:21

George B. McClellan by Bully King.

- Kitty Burch 2:24¼
- Winnifred 2:26¼

George Brooks.

- Ida B 2:17¼

George B. Swan.

- Little Wonder 2:24¼

George Chief by Milwaukee.

- Myrtle B 2:22½

George D. Patchen by Seneca Patchen.

- Kitty M. Patchen 2:30

George Fletcher by Albany Boy.

- Pronto, p 2:17½

George Gift by Fairy Gift.

- Minnie R., p 2:24¼

George Gordon by Gen. Hardee.

- Nettie Keenan 2:26½
- Rockdale .... ?:29¼

George Hall by Blue Bull.

- Dr. Frank 2:27½
- Jenny Hall, p 2:23¼
- Misty Morning, p 2:25¼
- Sam Hall, p 2:28½
- Toby, p 2:29¼

George H. Low by Florida.

- Eva 2:23¼

George H. D. by Lakeland Abdallah

- Belle W., p 2:26

George J. by Pasha.

- Nelly J 2:29¾

George K by Fisk's Mambrino Chief Jr.

- George W 2:24½
- Sherman 2:22½

George L. Napoleon by Louis Napoleon.

- Fred Judson 2:29¼
- Jim Corbett, p 2:23½
- Silver Thorne, p 2:26½

George Miller by Amboy.

- Billy Miller 2:26¼

George Milo by Louis Napoleon

- Louis C 2:28½
- Milo, p 2:27½

George M. Patchen by Cassius M. Clay.

- Charles E. Lowe 2:25½
- George M. Patchen 2:27

GEORGE FULLER, NASHVILLE, TENN.

(UNCLE GEORGE.)

An Ohio boy of the old Buckeye stock. Years touch him as lightly
as humming birds' wings. While at Glenview he gave Patron
a three-year-old world's record of 2:19½ and Elvira
a four-year-old world's record of 2:18¼.

GEORGE STARR, Terre Haute, Ind.

Starr placed the world's race record for teams at 2:15¼ with Rose
Leaf and Sallie Simmons at Columbus, Ohio, in 1894.

Lucy.......... ......2:18¾
Mary.... .. ..2:28
George M. Patchen Jr. (California Patchen) by Geo. M. Patchen.
Ben Ali......... .. 2:22
Big Lize...........2:24¼
James D. McMann... 2:28¾
Pond Lily.. ....2:29½
Sam Purdy. 2:20½
San Bruno..... ......2:25½
Star King. 2:22
Susie 2:26½
Tinker............ ..2:28
Vanderlynn. 2:21
Wells Fargo....... ...2:18¾
Floss, p...............2:28¾
Ruby Mac, p 2:21½
George M. Patchen Jr. (Wilson's) by George M. Patchen.
Easy Billy. 2:29½
George M. Patchen Jr. (Mc Crea's) by George M.-Patchen.
White Oak............2:30
George M. Van Norte by Mambrino Pilot.
Katie M...............2:25½
George O. by Lakeland Abdallah.
Algonquin...............2:29¾
Mary Lee. 2:29½
Prince T................2:29½
Vera....................2:29½
Ethel B., p 2:18
Henry O, p... ....2:20½
George P. Tucker by Charles Caffrey.
Dan Tucker 2:16¾
George Sherwood.
Marshall T 2:29
George Simmons by Simmons.
Gussie Leonard.......2:29¼
Yulo. 2:30
Ysi Della, p.. .... . .2:24¾
George Spalding by McKimmin's Columbus.
Simmie, p.............2:16¾
George Sprague by Governor Sprague.
Albert S 2:30
Edith Sprague. 2:15¾
Golden Sprague.......2:18¾
Maud 2:28¼
Molly Sprague.... ...2:16½
Onie Sprague..........2:26
Victor Sprague.......2:29¼
William B 2:26
Allesandro, p...........2:18
John Sprague, p 2:22¼
George Stanton by General Stanton.
Dick Mitchell.........2:27¼
George Steck by Strathmore.
Lady Van. 2:28
Charley Miller, p.....2:21¼
Orphan Boy, p.........2:18
George Washington by Ethan Allen.
Douglas. 2:25
Preston.................2:28½
Blue Dick, p 2:30
George Washington.
Harry Van, p. 2:22¼
George Wilkes by Rysdyk's Hambletonian.
Abby....... ....2:26
Albert France.........2:20¾
Alcantara.......... .. 2:23
Alcyone...............2:27
Alicia.......... ......2:30
Ambassador...........2:21¼
Anglin.................2:27½
Baron Wilkes.........2:18
Black Wilkes.........2:28½
Blondine...............2:24¾
Bob's Jug..............2:22¾
Bonnie Wilkes........2:29½
Brignoli Wilkes......2:14½
Brown Wilkes 2:21¾
Busbey.................2:29¼
Carrie........ ....2:29¾
Cuba... ....2:27¾
Daisy Wilkes..........2:30
Defender. 2:26
Early Dawn. 2:21½
Ellerslie Wilkes 2:22½
Empire Wilkes ...,...2:29¼
Fanny Wilkes.........2:26¼
Favorita..............2:25½
Favorite Wilkes 2:24½
Florence Elmore......2:26¾
Gambetta Wilkes.....2:19¼
Gen. Wilkes...........2:21¾
Georgiana 2:26¼
Guy Wilkes 2:15¼
Harry Wilkes..........2:13½
Howard 2:27¼
Ira Wilkes 2:28
Isaac...................2:25¼
J. B. Richardson......2:16¾
Jeff Wilkes. 2:29¼
Jimmy Temple. 2:22½
Joe Bunker 2:19¼
Kaiser..... ....2:28½
Kansas Wilkes. 2 30
Kentucky Wilkes 2:21¼
King Wilkes...........2:22¼
Kitty Wilkes..........2:30
Lizzie Wilkes..........2:22¾
Lumps. 2:21
Madison Wilkes......2:24¾
Magna Wilkes 2:23½
Mambrino Wilkes 2:28¾
May Bird.............2:21
Mike Wilkes 2:26½
Miss Wilkes...........2:29
Nelly L.................2:23¼
Onward... ... .2:25¼
Patchen Wilkes. . . . 2.29½
Prospect Maid 2 23¼
Queen Wilkes 2:23¾
Richard Wilkes.. ....2:26¼
Rosa Wilkes. 2:18¼
Rowena 2:24½
St. Gothard...........2:27
Sealskin Wilkes 2:29½
Sherman..............2.23½
Simmons 2:28
Sister Wilkes 2:22¾
So So...... ....2:17¼
Tennessee Wilkes.....2:27
The King, ...2:29¾
Tom Rogers............2:20
Wilkes Boy 2:24½
Willie Wilkes. 2:28
Wilson... . .. .2:16¼
Wilton... .. ..2:19¾
Young Wilkes.........2:28¼
Bud Crooke, p.........2:15½
Flora Wilkes, p.......2:19½
Honesty, p.......... 2:22
Ira Wilkes, p..........2:22¾
Jimmy Temple, p.....2:23¼
Macey, p...............2:29½
Mike Wilkes, p 2:15¾
Sir Wilkes, p..........2:24¾
Pilot Wilkes, p........2:23
Prophet Wilkes, p....2:21¼
Wilcox, p. 2:16
George Wilkes Jr. by George Wilkes.
Alice Wilkes 2:23¼
Donald................2.19½
Frank Wilkes.........2:27¾
George Wood by George Effner.
Belle Wilson... ......2:28¾
Rideau Belle..........2:23½
Georgia Wilkes by George Wilkes.
Billy Wilkes 2:20¼
Hancock Wilkes......2:29¼
Valentine.... ....2:18½
Bas-Blue Wilkes, p... 2 18¾
George W. Shakespeare.
Justinette. 2:28½
German Boy by Waverly.
German Girl. 2:27¾
Getaway by Gossip Jones.
George R. 2:27¼
Sue Grundy 2:25½
Getaway (Schmidlap's).
Little Joe, p 2:23½
Gibraltar by Echo.
Dora 2:29
Gibber 2:29¼
Homestake 2:14¼
Lottie G... .. ..2:25½
Our Dick., p......... 2:10¼
Gideon by Rysdyk's Hambletonian.
Badoura... ... .2:26¼
Bay..... ....2:27½
Boston Girl 2:25¼
Ezra L.................2:21¼
Gideon Chief by Gideon.
Likewise...... ..... 2.17½
Gift Jr. by Mambrino Gift.
Monk..................2:30
Sable Gift, p......... 2:13¾
Zeliah H., p...........2:26
Gilbirds Sprague by Gov. Sprague.
Charley Gilbirds......2:29¾
Joe Gilbirds...........2:29½
Kate C.... . ...2:27¼
Sarah Gilbirds 2:23½
Valentine Sprague... 2:29¼
Gilbreth Knox by Gen. Knox.
Capitola... . ...2:22½
Charles R 2:27
Gilbreth Maid....... 2:25½
Hambletonian Knox..2:28
Lothair 2:20½
Gilley.
Dave Boy, p.......... 2:29½
Gillig by Aristos.
King Gillig............2:26½
Rupert Gillig.........2:21¾
Sue Gillig 2:25¼
Gillis Horse by Tornado.
Confidence.......... 2:26
Gilman McGregor by Robert McGregor.
Lady McGregor 2:30
Gilroy by Johnny White.
T. A. K.. . .. .2:28½
Florence B.... ....2:25¼
Gilroy by Messenger Duroc.
Roy B.. ....2:24¾
Gilt Edge by Lyman.
Ben Bolt 2:27½

Flirt....................2:30
Grover C...............2:30
Lily D..................2:28¼
Mac.....................2:26¼
Norris N...............2:20¼
Rocket, p...............2:24½
Gilt Edge by White Cloud.
Grey Cloud............2:29¾
Gipsey Boy by Stonewall Jackson.
Billy Burton..........2:25¼
Lath.....................2:29¼
Lucy B..................2:22
Young Gipsy Boy.....2:28½
Gipsey Chief by Simmon's Seneca Chief.
Tipton Boy............2:24¼
Gladiator by George M. Patchen Jr.
Boss.....................2:29¼
James H...............2:21
Daminia, p............2:26¼
Snickelfritz, p........2:29½
Gladiator by Smuggler.
Fred Smuggler, p.....2:22
Glenair by Messenger Duroc.
Idlewild...............2:29¾
Glenalen by Ben Franklin.
B. F. Solon............2:24¼
Glenarm by Constellation.
Glenarma..............2:28¼
Glendale, p............2:26¼
Glencoe Golddust by Dorsey's Golddust.
George W. Davis.....2:26¼
Glencoe Jr.
Madge Hatton........2:17¼
Lady Pendleton, p....2:23¼
Scratch, p.............2:28¾
Uncle Jack, p.........2:16¼
Glencoe Wilkes by Alcantara.
George A..............2:29
Pansy Blossom........2:23
Whirlwind.............2:26¾
Jubilee Wilkes, p.....2:17½
Glencue by Glenarme.
Glenwood.............2:27
Glendale by Glenn's Hambletonian.
Mattie Hunter........2:30
Glen Knox.
Jalba...................2:29½
Glen Duroe by Messenger Duroc.
Clay Duroc............2:30
Glenelg by Baymont.
Lady Red..............2:24¼
Glen Miller by White Line.
Bryan Girl............2:26¼
Kate Ham.............2:28½
Kate Ham, p..........2:24¼
Glenview by Belmont.
Euclid..................2:28½
L. M. Wing............2:26½
Easter Girl, p.........2:27½
Glenwold by Nutwood.
Protien.................2:15½
Glenwood by Wapsle.
Maud Archibald......2:27¼
Gloster by Blue Bull.
Addie C., p............2:20
Dick C., p.............2:18¾
Sam Sharp, p.........2:26
Gloster by Phil Sheridan.
Lora J..................2:19½
Mabel C................2:25¼

Godfrey Patchen by George M. Patchen.
Cyclone................2:30
Ferd S..................2:27½
George H,.............2:25
Glamis.................2:22¼
Harry W. Genet......2:25½
Hopeful................2:14¾
Lady Snell.............2:23¼
Rex Patchen..........2:30
Wellesley Boy........2:26½
Gogebic by Red Wilkes.
All Right..............2:21
Trevor, p..............2:25
Goldbeater by Alcantara.
Marion.................2:19¾
George K, p...........2:18¼
Gold Boy by Gibson's Tom Hal.
Ada, p..................2:13¾
Blue Ridge, p.........2:20
Gen. Ewell, p,.........2:23¾
Golddust (Dorsey's) by Vermont Morgan.
Fleety Golddust......2:20
Indicator..............2:23¼
Lucille Golddust.....2:16¼
Rolla Golddust.......2:25
Golddust.
Red Cloud, p..........2:25¼
Golddust (McCracken's) by McCracken's Black Hawk.
Artist...................2:26¼
Golddust Jr. by Dorsey's Golddust.
Motion Golddust.....2:28½
Sleepy Tom, p.........2:25
Golddust (Thompson's).
Johnny Golddust.....2:17
Axtell, p...............2:16¼
Roy Golddust, p......2:30
Tennyson, p...........2:25¾
Goldemar by Princeps.
Abram..................2:25
Gold Bar...............2:20¾
Kenmar................2:29½
Lady B.................2:27
Natila..................2:25½
King Goldemar, p....2:25¾
Golden by Royal Lambert.
Fred Mac...............2:24¼
Goldenbow by Satellite.
Glitter..................2:22¾
Golden Girl...........2:28½
Jim Fuller.............2:19½
Octavia................2:29¼
Molly D................2:26
Pontiac Chief.........2:16¼
Prince Albert.........2:25¾
Vivian..................2:22
Golden Prince, p......2:18¾
Golden Seal by Satellite.
Billy Dolan............2:27
Golden Star by Bashaw Messenger.
Billy Bashaw.........2:29½
Gold King by Allie Gaines.
Henry L................2:28¾
Bessie B, p............2:21¼
Claremont, p..........2:21¼
Harry Gold King, p...2:27¾
Lady Claremont, p...2:24¼
Lila King, p...........2:22½
Golden Wing by Satellite.
Daisy J.................2:24¼
Gold Leaf by Nugget.
Greenleaf..............2:22½
Franklin...............2:27¾

Oakbourne............2:27½
Oakleaf.................2:28
Rose Leaf..............2:14¾
Goldleaf Jackson by Andrew Jackson Jr.
A. R....................2:27½
Goldmine by Aristos.
Natella.................2:25¼
Rockaway, p..........2:17¼
Goldsmith Pilot by Alden Goldsmith.
Robert Ryan..........2:21
Goodluck.
Boadicia, p...........2:28¼
Delight, p.............2:29½
Glidess, p.............2:26¼
Good Luck by Seymour's Davy Crocket.
Dale, p.................2:21½
Goodson by Smuggler.
Goodwin, Jr..........2:27½
Helen Goodson.......2:25
Sir Arthur............2:25¼
Goldstone by Masterlode.
Lew Wallace.........2:23½
Goodwin Hambletonian by Rysdyk's Hambletonian.
Goodwin, Jr..........2:29¾
Lady Collins..........2:30
Onawa..................2:22¼
Goodwood by Woodford Mambrino.
Greenwood............2:30
Goodwood, Jr.........2:23¼
Goodwood, Jr. by Goodwood.
Frank Irwin..........2:29¼
Gordon Windsor by Windsor.
Roger...................2:28¼
Gossip by Tattler.
Detractor, p..........2:26½
Gossip, Jr., p.........2:13¼
Gossiper by Simmons.
Gazelle.................2:16½
Ketcham, p...........2:17
Gossip Jones by Vanosdal's Whip.
Business..............2:28
Gov. Benton by Gen. Benton.
Gov. Hill...............2:25½
Governor Benton by Major Benton.
Benton M.............2:16¼
Bessie Benton........2:26¾
C. L. K.................2:29¼
Governor Boggs.
Chico, p...............2:21¼
Governor D.
Hugh G................2:28
Gov. Morrill by Knox Morrill.
Dr. Smith.............2:26½
Gov. Paine.
Orient..................2:27¼
Gov. Sprague by Rhode Island.
Agitator...............2:28½
Allen Sprague........2:30
Bertie Sprague.......2:24
Brinker Sprague......2:28
Bob Sprague..........2:24¾
Carrie Walton........2:23½
Charley P.............2:25½
Colvina Sprague......2:19¾
Dixie Sprague........2:25¼
Frank Sprague........2:29
Gilbirds Sprague.....2:21¾
Henry Esmond........2:30

James Morrison......2:25½
Kate Sprague . . .2 18
King Sprague 2:12
Lady Kate Sprague...2 27¼
Linda Sprague.. . . 2:17½
Lou Sprague..........2 27½
Lynn Sprague 2:28
Mary Karr...... .....2 24
Mary Sprague..... ...2 21
Mary W .. .. .2:·9¾
Maywood.... ....2.20
Medora............. .2 29¾
N. H. R 2:23¼
Pauline 2 27¼
Roscoe Conkling.... .2 30
Rowena Sprague 2:27¼
Sprague (Round's). .2 24½
Sprague Golddust ..2·15¼
Sprague Pilot . . 2·24
Susie T. 2:28¼
The Item 2:25¼
Theresa Sprague 2:25¼
Vincent Cromwell . . 2:30
Billy Sprague, p 2:28
Charley P , p 2:11¼
Vandal Wilkes, p..... 2:24

Gov. Sprague, Jr. by Gov. Sprague.
Charley Sprague......2.28¾

Gov. Stanford by Electioneer.
Clito, p............... 2:24¼

Gov. Wilkes by Geo. Wilkes.
Lieut. Wilkes, p 2.23½

Graduate.
Oliver Twist 2:29½

Granby by Princeps.
Granette .. .. 2·21¼
Mary Ferguson . 2.29½

Grand Duke by Iron Duke.
Sleepy Dan 2 29¼

Grandison.
Ella Graham, p...... 2 29½

Grandissimo by Le Grand.
Altissimo.... ....2:25¼
Myrtle Thorne. . . .. 2·20¾
Topsey . .. . .. 2·27

Grand Moor by The Moor.
Abdal 2:28
Myrtle T 2.27¼
Sadie Moor 2 29½

Grand Regent.
Mediator, p 2:30

Grand Sentinel by Sentinel.
Grace Darling 2 26
Grand Sentinel, Jr... 2:30
Lasella.............. .2.20
Nellette 2.26½
Samuel A 2:27½
Selene 2:29¾
Sentry 2:25
Shaefer 2:23¼
Signo Vinces 2:27¼
Sir Knight 2:23¾
Solferino.............2:26½
Sonnet 2:30
Strategist 2 22
Strathbridge........ .2·28¼
Strogoff...............2:24¼
Sumpter 2:25¼
Sutherland 2 24¼
Suzerain 2:29
Tosca 2.19¼
Shaefer, p 2.23¼

Grand Sentinel Jr. by Grand Sentinel.
Golden Boy 2:23½

Grand Wilkes by Lyle Wilkes.
Ike Wilkes....... ....2·17¼

Grantham Chief by Royal George.
Commodore Nut 2:29
Dan H . . .2 26½
Door Knob, p... ......2 21

Graphic by Mambrino Patchen.
Novelty....... ......2·29

Great Hope by Happy Medium.
Realization... ... . 2:26¾
Title Clear... .. .. 2:30

Great Tom by Pathfinder
Ben Davis... ... ... .2.19½
Etta B 2:25½
Etta B. p 2.17

Great Western by Masterlode.
Oliver West...... . .2:25¾
Phil W... .... .2.21

Greenback by Blue Bull.
Alaiedon 2:27¼
Counterfeit.. ... ..2 30
John M 2 27½
Fred Ager, p 2:24½
Ned Rawlin, p 2 30

Greenbacks by Princeps.
Bassora.. . . ..2·22¼
Choice 2:24½
Greenceps............2:18½
Greenwood...........2.20
Keno ... . .2·24¼
Loretta B 2.28
Mason 2:27½

Green Boy by John Green.
Charles Dorsey.... 2 20½
Daybreak. 2:25½
Green Boy Jr.. . . . .2.28¼
Harry C.............. 2:15
Lady Bug... . . .. 2 24¼

Greenbush by Woodbury,
Greenbush Star. 2:25½

Greenbush King by Greenbush.
Hinda W.... ..... 2 26
Greybush, p.. ....2:30
Judge B. p .. ..2·15¾

Greenfield by Black's Hambletonian.
Grayfield. 2:17½

Greenlander by Princeps.
Esquimo 2:18¾
Greenlander Boy 2:21¾
Greenlander Girl. .. 2.21
Greenway. 2:25
Kitty Greenlander. . 2 23½
Louisville..... . .....2.19¾
Orangelander....... .2 22¼
Otalgic 2.24½
Raola 2:28¼
Zingerelli, p 2 27

Green Mountain Banner by Black Banner.
Lady Pritchard... . 2:21
Vulcan 2:25

Green Mountain Morgan.
Bay Charley, p 2:23¾

Green Mountain Morgan by Ethan Allen
Honest Billy........ .2:29¼

Green Mountain Morgan (Dow's)
Sally B. p.............2:23

Greenwood.
Frank Allen..........2:30

Gregor McGregor by Robert McGregor.
Miss McLain........ 2:28½

Grenedier by Princeps.
Grandee.... . .. .2:29½

Grey Bill.
Kitty Grey...........2 29¼

Grey Comet.
Wallace 2.22¼

Grey Dan by Gideon.
Gov. Plaisted.... . .2:29¼
Hippona ....2·27¾
Maud L 2 30
St. Lawrence .. .. 2·23¼
Surprise.... ......2:28½

Grey Duke.
Billy Russel. p 2:16¼

Grey Eagle by Vermont Black Hawk.
Carrie K. 2:30
St. Charles 2.26

Grey Eagle.
Daisy B p........... 2:29¼

Grey Eagle (McKesson's) by Coman's Grey Eagle.
Charley Ford . . 2:16¾

Grey Eagle (Chenery's)
Ino 2 21¼
Red Bird 2:27¼
Aral, p 2:25½

Grey Eagle by Young Mountain Eagle.
New Berlin Girl.......2·29½

Grey Harry by Old Tempest.
Billy the Twister, p. 2 18¼
Black Diamond, p... 2:16
Florence J. p...... . 2:24½
Prairie Girl, p 2:20

Grey Jim by Morgan Tally-Ho
Cling............... 2:29¼
Pedro.... ....2·25¼

Grey McClellan by Gen. McClellan.
Blanche.... ....2:25½

Grey Messenger (Hoagland's) by a son of Sherman Morgan.
Blonde.. ....2 29½
Honest Dutchman. ..2 26½

Grey Messenger by Black Hawk.
Tom Walter. 2:29

Greystone by Nutwood.
Fedalma, p... ....2.22¼
Prince Elwood... .. 2:22¾

Griffard by Lepine Horse.
Balmoral Boy ...2 29½

Grimalkin by Princeps.
Nelly C 2:30

Grosjean by Belmont.
Grosis........... .. 2:25¼

Grosvenor by Administrator.
Lady Grosvenor.. . 2:27

Guarantee by Tom Patchen.
Dan Berry..... ..... 2·26½
Keystone.. ....2:28¼

Guardsman by Alcyone.
Nicola......... .... .2:23¼

Guelph by Princeps.
Guelph Jr.............2:26¾
Manette, p........ ...2:24
St. Croix, p. 2:18¾

Guide by Swigert.
Escort.................2:23
Guard.... ....2:27
Zig. 2:25

Guiderock, p 2:29
Guilford Boy by Dauntless.
Lucy K............... 2:25½
Cato, p 2:23½
Gulvallis by Conn's Harry Wilkes.
Bessie Cecil.......... 2:29½
Lucy K 2:30
Guy Darrell by King Rene.
Guy Rene.............. 2:25
Guy K by Guy Wilkes.
Dr Haile p............ 2:15¾
Guy Miller (Sayre's) by Guy Miller.
Blackstone 2:23½
Ella B................ 2:26¼
Josephine S 2:24½
Guy Wilkes by Geo. Wilkes
A. L. Kempland........ 2:26¼
Arthur Wilkes......... 2:28½
Atalanta Wilkes....... 2:29½
Auntie Wilkes......... 2:22½
Clio Wilkes........... 2:30
Earlie................ 2:27¾
Eclipse............... 2:25¾
Emin Bey.............. 2:21½
Etta Wilkes........... 2:25¾
Gulita................ 2:27¼
Guy Vernon............ 2:28
Hazel Wilkes.......... 2:11¼
Hulda................. 2:08½
Jean Wilkes........... 2:24¾
Leo Wilkes............ 2:29¾
Lesa Wilkes........... 2:11½
Lillian Wilkes........ 2:17¾
Linwood............... 2:20¼
Mary Best............. 2:12¼
May Wilkes............ 2:24¾
Millie Wilkes......... 2:26
Mustaph 2:23
Muta Wilkes........... 2:11
Nutwood Wilkes........ 2:19
Raven Wilkes.......... 2:15½
Regal Wilkes.......... 2:11¾
Sable Wilkes.......... 2:18
Silver Spray.......... 2:28
Siva 2:13¾
Ulee Wilkes........... 2:23
Una Wilkes 2:15
Venita Wilkes 2:13
Verona Wilkes......... 2:27
Vesta................. 2:30
Vida Wilkes........... 2:18¾
Alannah, p............ 2:11½
Blonde Wilkes, p...... 2:22¾
Chris Smith, p........ 2:14½
Rupee, p.............. 2:11
Seymour Wilkes, p..... 2:16

Hailstorm by Mambrino Patchen
Neckima............... 2:23
Quaker Girl 2:30
Jenny Wren, p 2:17½
Halbert by Egbert.
Maud Halbert.......... 2:30
Haldane by Mambrino Russell.
Haldan................ 2:22½
Hallidan.............. 2:28
Hallington............ 2:30
Halo 2:27
Howell 2:26¾
Hustler 2:20¼
Just Right............ 2:25¼
Howell, p............. 2:21¾
Hustler, p............ 2:27¼

Hall Colt by Bajardo.
Grey Duke 2:29¾
Hall Horse by Marshall Chief.
Little Sam............ 2:29
Ham (Culler's) by Baird's Hambletonian Prince.
Topaz 2:18¼
Hamblehawk by Rysdyk's Hambletonian.
Granger B............. 2:30
Tom Tinker 2:30
Hambleton by Florida.
Col. Briggs........... 2:22
May Queen............. 2:27
Hambletonian (Harris') by Bishop's Hambletonian.
Green MountainMaid.... 2:28½
Lady Shannon.......... 2:28¼
Hero, p 2:20½
Hambletonian (Green's) by Rysdyk's Hambletonian.
Nelly................. 2:30
Hambletonian (Black's) by Rysdyk's Hambletonian.
Avena................. 2:22½
Ben Kinney............ 2:21½
Blameless 2:19¾
Bruce 2:27¼
Lady M................ 2:23¼
McAllister 2:24¼
Tague O'Ragan......... 2:27¾
Hambletonian (Curtis') by Rysdyk's Hambletonian.
Andy Mershon 2:25½
Flora B 2:24½
Hambletonian Mambrino 2:21¾
Sunshine.............. 2:29¼
Hambletonian (Rysdyk's) by Abdallah.
Administrator 2:29½
Alma 2:28¾
Artillery 2:21½
Astoria............... 2:29½
Bella................. 2:22
Breeze................ 2:24
Bruno................. 2:29½
Chester 2:27
Deucalion............. 2:22
Dexter 2:17¼
Drift................. 2:29¾
Effie Deans........... 2:25½
Ella Madden........... 2:25¾
Enfield............... 2:29
Factory Girl.......... 2:29¼
Gazelle............... 2:21
George Wilkes 2:22
Hambletonian's Last... 2:25¼
Hamperion 2:29½
Harvest Queen......... 2:29½
James Howell Jr....... 2:24
Jay Gould............. 2:21½
Jerome................ 2:27
Kisbar................ 2:27¾
Lady Augusta.......... 2:30
Lady Banker 2:23
Lottery............... 2:27
Lottie 2:28
Madeline.............. 2:23¼
Marguerite............ 2:29
Mattie................ 2:22½
Maud.................. 2:29¾
Nettie................ 2:18
Orange Girl........... 2:20
Pickering 2:30
Rysdyk Maid 2:24¼
Scotland Maid 2:28½

Sentinel 2:29¾
Small Hopes........... 2:26½
Young Bruno........... 2:22¾
Hambletonian (Wood's) by Alexander's Abdallah.
Allegheny Boy......... 2:27¼
Ambler................ 2:30
Argo H................ 2:28
Argonaut.............. 2:23¼
Billy Ray............. 2:23¾
Billy Wood............ 2:20½
Blue Mare 2:23
Bucephalus............ 2:30
Chrystine 2:29¼
Dan S................. 2:24¼
Elda B................ 2:20½
Howard Jay............ 2:12¼
Ino................... 2:19½
Kilburn Jim 2:23
Kit Sanford........... 2:21¼
Kitty Wood............ 2:24¼
Mamie Wood............ 2:20
Maudie Belle 2:29¼
Nancy Hackett......... 2:20
Nancy S............... 2:27
R. B 2:29¼
Sam F................. 2:26¾
Spotted Sam........... 2:29¾
Telephone............. 2:22½
Spotted Sam, p........ 2:25¾
Hambletonian (Whipple's) by Guy Miller.
Ajax 2:29
Alameda Maid 2:27½
Cyclone 2:26¼
Empress 2:24
Graves 2:19
Lady Blanchard 2:26¼
Longfellow 2:24¼
Lou Whipple........... 2:26¾
Maggie C.............. 2:25
May Boy............... 2:23¾
Norman 2:28¾
Olivette 2:24
Rustic................ 2:30
Westfield............. 2:26½
Peacock, p............ 2:23¼
Hambletonion (Felter's) by Rysdyk's Hambletonian.
HambletonianBashaw.... 2:29½
Lady Tighe............ 2:29
Lucy.................. 2:26½
Star Hambletonian 2:23¾
Hambletonian (Parris') by Harris' Hambletonian.
Joker................. 2:22½
Hambletonian (McCurdy's) by Harold.
Alabama 2:15
Blontonian 2:22
Eleanor Malloy........ 2:29½
Fairest............... 2:18
Five Points 2:19
Io.................... 2:13
Lewe S................ 2:26¾
Lula Hambletonian 2:27
Macaroon.............. 2:21¾
McEwen................ 2:18¼
McVale 2:29
Mary R 2:24½
Miss McCurdy 2:28¾
Norwood Hambletonian............... 2:22¼
Play Boy.............. 2:18¼
Red Cedar 2:28¾
Red Fern.............. 2:27¾
Sally C............... 2:18¾
William Elkin 2:27¾

Alice McCurdy, p.....2:24¼
Den Ledyard, p......2:20
Dr. Miller, p.......2:21
Lula Mo, p..........2:25
McCurdy Jr., p......2:21½
Montrose, p.........2:24¼
Nannie Ward, p.....2:16

Hambletonian (Sackett's) by Rysdyk's Hambletonian.
Joseph A..............2:24

Hambletonian (Glenn's) by Volunteer.
Kitty Fisher..........2:29¼

Hambletonian (Powers') by Robert Bonner.
Jockey...............2:?0
Judge Parsons........2:23½

Hambletonian (Sherman's) by Rysdyk's Hambletonian.
Emma B..............2:29¼
Gold Edge...........2:26¼
Hulbert.............2:17½
Pembroke............2:27¼
Petitioner..........2:26¼
Silver Edge.........2:28¼

Hambletonian (Andrus') by Judson's Hambletonian.
Princess..............2:30

Hambletonian (Hough's) by Andrus' Hambletonian.
Spotted Colt..........2:25½

Hambletonian (Bell's) by Blue Grass.
Wonder...............2:22½

Hambletonian (Blackwell's).
Whitestockings......2:21

Hambletonian (Clark's) by Miller's Hambletonian.
Frank B., p..........2:18

Hambletonian (Sawin's).
Joe Ripley............2:25

Hambletonian (Clark's) by Duke of Brunswick.
Tom Jacobs...........2:21
Ben Morgan, p........2:17¼

Hambletonian (Frederick's).
Tod Crook, p..........2:14½

Hambletonian (Fleet's) by Goldsmith.
State Senator.........2:26
Princess H., p.......2:23¼

Hambletonian (Page's) by Edward Everett.
Coaticook Boy........2:26¼
Nicolet Boy...........2:29¾

Hambletonian Bashaw by Green's Bashaw
Duke..................2:25¼
Emma B...............2:29¼
Nabby G...............2:30

Hambletonian Bashaw by Felter's Hambletonian.
Bessie R...............2:29½
Daisy C................2:23¾

Hambletonian Chief by Middletown.
Elmbrook.............2:26¼
George O.............2:24¼
Chattie C., p........2:29¼

Hambletonian Chief by Thorne's Hambletonian.
Don Donaldo, p......2:24½

Hambletonian Chrisman by Whipple's Hambletonian.
Kate Agnew..........2:28½
Steve Whipple.......2:12

Hambletonian Don by Chester Dewey.
Walter Mac..........2:22½
Calvin C., p.........2:28

Hambletonian Downing by Miller's Hambletonian.
Bertha...............2:27¼
Charley Downing.....2:?9¼
Claytonia.............2:24¼
Claytonian...........2:27¼
Doctor E..............2:28
Dynamite.............2:27¾
Mamie Phillips.......2:28
Rag Baby.............2:22¼
Alert, p...............2:22½
Roadmaster, p.......2:26½

Hambletonian Gem by Rysdyk's Hambletonian.
Alfred...............2:26
Maria Theresa, p.....2:23½

Hambletonian George by Masterlode.
Ed. Mack.............2:26¼
George K.............2:22
George S., p.........2:19¼

Hambletonian Gift by Masterlode.
Mabel Parmeter......2:29½
Prince Gift, p........2:27¼

Hambletonian Jr. by Whipple's Hambletonian.
Hancock..............2:29

Hambletonian Jr (McCurdy's) by McCurdy's Hambletonian.
Ben H.................2:16½
Judge Austin........2:12¼

Hambletonian Knox by Gideon.
Combination.........2:29¼
Freeman..............2:29¼

Hambletonian Mambrino (Montgomery's) by Curtis' Hambletonian.
Big Four..............2:26¼
Haydon...............2:26½
Katie Cahill..........2:26½
Raven.................2:26¾
Wild Rake............2:22¾
Billy McCracken, p...2:24¾
J. J. C., p...........2:23¾

Hambletonian Mambrino (De Lashmutt's) by Menelaus.
Caryl Carne.........2:25
Fred Hambleton......2:26
Hamrock.............2:21
Hilda.................2:29¼
Jane L...............2:19½
Kitty Ham............2:26
Stella H..............2:29¾
Susie S...............2:18
Vanquish.............2:19
Cherry, p............2:27¾
King Priam, p........2:29
Stanwix, p...........2:29¾

Hambletonian Messenger.
Chepeta, p...........2:25½

Hambletonian Pilot by Guy Miller.
Signet...............2:26¼

Hambletonian Prince by Volunteer.
Harry Parker.........2:25
Little Eva............2:20½
T. G...................2:26

Hambletonian Prince (Baird's) by Rysdyk's Hambletonian.
Abbie.................2:29½
Baldy.................2:29¼
Billy Button.........2:18¼
Corona...............2:24½
Fanny Fairbanks.....2:30
Flavilla..............2:24½
Forest Prince........2:17¼
Gladys...............2:28
Guess Not...........2:27½
Happy Traveler.......2:27½
Helen.................2:28
Helene...............2:21
Monie................2:29¼
Musty................2:26½
Nelly.................2:29¼
Nelly Wilson.........2:30
Peralto..............2:26½
Prince................2:23
Princess.............2:27¼
Sylvia M.............2:25½
The Corporal.........2:28½
Trilly Willy..........2:25½
Tom Ellis, p.........2:26¼

Hambletonian Prince (Swanbrough's) by Menelaus.
Little Frank..........2:30
Prince.................2:26¼
Prince A..............2:26¼
Prince M.............2:29¼

Hambletonian Prince (Du-Bois') by Administrator.
H. Z. Leonard.........2:30

Hambletonian Rattler by Mambrino Rattler.
Sooner.................2:24

Hambletonian's Last by Rysdyk's Hambletonian.
Bill of Expense.......2:27½
Ernest.................2:27½
Gram C................2:23¾
Thorndale Prince, p..2:21

Hambletonian Tranby by Edward Everett.
Anna C.................2:27½
Clandins...............2:21¼
Cleveland Boy........2:29¾
Homewood............2:23½
John R. Wise.........2:28¼
Molly J................2:19¾
Perhaps...............2:30
S. J. Fletcher.........2:23½
Thad...................2:29¼
Allie C., p............2:13
Eclipse Tranby, p.....2:29¼
Templeton, p.........2:29¼
Tony R., p............2:26½
Whalebone, p.........2:18½

Hambletonian Wilkes by George Wilkes.
Arlene Wilkes.........2:22½
Aurora.................2:25
Bill Granger...........2:26
Grand George.........2:24½
Jack Spratt............2:23½
Phœbe Wilkes.........2:08¼
William Wilkes........2:30
Grand George, p......2:20½
Golden W., p..........2:29½
Guarantee, p..........2:23
New Era, p............2:13
Rocker, p..............2:11
Slipper, p.............2:28
Tammany Wilkes, p...2:24¼

Hambrino by Edward Everett
Almater................2:28
Alpine.................2:30
Baroness..............2:30

Belle Ure 2:19½
Ben Hur 2:24
Burlesque 2:22¼
Cresson 2:21½
Christine 2:25½
Delmarch 2:11½
Esmerelda 2:30
Fulda 2:19¼
Gladstone 2:28¼
Graydon 2:17¼
Hambrino Belle 2:25¼
Hambrino Pilot 2:29½
Hambrino Prince 2:26
Hamdallah 2:23
King Mambrino 2:30
Marea 2:22
Nelly T. 2:26¼
Olivia 2:24
Optimist 2:28¾
Pomona 2:25
Premier 2:29½
Roswall 2:24¼
Stet Brino 2:26½
Why Not 2:20¾
Wildbrino 2:19½
Wilkesbrino 2:23
Drelincourt, p 2:17¼
Fastwell, p 2:24¾
Hambrino Boy, p 2:24¾
Major Ham, p 2:25
M. L. Hare, p. 2:19
Tekla, p 2:26¾

Hambrino (Scott's) by Hambrino.
Tommy Brown, p 2:11½

Hambrino Pilot by Hambrino.
Hilda 2:29¾

Hambrino Star by Masterlode
Lorna Doone 2:24¼

Hamdallah by Hamlet.
Almo 2:30
Brittle Silver 2:25½
Dan Neville 2:28
Fanchon 2:19¾
Flight 2:24
Hamdallah (Aiken's) 2:24¾
Hamdallah Star 2:23
Jay Caldwell 2:22¼
King of the West 2:27
Maud D. N. 2:25
Minnie A. 2:29¾
Molly B. 2:26½
Nina Dinsmore 2:23¼
Rena N. 2:22
Seth Thomas 2:25¾
Shemdallah 2:25¾
Vera 2:22¼
Abdallah (Stiles') p. 2:23
Libbeas I., p. 2:13¾

Hamenger by Auditor.
Ben Wallace 2:19¾
Kate Dillard 2:22½
L. B. Curtis, p. 2:22¾

Hamilton by Rysdyk's Hambletonian.
Jerome 2:25¾
Tom Hamilton 2:21½

Hamilton by Mambrinotonian.
Prince Albert, p 2:28¾

Hamlet by Volunteer.
A. V. Pantlind 2:20
Brookside Flora 2:29
Lady M 2:23
Leontine 2:23¾
Loretta F. 2:18¾
Anna J. p 2:29¾
Truro, p 2:22¾

Hamlet by Hamlet.
Dave Wilson 2:24¾

Hamlin Patchen by George M. Patchen.
Sleepy Ned 2:26¼

Hampshire by Woodford Wilkes.
Bianca 2:29¼

Hampshire Boy by Hemingway Horse.
Susie 2:21
Etta C. p 2:29¼

Hampton by Rysdyk's Hambletonian.
Scott Ashton 2:25¾

Hampton by Smuggler.
Little Ned 2:29¼

Handy B. by Artemas.
Johnnie B 2:25¼

Handsome Harry.
Sibyl, p 2:23¾

Hannibal by De Lashmutt's HambletonianMambrino.
Hannibal Jr. 2:27¼
Volbrino H. 2:26¼

Hannibal by Woodford Mambrino.
Martin K. 2:18¼
Sleepy Ned 2:22¼

Hannis by Mambrino Pilot.
Arthuretta 2:29¼
Hannis Jr. 2:26¼
Jerry W 2:22¼
Lady Hannis 2:25
Linkwood Chief 2:18¾
Mamie W 2:30
Panic 2:21
Hannis Jr. p. 2:17¼
Mambrino Hannis, p 2:16½
Mountain Maid, p 2:27¼
Whitby, p 2:18¼

Hanover by Brougham.
Queen H 2:29½

Hanshaw Horse by Irwin's Blind Tuckahoe.
Sciola 2:23¼

Happy Chief.
Happy, p 2:27½

Happy Day by Happy Medium.
Blue Night 2:23
Harry B. p 2:20½

Happy Heir by Happy Medium.
Split Second 2:28
Plus, p 2:29½
White Socks. p 2:19½

Happy Home by Happy Thought
Happy Doctor 2:21½

Happy Medium by Rysdyk's Hambletonian.
Abdallah Medium 2:27¼
Ailse Medium 2:27¾
Albion Medium 2:30
Alexander 2:26¼
Alice Medium 2:29¾
Allie Rosebud 2:28¼
Almont Medium 2:18¼
Annie K. 2:28¾
Ashland Prince 2:26¾
Baron Luff 2:27
Belle Medium 2:20
Breeze Medium 2:22¼
Brigadier 2:21¼
Buzz Medium 2:20¼
Capitalist 2:29½
Camille 2:20¼
Celerrima 2:15
Champion Medium 2:22¾
Chief Medium 2:24½
Citizen 2:21¼
Country Medium 2:25¼
Carrie D. 2:26
Delaware Medium 2:30
Eddie Medium 2:29¼
Edith 2:22¾
Elwood Medium 2:24¾
Enchantress 2:26¾
Ernest Maltravers 2:22½
Ethel Medium 2:25½
Fairlawn Medium 2:25¼
Falkland 2:23¾
First Love 2:22½
Fleet Medium 2:29¼
Fleetwood 2:29
Folly 2:15¼
Frank Ellis 2:26¼
Fred Medium 2:23¼
Graceful 2:23¼
Happiness 2:29¾
Happy Courier 2:16¾
Happy Damsel 2:26½
Happy Day 2:29½
Happy Girl 2:27½
Happy Maid 2:30
Happy Princess 2:23¾
Happy Promise 2:16¾
Happy Thought 2:22½
Happy Wanderer 2:20½
Harry 2:26
Harry Medium 2:21½
Helen Houghton 2:29¾
Kildee 2:29½
Lady Fargo 2:24¾
Mambrino Medium 2:28½
Master Medium 2:29½
Maxie Cobb 2:13¾
Mediator 2:25½
Merry Thought 2:22¾
Millionaire 2:24½
Milton Medium 2:25½
Mott Medium 2:29¼
Nancy Hanks 2.04
Neta Medium 2:22½
Norman Medium 2:20
Ormond 2:27½
Paeony 2:22
Patchen Medium 2:29½
Pearl Medium 2:24
Poco Tempo 2:23½
Prince Medium 2:26
Rebel Medium 2:23¾
Robert Medium 2:29
Romancer 2:28½
Rose Medium 2:26½
R. P 2:22¼
Sauveur 2:29¾
Soudan 2:25
Spanish Maiden 2:29¾
Starin Medium 2:26¼
Storm King 2:25¾
Talavera 2:30
Time Medium 2:27½
Union Medium 2:18¾
Viola Medium 2:25
Ward Medium 2:25¼
Waymart 2:27¼
Crystal, p 2:29
Eddy C., p 2:20
Jerry Yetman, p 2:27½
King Medium, p. 2:20
Late Rose, p. 2:23¾
New Medium, p 2:30
Riley Medium, p. 2.10½

Happy Medium (Hickey's) by Happy Medium.
Gen. Mack............2:29¾
Happy Medium, Jr. by Happy Medium.
Carrie Medium........2:27¼
Lady Babcock........2:30
Happy Prince by Bayonne Prince.
Contento..............2:29¼
Happy...................2:27½
Happy Russell by Mambrino Russell.
Happy Bee............2:15¾
Happy Earl............2:29¾
Happy George.........2:24½
Happy Lady...........2:16¾
Happy Minnie.........2:17½
May Bee................2:25
Happy Thought by Happy Medium.
Ethel....................2:19¾
Go Some...............2:26¼
Happy Go Lucky......2:29
Happy Home..........2:24¼
Idle Thought.........2:29½
Little Sport...........2:25¼
Merriment............2:26½
Stoneridge............2:21¼
Happy Traveler by St. Elmo.
Bonnie B., p...........2:19¾
Happy Union by Woodbury.
Golden Girl, p.......2:25
Harbinger by Almont.
Ansel W...............2:29¾
Camille.................2:24½
Diana...................2:24½
Hallie...................2:20
Harvey Russell.......2:29½
St. Ives.................2:29¼
Silver Belle...........2:21½
Prince Harbinger.....2:30
Van Helmont.........2:26½
Hardee (Burton's) by Gen. Hardee.
Col. Hardee, p........2:29¼
Ida S., p...............2:15¾
Hard Tack.
Black Nell, p..........2:28
Hardwood by Blackwood, Jr.
Nelly Hardwood......2:18¾
Peter Hardwood.....2:20
Hardy Horse.
Fanny W..............2:25½
Harkaway by Stephen A. Douglass.
Tom Miller, p........2:25¼
Harkaway by Wilkins Micawber.
Hundley...............2:20¾
Roy......................2:26¼
Gertie Harkaway, p..2:26½
Jack, p..................2:10¼
J. C. R., p..............2:29
Nancy Harkaway, p. 2:19¼
Harlan by Dauntless.
Andrew C.............2:26¼
Harlequin by Hampton.
Joe L., p...............2:15
Haro by Harold.
Muggins...............2:20¼
Harold by Rysdyk's Hambletonian.
Altamura..............2:30
Calinda................2:26¼
Cammie L.............2:21
Cash Item............2:29¼
Chichester............2:25¼
Cora S.................2:25½
Daciana...............2:27½
Daireen...............2:21½
Disputant............2:18
Evermond............2:24¼
Gen. Turner.........2:26¾
Good Morning........2:28½
Hackberry............2:25¼
Hambletonian (McCurdy's).............2:26½
Harold Chief..........2:24¼
Harold, Jr..............2:24¼
Hartford...............2:22¼
Henry G................2:28
Hermes.................2:27½
High Tide..............2:30
Iowa Harold...........2:25½
Lorody..................2:24½
Mattie Graham.......2:21½
Maudlen...............2:25¾
Maud S................2:08¾
Meda...................2:25
Neva....................2:30
Noble Harold.........2:29¾
Noontide...............2:20½
Parapet................2:21
Pegasus...............2:30
Puella..................2:29
Russia.................2:28
Sisal....................2:23¼
Temple.................2:30
Valdemeer............2:28
Yazoo..................2:27½
Yuba....................2:24½
Zulu....................2:29½
Alturus, p.............2:12½
Belle Girl, p..........2:24
Gen. Turner, p........2:25¾
Hermit..................2:16½
Maud H., p.............2:20½
Slumber, p............2:13¼
Harold C. by West Liberty.
Bashaw Bill.........2:26
Harold C. by Harold.
George Mack, p........2:19¼
Harold, Jr. by Harold.
Godelia...............2:29¼
Haroldine............2:23¼
Haroldmont by Harold.
Hettiemont...........2:16¾
Rizpah.................2:24¼
Haroldmont by Harbinger.
Jack Wiman..........2:20¼
Harold Patchen by Harold.
Aunt Delilah.........2:12½
Haroldson by Harold.
Jonesville.............2:29¾
Sterling, p.............2:11½
Harold Thorne by Heptagon.
Woodbury Thorne...2:25¼
Harper by Harold.
Belle Harper..........2:29¼
Harper by Green's Bashaw.
Pride of Idaho........2:29¾
Harrison Chief by Clark Chief.
George L..............2:26½
Harrison...............2:28¼
Harry Chief...........2:30
Harry Arlington by Prince Albert.
Telegraph Girl........2:29¾
Harry B. by Blue Bull.
John T., p.............2:15
Harry Clay by Neave's Cassius M. Clay, Jr.
Clayton................2:19
Edwin Clay...........2:29½
No Hurry.............2:30
Shawmut..............2:26
Surprise...............2:26
Harry Clay by Joe Hooker.
Blanche Morrison.....2:27½
Harry Clay Jr. by Harry Clay.
Billy Bunker, p.......2:19¼
Harry Clay Jr. (Haven's).
Claytonian.........2:27¼
Harry F. by Compeer.
Tempest N., p..........2:19¼
Harry Franklin by Bergen.
Jim Graham...........2:26½
Harry Goldburg.
Tommy H., p.........2:21¼
Harry Golddust.
Goldmine, p...........2:17
Harry Green by Hiatoga.
Midnight Bell, p.......2:26¼
Min Young, p.........2:16½
Harry Hamilton by Knickerbocker.
J. M. D.................2:13¾
Harry Hamilton.
Fanny Miller..........2:22½
Harry Hontas by Pocahontas Boy.
Gertie K., p............2:25¾
Nettie E. Hontas, p...2:29½
Harry Hoyer by Pilot Champion.
Gladstone, p...........2:19½
Harry Knox by Gen. Knox Jr.
Billy I...................2:29¾
Maggie Miller.........2:26½
Maud Elenah, p.....2:19¼
Harry Lathrop by Blood's Black Hawk.
Henry...................2:20¼
Harry Mills by Milwaukee.
Marion Mills, p.......2:21¼
Harry Morgan by Royal Harry.
Minnie Grey..........2:30
Harry Noble by Frank Noble.
Belle Noble, p.........2:16
Harry Phelps by Cromwell Hiatoga.
Kitty Hiatoga.........2:18½
Harry Plummer by Harry Clay.
Little Mack...........2:29¾
MacIvor...............2:27
Harry Pulling by Menelaus.
Andy Pogue.........2:29¼
Don Pulling..........2:30
Gen. Buford..........2:24
Harry Scott.
Judge Black, p......2:28½
Harry Vane by Smuggler.
Loyalty.................2:27
Harry W. Genet by Godfrey Patchen.
Frances................2:27
Harry Wilkes (Conn's), by George Wilkes.
Bonnie Wilkes........2:29¼
Concord...............2:29¾
Fred Wilkes..........2:21½
Helena B.............2:27
Kathrina..............2:25¾
Rosaline Wilkes......2:14½
Sir Harry Wilkes, p...2:16
Twilight, p............2:28
Harry Wilkes (Letcher's) by George Wilkes.
Billy Wilkes..........2:29½

Harry Wilson by Jim Wilson.
Harry K., p 2:23¼
Hartford by Harold.
Robert A.. .... 2:29¼
Barb Wire, p.......... 2:24¾
Lily M., p.. ...... 2 24
Robert J., p 2:01½
Hartland.
Hartland.............. 2:29½
Harvester by Daniel Lambert.
J. Y. G 2.24¼
Haskew by Monte Christo.
Eagle Pass......... 2:29¾
Hatch Horse by Woodburn Pilot.
Pickwick.............. 2:27½
Haven Star by Conklin's American Star.
Lady Linda....... .. .2:26
Havoc by Thorndale.
Flora B. 2 30
Glenmore .... 2·23¼
Lady Havoc.......... 2:23
Lucy May 2.17
Hawkeye by Rice Graves.
Daisy Gardiner........ 2.28¼
Hawkeye.
Grey Hawk............ 2:28¾
Haw Patch by Rysdyk's Hambletonian.
Anna K .... 2·28¾
Eldine................ 2:28½
Eros 2:29
Gravel................ 2.29¾
Litta.................. 2·22
Magnolia.......... 2 09¼
Prince H.. .... 2 17¾
Robert L............. 2:26¼
Woodside Prince.. .2:24¾
Teaser D., p....... 2 30
Lucy J., p 2:27½
Hawthorne by Maine Hambletonian.
Belle Thorne......... 2·27
Hawthorne by Nutwood.
Bay Thorn 2 23½
Breastplate........ 2:23½
Bessie Thorne....... 2:22½
Brown Thorne 2 28
Hedgethorne......... 2 27
Ida May............. 2:28
John C. Shelly 2:29¾
Kilrain 2:22¾
Maj. Thorne 2:30
Moses S............ 2 19½
Paladin........... 2:29½
Pet Thorne......... 2:29
Sam Browne.......... 2:29¼
Tempest............ 2:19
Thornwood 2:19¼
A. W. Thorne, p..... 2 29½
Cap Thorne, p 2:18½
Chief Thorne, p...... 2:20
Hawthorne (Ladd's) by Thorndale.
Cyclone Jr 2 27
Hayward Hazzard.
Little Dick, p.. ...... 2.23
Haywood.
Henrietta, p 2:24¼
Hazel Bashaw by Bashaw, Jr.
Belle Truitt 2.25½
Doctor H., p.......... 2:22½
Hazel Heel.
F. M. B. A., p 2:22
Matt Wall, p 2:27½
H. B. Winship by Aristos.
Lady Winship 2:23½
Headlight by Blue Bull.
Billy Golden, p. 2 21
Heathwood by Nutwood.
Black Beauty.. ...... 2 24
Hector Wilkes by George Wilkes.
Fred S Wilkes .. 2·11¾
Thorn Wilkes........ 2:28½
Seaside. 2 18½
Superior Wilkes 2 24¾
Helmont by Mammont.
Caywood 2 19¼
Hemlock by Belmont.
Princess. .... 2·30
Waxford 2:26½
Henry.
Amelia S., p......... 2.25¾
Henry B.
Razor Blade, p........ 2:22¼
Henry Bell Colt by Cuyler.
Scott Newman....... 2 27½
Henry B. Patchen by George M. Patchen.
Idaho Patchen,....... 2:26½
Jerry.............. 2:28¾
Ki Ki. .... 2·28
Little Gem 2:29½
Nelly Rose 2 30
Patchen Maid. 2:30
Susie Parker....... 2:25¼
Billy Patchen, p..... 2:29¾
Henry C. by Ben Franklin.
Little Nancy 2:29
Henry Clay by Andrew Jackson.
Black Douglas 2:30
Jericho. 2:30
Henry Clay.
Charles D .... 2·29¼
Henry Clay Jr. by Henry Clay.
Bertha Clay 2 30
Henry Clay (Wilson's) by Vermont Black Hawk.
Newbrook.......... 2:30
Henry Clay by Romeo.
John C. Heenan, p . 2:25
Henry F
Lucy H.............. 2 25
Henry Gilbert by Clark Chief.
De Wulff.............. 2 21½
Future Gilbert........ 2·26¾
Henry Ham by Abdallah Woodford.
Lady, p............. 2:24¼
Henry Middleton by Bay Middleton.
Billy D., p 2.29½
Henry S. by Auctioneer.
Lucy P .... 2·27½
Opal. 2.30
Heptagon by Harold.
Amboy 2 13¾
Cleon.............. 2:22
Huntsman 2 30
Kate V............ 2 23
Hercules by Dorsey's Golddust.
T. L. D., p. 2:22¼
Hermes by Harold.
Early Bloom 2:29¾
Frank Ellis 2 29¼
Heckothrift......... 2.29
Heresy 2:27
Holmdel .... 2·18¾
Hoodwink 2:25
Homer 2.22¼
Mattie Bassett 2:26½
Thomas S. Harrison.. 2·29½
Ravelli, p.. .... 2.20¾
Hermit by Harold.
Albani. 2.21¼
Arona.............. 2:24¾
Dorking 2 24½
John L .... 2·27¾
Hermione, p........ 2:22½
Hernando by Almont.
Salando 2:26¼
Herod by King Herod.
King Grover 2 28½
Michael.. .... 2·28½
Kenoma, p 2 23
Herod Jr by Herod.
Nubbin. 2:17½
Hero by Stoner Boy.
Morris H 2.26½
Hero of Thorndale by Thorndale.
Alice Tyler.......... 2 30
Bob Johnson 2 28¾
Fairy Gift 2:30
Minnie Dale 2 29¾
Thorndale Jr. 2:30
Herschel by Belmont.
Alta May......... 2 27
Annabel 2:29¾
Frank Bellows 2:22
Frederick L.... ... 2:29¾
Hershon 2:29¼
Neva Seeley....... 2:20¼
Prince Herschel....... 2:13
Uranus, p 2:17¾
Virgie K., p...... 2 25
Hersey by Macedonian.
Baron 2.29¼
Hiatoga (Handley's), by Rice's Hiatoga.
Grand Duchess 2 26½
Twang 2:28½
Hiatoga (Scott's), by Handley's Hiatoga.
Duck.............. 2:30
Erebus. 2:28¼
Headlight.......... 2 30
Lew Scott 2:23
Tom Cameron ...... 2·23½
Belle Hammill, p .. 2:26¼
Dido, p 2:23¾
Estella, p....... 2:23¼
Gypsy, p 2:28½
Jenny Lind, p....... 2.28
Leviathian, p...... 2:23½
Marie Scott, p....... 2:24
Sorrel Billy, p...... 2.20
Hiatoga (Howser's) by Handley's Hiatoga.
Bay Dick 2:29½
Hiatoga (Bellew's).
Doctor H., p... 2.29¼
Hiatoga Chief by Scott's Hiatoga.
Tioga Belle........ 2:29½
Gypsy Boy, p 2 21¼
Hiatoga F., p.. ..... 2:28¼
Hibbard Wilkes.
May Murphy, p..... 2:29¾
Hickory, Jr. by Hickory.
Milton .... 2·16
Harrison Reed, p 2:23½
Hidalgo by Almont.
Carl .... 2·23¾
Miss May.......... 2 27¼
Red Line.......... 2:24½
Lady H., p.......... 2 25

Highland Beauty by Highland Boy.
Rockton..............2:25½

Highland Boy by Hamlet.
Gloucester...........2:23¼
Hamlet, p............2:23½

Highland Boy, Jr. by Highland Boy.
George S. James......2:22½

Highland Chief.
Belle W..............2:29¼

Highland Chief by Mayflower, Jr.
Lucky Boy............2:29
Mikado...............2:20¾
Jesse H., p..........2:18¼

Highlander.
Wm. H. Holliday, p...2:29¾

Highlander Boy.
Patsy K., p..........2:21¼

Highland Golddust by Golddust.
Barry Golddust.......2:24½
Novi.................2:29¼

Highland Grey by Darkey.
Don Carlos...........2:28¼
Emma B...............2:26¼
Florence.............2:23¾
Frank H..............2:21½
Highland Boy.........2:28¼
Highland L., p.......2:14¼
Katie L., p..........2:22½
Nelly June, p........2:24¼
Tim Cawley, p........2:27¼

Highland L. by Highland Gray.
Highland Lassie, p...2:19¾

Highlawn by Alcantara.
Alta Rose............2:28¾

High Jack.
Coupon...............2:26¾
High Jack, p.........2:25¼

High Private by Volunteer.
Fugleman.............2:27¼

Highwood by Nutwood.
Almira Highwood......2:23¼

Hillside Prince by Kentucky Prince.
Sunrise Prince.......2:13¼

Hi Miller.
Senator Maid.........2:30

Hi Monarch by Almonarch.
Tony Monarch, p......2:26¼

Hinder Wilkes by Red Wilkes
Chief Wilkes.........2:28½
Futurity.............2:19
Pat My Boy...........2:18¼
Penelope.............2:27½
Hindrance, p.........2:29¼

Hindoo by George M. Patchen.
Clover...............2:25¼
Timothy..............2:26¼

Hinkston Boy by Abdallah Clay.
Lady Savage..........2:25
Warren H., p.........2:26½

Hinsdale Chief by Edwin Forrest.
Larchleigh, p........2:23

Hinsdale Horse by Hinsdale Colt.
Deck Wright..........2:19¾
Grand Central........2:30
Ira..................2:27
Mattie K.............2:24¼
N. J. Fuller.........2:26¼
Wilbur F.............2:24½

Archie C., p.........2:30

Hiram.
Maud.................2:30

Hiram Woodruff by Rysdyk's Hambletonian.
Lenity...............2:29¼

Hiram Woodruff by Vermont Hero.
Lady Stillman........2:29¾

Hirsch Belmont by Belmont.
Bismarck.............2:22¼
Dora W...............2:30

Hoagland Horse by North American.
Betsey Ann...........2:22½

Hod Gregor by Hod Gregor.
Highland Tom.........2:24

Holliday by McMahon.
King Holliday........2:22¾

Holstein by Indianapolis.
Holcomb..............2:27

Homer by Mambrino Patchen
Lelah H..............2:24½
May Homer............2:18¾
Vivian...............2:27½

Homestead by Nutwood.
Lord Shelburne.......2:19

Honest Abe by Cassius.
Princeton............2:27

Honest Allen by Ethan Allen.
Bob Acres............2:28½
Lady Bonner..........2:24¼
Prince Allen.........2:26½
Tom Allen............2:22

Honest Allen (Davis') by Honest Allen.
Lady Martin..........2:29½

Honest Allen (Smith's) by Honest Allen.
Alton Boy............2:29½
Shakespeare..........2:30

Honest Charley by Charley B.
Gentle Harry.........2:30

Honest Dan by Vermont Hambletonian.
Charles W............2:29½
Forest King..........2:27
Sligo................2:30

Honest Dick by St. Lawrence.
Lizzie S.............2:30
George W., p.........2:22½

Honest John by Johnny White Horse.
Honest Jake..........2:27¼
Ace of Diamonds, p...2:24¼
Honest John, p.......2:23¼
Honest Prince, p.....2:27½

Honest John.
Bay Tom..............2:24¾

Honesty by Stier's Hiatoga.
Big Soap.............2:23
Nina K...............2:28½

Honor by Red Wilkes.
Upright Wilkes.......2:14¾

Hoosier Dick.
Frank Nevins, p......2:30

Hoosier Tom.
Bald Eagle, p........2:22¼
Dicer, p.............2:30
Miller Boy, p........2:18

Hope So by Hermes.
Belle B..............2:26¼
Hugo.................2:22½
Lady Powell..........2:25½

Horace by Dirigo.
Daisy Drew...........2:30

Hornell Wilkes by Red Wilkes
Red of Waranoke......2:22¾

Horne Horse by Blucher.
Willie D.............2:26

Horrey Mills.
Kitty Mills..........2:28¾

Hospodar by Belmont.
Horicon..............2:19¼

Hotspur by Rysdyk's Hambletonian.
Hotspur Chief........2:29
Lucy C...............2:30

Hotspur Jr. by Hotspur.
Hotspur Girl.........2:29¼
Hotspur King.........2:27¾
Little Ned...........2:29¼
Maud.................2:29½
Nickel Plate.........2:25½
Tommy B., p..........2:24¼
Prince M., p.........2:21¼

Hotspur Chief by Hotspur.
Billy G..............2:27½
Brewster.............2:26
Grey Dave............2:22¼
Tom Mackay...........2:26½

Howe Horse.
Guy C., p............2:27¼

Hubbell Horse.
Shellbark, p.........2:26

Hudson by Kentucky Prince.
Kitty Hudson.........2:25

Hughey Angus by Swigert.
Don Angus, p.........2:18½

Hugo Prince by Jefferson Prince.
Hugo H...............2:25½

Hull by Belmont.
Bay Hull.............2:29¼
Blancho P............2:26
Boxwood..............2:26
Fred Hull............2:29½
Hattie Hull..........2:30
Patience.............2:18¾
Vespasian............2:24¼
Ned Hull, p..........2:30

Humbird by Tom Jefferson.
Jack Draper..........2:27

Hummer by Electioneer.
Bouncer..............2:18½
Hustler..............2:20¾
Stately, p...........2:18

Hunter.
Black Hunter, p......2:29½

Hunter by Byron.
Lady K...............2:30
Ashton Boy, p........2:26

Hunter Chief by Lexington Chief, Jr.
Lexington King.......2:23½

Huon by Hamlin's Almont Jr.
Miss Huon............2:24¼

Hurly Burly by Rumor.
Wilber...............2:19½

Hurricane by Ringwood.
Iroquois.............2:25¼

Hussell Dan.
Hail Cloud, p........2:26½

Hutchinson Morrill by Morrill.
Fanny................2:27

Hylas by Alcalde.
Harry Hylas..........2:26¼
Hylas Boy............2:23
Hylas Maid...........2:29½
Susie S..............2:15½
Maggie J., p.........2:14¼
Sally Walker, p......2:28¼

Hylas Jr by Hylas.
- Daniel Boone, p.......2:20¾

Hyperion by Almont.
- Hyson ....2·26½
- Bright Hope, p.........2·25
- Hyson, p 2 18¾

Hyronomous.
- Senator, p 2 29¼

H. W Beecher by Phil Sheridan.
- Victor E 2 28¼
- Little Jeff, p..........2 23¼

H. Z. Leonard.
- Gypsey B, p...........2 30

Idaho Patchen by Henry B. Patchen
- Maud P 2 26½
- Maud Patchen.........2 19¼

Idler by A. W. Richmond.
- Rita, p 2 15½

Idol (Williams') by Elial G.
- Alexander D.........2 20
- Winifred ....2·24¾

Idol (Backman's) by Rysdyk's Hambletonian
- Capson 2 25¼
- Harry S ....2·27½
- Idolater...............2 28½
- Idolf 2:13¾
- Idol Jackson..........2:27¾
- Idol Stone............2 29¼
- Oxford Boy ....2·29½
- Pero 2:25
- Pickwick 2 29½
- Prince A..............2 19¼
- Silver Spray 2 27¾
- Taurus 2 30
- Fidol, p 2 10
- Harry S, p.............2 29½
- Idolator, p.............2·23¾

Idol (Akers') by Mambrino Chief
- Barbara Patchen.......2.24½
- Don 2 22½
- Idol Gift 2 24
- Iodine 2 29½
- John R 2 23

Idol Boy by Backman's Idol
- Vixen, p 2 13

Idolater by Backman's Idol
- Idleweise 2 24½
- Irene 2 30

Idol Gift by Akers' Idol
- Currito 2 17¾

Idol Wilkes by George Wilkes
- Ed Clarkson 2 20¾
- Lady Spencer 2 27
- Lady Idol..............2.25
- Spencer Wilkes 2 28½
- Willie E 2 24¼
- Idler, p ....2·20
- J H. L., p.............2 08½
- Wilkes J., p...........2·27

Ignaro by Princeps.
- Lady Spencer, p........2 27
- Toxie R, p.............2.16

Ignis Fatuus by Editor.
- Advolo 2.26½

I. J. by Wineman's Logan.
- Charley Boy 2 25¾
- Logan Chief 2 23¼

Illinois Chief.
- Davy Crockett, p.......2·20
- Noah the Kid, p.......2 28¼
- Stella H., p 2 28½

Iliad by Homer
- Pierron, p 2 15

Imaus by Princeps.
- Imogene 2 26¼

Imperial by Rysdyk's Hambletonian
- Crown Imperial 2 27½

Imprint by Onward.
- E. H. S, p 2 21¼
- Emma Nolan, p........2·24¾
- Jessie Wilkes p.........2.21¼

I. M. Singer by Two Bitts.
- Portugue Printz 2 29¼

Inca by Woodford Mambrino
- Conn 2 26½
- Geronimo 2 24½
- Inca Jr 2 29
- Incas 2 14½
- Jim Leach 2.28½
- Miss Foxie 2 22¼
- Pink 2 23½

Independence by Campbell's Andrew Jackson.
- John W Hall............2 25

Independence by Gen Knox.
- H R C 2 21¼

Independence by Young Hindoo.
- Blanche 2 29½
- Ruby 2 17¼
- Printer Boy, p.........2 29½

Independent (Mott's) by Rysdyk's Hambletonian
- Harry D 2 29¼
- Josh Billings...........2 29¾
- Uncle Dave 2 26½

Index by Keokuk.
- Bismarck 2 29¼

Index by James R Reese
- Chelsea D 2 18¾
- Sarah L 2 26

Index Jr. by Index
- Adam Index 2 29¼

Indiaman by Belmont
- Bellman 2 14¾
- Ben S 2 25
- Camilla ....2·24¼
- Ida S 2 24¼
- Lady M 2 21
- Martie G 2 28
- May Rose..............2 26½
- Wineshade.............2 23¾

Indiana Boy by Headlight.
- Minnie C, p 2 20

Indiana Chief.
- Dallas (Kissell's), p 2.10½

Indianap by Indianapolis.
- Pat McGinty...........2 23¾

Indianapolis by Tattler.
- Holstein...............2 26
- Indianap...............2·18¼
- Indigo 2.23¼
- Bonaventure, p........2 18
- Budd Doble, p 2 13½
- Colette p ....2·19¼
- De Jarnette, p 2 17
- Frank R, p ....2·28
- Gray Leaf, p 2 29¼
- Indianapolis Boy, p ...2.13½
- Regulator, p...........2 25

Indianapolis Chief by Indianapolis.
- Hazel 2:29¼

Indianapolis Jr. by Indianapolis
- Benny C...............2 22½

Indian Chief by Blood's Black Hawk.
- Lady De Jarnette 2 28
- Warrior 2 26

Indian Hill by Princeps.
- Naomi 2 25
- Orania 2 22

Indicator by Golddust.
- Fred G.................2:30
- King Golddust 2 30

Indus by Constellation.
- Quiver 2 28½

Inglewood by Onward.
- Rashleigh 2 28¼

Ingomar.
- Douglass, p 2 27½

Inheritance by American Volunteer.
- Goodwin 2 29¾

Inheritor, by Jay Gould
- Montgomery 2 21¼

Inspector by Contractor
- Loafer P 2 24¼

Instructor H. by Director
- Annapolis, p 2 25

Interior Boy.
- Interior 2 29¼

Intrigue by Jay Gould.
- Brother Jim 2 22¼
- Easter 2 23¼
- Jim F 2 26
- Miss Hunter 2 21¼

Invader by Onward.
- Minnie Wilkes 2 30
- Sam Hill 2 30

Inventor.
- Genius, p...............2·29½

Inveterate by Woodford Wilkes.
- Gladys..................2 29¾
- McGinty ....2·29¼

Invincible by Princeps.
- Invincible (Cory's)....2.27

Ion by Belmont
- Edgar Dudley..........2 17¾

Iowa Chief by Green's Bashaw.
- Bertie M...............2 27¾
- Charley Baldwin.......2 23¼
- Corisande 2 24½
- Lizzie S.................2 22½

Iowa Duroc by Messenger Duroc
- Lady Duroc, p 2:21½

Iowa Harold by Harold.
- Daisy B.................2.29¼

Iowa Mambrino by Mambrino Blitzen.
- Charley Hicks, p.......2.28¼

Iowa Star by Guiding Star.
- Biddy Boru 2 26¼
- Brian Boru 2 27¾

Ira by Piedmont.
- Iora 2 28½
- Lou 2 27

Ira Allen by Flyin Morgan
- Ripon Boy 2 25

Ira M
- Dick, p 2 29¼

Ira Nutwood by Ira Wilkes.
- Mason Nutwood 2 22

Ira Wilkes by George Wilkes.
- Hermetic ....2·23¼
- Jud Wilkes 2 29
- Little Frank 2 25
- Nelly G ....2·24
- Winnie Wilkes.........2 28½
- Berkshire Courier, p..2 14¼
- Ira King, p 2 24¼

Little Joe, p 2 15½
Minnie Wilkes, p... . 2·20½
Sir Maxwell p.. ... . 2·28
Track Wilkes, p... . 2 27
Iris by Eros.
Visalia 2 20
Cecilia, p 2 23½
Iron Duke by Rysdyk's Hambletonian.
Ben Williams... 2 29¼
Coriander 2.29¾
Duke 2 24¼
Fearless 2 29¼
Iron Duke Jr 2 25
Kelsie 2 23¼
Maud Cook . . 2 30
Monroe 2 27½
Silver Duke. ....2·28¾
Edwin T p . . 2 25
Iron Duke by Iron Duke.
Maggie H... ... .. 2.28¼
Iron Duke Jr by Iron Duke
Brown Daisy.......... 2 25
Little Mat 2 28¾
Island Chief by Dean Swift
Slippery Tom 2.25½
Island Chief by Daniel Lambert
Orono Boy 2 21¼
Phil Dwyer 2 29¼
Albert D , p.. . . ...2·26¼
Island Wilkes by Red Wilkes
Willits 2:29¼
Israel by Rampart.
Dinah 2 21¾
Mayflower 2 28

•

Jack Cook.
Flora L...... .. ..2.29
Jack Fowler by Ruby's Copperbottom
Roxie M ....2·28¾
Billy Hopper, p . .. 2·24
Buck Dickerson, p . . 2 25½
Jack Hawkins Jr. by Jack Hawkins
Coquette 2 28¼
Jack Lambert by Daniel Lambert.
Miss Cawley 2 23½
Jack Morrill
Adelaide M.. . .. 2:30
Jack Rapid
Jack Rapid, p....... 2 25
Jack Rapid Jr p . . 2:29¼
Jack Sheppard by Rysdyk's Hambletonian.
Arbogast 2 29¼
Clara M... . . .. 2·29¼
Jack Sheppard Jr.. .. 2 29¼
Minnie C. 2 25¼
Jack Stanton by Gen. Stanton.
John Shannon, p. . . . 2 28¼
Jack Stewart by Jack Stewart.
Brighton.. ....2 26¼
Jackson by Fine Cut.
Kitty Redbuck 2 29¼
Jackson (Young) by Andrew Jackson
Miller's Damsel........2:28¼
Jackson Temple by Volunteer.
Emma Temple.... ...2.21
Mattie P........ .... 2 26¼
Jacksonville Rhode Island by Rhode Island.
Black Slayer...........2:27½

Pisgah .... .2·30
Jalisco by Durango.
Mamie Case........ 2 28
James G. by Royal Chief.
Stella K., p 2 30
James A. Garfield by Hambrino Star.
Harry G 2.19½
James Madison by Anteeo
Bet Madison 2 30
Leila C., p 2 20½
James R Reese by Walkill Prince.
Index.. .... .. .2.21
Morocco 2 30
Janus by Green's Bashaw.
Maud M 2 23
Japan by Harold.
Nancy H 2 24¼
Jappo by Wood's Hambletonian
Laporte 2 26¼
Jasson by American Eagle.
Jasper . 2 26½
Jay Bird by George Wilkes.
Allerio... ... ... 2 22
Allen Wilkes 2 24¼
Allerton .. .2 09¼
Barnhart 2 22¾
Beconian..... .. 2 30
Bedouin 2 25¼
Bertie Girl. 2.23¾
Betsy Cotton .. 2 16¼
Billy Bird 2 26¼
Bird McGregor .. ....2·23¼
Blue Dawn . .2 21½
Blue Jay.... ... . 2.29¾
Blue Wing. 2 29¾
Border Wilkes .. .2 25½
Canary Bird .. 2·19½
Castalia.. .... 2.29¼
Col Lillard . . . 2 25½
Die Vernon . . ... 2·27¼
Eagle Bird .. 2 21
Early Bird........ 2.12½
Five Points 2 29¾
Isa Belle 2 17¾
Jackdaw 2 28¼
Jayfoot 2 28
Jayhawker 2 14¾
Kentucky Bird 2 26
King Bird. . 2:27¾
Knoxie Walker . 2 25¼
Leighton . . 2 24
Maud H 2:26
May Bird 2 21½
Merry Bird 2 16½
Minnie G 2 14¼
Pembroke.... . ....2 28¼
Queen Wilkes 2 26½
Shuck Wilson...... . 2.26¼
Sister Ethel 2.19¼
Twist 2.26
Wilkes Bird....... ....2 29½
Wilkes Bird 2 25
Za Za 2:27½
Jidex, p...............2:29¾
Little Jay, p 2 26¾
Jay Gould by Rysdyk's Hambletonian.
Adele Gould..........2 19
Aladdin 2 26½
Allen Boy..... . ..... .2 28¾
Ansonia........ ... 2 27¼
Blarney 2:27¾
Carrie R 2 28¼
Dude.... ....2:27½
Dundee . ... 2·25
Florence D 2:29¼

Harry Gould...........2 28¾
Janie, (Opal)........ ....2 21¼
Jessie Gould. 2 29¼
J. W. Gould..... ......2 28¼
King Phillip 2:21
Lady Dawson 2 28
May Gould...... . .. 2 24¼
Mecca.............. 2 28
Mill Boy.... .... 2 26
Mill Girl.. . ... 2 22¼
Mona 2 29
Otard 2 26¼
Panama ... . 2·24½
Pygmalion 2 25½
Patti..... .. .. 2 24
Pixley 2 08¼
Ray Gould 2 29½
Dude, p 2 28
Fortuna, p 2:19¾
George Gould, p........2:25
Jay Gould Jr , p... ....2:29¼
Keswick, p 2 18¼
Jay Gould Jr. by Jay Gould.
Mona, p.. .... 2 24¼
Jaywood by Nutwood
Cottonwood 2 28¼
Greenwood. 2 30
Jayhawk 2 29¾
Ira Band, p.. ....2.28¾
Mattie Warren, p . . 2.19¼
Jean Baptiste by Old Brandy.
Deceit 2 30
Jeb Stuart by Mambrino Patchen.
Kitty Patchen 2 21¼
Jefferson Mambrino by Woodford Mambrino.
Cherokee 2.29½
Jefferson Prince by Jim Scott.
Ben Hur 2 29¼
Cedric.............. .. 2 24½
Deacon 2 28
Eddie G....... ...... 2·23¾
Little Nell 2 19¼
Mambrino Prince 2 22
Shooting Star . .... . 2·25½
Winona 2 21¾
Black Prince, p 2 29¾
Gyp S , p 2 24¾
Leah K , p 2.23
Jefferson Star by Post's Conductor
Banner Boy......... . 2 23¼
Jerome Eddy by Louis Napoleon.
Adora.. .... 2.28½
Argo .... 2·25½
Arlino........ ...... 2 29½
Bertrina............ 2·23
Dick Eddy.......... 2 21½
Edifice 2 21
Edinia 2 25¼
Edleen 2 27½
Fanny Wilcox. ... . 2·13
Harry Eddy........... 2 29¾
Katherine..... ... .2.29¼
Lorella.... . ... 2 30
May Eddy .... 2·25½
Metamora.......... . 2 19¾
Octo 2.19½
Prince Eddy 2.29½
Tycho ....2·28¼
Venture 2.30
Ella Eddy, p. 2:12
Fraro, p ....2·28½
Lizziemont, p..... ....2 16¾
May Eddy, p.. ....2 22½
Rollo, p..................2·28½

Stelleta, p 2 25
Jerome Heath by St. Jerome
Maggie 2 29¼
Jerome Turner by Byerly Abdallah
Rose Turner 2 15½
Jerry by Swigert.
Billy Beverly 2 21
Jerry Ladd.
Hunter 2 25½
Jersey Prince by Kentucky Prince.
Gladys. 2 23¼
Ivy Princess 2 30
Jerseyman 2 23¼
Jersey Wood 2 27¼
John S . . 2 21¾
Little Jersey.... .... .. 2 29¼
Major F. 2 30
Jersey Star by Seely's American Star.
Sinbad 2 29¾
Tom Keeler . . 2 25
Jersey Wilkes by Geo. Wilkes.
Alice Black . .. 2 29¼
Chiquerita 2 16¾
Cythera 2.20¾
Elsinore . 2 25
Hussar . 2 18½
Inglewood . . 2·29½
Jersey Belle 2 18½
Jourdan Wilkes . 2 20¾
Minta Linder. .. 2 27¼
Nathalia 2 17
Nemoline 2 13¼
Nelly S 2 28½
Sparx ... . . . 2·24¾
Adlina, p. 2 29¾
Credo, p.... . . 2 29¾
Phenol, p .... 2·16¾
Rollo, p 2 21¼
Jesse James by Dean Sage
Betty Battaile....... .. 2 28¼
Jesse Lambert by Daniel Lambert
Flora O. 2 25
Jet by Blackwood Jr.
J. M K.. .... 2·18
J. H Welch by Sammis' Washington
Civilization 2 23¼
Urbana Belle 2 20¼
Jim Brister.
Billy Brister 2 27
Joe Brister. 2 25¾
Sally K . . .. 2·28
Roan Rattler, p . 2 28
Jim Crow by Manchester.
A. B. C .. 2 24¼
Jim Ervin by Clark Chief-
Bristol Girl 2 28¾
Ervin 2·26½
Nettie B.. . ... 2 25½
Pheon 2 24
Jim Fisk by Sackett's Hambletonian
Emma E. 2 19¼
Ruth S .. . 2 29¼
Bellevue Maid, p.. . 2 28
Cotton Queen, p.. 2 29½
Little Rhea, p 2 27½
Jim Fisk by Benedict Morrill
Magic 2 25¼
Jim Hawkins by Jack Hawkins
Belle B .... 2·26½
Tamarack 2.28½

Jim Hill by Whipple.
Stonewall . 2 28¼
Jim Lambert by Daniel Lambert
Eunice 2 24¾
Sallie.. .... .. 2 30
Jim Long by Petoskey
Lolla B., p.... .. 2 22¼
Jim Medium.
W. C. B., p 2.17¼
Jimmie by Leon
Maybird .. .. . 2·21¼
Jim Monroe by Alexander's Abdallah.
D. Monroe 2 28¾
Dread 2 27½
Flode Holden. ... . 2·29¼
Judge Hawes 2.24
Kitty Bates 2:19
Lady Monroe .. .. 2·26¼
Monroe Chief 2 18¼
Laverne, p.. . . 2 23¼
Jim Mulvenna by Nutwood.
Greywood 2 27
Lorena.. . 2.30
McGinty . . 2 26
Keno, p .. . 2 23¼
Jimmy Blaine by Hinsdale Chief
Swanton Boy . . 2 23¼
Jimmy Gift by Mambrino Gift
Go On . . . 2,28¾
Jim Schriber by Rhode Island.
Lettie Watterson...... 2 21¾
Yankee II 2 19¼
Lettie Sprague, p 2 23¼
Subscriber, p . 2 14¾
Jim Scott by Rich's Hambletonian.
Ed White 2 27
Scott B 2 29½
Jim Swigert by Swigert
Jim C... ... . 2 22½
Nancy Haas............ 2 29¾
Phil O.... .. .. .2 23¾
Topsy 2 28
Jim Wilkes by Young Jim.
Proctor W 2 26½
Dolly Spanker, p 2 11½
Jim Wilson (Fisk's) by Masterlode.
Nelly S 2 23¼
Jim Wilson Jr., p....... 2·18¼
Jim Wilson by Blue Bull
Belle Wilson 2 20
Boone Wilson. . 2 20½
Greenfield Girl...... .. 2 29½
Irma C. 2 23¼
Ironwood 2 23¼
Johnny Bull 2 27
Pawnee 2 21¾
Sly Chubby 2 24¾
Bonnie Wilson, p 2 26½
Boone Wilson, p .... .2·13
Cricket, p 2 25
Daisy C, p 2 17¾
Ed Valentine, p 2 30
Frank Wilson, p 2 22½
Irma C., p ... . 2·18
Jim Blaine, p......... 2 25
Minnie Martin, p ... 2 24¾
Montgomery Wilson, p 2·27
Walter D, p 2.30
Jim Wilson Jr. by Jim Wilson
Emick Wilson, p 2 23½
Joe by son of Vermont Black Hawk
Clifton Boy 2 23

Joe Bassett by Billy Bashaw.
Brother Dan 2 23½
Joe Bassett Jr ... . 2·18¼
Johnston, p 2 06¼
Joe Bates by Harris' Mambrino Chief Jr.
Little Joe. 2 25¼
Joe Blackburn by Sherman's Hambletonian
Billy Blackburn 2 26¼
Harry P., p .. . 2 21¼
Joe Bowers
Joe Bowers Jr.... 2 18
Joe Brister by Jim Brister.
Charley Foster, p .. 2 29¼
Joe Brister Jr p....... 2 24
King Brister, p ... 2 30
Joe Brister Jr, p 2 26¼
Joe Brown by Woodward's Rattler
Dan Jenkins. ...... 2·28
Judge Davis 2 18¾
Mary Russell. ... ... 2·23½
White Cloud... 2 25¾
Joe Brown Jr by Joe Brown.
Jenny Brown p.. .. 2 25
Joe Cool by Comet.
Joe M.. . ... 2 29½
Joe Coleman
Rambling Dick, p 2:27¾
Joe Downing by Edwin Forrest
Abe Downing.. 2·20¾
Dick Jamison ..... 2·26
Joe Downing Jr. by Joe Downing.
Nona Downing. 2 26¾
Joe Elmo by St. Elmo.
D C. S 2 22¼
Elmo Maid 2 23¼
Review 2 28¼
Lee Buoyant p 2 27½
Mark Wakefield, p.... 2 29¼
Joe Gavin by Messenger Duroc.
Ben-no-nie 2.25
Bismarck ... ... 2·28
Cora Belle . ... 2·29½
Fred Drake 2:26¾
Ollie Drake 2 25
Walter Drake 2.23½
Joe Hal.
Chester Boy, p 2 30
Joe Hooker by Mambrino Chief
Bushwhacker .. 2 29½
Maud Macey. 2·27¾
Joe Hooker by Dan Rice.
Finnigan, p . 2 20
Joe Hooker by Wolf's Tom Hyer
Jay Cook. . 2 27
Joe Hooper by Erie Abdallah
Jenny M 2 25½
Maggie C. 2 27¼
Maxie 2 27¾
Joe Howe.
Josie Howe, p . .. 2·25½
Joe Humphreys.
Hard Tack. . .. 2·26½
Joe Irving by Whitcomb's Fearnaught
Black Amble...... .. 2 26¼
Joe Johnson by Glencoe Jr.
Sleepy Joe 2 19¼
Joe Mack by Elial G
Fly-away . .. 2 29¼
Joe Pond by Don Carlos.
Diamond, p. 2 22

Joe Young by Star of the West.
Billy Young 2:29¼
Col Young 2:29¾
Joe-You-See 2:17¼
Leroy 2:25½
Bessie Young, p 2:24
Idol Duke p. 2:16¾

Joe You See by Joe Young.
Lady Russett 2:30
Lydi 2:30
Summer Queen 2:29¼
Joe Beppo, p 2:24½

John A. Allen by Bacon's Ethan Allen.
John Doddridge 2:23¼

John Adams
Seneca Maid .... ?:22¾

John A. Kasson by McKesson's Grey Eagle.
Charley Ross 2:29¾
Kasonis, p 2:25
Speed Waxy, p. 2:30

John A. Logan
Charley D. p 2:24¼

John A. Rawlins by Romulus
Rolo 2:23¼

John Bell by Pilot Mambrino.
Nicoll, p 2:19¼

John Bright by Volunteer
Beauty Bright 2:21¼
Bright Rattler 2:19¾
Maggie M 2:28¼

John B. Sprague by George Sprague.
Gov. Sprague Jr 2:30

John Burdine by Almont.
Lady Almont 2:27¾
Courier, p 2:27

John Carrier.
Grey Jack 2:28¼

John C. Breckinridge.
Minnie R 2:19
Minnie R, p 2:16½

John E. Rysdyk by Knickerbocker.
Big Fanny 2:24¼

John E. Wood by Knickerbocker.
Belle Hamilton 2:23¼
Elsie Wood 2:30
Katie Wood 2:26½
Leckwood 2:28½

John F. Payne by Bald Chief.
Bay Chieftain 2:28¼
Don Payne, p. 2:18
Little Wonder, p 2:21¼

John Goldsmith by Volunteer
Kemble Maid 2:28¼
Sid 2:23½
Trixie 2:26¼

John Green by Aberdeen.
Charley Thorne 2:25½
Green Boy 2:27¾

John Hadley.
Uncle Ned, p 2:23¾

John L.
John W. p 2:29¼

John Lambert by Daniel Lambert.
Goldfinder 2:23¼

John Morgan by Sherman Morgan Jr.
Wildair 2:23

John Morgan (Reynold's).
Maxwell Star, p 2:24¼

John Nelson by son of imp Trustee.
Aurora 2:27
Gov. Stanford 2:27½
Nemo 2:30
Nerea 2:23½

Johnny B by Wood's Hambletonian.
Taylor 2:26¼

Johnny Hawkins by New York.
Prairie Star 2:27

Johnny Mack
Olivette 2:29

Johnny Wonder.
Sarah Ann, p 2:28¾

John O'Rorke by Knickerbocker.
Red Weed 2:29½

John Sevenoaks by Nutwood.
Bay Rum 2:19½
Billy Oaks 2:30
Loupe, p 2:20¾

John Sherman by Wapsie.
Nelly Barrett 2:29½
Nelly Sherman 2:29¾
Sally Ranger 2:24¾

John W. Conley by Tom Wonder.
Drummer Boy 2:29½

John W. Daniel by Walker Morrill.
Little Betz 2:23½

John Wentworth by Major Davis.
John W 2:17¼

John Wilkes by Red Wilkes.
Minnie B 2:30

Joker by Memory.
Joe Wonder, p 2:21¾

Joker (Strang's) by Otsego Joker.
Billy Leach 2:29¾
Charley Van 2:29¼

Jolly, by Admiral.
Eclectic, p 2:14

Josh Bell.
Hugh L. McClung, p 2:27

Josh Billings by a St. Lawrence Horse.
Ossian Pet 2:29¼

Jot C. by Blue Bull.
Montephister 2:29
Hye Dye, p 2:21¼
Mascot, p 2:28¼
Natie, p 2:27¼

Journalist by Princeps.
Brazil 2:16¼

J. R. Shedd by Red Wilkes.
Belle B 2:24
Billy Shedd 2:30
Effie Wilkes 2:26
Rispee 2:30
Bessie Shedd, p. 2:23¼
Dupage, p 2:28
Woodshed, p. 2:13¼

Juanito by Tilton Almont.
Almont Patchen, p. 2:15
T. B., p 2:27

Jubilee, by Satellite.
Monte Christo 2:18½
Tootsie D., p 2:21

Jubilee Lambert by Daniel Lambert.
Jubilee De Jarnette 2:29¼
Jubilee Lambert Jr 2:27½
Juggler Boy 2:27
Jube, p 2:29½

Judge Advocate by Messenger Duroc.
Glassware Girl 2:19¼
Hortense 2:26½
May Not 2:27¼
Romulus 2:24¼
Thornburg 2:21½
Catherine H., p 2:27½
Hortense, p 2:19¼
Rhea, p 2:17¾

Judge Baldwin.
Quilsine 2:22½

Judge Craven by Blue Bull.
Carrie L 2:29
Tony Boy, p 2:20½

Judge Folger by Young Wilkes.
Capt. Watters 2:25½
Galen Prince 2:19

Judge Gould by Louis Napoleon.
Dido 2:21¼

Judge Hayes by Robert McGregor.
Addie Hayes 2:19¼
Emily 2:30
Flurry 2:28
Kitty Hayes 2:25½

Judge James by Ryskyk.
Judge Rysdyk 2:26

Judge Rysdyk by Judge James.
Twiggs 2:24¼

Judge Salisbury by Nutwood.
Bob Allen 2:27¼
Dandy Salisbury 2:24¾
Dave Salisbury 2:29¾
George Salisbury 2:30
Glendine 2:20
Muchado 2:20½
Tono 2:26½
Granberry, p 2:27½
Happiness, p 2:17¼
Paynestone, p 2:25¼
Roy O'More, p 2:17½
Spaulding, p 2:20¼

Judge Tranby by Hambletonian Tranby.
Tiny Moore 2:29½

Judge Trumbull by Leviathan.
Tim Kane 2:21¼
Trixy, p 2:25

Jud Wilkes by Ira Wilkes.
Galette 2:23½

Juggler Boy by Jubilee Lambert.
Alice G 2:29½

Jules Jurgensen by Gen. Knox.
Iron Age 2:19¼
Nelly Walton 2:26½

Jumbo.
Flora C, p 2:26

Junio by Electioneer.
Athanio 2:19¾
Bruno 2:19
Gilpatrick 2:29½
Salinas Maid 2:30
St. Joe 2:26

Junior by Constellation.
C. M. P 2:26½

Junius by Dictator.
Gipsey Girl 2:17¼

Jupiter by Long Island Black Hawk.
Harry Gilbert 2:24
Lady Emma 2:26¼
Lady Hughes 2:30
Lady Jupiter 2:30
M. R 2:28

Jupiter Abdallah by Jupiter.
Jupiter Jr. 2:23
Monopolist 2:29½
Prince 2:27

Result 2 25
Tom Moore .. . 2 28
Jura by Billy Wilkes.
Junetta, p .. . 2 20
Juror by Pilot Mambrino
Perette. . .2 22¼
Juryman by Bona Fide.
Jury Boy, p .. . 2 23¼
Justin Morgan by Lowe's Comet Morgan
Lady Lowe. .. 2 28
Wick 2 26½
J. W.
Flora A., p 2 25½
J. W. Bailey by Seneca Chief.
Dan Bailey 2 27½
Nina W., p.. . . ..2 25
J. W. South by Princeps.
J. S... . . . .2.16½

Kankakee by Mambrino Russell.
Royal David . . 2 26¼
Arkalon, p..... ...... 2 16
Iron Quill, p . 2 22¼
Kaiser by George Wilkes
Miss Wilkes 2 29½
Wilkesmont 2.20¼
Gretchen, p . . 2 20
Juliette, p ....2·30
Kansas Central by Rhode Island.
Haverly, p . 2·25
Kansas Rattler.
Captain 2 24
Karatas by Triton
Dandy 2 30
Eva, p 2 18¼
Kansas, p ... 2 10½
Karl by Messenger Duroc
Black Prince . . 2 25¼
Kearsarge by Volunteer.
Nelly G 2 28¼
Keeler by King Rene
Onoqua 2 11¼
Thad, p 2 26¼
Keene Wilkes by Red Wilkes
Orphan Wilkes. ...2:27½
Keller Thomas by Phil Duroc.
Billy Thomas 2 23
Little Snap. 2 17½
Kemble Jackson (Kleckner's) by Wilson's Kemble Jackson.
Penelope 2 27
Kemble Jackson Jr. (Kenyon's) by Young Kemble Jackson
Lola 2 30
Kenelm by Happy Medium
Al Cooper 2 28¼
Kenmore by Almont.
Daisy Kenmore 2 25½
Tony . .. 2·27
Walker J ... . 2·24¼
Kennebec by Independence.
Molly Mitchell.........2 26½
Kennebee Knox.
Dolly H.. . ...2.25¼
Kenney Wilkes by Lyle Wilkes.
Nancy Carr 2 25
Kensett by Rysdyk's Hambletonian.
Kaspar. 2.27¼
Kenneth 2 28
Kensett F. 2 22¼
Kensett Maid 2 30
Kepler 2 29¾
Keturah......... ..... 2 30
Lady Kensett 2 21¼
Mercurius 2 14¼
Kensingtan by Kentucky Prince.
McMillan 2 29½
Kent by Skipton.
Jaybird 2 30
Kent by Rysdyk's Hambletonian
Cora R.. ... . .2 29½
Doris 2 27¾
Glenny 2 29½
Jennie C........... 2 24½
Kendall 2.26½
Lady Barefoot 2 26½
Mary Kent 2.28½
Sister Barefoot .. 2 25
Kent (Clifton's) by Kent.
Julia M 2 26¾
Kenton Mambrino by Mambrino King.
Kenton George, p 2 20½
Kentucky by Whipple's Hambletonian.
Holly 2 28½
Kentucky by Joe Downing.
Lee Hope . .. 2 26
Kentucky Belmont by Belmont.
Harry Belmont . . 2.29
Lee Forester 2 22½
Vinco 2 30
Kentucky Black Hawk by Smith's Black Hawk.
Gen Garfield . . 2 21
Kentucky Clay Jr by Kentucky Clay
Kingsbury . . . 2 28¼
Leo, p 2 29½
Kentucky Clay Jr. by Kentucky Clay.
Valentine 2 22
Kentucky Dictator by Dictator.
Kingwood 2 17¼
St. Jonathan. 2 22½
Kentucky Jewell by Kentucky Prince.
Sadie Allen .. . 2 29½
Kentucky Prince by Clark Chief
Alsie 2 29
America . . 2 23½
Ana . . 2 28½
Annie Stevens 2 18¼
Bayonne Prince 2·21¼
Company. 2 19¾
Compeer 2 24½
Cora F 2 20½
Cornwal 2 20
Courtland 2 24¼
Cypress 2 18¼
Eloise 2 15
Elwood 2 26½
Encore . ... 2·2¼
Fred Folger 2 20¼
Gebhardt. 2 23
Gurney...... ....2.28¾
Guy 2 09¾
Jersey Prince 2 27¼
Josephine 2.24¼
Kenneth 2 28¼
Kentucky Blanche .. . 2 26¼
Little Ida 2 29¼
Noya 2 24
Prince Hogarth . . .2 27½
Problem .... 2·18
Punchellino 2 28
Shipman 2 24¼
Spofford . ... 2·18¾
Stevie 2 19
Sweepstakes....... ..2 24¼
Newcastle, p. 2 29¼
Prince Farlie, p . . . 2 30
St Cloud p 2 27
Kentucky Prince Jr. by Kentucky Prince.
J. Q. .. .2 17¼
Lemonade ... 2·27¼
Kentucky Ruler by Egbert
Burdetta. . 2 30
Jewel C . 2·24½
Rozinanti ..2 23¼
Kentucky Russell by Mambrino Russell
Brown Russell .2 29¼
Kentucky Volunteer by Volunteer.
Benteer 2 30
Harvey 2 21
S. S...... . ...2 29½
Vera 2 25
Maritani, p 2 20¼
Vollula, p ... 2 15
Kentucky Whip by Gill's Vermont
Longfellow Whip 2 20¼
Kentucky Wilkes by George Wilkes
Astoria . .. 2 30
Bravado 2.1½
Caprice 2 14¼
Celerity 2 19½
Penryn. 2 18½
Strephon 2 26½
Virginia Evans 2 15¼
Wilkesview...... . 2·28½
Crafty, p 2 13½
Riot p.... .... .. 2 27
Kenwood by Harry Clay.
Col. Kip. . . 2 20¼
Keokuk by Vermont Black Hawk.
Jerome 2 27
Kernwood by Wedgewood.
Dannemora .... 2·29
Keystone by Wood's Hambletonian
Bay Thornwood . 2 24½
Nettie B 2 27½
Keywood by Onward.
Tilly Q .. . .. 2·29¼
Kickapoo by Comas.
Rowdy 2 27¼
Kidnapper by Brigham Young.
Pauline H .. . 2 24
Pauline H , p...... ... 2:17¼
Kilbuck Tom by White Cloud.
Leopard Rose. 2 15¼
Alto, p........ . ...2 21
Charley P., p....... ...2.19¼
Comet, p 2 24¼
Evangeline, p 2 30
Jack Bowers, p 2:11¼
Lady, p 2 26¼
Maggie R., p . 2 14¼
Red Rock, p 2 25¼
Tommy, p 2.17¼
Tommy B., p.. . . . 2·25¼
Tom West, p 2 23¼
Trenton Girl, p . 2 26¼
Kilburn Jim Jr. by Kilburn Jim
Kitty Kilburn.... ....2:21

Kildare by King Rene.
Chiquita 2.30
Killan Horse.
Jim F., p 2:27¼
Killarney by Return
Killarney Girl, p 2:28¼
Kilmore by Black's Hambletonian
Pilot Boy 2:27¾
Kimball
Tony H., p 2:15¾
Kimball Morgan
Ned Hanlon, p. 2:26½
Kimo by Blue Bull
Retla Boy, p 2:19¼
Kilpatrick by Ahwaga Chief
Alice M 2:28
King by Mambrino King.
Irvington 2:29
King Almont by Almont
Delph 2:27½
Edith Almont 2:26½
H. C. T 2:17¼
Jewmont 2:30
Kitchen Belle 2:21½
Ladymont 2:28½
Queen Almont 2:27½
Tube Rose 2:30
Zembia 2:15½
Delph, p 2:24¾
King Ashland by King Rene.
Minnie Clay 2.27½
King Clay by Harry Clay
Clay King 2:27¾
Claymore 2:17¾
Eola 2:24¾
Marble 2:23¼
Miss Lida 2:10¾
Queen Clay 2:28
King Hal by Gibson's Tom Hal.
Count Hal, p 2:20¼
Emily Hal, p 2:25¼
Prince Hal, p 2:29¼
King Herod by Sherman Black Hawk
Billy Barefoot 2:28½
Foxie V 2:23¾
Herod. 2:24½
King Legacy by Legacy
Maud B., p 2:20
King Mac by Mambrino King
Billy Richbald, p 2.20½
King Mambrino by Mambrino Patchen.
Mambrino Payne 2:30
Cora D., p 2:26½
Dr M., p 2.13¼
King Monte Marlo by Mambrino King
Hazel King 2:21¼
King Nutwood by Nutwood
Queen Nutwood 2:27¼
King of Belair by King Rene.
Mad River Belle. 2:29¼
King of Salem, p 2:21¾
King Patchen by Mambrino King.
Hiatoga Chief 2:22¼
King Patchen by Tom Patchen
Forrest Patchen 2.19½
King Pharaoh by Seely's American Star.
Bawley, p 2.15
Daisy de Spain, p 2:12
Little Willie, p 2:23¼
Lyttleton, p 2.20½
Richball, p 2.12½

King Philip by Jay Gould.
Capt Ben 2:27
Speedress 2:25¼
King Philip by Mambrino King.
Lexington 2:24½
King Rene by Belmont.
Alacine 2:29½
Annette 2:27½
Arabesque 2:29¾
Aytoun 2:29¼
Balzarine 2:27
Chastelard 2:29¾
Conclave 2:30
Count Waldemar 2:26½
Dolly Rene 2:29
Etoile 2:26¼
Farandole 2:27
Fugue 2:19¼
Keeler 2.13¼
King Rex 2:26½
Laundry Girl 2:29¼
Lucy A 2:30
Mist 2:29½
Prince Edward 2:20
Prince Rene 2:23¼
Pythias 2:28¾
Rectitude 2:28
Rege 2:26¼
Rene 2:26
Renie Silver 2:24½
Renne 2:29¼
Samovar 2:28¾
Sarcenett 2:16¼
Savoyard 2:23
Serpolet 2:30
Valcour 2:28
King of Belair, p 2:24
King Richard by Peavine
Amelia Rives 2:27¾
King of the West by Hamdallah
Johnny Boggs 2:23
King Gaines 2:29¾
King Sprague by Gov. Sprague
Sanger, p 2:20¾
King Toska by Petoskey
Clay Toska 2:26¾
Kingston by Kinlock
Ben Harrison, p 2:18½
Kingston by Sterling.
Nogero 2:28½
King Wilkes by George Wilkes.
Ashby Girl. 2:25
Killona 2:20
King Darlington 2:16
Minnie Wilkes. 2:17
Monocacy 2:19½
Ollie K. 2:17¾
Oliver K 2:16¼
Purity Wilkes 2:15¼
Queen Susie 2:29¾
Wilkes D 2:29¼
Will Come 2:30
King Wagner, p 2:26½
Sclavonic, p. 2:23¼
King William by Rysdyk's Hambletonian
Col Burr 2:25½
Distaff. 2:28¼
Nancy K. 2.29¼
Gertie, p 2:26¼
King William by Washington Denmark.
King William 2:20¾
King William.
Louis D 2:24¾

King William L. by William L
G. W. Howe 2:25¾
King Wilson by Jim Wilson.
Bellado 2:25¼
Kinlock by Cuyler
Hudson 2:27¾
Bud Dille, p. 2:22½
Kirk.
Joe R 2:17¼
Kirkwood by Green's Bashaw.
Burns 2:30
Daisy Eyebright. 2:27
Mat Kirkwood 2:29¼
Kirkwood Jr.
Don Pedro, p 2:25
Kisbar by Rysdyk's Hambletonian.
Democrat 2:24½
Royal Kisbar 2:28½
Klux.
Kluxie 2:24¼
Knickerbocker by Rysdyk's Hambletonian.
Actress 2:26¾
Brookie 2:29¼
Dom Pedro 2:24¼
Grace 2:27
Hardiman 2:28¼
Lady Lemmon 2:27
Onward 2:20½
Stephen G 2:20½
Tribune 2:25½
Velox 2:30
Knick Wilkes by Alcantara.
Gen Herkimer. 2:24½
Harry P. 2:21½
Major S 2:29¼
Sitra Wilkes 2:28
Knight by Maryland Black Knight.
John W. 2:23¾
Knight Templar by Egbert
Katie 2:30
Knox by Gen Knox.
Edward K 2:23¾
Prescott 2:27½
Knox Boy by Gen. Knox.
Chub 2:27
Rocket 2:23¼
Sancho 2:29
Kokomis by Victor Bismarck
Kolena 2:22½
Konantz by Lyle Wilkes
Exit 2:24¼
Konie 2.28½
On Time. 2:25¼
Kossuth by John C Fremont.
Catskill Girl 2:28½
Kremlin by Lord Russell
Bither 2:28¾

Lace Dealer by Smuggler
Brown Jim, p 2:26½
Laclede by Happy Medium.
Frank H 2:25½
Highland Boy 2.30
Lisette. 2:22½
Rose Croix 2:28¼
Ruth H 2:24½
Ruth H., p. 2:22
La Crosse by King Rene.
Beulah 2:26¾
Fedora 2:18
La Crosse Jr 2:19¾
Lake Erie by Castellar
Jenny D 2:26¼

Lakeland Abdallah by Rysdyk's Hambletonion.
- Abdallah Clay 2:29¼
- Gail 2:26¼
- George O.........2:21½
- Sam Lakeland 2:26½

Lakeland Abdallah Jr. by Lakeland Abdallah.
- Leon Baker, p 2:21¾

Lakeside by Lakeland Abdallah
- Volney 2:24¼

Lakewood Prince by Wilkesonian.
- Princewood 2:21¼

Lambert (Ward's) by Daniel Lambert.
- Daisy Ward 2:23¾
- Harry Lambert 2:22

Lambert Chief by Daniel Lambert.
- Fanny B 2:29½
- Mabel H.......2:22¼
- Minnie Moulton 2:27¼

Lambertus by Daniel Lambert.
- C B. Kendall. 2:28¼
- Sir Thomas 2 24
- Sylvester K.......2:17¾

Lance by Flying Morgan.
- Birdie L., p 2:30

Lancelot by Messenger Duroc.
- Leone......2:28½
- Lyric 2:26¼
- Mesquite......2:29½
- Stelleria 2:26½
- Unkamet.......2:22¼

Lancewood by Rysdyk's Hambletanian.
- Lancewood. 2:29¼

Lancewood Jr.
- Emaline K 2:29

Landmark by Volunteer.
- Anson 2:25¾
- Clara J.......2:23¾
- Claudius 2:25
- Eye See.......2:30
- Gracie 2:27
- Guess 2:16¼
- James M. 2:21¼
- Jessie K......2:26½
- John L.......2:29¼
- Jose S 2:22½
- Julia L.......2:25¼
- Katie R......2:21½
- Kitefoot 2:17¼
- Landmark Maid. 2:23¼
- Mabel S.......2:22½
- Mamie A......2:25
- Maud C 2:28¼
- Maud H.......2:29¼
- M. J. Henderson......2:22¼
- Otto.......2:25
- Dolly Quinn, p 2:29½

Land Pilot.
- Possell 2:16¼
- Billy F., p 2:20½
- Landlord, p........2:25¾

Landseer by Gen. Knox.
- Khedive 2:24½
- Willis.......2:28½

Lapadist Chief by imp. Lapadist.
- Little Pitt, p.......2:13¼
- Maud L., p.......2:24½

Larry W. by Louis Napoleon.
- J. I. R., p 2:24¾

Latitude by Walsingham.
- Latimer, p 2:27¼

Lavalard by Director.
- Prince Lavalard 2:29¼

Lawrence by Kentucky Prince
- Brooklyn........2:24
- Daisy L 2:27¾

Lee by Gen. Lee.
- Pomp 2:30

Ledger by Robert Bonner.
- Adele Clark......2:25¼
- Tempest......2:29¼
- Harry M., p......2:27½

Ledger by Crown Chief.
- Belle K......2:28½

Ledger Jr.
- Ryland T.......2:07¾

Ledo by Ledo.
- Miss Ledo......2:29

Legacy by Goldsmith's Star.
- Maria Legacy......2:22¼
- Miss Legacy......2:24½
- Islander, p 2:22¼
- Lucy B., p 2:18¼

Legal Note by Legal Tender Jr.
- Blue Note, p......2:22¼
- Jersey Girl, p......2:20

Legal Star by Legal Tender Jr.
- Jim Blaine, p.......2:25

Legal Tender by Moody's Davy Crocket.
- Harry Lee......2:26
- Katie B.......2:28¼
- Legal Tender......2:27¼
- Red Cloud......2:18
- Black Bassinger, p....2:29¾
- Legal Tender, p......2:28

Legal Tender Jr. by Legal Tender.
- Charles Z.......2:28¼
- Harry Laird 2:29¼
- Lady Elgin......2:25¼
- Legal R......2:30
- Lewand......2:25¾
- Lowland Girl......2:19½
- Pearl Winship......2:23¼
- Ada, p.......2:17¼
- Alhambra, p 2:14½
- Burley F., p 2:18½
- Bob Ingersoll, p......2:26¼
- Dandy Boy, p......2:23¼
- Davy Crockett, p......2:24¼
- Elgin Girl, p......2:20½
- Elgin Girl. p 2:27¼
- Elsie Mack, p......2:29¼
- Joe B., p......2:17¼
- Joe Hooker, Jr., p ...2:24½
- J. C. C., p......2:16
- Laura J., p 2:27½
- Legal Vein, p......2:24½
- Lex, p......2:23¼
- Luella, p......2:19¼
- Maggie H., p 2:25
- Minnie H., p......2:24¾
- Nelly McCrory, p......2:18¼
- Violet, p 2:30
- Vitello, p......2:11¼
- Wonderful, p......2:25½

Le Grand by Almont.
- Anita......2:25¼
- Beaumont......2:22½
- Belle Grand......2:21½
- Charles James......2:22¾
- Grandee......2:23¼
- Grandissimo 2:23¼
- Le Grand......2:28½
- Hattie F., p......2:18

Leighton Horse by Joe Smith
- Charles A.......2:27¼

Leland by Rysdyk's Hambletonian.
- Barrmore.......2:29¾
- Clara......2:21
- Geneva......2:14
- Hades.......2:27¾
- Madison 2:24
- Miss Leland......2:25¾
- Prosperity......2:23
- Young Leland 2 24¾

Lemont by Almont.
- Blondie......2:19½
- Lady Mac......2:23½
- Pilot Lemont......2:21¾
- Blondie, p. 2:15

L'Empreur by Alcyone.
- L'Empress......2:20½

Lenawee Chief by Masterlode
- Gen. Custer, ...2:20¼

Len Rose by A. W. Richmond.
- Barbero 2:29½

Leo by Administrator.
- Little Leo.......2:26¼

Leon by Anthony Wayne.
- Badger Boy 2:29
- Olivette 2:28¾

Leroy by Amboy,
- Charm, p 2 24½

Leroy Horse.
- Dave R., p......2:26¼

Levi Aristos by Aristos.
- Buckshot, p.......2:28½

Lewiston Boy by Pollard Morgan.
- Despatch 2 24¼

Lew Scott by McCurdy's Hambletonian.
- Musette......2:17½

Lew Wann by Egmont.
- Josie B 2:17¾

Lex by Lexington.
- Clipper......2:23½
- Six-Forty, p......2:30

Lexington.
- Grace......2:27¼

Lexington (Keene's) by Brandywine.
- Arthur......2:28¼

Lexington Boy by Egbert.
- Esca......2:25½

Lexington Chief by Regular.
- Fred S., p 2:16
- Joseph L., p......2:24¼

Lexington Chief Jr. by Lexington Chief.
- Daisy R 2:25½
- Lexington Belle......2:24¼
- Lynx......2:28
- Michael......2:29¾
- Model 2:30
- Waiting 2:24¼
- Frank F., p 2:21½
- Meacham, p......2:20
- Spider, p......2:14¼

Lexington Golddust by Golddust.
- Sir Roger......2:23¼

Lexington Wilkes by George Wilkes.
- Wilkes......2:25¼
- Laura Wilkes, p......2:30

Liberty Sontag by Piedmont
- Surprise, p 2:16½

Lightning (Doble's) by Black Bashaw.
- Gen. Hancock......2:24¼

R. C. STINSON, HAMILTON, ONT.

Canada's most successful trainer. He gave Patron 2:14¼ and Houri
2:17 their first lessons, marked Geneva 2:14 and cut the
world's race record for yearlings to 2:26½.

DICK WILSON, BINGHAMTON, N. Y.
A young man from the Blue Bull country who marked Henry F. 2:10¼,
Allen Lowe 2:12, Allegro 2:14¼, Gambrel 2:15 and Emma 2:16¼.

Lightwood by Blackwood.
Mary Anderson 2:26
Limber Bill by Red Buck.
Buffalo Bill 2:29½
Limber Jim by Richmond Chief.
Hal J. 2:29
Tom Covington . 2:28¼
Lincoln by Cortland Wilkes.
Independent ... 2:28½
Lincoln Abdallah.
George W. 2:30
Linkwood Chief by Hannis.
Judge Fisher 2:14
Miss Ida 2:27¼
Miss Patchen 2:25
Linkwood Patchen, p 2:12½
Little Ben by Port Leonard.
Edith V 2:24
Maud White 2:22
Little Billy by Clear Grit.
Billy B 2:19¼
Bradford 2:29¼
Dinah 2:27½
Kapolina 2:25¾
Bessie M., p 2:23½
Little Burl.
Kate Bender, p 2:20½
Little Dan.
Della 2:28
Little Dave Jr. by Dave Jennings.
Hadley Jr., p 2:15¼
Little Eastern by Gen. Benton.
Blanche 2:30
Eastern Boy 2:27¼
Little Frank by Goldenbow.
Little Goldie 2:27
John W., p 2:29¼
Little Gift by Fairy Gift.
Seneca See, p. 2:24½
Little Grant by Bay Chief Jr.
Nelly C 2:29½
Bob Cotton, p 2:29¼
Little Hamilton by Bay Middleton.
Dick French 2:19½
Maud M 2:28¼
Nelly 2:28
Nina C 2:26½
Little Henry by Blue Bull.
Susie G., p 2:11¼
Little Jack.
Sara B 2:29¾
Little Johnny.
Little Dock 2:25
Little Logan by Gage's Logan
Harry Z., p 2:17
Little Mack.
Little Mack Jr 2:27½
Little Pete C.
Crusader 2:23½
Little Rock by Swigert.
Big Rock 2:29¼
Minnie Whitestone 2:24¼
Little Washington by Tecumseh.
Pocahontas, p 2:22½
Little Wonder by St. Elmo.
Leopard Bob 2:28
Little Wonder by Blue Bull.
Lady Wonder 2:25
Everett M., p 2:19¼
Monte Christo, p 2:18½
Lively.
Lamp 2:26

L. J. Sutton by Castellar.
Jim Smith 2:22¼
Lochinvar.
Miss Ridgeway, p 2:29½
Lockeibie by Blue Bull.
Maud Muller 2:20¾
Allie L., p 2:10½
Lockheart by Nutwood.
La Belle, p 2:09
Locksmith by Goldsmith.
Perplexed 2:24¼
Lockwood by Aberdeen.
Galatea 2:27¾
Locomotive.
Elgin 2:27
Locomotive by Robert E. Lee.
Capt. Smith 2:29
Locomotive (Gray's) by Gibson's Tom Hal Jr
Cedar Snag, p 2:25¾
Engineer, p 2:17½
Frank Dortch, p. 2:15¾
Rebellion, p 2:25
Locomotive (Moore's) by Gray's Locomotive.
Henry Drane, p 2:23½
Logan (Gage's) by Rysdyk's Hambletonian.
Skinkle Hambletonian 2:28¾
Logan (Wadleigh's) by Logan.
Logan (Wineman's) 2:28
Logan (Wineman's) by Wadleigh's Logan.
Logan B 2:22¾
Logan by Shoreham Black Hawk.
Geo. Storms 2:27½
Logan Chief by I. J.
Logan K., p 2:27½
Logan Hambletonian by Skinkle Hambletonian.
Prince Mac, p 2:19¾
Logan Jr.
Carbolic 2:24¼
Logue Horse by Golding Horse.
Lady Daggett 2:26
Long Branch by The Commodore.
Molly Mc. 2:18¼
Longfellow by Mormon Chief.
Johnny Weigle, p 2:20½
Longfellow by Mambrino Patchen.
Gense 2:19
Longfellow Golddust by Golddust.
William H 2:25
Longstride by Sweepstakes.
Jacksonian 2:22½
Longstrider.
Flora Temple, p 2:18¾
Jenny Lind, p. 2:17
Lilly H., p 2:25¼
Lizzie H., p 2:22
Nettie Hoppin 2:20
Peter V., p 2:16½
Lon Morris by Gen. Knox
Kitty Morris 2:30
Look by Nutwood.
Adah Look 2:20¼
Lookaway 2:22½
Flosswood 2:23¾
Jean Look 2:30
Teddy Look 2:28¾
Lynnwood 2:27¼
Bessie B., p 2:18¼

Lookout by Bourbon Chief.
Keene Jim 2:19¼
Lord Almont by Almont.
Erie Girl 2:23
Lord Byron by General Benton.
Bitter Root 2:25
Lord Eldon by Mansfield
Cute, p 2:21¼
Lord Harold by Harold.
Ogle Boy 2:30
Jim Quay, p 2:24½
Lord Jenkinson by Cuyler.
Jokton 2:24¾
Lord Nelson by Lord Wellington.
Nelson D 2:26½
Lord Cope.
Dandy, p 2:29½
Lord Nelson by Lander's Knox.
Katie B 2:22¼
Lord Russell by Harold.
Ada de Clare 2:26½
Alencon 2:23¼
Elite Russell 2:29¾
King Russell 2:26¼
Kremlin 2:07¾
Lee Russell 2:16¼
Matanzas 2:27½
Pastime 2:27¼
Redwald 2:23½
Rurik 2:23
Russellmont 2:14¼
Sineus 2:27¼
Tonquin 2:28
Typhoon 2:28
Yuletide 2:28¼
Lord Egbert, p 2:30
Hustler Russell, p. 2:12¼
Seabird, p 2:18¼
Sea Shell, p 2:20
Lord Wellington by Cuyler.
Agate Wellington ... 2:27
Alahambra G 2:24½
Regret 2:15¼
Wellington King 2:27¾
Lothair by Gilbreth Knox.
Eli 2:28¼
Fred Lothair 2:29¾
Lothair Jr 2:30
Lothair Chief by Lothair.
Prince Henry 2:23¼
Lothair Jr. by Lothair.
Cleveland Boy 2:28
Eldin 2:24¼
Resolute 2:26¾
Erwin M., p 2:20¼
Ida K., p 2:25
Lazy Jim, p 2:28
Lothair Boy, p 2:19
Lotus by Rysdyk's Hambletonian.
Aggie 2:19½
Francis C 2:28¼
Louis Napoleon by Volunteer.
Ben Hulett 2:26¼
Chandler 2:28
Charles Hilton 2:17½
Cora Barlum 2:23½
Dr. Morland 2:28½
Edmore 2:29¼
George L. Napoleon 2:24¼
Grace Napoleon 2:14½
Jerome Eddy 2:16½
Letitia 2:27½
Louis R 2:26¼
Louis Owosso 2:25

Lulu B..............2:29¼
Mattie B..........2:28¼
Myrtie.....2:22¼
Reno Defiance......2:29¼
Spinella 2:21¾
Tipseco...........2:19½
Uncle Sam........2:22
Beechnut, p......2:23¼
Benson H., p... ....2:17¾
Dr. Perkins, p.......2:26¼
George Swift, p......2:30
John S., p 2:20¼
Judge Wolsley, p... 2:27¾
Louis Napoleon by Ticonderoga.
  Col. Russell..........2:25¾
  Grey Chief..........2:24¾
Louis R. by Louis Napoleon.
  J. P..........2:26¼
  Lucy M..........2:20½
Louisville by Greenlander.
  Girard..........2:26¼
L. P. Thompson by Sterling.
  Paul Pinkham.......2:24
Lou Scott by McCurdy's Hambletonian.
  Musette...........2:23
Lowell Chief by George H. Low.
  Morris H..........2:22½
Lucas Brodhead by Harold.
  Green Bird 2:24¼
  Kate B 2:26
  Prairie Boy........2:28
  Prince M 2 16¾
  Comus....2:30
  Effie O., p 2:19
  Pearl R., p 2 17½
  See Saw, p 2:22¼
Lucifer by Lightning.
  Aubertine..........2:26¼
  Civilian............2:26
Lucky Cross by Belmont.
  Merron............2:28¼
Lucy Horse by Mambrino Tuckahoe.
  Dave R., p.........2:28½
Luke Brodhead by Belmont.
  Dan Jennings.......2:25
  Dick Smith........2:17
  Hal Pointer........2:18¾
Lumber by Ericsson.
  Lady Lumber....2:29¼
Luminator by Lumps.
  Lottie 2:25½
Lumps by George Wilkes.
  Bamboo....2:20¼
  Bessie P.....2:29½
  Bullet......2:5¾
  Bumps......2:29½
  Classmate.......2:19¾
  Col. Tom...2:22
  Elko.......2:17
  Inis Wilkes....2:29
  Lady Williams.....2:29¾
  Lumpson 2:29½
  La Grippe......2:17¾
  Lunette.......2:25¾
  Lycurgus..........2:25
  Mambrino Lumps....2:28¼
  Mary Mac 2:18½
  Modred......2:29¼
  Royal Wilkes....2:25¼
  S. and E. 2:26¼
  Annie Dickinson. p. 2:15½
  Tom Porter, p......2:24
Lyle Wilkes by George Wilkes.
  Danville Wilkes. ...2:27

Konantz 2:28
Mattie Wilkes....2:30
Raven Wilkes....2:29¼
Sir Bell....2:20¼
Wood Wilkes.....2:25
Lynwood by Nutwood.
  Lynette..........2:22½
Lysander by Rysdyk's Hambletonian.
  Lysander Boy........2:20¾
  Prince....2:20¼
  Watt.....2:24¾
  William Kearney....2:20½
  Robin E., p.....2:27¼
Lysander Chief by Lysander.
  Roanoke.....2 30

McBeth.
  Gipsey M., p 2:13½
MacCallummore by Robert McGregor.
  Mary.....2:20¼
McCurdy by McCurdy's Hambletonian.
  Grapevine, p.....2:26½
  Nellie G..p.....2:27¼
McDonald Chief by Clark Chief.
  Catharine.....2:28¾
  Columbus S ...2:27½
  Maud.....2:29¾
McEwen by McCurdy's Hambletonian.
  Merman.....2:16
  Penelope.....2:20¾
  Squeezer.....2 23⅜
  Calera, p.....2:18½
McFarland Hambletonian.
  Olive K.....2 29¼
McGregor (Howe's).
  Black Nelly 2.30
  Delmont 2.30
McGregor Boy by Robert McGregor.
  A. D. McGregor.....2:28
McGregor Chief by Robert McGregor.
  Billy McGregor 2:21¾
  Nelly McGregor....2:26¼
  Surprise.....2:23¾
McGregor Jr. by Robert McGregor.
  McKelvey.....2:29¼
McKean by Volunteer.
  Elbert K.....2.28¼
McKinney by Alcyone.
  McZeus.....2:29¼
  Osito.....2.30
  Sir Credit.....2:28¾
  Harvey Mc. p.....2:18
McLeod by Iron Duke.
  Jim Sneaks.....2:23½
McMahon by Administrator.
  Auburn H.....2:24½
  Big Mc.....2:25¾
  Frank McMahon.....2:30
  Gladys.....2:30
  Prince McMahon....2 21
  Ted McMahon.....2:28
McVeigh by Winthrop Morrill.
  Currier.....2:27
Macdonough.
  G T. Pilot.....2.24
Macedonian by Rysdyk's Hambletonian.
  Freeman 2 29
  Hersey.....2 25¾

Macey by George Wilkes
  Capt. Macey....2:19¼
  Gen. Macey.....2:25½
  Lucy Macey..2 26¼
  Tillie Macey.....2 26¼
  Tot Macey, p.....2 26¼
Macon by Belmont.
  Susie H.....2 29¼
Madison by Leland.
  Clara Madison......2 27½
Madison Smith by Supervisor.
  Manchester C.....2 28¼
  The Parson, p.....2.19
Madison Wilkes by George Wilkes.
  Linden.....2:17¼
  Madison Chief.....2:21½
  Marble Chief.....2 29¼
  Addie Wilkes, p ..2:23¼
  Linden, p . .2 15
Madrid by George Wilkes
  Charley R.. .....2:30
  Cortis.....2:30
  Coxcomb.....2 25½
  Crossman.....2.26
  Deposit.....2 29¾
  Frank S.....2:18¼
  La Tosca.....2 15¾
  Madras.....2 25¾
  Pelerine.....2.19
  Boodle, p.....2 26
  Cigarette, p.....2 18¾
  Cognac, p.....2 20½
Magic by American Clay.
  Clemmie G.....2:15½
  Keno.....2:23¼
  Mystery.....2 25¼
  Post Boy 2.23
Magic by Elmo.
  Keno R.....2:20½
Magna Charta by Morgan Eagle.
  Belle of Lexington..2 26¾
  Hannah D.....2:22¾
  Molly.....2:27
  Sally Scott.....2:28¾
  Young Magna.....2 29
Magna Chief by Magna Charta.
  Kitty B.....2:27¼
Magnet by Magnolia.
  Knoxie Magnet.....2:30
  Stella Magnet .....2·24½
  Jenny McCoy, p. . .2:22
Magnolia by Seely's American Star.
  Magnet.....2:27¼
  Magnolia.....2:26¼
Maitland by Blackstone.
  Lady McCune.....2 28¼
  McClellan, p.....2 28¼
Majesty by Alcoran.
  Timbuctoo, p..... 2.28
Maj. Benton by Jim Scott.
  Gov. Benton.....2:22¼
  Dick.....2 26¼
Maj. Doke by Seafoam.
  Dexter Power, p.....2 24¼
  Sea Foam Jr., p. ..2.17¼
Maj. Edsall by Alexander's Abdallah.
  Clayton Edsall.....2:23¾
  Major A.....2 20
  Robert McGregor.....2:17½
  Daisy Dean, p.....2:26

Maj. Edsall Jr. by Maj. Edsall.
Major Wonder, p. . .2 09¾
Maj Flower by Florida.
Bessie Wilkes 2:24¼
Maj. Grant by Delmonico.
Granite.. ....2:24¾
Nelly Grant 2 28¾
Major H. by Dictator.
Tenny C 2:26½
Maj Miller by Guy Miller
Ida Bell 2 23
Prince A.... . ...2.22¼
Prince Miller 2:20½
Maj. Ringgold.
Fanny. 2:29¼
John A. Logan .. . 2 30
Fanny, p 2:29¾
John A. Logan, p . . 2:29½
Richard, p 2:16¾
Major. White by Stephen A. Douglas.
Grey Dawn 2:20
Majer Sommers.
John L., p. . . 2 26½
Major Winfield Jr. by Edward Everett.
Clifton Boy.. .. .. .. 2 30
Maj. Strathmore by Strathmore.
Harry Strathmore, p. 2 24¼
Major Wonder by Major Edsall Jr.
Monkey Wonder, p 2:29¾
Malta by Swigert.
Monte Christo.. ....2 29
Marmaduke.
Madge W.... ....2:28¾
Mambrino (Graham's) by Mambrino Bashaw.
Tim C............ . .2:24¼
Mambrino by Mambrino Patchen
Lady Ellen...... .. 2.29¼
Maud H... ....2 24
Mambrino Abdallah by Mambrino Patchen.
Elastic 2:21¼
Flossie Reed, p 2 26¾
Mambrino Prince, p..2 23¾
Mambrino Barker by Woodford Mambrino.
Prince Brino. 2 29¾
Mambrino Bashaw by Mambrino Pilot.
Nancy V. 2 24¼
Mambrino Bashaw by Mambrino Abdallah.
Mambrino (Grah'ms).2 27¾
Mambrino Black Hawk by Stockbridge Chief.
Columbia Chief 2 28¾
Mambrino Blitzen by Mambrino Patchen.
Blitzen Jr. 2:29¾
McLeod 2:21¾
Mambrino Boy by Mambrino Patchen.
Chicadee.............2:29
Five Points..... ... 2:30
Julian 2:30
Lizzie R............ 2:23¼
Louis T 2:30
Mambrino Archy..... 2:24¾
Merva K............. 2.27½
Rhoderick Dhu.... . 2:20
Sadie..................2:29½

Mambrino Brave by Mambrino Chief.
Rip Rap. 2 26
Mambrino Bruce by Alcalde.
Belle Wilson......... 2:24¼
Kit Curry 2 18½
Col Bruce, p 2 25
Mambrino Champion by Eureka.
Champion Jr.. ..... 2 24
Mambrino Champion by Mambrino Chief.
Molly Long . . 2 29¼
Mambrino Chief by Mambrino Paymaster.
Bay Henry......... 2:28½
Brignoli.. . . 2 29¾
Lady Thorn 2:18¼
Mambrino Star.. .. 2 28½
North Star Mambrino.2:26½
Woodford Mambrino 2.21½
Mambrino Chief (Ward's) by Mambrino Chief.
Blackstone 2:29¼
Mambrino Chief Jr. (Fisk's) by Mambrino Chief.
Mambrino Belle.... . 2:23
Mambrino General 2:25¼
Mambrino George ...2 30
Mambrino Sparkle....2:17
Silver Cloud 2 22¾
Woodchuck.......... 2 30
Peter T., p.. . .. 2:29¼
Mambrino Chief Jr. (Harris') by Mambrino Chief.
Proctor. 2 23
Mambrino Chief Jr. by McDonald Chief.
Solana Chief 2:29¼
George Washington 2 16¾
Frankie D., p.. ...... 2:24¾
McCleery, p 2:18½
Mambrino Chief Jr. (Williams') by Mambrino Patchen.
Ottumwa Maid 2:27¾
Mambrino Clay by Kentucky Clay.
Mambrino Clay Jr. . 2:25
Mambrino Clay Jr. Mambrino Clay.
Mahommet. 2 20
Mambrino Clark by Mambrino Dudley.
Arias 2:29¾
Newport. 2:26¼
Mambrino Davis by Dr. Herr.
Brinoda, p 2 15¼
Mambrino Diamond by Mambrino Patchen.
Dolly 2:25
Kate Sparks 2 19
Dr. Kelly 2 15¾
Mambrino Dick by Mambrino Time.
Billy H 2 29½
Doctor H. 2 28
Mambrino Dix.
Reginald.. . .. .. . .2 30
Mambrino Dudley by Woodford Mambrino.
Crescendo...... ....2:24
Dud Bonum......... ... 2:26
Gretna 2:22¼
Master Dudley ...2:29¼
Rinaldo 2:27¼
Rintoul. 2 24¼
Tracy. 2:26½

Mambrino Duke by Mambrino Paris.
Mambrino Maud. . 2 28½
Raven Boy.. .. .. . 2 29¾
Mambrino Duncan.
Oscar W 2 25¼
Mambrino Excelsior by Mambrino Patchen.
Thalberg . 2.20
Mambrino George.
Grey Elsie, p 2:20¼
Mambrino Gift by Mambrino Pilot.
Alfretta.. . . 2 26¼
Faro. 2:23¼
Gift Jr. 2:27½
Mambrinette. . 2.21
Mambrino Sotham. 2.26¾
Molly Talbert 2 29¼
Tecumseh 2:28
Mambrino Hambletonian by Mambrino Pilot.
Lilly Langtry 2:23¼
Parana 2.19¾
Mambrino Hambletonian by Ashland.
Stranger . . . 2.22¾
Mambrino Harold by Mambrino Russell.
Winfield, p... ... . . 2:26¼
Mambrino Hannis by Hannis.
Bran Slack 2:27¼
Mambrino Hassan by Mambrino Pilot.
Lady Hassan 2:30
Mambrino Hippy by Garrard Chief.
George W.. . .. .. 2:24½
Miss Annie, p.. ....2:24¼
Mambrino Jackson.
Monarch.. .... 2:25¼
Mambrino Jester by Highland Chief.
Dexter.. ....2:27¼
Mambrino Joe by Mambrino Patchen.
Woodard and Harbison.. .... 2.27¼
Mambrino King by Mambrino Patchen.
Amy King 2:22¼
Bozeman. 2 17
Carleton 2 28
Comanche.. ....2:24¼
Egyptienne.. .... 2:18
Elyria 2:25¼
Emerson King.... .. 2 27¼
Excellence... ......2:19½
Germaine.......... 2 20
Gimcrack............. 2 27
Heir-at-Law 2:12
Henrietta.. ... . 2:17
Iron Worker..... ... 2 29½
J. D. L.... .. .. . 2:29¾
King Patchen. 2 23½
King of Wales 2:30
King Philip 2:26¾
Lady Mac...... . .. 2 25¼
Mandame.. .... 2.29¾
Miss Olive 2.27½
Mocking Bird . . . 2 16¾
Nettie King. 2:20¼
Nightingale...........2:10½
Nutting King...... .. 2 19½
Olaf 2 21¼
Oney 2:19¼
Oscar King. 2 26½
Prince Regent 2.16½

Royal King..........2:25¼
Silver King........2:26¼
Tillie Green........2:27
Harleigh, p........2:28
Jocko, p...........2:16½
King's Protector, p..2:18¾
Moonstone, p........2:09¾
Wisdom, p...........2:27
William Wallace, p..2:22¼
Mambrino Lance by Mambrino Patchen.
Lady Alert.........2:24½
Mambrino Lexington by Lexington Chief.
Betty K............2:26¼
Mambrino Logan by Gage's Logan.
Callie S., p.......2:23¼
Minnie Barb, p.....2:26
Pearl Logan, p.....2:26¼
Mambrino Messenger (Turner's) by Mambrino Prince
Bushnell Chief......2:29¾
Mambrino Messenger by Mambrino Monarch.
Speculation........2:25
Mambrino Messenger (Herr's) by Mambrino Pilot.
Lewinski...........2:25¼
Mambrino Morgan
Nelly T............2:29¾
Mambrino Motor.
Billy Breen, p.....2:26¾
Mambrino Paris by Mambrino Patchen.
Bowman.............2:30
Mambrino Patchen by Mambrino Chief.
Banquet............2:24
Billy Marshall.....2:27¼
Decorah............2:26¾
Forest Mambrino....2:29¾
Gold Star..........2:29¾
Harry C. Midnight....2:29½
Jessie Dixon.......2:28¾
Katie Middleton....2:23
Kitty Silver.......2:27¾
Lady Stout.........2:29
London.............2:20¼
Lottie Prall.......2:28¾
Lottie Thorn.......2:23¾
Mambrino Boy.......2:26½
Mambrino Diamond...2:26
Mambrino Kate......2:24
Mistletoe..........2:30
Nymphia............2:26¼
Ogdensburg.........2:28½
Pericles...........2:30
Pretty Boy.........2:29½
Richwood...........2:27
Secure.............2:30
The Banker.........2:29½
The Jewess.........2:26
Turner.............2:28½
Mambrino Patchen (Smith's) by George M. Patchen.
Highland Stranger...2:25¼
Orient.............2:24
Mambrino Payne by John F. Payne.
Effie Payne........2:25¼
Cedar Rapids, p.....2:24
Mambrino Pilot by Mambrino Chief.
Æmulus.............2:25
David Wallace......2:28
Frank C............2:27¼
Hannis.............2:17¾

James D............2:28¼
Mambrino Gift......2:20
Mayflower..........2:27¼
Morning............2:30
William Gee........2:29½
John, p............2:29½
Mambrino Pilot Jr.
Marvel.............2:21½
Mambrino Pilot Jr. by Mambrino Pilot.
George W...........2:23½
Old Judge..........2:29¾
Mambrino Redmon by Mambrino Patchen
Pat Legg, p........2:25
Mambrino Rescue.
Orphan Alice, p....2:27¼
Willie Bee, p......2:20
Mambrino Rule.
Rustic Lady........2:30
Mambrino Russell by Woodford Mambrino.
Bourbon Russell....2:30
Col. Moss..........2:27¾
Duchess Russell....2:26½
Haldane............2:26½
Kentucky Russell...2:18½
Rustic Maid........2:27½
Stoner Boy.........2:26¼
Alley Russell, p...2:22¾
Great Heart, p.....2:13¼
Happy Russell, p...2:21½
Russell Chief, p...2:22¾
Wilkie Russell, p..2:15
Mambrino St. Lawrence by Darlbay
J. J. Douglas......2:20½
Mambrino Sample by Sam Sharpley.
Flora P............2:23¼
Mambrino Smuggler by Mambrino Patchen.
Billy Carr, p......2:27
Stella R., p.......2:17½
Willard M., p......2:14
Mambrino Star by Mambrino Chief
Cottage Girl.......2:29½
Iris...............2:29¼
Mambrino Startle by Mambrino Patchen.
Jim Dunn...........2:20¼
Mambrino Startle by Startle.
Boulanger..........2:28½
Capt. Lee..........2:25
Collinwood.........2:21¼
Earldon............2:30
Julia Jackson......2:25¾
Lord Palm..........2:29½
Mambrino Maid......2:15¾
Mambrino Startle...2:26¼
Mira Startle.......2:21¼
Sir Albert.........2:20¾
Startler...........2:25
Daisy B., p........2:18¼
Yeiser Boy, p......2:29¾
Mambrino Swigert by Swigert
Bay Henry..........2:29¼
Black Frank........2:27¼
Carrie B...........2:20¾
Grey Swigert.......2:29¼
Lady Jane..........2:17¾
Libretto...........2:30
Mambrino Temple by Pilot Temple.
Billy Boy..........2:26¼

Mambrino Templar Jr. by Mambrino Templar.
Long John..........2:28½
Mambrino Time by Mambrino Patchen
Emmett.............2:29½
Four Corners.......2:20¼
Mambrino Dick......2:24
Sorrel Kate........2:29¼
Mambrino Wagner by Mambrino Patchen.
Glendale...........2:20½
Mambrino Wilkes (Ayer's) by George Wilkes.
Alpheus............2:25
Balkan.............2:15
Bay Wilkes.........2:16¼
Clara P............2:29½
Gus Wilkes.........2:22
Hera...............2:23½
Brino Tricks, p....2:18½
Flora B., p........2:22½
Molly Allen, p.....2:20½
Mambrino Wilkes (Clark's) by George Wilkes.
Arthur Wilkes......2:19
Col. Arthur Wilkes....2:29½
Dan Wilkes.........2:24¼
Fanny Wilkes.......2:30
Homer Wilkes.......2:29½
Ira Wilkes.........2:29¾
Mischief...........2:17¾
R. M. Wilkes.......2:25¼
Thetis.............2:16¼
Union Wilkes.......2:29½
Daisy C., p........2:26¾
Myra Wilkes, p.....2:24¾
Mambrino Wilkes by Bourbon Wilkes.
Dr. Wood, p........2:29¼
Mambrino Yorick by Woodford Mambrino.
Manawa.............2:20
Mambritonian by Belmont.
Augusta............2:29¼
Belfast............2:29¼
C. O. B............2:26¼
Nankeen............2:28
Prinsonian.........2:20½
Senatress..........2:22
Tony Klock.........2:18¾
Klick Klock, p.....2:14¾
Mambrunello by Mambrino Chief.
Sadie Howe.........2:26
Tom Britton........2:26
Mammont by Almont.
Dan Mack...........2:27¾
Goldmont...........2:23½
Lewis R............2:23
Molly C............2:29¼
S. Montgomery......2:25½
Mammonteer.
Prairie Maid, p....2:30
Manchester by Fearnaught.
Paul M., p.........2:24¼
Manchester by Hetzel's Hambletonian.
Vernette...........2:23¾
Manchester Tuckahoe by Blind Tuckahoe.
Lady H.............2:27
Lady Voorhees......2:23½
Jim Crow, p........2:26
Paul M.............2:28¾
Mandarin by Administrator
Fanny S............2:29¼

Manetho by Harold.
Lizzie Harold........2:28¾
Mansfield by Messenger Duroc.
Borden.............2:29½
Dawson.............2 19¼
Foxie. 2 28½
Litchfield..........2:29¾
Remsen 2 24¼
Mansfield Medium by Happy Medium.
Fanny D.............2 28¾
Langford 2 28¼
Manville by Meander.
Anvil. 2 23¾
Mapes Horse by Rysdyk's Hambletonian.
Lady Thornton 2:26¼
Maplehurst by Allie West.
Cumberland.........2:21¾
Diamond Joe........2 18
Mapleton by New York.
Lady Mac...........2.29½
Maplewood Chief by Polonius
Joker H.............2 30
Miss McGinty, p......2:24
Marco by Morrow's Elector.
Joe 2:29¼
Marin by Quinn's Patchen.
Marin Jr 2.13
Mario Jr. by Marion.
Alice 2 29
Mark Anthony by Hamlet.
Susan B 2:29¼
Mark Field by George Wilkes
Called Back.........2:27¼
Mark Field Jr........2.29¼
Veritas..............2·16¼
Vindex 2 29¼
Mark Monroe by Victor Bismarck.
Mark W.............2:28¾
Minnie Monroe.......2:25¼
Mark Sirius by Sirius.
Minnehaha, p........2 27¼
Marksman by Thorndale
Marksman Maid 2 21¼
Misty Morning 2 21
Marksmaid, p........2 21
Marksman by Frank Forrester.
Frank Forrester......2 27½
Mark Time by Robert McGregor.
Good Time............2.18
Mark Twain by Moonstone.
Minnie May 2 29¾
Marlborough by Rysdyk's Hambletonian.
Avalon...............2 25
Judd Boy 2:20¼
Sheridan Girl.........2:29¼
Oliver C p............2:26¾
Marmaduke by Marion.
Bessie 2 26¼
Marmaluke.
Madge W. p..........2 25¼
Marmion Golddust by Golddust Jr.
Kioto 2:20¾
Marquette by Victor Bismarck
Mamie Hayward 2:29½
Marshall Chief by Kilburn's Hero.
Dr. Lewis. 2 24
Marshall Kieber by Cuyler.
Mistake 2:29½

Marshal Ney by Mambrino Pilot.
Cyclops. 2 27
Westover.............2·26¼
Marshall Ney by Stonewall Jackson.
Indian Pet...........2 28½
Martine by Triumvir.
Alice E 2 29¼
McElree 2 24¼
Elyton, p 2:22
Martin McGregor by Robert McGregor.
Harry McGregor......2 28
Maryland Volunteer.
Garrett, p...........2:26½
Marvin by Electioneer.
Bramblette.........2 24½
Masker.
Domino ....2·19½
Mar's Pointer, p.....2.27¾
Masterlode by Rysdyk's Hambletonian.
Ara 2:29¼
Beechnut. ....2·29
Belle F 2:15¼
Belle Noble 2:28
Betsy Braun..........2:21¾
Clara Belle 2 29¾
Decorator 2 22½
D. N. T 2:27¾
Edward 2:19
Fanny K.............2:30
George V ....2·20
Goldstone.............2:27¼
Hambletonian Gift....2·29
Ham Morrison 2:30
Happy Man ....2·27¼
Jenny Star 2:24¼
Lassie 2 30
Master 2.27½
Peek-a-Boo 2 27
Phillis...............2 30
Plush 2:19¼
Princess ....2·29½
Ruby 2 25¼
Sickle Hambletonian 2:29¼
Sierra La Salle 2:28
Sweetheart ....2·29¼
Phillis, p 2:17½
Matadon by Onward.
Athadon 2:27
Matchless by Prince Albert.
Palma...............2 22¾
Matterhorn by Nutwood.
Balzac Chief.........2:26¼
Jungfrau 2 28¾
Merodock............2:22¾
Mount Blanc, p......2.30
Maury Chief by Old Traveler
Billy White..........2·28½
Maxie Cobb by Happy Medium.
Maxie Cobb, Jr......2·28½
Maxie Cobb, Jr. by Maxie Cobb.
Nina Cobb 2:25
Maxim by Belmont.
Freedom 2:28½
Ida D 2 17¾
Lady Maxim ....2·26½
Mikado, p 2:13
Motto, p 2:20
Maximus by Almont.
Avelloni 2:26¼
Brown Mat 2 29¼
Aldabaron B., p 2 27¼

Bandella, p...........2 25
Tom Shirley, p.......2:20½
Maxwell by Brougham.
Marengo Chief.......2:30
May Boy by Whipple's Hambletonian.
Col. May 2:17
Vernon. 2:26¼
Bess H., p............2·21½
May Day by Henry.
May Queen 2:26
Mazeppa by Rysdyk's Hambletonian.
Black Captain........2:29¾
Mazeppa by Taggart's Abdallah
Spotted Beauty......2:29¼
Mazeppa.
Happy................2:27
Mazeppa by Winthrop Morrill.
Slippery Dick.........2:30
Meadowbrook by Cuyler.
Red Brook............2:22
Meander by Belmont.
Amender..............2:25¼
Kit Baker 2:27¼
Manville 2.26
Pamlico. 2.10
Stephanie. 2:22¼
Dapignac, p. 2:22¼
School Boy, p........2 22½
Mecca by Nutwood.
Rosewood 2:28¼
Medonius by Pilot Modium.
Madelle, p 2:18¼
Meeker Hambletonian by William M. Rysdyk.
Nelly P 2:28½
Meeker Horse.
Fearless 2:28
Melbourne King by Mambrino King.
Jubilee 2 25¼
Sea King 2:18¼
Belle, p................2 15
Helen, p 2:16½
Melrose by Victor Bismarck.
Annie C 2 27½
Ebony Job ....2·28¼
Eli......................2 26
Ella 2:28¼
Felix...................2 23¼
J. T.....................2·24½
Olivia 2:29¼
Primrose...............2.29¼
Rose Filkin............2:22
Tom Judge 2 25¼
T. T. S. 2:19½
Melville Chief by Tattler.
Clipper ....2·24¼
Memento Wilkes by Red Wilkes.
Allie B 2:30
Lone Star 2 29½
Rabb Wilkes...........2 26
Ruby Wilkes ....2·25
Memory by Mambrino Gift.
Harmonia 2 25¼
Menelaus by Rysdyk's Hambletonian.
Altona.................2:22¾
Belle S................2·25
Black Pilot............2:29
Cleora 2:18¾
Harry Pulling..........2·29¾
Maggie F..............2:27
Romeo.................2 29¼

Silver Leaf ... . 2·23
Altoona, p... . . 2 16¼
Black Hawk Mene-
laus, p 2:22¼
Menelaus Jr. by Menelaus.
Menogain, p... .. 2·15
Menlo by Nutwood.
Menlo Belle 2:30
Merchant by Belmont.
Frank. p..........2:28
Nettlewood. p ... . 2·23
Mercury by Rysdyk's Ham-
bletonian.
Chester F 2 30
Linwood 2:30
Mamie 2 28¼
Meredith by Kearsarge.
Darwinna 2:23½
Meredith by Rysdyk's Ham-
bletonian.
Nelly Mambrino 2:18¼
Meriton.
Zip M., p ... 2 26¼
Merriworth by Wedgewood
Princess M 2 26¼
Kitty Clinker, p. .2·28
Merrow Horse by Witherell
Messenger
Belle Strickland . 2:26
Merry Boy by Mambrino Boy.
Mambrino Lambert 2:29½
Messenger by Mountain
Slasher Jr.
Slasher 2:18¼
Messenger (Logan's) by State
of Maine.
Crown Prince. 2:25
Messenger Chief by Abdallah
Pilot.
Abel 2 24¼
Earncliffe 2.29
Elite 2 30
Hooka 2:30
Jake 2 22
Katherine S. 2 17¾
Manning 2:18¼
Marvel 2 28
Maud Messenger. . 2 16¼
Maumejan 2:26½
Mimic 2 21
Prette Belle .2 26¼
Quarryville Boy.. 2:26
William H.. .2·22¼
Frank E , p .2:19¼
Neddie H., p 2:17¼
Ruby Messenger, p . . 2.23
Messenger Chief.
Bessie M 2:30
Messenger Chief Jr.
J. K., p. 2:28
Messenger Clay by Karl.
Kitty B., p 2:11
Messenger Duroc by Rysdyk's
Hambletonian.
Antonio.. ... .2 25¾
Bergen 2:26¾
Charley Champlin . 2 21¾
Dame Trot 2.22
Duroc Maid 2 29¼
Elaine . . . .2·20
Elina 2:28
Elista .2:20¾
Gilroy 2 28¾
Griffen...........2:29¼
Hogarth.... ...2 26
John D.. ....2:23¼
John W............2·24¼
Lancelot 2:23

Maclure 2:30
Mansfield 2.26
Nettie D 2:30
Paul 2:23½
Praetor 2.29¼
Prospero 2 20
Star Duroc 2 25¾
Troublesome . ..2:25½
Daisy L., p 2:29¼
Lady Hill, p.... 2 22
Messenger Duroc (Wilson's)
by Messenger Duroc.
Josh Morse.. .. .2 29¼
Messenger Golddust by Gold-
dust.
Kate Keener 2:29¼
Billy Dohrman, p.....2 24¼
Messenger Hunter.
James G. Blaine. ..2.28¾
Messenger Wilkes by Red
Wilkes.
Eiffel T. Wilkes . .,2 24¼
Gene Briggs 2:19¼
Grenadier.... .2:26¼
Narcus 2 25½
Narka ....2·29
Palm 2 28¼
Mordica. p .....,2 20¾
Metacomet by Morrill.
Winthrop Morrill Jr .2:27
Michie by Young Cassius M.
Clay.
Mink 2:29¼
Michigan Boy.
A. C. K 2 29¼
Midas by Onward.
Henry C . . 2 26¼
Kiowa.............2:29¾
Misdeal.. ... .2:20½
Miss Edith. 2.19
Middletown by Rysdyk's Ham-
bletonian.
Fancy 2 24¾
Lady Blessington...2:28
Marionette....... 2 27½
Mentor.. . ...2 27
Middletown Jr 2:27¼
Mogul....... . 2·19¼
Music 2.21½
Nelly Irwin 2.25
Orange Blossom 2 26½
Orange Bud . 2 21¼
Piloton 2:30
Storm . .. 2 26¾
Susie D . .. . 2·29¼
Middletown Jr. by Middle-
town
Billy C. 2.20¼
Pilot 2 22¾
Nelly Bly 2 23½
Sylvia. 2:27¼
Billy C., p 2 29¼
Blanche, p .... .2·20½
Middlesex by Seneca Chief.
Midway 2 29¾
Mikagan by Onward.
Ross ....2·28½
Angie D., p . . . 2.11¼
Frank Agan, p ... 2 10¼
Mike by Vermont.
Barney... .... 2 25¾
Mike Logan by Jules Jurgen-
sen.
Billy F 2:28¾
Lady Underhill 2:29¼
Plumed Knight 2 26¾
Mike Logan Jr., p....2:23

Mike Snyder by Ben Snyder.
Belle Durland, p . 2 19¼
Milo by Golddust.
Bay Diamond, p 2:23½
Milo by Milwaukee.
Scotsman . . 2 27½
Milton Medium by Happy
Medium.
Palatina 2 22¼
Warwick Medium ...2 27½
Johnny Skelton .. 2 29½
Milton R by Milton Medium.
Hanford Medium, p . 2 14
Milwaukee by Rysdyk's Ham-
bletonian.
Adelaide.... ..... . 2:18
Milo 2:21
Ticonic 2:26½
Milwaukee Jr. by Milwaukee.
Mystery 2.26½
Mimic by Messenger Chief.
Kitty M , p. 2:23¾
Mink by Michie.
Pansy.. ... . 2·28¼
Mistake.
Hickory Boy, p ...2 24
Missouri Chief by Tom Ben-
ton.
Prince, p 2:23¾
Nimrod, p 2.19¾
Model.
Granville K.. ......2:30
Modoc.
Oxford Chief 2 28¼
Modoc Chief by Mountain
Chief.
Pat Quinn. ....2·25½
Mogadore by Eli Abdallah.
Maj. Lacey .. . 2 30
Mohawk.
Pomp A , p .. 2 24¾
Mohawk by Long Island Black
Hawk
Elmo 2:27
Mohawk Jr. .. . 2.25
Mohawk Jr. 2 26
Gork O., p. 2 27¼
Mohawk (Goff's) by Clark's
Mohawk Jr.
Major.. ....2:22
Mohawk (McMullen's).
Free Trader ... 2 25¾
Mohawk (Pratt's).
Lew Wallace, p . 2 28¼
Mohawk Island by Mohawk.
McCue's Mohawk . 2 29½
Mohawk Jr. (Clark's) by Mo-
hawk.
Fashion. 2 23½
Lady Clark 2.27
Yellow Dock 2 20¾
Mohawk Jr. by Clark's Mo-
hawk Jr.
Thomas H... .. . 2:30
Mohawk Jr. (Hall's) by Mo-
hawk.
Belle Hyler.........2 22¼
Belle Ogle. 2 21½
Mohawk Blondi.... 2 24¾
Mohawk Chief 2 30
Mohawk Gift.......2:21¼
Mohawk Kate. .. 2 26¾
Mohawk Chief (Grove's).
Little Jimmy, p......2:30
Mohawk Chief by Confeder-
ate Chief.
Belle of Montour... 2:29¼

Mountain Boy by Daniel Lambert.
Daisy C 2:22¼
McIntosh... ....2:27½
Bessie Braddock, p. .2:25¼
Mountain Chief by Morrill.
Haviland..............2:29½
Mt Morris by Smuggler.
Chester Morris.......2:27¼
Mount Vernon by Nutwood.
Daisy Mc, p...........2:24
Geraldine, p 2:16¾
Muggins by Elial G.
Fred R. 2 25½
Munsey by Rebel Chief
Kate Isler... ......2:22¼
Muscatine by Green's Bashaw
Eldine.. . ...2:29½
Muscovite by Nutwood.
Abel Muscovite 2:29¾
Auora............ .....2:30
Galatana 2:24½
Lion Moscow.. ...2:21¼
Music by Orion.
Red Wing, p........ 2:13½
Myron Perry by Young Columbus.
Gen. Tweed 2:26¼
Myrtleton by Red Wilkes.
Mechanicsville 2:28¼
Myrtle Boy..... ......2:25½
Myrtle Twig...........2:28½

Naaman by Harold.
Barb Wire, p.......2:24¾
Nabob by Blackwood.
Emma Balch.   2:20¾
Naham by Hambrino.
Abraham L 2:18
Nantucket by Nutwood.
Jack Offutt.. ....2:26
La Mode 2:26
Lizzie Hunter, p 2:22
Peter Piper, p 2:14¼
Narragansett by Rhode Island
Narragansett.. .....2:23½
Typhoon 2:28¼
Nathan Mills by Imperial.
Black Mack 2:24¼
Fred Mills, p. ?......2:21¾
Nate C.. p 2:24¾
Naubic by Toronto Chief.
J. H. S................2:30
Navarro by Nutwood.
Marcus 2:21
Navigator.
Pasadena Belle 2:18
Neatwood by Nutwood.
Roywood.. ....2:21¼
Neatbud, p 2:26
Ned Forrest by Dave Hill.
Jessie Hayes   .. 2:24
Ned Forrest by Joe Downing.
Edwin Forrest 2 18
Tom Rogers, p........2:29¾
Ned Hastings.
Nellie Hastings, p....2:27¾
Ned Patchen.
Allen H............ ....2:25¼
Nelly Gray 2:21¼
Ned Warfield by Foreman's Warfield.
Billy B., p 2:29
Ned B., p.. ....2:18¼
Ned Wilkes by Alcantara.
Berwick...... ......2:30
Capt. Bowman 2:28¾

Neighbor Ups by Thorndale.
Matthew W....... .. 2:30
Nelson by Young Rolfe.
Amber... ... . .2:24
Brenda... .. ..2:28¼
Conkling. 2:26¾
Damosella 2:25
Donna... ....2:27½
Haley ....2·18¾
Hilda.............. ..2:28¾
Lady Nelson 2:21½
Nelson Jr .... 2·26¼
Polly Nelson 2:30
Queen 2:19¾
Silver Street........2.19½
Slick Nelson..........2:27¼
Theresa.......... .2.25¾
Trafalgar 2:2¾
Cashier, p...........2:25½
Cylex, p.. ....2:24¼
Edmond, p... ....2:17¼
Merrill, p 2:24½
Nelson Allen, p.......2.29¼
Parker, p 2:19½
Selim, p.. ....2:19¼
Nephew by Hambrino.
Ameer................2:27
Baby Mine 2:27
Beury Mc. 2:14¼
Chantilly 2:29¼
Ecru 2:30
Elden 2:19½
Ella May..............2:28
Geneve 2:26¾
Ha Ha 2:22¼
Lord Stanley.........2:28¼
Lottie M..............2:24
Lucilla 2:28¼
Lexon 2 27¾
Newflower .. ..2...3¾
Ruler..... ....2:23
Vina Belle............2:15¼
Voucher 2:22
Barney Horn, p........2:23¾
Bracelet, p. 2.21
Nephew(Dorsey's)by Nephew
Ottinger........ .....2:11½
George N., p 2.22½
Nephew Jr. by Nephew.
Gold Medal p,. 2:14½
Nero by Winoo.ki.
Maggie H. 2:27¼
Nest Egg by Amboy.
Huxham. 2:18½
Nestor by Alden Goldsmith.
Don S 2 28¾
Nestwood 2:23¾
Netherland by Manhattan.
Nonesuch 2.30
Young Netherland. ..2:29
Nettle Keenan by George Gordon.
Brooks, p 2:15¼
Nevada by Blackbird.
Nevada .. .. .2·23
Nevins by Volunteer.
Nevins' First. 2:19
New Jersey by George M. Patchen.
Grace Bertram 2:29
New Jersey Volunteer by Standard Bearer.
Gen. Marion 2:27¼
Newman Horse by Rollins Horse.
Emperor 2:29¼
Newmont by Belmont.
Charles H. Hoyt......2:21¼

Charles H. Hoyt, p...2:15½
Newry by Lexington.
Maggie F.... .. ...2:26
New York by Rysdyk's Hambletonian.
Cad Wade 2:20
George W 2:23¼
New York Dictator .2:29¼
Novelty.. .. ..2:28¼
Reveille....'' 2:21¾
New York Dictator by New York.
Dr. Carver............2:29¼
York Wilkes, p......2.25
Niagara.
Fairmont, p 2:22¼
Niagara Champion by imp. Grand Exhibition.
Harry, p.............2:19¾
Niagara Chief by Toronto Chief.
Ben Flagler 2:26¼
Bucephalus 2:28¾
George F. Smith.... 2:28
Nick A. by Hadley's Fearnaught.
Harry R., p 2.21¼
Nick Wall.
Big Ike. 2:29¼
Nicotine by Clark Chief.
Susie Mac.. .. 2:29
Nigger Baby.
Bay Fanny 2:28
NiggerBoy by Plymouth Rock
Midnight, p 2:17¾
Nigger Doctor by King Dave.
Trouble. 2:24¾
Night Hawk by Jay Bird.
Shadow 2:28
Night Hawk by Grinnell's Champion.
Red Cross 2:26¾
Minnie Warren 2:27¼
Nihilist by Strathmore.
Maggie T., p....... 2:18¼
Nil Desperandum by, Belmont.
Dancer 2:24
De Barry 2:18¼
Desperation 2:30
James H.. ....2:28½
Matchless.. ....2:24¾
Ranger..............2:24¼
Thorn Rose 2:24¼
Top Royal.. ....2.27
Watchword 2:20
Niles.
Maggie, p...........2:28
Nimble Dan.
Joe S., p............2.20¼
Nitrogen by Robert McGregor
Electricity............2:30
Hydrogen .. .. .   2·27¾
Nobby by Garrard Chief.
Mambrino Queen. 2:26¼
Nobby.... ....2:18¾
Noble Harold by Harold.
Arline..................2:25
Nonpareil by Long Island Black Hawk.
Western New York....2:29
Nonpareil by Cassius M. Clay
Commodore Perry..2:27½
Nonpareil by Wood's Hambletonian.
Minnie D.... ....2:23½
Noonday by Wedgewood.
Thursday 2:25

Norfolk by Nutwood.
Miss Nelson..........2.12¾
Presguile.............2:29¾
Norman (Alexander's) by Morse Horse
Lula 2:15
May Queen.........2.20
Norman (Palmer's) by Alexander's Norman.
Nelly Bryant.....2:25¼
Norman (De Witt's).
Regardless, p 2:16¼
Norman Medium by Happy Medium.
Gov. Riddle.......2:23
Silver Threads, p.....2:19
Norman Temple Jr. by Norman Temple.
Frances C 2.29¼
NormanWilkes byGeo.Wilkes
West Wilkes........2:27
Norton McGregor by Robert McGregor.
Gonzales McGregor...2:16¼
Norval by Electioneer.
Countess Eve......2.29¼
Interval 2.25¼
John G. Carlisle . 2:27
Lakeside Norval.....2.15
Norhawk..........2·15½
Norvadine 2.25½
Norvalson ....2·28½
Norvin G.........2:20½
Novelett............2:29¼
Novelist 2:27
Orphina.. ....2:17¼
Villiers..........2·27¾
Voyager 2:30
Norway by Almonarch
Nornette..........2:30
Norway Knox by Phil Sheridan, Jr.
Dinah...........2·28½
Margaret Knox....2:28¼
Norwood by Rysdyk's Hambletonian.
B. L. C 2:28¼
Ella Norwood 2:22¾
Hickorywood.......2:29
Ida Norwood.......2:26½
Lakewood 2:23
Tommy Norwood...2.26½
Wild Oats.......2:16½
Will Hamilton.....2:28½
Norwood Chief by Norwood
Caesar 2:23¼
Daisy G.........2:25½
Norwood Star by Norwood.
Daconia..........2.24
Jessie Clark.......2:27¾
Zoe Hammond.......2:26¼
Nora L., p........2.29¼
NorwoodWilkes byAmbas dor
Clifford K.........2:29¼
Nix.............2:22½
Notable by Chosroes.
Nelly B., p.........2:14¾
Notary by Attorney.
Seal, p............2:08¾
Nugget by Wedgewood.
Bon Ami.......2:23¾
Carilla..........2:22¼
Gold Leaf.......2:16½
Ingot.........2:26¼
Nettle Leaf......2:23¼
Newton.......2:22
Nuggetta.......2:24¼
Nugget, Jr.......2:28

Numero.........2·27
San Malo.......2:16½
Saboya, p.........2:19½
Nuncio by Nutwood.
Irl N.........2:24¼
A K. R., p 2:22½
Nutalwood by Nutwood.
George Anthony..,2:29¼
Linewood, p........2.21
Nutbourne by Belmont.
Arnutta.........2:27¼
Cheyenne.........2:14¼
Clontarf.........2:22
Newbold.........2:27½
Nunmont 2:22¼
Nuttalite.........2.26¾
Nutbreaker by Nutwood.
Aura D......2:27¼
Hassicla.........2:27½
Barada.........2:22½
Edgar P.........2:24¾
May Breaker.......2 17½
Moses.........2:29¾
Nutmaid.........2:29¼
Nutpick.........2.25¾
Colletta, p.......2:19½
Dawson Lake, p....2:20¼
Earnest B., p......2:27½
The Princess, p.....2:19
Nutgrove by Nutwood.
Bellwood.......2 30
Christine.........2:25¾
Nuthunter by Nutwood.
Charley Moore.....2:21¾
Eastwood.......2.24¾
Dick Mason, p. ..2:14¾
Nuthurst by Nutwood.
Garland H. 2:29¾
Dan Robinson, p...2:25¼
Little Doubtful, p...2:29½
Nutland by Nutwood.
Georgia.........2.29¾
Nutman by Nugget.
Shylock, p 2:20
Nutmeg by Nutwood.
Damania.........2:22¾
Hilberry.........2.27¼
Maud V.........2:29¾
Nutant.........2:26½
Nutmont by Nutbourne.
Navarro.........2:22
Nutgold by Nutwood.
Kitty B.........2:29¼
Nutpatch by Nutwood.
Albert Darling, p. 2:21¾
Nuttingham by Nutwood.
Col. Nuttingham....2:22½
Laura Nuttingham. .2:21¾
Nutwood by Belmont.
Addie D....2:25¾
Aegon. 2:18¼
Algy.........2:19¾
Antelope..........2:23½
Æolian...........2:28¼
Atwood.........2:27¼
Bamboo.......2:29¼
Baywood.........2.27
Bessie Burton.. 2:22½
Bedah. 2:27½
Blake..........2:18¼
Blanche N 2:25¾
Bonnie Nutwood 2:29¾
Brilliantine.......2:29½
Capt. Mack.......2:29
Cedarwood.......2:28
Chancewood.......2:25
Com. Porter.......2:13
Cyrus R.........2:17¾

Daisy N.........2:26½
Dalphia D 2:29¼
Dawn.........2:18¾
El Capitan.........2:26
Elfinwood. 2 15¼
Emma Nutwood.....2:24
Enright.........2:18¼
Esmond.........2:29¼
Estelle.........2 19
Eva W.........2:25½
Felix 2:18¾
Florence R.........2.26¾
Foxwood.........2:24¼
Glen Mary.........2:25½
Glenview Belle 2:20½
Glenwood 2 29½
Gotham 2:29¾
Gracewood.........2:27½
Hagar.........2.25
Herman Nutwood....2:22½
Highwood 2:21½
Homestead. 2:30
Jeanie C.........2:22
Jim Mulvernna.....2:19¾
Lady Nutwood . 2:25¾
Lightwood 2:25¾
Lilly H 2:29
Lizzie Mac 2:24
Lockheart 2:13
Lulie C.........2:16½
Maggie E.........2:19¾
Madwood.........2:29¾
Mamie Comet.....2:24¾
Manipulator.... ....2 29¾
Manon 2 21
Matilda.........2:30
Melissa.........2 25
Miner.........2:19¾
Menlo 2.21½
Monte Vista 2:28¾
Mount Vernon.......2:15¾
Muscovite ....2 .18
Nemesis............2 28
Neponset ...'.....2·24¼
Newcomb.........2·29¾
Nina D. 2:26½
Nuncio.........2 29
Nutallee.........2 29
Nutbreaker 2:24½
Nutcoast.........2:19
Nutgall 2 29
Nuthunter 2 30
Nutland. 2:29
Nutling.........2:29¼
Nutmeg 2.16
Nutrition.........2:24¼
Nutwith.........2 29¾
Nutwood Chieftain..2 29¾
Nutwood Jr 2:29½
Nutwood Prince....2 28¾
Parkwood.........2:26½
Prince Nutwood...2:26
Red Nutwood.....2.27
Redwood.........2:27
Rockbridge.........2·29
Roloson.........2:30
Ross S.........2:19¾
Rowood 2:29¼
Russia 2:29½
Ruth Nutwood.....2 24¾
Sagasta 2:29½
Sally Graham.....2 29¾
Shadeland Bellwood.2:25¾
Silena F.........2:20
Sol 2:30
Sulfonal.........2:16¾
Sylvan 2:23¾
Teakwood.........2:30

Tom Scott 2:26
Trousseau 2:28½
Wilkeswood 2:23¼
Woodbird 2:27
Woodbrino 2:25½
Wood Boy 2:25
Woodline 2:19
Woodnut 2:16½
Wormwood 2:25
Acmon, p 2:29½
Belmont Boy, p. 2:15
Birchwood, p 2:15
Foxglove, p 2:24½
Glenwood, p 2:13¾
Harry T., p 2:25¼
Irma, p 2:18½
Jaywood, p 2:29¼
Lida W., p 2:18¾
Manager, p 2:06¾
Matterhorn, p 2:16¼
Mecca, p 2:19¾
Nutcoal, p 2:24
Nuthurst, p. 2:12
Nutpan, p 2:19¾
Nutpine, p 2:15¼
Nutrose, p 2:22
Nutwood Wilkes, p 2:25¼
Reserve Fund, p 2:26
Stockwell, p 2:21¼
Strongwood, p 2:16¾
Waif, p 2:27¼
Wilkes Nutwood, p 2:24¾

O. A. C. by Knickerbocker.
Highland Girl 2:29½
Oak Hill by Rysdyk's Hambletonian.
Nickle 2:21
Oakhill by Woodford Mambrino.
Charley K. 2:29¾
Oberlin by Harold,
Dodgeville 2:14¼
Marie B. 2:30
Obediah 2:25
Summit 2:29¾
Oberon by Messenger Duroc.
Nelly 2:23¼
Obstacle by Onward.
Gov. Hogg 2:29¼
Oceana Chief by Aldrich Colt.
Maggie Knox 2:24¼
Oceana Prince, p 2:25
Octibbeha by Jeff Davis.
Echo Chief 2:21¼
Odd Fellow by Echo.
Danger 2:26¼
Ricetta 2:22½
Odd Ringham by King Herod.
Capt. Herod 2:25¾
Odessa by Onward.
Ella G. p 2:23¾
Odin Bell by Samson.
Sadie Bell 2:24
O. F. C. by Onward.
Fred Nelson 2:24½
Ohio by Hotspur
Jeff Smith 2:27¼
Jeff Smith, p 2:29¾
Ohio Knickerbocker by Knickerbocker.
Quaker Boy 2:24
Zenobia 2:29¼
Nicholas, p. 2:19¼
Old Charley.
Charles H. 2:21½
Old Joe.
Desdemona 2:27
Old Nig.
German Boy 2:28¼
Old Rocket.
Rocket, p 2:28½
Ole Bull by Pacing Pilot.
Chicago 2:24¾
Ole Bull by Antar.
Solo, p. 2:29¼
Ole Bull Jr. Ole Bull.
Steve Maxwell 2:21½
Olmedo Wilkes by Onward.
Cash 2:26¼
Fancy Bess 2:27¼
Flora Wilkes 2:23¼
Olney Wilkes 2:25¼
Tennyson 2:27¼
Mercurius, p 2:22¼
Play Fair, p 2:24½
Olympus by Almont.
McKusick 2:26¾
Rose L 2:27¼
School Marm 2:20
Vishmont 2:30
Onawa by Goodwin Hambletonian.
Beulah 2:26
Daisy W. 2:25¼
Flossie M 2:29¼
Onawa Jr 2:30
Owoissa 2:29¼
Otto, p 2:23¼
Oneco by Altamont.
Delcho 2:23¼
Oneida.
Margaret M p. 2:25½
Oneida Chief by Kentucky Chief.
Maud F 2:30
Onmore by Onward.
Crete 2:29¾
Onslaught.
On Set 2:26¾
Onslaught by Onward.
Al Q. Chase 2:24¾
Big Fox 2:22½
Black Hal. 2:29¼
Clara Wilkes 2:26½
Eilers 2:29¼
Lady Washington 2:25¼
Rinaldo, p 2:14¼
Onward by George Wilkes.
Acolyte 2:21
Action 2:28
Advance 2:22½
Alcolyte 2:27¼
Allandorf 2:19½
Anderson Wilkes 2:22¼
Aparka 2:22
Artisan 2:18½
Ballast 2:29¼
Beuzetta 2:12¾
Boaz 2:17½
Braxton 2:30
Bohemian 2:22½
Catherine Leyburn 2:16¼
Carthage 2:29¾
Charter 2:24
Christabel 2:29¾
Church Belle 2:27½
Circuit 2:27
Clara Wilkes 2:17
Counsellor 2:21¼
Count Folsio 2:26¾
Cut Glass 2:17
Daphne 2:25
Dessie Wingate 2:28
Elkhorn 2:28¾
El Mahdi 2:25½
Emulation 2:21
Energy 2:24¼
Eros 2:30
Gazette 2:23¾
Gen. Bartholomew 2:27½
Glycera 2:20¾
Grit 2:29¾
Henry Bruce 2:26½
Helen Leyburn 2:14
Holland 2:29¼
Houri 2:17
Ideal 2:29¼
Inglewood 2:24
Irma H 2:29¼
Keywood 2:21
Lena Miller 2:26¼
Linnetta 2:29¼
Lulu Wilkes 2:26½
Magic Wilkes 2:29¼
March Onward 2:28½
May Morgan 2:19½
Mikagan 2:19¾
Motor 2:29½
Nelly Mason 2:14
Norther 2:15¼
Oasis 2:29½
Oima 2:25¼
Old Crow 2:22
Olmedo Wilkes 2:26¼
Onslaught 2:28½
On Time 2:29¾
Onward Boy 2:30
Onward Jr 2:29½
Orianna 2:17¾
Ouray 2:28¾
Prelude 2:28¼
Proth 2:29½
Rapid Transit 2:18½
Rex Americus 2:11¼
Rutledge 2:27¼
Shadeland Baron 2:27¾
Shadeland Onward 2:18½
Southward 2:28½
Success 2:26¾
Susette 2:26½
Toinette 2:30
Token 2:14½
Ursula 2:28½
Victoria Wilkes 2:19½
Westward 2:29¼
Wheatland Onward 2:16¼
Wilkesward 2:18½
Valse 2:30
Zuletta 2:23½
Andy Wilkes, p 2:18½
Attraction, p 2:28¼
Bud Onward 2:21¼
Carrie Onward 2:18¾
Colbert, p 2:12¼
Col. Thornton 2:11
Dumas 2:18¾
Empress Wilkes, p 2:25¾
Evonward, p 2:28½
Gazette, p 2:09¾
Hugh Gay, p 2:22
Interest, p 2:18
Judge Hines, p 2:20
Leeward Wilkes, p 2:19¼
Macklin, p 2:28½
Odella, p 2:24½
Rose Leyburn, p 2:15¼
Tangent, p 2:18½
Tom Exum, p 2:19¼
Onward King by Onward.
Lord Tennyson, p 2:24¼
Opal by Swigert.
Moxie 2:29¼
Agate, p 2:21

You Tell.... 2:19¾
Orange Blossom by Middletown.
Garrison.... 2:25½
Hunter Rye.... 2:26¾
Orange Bloom.... 2:25¾
Orange Boy.... 2:18¾
Orange Chief.... 2:16¾
Orange Leaf.... 2:29¼
Sir Blossom.... 2:29¾
Prince Orange, p.... 2:25
Orange County by Rysdyk's Hambletonian.
Lem.... 2:27½
Lizzie H.... 2:28½
W. M. Mallory.... 2:30
Welter.... 2:20¾
Orange Duroc by Messenger Duroc.
Bob M.... 2:26¼
Oregon Pathfinder by Morrill.
Blaine.... 2:26¾
Young Rattler.... 2:30
Orient.
Boston.... 2:29½
Oriole by De Graff's Alexander
Tulu.... 2:24¾
Orion by Rysdyk's Hambletonian.
Rex.... 2:22¾
Verlinda B.... 2:20
Oran C., p.... 2:22¾
Orion by Guiding Star.
Bonnie B., p.... 2:19¾
Orphan Boy by Potter Clay.
Black Hawk.... 2:20¼
Orpheus by Strader's Cassius M. Clay Jr.
Alvin.... 2:11
Orra Drew.
Joe B., p.... 2:29½
Orton by Princeps.
Livia, p.... 2:22¾
Oscar by Masterlode.
Oscar Jr.... 2:28¼
Osceola by Drennon.
W. K. Thomas.... 2:26
Oshkosh by Milwaukee.
Cato Boy.... 2:26½
J. C.... 2:29¼
Winnebago.... 2:24¼
Oshkosh Boy.
Little Johnnie, p.... 2:19½
Vinnie, p.... 2:23¼
Osier Horse.
Lee M.... 2:28¾
Osman by Strader's Cassius M. Clay.
Oreide.... 2:26¼
Longitude, p.... 2:18
Osric by Middletown.
Miss Hoke.... 2:29¾
Ossian by Tyrant.
Annie Ossian.... 2:25
Ossidine by Hambrino.
Osman.... 2:27
Otego Chief by Victor.
Effie B.... 2:27
Hector.... 2:23
Othello by Mambrino Pilot.
Agnes M.... 2:24¼
Charles F. Iseminger. 2:19¾
Maud.... 2:29½
Ottawa Chief by Byron.
Harrison.... 2:18¼
Wayside.... 2:21¼
Wilber Chief.... 2:21
Otta Nelly, p.... 2:28
Harrison, p.... 2:19½
Outcross by Jeb Stuart.
Odin.... 2:29¼
Overland by Stevens' Bald Chief.
Ned.... 2:29¼
Overseer by Supervisor.
Blue Bell.... 2:30
Overstreet Wilkes by George Wilkes.
Salute.... 2:26¼
Joy Wilkes, p.... 2:21½
Oxford Boy by Backman's Idol.
Maby.... 2:16¼
Oxford Boy.
Molly S., p.... 2:27¼
Oxford Boy by Hampton.
Myrtle.... 2:30
Oxmoor by Princeps.
Cheltenham.... 2:28
Octavius.... 2:26¼
Orpheus.... 2:30
Hermod, p.... 2:27¼
Ozark by Swigert.
Ben K.... 2:27¾
John M. p.... 2:25

Pacing Abdallah by Alexander's Abdallah.
Bay Mate.... 2:30
W. B. H.... 2:28¼
Abbie H. p.... 2:26½
Doctor G. p.... 2:25¼
Pacing Almont by Cardinal
Glidemont, p.... 2:21½
Pacing Pilot.
Kate Preston.... 2:27¼
Pactolus by Patronage.
Packet.... 2:27
Paddy Magee.
Kitty L.... 2:27¼
Paganni.
Blossom.... 2:26¼
Paladine.
Morgan Wheeler.... 2:29¼
Palmer Bogus by Ballard's Bogus.
Damon.... 2:23¾
George Palmer.... 2:19¼
Palmer Horse.
Walter D.... 2:25
Palmer Knox.
Jim Knox, p.... 2:29¾
Palmetto by Red Wilkes.
Ali.... 2:29¾
Pat Murphy, p.... 2:20
Palatka by Nutwood.
Delta, p.... 2:21¼
Palo Alto by Electioneer.
Avena.... 2:19½
Fillmore.... 2:21¾
Palatine.... 2:18
Rio Alto.... 2:16½
Palo Alto by Barkis
Alma Alto.... 2:30
Pamlico by Meander.
Little Tobe.... 2:19¾
Maggie Campbell.... 2:25½
Pan by Pancoast.
Mattie G.... 2:22½
Lucy Pan, p.... 2:17
Pansy L. p.... 2:23½
Panama by Jay Gould.
Panama Maid, p.... 2:20
Can Clare by Pancoast.
Pendelum.... 2:30
Pancoast by Woodford Mambrino.
Aquarius.... 2:26
Arpansa.... 2:30
Bluecoast.... 2:29¼
Breadwinner.... 2:29¾
Cuylercoast.... 2:16½
Garnet.... 2:13½
Issaquena.... 2:21¼
Lucy Pancoast.... 2:29
Nita Pancoast.... 2:24¼
Pall Mall.... 2:22¼
Pan.... 2:28½
Panclare.... 2:23¼
Pangold.... 2:24½
Patenter.... 2:27¼
Patron.... 2:14
Pointer.... 2:26¾
Ponce de Leon.... 2:13
Prodigal.... 2:16
Arpansa, p.... 2:23¼
Dodd Peet, p.... 2:18
Proctor, p.... 2:17
Pronto, p.... 2:24
Pandect by Pancoast.
Paudetta.... 2:29¾
Panic by Ethan Allen.
Barney Allen.... 2:26½
Butterscotch.... 2:20
Twinebinder.... 2:29¼
Wanetah.... 2:18¾
Panic by McGregor's Warrior.
Empress.... 2:30
Pappalee by Pocohontas Boy.
Maggie's Last.... 2:29¼
Paragon by Andrew Jackson.
Frank Munson.... 2:25
Paragon by Womack's Messenger.
Gussie T.... 2:26½
Sunrise, p.... 2:27¼
Paragon by Bailey's Paragon.
Belle of Fitchburg.... 2:30
Paramount by Swigert.
Baby Mine.... 2:22
Col. P.... 2:24¼
Jay See Bee.... 2:28½
Lurline.... 2:17¼
Parisian by Happy Medium.
Yellow Yam.... 2:30
Paris by Mohican.
Dixie Van, p.... 2:24¾
Paris Medium by Happy Medium.
Prince Medium.... 2:29½
Parkville by Electioneer.
Sub Rosa, p.... 2:23¾
Parmenus by Woodford Mambrino.
Daisy D.... 2:30
Parsons Horse by Ball Horse.
Lady Williams.... 2:28½
Pasacas by Almont.
Agnes.... 2:29½
Cenateur.... 2:21¾
Eva S.... 2:30
Hyacinthe.... 2:20½
Huron Boy.... 2:16¼
Lucille.... 2:29¼
May Mitchell.... 2:22¼
Nestor.... 2:26¼
Tillie S.... 2:27½
White Oak.... 2:24¼
Greenfield Maid, p.... 2:20¼

Lady Belle, p 2:28¾
Passmont, p.......... 2:28¼
Woodmont, p.......... 2:22¾
Pascarel by Almont.
Harry P............ 2.25¼
Modesty.............. 2 30
Pascolette.
Pascal. 2:27½
Pasha by Sultan.
Moro.................. 2.25
Pat.
Jack the Ripper, p.. 2:26¼
Patchen (Thibbett's) by Patchen Boy.
Screwdriver 2:24¼
Patchen (Quinn's) by George M. Patchen Jr.
Marin............... 2:22½
Patchen (Marshall's).
John L................ 2:29¼
Patchen by Mambrino Patchen.
A. H. F................ 2:26
Patchen (Monahan's).
Mabel F.............. 2:29¾
Patchen (Osgood's) by Pat McCrea.
Nightingale............ 2 10½
Patchen (Goodhue's).
Grey Ned.............. 2 25
Patchen (Dean's) by Mambrino Patchen.
Surpass, p.......... 2 21¼
Patchen.
Little Maud. 2:26½
Patchen (King's) by Young Red Rover.
Patchen 2 18¾
Patchen Chief, Jr. by Chas. E. Loew.
Revenge............... 2:24¼
Patchen Mambrino by Mambrino Patchen.
Walter E............ 2:10
Patchen Vernon by George M. Patchen, Jr.
Allan Roy..... ...... 2:17½
Patchen Volunteer by Godfrey Patchen.
Annie P.............. 2:25¾
Nettie D., p........... 2:24¾
Patchen Wilkes by George Wilkes.
Corna................. 2 26¼
Favora............ 2.12½
Henrico...... .... 2.15
Jaco.................. 2 29
Juliana 2:30
Lauretta............ 2:30
Lissa................. 2 16¾
Liva.......... ...... 2:25½
Patchen Wilkes Maid 2:22½
Westbrook.. ...... 2:23
Blackie, p.............. 2:20
Divan, p............. 2:15
Joe Patchen, p 2:04
Lauretta, p........... 2:24¼
Mary West, p......... 2:21½
Monita, p............ 2:19¼
Pathfinder (Buell's) by Benedict's Pathfinder.
Addie Pathfinder....... 2:25
Pathfinder, Jr 2:27¾
Western Pathfinder... 2:28
Pathfinder (Hayner's) by Buell's Pathfinder.
Richard H 2 30

Pathfinder, Jr. by Buell's Pathfinder.
Escalanti 2:29½
Patoka by Despatch.
Patoka Boy 2.30
Patrick Henry by Vermont Black Hawk.
Chester................ 2 28¼
Maggie M 2:27½
Patron by Pancoast.
Helen K............... 2 22½
Luzelle 2:16¼
Marie D............... 2 25¾
Nancy W............... 2:26¼
Parole................ .2 16
Patroon............... 2.23½
Patroness.. .... 2:27¼
Peeler.................. 2:27
Stamina 2:26½
Hyannis, p........... 2:11¼
Phylie, p 2:19¼
Patronage by Pancoast.
Alix..................... 2:03¾
Pactolus.... .... 2:12¾
Patroness 2:26½
Pearwood........ ...... 2:25
Pontoon 2:30
Pat Silver by Ben Patchen.
Flora Silver, p....... 2:25
Patterson Medium by Happy Medium.
Dot 2 28¼
Paul Jones by Gossip Jones.
Annie Collins... ... .2:23½
Paul Jones, Jr. by Bennett's Paul Jones.
Billy R., p 2:27¼
Jersey Boy, p 2 22¼
Perine, p............... 2:24¼
Peacemaker by Rysdyk's Hambletonian.
Alroy........ .... 2:22¼
Kitty Frazier... .... 2:21¼
Lady Moore 2.25
Midnight........ .... .2:18¼
Frank Burgess, p.... 2:20½
Nodine, p 2:19¾
Peacock by Hamlin's Almont, Jr.
Hartford............ 2:30
Peacock by Whipple's Hambletonian.
Sensation 2:22
White Cap, p...... .... 2.15¼
Peacock.
Fox 2:30
Peacock.
Tip O' Tip, p 2:12¼
Pearsall by Jupiter.
Capadura........ 2:30
Charley Hood......... 2:29½
David Jones 2.17¼
W. T. Allen 2 29
Peavine by Rattler.
Lucy Fleming. 2 24¼
Nettie Ward 2:29½
Peddlar by Electioneer.
Elspeth, p............ 2 27¼
Pedo by Wagner Bashaw.
Maud S. M 2:22
Pegasus by Lexington Golddust.
Black Diamond.... .2:19½
Pegasus by Harold.
Happy Tom, p....... 2:23½
Pelham Tartar by Toronto Chief.
Namouna.. .... 2:28¼

Pelletier by Lord Russell.
Armenian. 2:27¼
Harry T................ 2:28¾
King Goldmar 2:25¾
Secure................. 2:29¼
Billy Pierce, p......... 2:22¾
Lenatier, p........... 2:16¼
Valid, p.............. 2:17½
Pennant by Abe Downing.
Fair Rosamund....... 2:30
Nerissa.............. .2:21¾
Umbria 2:25¼
Pennypack by Mambrino Pilot.
Blossom 2:20
Nora Lee.............. 2:29¼
Star.............. .... 2:30
Penrose by Onward.
Cecie Lewis 2:30
Tirzah............... . 2:26
Albert E., p........ 2:10¾
Arbor Wilkes, p....... 2:18½
Ring Rose, p........ 2:14¾
Tonsorial, p.......... 2:23¾
Weber Wilkes.. ...... 2:13¼
Zelpha Burns.......... 2.15¼
Peoria by Arnold.
Dick Dimple.. .... 2:30
Smith, p.............. 2:13¼
Pepper by Harold.
Belle Pepper......... 2:28¾
Pequa Prince.
Pequa Princess 2:27½
Pequawket by Gideon.
Sadie S............... 2:28½
Stella Blake. 2:25¼
Sweetness 2:26½
Perduro by Durango.
Clayton... .... 2:20½
Perduro K........... 2.19¼
Joe Nelson, p 2:17¼
Perkins Morrill by Young Morrill.
Glide.................. 2:24
Pero by Backman's Idol.
Multiform........... .2:28
Robert S............. 2:28
Pete (White's).
The Colonel......... 2:26¼
Peter by Rysdyk's Hambletonian.
Iola.................... 2:29¼
Peter Everett.
Sleepy Dave, p 2:28¼
Peter Blair.
Dexter............... 2:25
Peter G. by Wood's Hambletonian.
Walker H..... ...... 2:26¾
Peter Jefferson by Thomas Jefferson.
Nelly C................ 2:27½
Peter Pinder by Return.
Lady Passmore...... 2:25½
Peter Story by Rysdyk's Hambletonian.
Story Teller........... 2:27¾
Westchester Girl.... .2:26¼
Petoskey by George Wilkes.
Jadie Allen............ 2:17½
Nelly O'Neill.. ...... 2:22½
Prohibition.......... 2:27¼
Sylvan................ 2:28½
Allie Wilkes, p....... 2:18¼
Alphonso Wilkes, p.. 2:25
Alta Wilkes, p....... 2:28¼
Dora Martin, p..... 2:19¼
Jewell, p........... 2:10¼

Kingtoska, p... .2 17
Lady Long, p ... 2:20¼
Lennie Striker, p ... 2:20
Long Wilkes, p ... 2 23
Mary Lou, p ... 2 19½
Tip Top, p ... 2 19
Phallamont by Phallas.
Dan Phallamont ... 2·24½
Esperanza ... 2.23¾
Harry Phallamont ... 2:30
Kate Phallamont ... 2:17¼
Kitty Clyde ... 2 28¾
Luna ... 2 21¾
May Belle ... 2.29½
Massasoit ... 2.25¾
Phallamiss ... 2:29½
Phallamont Boy ... 2:18
Phallamont Chief ... 2 30
Phallamont Girl ... 2 27¾
Phallamont Sprague 2.27¼
Phallamont Swigert. 2:28
Phallene ... 2 30
Therese Phallamont 2 29¾
Virginius ... 2.19¾
Phallas by Dictator.
Bonnie Phallas ... 2 29
Gov. Rusk ... 2 27¾
Gus Voltz ... 2:29¾
Hattie K ... 2 24¾
Hellas ... 2 24½
Jenny K ... 2:15¼
Merlin ... 2:27¼
Mystery ... 2:21¼
Pacolet ... 2 29¾
Patriot ... 2.24
Puzzle ... 2 30
Ripplet ... 2:29¼
Trotwood ... 2:27½
Pharos, p ... 2 21½
Phantom by Mambrino Paris.
Frank M. ... 2:27
Pharaoh (Pepper's).
Maud P., p ... 2:15¼
White Billy, p ... 2:27
Pharon by Pharos.
Daisy, p ... 2:27¼
Pharos by Phallas.
Fred Douglass, p ... 2.17¼
Pat Heron, p ... 2·17¾
Pharon, p ... 2:16¾
Phil by Arlington Tuckahoe.
Spider, p ... 2·25
Phil Fortune by Fortune Boy.
Flora S ... 2:27¼
Clara H., p ... 2:24¾
Phil Sheridan by Young Columbus.
Adelaide ... 2·19¾
Bessie Sheridan ... 2 23½
Commonwealth ... 2:22
Faustina ... 2.28¼
Hiram Woodruff ... 2 25
H. W. Beecher ... 2:28¼
Julia C ... 2:23¾
Phil Sheridan Jr ... 2:28½
Phyllis ... 2 15½
Tom Malloy ... 2 30
Valley Chief ... 2:25
Phil Sheridan (Thurlew's) by Gen. Knox.
Fanny M. ... 2 29¾
Phil Sheridan Jr. by Thurlew's Phil Sheridan.
Mattie B ... 2:27¾
Norway Knox ... 2·29¼
Phil Sheridan Jr. by Phil Sheridan.
Fleetwood ... 2:27¼

Irish Pullet ... 2:28
Phil Mack ... 2:29¾
Phil Sheridan Jr. by Stockholm.
Nettie D ... 2 25¾
Commonwealth, p ... 2 24¾
Daisy, p ... 2 23½
Philosopher.
Major Brown ... 2.28
Phœnix by Stony Ford.
Kate C. ... 2.24
Phurah by St. Gothard.
Cinch, p ... 2·26
Pickering by Rysdyk's Hambletonian.
Lonsbury ... 2 28¾
Louis P ... 2:21¾
Phillis ... 2 25¾
Phillios, p ... 2·27½
Picco by Parmenus.
Griever ... 2:23¾
Lady Picco, p ... 2 30
Picket by Aberdeen.
Helen R ... 2:27¼
Molly G ... 2.20¾
Nelly S ... 2:21¾
Picket ... 2:16½
Verona ... 2:21½
Woodlawn ... 2:22½
Nelly S., p ... 2·16¾
Pickpocket by Pequawket.
Mamie W ... 2:27½
Pickpania ... 2:14¾
Margaret M ... 2 19
Piedmont by Almont.
Carlisle ... 2:22¼
Esparto Rex ... 2.29¾
Highmont ... 2:29¼
Hyperion ... 2:21¾
Ira ... 2:24½
King Piedmont ... 2.30
Limonero ... 2:15¾
Lorita ... 2 22¾
Marion ... 2:26¾
Marston C ... 2:19¾
Pequot ... 2 26
Sport ... 2 22¾
Stanford ... 2.26½
Wanda ... 2 22½
Wavelet ... 2 28
Wild Bee ... 2:29
Wildmont ... 2:27¼
Charley C., p ... 2 18¾
Pilot by Pilot Medium.
Daisy Norwood, p ... 2:23¼
Pilot (Heinsohn's).
Roanoke ... 2:26
Pilot (Miner's).
Miss Maybee ... 2:29¼
Pilot Jr. by Canadian Pilot.
Dixie ... 2 30
Gen. Sherman ... 2:28¾
John Morgan ... 2:24
Pilot ... 2:28¾
Pilot Temple ... 2 24½
Queen of the West ... 2 26¼
Tackey ... 2:26
Tattler ... 2.26
Pilot Almont by Bostick's Almont Jr.
Duchess ... 2 30
I. S. French ... 2:12¾
Gipsy Girl, p ... 2:15
Mattie Graham, p ... 2:21
Pilot Chief by Bayard.
Mugwump, p ... 2:20½
Pilot Champion by Argonaut
Alpha ... 2.25¾

Charley R., p ... 2:25¾
Harry Hoyer, p ... 2:28
Pilot Duroc by Pilot Jr.
Big John ... 2 24¾
Kellar Thomas ... 2:12¾
Pilot W ... 2 24¾
Shiloh, p ... 2 20½
Pilot Duroc Jr. by Pilot Duroc
Daisy Holmes, p ... 2 28½
Pilot Gift
Mamie Gift, p ... 2 29¾
Pilot Knox by Black Pilot.
Pilot Bird, p ... 2:22¾
Piloteer by Bayard.
Prize ... 2·22¼
Pilot Mambrino by Pilot Jr.
John Henry ... 2.26½
Juror ... 2·24¾
N. T. H ... 2.17½
Wee Wee ... 2:23
Pilot Medium by Happy Medium.
Alphington ... 2:16½
B. B. P ... 2 13½
Belle Medium ... 2 18½
Berwick Boy ... 2:24½
Bohemian ... 2:24½
Buckshot ... 2 20¼
Calhoun ... 2 24¾
Chancert ... 2:29¼
Cherokee ... 2.29½
Clarence ... 2.24½
Col. Dickey ... 2 16¾
Delevan ... 2:25¼
Florinda ... 2:29¼
Galatea ... 2·25¾
Georgie ... 2:28¾
Girflue ... 2:22¼
Gognac ... 2.27
Happy Pilot ... 2.22¼
Helmsman ... 2·28¾
Jack ... 2:11½
Knight ... 2.29¼
Lady Belle ... 2 14¾
Lady Bullion ... 2 16¾
Lottie Williams ... 2:27
Max ... 2:20¼
McLane ... 2 28¾
Medio ... 2:14½
Medonias ... 2:30
Minerva ... 2 18
Minnie Brown ... 2 29¼
Overholt ... 2:19
Pabst ... 2.21
Piletta ... 2:14¼
Pilot (Lee's) ... 2:12½
Pilot H ... 2:29½
Pilot Middleton ... 2·26½
Piloteen ... 2:28½
Pilot W ... 2:24
Quickstep ... 2 27¾
Racine ... 2:14
Star Medium ... 2:26¼
Stewart ... 2 19½
S. W. Bennett ... 2:19½
Tentabit ... 2:29¾
Tyrolean ... 2 20½
Vestibula ... 2 25
Vesta Medium ... 2:29¼
Wapokisko ... 2·26
Will Carleton ... 2 25¼
Allison, p ... 2:24½
Michigan Mattie, p 2 26¾
Molly Slimmer, p ... 2 23½
Valley, p ... 2:19¾
Victor, p ... 2:23¼

Pilotown by Middletown.
Max T. 2:29½
Pilot Wilkes by George Wilkes.
Clara Wilkes 2:29¼
Jessie Wilkes 2:28½
Jim Riddle 2:25¼
Ramona 2:26¼
Tavernier 2:26½
Blinky Morgan, p. 2:26¾
Lady M., p 2:20¼
Rock Wilkes, p 2:20¼
Pineapple by George Wilkes.
Lady Thistle 2:27¼
Pioneer Clay by Pioneer.
Frontier 2:29¾
Pistachio by Belmont.
Sarah C 2:22¼
Guiado 2:30
P. J. Purcell by Squire Talmage.
C. H. Purcell 2:19¼
Planet.
Sarah B 2:30
Planter by Pancoast.
Pandora 2:27
Pauline 2:29¾
Plato by Gen. Knox.
Golden Boy, p 2:13¾
Plato Jr. by Plato.
Eddie B 2:29¾
Platte by Gustavus.
Emma J 2:27¾
Billy L 2:18¾
Platte Allen.
Lydie Allen, p 2:30
Play Boy by Hamlin's Almont Jr.
Playful 2:26¾
Plow Boy by Long Island Black Hawk.
Bashaw Maid 2:30
Plow Boy by Excelsior.
Dan Bryant 2:24
Plumas by Rattler.
Ashley 2:25½
Wallace G 2:23¼
Plumstone by Harry Plummer.
B G 2:24½
Panstone 2:19½
Pluto by Wedgewood.
Clarence 2:30
Kluto 2:28¾
Leo 2:22½
Poco 2:29½
Plutrusse 2:30
Blue Wing, p 2:27
Plutowood, p 2:29¾
Plymouth by Mambrino Patchen.
Erminie 2:13¼
Pocahontas Abdallah by Pocahontas Boy.
Mabel Flood, p 2:19
Nelly Mayo, p 2:28
Pocahontas Boy by Tom Rolfe.
Highland Maid 2:29¼
Highland Mary 2:26
King Charles 2:29½
Pocahontas Prince 2:20½
Polka Dot 2:28
Twilight 2:28½
Al Donis, p 2:28
American Boy, p 2:26½
Butcher Boy, p 2:26¼
Clayhontas, p 2:11¼
Candidate, p 2:29¾
Daisy V, p 2:23¼
Gurgle, p 2:20
Harry Hontas, p 2:24¼
Legal Hontas, p 2:24
Nelly B. p 2:21
Pocahontas Sam, p 2:27¾
Pocahonsas Prince, p 2:19¼
Princess, p 2:19¼
Raven Boy, p 2:15¾
Sancho, p 2:20
Pocohontas Chief.
Tommy R. p 2:20
Pocohontas Boy Jr. by Pocohontas Boy.
Sleepy Frank, p 2:24¼
Pocohontas Sam by Pocohontas Boy.
Billy E. p 2:29½
Nels Randall, p 2:20¾
Pixley Boy, p 2:12
Poca Eagle, p 2:21½
Royal Jim, p 2:26½
Touch-Me-Not, p 2:13¼
Zigler, p 2:13¼
Poco Tempo by Happy Medium
Queen Tempo 2:28¼
Polonius by Rysdyk's Hambletonian.
Bob Pinkerton 2:30
Button 2:26
Furniture Boy 2:22½
Fred 2:28
Horton 2:25¾
On Time 2:29
Philosee 2:22¼
Reality 2:20¼
Van Cott, p 2:20¼
Pomeroy.
Pearl, p 2:19¾
Pompadour by Princeps.
Charley H 2:22¼
Pompey Smash by Cuyler.
Sam B 2:26¾
Ponce de Leon by Pancoast.
Larry C 2:29½
Periwinkle 2:28¾
Pontiac by Happy Medium.
Molly Green 2:26¼
Pony Frank by Frank.
Black Frank, p 2:30
Porter Stanton by Gen Stanton.
Senator 2:26¼
Portion by Planet.
Minnesota 2:27¾
Portland Pilot by Mambrino Pilot
Winthrop Pilot 2:27
Port Leonard by Ben Patchen.
Annie D 2:29½
Dick Roach 2:24¼
Minnie P 2:29½
Poscora Hayward by Billy Hayward.
Johnny Hayward 2:26
Post Boy.
Fanny Otis 2:28¾
Post Boy by Magic.
Clemmie G. II 2:18½
Luby 2:20
Puella 2:29
Post Boy Frank by Post Boy.
Neome 2:24
Potter Hambletonian by Lysander.
Little Harry 2:29¼
Potter Horse.
Brother Jonathan 2:24
Potter Horse (Young) by Potter Horse.
Falmouth Boy 2:29½
Prætor by Messenger Duroc.
Charley Green 2:19¼
Prairie King by Chester Chief.
Garnishee 2:22¼
King Chester 2:19¾
Prairie Star by Johnny Hawkins.
Astrione 2:30
Laura B 2:27½
Reddy 2:29¾
Tiny Rogers 2:30
Premier by Daniel Lambert
Blondin 2:28¾
Prescott by Harold.
Haroldson 2:25¾
President Garfield by Masterlode.
Star Lily 2:20
President Sprague by George Sprague.
Granger, p 2:18¼
President Wilkes by Ashland Wilkes.
P. J., p 2:23¾
Pretender by Dictator.
Benoni 2:22¼
Blue Dick 2:30
Dick Richmond 2:27½
Eula G 2:24
Ferguson Wilkes 2:26
Frankfort 2:27¾
Lindie 2:20¼
Reality 2:26
Ruby Macklin 2:22¼
Westfall 2:29¼
George Hayes, p 2:22¾
Hermitage, p 2:19
Pretension, p 2:24½
Red Rover, p 2:21
Priam by Whipple's Hambletonian.
Frank M 2:17¼
Honesty 2:25¾
Harry M., p 2:22¼
Primmont by Belmont.
Prescott 2:27
Prior 2:29½
Primo by Hambletonian Wilkes.
Prime 2:21¼
Primus by Marshall Chief.
Ewing 2:21¼
Magdallah 2:23½
Tump Winston 2:24½
Prince
Princess, p 2:17¼
Prince by William Tell.
Flora Belle 2:29¾
Prince by Tom Crowder
Granger, p 2:24
Prince Albert by Handy Andy.
Harry Arlington 2:29¼
Don Q., p 2:26
Fanny D., p 2:27
Prince Albert.
Bessie S. 2:29¼
Prince Ali by Almont.
Alexis 2:21¼

Prince Aldine by Major Benton.
Marion H.... 2:24¼
Prince Allen by Honest Allen.
Robert B. Thomas.... 2:25
Prince Almont.
Maud Lightfoot..... 2:25½
Prince Bismarck by Victor Bismarck.
Merrimark, p.... 2:18¾
Prince Charles by George Wilkes.
Frank Jones.... 2:19¼
Prince Columbia.
Reform, p.... 2:26
Prince Dictator by Dictator.
Dictator G.... 2:30
Princeer by Kentucky Prince.
Freda.... 2:30
Ida A.... 2:25
Warren Guy.... 2:25
Prince Echo by Cloud Mambrino.
Hettie Hood, p.... 2:24¼
Prince Edward by King Rene.
Princeonia.... 2:28¼
Prince Elma by Stephen A. Douglas.
Ella E.... 2:22¼
Prince Fearnaught by Fearnaught Jr.
Parole.... 2:26½
Prince George by Kentucky Prince.
Gregorian.... 2:29¾
Princess Clara.... 2:26½
Prince Hal by Gibson's Tom Hal.
Houck, p.... 2:27
Hugh A., p.... 2:20
Lady B., p.... 2:29¼
Prince Imperial by Gen. Stanton.
Dick Smith, p.... 2:19½
Prince Imperial by William Welch.
May Temple, p.... 2:30
Prince Jr. by Jefferson Prince.
Hat Rack, p.... 2:29¼
Prince L. by Bourbon Wilkes.
Burt G.... 2:25¾
Topsy C.... 2:29¼
Prince Medium by Happy Medium.
Ivy Medium.... 2:24¼
Sam Medium.... 2:30
Razzle Dazzle, p.... 2:22
Prince Monroe by King Rene.
Jack Slade.... 2:29¼
Prince Orloff by Messenger Duroc.
Annie L.... 2:29¾
Little Mag.... 2:26
Nelly Orloff.... 2:26¼
Princess Orloff.... 2:29¼
Rigmarole.... 2:29¼
Sadie M.... 2:17¼
Prince Phallas by Phallas.
Royal Phallas.... 2:30
Princeps by Woodford Mambrino.
Earl.... 2:23¾
Editor.... 2:25¼
Epithet.... 2:29¾
Farce.... 2:29¼
Femme Sole.... 2:20
Fugleman.... 2:28¾
Geneva.... 2:17½
Granby.... 2:19¼
Grasshopper.... 2:29½
Greenbacks.... 2:23¼
Greenlander.... 2:12
Guelph.... 2:16¼
Guitar.... 2:29¾
Guyon.... 2:27¼
Hebron.... 2:30
Hetty Pearl.... 2:27¼
Ibis.... 2:27
Ignaro.... 2:25½
Imogene.... 2:22
Invincible.... 2:19¾
Jacobin.... 2:27
James P.... 2:28
Jubilant.... 2:22
Jubilee.... 2:26
Judean.... 2:29¾
J. W. South.... 2:29¼
Lady Washington.... 2:24¾
Lucille's Baby.... 2:20½
Oddity.... 2:30
Opus.... 2:30
Predicate.... 2:23½
Prince Dudley.... 2:29¾
Prince Edsall.... 2:18¼
Princeton.... 2:19¾
Princewood.... 2:18¼
Prince N.... 2:30
Princeno.... 2:30
Princeps Jr.... 2:26¼
Principe.... 2:24½
Romance.... 2:29½
Star Princeps.... 2:16¾
Talisman.... 2:30
Trinket.... 2:14
Count Princeps, p.... 2:20¼
Greenhorn, p.... 2:22½
Inkle, p.... 2:26½
Le Clede, p.... 2:18¼
Patoche, p.... 2:27¼
Princeptor by Princeps.
Prince A. G.... 2:29½
Cora Mack, p.... 2:22¾
Prince Pulaski.
Henry Clay, p.... 2:25½
Mattie Hunter, p.... 2:12¾
Prince Columbia, p.... 2:20
Prince Pilot, p.... 2:22½
Prince Pulaski Jr. by Prince Pulaski.
Ella Brown, p.... 2:11½
Flying Prince, p.... 2:24½
Prince Red by Red Wilkes.
Best Way.... 2:29¾
Prince Regent by Mambrino King.
Zenobia.... 2:22
Princeton by Princeps.
Autrain.... 2:16¼
Guy Princeton.... 2:28¼
Lizzie Lansing.... 2:22¼
Marquis of Eden.... 2:23½
Roy Princeton.... 2:29¼
Spray.... 2:28½
Daisy C., p.... 2:22
Guy Princeton, p.... 2:19¼
Henry F., p.... 2:10¼
Lady Princeton, p.... 2:15½
Rex Princeton, p.... 2:23½
Principe by Princeps.
Dirego.... 2:18½
Green River.... 2:22¼
Irene White.... 2:25½
Polk Laffoon.... 2:21¼
Prince Belmont.... 2:29¼
Red Clover.... 2:26¾
Tom Dixon.... 2:24¼
Prinmont.
Mite, p.... 2:26¼
Privateer by Grey Messenger.
Moscow.... 2:26¼
Proclamation by Hiatoga Jim.
Moxie Hiatoga, p.... 2:21¼
Prodigal by Onward.
Onward Boy, p.... 2:24¼
Prompter by Blue Bull.
Apex.... 2:26
Gazelle.... 2:25
Lucky B.... 2:20½
Transit.... 2:26½
Creole, p.... 2:15
Walker, p.... 2:23½
Prophet Wilkes by George Wilkes.
Karl K.... 2:28¾
John H., p.... 2:24¼
Prospect by Messenger Duroc.
Commodore.... 2:24¼
Prospect by Reno Refiance.
Goldenrod.... 2:29¾
Prospect by Blood Chief.
Turk Franklin, p.... 2:16¼
Prosper by Rysdyk's Hambletonian.
Martha.... 2:30
Prosper Merimee by Fritz.
Ayers P.... 2:21¾
Pure Gold by Mambrino King,
Poser.... 2:26½
Pure Wilkes by Red Wilkes.
Prue.... 2:21¼
Puritan by Happy Medium.
B. G.... 2:27½
Puzzler.
Gloriana.... 2:25¼
Joe Dayton.... 2:25¾
Pyramid by Almont.
Maud A.... 2:19½
Latimer Girl, p.... 2:29¼

Quaker Boy by Ohio Knickerbocker.
Elma.... 2:29¾
Quaker General by Gen. Knox
Lula H.... 2:24¼
Quartermaster by Alcyone.
Bellaire.... 2:28
Blue Bells.... 2:18¼
Frisco.... 2:27¾
Hortense.... 2:21½
Lady Juno.... 2:30
Leesee.... 2:23¾
Lenox.... 2:22¾
Leola.... 2:30
Melophene.... 2:28
Nyanza.... 2:30
Penelope.... 2:29½
Quartermain.... 2:29
Quartermarch.... 2:19¼
Quarterstretch.... 2:15
Reveille.... 2:27½
Stanley.... 2:24¼
Sunbeam.... 2:28
Woodwine.... 2:28½
Queechy by Alcyone.
Miss Woolsey.... 2:22½
Queen's Phallas by Phallas.
Tommy G.... 2:25
Quicksilver.
George Jones, p.... 2:24½
Quilna Chief by Pocahontas Boy.
Bay Leaf, p.... 2:24¼

Ben F., p.. .. ..2:24¼
David Copperfield, p 2·16
Deck Wright, p 2.18¼

Railsplitter by Young Morrill
  Blanche 2:23½
Rainbow.
  Red Cloud, p...... 2 19¼
Rainbow (Kremer's) by Tucker's Rainbow.
  Nelly Davis, p. . 2 24¼
Ralston by Romulus
  Lady Hamilton...... 2 25¾
  Rena .... 2 ·25
Rampart by Almont.
  Arc Light 2 19¾
  Deceiver........ . 2 30
  Israel............. ...2:19¼
  Rampart Jr . . 2 29
  Resolution........... 2 ·28¾
Ranchero by Clark Chief Jr.
  De Soto...... .....2 24
  Fantasia........ .....2 25
Rappahannock by Ethan Allen.
  Brushy John... .... 2:27
Rare Ben by Ben Franklin.
  Rare John. 2 18½
Rattler (Werner's) by Biggart's Rattler
  Mary Davis 2 26¾
Rattler by Stockbridge Chief.
  Gen Picton 2.30
  Sophia Temple..... ..2.27
Rattler.
  Sagwa. p..... ... 2:25¾
Rattler (Woodard's) by Biggart's Rattler.
  Joe Brown .. . 2:22
Rattler (Whitehead's) by Judge F.
  C. W. L., p............2:25
Rattler.
  Mead 2:25
Rattler Jr. by Rattler.
  Esmeralda 2:29¾
Rattler Brooks by Earnhart's Brooks.
  Clara J.. p. 2:17½
  Edward, p.............2:29½
  Lucy K.. p 2.21½
  Minnie Holden, p. .. 2.15½
Rattler Tuckahoe.
  Kitty D. 2 26¾
Raven by Hambletonian Mambrino
  Glaucus.. ... 2 25¾
Raven by Milton.
  Bo Peep. p 2 16¾
Raven Golddust by Golddust.
  Lou White .... 2 ·21¾
  M. R. 2.19¾
  Nelly H............2.24½
Raven Wilkes.
  Nellie W., p. ../. . 2:27¾
Ravenswood by Blackwood Jr.
  Kate Hamilton 2 30
  Kissel's Pointer, p .. 2.16½
Ray Almont by Bostick's Almont Jr.
  Gretchen H., p 2:23¾
Raymond by Simmons.
  Raymond Wilkes.....2:26
Raymond by New York.
  Idler.. .... 2:28

R. C. Brown by Florida.
  Mary Centlivre, p .. 2:12
Ready Money by Red Wilkes.
  King Wilkes 2:25¾
  Sibyl, p. 2:29¾
Rebel Medium by Happy Medium.
  Confederate Medium 2·27
Reconstruction by Vermont Boy. ·
  Black Jim. 2 29¾
  Little Crow . ..2:28¾
Recorder by Alcantara.
  Investigator 2:19¼
  Naiad King 2:23
  Zilhca 2.20½
  Leila May, p... 2 18¼
Red Bank by Iron Duke
  Gautier 2:27¾
Red Bill.
  Longfellow, p.. . 2 19¼
Red Bird by Henry 2d.
  Red Bird ... 2 30
Red Bird by Eagle Bird.
  Phillip H 2:27¾
Red Bird by Norman.
  Planter................2.24½
Red Bird.
  Tolu Maid.... .... 2.23¾
Red Blossom by Red Wilkes
  Red Grant, p 2:27¾
Red Buck (Arnold's) by Noah Day's Copperbottom
  Chestnut Star, p.... . 2·22
  Capt. Jack, p.... .. 2 24¾
  Columbus Girl, p. . 2 25¾
Red Buck.
  Janie Woody, p. 2 26¾
Red Buck (Hale's) by Arnold's Red Buck.
  Sorrel Dan, p ... 2 14
Red Buck (Taylor's) by Arnold's Red Buck.
  Harry C 2 21
Red Buck (Lafolette's) by Arnold's Red Buck.
  Belle Lawrence 2.28
Red Buck.
  Frank F., p . . 2.30
Red Buck (Stone's) by Arnold's Red Buck.
  Ada Paul 2 26
Red Buck.
  Van Zant, p . 2 29
Red Buck.
  Little Joe, p........ 2 29½
  Rockaway, p. . . 2 26¼
  Silver Buck, p.. . 2 29½
Red Cedar by Red Wilkes.
  Bay Cedar 2:30
  Brown Cedar.. .... 2:22
Red Chief by Red Wilkes.
  Wilkes Chief.... 2 23¾
Red Cloud by Night Hawk.
  Nelly R........ .. 2.28
  Red Belle.... ... 2 29¾
  Hazel Kirke, p 2 29¾
Red Dick.
  Belle N., p 2:27¾
Red Eagle by Grey Eagle.
  Daniel the Prophet .2:27
  Jenny. 2.22½
Red Eagle by Volunteer.
  Vernet 2 27¾
Red Fern by McCurdy's Hambletonian
  Fern Slip. 2 27¾
  Lady Fern . 2:29¾

Red Bird 2 17
Red Bud. .... 2·14¼
Redfield by Red Wilkes.
  Cardinal...... ..2·27
  Brookfield, p.... ... 2.22
  Charley Wilkes, p ...2·18
  Elbertfield, p.... ·. .2.19½
  Red Rover, p . . . 2:24¾
Red Flame by Enfield.
  Red Flame, Jr . 2 24¼
Red Jacket.
  Cannon Ball, p . 2 19¾
  Roadmaster, p .2.22
Red Joe.
  Charles S., p.... .. 2:21½
  Pickaway, p . 2 16¾
Red King by Red Wilkes
  King Harry 2 22
  Red Lake . . . 2.24½
Red Lambert by Red Wilkes.
  Marion Wilkes ... 2:22¾
Red Luke by Red Wilkes.
  Joe McLaughlin 2 26½
Red Mark by Pinafore
  Bright Pat. p . 2 23¾
Redmond C. by Joe Thorne.
  Red Bells . 2 26¼
Redmond Wilkes by Victor Bismarck.
  Bessie R., p 2:23¾
Redmont by Atlantic.
  Lottie Rocket, p .2 18¾
Red Oak by Blue Bull
  Moscow, p .. ..2·20
Red Pilot by Brown Trigham.
  Jeffie Lee....... 2·22
  Bay Pilot, p.. . 7 21½
  Monogram, p 2 20¼
Red Prince by Red Wilkes
  Allie Wilkes........ 2 28
Red Wilkes by George Wilkes.
  Allie Wilkes. . . 2·15
  Aristides....... .. 2 20¾
  Ashland Wilkes ..2·17¾
  Barney Wilkes .. 2:24¾
  Bell Red...... 2 28¾
  Bellevue Wilkes . 2 27¾
  Ben V 2 29¾
  Bessie C ...... 2·30
  Billy Bell .. 2 25¾
  Billy Red .2·28½
  Bonhommie.......2·17¾
  Boston Globe . 2 24
  Butte 2 29¾
  Charley Wilkes......2.21¾
  Chestnut Wilkes... 2 26¾
  Claimant 2 28½
  Clara T. . 2 28¾
  Clinton Wilkes ..2 26
  Dallie Wilkes... ..2.14
  Domineer .. 2:18¾
  Don Wilkes... . 2:29½
  Etta Wilkes .. .2.28¾
  Fred Wilkes . 2:26½
  Giovani ......2·28¾
  Harvey Wilkes.... 2.26½
  Hinder Wilkes .. 2:20¾
  Hornell Wilkes ... 2 27¾
  Island Wilkes... 2:13¾
  Ithuriel 2 29¾
  Janifer... ... 2 22
  Jean Wilkes . 2 27¾
  J. R. Shedd .. 2:19¾
  Kadijah.... .. 2 28¾
  King D . . 2:29¼
  Lady Gilbert 3 25¾
  Lady Mascotte 2:25¾

R. BEVER, ROCHESTER, N. Y.

A Cleveland graduate who marked Vitello 2:11¼ and
Clayhontas 2:11¼.

GEORGE SAUNDERS, Cleveland Ohio.

One of the world's cleverest race drivers. He marked Clingstone 2:14,
Evangeline 2:11¾, and was out in 1894 with Sable Gift 2:13¼.

Lady Wilkes 2:29¾
Lilly Moreland 2:26½
Lottie Moore 2:29¾
Memento Wilkes 2:24½
Messenger Wilkes 2:23
Nathan Wilkes 2:25¼
Midvale Prince 2:25
Nelly Wilkes 2:18½
Orianna 2:27¼
Passenger 2:30
Petrolia 2:27½
Phil Thompson 2:16½
Prince Wilkes 2:14¾
Prince Wilkes 2:29¼
Pure Wilkes 2:17½
Ralph Wilkes 2:06¾
Redalia 2:26¼
Red Cherry 2:22½
Reddie Clay 2:28¼
Red Girl 2:23¾
Red Hawk 2:28½
Red Heart 2:19
Red Hot 2:26¼
Red Lambert 2:28½
Red Lassie 2:20
Red Line 2:15
Red Mack 2:27¾
Red Queen 2:27¾
Red Star 2:23
Redstone 2:26¾
Red Wedge 2:29½
Red Wilkes(Kitchel's) 2:19¼
Reed Wilkes 2:25¼
Repetition 2:19¼
Red Wing 2:29¼
Richard 2:30
Riverside 2:20¾
Roseline 2:22
Royal Red 2:21½
Ruby 2:22½
Sentinel Wilkes 2:20¼
Sour Mash 2:24¾
Stanhope 2:25½
Tom Pugh 2:30
Trafford 2:27¼
Vrowsky 2:18¼
Wabash 2:20
Werther 2:20½
Whipsaw 2:27¾
Wilkeslona 2:24½
Abbott Wilkes, p 2:12½
Bellevue Wilkes, p 2:29¼
Blanche Louise, p 2:10
Burback, p 2:29¼
Edna Wilkes, p 2:23
Effie G. p 2:24½
Ernestine, p 2:24
Grover Wilkes, p 2:24¾
Ithuriel, p 2:29¾
Lady Belle, p. 2:27¼
Lydia Wilkes, p 2:17½
Molly Malloy, p 2:20
Montana Wilkes, p 2:17
Nannie W. p 2.22
Natalie Wilkes, p 2:26¼
Red Bell, p 2:11¼
Red Bud, p 2:24½
Red Lady, p 2:16¾
Redfield, p 2:19¾
Robert Red, p 2:26¼
Scarlet Wilkes, p 2:27½
Trafford, p 2:23½
Wayne Wilkes, p 2:16
Whipsaw, p 2:26¼
Wilkeslona, p 2:28
William Red, p 2:27

Redwood by Belmont.
Grace 2:26½
Grover Cleveland 2:18¾
Lady Redwood 2:27
Lamont 2:19
Orrville 2:27¾
Red Oak 2:21
Rosewood 2:25¾
Scipio 2:26½

Redwood by Nutwood.
Carl Redwood 2:20¾
George Gray 2:27
Gertrude G., p 2:22
Our Dick, p 2:22¾

Redwood Boone by Redwood.
Thompson 2:27¾

Re-Election by Electioneer.
La Haute 2:24¼

Referee by Administrator.
Big Brown Jug. 2:29½
Hambrino Pilot 2:29
Metal 2:27¼
Reference 2:18

Regalia by Jay Gould.
Country Boy 2:23¼
Hathaway 2:20¼
Flossy L., p 2:23
Fullerton D., p 2:19¾
Merit, p 2:23

Regal Wilkes by Guy Wilkes.
Last Chance 2:26¼

Regent by Onward.
Elsie 2:26½
Zebu 2:29

Rego by Bayard.
Kitty B 2:29¼

Regulator by Mapes Horse.
Bonnie G 2:28
John Carter 2:30
Dan Mitchell, p 2:22¾

Regulus by Rysdyk's Hambletonian.
Billy S 2:28¼
Echo 2:28½
Jessie Maud 2:29
Pearl 2:23½

R. E. Lee.
Goldbud, p 2:25½

Reliance by Cassius M. Clay.
Mystic 2:22

Reliance by Alexander.
Adrian 2:26½
Ed Marsh 2:23¼
Reality 2:19¼
Tippo Tib 2:24½
Daughter, p 2:23½

Rene by King Rene.
Belle Archer 2:12¾

Reno Defiance by Louis Napoleon.
Huseholt 2:25
Peleg 2:23¼
Prospect 2:18¾
Reno's Baby 2:25½
Richelieu 2:23½
Barbara Riddle, p 2:22½
Dolly W., p 2:24¼
George Campbell, p 2:17
Nannie E., p 2:17¼
Peleg, p 2:12¼
Reno's Baby, p 2:14
Reno Clipper, p 2:20½

Reno's Baby by Reno Defiance
Reno M., p 2:20

Renshaw.
Senator L 2:25½

Repetition by Red Wilkes.
Repetition Jr 2:26
Grace Wilkes, p 2:20½
Little Barefoot, p 2:27½

Repolee.
Maggie's Last 2:29¼

Reporter by Rysdyk's Hambletonian.
Dan Smith 2:21¼

Reporter by Dictator.
Byron Smith 2:29¾
James F 2:22½

Republic by Mambrino Patchen.
Freestone 2:25

Republican by Almont Wilkes.
Pat L 2:27¾

Rescue by Satellite.
Minnie R 2:25
Nominee 2:25
Olivette 2:18½
Roscoe 2:30
Tommy Lee 2:25¾
Willis Woods 2:25
Billy C., p 2:27¼
Joe Taylor, p 2:23
Minnie R., p 2:20¼
Red Thorne, p 2:15½

Reserve by Rysdyk's Hambletonian.
Oscar 2:30

Reserve Fund by Nutwood.
Equivalent 2:29¼
Gold Bond 2:28
Tezuca 2:15

Resolute by (Fisk's) Mambrino Chief Jr.
Henry O 2:25¼

Retter by Hamdallah.
Captain Retter 2:26¼

Reveille by New York.
Capt. Wade 2:30
Cappille 2:30
Fred B 2:16¼
Grey Cloud 2:25
Harry Baldwin 2:24¼
Harry Wade 2.19
Henry W 2:29½
Linnette 2:28¾
Racer 2:19¼
Red Leaf 2:29½
Revel 2:29½
Revolt 2:19
Rinaldo 2:27
Theodore 2:26¼
Vendetta 2:20½
Butler Chief, p 2.25
Lulu N., p 2:24½
Recall, p 2:26½
Revenue, p 2:29¼
Sir Thornton, p 2:20¾
Theodore, p 2:18½

Revenge by Napoleon.
Callahan Maid 2:25
Observer 2:24¼
Troubadour 2:19½

Revenue by Smuggler.
Rena Rolfe 2:19¾
Reve So 2:28¼

Revolution.
Sidney J. 2:26¼

Rex Hiatoga by Scott's Hiatoga.
Lucy Page 2:29¼
Newton B 2:17¾
Frank A., p 2:22
George A., p 2:27
George Steece, p 2:28½
Gray Jack, p 2:29
Hattie P., p 2:28¼

Minnie L., p ... 2:29¼
Rex King, p ... 2:25
Rex Patchen by Godfrey Patchen.
Ned Allen ... 2:29½
Nelly F ... 2:23¼
Raymond ... 2:17¼
Rex ... 2:28½
Roadster ... 2:30
Humming Bird, p ... 2:19½
R. F. Galloway by Mambrino Duncan.
Enola ... 2:21½
Neddie D ... 2:26
Rhode Island by Whitehall.
Gov. Sprague ... 2:20½
Jim Schriber ... 2:21½
Wilmar ... 2·29¼
Richard Alden by Alden Goldsmith.
Alden G., p ... 2:19¼
Richard Scobell by Wood's Hambletonian.
Belle B., p ... 2:19¼
Belle McGee, p ... 2:24½
Daisy B., p ... 2:21¼
Sheriff, p ... 2:15½
Tony, p ... 2·24¼
Richmond by Mambrino Pilot
Molly S. Lightfoot ... 2:21¼
Moonlight ... 2:25½
Nettie H ... 2:26½
Richmond Chief.
Lucy B ... 2:27
Richmond Chief.
Limber Jim, p ... 2:30
Richmont by Almont.
Pattie P ... 2:27
Ella Winters, p ... 2:29
Rich Wilson by Blue Bull.
Kitty White, p ... 2:27¼
Richwood by Rysdyk's Hambletonian.
Actor ... 2.26¼
Jenny ... 2:18½
Lady Richwood ... 2:29½
Norrick ... 2:29½
Quartette ... 2:22¾
Reporter ... 2:29¾
Triumph ... 2:29¾
Nutmeg, p ... 2:27¼
Richwood by Squire Talmage.
Bon Ton ... 2·29¾
Richmont p ... 2:27½
Richwood by Clark's Mohawk Jr.
Morefield ... 2:29¼
Ridgeway.
Ina ... 2:25¾
Ridgewood by Rysdyk's Hambletonian.
Belle of Kalmia ... 2:29¾
Ben B ... 2:17½
Wanda ... 2:25¾
Ridley Horse.
Robert Lee ... 2:23¼
Rienzi by Belmont.
Dunnette ... 2:22¼
Josephine ... 2:24¼
Pence ... 2:24¼
Rifleman by imp. Glencoe.
Col. Lewis ... 2:18¾
Rifleman by Rexford's Black Hawk.
Rifleman ... 2:27¼
Right Onward by Onward.
Chief Onward ... 2:22½

Darkwood ... 2:27¼
Red Express ... 2:22½
Riley Medium by Happy Medium.
Bernice Medium ... 2·27¾
Nina Medium ... 2:14
Riley S ... 2:21½
Tom Medium ... 2:29¼
Aurelian, p ... 2:29¼
Rinaldo by Mambrino Pilot.
Frenaldo ... 2:27¼
Ringgold by Tobe Drum Jr.
Mondace ... 2:27¼
Romeo ... 2:19½
Rocea ... 2:24
Ringwood by Edward Everett
Hurricane ... 2:29¼
Baby Girl, p ... 2:26¼
Redwood p ... 2:28½
Ripple by Romulus.
Col. Crockett ... 2:29¼
Ripton.
Lucky Jim ... 2:26½
Rising Sun by Rising Sun.
Naboklish ... 2:29½
Roanoke by Jupiter.
Roanoke Maid ... 2:22¼
Robb Wilkes by Ambassador
Santa Clara ... 2 29
Robber Boy by Mambrino King.
Tandy ... 2·28¼
Robert B. by Squire Talmage.
Lucy C., p. ... 2 20½
Robert Bonner by Rysdyk's Hambletonian
Chauncey H ... 2:27¼
Lady Dahlman ... 2:28
Robert Bonner Jr.
Helen Luce ... 2:26½
Robert Bonner, p ... 2:24¼
Robert Burns by Green's Bashaw.
Ben Haden ... 2·30
Fauntine ... 2:29½
Robert C. by Swigert.
Beulah Boy, p ... 2:23¼
Robert Fillingham Jr. by George Wilkes.
Dr. W. p ... 2:24½
Robert Fulton by Blanchard Morrill.
Janesville ... 2.29¼
Robert Fulton.
Julia D ... 2.27
Robert H ... 2:17
Robert L. by Haw Patch.
Lady Robert ... 2:17¼
Robert McGregor by Maj. Edsall.
Annie Hazen ... 2·22¼
Anna Mace ... 2·29¼
Annie McGregor ... 2:24
Black HawkM'Greg'r ... 2:28
Billy McGregor ... 2:28½
Bonnie McGregor ... 2:13½
Bryan McGregor ... 2:23¾
Burns McGregor ... 2:29
Buck McGregor ... 2.29½
Corle McGregor ... 2·21
Corinne ... 2:14½
Count Robert ... 2:13½
Dollikins ... 2:26½
Don McGregor ... 2 27¼
Earl McGregor ... 2·21½
Ethan McGregor ... 2:29¼
Eulalia ... 2:29¼
Frank McGregor ... 2.24½

Fred McGregor ... 2:29¼
Fred McGregor ... 2·30
Hixie McGregor ... 2:28½
Ida K ... 2:29¾
Jim Anderson ... 2·28½
Joe Eastman ... 2:29¼
Katie Mac ... 2:26¼
Lady McGregor ... 2:25½
Laura McGregor ... 2:22
Mac D ... 2:30
Mark Time ... 2 19
Mazie McGregor ... 2:28
McCullough ... 2 30
McGregor (Hood's) ... 2:26¾
McGregor Boy ... 2:29½
McGregor Time ... 2 30
McGregor Wilkes ... 2:27¼
McGregor Wilkes ... 2·21
Miss McGregor ... 2:19¼
Mohaw McGregor ... 2.29
Nelly McGregor ... 2:14
Notre Dame ... 2·23¾
Novia ... 2:27¼
Nyanza ... 2:15¾
Pearl McGregor ... 2·23¾
Prelude ... 2:29
Robert McGregor Jr. 2:30
Roslyn ... 2:15
Roxy McGregor ... 2:20¾
Sacaza ... 2:29¾
Sappho ... 2:15¾
Sidner McGregor ... 2.18½
Silver Bow ... 2·16
Silver King ... 2:30
Silver Wing ... 2:28
Velmar ... 2.28¾
Victor McGregor ... 2:19¼
Warren McGregor ... 2:20¾
Wilksie G ... 2:22¼
Wildstar ... 2:23½
Woodstock ... 2:17¼
Kentucky Star, p ... 2:17¼
Tom McGregor, p ... 2:12
Robert R. Morris by Independent.
J. P. Morris ... 2.20¼
Senator ... 2:26½
Robert Ryan by Goldsmith's Pilot
Belle Calley, p ... 2:27¼
Robert Rysdyk by William Rysdyk.
Guy ... 2 15¼
Eliza K ... 2·19½
Jap, p ... 2:25¾
Robert St. Clair by Jack Roberts Jr.
Howard St. Clair, p ... 2:18
Robert Smith by Rysdyk's Hambletonian.
Broadway ... 2·29¼
Robert Whaley by Night Hawk.
Adelene ... 2:26¾
Luzerne ... 2:23¼
Razor B ... 2:25
Robin Clay by Star Clay.
Bill Thunder ... 2:25
Robin Hood by Balaklava.
Quiz, p ... 2:17¼
Robinson by Swigert.
Alexander ... 2:25
Robinson D. by Daniel Boone.
Black Nathan ... 2:23¼
Nelly D ... 2:27
Belle Chase, p ... 2:21¼
Evelyn, p ... 2:23¼

Robinson Horse by S. E. Mudgett.
Sir William Wallace. 2:27½
Rob Roy McGregor by Robert McGregor.
Bob 2:30
Waldo McGregor 2:29¼
Rockaway.
Sucker Maid 2:29¼
Danness, p 2:26¼
Rockdale by George Gordon.
Rockbottom, p 2:16½
Socks, p 2:14¾
Rockefeller by Electioneer.
Granieta 2:25½
Leola 2:30
Rockford.
Grover Cleveland, p 2:28
Rockwell Success by Glencoe Jr.
Una Forrest, p 2:20
Rochester by Aberdeen.
Dinnie 2:25
Florestine 2:26¼
Minot 2:26¼
Oriana 2:25
Sensation 2:29½
Surah 2:29½
Bell Boy, p 2:20½
Rocket by Cyren Joslyn Horse.
India Rubber 2:29½
Rocket by Blue Bull.
True 2:23¾
Rocket Jr. by Rocket.
Dandy White Stocking 2:27¼
Rockwood.
Little Maid, p 2:26
Rockwood by Fleetwood.
Blackwood 2:21½
Katie Lee 2:29¾
Lady Maud 2:23½
Nantilla J 2:30
Rickreel 2:29
Rockwood Jr. by Rockwood.
Anita 2:23½
Rocky Ford.
Bob Ford 2:28¾
Roger Hanson by Alta.
Billy Worthington 2:27½
Jessie Hanson 2:13¾
Frank Hanson, p 2:27¼
Roger, p 2:23¼
Rhomer by King Rene.
Mary Crit 2:23¾
Gertie Ayer, p 2:28¾
Mary Crit, p 2:19
Roland by Crown Chief.
Maggie S 2:30
Rolf Duke by Tom Rolf.
Brogan 2:29½
Rolla Golddust by Arabian Golddust.
Nelly W 2:14¾
Pauline C. 2:29
Rolling Wave by Messenger Chief.
Mary Spillman 2:30
Rollins Horse by Rising Sun.
Emperor 2:30
Roman Chief by Walkill Chief.
Pat Dempsey 2:29¾
Whitesboro Chief 2:28¼
Honest Abe, p 2:24¼
Sangerfield, p 2:30

Romping Prince.
Prince S 2:22¼
Romulus by Rysdyk's Hambletonian.
Almont Hambletonian 2:23½
Little Nell 2:29½
Louetta 2:24½
Rooker by Stranger.
Bonnie Annie 2:26
Bonnie Donne 2:29¼
Dictator 2:27¾
Lady Rooker 2:26½
Nelly Woodruff 2:30
Regulator 2:27½
Reil Rooker, p 2:28½
Rocky Ford, p 2:18¼
Roscoe by Charley Ball.
Wizz 2:23¼
Roscoe by Pilot Jr.
Black Pilot 2:30
Roscoe by Brigadier.
Pilot W 2:24½
Roscoe Jr. by Roscoe.
Daisy Wood, p 2:26¼
George G., p 2:20¾
Roscoe Boy.
Brandywine, p 2:29¼
Roscoe C. by Highland Grey.
J. D. C 2:30
Roscoe C. by Blue Bull.
Tommy P., p 2:23
Roscoe Conkling by Gov. Sprague.
Judd's Baby 2:19¼
May Conkling 2:28
Senator Conkling 2:12¾
Dan Conkling, p 2:18¼
Roseberry by Strathmore.
Blazeberry 2:18
Cornelius, p 2:29½
Judge T., p 2:20¼
Noxall, p 2:18
Strathberry, p 2:06½
Rosedale by Col. Hambrick.
Breast Plate, p 2:20
Ross Colt by Burke Colt.
Anodyne 2:25
Ross S by Nutwood.
Booth Barrett 2:29½
Ross Wilkes by George Wilkes.
Exchange Boy, p 2:30
Jack Shiel, p 2:21¾
Rough and Ready by Vermont Black Hawk.
Cattaraugus Chief 2:29
Derby 2:25½
Roulette by Mambrino Russell.
Chimes C 2:26
Brownie, p 2:22¾
Rowdy Boy by Honest Frank.
Dell 2:27
Royal Almont by Almont.
Purity 2:28
Royal Chief by Niagara Chief.
James G 2:20
Royal Duke by Silver Duke.
Lulu Judd 2:26½
Royal Fearnaught by Fearnaught.
Ben Wright 2:30
Chance 2:23¼
Gladys 2:23
Grace Walker 2:23½
Gula 2:27½

Hazel 2:30
Home Maid 2:25¼
Lady Walker 2:30
Lady Warren 2:29¾
Laputa 2:27¼
Pete Lindley 2:27¼
Peter K 2:29¼
Roy 2:21¼
Royal 2:20¾
Shellbark 2:29¾
St. Elmo 2:16¼
Topsey 2:28
Young Frank 2:30
Lora, p 2:14¾
Royal Belle, p 2:23¼
Silverthread, p 2:15½
Royal George by Black Warrior.
Lady Byron 2:28
Royal George (Fields') by Royal George.
Byron 2:25½
Gen. Love 2:30
Royal George (Henderson Horse).
Hortense, p 2:25
Royal George (Howe's) by Royal George.
Caledonia Chief 2:29½
Royal George.
Gen. Beamish 2:26¼
Royal George (Murphy's) by Howe's Royal George.
Russian Spy 2:26½
Royal Jim by Pocahontas Sam.
Red Skin, p 2:17¾
Royal Lambert by Daniel Lambert.
Golden 2:29¼
Royal Revenge by Toronto Chief.
Fred Hooper 2:23
Lucy 2:20¼
Prince 2:21¼
Royalston by Maj. Edsall.
John D 2:28¾
Loyalton by Royalty.
Bovee K., p 2:15¾
Royalty by Swigert.
Carrie W 2:26¼
Governor F 2:21
Carrie W., p 2:20
Royalton, p 2:18¼
Roy Wilkes by Adrian Wilkes.
Marr, p 2:26
Royal Sid, p 2:24½
Royal Windsor by Windsor.
Clay Cross 2:30
Roy Executor by Administrator.
Mira 2:28¼
Ruby by Red Wilkes.
Lump 2:26½
Rumor by Tattler.
Boyer 2:29¼
Calvo 2:29¼
Digma 2:25¾
Dupree 2:29½
Edgardo 2:13¾
Hurly Burly 2:16½
Lammermoor 2:19¼
Lugano 2:21¾
Maestro 2:29½
Martyr 2:23
Oxide 2:29½
Thornley 2:29½

Trapeze 2 27
Verdi 2:25½
Zigzag 2:30
Flask, p 2:19
McBride, p 2:17¼
Rupert Medium by Happy Medium.
Comet Medium 2:27¼
Star Medium. 2:28½
Rural Chief.
Prairie Chief 2:27
Rusco by Hambletonian Downing.
Harry Wood, p. 2:16
Russell (Miller's) by Col. H. S. Russell
Russell T., p 2:19¼
Rushville by Blue Bull.
Blucher 2 29¼
Dusty Heels. 2:27¼
Gipsey Queen 2:19¾
Russ Denmark by Oatt's Stonewall.
Tom Arden 2:16¼
Russia by Nutwood.
Czar 2:12½
Oakley Maid 2.24
Russia White 2:29¼
Woodbird 2:25½
Rustic by Whipple's Hambletonian.
Amelia 2:22½
Nighttime. 2:29¼
Rustler
Hustler. 2:29¼
Ryland by Hamlet.
Blanche Clemons 2:27½
Rysdyk by Rysdyk's Hambletonian.
Bertrace .... 2·27½
Billy K 2 25¼
Clingstone 2:14
Clingstone 2d 2:29½
George M. Rysdyk 2:25
Maud A. 2:26¼
Mauston 2:25¼
Royal Rysdyk 2:28¼
Thomas Rysdyk 2:29¼
Victor 2:21½
Rysdyk Chief by Squire Talmage.
St. Louis Maid 2:24½
Ryse Duke by Rysdyk's Hambletonian.
Addie C 2:30
Van Duke 2 30
Addie C., p .... 2·29
Ryswood by Bellwood
Silver Wood. .... 2·21

Sable Wilkes by Guy Wilkes.
Beverly. 2:24½
Buffington. 2.20¼
Chris Lang. .... 2·26½
Deborah 2:21½
Double Cross 2:18¾
Freedom 2:29¾
Kent. 2:28
Lallah Wilkes 2:26
Lou Wilkes 2:19¾
Macleay 2:22¼
Native Son 2 26½
Oro Wilkes 2 11
Puritan 2:29½
Sabina 2:15¼
Sabledale 2 18½
Sablehurst 2:25
Sablenut 2 22¼
Sir Wilkes 2:29
Whalebone 2:24
Macleay, p 2:29¼
Sacramento by Woodford Mambrino.
Bob Henderson 2:29¼
Nelly Rose 2:25¼
Scotia 2:21¼
Saddling Buck by Chad's Red Buck.
Frank Landers 2:18¾
Sagerser by Jim Monroe.
Daily News 2 25
Lady Monroe 2 29
St. Almo by Almont.
Maggie C. 2.29¾
Nelly G. 2 29½
St. Arnaud by Cuyler.
Grover Cleveland 2:30
Hanen. 2:29½
Judge Keeler 2.21¼
Reina 2:12¼
Ruby 2:28½
St. Regis 2:29½
St. Bel by Electioneer.
Allibel 2:19½
Amoral 2:26
Bellman 2.28¾
Bell Town 2 25½
Benzoni 2:30
Bel Onward 2.23
Bessie Bel 2 29¾
Comet 2:28¼
Election Bel 2:22¼
First Bell .... 2·28¼
Favora .... 2·23¼
Flora Belle 2 29¼
Free 2:25
Gold Point .... 2·29¾
Honey Dew 2:29½
Honey Wood 2:19½
Katrina Belle 2 26¼
La Bel 2:27
La Petite Bel 2:29½
Legacy 2:30
Lynne Bel 2 23
Miss Zura Belle 2:26½
Robert Bell 2:30
Santa Belle 2:28
St. Aubin 2 28½
St Croix .... 2·28½
St. Felix 2:25½
St. Minx 2 26½
Silver Ore .... 2·19½
Tempter 2:24¾
Almabel, p 2 17½
Baron Bel, p .... 2·11½
Fail Not, p 2 16½
Monabel, p 2 18
Notion, p. 2:16
Silver Bell, p 2:29¼
St. Clair by Comus.
Belva Maid 2:29½
St. Clair (Fred Low) by St. Clair.
Adalia 2:27
Clay 2 25½
St. Clair.
Ben Butler, p 2.19¾
Humming Bird, p 2 30
Jim McCue, p 2:30
Lady St. Clair, p 2 20
St. Cloud by St. Elmo.
Col. Walker 2:24¼
St. Cloud by Swigert.
Brown Dick .... 2·12
Dick C 2:30
Senator 2 30
St. Cloud Jr .... 2·26¾
Kate Poverty, p 2:24½
St. Croix by Wilkes.
St. Croix, Jr. .... 2·30
St. Elmo by Gen. Knox.
Elmo 2 27¼
St. Elmo by Guynn Clipper.
John Had 2 26½
Dr. Elmo, p 2.22
St. Gothard by George Wilkes
Althard 2 28¼
Berthard 2 29
Don Gothard 2.27
Duroc Gothard 2 29¼
Frank S 2:30
Fritz 2.29¼
George T 2 28¼
Grace Gothard 2:20
Happy Gothard. 2 29¾
Lizzie O .... 2·27½
Phurah 2:30
Rosa Gothard 2 25
Sir Gothard 2 29¼
Stathard 2:27½
Willie Gothard 2 29¼
Heron Wilkes, p 2:24¼
Magoth, p .... 2·29¼
Queen Gothard, p .... 2·14½
T. C. B., p 2:27½
St. James by Damon.
Big Charley .... 2·23¼
Alvin Green, p 2:23
St. Jerome by Hambletonian Wilkes.
Wilkes 2:17¼
Jerome Taylor, p .... 2·21½
St. Just by Electioneer.
Adjutant .... 2·29¾
Lanier 2,27
Mary 2:14¼
St. Lawrence (Foster's) by Old St. Lawrence (Canadian).
Harry Mitchell 2:28¾
St. Lawrence (Finch's).
Belle Mahone, p 2:24½
St. Lawrence (Price's) by St. Lawrence.
Sadie H 2.30
St. Lawrence by St. Lawrence (Canadian)
Cooloo 2:30
St. Lawrence (Douglass) by Bett's St Lawrence,
Joe Mowat, p. 2:19½
St Leon by Volunteer.
Tomoka 2 28¼
St. Louis by Belmont.
Tartar .... 2·26½
St. Mark by St. Elmo.
Laura Belle, p 2 27
Rattler, p 2:19¼
St. Nicholas by Blue Bull.
St. Lewis 2:19
St. Nick, p 2 27¼
St. Omer by Blue Bull.
Johnny B 2.27¼
Chapman, p 2 19½
Harry Omer, p 2:23¾
Mentor Maid, p. 2.27¾
St. Patrick by Volunteer.
St Patrick, Jr 2:28¾
St. Vincent by Wilkes Boy.
Dresch 2:30
Salamon.
Little Kahn 2.27¾

Saltram by Webber's Kentucky Whip.
Highland Maid 2:27

Sam B.
Tom Bailey 2:28¼
Sorrel John, p 2:29¼

Sambo.
Charley E., p 2:24

Sam.
Turk, p 2:18½

Sam Hazard.
John Hazard, p 2:27½
Sneak, p 2:25

Sam Kirkwood by Kirkwood.
Centella 2:21
Kitty Clyde 2:29¼

Sample by St. Elmo.
Elsie Manager 2:30

Sammy J.
Robert Elsmere, p 2:25

Sam Purdy by George M. Patchen Jr.
Calhoun 2:29¼
Charley C 2:13¼
Charley H 2:20¼
Sam Hickson 2:30
Strontia 2:14¼
Three Tips 2:25¼
Buster, p 2:27¾
Miss Woodford, p 2:19¼

Sam Sharply by Bashaw Jr.
Gypsey H 2:29¼

Samson by Rysdyk's Hambletonian.
Shamrock 2:28
William H 2:29

Sanborn by Gen. Washington.
John Schumacker, p 2:29¾

San Diego by Alcona Clay.
Lottie B 2:26¼

Sandwich by Lord Russell.
Yarmouth 2:25¾

Sandy Lake.
Sankey, p 2:25

Sandy Morris.
Sandy Morris Jr, p 2:28¼

Sandy Short by Grey Charley.
Blizzard, p 2:12¾

San Gabriel by Sultan.
Viola, p 2:25¼

Sankey.
Lulu P 2:29¾

Santa Claus by Strathmore.
Claus Almont 2:26½
Doric 2:29½
Kris Kingle 2:28¼
Merry Christmas 2:27
Nelly R 2:21½
Miss Carroll 2:22½
Pilot Claus' 2:26¼
San Mateo 2:28¼
Santie 2:25
San Jose, p 2:30
William Penn 2:12½
Sidney, p 2:19¾

Satinwood by Nutwood.
Marcus Daly 2:22¼

Sarcenet by King Rene.
Grover C 2:26¼

Satellite by Robert Bonner.
Electric 2:30
Goldenbow 2:29¾
Golden Eagle 2:28¾
Golden Wing 2:24¾
Jubilee 2:28
Sharpland Lena 2:28¾

Satrap by Dictator.
Excellence, p 2:25

Saturn by Satellite.
Byron Sherman 2:28
Consul 2:22½
McLeod 2:19½
Great Western, p 2:25

Saxony by Happy Medium.
Garret L 2:19½
Howard Medium 2:19¼

Scarlet Wilkes by Red Wilkes.
Elsie Harris 2:25½
Captain White 2:29
The Duke, p 2:24¾

Schuyler by Seneca Chief.
Gretchen 2:16¼

Schuyler Colfax by Rysdyk's Hambletonian.
Jacksonian 2:22½
Vivid C 2:28¼
Maggie H, p 2:27½
Smiler Colfax, p 2:16½

Scotch Prince by Baird's Hambletonian Prince.
Doc F 2:26
Lucy Hayes 2:29¼
Weazel 2:29¼

Scotia Horse by Miner Horse.
Roachmane 2:27½

Scotland by Star of the West.
Lily Kahn 2:27¾

Scott by Egbert.
Black Diamond 2:18¾

Scott Chief by Egmont.
Lou Scott 2:29¾
Lucky Baldwin 2:22
Queen of Scotts 2:28

Scott's Thomas by Gen. George H. Thomas.
Buccleuch 2:29½
George 2:20¼
Largesse 2:25
J. W. Thomas 2:27½

Scriba Boy.
Marvin, p 2:21¾

Sea Bird by Lord Russell.
Piquant, p 2:29¼

Sea Foam by Blue Boy.
Belle Mahone, p 2:10¼
Blue Belle, p 2:17
Bessie B. p 2:22
Blue Bell, p 2:19¾
Cricket, p 2:30
Kosciusko, p 2:27
Little Lulu, p 2:23¼
Maggie May, p 2:24¾
Maud Neff, p 2:19
Sir Edward, p 2:27

Sealskin Wilkes by George Wilkes.
Bessie Wilkes 2:24
Emoleta 2:24½
Miss Pilot 2:30
Orlie Wilkes, p 2:27

Sea Side.
Maud L 2:29¼

Secretary by Director.
Secret 2:26½
Josephine 2:28½

Sefton by Blue Bull.
Jewell, p 2:21¼

Sedgewick by Allie West.
Edison, p 2:24

Selenite by Satellite.
J. M. B 2:26¾

Selim by Kenny Horse.
Stranger 2:28

Selkirk.
Belle W 2:19¼
Cricket 2:24½

Senator.
Sally C. p 2:17¼

Senator.
Favorite 2:30

Senator by Echo
Jenny Thomb 2:25½
Leland 2:29¾

Senator N. by Wapsie.
Forest D 2:27¾
John W 2:29¾

Senator Rose by Sultan.
Senator Boy 2:24¾

Senator Updegraff by Simmons.
Reita U 2:25¾

Seneca Chief by Rysdyk's Hambletonian.
Lottie C 2:29¼
Mattie C 2:28¼
Middlesex 2:24
Schuyler 2:26

Seneca Patchen by George M. Patchen
Alta Patchen 2:24½
Bartholdi Patchen 2:22¾
Bertrace Patchen 2:29
Blew 2:27
Dr. Day 2:27
Fleety Patchen 2:29¼
Frank Patchen 2:24¾
Lucky Baldwin 2:24
Monk 2:26¼
Opal Patchen 2:29½
Rex Patchen 2:29¼
Patchen (Gidding's) 2:27¼
Sunrise Patchen 2:19¼
Sunset Patchen 2:23½
Sunshade Patchen 2:28
Victor Hugo 2:23¼
Sunset Patchen, p 2:18¾

Seneca Prince by Seneca Chief
John F 2:30

Sensation by Rochester.
Sartwell 2:28¾

Sentinel by Rysdyk's Hambletonian.
Annette 2:25¼
Capoul 2:28
Grand Sentinel 2:27¼
Mignon 2:27¼
T. A. 2:26
Vivandiere 2:21½
Von Arnim 2:19½
Young Sentinel 2:26

Sentinel by Sentinel.
Hattie Hawthorne 2:23½

Sentinel Wilkes by George Wilkes.
Brother G 2:25¼
Dashwood 2:22
Dick Wilkes 2:30
Frank L 2:14½
Western Wilkes 2:29¾
Thistle Dew, p 2:17¼

Seth P. by Swigert.
Charles F 2:20¾
Kesterson 2:27

Seth Warner by Ethan Allen.
Sontag Clay 2:24

Shadeland Onward by Onward.
Chantward 2:21
Edith Gard 2:27½
Onetta 2:23

Wanita 2 29¼
Belle Acton, p. 2:16¼
Fred K., p. 2:09¾
Online, p 2 04
Ontonian, p. 2 07½
Shadow by Goldsmith's Abdallah.
Patchen T., p. 2:24¼
Shaker Boy.
G. W. Huey, p. 2 24¼
Shaker, p. 2:21¼
Shannon Medium.
Lovely Medium. 2:28
Sharatack Jr. by Sharatack.
Slow Go 2:18½
Sharon Benton by Gen. Benton
Patrick's Pacer, p. 2 21¾
Sharper by Bourbon Wilkes
Mable Sharpe, p. 2:23½
Shawmut by Harry Clay.
Dick Hardin 2:29
Fire Clay 2:30
Maggie S 2 29
Red Shawmut 2:25¾
Stella 2 21
Shelby Chief by Alexander's Abdallah.
Cascarilla 2 25½
Grand Duke 2:29¼
Rolla 2:24½
Shelby Maid 2:29
Shelbyville Chief by Clark Chief.
Maggie B. 2:20
Shelden Messenger by Alexander's Abdallah.
George Wolf 2:30
Shennan Medium by Happy Medium.
Fred K 2.24½
Medium Boy 2 29¼
Tony Medium. 2:24¼
Shepherd F. Knapp by Eaton Horse
Shepherd Knapp Jr. 2:27¾
Sherman by George Wilkes
Alexie Sherman 2 25¼
Archie Sherman 2:29¼
Ashmaid 2:18¼
Ashman 2:18¼
Eddie Sherman 2 29½
Grant Sherman 2.29
Helen M. 2 29¼
Sherbet 2:20
Win Sure 2:25¼
Zyco. 2:26¼
George Sherman, p 2:18¼
Heilo, p 2:20½
Sherman Aristos by Aristos.
Maid of the Wilderness 2:25¾
Sherman Black Hawk by Vermont Black Hawk.
Chicago Jack 2 30
Panic 2 28
Sherman Morgan, Jr. (Slicer's) by Napoleon Morgan
Sherman Morgan, Jr 2:29
Sherman Wilkes by George Wilkes.
Dean Wilkes 2:25¼
Duroc Wilkes 2:28½
Ruskin Wilkes, p 2:17
Shermont by Almont Eagle.
Enigma 2:21
Shibboleth.
Elder Lucas, p 2:26

Shiloh.
Guy, p 2:06¾
Shilton.
Tola 2.29¼
Shoo Fly by Kramer.
Henry H., p 2:22½
Shungamunga by Mazeppa.
Ionia 2 29¼
Sickle Hambletonian by Masterlode.
Lenawee 2.22¾
Sidmore by Sidney.
Marchioness 2 29
Sidney by Santa Claus.
Birdie 2:28
Carmello 2:21¾
Cassie 2:28½
Cupid 2:18
Dictator Sidney 2:25
Duchess 2.20¾
Elegance 2:30
Faustino 2:14¾
Fleet 2 18¾
Fleet Boy 2 24¼
Frou Frou 2:22
Grace 2:29
Highland Lass 2 27¼
Highland Sidney 2:29½
Idah 2 30
Judge G 2 21¼
Kitty B 2:24½
La Belle 2.16
Lea 2.24¼
Montana 2:30
Sanders 2:26¼
Moorzouk 2 26
Sans Souci 2:28¼
Sedina 2.28½
Serena 2.29½
Sid Fleet 2:26½
Sidlette 2:22
Sidney Boy 2 29
Sidney Maid 2 27
Sidney Smith 2:24½
Sidnut 2:25¼
Sister V 2:18½
Sibyl 2:27½
Adonis, p 2:11½
Edna R, p 2:17½
Fausta, p 2:22¾
Gold Leaf, p 2:11¼
Hummer, p 2:18½
Lady H., p 2:15
Longworth, p 2 19
Maggie McDowell, p 2:21¼
Mephisto, p 2.21¼
Mercury, p 2.21
Ramon, p 2:17¼
Rosedale, p 2:22
Santa Rita, p 2:24¼
Sidmont, p 2:10½
Sidmoor, p 2.17¾
Sidwood p 2:16
Smilax, p 2.21¼
Thistle, p 2:13¼
Tho, p 2:23
William Sidney, p 2:25
Sierra Boy by Plumas.
Robert L. 2:21
Sigma Nu by Bourbon Wilkes.
Daisy Dee 2 27
Eddie R., p 2 24¾
St. Francis, p 2:23½
Secret. p 2:22½
Signal by Bunday's Rob Roy.
Carrie T., p 2 20½
Dan Rice, p 2:20½
Handy Andy, p 2.29¼

Prussian Maid, p 2.19
Signal by Sentinel.
Eli 2:18¾
Green Light 2:24¾
Jessie Hammond 2:25½
Red Light 2:27¼
Sighlight 2:22¼
Signet by Hambletonian Pilot.
Clifton 2:27
Silas Wright by Degraff's Alexander.
Maggie Wright 2:15¼
Maud Wright 2:25¼
Badge, p 2:13¼
Colon, p 2.17¼
Lottie Wright, p 2.27½
Silkwood by Blackwood Mambrino.
Daisy Wood 2:27
Silliman Morgan.
Alexander S. 2 28¼
Silver Bow by Robert McGregor.
Silver Bee 2:27¾
Silver Chief.
Silveretta, p 2:23¾
Silver Chimes by Alcyone.
Silver Lace 2 22½
Silver Cloud by Fisk's Mambrino Chief, Jr.
Silver Plate 2 17¼
Silver Star 2 30
Silver Bar, p 2:24¼
Silver Cloud, Jr., p 2:16¼
Silvermaker, p 2.27½
Silverheels.
Kitty B 2:29¼
Silver Heel.
Mc O'Donnell, p 2.28½
Silver Heels Jr. by Silver Heels (Canadian).
Silver Dick, p. 2:13
Silver King by Whipple's Hambletonian.
King of the Ring 2:23¼
Silver King by Robert McGregor.
Robert T. McGregor 2:29¼
Silver Mine by Grand Sentinel
Quicksilver, p 2.26½
Silvertail by Legal Tender.
Dutch Girl 2 27
Silver Maid 2:30
Silvertail by Belmont.
Frank S., p 2 22½
Silver Bow by Robert McGregor.
Rainbow 2 24¼
Simcoe Wilkes by Idol Wilkes
Samuel G. 2:29
Simmocolon by Simmons.
Ferndale, p 2:16½
Simeta, p 2:23¼
Simmons by George Wilkes.
Adelaide Simmons 2.14½
Adino 2:30
Agnes Huntington 2 28¾
Al B 2:28¾
Alice Simmons 2:30
Black Raven 2:17½
Black Storm 2:17¼
Blanton 2:20¾
Bon Bon 2:26
Bryson 2:20¾
Carter 2:29¾
C. O. D 2:30

Col. Simmons.........2:22¾
Coralloid..............2:13½
Dashwood...............2:30
Ersilla......... . ..2:26¼
Fanny G......... . ...2:22¾
Garnet Girl.............2:27
George Simmons..... 2:28
Gossiper................2:14¾
Grace Simmons 2:19½
Greenleaf 2:10½
Lady Thompson...... 2:23¾
Le Simmons 2:26
Mattie S. Wilkes 2:26½
Megibbon..... ......2:28
Miss Simmons,.........2:29½
Miss Van S............2:27¼
M'liss. ....?:27¾
Myra Simmons........2:20¾
Nathalie 2:28¾
Nanny Wilson........ 2:28½
New York 2:13½
Ophir,.... ....2:26½
Orinoco................ 2:19¾
Oscar William 2:18½
Persimmons 2:29¾
Prospect Simmons.. .2:23¾
Raymon 2:27¼
Sally Simmons. 2:13½
Senator Updegraff ...2:27½
Simbrino 2:22¼
Simmocolon 2:13¾
Simoda..................2:28
Spray.......... ....2:28½
West Wilkes..........2:22¼
Ellen C, p...............2:21¾
Sadie Gray, p.. ......2:29½
Snow Bird, p...........2:22
Simmons Boy by Simmons.
Simmonette.. .....2:17½
Simmons Jr. by Simmons.
Ripple P...............2:28¼
Simon Strader.
Grey Joe, p 2:28¼
Simontie by Simmons.
Nubbin W...............2:26¼
Sim Watson by Harry Clay.
Lady Watson.. ..... 2:20¾
Sim Watson Jr. . .. 2:21½
Sinbad by Strader's C. M. Clay Jr.
Donna Inez... ....2:26½
Chautauqua Prince,p.2:28¾
Singleton by Willie Schepper.
Maud Singleton.......2:28½
Lota, p....... .....2:29
Sir Archie.
Thurston.............2:29¾
Sir Archie by Swigert Dewdrop.
Shawano Girl, p......2:21¼
Sir Charles by Mambrino Charta.
King Charles 2:22¼
Maggie T...............2:18½
Maud C............. 2:27½
Mattie K., p..........2:25½
Sir Denton by Satellite.
Ada 2:29¼
Tony Denton.........2:22
Sir Folko by Embassador.
Frank F....... ....2:20½
Fred Ensign. 2:26½
Sir George by Silver Dick.
Pat McCann 2:28¾
Sir Henry by Seely's American Star.
Lady Star... ....2:24
Sir Henry by Honest John.
Rufus 2:24¾
Sirius by Hambletonian Tranby.
Mark Sirius ..../ 2:13
Sir John Dean.
Stranger 2:25¼
Sir John by Clear Grit.
Babette... ....2:22¼
Babette, p...............2:14¼
Sir John Franklin.
O. S. B.. ....2:27
Sir Knight by Grand Sentinel
Karta.... ... . 2:28
Knita... .. ..2:23½
Knightmare... . ....2:12½
Knightmont... ......2:24
May B 2:30
Mike Knight. 2:28¼
Red Knight 2:23
Glen, p 2:26¼
Kaota, p.. ....2:15¼
Knight L., p...........2:27¾
Sir Nutwood by Nutwood.
Francis, p 2:28¼
Sirocco by Jerome Eddy.
Siretta, p............2:25¾
Sir Peter by Alden Goldsmith.
St. Catherine, p 2:22¼
Sir Thomas by Lambertus.
Guy Lambert 2:22
Sir Walkill by Rysdyk's Hambletonian.
Claudia................2:29
Frank Walkill........2:24¼
Judge Purple 2:28½
Jura.. ....2:26¼
King Walkill 2:24¼
Nelson....... ....2:26¼
Sultana...... ....2:29¾
Walkill Boy..........2:24
Warren E...............2:30
Sir Wallace by Sir Walkill.
John Cody Jr..........2:29¼
Sir Walter by Aberdeen.
Cleveland..............2:26½
Felina...... ...... .2:29½
Joe Holmes 2:26½
Lady Gay 2:27¼
Lucy Walter.. .....2:29
Sir Walter..............2:18¼
Walter Herr 2:19¼
William M. Hill..... 2:20
Sir Walter Jr. by Sir Walter.
Alcidalia...............2:30
Walter D. p 2:24¼
Sir Walter Scott by Jim Scott.
Daisy Queen 2:24¼
Sirius by Hambletonian Tranby.
Mark Sirius...........2:17½
Sir Wilkes.
Mamie Wilkes, p..... 2:29¼
S. J. Fletcher by Hambletonian Tranby.
Jim Deyo..............2:29
Skedaddle by Whiteside's Black Hawk.
Frank Reeves.........2:23¼
Skenandoah by Broken-Legged Kentucky Hunter.
Daisy Burns..........2:29¾
Skinkle Hambletonian by Gage's Logan.
Topsey..................2:30
Slander by Tattler.
Dazzle...................2:29½
Kerwin....................2:20¾
Ember, p...............2:20½
Fife, p....................2:17½
Slasher by Ashland Young.
Tommy Thompson, p 2:29½
Sleepy Dutchman by Jim Welch.
Fanny C. p.............2:24½
Smith Burr by Burr's Napoleon.
Gen. Butler 2:23¼
Smuggler by Blanco.
Lace Dealer....... ....2:25
Milton 2:30
Mount Morris..........2:19½
Nomad. 2:29½
Ouida 2:25¼
Revenue 2:22¼
Smuggle 2:24
Smuggler's Daughter...2:24¾
Tom Corwin....... .. .2:25
Young Smuggler 2:29¼
Flossy p... ....2:26¾
Grey Billy p.......... 2:23¼
Silver King, p...... .. 2:29½
Smuggler by Munsey.
Dan R., p 2:19½
Smuggler Gift by Smuggler.
Free Trade... .. ...2 24½
Smuggler Jr by Smuggler.
Sailor Boy, p 2 17¼
Smuggler Boy, p.......2:28
Smuggler Jr by Smuggler.
Albany Boy..........2:23
Smuggler Jr. by Smuggler.
J. S. A., p............ 2:20¼
Snowstorm by Steele's Snowstorm.
Jim Irving 2:23
Socrates by Rysdyk's Hambletonian.
Emma T. 2:17½
Socrates 2:27¼
Socratist 2:26
Soldier 2:28½
Student 2 21¼
Lochinvar, p . .2:28
Lucille H., p 2:12
Solicitor by Belmont.
Justinian. 2:27
Edmund Burke 2 30
Tiny..... .... 2 29¼
Solon by Harry Clay.
Alda, p... ....2.14¼
Sol Smith.
John B , p . 2:27½
Somonauk by Green's Bashaw.
Rex M 2:26¼
Sorrel Tom (Shawhan's Tom Hal) by Bald Stockings.
Hoosier Tom, p........2.19½
Sorrento by Woodford Mambrino.
Gordon 2:26¼
Lucina... ....2:29¼
Marcus. 2:29½
Somerset..... ... .2:2?¼
Sortie by Onward.
Aerolite 2:25¼
Soudan by Sultan.
Nubia 2:24½
South Jersey Patchen.
L D.....................2.25¼
Peachblow 2:29¼
South Jersey Patchen Jr 2:14¼
William S... .... 2:22¾
South Side.
Plain Dick. 2:29

Sovereign by Sterling.
Molly B. 2.25¼
Spartan.
Spartan, p 2 26¾
Spartacus by Almont.
Marie M.... ....2 19¼
Head Centre 2 25
Spectator by Dictator.
Charmion 2 20½
Kay S 2 29¼
Speculation by Rysdyk's Hambletonian
Crown Point . .. 2·24
Gracie S 2.22
Gus Spreckles . . . 2 30
Oakland Maid . . 2 22
Sphinx by Electioneer.
Altoneer 2.25
Baker . . 2 19¼
Belle of Abscota. 2:30
Borneo 2.23
Cervus 2 23½
Gen Sphinx .. 2 28¾
Gift O'Neer 2 20
Islam 2 26
Magna Sphinx .. 2 29
Peru . 2 19½
Rocko .. 2 29¼
Sibyl . . 2 29¼
Sylva C. 2 29¾
Uncle Tom .. 2 18¼
Valtullo 2·25
Valley Queen 2 28½
Water Lily .. . 2 19¾
Como, p 2 17¼
Cantab, p 2 14¾
Princeton R., p . 2 25¼
Sphinxetta, p 2 14¼
Syrena, p ....2·14¼
Spink by Andy Johnston.
Capt Lewis .. 2 20¼
Clara P. 2 17
Ebony Spink. 2 29¼
Frankie H 2 27¼
Splendor by Dauntless.
Broadway, p . 2 21½
Splendor (Reed's) by Glenn's Splendor
Kitty Clyde . 2:30
Sponseller Tuckahoe by Irwin's Tuckahoe.
Lynn W. . . 2 21¼
Sportsman by Tippo (Canadian.)
Tacony..................2 27
Sportsman.
Ella P., p 2.24¼
Sprague (McQuaid's.)
Peter Whetstone. . 2 29¼
Sprague (Round's) by Gov. Sprague.
Bill Cody. 2 29
Eldridge . . 2:23¼
Elsie Sprague 2 18½
Hat Sprague. . . 2 24¾
Jay-See-Ell. 2 24½
Jenny Sprague. . .. 2 15½
Mathewson Sprague ..2 29¼
Miss Grant 2 27¼
Raven Sprague .. . 2·19½
Victor Sprague. 2 26½
Yula . . . 2 27½
Gipsey Golddust, p.. ...2.24¾
Blanche, p. 2 24½
Frank Logan, p 2 25
J. F R., p 2:18¼
Nora Marks, p 2 23
Sprague, p 2 28¾

Tempest, p 2 17
The Judge, p . 2:22¾
Sprague Golddust by Governor Sprague.
Ora. . . 2 16¼
Mamie Golddust p. . 2 26½
Springfield by Kentucky Clay.
Annie Rooney . 2 24¼
Springhill by Dictator
Careless, p .. . 2 23¼
Springtime.
Lady B 2 25¾
Springville Chief by Field's Royal George
Leon Boy 2 29¾
Nora 2 28½
Spurgeon by Charley B
Fanny B.. .... . . 2 27½
Square Dealer by Knickerbocker
Utell 2 24¾
Squire Talmage by Rysdyk's Hambletonian
Avana . . . 2 29¼
Arctic B . . 2 17¾
Baldy T 2 29¾
Billy Ackerson . 2 24½
Billy D. . . . 2 19¼
Cadmus Hambletonian..2 29¾
Clifton Boy 2 26¼
Col. Bullitt. ... 2 18¼
Col. Neal..... . . 2 25¾
Hambletonian (Wooley's).. , 2 28½
Lottie K . 2.26¾
Mamie Tyler. . 2 27¼
Miami Chief 2 28
Neva . 2.23½
Richwood . . 2 24¼
Robert B 2 29½
Strader H 2 09½
Wood Talmage ... 2 30
Frank H, p.. . . 2 22½
S. R. Lamont by Hambletonian Prince
Headlight 2 26¾
Stamboul by Sultan.
Baron Rose . 2 29¼
Comrade 2 24¾
Daghestan 2.25½
Dorcas Pratt . 2.25
El Trebizond.. .... 2·26½
Falka . . . 2.24¼
Galata .. 2 26
Harry Winchester 2 27
Hilda S 2 19¼
Mascot . . .2 25¾
Murtha . . 2 18
Nadjy . . 2 26
Nehushta. . .. 2·30
Pawnee 2 26½
Redondo . 2 23
Rosita 2 27¼
Stammont . . 2 29¼
Stamnal.. . .... 2 25½
Sweetwater. .. . 2·26
Vera 2 18¾
Vesolia.. .. .2.29½
Voodoo 2 27½
Stamboula by Stamboul.
Precieuse..... .. 2:25
Standard Bearer by Volunteer.
Banner Bearer. 2 28½
Banner Boy. . .2 25
Contender, p. 2 30
Marlowe, p.. 2.15
Stanford Belmont.
Sargeant. . 2.29¼

Stanley by Strathmore.
Bonnie A .. . 2 25½
Bay Dan, p.. 2 22½
Stanton (Hager's). by General Stanton
Grimsby Girl. .. 2 26¾
Stanton Jr, by Gen Stanton.
Joe W. . 2 26¼
Star (Dunn's), by Monitor.
Sussex . . 2 30
Star Almont by Almont
Estelle.. ..... 2·26½
Star Bashaw by Bashaw Campbell
Golddust Prince 2.24¼
Star Duke by Iron Duke.
Lady Peek 2 26
Star Duroc by Messenger Duroc.
Gabrielle 2 20¼
Star Edmund by Seely's American Girl
Gov. Hill 2.18¼
Starguard by Strathmore.
Eldon, p .. . 2 29¼
Star Ethan by Daniel Lambert
Allen 2 30
Ben H , 2 30
Little Dan. . .2 19¼
Little Wonder . 2 24½
Pearl 2 25½
Split Ears . . 2 29¼
Swanton Boy. . 2 27¼
U. Tell . .. 2 29¼
Ethan Boy, p 2 24¾
Flying Morgan, p . . 2 28¼
Star Hambletonian by Rysdyk's Hambletonian
Clingstone . 2 30
Bacillus p...... .. 2 23¾
John McKay, p. . 2:23
Lady, p 2 23½
Star Hambletonian by Felter's Hambletonian.
Blanche 2 30
Snowball . 2 19½
Star Harold by Star Hambletonian
Uncle Sile .. 2 25
Starin Medium by Happy Medium
Echo 2 21¼
Star Lambert
Star Girl. . . 2 29½
Starlight by Kentucky Prince.
Daylight 2 19¼
Extralight .. 2 27
Greylight 2 16½
Morelight 2:28
Starletta 2 21¼
Starlight by McNasser's Golddust
Col McNasser . 2 19
Starlight by Star of the West.
Bird .. . 2 22
Starmont by Almont.
Emma Armstrong.. .. 2·28¾
Neri Newcombe . 2 28¾
Starmont Jr by Starmont.
Laura S 2 23¼
Star of Catskill by Seely's American Star.
Bonner 2.23
Ellen Cooper . . ·29¼
Star of the West by Flying Cloud.
Gipsey A.. . . . 2·25¾
Jim Raven. 2.30
Jim Star 2 29

Joe Young 2 19½
John J. Cook ....2·29½
Lady Groesbeck 2 25½
Little Fred... ...... 2:30
Maggie Kevin . ....2·25½
Star Bashaw 2 24½
Star Hawk . , ...2.17¾
Star of the West Jr. 2·29½
Vanadis...... ...... 2:26½
Idlewild, p....... ..2:2¾
Star Patchen by Henry Patchen.
Lady Finch 2:30
Startle by Ryskyk's Hamble-
tonian.
Alley Bonner .. . 2:23¾
Grey Dawn 2:22½
Instant 2:14¾
King Star 2.26½
Majolica . 2 15
Miss Majolica 2.24½
Portia 2 29½
Tural. ... .2·23½
Genevieve, p . 2 23½
Star Wilkes by George Wilkes
Actress... ...... 2·27½
Dandy Wilkes 2 29½
Eva Wilkes .... 2·22½
Irene 2.16½
Dennison Wilkes, p....2.27½
Fargo, p.. ....2.22½
Irene, p .. .. 2·11¾
Sailor Wilkes, p. ...2·25½
Statesman by Satellite.
Barney C.. p....... 2.21¼
State of Maine by Elmo.
Queen Anne .. . 2·28
Steele by Startle.
Arago .... 2·22½
Bonner Steele . 2·30
Puritan. 2 25
Speedwell...... ....2 26½
Silverone, p 2:28
Steinway by Strathmore.
Alamo 2 29½
Baden... ....2:24½
Cassidy. ....2·30
Charles Derby 2 20
Covey.............. 2.25
Neva 2.27
Steineer 2 29¼
Strathway...... ... 2:19
Caesar. p...... ....2 16½
Cricket, p 2.10
Critt, p........ .... 2.24¾
Free Coinage. p .. . 2 11¾
Lilly C , p....... ..2 20½
W. Wood, p 2:07
W. W. Foote p. 2.15½
Stephen A. Douglas by Rysdyk's
Hambletonian.
Dave Young 2:23
Douglas Girl.......... 2 29½
Edith F 2 28½
Frank K.............. ..2:28
Handicap........... 2 22
Idol 2 23
Lena D.. ...... 2·30
Nelly R...... ...2.22½
Versailles Girl..........2:25½
Western ... ... 2·30
Kate Craig, p .....2·25¾
Sterling by Patchen Boy.
J. B Thomas 2.18½
Sterling by Egmont
Argent 2.24½
Rattle Bones...........2 28
Sterling .. ....2·24
Acrobat, p 2:18¼

Haviland, p.............2:27
Vigor, p 2.28
Sterling by Volunteer.
Col Sterling ...... 2·28½
Dr. McFarland 2.21¾
Freddy J. 2.26½
Sterling Boy by Bellwood.
Belle Peters........ ...2 29
Cora Sterling. 2.26½
Steve Whipple by Hambletonian
Christman.
Needham's Whipple....2.27¾
Steve.... .... 2.19¼
Stillman by Louis Napoleon.
Jube....... ....2:26
Jupiter. ... .2·30
Stillson by Messenger Duroc.
Alice C. 2:27
Alvira.. . ..2·29¼
Baby Mine .. . 2.29½
D. G. B. 2 29¼
Maud Stillson.. .....2:29¼
Nelly Stillson . 2 24
Orphan Boy. 2:22½
Zeno 2:26½
Charley Stillson, p.....2:2½
Irene B., p 2:23¾
Stillson Jr. by Stillson.
Minnie G., p. .. 2.27½
Stockbridge Chief Jr. by Stock-
bridge Chief.
Abe Edgington. . .2.23¾
Stockbridge Chief Jr by Magic.
Young Stockbridge . 2:27
Stockholm by Phil Sheridan.
Larry Boy 2 29½
Poughkeepsie 2:29½
Triumph 2:27¼
Brown Nell, p...........2:23
Fred Holcomb, p 2 23
Stocking Chief by Clark Chief.
Annie Pixley........ 2 29½
Humboldt 2.20
Stockwell by Nutwood.
Immense 2:25½
Stoner Boy by Strathmore.
Hero 2 28
Wayne Wilson... .....2 29½
Stonewall Jackson by Mambri-
no Chief.
Gipsey Boy .. . 2 28
Stonewall Jackson by Len Rog-
ers.
Baby Mine 2 27½
Stonewall Jackson Jr by Stone-
wall Jackson.
Jerry L. 2 15¾
Storm by Masterlode.
Johnson... .... .. 2 27
Storm King by Happy Medium.
Paragon 2:13½
Stormer............ 2 26½
Stoughton J. Fletcher by Ham-
bletonian Tranby.
Elmo Echo 2:30
Fairplains .... 2·26¾
Strader by Strader's Cassius M.
Clay Jr
Rabe .... .2·24
Will Collender.... . 2 21½
Strader Jr. by Strader.
Leander, p 2 22
Straight Flush by Fearnaught
Jr.
Fearnaught. ..... 2·17¾
Stranger by Gen. Washington
Ballona.............2 11½
Boodle............... .2:19¼

Broomal . ...2·15
Col. Kuser 2:16½
Cebolla 2.18½
Hazel Dell.. .. ....2 24¾
Kathleen .. . 2·25½
Maggie Lewis . 2 28½
Moloch. 2:17
Myriad 2.28½
Nominator.. ......2:17½
Nominee... ....2:17½
Penhorn 2 24½
Spokane 2.26
Stanza 2 22½
Stranger Boy........ 2 29½
Strangler......... 2.2b½
Sylvia 2:29½
Wilder Boy .... 2·29½
Stranger by Ohio Stranger.
Kinsman 2:23½
Kinsman, p. ..... 2·17¾
Stratagem by Grand Sentinel.
Molly Gibson, p. 2.23½
Stratford by Strathmore.
Mistrea, p.. . . 2 23¾
Strathboy by Strathmore.
Wesley R , p... .. . 2 19½
Strathearn by Echo
Plunkett, p.........2:13¼
Strathlan by Strathmore
Freddy B...............2.29¾
Glamour.... ....2:26½
Kenneth....... ...2:29½
Strathmore by Rysdyk's Ham-
bletonian.
Algomah 2 29½
Alice Stoner ...... 2·24½
Ashmore . .. 2 29½
August Haverstick ..2.29½
Avonmore.. . 2 29½
Bedford. 2 30
Chandos.... ...... 2·28½
Chestnut Hill.. .2 22½
Cyprus.............2.22½
Deronda.... ......2.27½
Duchess.... .... 2.20½
Emmett B 2 29½
Frantic 2 22¼
Georgie Moshier .... 2·22½
Harkaway.. ....2.22½
Henderson........... 2 27¼
Herzog. . .. 2 29½
Leland Stanford. 2:21½
Loretta ... .. ·· 2 30
Major Ewing ·. 2 18¼
Milkshake 2 28
Miss Strathmore ... 2 29¾
Monitor 2 29½
Nannie Talbott. 2:29½
Ollie 2.24
Patience 2.26¼
Paul Hacker... ......2.24½
Phantom.............2 29¼
Poneto. 2.25½
Prince Albert. 2.26
Roseberry..........2.15¾
Santa Claus........2:17½
Secret............2.20½
Sim Brown...... ...2.26¼
Skylight Pilot 2:19
Snap 2 30
Snowden 2:16½
Solo 2:18½
Spartan............2:24½
Steinway.... ...... 2.25½
Stratford ....,....2.22½
Strathalan.............2:24¼
Strathboy .... 2·22½
Strathlan .. ..2·21¾

Strathmore Abdallah. 2 28
Strathwood 2:25½
Stuart. 2.25
Takina 2 30
Tucker 2:19
Carrie Strathmore, p. 2:17¼
Cutler, p. 2:24½
Esther, p 2 26¼
Jewetta Strathmore, p 2 21¾
Lower Stoner, p. 2.21
Lutie Strathmore, p 2 15¼
O. B., p. 2 26¼
Rockmore, p. 2.20½
Rosebug, p 2 15
Sand Boy, p 2·21
Strathso 2 13
Strathwayne, p 2 23¼
Senator Bell, p 2 26¼
Strathmore by Ericsson
Silver King 2.28¾
Strathmore (Morgan's) by Strathmore.
Harry Strathmore, p 2 24¼
Strathmore Jr by Strathmore.
Chesterfield, p. 2 11¼
Strathroy by Strathmore.
Mary Maderia 2 27¼
Strathway by Steinway.
Anerone, p. 2 29
Annie Rooney, p... 2 24¾
Stoneway, p 2 23¾
Strawn by Mammont.
Carrie Strawn 2 29¾
Grey Jim 2 22
Strideaway by Black Hawk Telegraph
Pratt 2 28
Strideaway.
Harry Strideaway 2.24¼
Strideaway Jr. by Strideaway.
Mattie Hunter 2 21¼
Stride Wilkes.
Charley D., p. 2 19½
Strike by Jay Gould
Mamie Strike 2·26¾
Strogoff by Grand Sentinel
Elsie Groff, p 2 16¼
Strong Horse
Whiteline 2 30
Studer by Durango.
Big Mike, p 2 19
Subscriber by Jim Schriber.
Charles M 2 29¼
Isabelle, p. 2 27¼
Soubrette, p 2·26
Suitor by Blackwood.
Suitor Jr., p. 2 24½
Sultan by The Moor.
Alcazar 2 20½
Amurath 2 26
Bay Rose 2 20½
Bay Sultan 2 29½
Big Frank 2·30
Centre 2 29½
Contractor 2 22
Dubec 2 17
Eva 2 23½
Florence Sultan 2 20¼
Hidalgo 2 27
Jaunita 2 29
King Sultan 2 23
Kismet 2·25½
La Grange 2 23½
Lucy R 2 18¼
Maggie Sultan 2·30
Margaret 2 28
Melrose 2 27
Moonstone 2:28½
Nailor 2 29
Othello 2 28
Rajah 2 29¼
Ruby 2 19¾
San Gabriel 2 29¾
Senator Rose 2 18
Soudan 2 27½
Stamboul 2 07½
St Lookout 2 26
Sultandin 2 29½
Sulwood 2 20
Sweetheart 2 22½
The Turk 2 30
Saladin, p 2.05¾
Sunny Slope, p. 2 29½
Summit by Attorney.
Mercury, p 2 24¾
Sunolo by Electioneer.
Baptism 2 30
Sunalto 2 26¼
Sunrise Patchen by Seneca Patchen.
Bob Volunteer, p 2 19¼
Sunshine by Brignoli.
Kid, p 2 25¾
Sunshine by Curtis' Hambletonian
Tempest 2 27¾
Superb by Ethan Allen.
Great Western 2 29
Harry Conklin 2 26
Superior (James') by Wood's Hambletonian.
Miss Superior 2 23
Superior (Du Bois') by Egbert.
Elsie S. 2.21½
Mary Magdalene 2 27¾
Beulah, p 2:14½
Carbonate, p. 2 09
Superior (Strait's) by Warwick Boy.
E. J S 2.22½
J B C. 2 27¼
Supervisor by Administrator.
Advisor 2:25¼
Surprise by Cutter's Comet.
Stormer 2 29¼
Sussex Chief
Lady Crossan 2 28
Sut Lovingood by Shelby Chief.
Sut 2 28½
Sutton D.
Merry Boy, p. 2 24¼
Sutton Boy, p 2 24½
Sweep by Sweepstakes
Minnie, p. 2 29½
Sweepstakes by Rysdyk's Hambletonian.
Argentine 2 21¼
Black Jack 2 22¼
Capt Lyons 2 17¼
Charley Kaile 2 28
Concentrator 2 30
Cranston 2 27½
Frank G. 2 27½
Frank M. 2:29¼
George C 2.23¼
Great Eastern 2 23½
Harry H. 2·23¾
Harry Mills 2.25½
Huzzar 2·29½
Inez 2 22¼
Jack Sailor 2 25¼
Joe 2 30
Le Count 2·29
Mabel Mack 2 25
McMullen Boy 2 29¼
Montgomery Boy. 2:28¼
Mustache 2 30
Nelly W. 2 23¾
Onida 2 29¼
Packer 2.23¼
Rex 2 24¼
Prince H 2 26½
Smith O'Brien 2 29¼
Taylorson 2 27¼
Willet 2 27½
Willie Brooks 2 29¼
Young Sweepstakes 2 30
Cleveland, p 2 23¾
Jim Wilson, p 2.26¾
Lenore K, p 2 23¼
Tommy K., p. 2.26½
Sweetmeats.
Kitty B. 2 25
Swigert by Alexander's Norman
Allegro 2 30
Badger Boy 2 27¼
Baybrino 2 28
Ben Gage 2 30
Bob Swigert 2 30
Brilliant 2 17½
Calamus 2 24¼
Chippewa Chief, 2 20¼
Cicero 2 26¼
David R 2 29¼
Dick Johnson 2 29¾
Doctor C 2 27½
Fashion 2 29
George K 2 25¼
Gen Sibley 2 30
Governor D 2 21
Harry Howe 2 27
Jessie Fly 2 29¼
Lady Richards 2 21¼
Laura E 2 28
Mambrino Swigert 2 30
Molly O'Connor 2 25¼
Moody 2 18½
Nickle Plate 2 20¾
Placida 2 30
Racine 2 30
Resolute 2 27¾
Richard E 2 28¾
Robbins 2 29¼
Royalty 2 25
St Cloud 2 23¾
Silvernale 2 25
Swigert Bellfounder 2 25¾
Swigert, Jr 2 22¾
Swigert K 2 22¾
Tirzah 2 30
Trotwood 2 22½
Winnie Wick 2 24¼
Yuca Solis 2 29¼
Jim Wilson, p 2 24½
President, p 2.23¼
Swigert Chief by Swigert.
Ice Cream 2 26

Tacoma by Gen Washington.
Puck 2 17¾
Talavera by Happy Medium.
Ely See 2 27½
Kitty Vera 2 23½
McVera 2 21¼
Tallett by Templar.
Don Pedro 2 25¾
Tallmage by Byerly Abdallah.
Newago 2 28
Tall Leon 2 29½
Tamarisk by Almont Rattler
Tina F. 2 25
Tangent by Onward
Radius 2 28½

Effie R., p 2:24¼
Tangle by Wood's Hambletonian.
Larry 2:29¼
Tarantalus by Strader's C. M. Clay Jr.
Billy D. 2:21¼
Tariff by Clarion Chief.
Sargent 2:29¼
Tariff Jr. 2:26
Tasco by American Boy.
Robert A. 2:29¼
Sunlight 2:27
Jessie L., p. 2:14¾
Julia R., p 2:22½
Nelly Tasco, p 2:23½
Lorine, p 2:27
Stephen W., p 2:25
Tasco Jr., p 2:23½
Tattler by Pilot Jr.
Indianapolis 2:21
Rumor 2:20
Slander 2:28½
Voltaire 2:20¾
Gossip, p 2:18
Tattler Jr. by Tattler
G. D. S. 2:29¼
Manson E., p 2:24¼
Taunton by Bay State.
Terragon 2:23
Sabatia, p 2:18¼
Taylor by Florida.
Nelly D 2:27¾
Taylor Horse.
Frank S. 2:22
Teak Blackwood by Blackwood.
Cinderella 2:22
Teak Blackwood Jr. by Teak Blackwood
Dynamite 2:30
Tecumseh.
Pat Hunt 2:25
Hiram Tracy, p 2:22½
Tecumseh by Mambrino Gift.
Daisy 2:23¼
Minnie Irene, p 2:25
Telegraph.
Hope 2:28
Telegraph
John D., p 2:20¾
Rowdy Joe, p 2:08
Telegram, p 2:12½
Telephone by Tom Lang
Tom Knox 2:28¼
Teller by Alcalde.
Tommy Root 2:25¼
Temperance by Young Wilkes
Jim Burns 2:25½
Tempest by Almont.
Gloster 2:26
Ilton 2:28½
Leap Year 2:26¾
Tempest Jr., by Tempest.
Billy G., p 2:21¼
Black York, p 2:18
Grey Harry, p 2:15¼
Humming Bird, p 2:25¼
Jimmy Temple, p 2:29½
Lincoln, p 2:23¾
Little Hope, p 2:21¼
Minnie Palmer, p 2:30
Monkey Rolla, p 2:15½
Ollie Belle, p 2:29½
Silvertail, p 2:16½
Thomas L., p 2:27¾
Temple Bar by Egbert
Iron Bar 2:24¾

Tennessee Dictator by Dictator.
Dyersburg, p 2:24½
Plaza, p 2:22¾
Tennessee Wilkes by George Wilkes.
Cantrell 2:29¾
Chiquita 2:26
Major Brown 2:27
Mary Wilkes 2:19
Meteora 2:20½
Optimist 2:27
Argot Wilkes, p 2:14¼
Bastion, p 2:27½
Cassie, p 2:12¾
Ialene, p 2:14
Morena, p 2:24
Monreo, p 2:26¼
Novice, p. 2:24¼
Paul Clifford, p 2:29½
Roan Wilkes, p 2:11¾
Turk, p 2:19½
Terhune Horse
Jenny L 2:27¼
Texas Jack Sr. by Judge Durell.
Corncracker, p. 2:18½
Jack the Ripper, p 2:18¼
Texas Jack Jr., p. .... 2:2?¼
Texas Joe, p. 2:29½
Texas Mike, p 2:27¼
Texas Rooker, p 2:24½
Texas Prince.
Duke, p 2:28¾
Thacher Hambletonian by Masterlode.
Lady H. 2:24¼
Nettie T. 2:27
William T. 2:25¼
The Baron.
Maumee S., p 2:28¾
The Banker by Mambrino Patchen.
Little Dick. 2:29¼
The Commodore by Guy Miller.
Mohawk Prince 2:28
The King by George Wilkes.
Bethlehem King 2:24¼
Berk King 2:29¼
Bruce King 2:28¾
Famous 2:28
Fred Wilkes. 2:25
Harriet 2:28¾
Jay 2:24¾
Jeanette 2:24½
Josie King 2:29¼
King 2:28¾
Kingbolt 2:27½
King Patchen 2:16¼
Limestone 2:19½
Nettie 2:19¼
Pattie Moore. 2:30
Sheik. 2:29½
Eximus, p. 2:23¼
The Marquis by Edward Everett.
Harry Watch. 2:16½
Marquis 2:19¼
William R 2:29¼
The Moor by Clay Pilot.
Beautiful Bells. 2:29½
Del Sur 2:24
Inez 2:30
Sir Guy 2:28½
Sultan 2:24
Tommy Gates 2:24
Theron by Adrian Wilkes.
Nathan P., p 2:28

The Seer by General Benton
Seersucker 2:30
Theseus by Administrator.
Templemore 2:29¾
Thistle by Sidney.
Dave Hyland 2:30
Oriole 2:20
Della S., p. 2:21
To Order, p 2:12¾
Thomas A. Scott by Mambrino Patchen.
Pat. 2:26¾
Thomas Carlyle by Gen. Withers.
Lizzie L 2:27¼
Thomas Jefferson by Toronto Chief
Fanny Jefferson 2:29
Farmer Boy 2:19½
Flora Jefferson 2:28¾
Green Mountain Boy 2:28¼
Harry Pelham 2:28½
John S. Clark 2:19¾
Kate Clark. 2:29½
Lady Jefferson 2:22¼
Lizzie M 2:20¼
Mambrino Jefferson. 2:30
Mike Jefferson 2:29½
Neli 2:27
Patrician 2:26¼
The Bull 2:30
Tom Carpenter 2:23½
Joe Jefferson, p 2:19¾
Thomas K. by Edward Everett.
Bosque Bonita 2:26¼
Col. Taylor 2:21½
Cordie Macey 2:25¼
Dearest 2:26¼
Eliza Jane 2:26½
Hambletonian (Bailey's) 2:29¼
Louise Macey. 2:27½
Mary Cecil 2:22½
Oscar J. 2:28¾
Russell R. 2:29½
Thompson.
Lottie 2:21
Thorndale by Alexander's Abdallah.
Daisydale 2:19¾
Edwin Thorne 2:16¼
El Capitan 2:24
May Thorne 2:24¾
Nettie Thorne. 2:25¼
Rosy Thorne 2:27¾
Thorndale Maid 2:30
Dalgetty, p 2:17¼
Thorndale Chief by Thorndale.
Thorndella 2:27¼
Thorndale F. 2:30
Molly Pitcher, p 2:23¼
Thorndale Idol by Thorndale.
Skipper. 2:28¼
Robert C., p 2:13¼
Thorndyke by Stockbridge.
Troublesome 2:19¼
Thorn Wilkes by Hector Wilkes.
Elsie Wilkes 2:24¾
Thorr by Alcazar.
Thelma 2:29
Thought by Daniel Lambert.
Archie B. 2:18½
Mabel W 2:27¾
Mack. 2:20½
Thunder by Middletown.
Independence B 2:29¾
Tiger by Canadian Lion.
Montreal Girl 2:30

Tilton Almont by Almont.
Almonta........2:25
Annie E........2:23
Belle A........2:29
Daisy S........2:23½
Kittie Almont,........2:22¾
Stranger........2.17
Tilton B........2:24¾
W. W........2 29¾
Time Medium by Happy Medium.
Rowland........2 24½
Tinder.
Jack Spratt........2 27¼
Tippoo.
Hudson........2.29
Tippoo.
James H Burke........2.27½
Tippoo Bashaw by Doble's Black Bashaw.
Duquesne........2 17¾
Tobe Jr by Blue Bull.
Franklin........2.19½
Token P.
Melson, p........2:28½
T. O. M. by Anteeo.
Lady O........2·24
Tom by Scott's Hiatoga.
Charley Douglas........2·30
Tom Allen.
Sinful, p........2 28¼
Tom Allen.
Frank J., p........2:19½
Tom Benton by Gen. Benton.
Mary Lou........2 17
Shylock........2.15½
Ned Winslow, p........2·12¾
Tom Brown Jr by Tom Brown.
Dandy Brown, p........2 23½
Fedora p........2 15
Tom Corwin by Smuggler.
Belle Martin........2:25
Anderson A. L, p........2:24¾
Johnny Corwin, p........2:24¼
Sherman, p........2·28½
Tom Crowder (Brown's) by Old Tom Crowder.
Judge Pollard........2·29½
Tom Crowder (Jamison's) by Tom Crowder.
Marion........2 23½
Tom Crowder (Gosnell's) by Wilson's Tom Crowder.
Bay Sally, p........2 20
Sweetzer, p........2 15
Tom Hal (Gray's) by Sorrel Tom
Little Gipsey........2·22
Limber Jack, p........2 18½
Tom Hal (Gibson's) by Kittrell's Tom Hal
Amorita, p........2·14¼
Blue Hal, p........2:23
Bob Taylor, p........2 18½
Brown Hal, p........2·12½
Chestnut Hal, p........2·27
Elma, p........2:18¼
Glide, p........2.19¾
Hal Index, p........2:20¼
Hal Pointer, p........2 04½
Imperial Hal, p........2 26¼
Jim Friel, p........2:20¾
John L., p........2:18½
Little Brown Jug, p........2:11¾
Plunger, p........2 27
Tom Hal, Jr........2.30
Trixy Hal, p........2:19½

Tom Hal, Jr., by Gibson's Tom Hal, Jr.
Brac, p........2 25¼
Brown Frank, p........2 16¼
Doctor H, p........2 14½
Gyp, p........2 27¾
Sleepy Tom, p........2 23¼
Tom Hal (Martin's) by Gibson's Tom Hal, Jr.
Brookside, p........2 11½
Red Hal, p........2·13¾
Tom Hazzard by Pelton's Hazzard.
Ben Starr........2 21¾
Ben Starr, p........2·19¼
Tom Hunter by Secor's Black Hawk.
Albemarle........2:19
Harvey........2·24¼
Joe........2 30
Tom Hendricks........2 30
Tom Jackson.
Daisy Dean, p........2:18¼
Tom Jefferson by Murphy's Royal George.
Honest Billy........2:27½
Tom Kimball by Tom Kimball (Canadian).
Hiram Miller........2 22¾
Tom Kirkwood by Green's Bashaw.
Bluewood........2 24½
Tom Moore (Minchin's) by Warlock.
Roxie, p........2.29¼
Tom Moore by Ethan Allen
Emma E........2 29
Tom Scott.
Tom H........2 27¼
Tommy Wilkes by Harry Wilkes.
Baby Wilkes, p........2·24
Doty, p........2:11½
Sprague Wilkes, p........2 18½
Tom Patchen by George M Patchen.
Captain........2·21½
Gladiator Jr........2:27½
Jack Spratt........2 22¼
Tom F. Patchen by Tom Patchen.
Stargazer........2.24¼
Tom Pugh by Red Wilkes.
Ambrosial........2.17¼
Tom Rolfe by Pugh's Aratus.
Lady Rolfe........2:22¼
Tom Hendricks........2·25
Tom Rolfe........2:22¼
Young Rolfe........2:21¼
Gem, p........2:13¾
Lady Rolfe, p........2 23
Sleepy Tom, p........2 12¼
Tom Rogers by George Wilkes.
Edgewood........2 21
Tom Rogers, Jr by Tom Rogers.
Adelia Wilkes, p........2 26
Tom Scott by Hambrino.
Hammond........2 26½
Taylor........2 28½
Tom H........2 27¼
Tom Wonder by Tom Crowder.
John W. Conley........2:24
John Stewart........2.30
Little Wonder........2:30
Modesty........2 26½
Lizzie Wonder, p........2:29¾

Tom Wonder Jr. by Tom Wonder.
Flora W., p........2·24¾
Tony Ensign by Skinkle Hambletonian.
Cyclone........2:25
Henry L........2:29¼
Tony R.
William Penn, p........2 24¼
Toodles Jr by Odin Bell.
Miss Thompson........2 20½
Nellie D........2 22¼
Tornado (Ely's) by Son of Long's Tornado
Modoc........2:25
Silky B........2:30
Tornado by Index.
Bay Frank........2·20
Tornado.
Maggie Dot........2 24¼
Tornado M. by Fortune.
John A. Logan........2:25
Toronto Abdallah by Toronto.
Polly B........2:28½
Toronto Chief by Royal George.
Belle of Toronto........2 30
Lady Hamilton........2:30
Thomas Jefferson........2:23
Toronto Chief.
Buzz........2.28½
Toronto Chief (Jones') by Toronto Chief.
Toronto Chief Jr........2·26¼
Toronto Chief Jr.
Harry Arthur........2·25½
Toronto Chief Jr. by Toronto Chief.
Johnny Gordon........2:25¼
Minnie Moore........2:27¼
Volunteer........2:25¼
Cyclone, p........2:27¼
Toronto Patchen by Ellis Patchen.
Belle Wythe........2 27½
Catalpa........2:27
Fidget........2..6½
Willie C........2:25½
Totoway by Aberdeen.
Queen Anne........2.25
Johnny Smoker, p........2:16¼
Touchstone by imp. Lapidist.
Frank Hull........2·27
Touchstone by Knickerbocker
Red Weed........2 29½
Tradewind by Nutwood.
Trader, p........2:25
Tramp by Gage's Logan.
Blue Bell........2:30
Brocade........2:28
Capt. Seth........2:27
Content........2:24¼
Dick Garret........2 29¼
Farmer........2.29¼
I, Jay S........2:24¾
Princess........2:29½
Sunshine........2:29¾
Tramp Jr........2 30
Trampoline........2:23
Tramp S........2:21¼
Velvet........2:28
Billy Hayes, p........2:29¼
Mandolin, p........2 15¾
Travilla, p........2:24¾
Tramp by Burger.
Miss Charley Joe John, p........2:29¼

Tramp Dexter by Tramp.
Western........2:25¼
Tramp Jr. by Tramp.
Don H........2:30
Tramp Panic by Tramp.
Senator A........2:13¼
Minnie T., p........2:30
Trample.
Leroy........2:29¼
Traveler.
Jack Curry, p........2:21¼
Traveler (Thompson's) by McMean's Traveller.
Sam Jones, p........2:18¾
Treewood by Nutwood.
Rockwood........2:25½
Trego by Egmont.
Bessie Trego........2:26½
Tremont by Belmont.
Bellerene........2:26¾
Home Brewed........2:24¾
Junemont........2:14
Loumont........2:23¼
Maymont........2:28½
Regmont........2:29¼
Tennyson........2:27¼
Wilkesmont........2:27
Tribune by Knickerbocker.
Tribune Jr........2:30
Tribute........2:25¾
Tribute by Tribune.
Dempsey, p........2:16½
Triceps by Dunbarton.
Actress........2:28¼
Dusty Miller........2:20¼
Lady Triceps........2:28
Mascot........2:24¼
Otis N........2:26¾
Trident by Almont Mambrino
Trident Jr........2:27¼
Tripolitan Chief by Bashaw Jr.
Linkwood Maid........2:20
Triton by Princeps.
McDowell, p........2:25
Trojan by Flying Cloud.
Ella Wright........2:24¾
Hattie........2:30
Trojan Boy by Rysdyk's Hambletonian.
Topsey M........2:30
Trojan Jr by Trojan.
Billy Briggs, p........2:21
Trouble by Almont.
Chartamount........2:28
Lizzie 2d........2:23½
Trifle........2:29¼
Abe Lincoln, p........2:26
Trouble by Paw Paw Chief.
Gyp........2:26¾
Troy by Menelaus.
Maud F........2:25¼
True Bred by Walkill Chief.
Katie L........2:23¾
Truxton by George Wilkes Jr.
Belle Truxton........2:30
Tuckahoe Post Boy.
Joe Kellogg........2:30
Turk by Arthur S.
Crepe McNett........2:28¼
Tuscarora Sea King by Lord Russell.
Cecil M........2:28¼
Louis Victor........2:23¾
Twilight by Rysdyk's Hambletonian.
Dr. Tilton........2:25¼
Morelight........2:30
Northlight........2:28
Oakwood........2:29
Twilight........2:30
Darklight, p........2:23½
Shawhan, p........2:16
Tybalt by Altamont.
Juliette, p........2:22
Typhoon by Narragansett.
Ranger H........2:27
Loafer, p........2:14½
Tyrant by Dictator.
Tyrant Chief........2:26¾
Tyrone by Scott's Hiatoga.
Stubby S. p........2:25

Ulric Wilkes by Young Jim.
Margaret L........2:16¼
Ulster Chief by Rysdyk's Hambletonian
Nile Beauty........2:19
Ulster Prince by Sweepstakes.
Mott........2:25½
Ultimus by Rysdyk's Hambletonian.
Mattie J. p........2:19
Pappoose, p........2:18¼
Pattie D. p........2:12¼
Uncle Ned by John Hadley.
Pull Back, p........2:26¼
Uncle Sim by Privateer.
Gordon Sim........2:20½
Union by Young Morrill.
Miss Murray........2:28½
Union Medium by Happy Medium.
Happy Glen........2:30
Star Medium........2:29¾
Updegraff.
Frankie Folsom, p........2:28¼
Upright by Whipple's Hambletonian.
Orlando, p........2:[illegible]3¼
Uwharie (Onion's) by Steven's Uwharie.
Billy the Kid, p........2:21
Uwharie (Stevens') by Farlow's Uwharie.
Flora Belle........2:22¾

Vacher by Woodford Mambrino.
Prosperous........2:29¾
Wauseon........2:22
Valdameer by Harold.
Corinne........2:29½
Dave Cook........2:24¾
Morning Star........2:27
Valley Girl........2:29½
Vanity........2:29¼
Valensin by Crown Point.
Hibibi, p........2:15¼
Valentine by Gibson's Tom Hal.
Veni, p........2:24½
Vestigie, p........2:15¾
Waste Ferris, p........2:27¼
Valentine (Langley's) by Erin Chief.
Prince Frederick, p........2:24¼
Valentine Swigert by Joe Dimmick.
Stanley........2:27
Valentine Chief........2:29½
How, p........2:17¼
Onyx, p........2:20¾
Stanley, p........2:27½
Valiant by Enchanter.
Ollie B........2:24¼
Antoinette, p........2:28¾
Valley Chief by Phil Sheridan.
Nero........2:25½
Valley Chief Jr. p........2:24¼
Van Also by Also.
Lady Van, p........2:24½
Vandergriff Colt by Brutus Jr.
Diamond........2:15¼
Vandergrift by Woodford Mambrino.
Robert Bonner Jr........2:29¼
Agnes M., p........2:24½
Van Helmont by Harbinger.
Caywood........2:17¼
Van Zandt by Florida.
Volk, p........2:28
Vandalia Wilkes.
Lenwood, p........2:30
Van Morgan.
Morgenthaler, p........2:29¾
Vasco by Harold.
Bill Lindsay........2:17½
Vadel........2:29¾
Val........2:18
Valissa........2:19
Ed Rosewater, p........2:16¾
Isa B. p........2:23½
Vasto, p........2:16½
Vatican by Belmont.
Ashby........2:19¾
Belle Vara........2:08¾
Brown Velvet........2:28¼
Doctor Hooker........2:23¾
Huguely........2:24
June Light........2:29¼
Light Hall........2:25¾
Tulu........2:21¾
Tony V........2:27¾
Van Robin........2:19¼
Vassar........2:21¾
Virus........2:29¼
Robin, p........2:20½
Vassar, p........2:07
Velox by Young Morrill.
Harry Velox........2:24½
Venango Chief by Venango.
Fanny C........2:27¼
Venture (McRoberts) by Belmont.
Venturer, p........2:26½
Venture Boone by Daniel Boone.
Stanley........2:17
Velocity.
King of Diamonds, p........2:22
Vere de Vere by Onward.
Iras, p........2:19½
Vergennes Black Hawk by Vermont Black Hawk.
Lady Ross........2:29¾
Vermont (Gill's) by Downing's Vermont.
Bonner Boy........2:23
Vermont by Independence.
Ella Lewis........2:27
Lollie T........2:28¼
Parrott........2:26
Vermont Abdallah by Young America.
Fanny A........2:29
Howard........2:20

Jay U. See 2:25¾
Maj. Ulrich 2:24¼
Vermont Hero by Sherman Black Hawk.
Lady M 2:30
Vermont Hero by Hale's Green Mountain Morgan.
Lady Douglas 2 30
Princeton Boy 2 28
Vermont Ranger by Morrill.
Champion Morrill 2 27
Vernon Boy by Tom Vernon.
Our Boy, p 2:17½
Vero by Swigert.
Wild Idol 2 28½
Winnie Winsome 2:22¾
Ben Swigert, p 2:30
Veto Jr.
B. B., p 2:12½
Viceroy by Viscount.
John W., p 2 25
Lady Vice, p 2 17
Viceroy (Snyder's), p. 2:20
Victor by Cassius M. Clay.
Bay Jack 2:30
Victor by Young Darkey.
W. C. B. 2.26½
Victor by Echo.
Pascal, p 2:21¾
Victor by Gen. Knox.
Iolanthe 2 30
Victor by Gen. Putnam.
Flossy 2:25½
Lady Wellington 2:25¼
Victor Bismarck by Rysdyk's Hambletonian.
Bannermark 2.17¾
Bismarck Monroe 2:25
Bismont 2.18½
Blue Grass Hambletonian 2:19¾
Brightmark 2·24¾
Brownmark 2:24
Col. Bismarck 2:24
Edgemark 2:16
Escape 2·26½
E. T. H 2:16¼
Fanny Mark 2 29¾
Joe Mark 2 28¼
Kentucky Boy 2:28
Kentucky Hambletonian 2·27
Kokomis 2:21
Last Chance 2:28¾
Lucetta 2:22¼
Mambrino Girl 2:30
Mark Monroe 2:25½
Marquette 2:20
Melrose 2:29½
Merle Moore 2.25¾
Oakhurst 2:26
Orange Blossom 2:26½
Queen Mark 2·27
Red Mark 2:26¾
Seneca Bismarck 2:22¼
Victor Hambrino 2.20
Victor Wilkes 2:29½
Emma L., p 2 21¼
Markland, p. 2:18½
Milan, p. 2 29
Victor Denmark by Grey Denmark.
Billy 2:29¼
Victor Knight by Satellite.
Colored Girl 2:25½
Victor Mohawk by Mohawk Chief.
Miss Sontag 2:28
Victor Clay 2:26¼
Victor Duroc 2 28
Victor Napoleon by Louis Napoleon.
Brighton Girl, p 2·21¼
Victor Patchen by Tom Patchen.
Nicholas 2.29¼
Byrl C., p 2:23¼
Victor Wilkes by Victor Bismarck.
Bachelor Wilkes 2:30
Contestor Wilkes 2.29¾
Dana Wilkes 2 29½
Decorum 2:28½
Jumbo Wilkes 2:22¾
Juno Wilkes 2:29
Madge Wilkes 2 21¾
Ruth Wilkes 2 17½
Vidette Boy Jr. by Vidette Boy.
W. H. Bailey 2·20¼
Vigil Rene by King Rene.
Geb. 2:20¼
Viking by Belmont.
Bellwether 2:19¼
Brinhilde 2 19¾
Earl King 2:27
Queen Esther 2:29¾
Vera 2:25¼
Vida 2 23½
Rosebud, p 2 23
Virgil by Green's Bashaw.
Alkali 2·29¼
Virgo Hambletonian by Rysdyk's Hambletonian.
Charley Hogan 2·18¾
Cunarder 2:26¼
Lilly Irwin 2:30
Same Kind 2:25½
Vitalis by Belle Morgan.
Moss Rose 2:30
Vitalis Jr. by Vitalis.
Black Vitulis, p 2 25
Vittoria by Administrator.
Enderby 2:29¾
Vitruvian by Stillson.
Black Vic 2:29¼
Volante by Selim
King Clifton 2 22
Volevant
Island Belle, p 2 24¾
Volley.
Billy C 2:23¼
Volmer by Gambetta.
Brown Lace 2:28½
Volney by Volunteer.
Edward 2.21¼
Lottie P. 2:30
Voltaire by Tattler.
Brown Jim 2.27¾
Volney 2.26½
Young Voltaire 2:30
Bessemer, p 2·13¼
Volume by Volunteer.
H. M. B., p 2 29½
Volunteer by Rysdyk's Hambletonian.
Abdallah (Goldsmiths) 2·30
Alley 2:19
Amy 2,20¼
Autumn Queen 2:29
Bodine 2:19¼
Carrie 2·24¼
Carver 2:27¼
Dexter 2 27
Domestic 2:20½
Driver 2 19½
Frank Wood 2:24
Gloster 2 17
Happy Volunteer 2:27¾
Hillcrest 2·29
Huntress 2.20¾
John Goldsmith 2:28½
Lady Morrison 2.27½
Louise 2·29¼
Maggie May 2.29½
Mary A. Whitney 2:28
McKeen 2 27½
Powers 2 21
Prince Arthur 2:29
St. Julien 2 11¼
St. Remo 2:28½
Susie Collins 2.26¼
Sweetness 2·21¼
Trio 2:23¼
Unolala 2.22¼
Volney 2 23
Volunteer Chief 2:29½
Volunteer Maid 2·27
William H. Allen 2.23¼
St. Patrick, p 2:14½
Shamrock, p 2:27¼
Volunteer by Gen. Dana.
Connemara 2:30
Volunteer Boy by Volunteer.
Linda 2·29½
Volunteer Clay by Harry Clay
Viola Clay 2:24¼
Volunteer Duroc.
Maurice Mullins, p 2:26½
Volunteer Goldsmith by Goldsmith.
Hambletonian (Ayres') 2.29½
Volunteer Jr. (Dunbar's) by Volunteer
Vilette 2 22½
Volunteer Jr. by Volunteer.
Country Girl, p 2:21½
Volunteer Star by Volunteer.
Alaric 2:21¾
Bethlehem Star 2:20¾
Kentucky Star 2.21½
Valkyr 2:19¾
Volunteer Swigert by Swigert
First Born 2:29¼
Kitty B. 2 29½
Prince S 2:20¼
Cisco Queen, p 2:23
Von Arnim by Sentinel.
Von R 2·29½
Von Mark by Victor Bismarck
Lelah W., p 2 23¾
Von Moltke by Morrill Colt
Cunard 2:30
Dotty D 2:25¼
Flora 2 25½
Mermaid 2:26¼
Vosburg by Mambrino Pilot.
Ike Shultz 2 30
Voucher by Volunteer.
Windsorina, p 2 22

Wabash by Red Wilkes.
Dembert 2:30
Wade Hampton.
Jennie Wynn 2:26¼
Rolo Ryan 2:21½
Grey Goose, p 2.25¼
Nancy B. 2·29¼
Ilderim, p 2:19¾
Wagner Bashaw by Green's Bashaw.
Ida T 2:27

J. H. McCormack.... 2.29
Mary C.... .... 2 30
Oliver W...... ..2:24
Ashby, p... . .. 2:26¾
Minnie Roberts, p 2:22¼
Waldensian by Holabird's Ethan Allen
Harry B., p 2:20¼
Waldstein by Director.
Humboldt Maid......2:27
Native Son...... ...2:29½
Walker Morrill by Winthrop Morrill.
Forest Boy.... ... . .2:26½
I. X. L.......... .... .2:25¼
Kitty Van.............2:24
Molly Morrill.........2:28¼
Vortex 2:21¼
Marendes, p. 2:17¼
Omega, p..............2:23½
Orphan Boy, p.. ....2:24¼
Walker Sprague by Gov. Sprague.
Arthur Sprague.......2:27½
Walkill by Rysdyk's Hambletonian.
Nora...................2:27¾
Walkill (Steele's) by Walkill Chief.
Gen. Grant.... ....2:26¼
Gaiters, p..... ...... 2:23¼
Peter Cooper, p. 2:21¼
Phantom, p............2:26½
Zandora, p... ....2:22½
Walkill by Walkill Chief.
Mayflower...... . . .2.21¼
Whalebone. 2:23½
Walkill by Walkill Chief.
Messina Boy, p .. . 2:16¾
Walkill Chief by Rysdyk's Hambletonian.
Billy Burr. 2:29½
Dick Swiveller. 2:18
Great Eastern 2:18
Topsey...... .. ..2:21¾
Valley Girl...........2:30
Walkill Chief 2d by Walkill Chief.
Young Vermonter 2.30
Walkill Jr. by Walkill Chief.
Frank P., p...........2:17¾
Nellie I., p. 2:25½
Walkill Prince by Rysdyk's Hambletonian.
Athalia Prince. 2:26¾
Brunswick 2:25
Della McGee..........2:28
Demonstrator 2:30
Eagle Lake 2:27½
Eura 2:18¼
Glenwood Prince.....2:21
Letta C. 2:16¼
O. K....................2:26¼
Silverdale.............2:25½
Walsingham by Geo. Wilkes.
Fay Gordon.......... 2:26½
Jellyby 2:26
Latitude................2:15
Linkwood..............2:29¼
Louise Watt.........2:27
Lovell.... ....2:26¼
Mount Airy 2:19¼
Naboth.... .. . 2:19¼
Neville 2:29½
Niblo...... .. ..2:27¼
Novice 2:26½
Birentha, p.... .... . 2:25
Long Shot, p... ......2:26½

Walter Lewis by Corsair.
Belle Underhill 2:26¼
Walter V.
Plano Prince. 2:28½
Wanderer by Gen. Knox.
Oakdale Dot 2:23¼
Wapsie by Green's Bashaw.
Blue Charley..........2:22
Gen. Grant 2:21
Glenwood 2:27¾
Senator N..............2:25
Star Bashaw..........2:27
Wapsie B........ ......2:29
West Liberty.........2:28
Wonder................2:21¼
Yellow Ochre.... ....2:28½
J. F. G., p 2:25¼
Minnie M., p...... ..2:24¼
Wapsie L., p 2:29
Ward B. by Eros.
Letter B................2:27½
War Eagle by Alden Goldsmith.
Winnie H 2:18¼
War Eagle by Prompter.
Eagle, p 2:19½
Warfare by Aberdeen.
Margery H., p.........2:26½
Warlock by Belmont.
Annine 2:21
Bertha C...............2:29¼
King Warlock. 2:24¼
Moloch.................2:26¼
Rachel 2:25¼
Templeton. 2:25½
Warcliff 2:29¾
Wardship. 2:23¾
Warwitch 2.18¼
Warwitch, p 2.25¼
Warrior Jr. by Warrior.
Headlight, p...........2:22½
Lizzie Mack, p........2:14¼
Soldier, p. 2:23
Warwick Boy by Middleton.
Midnight, p 2:28¼
Warwick Boy by Iron Duke.
A. B. C 2:29¼
Addie L 2:18¼
Belle D... ....2:29¼
Bert Sheldon 2:29¾
Bert Sheldon Jr.......2:16¼
Class Leader. . 2 22¼
Ed Cook....... . .....2:24½
Edna C..................2:29½
Jenny R... ......2:29¼
Lady B.... .....2:23½
Myrtle..................2 28½
Okalona 2:27¾
Sam Webber . . .2:25¼
Superior 2:18½
Tom Barry 2:26¼
Lady Mac, p....... 2 25¼
Moxie, p 2:27¼
Onie D., p...............2:20
Warwick Girl, p.. ....2:26¼
Washburn by Volunteer.
Johnny B., p..........2:15
Washburn Horse.
Moose 2:19½
Washington (Burr's) by Burr's Napoleon.
Lady Woodruff 2:29
Washington.
Stevie H...............2:22¼
Washington by George M. Patchen.
Laura M.............2:27

Fred Ackerman, p . 2:23
Washington Jackson by Andrew Jackson.
Twilight 2:27
Watchmaker by Winthrop Morrill.
Hamoun...............2:28¾
Josie B 2:28¼
Young Watchmaker..2:30
Waterloo by Belmont.
Benedicta.... ....2:29½
No Trouble............2 21¼
Water Bird, p,........2:29¼
Waveland Chief by Ericsson.
Joan....................2:30
Olaf....................2:22
Syenite 2:29¼
Waveland.............2:26¼
Wildey. 2:29
Waxford by Hemlock.
Baby Bunting 2:28½
Belmont Prince.......2:17¼
Prince..................2:28¾
Wax.... ....2:24
Waxey by Berthune.
Grafton 2:22¼
Waymart by Happy Medium.
Low Mark, p..........2:19¾
Waymark, p.... .....2:10¼
Wayne Wilkes by Red Wilkes
Centlivre Wilkes......2:28
Hazel Wilkes 2:21¾
Wayne Chief......... 2:25
Cash Boy, p...........2:27¼
Kaiser Wilkes, p......2:27¼
Nidia, p 2.13¼
Wayne Wilson by Stoner Boy.
King Wilson, p........2:25½
Quaker K., p..........2·22½
Wayward by Onward.
Importer, p...........2:22½
J. H. K., p............2:24½
Wedgebrook.
Honeymoon, p........2:30
Wedgewood by Belmont.
Connaught............2:24
Ethelwyn 2:29¾
Favonia..............2:15
French Plate.........2:26¼
Jeff Davis 2:27½
Malabar...............2:21¼
Miss Kirkman. 2:17
Myrtlewood...........2:25¼
Noonday 2:30
Nugget.... ... .2:26¾
Pagan 2:30
Queensware. 2:25
Ulva....................2:27
Wistful................2:13¼
Woodnote.............2:28
Blairwood, p.........2:15¼
Conway p.............2:18¾
Frank Wood, p.......2:25½
Halwood, p 2:27½
Harpeth, p 2:21½
Ironwood, p...........2:26¾
J. W. C., p............2:24½
Laredo, p. 2:19½
Lilly, p. 2:28¼
Lucille, p. 2:14½
Rosewood, p..........2:22
Well Ahead, p.........2:19¼
Weige.
Mountain Quail......2:25½
Weisbaden by Belmont.
Goldbaden............2:25¼
Lady W........... ..2:18¾

Red Bird.............2:25¼
Wellington by Kentucky Prince.
Black Bess......2.22¼
Daddy K........2:28½
Darlington........2:18¼
Daisy........2 28¼
Duke of Wellington 2 20
H. C 2:22
Lord Nelson ...2 26¼
National 2 20¼
Robert L 2:28
Rose 2 29¼
Walton Boy ...2 20¾
Westman by Col. West.
Emma Westman ..2 29¼
West Cloud by Abdallah West.
Wild Rose, p .2 16
Westchester by Hasbrouck's Hambletonian Chief.
Brookside 2:26
Fantine 2:26
West Egbert by Egbert.
Halifax......2 25¼
Easter Girl, p. .2:28¼
Eggleton, p....2.16¾
Joe Egbert, p....2:15¼
Westland
Waveland. p 2.26¼
Western by Hambletonian Jr.
Chapman, p ...2 22¼
Western Boy by Empire.
Howard S ...2 28¼
Tom Thorn ...2:20½
Zulu Girl ..2 27¼
Western Chief by Curtis' Hambletonian.
Cottonette ...2 25
Western Fearnaught by Danville Boy, Jr.
Alley W . 2.22¼
Billy Freer ...2:24¼
Carrie H.... 2:29¼
Lady Brownell .2:25¾
May Queen ...2:29¾
Prince Arthur.....2:18
Jessie C. p ...2:29¼
Western Sprague by Gov. Sprague.
Four Lines ... 2 29½
Westfield Boy by Black Prince.
George M . 2.24
Westmont by Col. West.
Monte West ...2:25¾
Lady Westmont, p..2 25¼
Westmont (Sperry's) 2.27¼
Westmont (Sperry's) by Westmont.
Sandy ... 2 23¾
Westwood by Blackwood.
St. Valentine ...2:16¼
Whalebone by Hambletonian Tranby.
Billy Jay, p.......2 17¾
Billy Walters, p .2 18¼
Guy Wonder, p . 2.24¾
Quaker Boy, p.. 2.14¼
Thornton Girl, p.....2 26¾
Whalebone by Sherman Morgan.
Blackstone Belle .2:28¼
Whalebone.
Phil Caswell .. 2 28

Whalebone Knox by Gen. Knox.
Alpha......2:29¼
John S Heald...2:27¼
W. H. Cassidy by Young Jim.
Jessie Hood.. 2:25½
Wheelock by Romulus.
Rome 2 29¼
Whip Clay by Strader's Cassius M. Clay Jr.
Will Benham 2 24¼
Whipple by Whipple's Hambletonian
Glaucus .. 2 27¼
Retta ...2 28¼
Whippleton by Hambletonian Jr.
Flora B......2 27
Frank O'Neil....2.29
Glaucus .. 2 30
Lilly Stanley...2.17½
Molly Patten ...2:29½
Oakville Maid. 2 26
Cora C. p ...2.22½
Homestake, p...2.16½
Like Like, p ...2 25
Whip (Hunt's).
Hoosier Dick, p 2 30
Whips by Electioneer.
Azote .2.08¼
Cobwebs .. 2 12
Manille . 2 29¼
Navidad ... 2 21½
Warlock .2 24
Whirlwind.
Bay Whalebone.. ...2:26½
Whirlwind.
Barkis ...2:25½
Elsie Y . 2 29¾
Lady Mac .. 2 23
Whirlwind Chief by Whirlwind.
Birdie .2:28¼
Ray Jackson ...2 29¼
Whirlwind Jr. by Whirlwind.
Jimmy Puzzler ...2.30
Whirlwind Jr.
Little Dan, p 2 28
Whistle Jacket by Strader's Cassius M. Clay Jr
Brown Sam, p.....2 29¼
Whitby by Hannis.
Angelus .2:23½
White Cloud by Telegraph.
Bessie Ann, p 2:29¼
Bessie M, p..... 2 14
Flora Belle, p .2.13¾
Logan, p ...2:26
Rocktown, p ...2:25
T. N. B ...2:10½
Josephus, p.. .. 2 25
White Ghost by Simpson Messenger.
Ed Eaton... 2:28
Whitehall by North American.
Rhode Island ... 2:23½
Whiteline by Strong Horse.
Belle Whitney... 2:30
Glen Miller... 2 18
J. M. G... 2:20
Star Line 2.27
Star Line ...2:29¾
Lady L. p ...2 26¼
Whiteline Jr. by Whiteline.
Maggie B......2 26

Whiteline Chief by Whiteline.
Castor . 2:30
Whitney by Mambrino Russell.
Ramona ...2 16¾
W. H. Maxwell by Baird's Hambletonian Prince.
Merzalia......2 29¼
Tricotrin 2:25
Wichita by Mambrino Patchen.
Arthur... 2.26¼
Wiggins.
Gentle Annie. 2:26
Wildair by Ethan Allen.
Rustic. 2:27
Wideawake by Spalding's Abdallah.
Lady Spanker 2:26½
Wild Bashaw by Green's Bashaw.
Diamond 2:28
Wild Billy by son of Vermont Black Hawk.
Fairmont ... 2 29¼
Wild Boy by Gen. Benton.
Donchka. 2.24
Wild Deer by Old Tippoo
Tartar. 2 25½
Wildbrino by Hambrino.
Callino 2:20½
Little Jim. 2 23¼
Wild Crocus.... 2:25¾
Attar, p. 2:23¾
Little M.. p 2 22
Sweet Violet, p 21¾
Wilder by Bayard.
Trifle . 2 26¼
Wilder by Middletown.
William 2 18¾
Wilder Wilkes.
Daisy C , p 2.22
Wildfire by Volunteer.
Lizzie S 2 22¼
Wildmont by Egmont.
Chloe. 2:22¼
Wildnut by Woodnut.
Arial. 2 27¾
Bedworth 2:27
El Rami. 2:29¾
Wild Tom by Old Wild Tom.
John R . p 2 12¼
Wild Wagner (Hiatt's)
Leon, p. 2 23¼
Wiley, p 2 30
Wild Wagoner by George M. Patchen.
Black Frank 2 24½
Essex Maid ... 2 30
Lady Wilson . 2 29¾
Lizzie S 2 27¼
Lydia Thompson . 2 26¼
Wilgus Clay by Neaves' Cassius M Clay Jr.
Ella Clay......2 23¼
Lillian D. 2:30
Wilkerson by Favorite Wilkes
Mamie Allen. 2.30
Grover Cleveland, p 2 15¼
Wilkes by Alcyone.
Brownie.. .... 2 29¼
China Boy 2:29¾
Col. Pitt - 2:22¼
Col. Osgood 2:18¼
Fred Wilkes .. 2 17¾
Glimmer. 2.23½

CRIT DAVIS, Harrodsburg, Ky.
There are few who do not remember how he swept the deck
with Prince Wilkes 2:14¾.

GILL CURRY, Nashville, Tenn.

The master mechanic from the Sunny South who earned his share
of the money in 1894 with Red Bud 2:14¼.

Hazel 2:28¼
Johnny Wilkes 2:27½
Mattie Merrill 2:27¼
St. Croix 2:14¾
Wilkes by Favorite Wilkes.
Walter Wilkes, p 2:14½
Wilkes (DeLong's) by Hambletonian Wilkes.
Midget Wilkes 2:29¾
Wilkes Boy by George Wilkes.
Abbadonne 2:23¼
Albert S 2:30
Albion 2:25½
Angelina 2:12
Angis 2:29¼
Bessie Wilkes 2:29¼
Cleta Wilkes 2:29¼
Constantine 2:12½
Ella O. K 2:29
Emsie 2:28
Glen Wilkes 2:25
Grattan 2:13
Homer Wilkes 2:28
Julia Coulter 2:27
Kentucky Lew 2:28½
Mary Caldwell 2:20
Nelly A 2:16¼
Nelly Aldine 2:21¾
Preston 2:27¾
St. Vincent 2:13½
Sternberg 2:15¾
Wilbooka 2:19¾
Wilkes Boy Jr. 2:29¾
Wilkesman 2:26¼
Willelah 2:27¼
Winston 2:25
Judge Swing, p. 2:11¾
Warburton, p 2:18½
Wilkes Chief by Bourbon Wilkes.
Charley Anderson 2:22½
Wilkesdale by Alcantara.
Hurlingham 2:19½
Wilkes Golddust by Young Jim.
Psyche 2:15¾
Fanny S., p. 2:23¾
Wilkesmont by Tremont.
Andy Wilkes 2:28½
La Bessa, p. 2:24¼
Lizzie N., p 2:21¼
McKinley, p. 2:24¼
Wilkes Nutwood by Nutwood
Shadeland Acme 2:28¾
Shadeland Almeda 2:27¼
Shadeland Lamott 2:29¼
Wilkesonian by George Wilkes
Dick Wills 2:25¾
Emma Wilkes 2:23¾
Joe Bluffer 2:27¼
Lakewood Maid 2:29
Lakewood Prince 2:13½
Miss Q 2:29¾
Myrtie Peak 2:29¾
Pittsburg Wilkes 2:16¾
Dick Wills, p. 2:16½
Joe Bluffer, p 2:29¾
Minnie C., p. 2:29¼
Wilkes Spirit by George Wilkes.
Cornelia Wilkes 2:23¾
Morton 2:29½
Preston Wilkes 2:29¾
Sarah Coin 2:29¾
Wilkes Spirit Jr. by Wilkes Spirit.
Chester 2:17¼
Easter Wilkes 2:21¾
Jerry Wilkes 2:30
Pearl Wilkes 2:22¾
Sam Hill 2:20¼
Barrington Wilkes, p 2:25
Wilkes U.
Bessie Wilkes, p. 2:23¼
Wilkeswood by Nutwood.
Bessie Wilkeswood 2:20
Ergot 2:23½
Fleety Wilkeswood 2:28
Maggie Wilkeswood 2:28
Mattie Mosier 2:27¼
Vernwood 2:26
Capt. Wood, p. 2:16¾
Wilkie Collins by George Wilkes.
Aberdeen Wilkes 2:26
Administrator Wilkes 2:25¼
Almont Wilkes 2:20
Annie Wilkes 2:21½
Bella Wilkes 2:18½
Catapult 2:21½
E. N. Cook 2:26¼
Harry Bacchus 2:23¼
John Bascomb 2:25
Plutone 2:23¼
Pluto Wilkes 2:26¾
Balsora Wilkes, p. 2:17¾
Nelly Green, p 2:29
Teddie Collins, p 2:24¼
Wilkie Collins by Ahawaga Chief.
Midge 2:27¾
Wilkesmont by Alcantara.
Quiz 2:23¾
Wilkie Russell by Mambrino Russell.
Primus 2:29
Willard Russell, p 2:15
Wilkins by Wilkins Micawber
Gavaroche 2:28¾
Wilkins Micawber by Rysdyk's Hambletonian.
Black Prince 2:25½
Kingsley 2:26¼
Victoria 2:30
Wilko by Simmons.
Whirligig, p. 2:10
Wilkomont by Almont Pilot.
Bertie R 2:15¾
Will Crocker by Electioneer.
Irene Crocker 2:20
Little Crocker 2:30
Willet by Rochester.
Nabob 2:30
Will Go.
Daisy E., p 2:24¼
William Clay by Little Billy.
Wilson, p 2:12¾
William Corbitt by Arthurton.
Ben Corbitt 2:21
Dot, p 2:27¼
William H. Allen by Volunteer.
Allen's Best 2:28½
George Allen 2:28
Walter A 2:25¼
Warren T 2:26
William H. Ripley by Woodpecker (Canadian).
Royal George 2:26¼
Dan Ripley, p. 2:24¾
William Irvin by Lyle Wilkes.
Little Billy 2:30
William H. Vanderbilt by Masterlode.
Alleta 2:26½
Bonnie M. George 2:30
Conway 2:18¾
Dick 2:29
Lena V. 2:28¼
S. W. G 2:26¾
Dick R., p 2:27½
William L. by George Wilkes.
Axtell 2:12
Emperor Wilkes 2:20¾
Erica 2:24
Margaret C 2:19¼
Alexis, p 2:18
Bonecher, p 2:26
Lucra, p 2:23¼
William M by William M. Rysdyk.
Frank B 2:23½
William M. by Messenger Chief.
Gen. Denver 2:22½
Zebidee 2:29¾
Woodland Maid, p 2:30
William M. Hill by Sir Walter.
Judge Hurt, p 2:14¾
Lena Hill, p 2:12
William Miner (Canadian).
Chieftein 2:25½
Frank McCune 2:25¼
William M. Rysdyk by Rysdyk's Hambletonian.
Lady Whitefoot 2:18¼
William Penn.
Georgie H., p. 2:29
William Rysdyk by Rysdyk's Hambletonian.
Beulah 2:29¼
Billy Rysdyk 2:27½
Charley Ellis 2:27¼
Defiance 2:27¼
Lily Rysdyk 2:25½
Priscilla 2:27¼
Robert Rysdyk 2:18¾
Umber 2:25¼
William Rysdyk, Jr. by William Rysdyk.
Nellie B., p 2:29¾
Williams by Combat.
Tom Williams 2:23¾
Miss Williams, p 2:16¼
William Tell by Plumas.
Maxwell 2:28¾
William Wallace by Duke of Brunswick.
Lady Cummings, p 2:29¼
Lady Wallace, p. 2:22½
Prim Wallace, p. 2:27½
William Wallace Scribner, p 2:26¼
William Welch by Rysdyk's Hambletonian.
Jeremiah 2:21½
Violin 2:25¼
William Wheeler by Iowa Duroc.
Green Stotts, p. 2:22¾
Willie McMahon by McMahon
Bonnie F. 2:26
Molly B. 2:29½
Willie Schepper by Rysdyk's Hambletonian.
Laura B 2:27
Willie Wilkes by Young Wilkes.
Iola Wilkes, p. 2:22½
Wilmont by Almont Rattler.
Gladstone 2:28¾

Willoughby by Ned Forrest.
- Belle Cassett......... 2:13¼
- Belle M., p 2:19¾

Wilmar by Rhode Island.
- Sprague Superb...... 2:29¼
- Sprague Winship 2:29¼

Wilmore by Strathmore.
- Bonnie Wilmore 2:14½

Wilson Horse by Morse Horse
- Mary C 2:24½

Wilton by George Wilkes.
- Adelia 2:25¾
- Amani 2:28¾
- Antecedent....... 2 29½
- Axminster 2:21¾
- Bernadotte....... 2·29½
- Billy Wilton........ 2:30
- Bon Ton......... 2·28½
- Bucyrus 2 23¾
- Cornelia........... 2:20
- Cornelia Wilton 2 25¼
- Ernest Wilton......... 2 27¾
- Fairhaven............ 2:19¼
- Freckles 2:30
- Georgia H............. 2:26½
- Goblin 2:26½
- Kate Wilton........... 2:27
- Lady Wilton......... 2.21¼
- Maggie Wilton..... 2·28½
- Maggie Wilton....... 2:30
- Mike Bowerman 2:29¼
- Miss Wilton 2:25
- Moquette .... 2·30
- Moquette 2:10
- Ortolan .... 2·28½
- Red Wilton .... 2·29¼
- Royal Wilton ...... 2·21½
- Scourine 2 23½
- Sea Girl 2:18¼
- Silk Velvet........... 2:26
- Silicon .... 2·13½
- Silurian 2:25¼
- Silvertone............ 2:30
- Tip Tyler ...... 2·22
- Walter King 2 24¼
- Watson.............. 2:27¾
- Wilmarch 2:17¼
- Wilto 2.22½
- Wiltonette......... 2:24
- Wiltonian 2:28¼
- Wilton, Jr. 2 25
- Winchester........... 2:19¾
- Vera Capel, p 2:10¼
- Walter Wilton, p 2.19½

Windsor by Maj. Anderson
- Flora Windsor......... 2:30
- Gen. Ewing......... 2:27¼
- Lady Marie........... 2:29
- Lizzie F.............. 2 27¾
- Windsor H 2.25¾
- Windsor M 2 20¼
- Frank Finch, p....... 2 24¼
- Windsor H., p ...... 2·22½

Winfield Scott by Edward Everett.
- George B 2:29¼
- Maud J 2:25¼
- Mike Scott 2:23¼
- St. Simon............ 2:24¼
- Jennie Scott, p 2:29¾
- Theresa Scott, p 2:25

Winnebago Chief by Mountain Chief.
- J. C 2:20
- Jack Jewett, p........ 2.13¼
- Salol, p 2:21½

Winooski by Walkill Chief.
- Albion 2:27¼
- Grand Isle........... 2·24¼
- Lizzie H 2:24¼
- Orphan Boy 2 29¾

Winship Jr.
- H. B 2:18¾

Winslow Boy.
- Daisy Rolfe, p......... 2.30

Winthrop by Drew Horse.
- Molly Drew.......... 2 27
- Corette, p .... 2·19
- Oakland Boy, p 2:29

Winthrop Knox by Gen. Knox
- Maud Knox 2:27
- St. Joe 2 18

Winthrop Morrill by Young Morrill.
- Baby Boy 2 30
- Ben Morrill 2.27
- Ed. Getchell. 2:27
- Fleetwood 2 29
- Glengarry. .... 2·27
- Honest Harry 2:22½
- John Morrill 2 27½
- J. G. Morrill 2:29
- Sam Curtis 2 28

Winthrop Morrill Jr. by Metacomet.
- Gipsey 2:24¼

Wistrel, an Orloff.
- Wzmakh 2:26¼

Witchcraft by Brown Wilkes.
- Sorceress 2 24¼

Witherell Messenger by Winthrop Messenger.
- Belle of Portland 2 26

Woful Allen by Young Wofnl.
- Mamie D 2.26¼

Wolferl by Calamity Dick.
- Agamemnon, p 2 19½

Wonder by Post's Hambletonian
- Gertie J., p 2 24¾

Wonder by Blue Bull.
- John B., p 2:28½
- Susie Wonder, p 2:19½

Woodbridge Jr. by Woodbridge.
- Kate............. 2 22¾

Woodbrino by Nutwood.
- Caprivi.............. 2 28
- Ezra T 2 30
- Lord Brino 2:25½
- Matchwood 2 27
- Marvelous 2:23
- Vega 2:15¾
- Vollery .... 2·21¼
- Zerbrino 2:27¼

Woodburn by Lexington.
- Monarch 2 28¼

Woodburn by Autocrat.
- Joe Moreland 2:22

Woodburn Chief by Roscoe.
- Lady Helen 2:22

Woodburn Hambletonian by Belmont.
- Lola Anderson...... 2.29½
- Branchwood, p...... 2.25

Woodburn Pilot by Pilot Jr.
- Vladimir 2.28¾
- Woodburn Boy........... 2.27¼
- Bob R., p 2:29¼

Woodcraft by Menelaus.
- Woodlark 2 20½

Woodford by Woodford Mambrino.
- Auburn. 2:30

Woodford Abdallah by Woodford Mambrino.
- Kenilworth 2 18¼
- Sparkle, p.............. 2:29¼
- Wilshire, p......... 2 26½

Woodford Boy.
- Logan F., p 2 26½

WoodfordKnox by Gen Knox.
- Forest King 2:30
- E. W. S., p 2.23½
- Honesty, p 2.17¾
- Willie F., p 2:27¼
- Woodie, p....... 2:29¼

Woodford Mambrino by Mambrino Chief.
- Abbottsford.. ...... 2:19½
- Convoy 2 22½
- Dacia. 2:29½
- George A. Ayer....... 2·30
- Inca 2:27
- Lady McFatridge 2:29
- Magenta 2.24½
- Mambrino Dudley ..... 2·19¾
- Mattie Price 2.29¼
- Nora Lee 2 29¼
- Pancoast............ 2:21¾
- Rachel .... 2·26¾
- Woodford Pilot...... 2 23¼

Woodford Pilot by Woodford Mambrino.
- Belford............ 2 21
- King Midas 2:28¼
- Pana 2.30
- Prohibit .... 2·25½
- Rockburn 2:19¼
- Woodford Pilot Jr. .. 2·27½

Woodford Wilkes by George Wilkes.
- Hampshire.......... 2 22½
- Heiress 2.27
- Inveterate 2 29¾
- Jenny Wilkes.......... 2 12½
- Jewel Wilkes 2:28½
- Jocta Wilkes 2 29¾
- Joy Wilkes.......... 2:23¼
- Knight............ 2 28½
- Lavina............ 2 28
- L. L. D 2.24¼
- Linden Wilkes 2 25
- Marie Wilkes....... 2 30
- McGinty, p 2:28
- Woodford (La Due's). 2.16¼

Woodland by Woodlawn.
- O'Connell, p. 2:30

Woodlark by A. W. Richmond.
- Los Angeles........... 2:23½

Woodlawn.
- Hiatoga Boy, p...... 2 29¾

Woodline by Nutwood.
- Cappie Wooline...... 2 28¼
- Ella Woodline....... 2:23½

Woodman by Wedgewood.
- Maud G 2:28¼

Woodmont by Woodford Abdallah.
- Charlie Mozee, p 2:20½

Woodnut by Nutwood.
- Extravagant......... 2:28½
- Hawwood 2 30
- Baywood, p........ 2·14¾
- Wasatch, p......... 2 26¼

Woodpecker.
- Silverspray, p ...... 2·29¼

Woodstock by Young Morrill.
- Royal John. 2:26

Woolsey by Electioneer.
- Loyaleer.. .... 2.30

Nelly W 2:17¼
Princess 2:19¾
Sir Gird 2:26½
Wehina 2:26¼
Abeto, p. 2:21¾
W. P. Maxwell by Squire Talmadge.
Billy Terrill 2:28¼
Wyandotte Chief.
Bennie C., p. 2:30
Wyoming Chief.
Dick Kitchen, p. 2:27½

Yankee Bill by Peck Horse.
Nigger Baby 2:27¼
Yatagan by Lord Russell.
Yaqui 2:28¾
Yellow Jacket.
Doubtful, p. 2:25¼
Yellow Jacket (Wells') by Pyle's Yellow Jacket.
Thomas L. Young 2:19½
Young Alarm by Alarm.
Fieldmont, p 2:19
Young Abner.
Bob, p 2:23¾
Young Almont by Alburn.
Dan S 2:20
Young America by Grey Messenger.
Hazor 2:27
Young Banner by Fish Horse.
Little Harry 2:29¼
Young Bashaw by Capt. Grant
Maj. Lynn 2:23¼
Young Cassius by Jones' 2d Cassius M. Clay.
Col. Pike 2:29½
Nelly Gray 2:26½
Young Columbus Jr. by Young Columbus.
Tot 2:24
Young Darkey by Darkey.
Victor 2:26¼
Young Denmark (Kinney's) by Denmark.
Trim 2:16½
Young Detective.
Molly H 2:29¼
Young Dirigo by Dirigo.
Molly C 2:23½
Tom Drew 2:27¾
Young Flying Cloud by Flying Cloud.
Dinah 2:30
Young Forrester.
Ned Forrester, p 2:23½
Young Frenchman.
Virginia, p 2:18½
Young Fullerton by Edward Everett.
Angelica 2:25¼
Full Prince 2:23¼
Lady Potter 2:27
Louise B. 2:29¼
Madge Fullerton 2:30
Miss Fullerton 2:19¾
Young Harry Clay by Harry Clay.
Veva 2:26¾
Young Highland Gray by Highland Gray.
Highland Lassie 2:20¼
Young Highlander.
Dan Howell 2:29½
Young Hindoo by Hindoo.
Independence 2:23¼
Young Jim by George Wilkes.
At-A-Lanta 2:24½
Butterfly 2:19¾
Caneland Wilkes 2:29
Col. Young 2:23¼
Dandy Jim 2:10½
David B 2:10¼
Drum Major 2:25¼
Garnet 2:19
Incense 2:17¾
Jim Matt 2:28¼
Jim Wilkes 2:19¼
Jim Wilkes 2:15¾
Jim Young 2:26½
Maggie F 2:22¾
Mattie Swope 2:30
Mayflower 2:29¼
Minneola 2:20½
Minnie Keene 2:24¾
Molly Wilkes 2:22¼
Narka 2:27¾
Naughty Clara 2:28¼
Ruby Wilkes 2:25½
Sally B 2:20
Shadeland Delmonia 2:15
Trevillian 2:08¼
W. H. Cassidy 2:29¼
Wilkes Golddust 2:23¼
Caneland Wilkes, p 2:12
Dan Murphy, p 2:25
Jim Finch, p 2:25
Major Wilkes, p 2:16¼
Young Joe by Joe Gavin.
Bismarck 2:26¼
Young Josephus (Young's) by Hughes' Josephus.
Kansas Chief 2:21¼
Young Kirkwood.
Little Daisy, p 2:16¼
Young Mambrino Chief by Border Chief.
Flora Belle 2:29¼
Young Moscow (Jordan's) by Fleming's Moscow.
May 2:25
Young Napoleon by Bay Chief.
Maud 2:18½
Young Oneida by Benedict's Pathfinder.
Frank 2:20
Young Padlock.
K. P 2:29¼
Young Plenipo.
Joe 2:25¼
Young Post Boy by Campbell's Young Andrew Jackson.
Commodore 2:23
Young Priam by Priam.
Silas Rich 2:24¾
Young Prince by Prince Imperial.
Lady O 2:28½
Young Rex.
Gen. George A. Ballard 2:30
Young Rolfe by Tom Rolfe.
Aubine 2:18
Blue John 2:26¼
Daisy Rolfe 2:26¼
Jennie Rolfe 2:27¼
Medora 2:20½
Mountaineer 2:23¾
Nelson 2:09
Present 2:23½
Sadie L 2:26¼
Young Sportsman by Sportsman.
Clara 2:27
Young Swindler.
Juno, p 2:27
Young Thorndale.
Joe Thorndale 2:30
Young Volunteer by Volunteer.
Addie G 2:28¼
Billy R 2:24½
Dr. Miller 2:27½
Jersey Boy 2:21¼
Minnie O. 2:21¼
Sweetness 2:22¾
Yorktown Belle 2:20½
Young Wilkes by George Wilkes.
Bessie Wilkes 2:29¾
Capitana 2:20½
David H. 2:29¾
Duster Wilkes 2:27¼
Ed Wilkes 2:26¼
Free Trade 2:29¾
Jean Wilkes 2:29¼
John Wilkes 2:27
Leon H. 2:29¼
Lida Wilkes 2:29½
May Wilkes 2:26½
Michigan Prince 2:26¾
Mink Wilkes 2:28½
Nettie Wilkes 2:17½
Tariff 2:20¾
Tommy Wilkes 2:22
Tyranus 2:21¼
Van Buren Wilkes 2:21½
Victor Wilkes 2:26¾
Wilkes Girl 2:19½
Wilkes Maid 2:25½
William C 2:22¾
William H 2:18½
Madge Miller, p 2:20¾
Tyrannus, p 2:22¼
Young Wilkes (Olmstead's') by George Wilkes.
Belle Wilkes 2:28¼
Evaline Wilkes 2:27¼
Dick Wilkes, p 2:23½
Young Woful by Woful.
Carrie N 2:27
Larkin 2:30

Zachariah by George Wilkes.
Eph 2:24¾
Zack Chandler by Blue Bull.
Ellis 2:26¼
Zeno by Stillson.
Zulu 2:25
Zilcaadi Golddust by Golddust.
Cleveland 2:29½
Estelle 2:26
Frazier 2:27¾
Gold Zil 2:30
Whirlwind 2:24
Fanny Golddust, p 2:25¼

Lightning Source UK Ltd.
Milton Keynes UK
UKOW030934020513

210075UK00004B/25/P